THE MOST TRUSTED NAME IN TRAVEL: FROMMER'S

FROMMER'S EasyGuide to TOKYO, KYOTO & WESTERN HONSHU

2nd Edition

By Beth Reiber

FROMMER'S STAR RATINGS SYSTEM

Every hotel, restaurant, and attraction listed in this guide has been ranked for quality and value. Here's what the stars mean:

★	Recommended
★★	Highly Recommended
★★★	A must! Don't miss!

AN IMPORTANT NOTE

Kyoto's Kiyomizu Temple, founded in 778, in spring's cherry blossom season.

CONTENTS

Autumn in Shinjuku Park in Tokyo.

A LOOK AT TOKYO, KYOTO & WESTERN HONSHU

Japan is a trip, one of those indelibly singular destinations, that is tonic for the body, mind, and soul. But as you'll see in the following pages, it's also a feast for the eyes. In this dazzling, rainbow-hued milieu, white-powdered geisha twirl parasols on gaudily lit urban streets. Cherry blossoms dress the landscape in feathery clouds of pink and white. Tokyo's neon nightscape pulses as the skyline stretches higher, bolder. Japan is a place where you can time-travel backward and forward, from the ancient palaces and misty gardens of the *shogunate* to the supercharged toys of the digital era. High-tech bullet trains rip across the countryside at speeds up to 187 mph, while guests at traditional *ryokan* dine on tatami mats in hushed rooms with rice-paper sliding doors. Nature and the seasons are revered here—the Japanese live it up in the moment better than just about anyone. Add some of the most delicious food on the planet, 18 World Heritage Sites (12 in western Honshu alone), and breathtaking landscapes, from mossy mountains to sapphire seas, and you'll see why people come from around the world (28 million in 2017) to experience it for themselves.

Built to honor Kannon, the Buddhist goddess of mercy and happiness, Tokyo's Sensoji-ji Temple is beautifully illuminated after sunset.

TOKYO

One of the world's busiest crosswalks, Shibuya Crossing is known for its "scramble" crossing, giant TV screens, and statue of Hachiko, the real-life dog celebrated in Japanese culture for its loyalty.

The Japanese sense of whimsy is on colorful display with these girls dressed as *anime* characters at a cosplay (costume play) gathering.

Two geisha in traditional Japanese kimono stroll the lanes of Sensoji Temple in Asakusa, Tokyo.

Each of the cheerful figurines known as *maneki neko* ("the beckoning cat"), here at Gotokuji, the "cat temple," is a good-luck charm.

Taiko drum performers at the Tsukiji Hongan-ji Bon Odori Matsuri, a traditional Buddhist cultural festival honoring ancestral spirits.

Shop selling fresh seafood at the Outer Market (*Jogai*) of the Toyosu (formerly Tsukiji) Fish Market.

Young Japanese girl in traditional kimono poses in Asakusa.

Hashimake (*Okonomiyaki* rolled on chopsticks) is a popular Japanese street food.

Cooking *takoyaki*, a popular ball-shaped savory snack in Japan.

Stalls in Tokyo's Ameyoko market sell everything from vegetables to handbags to watches. The street was the site of a black market in the years following World War II.

Customers dine on traditional *tatami* while seated in this tempura restaurant in Tokyo.

A leisurely ride in a traditional riverboat in Arashiyama, Kyoto, is a popular pastime in *Koyo* (autumn).

The hushed rustlings of the otherworldly Sagana Bamboo Forest in Arashimyama, Kyoto, has put it on the Japanese Ministry of Environment's "100 Soundscapes of Japan."

One of the most popular landmarks in Kyoto is the Fushimi-Inari Shrine, where pathways are lined with rows of thousands of vermilion-hued *torii* (gates).

Symbolizing the Big Dipper constellation, a Zen garden of raked sand and pebbles surrounds cylindrical standing stones in the Tofukuji temple complex.

The art of making traditional sweet treats, known as *wagashi*, is often handed down through generations.

A UNESCO World Heritage Site, historic Toji Temple has Japan's tallest pagoda and is also the site of the country's biggest flea market, held on the 21st day of each month.

Founded in 778 and rebuilt in 1633 by the third Tokugawa shogun, Iemitsu, Kiyomizudera Temple is one of Eastern Kyoto's most famous shrines, with glorious views from its perch atop Mount Otowa.

A *maiko* (apprentice) geisha, in full ceremonial garb and white makeup, in Gion Kyoto, the city's famed geisha district.

Celebrants dressed in traditional Heian-period garb parade during Aoi Matsuri, the "Hollyhock Festival," held in May and one of the Kyoto's three main festivals.

Marchers pull massive floats in downtown Kyoto during the grand parade for Gion Matsuri, a popular festival held in July.

WESTERN HONSHU

The massive red *torii* gate guarding the Itsukushima Shrine appears to float atop the shallows of the Seto Inland Sea on Miyajima Island.

Naoshima Island is famed for its art-centric landscape, where sculptures and outdoor installations are strewn about the island, including Karel Appel's playful "Frog and Cat."

The gardens of Daisho-in Temple on Miyajima Island are filled with 500 small dedicated statues of *arhat* (Buddhist enlightened beings), each with its own individual expression and knitted cap.

The A-Bomb Dome, the skeletal ruins of the former Industrial Promotion Hall, in the Peace Memorial Park, is a stark reminder of the atomic bomb's devastation in Hiroshima.

The shimmering lavender blooms of the Great Wisteria Flower Arch, in Okayama, peak in May.

The Japanese garden in the Adachi Museum of Art has been named the best garden in Japan every year since 2003.

Guides offers tours of scenic Miyajima Island in traditional rickshaws, like this one.

A boatman takes riders along a willow-fringed canal in Kurashiki, one of Japan's most picturesque cities.

The 100,000-year-old Tottori Sand Dunes are the only large dune system in Japan.

Yayo Kusama's giant pumpkin art piece is a striking fixture on art-obsessed Naoshima Island.

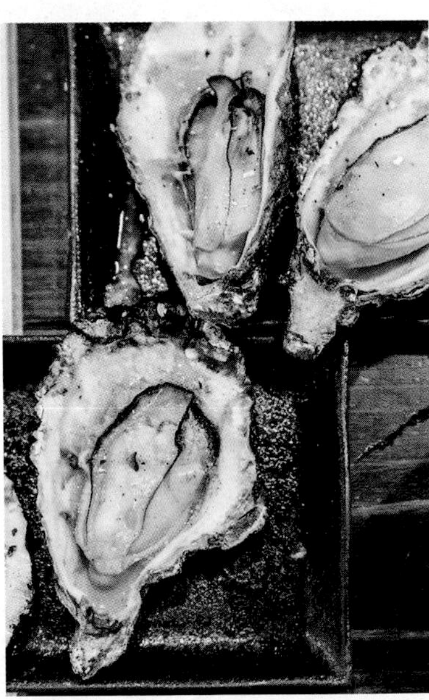

Fresh oysters, here grilled, are a local specialty on Miyajima Island, which is known for its many oyster farms.

THE BEST OF TOKYO, KYOTO & WESTERN HONSHU

1

Japan, a nation modern and dynamic and yet historic and deeply cultural, is a stunning travel experience. It fascinates every kind of visitor, from digital engineers to theater buffs engrossed in *kabuki,* from naturalists enchanted by the country's awesome mountain scenery to lovers of sushi and sashimi, or Japanese gardens, or hot-spring spas. Its greatest number of rewards are found on the largest and most heavily populated island, Honshu, whose western half includes Tokyo, Kyoto, Hiroshima, and many other captivating and trend-setting towns.

Although Tokyo and Kyoto offer plenty to keep visitors fully occupied, this guide also introduces a treasure trove of easily reached destinations throughout western Honshu, from mountaintop temples and exquisite inns to hip restaurants and vibrant neighborhoods. And to begin our journey, I've compiled a list of what I consider the best Japan has to offer, based on years of traveling the country. From the weird to the wonderful, the profound to the profane, the obvious to the obscure, these recommendations should fire your imagination and launch you toward discoveries of your own.

THE best AUTHENTIC EXPERIENCES

- **Feeling the Adrenalin Rush of Tokyo:** Tokyo is Japan's showcase for all that's high-tech, sophisticated, zany, and avant-garde, making this a must-see for just about everyone. Visiting the city's main sights, such as the Tokyo National Museum and Sensoji Temple, tops the list, but wandering the metropolis's many neighborhoods adds a totally new dimension to the Tokyo experience. See chapters 4 and 5.
- **Living the Past in Kyoto:** If you see only one city in Japan, Kyoto should be it. Japan's capital from 794 to 1868, Kyoto

boasts some of the country's oldest and best temples, imperial villas, Japanese-style inns, traditional restaurants, shops, and gardens. It's also one of the country's most beautiful cities. See chapter 8.

- **Making a Pilgrimage to a Temple or Shrine:** From mountaintop Buddhist temples to neighborhood Shinto shrines, Japan's religious structures rank among the nation's most popular attractions. They're often visited for specific reasons: Couples wishing for a happy marriage, for example, head to Kyoto's **Jishu Shrine** (p. 256), devoted to the deity of love.
- **Taking a Communal Hot-Spring Bath:** No other people on earth bathe as enthusiastically, as frequently, and for such duration as the Japanese. Their many hot-spring baths—thought to cure all sorts of ailments as well as simply make you feel good—range from elegant, Zen-like affairs to rustic outdoor baths with views of the countryside. See "Bathing," in chapter 2.
- **Riding the Shinkansen Bullet Train:** One of the world's fastest trains whips you across the countryside at up to 300km (187 miles) an hour as you relax, see Japan's rural countryside, and dine on boxed meals *(bento)* filled with local specialties. See "Getting Around Japan," in chapter 12.
- **Strolling Through a Japanese Garden:** Most of Japan's famous gardens are relics of the Edo Period, when the shogun, *daimyo* (feudal lords), imperial family, and even samurai and Buddhist priests developed private gardens for their own viewing pleasure. The garden at **Katsura Imperial Villa** (p. 252) in Kyoto is, in my view, Japan's most beautiful, but other personal favorites are **Rikugien** in Tokyo (p. 131), **Kenrokuen** in Kanazawa (p. 188), and several in Kyoto, including Ryoanji Temple's rock garden and those at the Golden and Silver Pavilions (see chapter 8).
- **Watching the Fat Guys Wrestle:** There's nothing quite like watching two monstrous sumo wrestlers square off, bluff, and grapple as they attempt to throw each other on the ground or out of the ring. Both Tokyo and Osaka have annual 15-day tournaments, but even if you can't attend one, you can watch them on TV. For more information, see "Sumo," in chapter 2, and "Spectator Sports," in chapter 5.
- **Staying in a Ryokan:** Japan's legendary service reigns supreme in a top-class *ryokan,* a traditional Japanese inn. You'll bathe in a Japanese tub or hot-spring bath, feast your eyes on lovely views past *shoji* screens, dine like a king in your *tatami* room, and sleep on a futon. See "Tips on Accommodations," in chapter 2.
- **Attending a Kabuki Play:** Based on universal themes and designed to appeal to the masses, *kabuki* plays are extravaganzas of theatrical displays, costumes, and scenes—but mostly they're just plain fun. See "Japanese Arts in a Nutshell," in chapter 2, and the *kabuki* section of "Tokyo After Dark," in chapter 5.
- **Browsing for Antiques at a Flea Market:** Flea markets are great for inexpensive used kimono, old woodblock prints, iron tea kettles, folk toys, hair ornaments, and much more. Tokyo's **Oedo Antique Market** (p. 144) and markets held at **Toji Temple** in Kyoto (p. 261) are among the best.

- **Shopping in a Department Store:** Japanese department stores are microcosms of practically everything Japan produces, from the food halls in the basement to the floors selling clothing, accessories, souvenirs, and pottery to the rooftop garden centers. What's more, service is great, and purchases are beautifully wrapped. If you arrive when the store opens, staff will be lined up at the front door to bow as you enter. You'll be spoiled for life.

THE best HOTELS & INNS

- **Most Famous Setting: Park Hyatt Tokyo** (Tokyo): Occupying the 39th to 52nd floors of a skyscraper designed by famed architect Kenzo Tange, this gorgeous property offers stunning views of the city, one of Tokyo's hottest restaurants, rooms you could live in, and legendary service. No wonder it has many imitators and was featured in *Lost in Translation.* See p. 85.
- **Best Views Without Spending a Fortune: Park Hotel Tokyo** (Tokyo): With a great location near the Ginza, a light-filled lobby filled with art, and rooms with outstanding views (including some designed by Japanese artists), this contemporary high-rise hotel delivers plenty but doesn't break the bank. See p. 77.
- **Best Historic Hotel: The Fujiya Hotel** (Hakone): Established in 1878 and nestled on a wooded hillside, the Fujiya is one of Japan's oldest, grandest, and most majestic Western-style hotels. Resembling a Japanese *ryokan* from the outside, it has a comfortable interior of detailed woodwork; old-fashioned, antiques-filled guest rooms; a delightful 1930s dining hall; hot-spring baths; and extensive landscaping. A stay here makes you feel as though you've traveled not just to Hakone but to another century. See p. 179.
- **Best Japanese Inn Experience: Hiiragiya Ryokan** (Kyoto): If ever there was an example of the quintessential *ryokan,* Hiiragiya is it. Located in the heart of old Kyoto, it's the ultimate in *tatami* luxury: a dignified enclave of polished wood and rooms with antique furnishings overlooking private gardens. Six generations of the same family have provided impeccable service here since 1861. See p. 218.
- **Best Youth Hostel: Kyoto Utano Youth Hostel** (Kyoto): With a lovely lodgelike ambience, free nightly events, and rooms ranging from twins to dorms, this is certainly Japan's most attractive youth hostel. See p. 227.
- **Best Contemporary Digs: Osaka Marriott Miyako Hotel** (Osaka): Opened in 2014 in Japan's tallest building, this is the most unhotel-like hotel I've seen in Japan, where the emphasis is clearly on the views and the experience, whether it's gazing at the horizon or celebrating at the 57th-floor restaurant. See p. 276.
- **Best Rural Experience: Staying at a Minshuku in Shirakawa-go:** Nestled in the Japan Alps, Shirakawa-go is a narrow valley of paddies, irrigation canals, and 200-year-old thatched farmhouses, several of which offer simple *tatami* accommodations and meals featuring local cuisine. This is a great, inexpensive escape. See chapter 7.

- **Best Temple Stay: Mount Koya:** If your vision of Japan includes temples, towering cypress trees, shaven-headed monks, and religious chanting at the crack of dawn, head for the religious sanctuary atop Mount Koya, where some 50 Buddhist temples offer *tatami* accommodations and two vegetarian meals a day. See chapter 10.
- **Best Backpacker Hostel: Cuore Kurashiki** (Kurashiki): Virtually nonexistent a decade ago, inexpensive guesthouses are now found virtually everywhere. This one, opened in 2014, proves just how far hostels have come, with a hip lounge/restaurant complete with hammocks and both private and dormitory rooms (including one just for women). See p. 304.

THE best FOOD & DRINK EXPERIENCES

- **Experiencing a Kaiseki Feast:** The ultimate in Japanese cuisine, *kaiseki* is a feast for the senses and spirit. This multicourse meal offers a variety of exquisitely cooked and arranged dishes, prepared with seasonal ingredients and served on complementary tableware. Japan has hundreds of exceptional *kaiseki* restaurants, from old-world traditional to sleek modern. Traditional *ryokan* also serve *kaiseki.* See "Eating & Drinking in Japan," in chapter 2.
- **Rubbing Elbows in an Izakaya:** *Izakaya* are pubs in Japan—usually tiny affairs with just a counter, serving up skewered grilled chicken, fish, and other fare. They're good places to meet the natives and are inexpensive as well. You'll find them in every nightlife district in the country.
- **Dining on Western Food in a Memorable Setting:** The **New York Grill** (p. 101) epitomizes the best of the West with its sophisticated setting, spectacular Tokyo views, and great food. In Kyoto, personal favorites include **Misoguigawa** (p. 231), serving French *kaiseki* in a former teahouse and with an open-air pavilion in summer, and the **Sodoh** (p. 237), an Italian restaurant in a 1929 villa.
- **Listening to the Shamisen at Waentei-Kikko** (Tokyo): Just steps away from bustling Sensoji Temple, this charming restaurant in a rustic farmhouse offers *kaiseki* and bento meals and live *shamisen* performances. See p. 99.
- **Dining Like a Monk on Buddhist Vegetarian Cuisine:** Mount Koya's temple lodgings (see chapter 10) are among the most memorable places to dine like a monk, but I also like **Kotobuki-Ya** (p. 187), which occupies a 170-year-old merchant's house in Kanazawa, and, in Takayama, **Kakusho** (p. 202), offering *kaiseki shojin-ryori* in a historic setting with views of a garden.
- **Watching Short-Order Okonomiyaki Cooks at Work:** A perch at the counter gives you a ringside seat as cooks prepare *okonomiyaki,* a savory Japanese pancake. Osaka and Hiroshima are famous for their okonomiyaki, though the styles of preparation are different in each. See chapters 9 and 11.

- **Slurping Noodles in a Noodle Shop:** You're *supposed* to slurp when eating Japanese noodles, which are prepared in almost as many different ways as there are regions. Noodle shops range from standup counters to sit-down restaurants.
- **Making a Meal of Tofu:** You may have had tofu before, but you've never had it like this. **Tokyo Shiba Toufuya Ukai** (p. 110) specializes in tofu prepared many different ways, in a restaurant surrounded by a garden. Elsewhere, Nikko is famous for *yuba,* delicate layers formed by boiling soymilk (see chapter 6), while Kyoto restaurants offer *yudofu,* a one-pot stew with tofu and vegetables (see chapter 8).
- **Feeling Adventuresome in the Hinterlands:** Virtually every region in Japan has its own local specialties, from oysters in Hiroshima to mountain vegetables in Takayama to *jibuni* in Kanazawa. You can even enjoy local specialties by ordering box lunches *(bento)* on the Shinkansen bullet train. See individual chapters.

THE best FREE THINGS TO DO

- **Sitting Pretty Above Tokyo:** On the 45th floor of the Tokyo Metropolitan Government Office (TMG), designed by Kenzo Tange (the architect behind the Park Hyatt Tokyo), this observatory offers a bird's-eye view of an endlessly stretching metropolis and, on fine winter days, Mount Fuji. See p. 126.
- **Joining a Free Guided Tour of Iconic Landmarks:** English-speaking volunteers lead free tours at many of Japan's iconic landmarks, including the Asakusa and Ueno areas in Tokyo, Nara Park, Kanazawa Castle Park, and Himeji Castle. See individual chapters.
- **Browsing the Electronics & Anime Shops of Akihabara:** Even if you don't buy anything, it's great fun—and very educational—to check out the latest in gadgetry in Japan's largest electronics district. In recent years, shops specializing in *manga* (Japanese comic books and graphic novels) and *anime* (Japanese animation) have also opened, along with so-called maid cafes. See p. 136.
- **Joining the Crowds at a Festival:** With Shintoism and Buddhism as its major religions, and temples and shrines virtually everywhere, Japan abounds in festivals. Celebrations range from those featuring horseback archery to parades of huge fake phalluses; you may want to plan your trip around one (and book early for a hotel). See "Calendar of Events," in chapter 2.
- **Walking to Kobo Daishi's Mausoleum on Mount Koya:** Since the 9th century, when Buddhist leader Kobo Daishi was laid to rest at Okunoin on Mount Koya, his faithful followers have followed him to their graves—and now tomb after tomb lines a 1.5km (1-mile) pathway to Daishi's mausoleum. Cypress trees, moss-covered stone lanterns, and thousands upon thousands of tombs make this the most impressive graveyard stroll in Japan, especially at night. See chapter 10.

- **Visiting a Local Market:** Tokyo's Toyosu Fish Market is Japan's largest, but there are local seafood and produce markets virtually everywhere. Those in Kyoto, Kanazawa, and Takayama are among my favorites. See p. 259, 192, and 203.
- **Seeing the Cherry Blossoms:** Nothing symbolizes the approach of spring so vividly to Japanese as the appearance of the cherry blossoms—and the Japanese celebrate the season with spirited gatherings of food, drink, and dance under the blossoms. See "Calendar of Events," in chapter 2, for cherry-blossom details.

THE best FOR FAMILIES

- **Joining the Throngs at Sensoji Temple:** Tokyo's oldest temple is also its liveliest, with throngs of visitors and stalls selling both traditional and kitschy items, giving it a festival-like atmosphere every day of the year. There's enough excitement to keep everyone entertained. Top it off with a stop at nearby **Hanayashiki amusement park** for its old-fashioned kiddie rides. See p. 120.
- **Learning History at the Edo-Tokyo Museum:** Housed in a high-tech modern building, this ambitious museum chronicles the fascinating and somewhat tumultuous history of Tokyo (known as Edo during the Feudal Era) with models, replicas, artifacts, and dioramas. Not only can children climb into a palanquin and a rickshaw, but volunteers stand ready to give free guided tours in English. See p. 129.
- **Traveling in Hakone:** With its mountain railway, cable car, ropeway, and sightseeing boat outfitted like a pirate ship, this circuitous route through scenic Hakone is a great excursion for families. The best place to stay? The historic **Fujiya Hotel,** hands down my favorite hotel in Japan. See p. 171.
- **Spending Sunday in the Park:** Parks are popular Sunday destinations for families with kids and young couples on dates, making for great people-watching and a restorative afternoon. Among my favorites: **Ueno Park** (where you'll also find the nation's oldest zoo) and **Yoyogi Park** in Tokyo and the extensive park surrounding **Osaka Castle.** See p. 124 and 280.
- **Communing with Deep-Sea Creatures in an Aquarium:** Japan is surrounded by sea, so it's no surprise that it has more than its share of aquariums, many with innovative displays that put you eye-to-eye with the creatures of the deep. Among the best is the **Osaka Aquarium** (p. 282).
- **Hanging Out in Harajuku:** For teens and tweens, nothing beats a day in teenybopper heaven, with its many clothing and accessory stores lining narrow streets packed with a never-ending flow of humanity. Lots of restaurants in this vibrant Tokyo neighborhood are geared to the younger generation, too, but for a bit of culture (and quietude), head to nearby **Meiji Shrine,** enveloped in woods.
- **Exploring a Japanese Castle:** The past comes alive when you tromp the many wooden stairs in a Japanese castle, gaze upon samurai helmets and gear (and even try them on), and pretend you're the feudal lord viewing his

domain from the keep's top floor. **Himeji Castle** (p. 298) is Japan's most famous, but even **Osaka Castle** (p. 280) and **Hiroshima Castle** (p. 318), both resurrected after being destroyed during World War II, are impressive and boast good museums.

- **Testing Your Skills at a Game Arcade:** Older kids can battle dinosaurs or test their fishing skills at **VR Zone Shinjuku** (p. 125), while the challenges and games at **One Piece Tower theme park** in Tokyo Tower (p. 128) are meant to appeal to younger children.
- **Cycling Through History in the Kibiji District:** Just a short train ride from Kurashiki is the ancient Kibiji District, where you can rent bicycles and cycle your way past ancient burial mounds, temples, and paddies on a marked trail. See p. 307.
- **Feeding the Deer:** Deer, considered divine messengers, roam freely in Nara Park and on the island of Miyajima. But they're just the bonus to exploring the World Heritage Sites at both locations. See chapters 9 and 10.

THE best NEIGHBORHOODS

- **Asakusa** (Tokyo): Asakusa is the best place to experience Tokyo's old downtown, with its popular Sensoji Temple, Nakamise shopping lane crammed with crafts and kitsch, and casual traditional restaurants. As in days of yore, arrive by boat on the Sumida River. See chapters 4 and 5.
- **Ni-Chome** (Tokyo): With its 300 bars, dance clubs, shops, and other establishments, Ni-Chome is Japan's largest gay nightlife district and boasts the country's liveliest street scene. Many bars welcome people of all persuasions. See chapter 5.
- **Higashiyama-ku District:** Kyoto's eastern sector is a lovely combination of wooded hills, temples, shrines, museums, shops, and traditional restaurants, making it one of the best neighborhoods in Japan for a stroll. See "A Stroll Through Higashiyama-ku," in chapter 8.
- **Sanmachi District in Takayama:** Nicknamed "Little Kyoto" of the **Hida Mountains,** Takayama has a downtown lined with traditional wooden buildings and shops, a morning market, Japanese inns, and a wealth of museums. For a more rural setting, Takayama's **Higashiyama Walking Course** is a hiking path that leads past temples and shrines and provides a different perspective on the city. See chapter 7.
- **Bikan Historic Quarter** (Kurashiki): With its willow-fringed canal and old black-and-white granaries, the historic district of this former merchant town is a photographer's dream. See chapter 11.

2 JAPAN IN CONTEXT

Hardly a day goes by that you don't hear something about Japan, whether the subject is travel, traditional Japanese cuisine (placed on UNESCO's Intangible Cultural Heritage list in 2013), the arts, *anime,* the upcoming 2020 Olympics in Tokyo, or the ongoing clean-up efforts from the 2011 Great East Japan Earthquake. Yet this dynamic Asian nation remains something of an enigma to people in the Western world. What best encapsulates Japan? Is it the land of cutting-edge cars and robots? Or is it the land of geisha and bonsai, the punctilious tea ceremony, and the delicate art of flower arranging? Has it become, in its outlook and pop culture, a country more Western than Asian? Or has it retained its unique ancient traditions while forging a central place in the contemporary post-industrialized world?

Japan eludes easy definition. Its cities may look Westernized—often disappointingly so—but beyond first impressions, there's very little about this Asian nation that could lull you into thinking you're in the West. In fact, the country has long adopted the best of the West (and the East, for that matter) and then adapted it to its own needs. That modern high-rise may look Western, but inside you might find a rustic-looking restaurant with open charcoal grills, corporate offices, a pachinko parlor, a high-tech bar with surreal city views, a McDonald's, an acupuncture clinic, a computer showroom, and a rooftop shrine. This unique synthesis of East and West has produced a culture that is distinctly Japanese.

Japan also differs greatly from its Asian neighbors, mostly because the island remained steadfastly isolated from the rest of the world throughout much of its history, usually deliberately so.

Discovering Japan today is like peeling an onion—you uncover one layer only to find more layers underneath. Thus, no matter how long you stay in Japan, you never stop learning something new—and that constant discovery is one of the most fascinating aspects of being here.

JAPAN TODAY

You can't talk about Japan today without mentioning its biggest earthquake in recorded history, known as the Great East Japan Earthquake, which struck off the Tohoku coast on March 11, 2011. While all the consequences of the triple whammy—earthquake, tsunami, and meltdown of the Fukushima nuclear power plant—may not be entirely evident for years to come, it seems safe to say that for Japan, 3/11 will remain a defining moment in its history and its future.

Although much of Japan, including western Honshu, was not directly affected by the Great East Japan Earthquake, tourism to the country plummeted following the disaster, dropping from 8.6 million visitors in 2010 to 6.2 million in 2011. Since then, however, international tourism to Japan has risen dramatically, with more than 28 million people visiting in 2017, the most ever recorded. Approximately 75% of those visitors hailed from China, Taiwan, Hong Kong, and South Korea, a statistic that has changed the face of tourism in Japan. Whereas just two decades ago I used to see other Asians (mostly South Koreans) primarily on the southern island of Kyushu, I now see busloads of Asian tourists everywhere, from the narrow streets of Kyoto (sometimes decked out for the day in rented kimonos) to designer shops in Tokyo's fashionable Ginza to the tiny mountain village of Shirakawa-go, plus everywhere in between. North Americans are also arriving in record numbers, with 1.3 million visiting Japan in 2017, topping the list of long-haul visitors to the nation.

The upside of increased tourism to Japan is more information in English and other foreign languages than ever before, from bus schedules to signage, as well as better services and infrastructure to lure and accommodate visitors—including more frequent runs of rural buses that used to be few and far between, the rise of inexpensive guesthouses, longer hours for tourist information offices, and a decrease in the amount of money you need to spend to qualify for duty-free allowances.

The downside, of course, is that transportation and accommodations are more crowded than I've ever seen them, especially during peak seasons like cherry-blossom time in spring and autumn leaf viewing, which have always been huge tourism draws, and during Chinese holidays. I expect tourism only to grow in the years ahead, especially since the Japanese government has set a goal of attracting 40 million annual overseas visitors by 2020, when Tokyo hosts the Summer Olympics.

THE HISTORY OF JAPAN

ANCIENT HISTORY (CA. 30,000 B.C.–A.D. 710) Although the exact origin of Japanese people is unknown, we know the territory of Japan was occupied as early as 30,000 B.C. According to mythology, however, Japan's history began when the sun goddess, Amaterasu, sent one of her descendants down to the island of Kyushu to unify the people of Japan. Unification, however, was not realized until a few generations later when Jimmu, the great-grandson of the goddess's emissary, succeeded in bringing all of the country under his rule. Because of his divine descent, Jimmu became emperor in 660 B.C. (the date is mythical), thus establishing the line from which all of Japan's emperors are said to derive. However mysterious the origin of this imperial dynasty, it is acknowledged as the longest-reigning such family in the world.

Legend begins to give way to fact only in the A.D. 4th century, when a family by the name of Yamato succeeded in expanding its kingdom throughout much of the country and set up court in what is now Nara Prefecture. At the core of unification was the Shinto religion. Indigenous to Japan, Shintoism is marked by the worship of natural things (like rivers and foxes) and of the spirits of ancestors, as well as the belief in the emperor's divinity.

Eventually, Yamato (present-day Japan) also began pointing cultural feelers toward its great neighbor to the west, China. In the 6th century, Buddhism, which originated in India, was brought to Japan via China and Korea, followed by the importation of Chinese cultural and scholarly knowledge—including art, architecture, and the use of Chinese written characters. In 604, the prince regent Shotoku, greatly influenced by the teachings of Buddhism and Confucianism and still a beloved figure today, drafted a document calling for political reforms and a constitutional government. By 607, he was sending Japanese scholars to China to study Buddhism, and he started building Buddhist temples, including Shitennoji Temple in what is now Osaka and Horyuji

SHRINES & TEMPLES: religion IN JAPAN

The main religions in Japan are Shintoism and Buddhism, and many Japanese consider themselves believers in both. Most Japanese, for example, will marry in a Shinto ceremony, but when they die, they'll have a Buddhist funeral.

A native religion of Japan, **Shintoism** is the worship of ancestors and national heroes, as well as of all natural things—mountains, trees, stars, seas, fire, animals, even vegetables—as the embodiment of *kami* (gods). There are no scriptures in Shintoism, nor any ordained code of morals or ethics. The place of worship in Shintoism is called a *jinja*, or shrine. The most obvious sign of a shrine is its *torii*, an entrance gate, usually of wood and sometimes painted vermillion, consisting of two tall poles topped with either one or two crossbeams. Another feature common to shrines is a water trough with communal cups, where the Japanese will wash their hands and sometimes rinse out their mouths. Purification and cleanliness are important in Shintoism because they show respect to the gods. At the shrine, worshipers will throw a few coins into a money box, clap their hands twice to get the gods' attention, and then bow their heads and pray for whatever they wish—good health, the safe delivery of a child, or a prosperous year.

Founded in India in the 6th to 5th centuries B.C., **Buddhism** came to Japan in the A.D. 6th century, bringing with it the concept of eternal life. Whereas Shintoists have shrines, Buddhists have temples, called *otera*. Instead of *torii*, temples will often have an entrance gate with a raised doorsill and heavy doors. Temples may also have a cemetery on their grounds (which Shinto shrines never have) as well as a pagoda.

Temple near Nara, the latter said to be the oldest existing wooden structure in the world. Even today, both Buddhism and Shintoism are driving influences in Japanese life.

THE NARA PERIOD (710–84) Before the 700s, the site of Japan's capital changed every time a new emperor came to the throne. In 710, however, a permanent capital was established at Nara. Although it remained the capital for only 74 years, seven successive emperors ruled from Nara. The period was graced with the expansion of Buddhism and flourishing temple construction throughout the country. Buddhism also inspired the arts, including Buddhist sculpture, metal casting, painting, and lacquerware. It was during this time that Emperor Shomu, the most devout Buddhist among the Nara emperors, ordered the casting of a huge bronze statue of Buddha to be erected in Nara. Known as the Daibutsu, it remains Nara's biggest attraction.

THE HEIAN PERIOD (794–1192) In 794, the capital was moved to Heiankyo (present-day Kyoto), and, following the example of cities in China, Kyoto was laid out in a grid pattern with broad roads and canals. Heiankyo means "capital of peace and tranquillity," and the Heian Period was a glorious time for aristocratic families, a period of prosperous luxury during which court life reached new artistic heights. Moon viewing became popular. Chinese characters were blended with a new Japanese writing system, allowing for the first time the flowering of Japanese literature and poetry. The life of the times was captured in works by two women: Sei Shonagon, who wrote a collection of impressions of her life at court known as the *Pillow Book;* and Murasaki Shikibu, who wrote the world's first major novel, *The Tale of Genji*

Because the nobles were completely engrossed in their luxurious lifestyles, however, they failed to notice the growth of military clans in the provinces. The two most powerful warrior clans were the Taira (also called Heike) and the Minamoto (also called Genji), whose fierce civil wars tore the nation apart until a young warrior, Minamoto Yoritomo, established supremacy.

THE KAMAKURA PERIOD (1192–1333) Wishing to set up rule far away from Kyoto, Minamoto Yoritomo established his capital in a remote and easily defended fishing village called Kamakura, not far from today's Tokyo. In becoming the nation's first shogun, or military dictator, Minamoto Yoritomo laid the groundwork for 700 years of military governments—in which the power of the country passed from the aristocratic court into the hands of the warrior class—until the imperial court was restored in 1868.

The Kamakura Period is perhaps best known for the unrivaled ascendancy of the warrior caste, or **samurai.** Ruled by a rigid honor code, samurai were bound in loyalty to their feudal lord *(daimyo),* and they became the only caste allowed to carry two swords. They were expected to give up their lives for their lord without hesitation, and if they failed in their duty, they could regain their honor only by committing ritualistic suicide, or *seppuku.* Spurning the soft life led by court nobles, samurai embraced a spartan lifestyle. When **Zen Buddhism,** with its tenets of mental and physical discipline, was introduced into Japan from China in the 1190s, it appealed greatly to the samurai.

Weapons and armor achieved new heights in artistry, while *Bushido,* the way of the warrior, contributed to the spirit of national unity.

In 1274, Mongolian forces under Kublai Khan made an unsuccessful attempt to invade Japan. They returned in 1281 with a larger fleet, but a typhoon destroyed it. Regarding the cyclone as a gift from the gods, Japanese called it *kamikaze,* meaning "divine wind," which took on a different significance at the end of World War II when Japanese pilots flew suicide missions in an attempt to turn the tide of war.

THE AGE OF THE WARRING STATES (1336–1603) After the fall of the Kamakura shogunate, a new feudal government was set up at Muromachi in Kyoto. The next 200 years, however, were marred by bloody civil wars as *daimyo* staked out their fiefdoms. Similar to the barons of Europe, the *daimyo* owned tracts of land, had complete rule over the people who lived on them, and had an army of retainers, the samurai, who fought his enemies. This period of civil wars is called Sengoku-Jidai, or Age of the Warring States. Yet these centuries of strife also saw a blossoming of art and culture. Kyoto witnessed the construction of the extravagant Golden and Silver pavilions as well as the artistic arrangement of Ryoanji Temple's famous rock garden. *Noh* drama, the tea ceremony, flower arranging, and landscape gardening became passions of the upper class. At the end of the 16th century, many mountaintop castles were built to demonstrate the strength of the *daimyo,* guard their fiefdoms, and defend themselves against the firearms introduced by the Portuguese.

THE EDO PERIOD (1603–1867) In 1600, power was seized by Tokugawa Ieyasu, a statesman so shrewd and skillful in eliminating enemies that his heirs would continue to rule Japan for the next 250 years. After defeating his greatest rival in the famous battle of Sekigahara, Tokugawa set up a shogunate government in 1603 in Edo (present-day Tokyo), leaving the emperor intact but virtually powerless in Kyoto.

In 1639, fearing the expansionist policies of European nations and the spread of Christianity, the Tokugawa shogunate adopted a policy of total isolation. Thus began an amazing 215-year period in Japanese history during which Japan was closed to the rest of the world. It was a time of political stability at the expense of personal freedom, as all aspects of life were strictly controlled by the Tokugawa government. Japanese society was divided into four distinct classes: samurai, farmers, craftspeople, and merchants. Class determined everything in daily life, from where a person could live to what he was allowed to wear or eat. Samurai led the most exalted social position, and it was probably during the Tokugawa Period that the samurai class reached the zenith of its glory. At the bottom of the social ladder were the merchants, but as they prospered under the peaceful regime, new forms of entertainment arose to occupy their time. *Kabuki* drama and woodblock prints became the rage, while stoneware and porcelain, silk brocade for kimono, and lacquerware improved in quality. In fact, it was probably the shogunate's rigid policies that actually fostered the arts. Because anything new was considered dangerous and quickly suppressed, Japanese were forced to retreat inward, focusing their energies on the arts and perfecting handicrafts down to the minutest detail whether it was swords, textiles, or lacquered boxes. Only Japan's many festivals and pilgrimages to designated religious sites offered relief from harsh and restrictive social mores.

To ensure that no *daimyo* in the distant provinces would become too powerful and a threat to the shogun's power, the Tokugawa government ordered each *daimyo* to maintain a second mansion in Edo, leave his family there as permanent residents (effectively as hostages), and spend a prescribed number of months in Edo every year or two. Inns and townships sprang up along Japan's major highways to accommodate the elaborate processions of palanquins, samurai, and footmen traveling back and forth between Edo and the provinces. In expending so much time and money traveling back and forth and maintaining elaborate residences both in the provinces and in Edo, the *daimyo* had no resources left with which to wage a rebellion.

Yet even though the Tokugawa government took such extreme measures to ensure its supremacy, by the mid–19th century it was clear that the feudal system was outdated and economic power had shifted into the hands of the merchants. Many samurai families were impoverished, and discontent with the shogunate became widespread. In 1853, American Commodore Matthew C. Perry sailed to Japan, seeking to gain trading rights. He left unsuccessful, but returning a year later he forced the Shogun to sign an agreement despite the disapproval of the emperor, thus ending Japan's 2 centuries of isolation. In 1867, powerful families toppled the Tokugawa regime and restored the emperor as ruler, thus bringing the Feudal Era to a close.

MEIJI PERIOD THROUGH WORLD WAR II (1868–1945) In 1868, Emperor Meiji moved his imperial government from Kyoto to Edo, renamed it Tokyo (Eastern Capital), and designated it the official national capital. During the next few decades, known as the Meiji Restoration, Japan rapidly progressed from a feudal agricultural society of samurai and peasants to an industrial nation. The samurai were stripped of their power and no longer allowed to carry swords, thus ending a privileged way of life begun almost 700 years earlier in Kamakura. A prime minister and a cabinet were appointed, a constitution was drafted, and a parliament (called the Diet) was elected. With the enthusiastic support of Emperor Meiji, the latest in Western technological know-how was imported, including railway and postal systems, along with specialists and advisers: Between 1881 and 1898, about 10,000 Westerners were retained by the Japanese government to help modernize the country.

Meanwhile, Japan made incursions into neighboring lands. In 1894 to 1895, it fought and won a war against China; in 1904 to 1905, it attacked and defeated Russia; and in 1910, it annexed Korea. After militarists gained control of the government in the 1930s, these expansionist policies continued; Manchuria was annexed, and Japan went to war with China again in 1937. On December 7, 1941, Japan bombed Pearl Harbor, entering World War II against the United States. Although Japan went on to conquer Hong Kong, Singapore,

Burma, Malaysia, the Philippines, the Dutch East Indies, and Guam, the tide eventually turned, and American bombers reduced every major Japanese city to rubble with the exception of historic Kyoto. On August 6, 1945, the United States dropped the world's first atomic bomb over Hiroshima, followed on August 9 by a second over Nagasaki. Japan submitted to unconditional surrender on August 14, with Emperor Hirohito's radio broadcast telling his people the time had come for "enduring the unendurable and suffering what is insufferable." American and other Allied occupation forces arrived and remained until 1952. For the first time in history, Japan had suffered defeat by a foreign power; the country had never before been invaded or occupied by a foreign nation.

POSTWAR JAPAN (1946–89) The experience of World War II had a profound effect on the Japanese, yet they emerged from their defeat and began to rebuild. In 1946, under the guidance of the Allied military authority headed by U.S. Gen. Douglas MacArthur, they adopted a democratic constitution renouncing war and the use of force to settle international disputes and divesting the emperor of divinity. A parliamentary system of government was set up, and 1947 witnessed the first general elections for the National Diet, the government's legislative body.

Avoiding involvement in foreign conflicts as outlined by its constitution, Japanese concentrated on economic recovery. Through a series of policies favoring domestic industries and shielding Japan from foreign competition, they achieved rapid economic growth. In 1964, Tokyo hosted the Summer Olympic Games, showing the world that not only had Japan recovered from the war's destruction but had also transformed into a formidable industrialized power. By the 1980s, Japan was by far the richest industrialized nation in Asia and the envy of its neighbors, who strove to emulate Japan's success. Sony had become a household word around the globe; books flooded the international market touting the economic secrets of Japan, Inc. After all, Japan seemed to have it all: a good economy, political stability, safe streets, and great schools. As the yen soared, Japanese traveled abroad as never before, and Japanese companies gained international attention as they gobbled up real estate in foreign lands and purchased works of art at unheard-of prices.

In 1989, Emperor Hirohito died of cancer at age 87, bringing the 63-year Showa Era to an end and ushering in the **Heisei Period** under Akihito, the 125th emperor, who proclaimed the new "Era of Peace" (Heisei). When Akihito abdicates in April 2019, Crown Prince Naruhito will ascend to the throne.

AFTER THE BUBBLE BURST (1990–PRESENT) In the early 1990s, shadows of financial doubt began to spread over the Land of the Rising Sun, with alarming reports of bad bank loans, inflated stock prices, and overextended corporate investment abroad. In 1992, recession hit Japan, bursting the economic bubble and plunging the country into its worst recession since World War II.

Although Japan, whose foremost trading partner had shifted from the United States to China, seemed to be on the economic mend by the mid-2000s, the

2008 global financial meltdown (referred to in Japan as the "Lehman Shock") hijacked its recovery by causing a downward spiral in foreign trade as demand for Japanese cars, electronics, and other exports dropped dramatically around the world. For Japan's young generation, economic stagnation was all they'd known. Instead of being envied as an Asian superpower, Japan had become an example of an economy other nations wished to avoid. Furthermore, Japan continued to suffer a declining birthrate, coupled with one of the most rapidly aging populations in the world.

On the international front, Japan's most immediate worry has long been its neighbor, North Korea, which lobbed its first missile over Japan in 1988 and launched its first satellite rocket over Japan in 2008. Relations with other neighboring countries are strained too, thanks to territorial disputes over several islands and Japan's revisionist views of its wartime aggression and war crimes, including its denial of forcing so-called "comfort women" to work in brothels established by Japanese military. Even Japan's Prime Minister Shinzo Abe has questioned whether comfort women were coerced and has angered the rest of Asia with visits to Tokyo's Yasukuni Shrine, dedicated to war dead.

But all of Japan's woes paled to what happened on March 11, 2011, when Japan's strongest quake in recorded history struck off the Tohoku coast with a magnitude of 9.0, unleashing a massive tsunami up to three stories high that raced up to 10km (6 miles) inland. More than 19,000 people died or vanished, entire towns and villages along the Tohoku coast (in eastern Honshu) were obliterated, and the Fukushima nuclear power plant was severely crippled. Although most of Tohoku has recovered, cleanup and decontamination in Fukushima continues. Experts say it could take 40 years to fully decommission the Fukushima power plant; 110,000 houses were contaminated in Fukushima Prefecture alone. Just as 9/11 remains seared in American minds, 3/11 is the day that for most Japanese changed their nation forever.

For now, the biggest changes in Japan are related to the 2020 Summer Olympics. Preparations for increased services for international tourists include everything from no-step buses in Tokyo to temples offering overnight stays.

TRADITIONAL ARTS

KABUKI Japan's best-known traditional theater art, *kabuki* is also one of the country's most popular forms of entertainment. Visit a performance and it's easy to see why—*kabuki* is fun! The plays are dramatic, the costumes are gorgeous, the stage settings are often fantastic, and the themes are universal—love, revenge, and the conflict between duty and personal feelings. Plots are easy to follow, though some theaters have English-language programs and earphones that describe everything in minute detail. Probably one of the reasons *kabuki* is so popular even today is that it developed centuries ago as a form of entertainment for the common people in feudal Japan, particularly the merchants. And one of *kabuki*'s interesting aspects is that all roles—even those depicting women—are played by men.

Altogether there are more than 300 *kabuki* plays, dating mostly from the 18th century. *Kabuki* stages almost always revolve and have an aisle that extends from the stage to the back of the spectator theater. For a Westerner, one of the more arresting things about a *kabuki* performance is the audience itself. Because this has always been entertainment for the masses, the audience can get quite lively with yells, guffaws, shouts of approval, and laughter. The best place to enjoy *kabuki* is Tokyo, where performances are held throughout the year.

NOH Whereas *kabuki* developed as a form of entertainment for the masses, *Noh* was a much more traditional and aristocratic form of theater. Most of Japan's shogun were patrons of *Noh;* during the Edo era, it became the exclusive entertainment of the samurai class. In contrast to *kabuki*'s extroverted liveliness, *Noh* is very calculated, slow, and restrained. The oldest form of theater in Japan, it has changed very little in the past 600 years, making it the oldest theater art in the world. The language is so archaic that Japanese cannot understand it at all, which explains in part why *Noh* does not have the popularity that kabuki does.

As in *kabuki,* all *Noh* performers are men, with the principal characters consisting mostly of ghosts or spirits, who illuminate foibles of human nature or tragic-heroic events. Performers often wear masks. Spoken parts are chanted by a chorus of about eight; music is provided by a *Noh* orchestra that consists of several drums and a flute. In between *Noh* plays, short comic reliefs, called *kyogen,* usually make fun of life in the 1600s, depicting the lives of lazy husbands, conniving servants, and other characters with universal appeal. In addition to Tokyo's National Noh Theatre, Noh is staged throughout the country, including at shrines and private Noh venues.

BUNRAKU *Bunraku* is traditional Japanese puppet theater. But contrary to what you might expect, *bunraku* is for adults, and themes center on love and revenge, sacrifice and suicide. Many dramas now adapted for *kabuki* were first written for the *bunraku* stage. Popular in Japan since the 17th century, *bunraku* is fascinating to watch because the puppeteers are right onstage with their puppets, dressed in black and wonderfully skilled in making puppets seem like living beings. Usually, there are three puppeteers for each puppet, which is about three-fourths human size: One puppeteer is responsible for movement of the puppet's head, the expression on its face, and the movement of the right arm and hand; another puppeteer operates the puppet's left arm and hand; while the third moves the legs. Although at first the puppeteers are somewhat distracting, after a while you forget they're there as the puppets assume personalities of their own. The narrator, who tells the story and speaks the various parts, is accompanied by a *shamisen,* a three-stringed Japanese instrument. The most famous *bunraku* presentations are at the Osaka Bunraku Theater, but there are performances in Tokyo and other major cities, too.

THE TEA CEREMONY Tea was brought to Japan from China about 1,200 years ago. It first became popular among Buddhist priests as a means of staying awake during long hours of meditation; gradually, its use filtered down

sumo

The Japanese form of wrestling known as **sumo** was first mentioned in written records in the 6th century but was probably popular long before that. Today it's still popular, with the best wrestlers revered as national heroes, much as baseball or basketball players are in North America. Often taller than 1.8m (6 ft.) and weighing well over 136kg (300 lb.), sumo wrestlers follow a rigorous training period, which usually begins when they're in their teens and includes eating special foods to gain weight. Unmarried wrestlers even live together at their training schools, called sumo stables. Many sumo wrestlers nowadays are non-Japanese, with the majority from Mongolia.

A sumo match takes place on a sandy-floored ring less than 4.5m (15 ft.) in diameter. Wrestlers dress much as they did during the Edo Period—their hair in a samurai-style topknot, an ornamental belt/loincloth around their huge girths. Before each bout, the two contestants scatter salt in the ring to purify it from the last bout's loss; they also squat and then raise each leg, stamping it into the ground to crush, symbolically, any evil spirits. They then squat down and face each other, glaring to intimidate their opponent. Once they rush each other, each wrestler's object is to either eject his opponent from the ring or cause him to touch the ground with any part of his body other than his feet. This is accomplished by shoving, slapping, tripping, throwing, and even carrying the opponent, but punching with a closed fist and kicking are not allowed. Altogether there are 48 holds and throws, and sumo fans know all of them.

There are six 15-day sumo tournaments in Japan every year: Three are held in Tokyo (Jan, May, and Sept); the others are held in Osaka (Mar), Nagoya (July), and Fukuoka (Nov). Each wrestler in the tournament faces a new opponent every day; the winner of the tournament is the wrestler who maintains the best overall record. Tournament matches are also widely covered on television.

among the upper classes, and in the 16th century, the tea ceremony was perfected by a merchant named Sen-no-Rikyu. Using the principles of Zen and the spiritual discipline of the samurai, the tea ceremony became a highly stylized ritual, with detailed rules on how tea should be prepared, served, and drunk. The simplicity of movement and tranquility of setting are meant to free the mind from the banality of everyday life and to allow the spirit to enjoy peace. In a way, it is a form of spiritual therapy.

The tea ceremony, *cha-no-yu,* is still practiced in Japan today and is regarded as a form of disciplinary training for mental composure and for etiquette and manners. In Kyoto, I once met a fellow guest in an inexpensive Japanese inn who asked whether she could serve me Japanese tea and a sweet after breakfast. She apologized for her ineptitude, saying she was only a mere apprentice of tea. When I asked how long she'd been studying *cha-no-yu,* she replied 7 years. That may seem like a long time, but the study of the tea ceremony includes related subjects like the craftsmanship of tea vessels and implements, the design and construction of the teahouse, the landscaping of gardens, and literature related to the tea ceremony.

Several of Japan's more famous landscape gardens have teahouses on their grounds where you can sit on *tatami,* drink the frothy green tea (called *maccha*), eat sweets (meant to counteract the bitter taste of the tea), and contemplate the view. Tea pottery changes with the seasons and are often valuable art objects.

IKEBANA Whereas a Westerner is likely to put a bunch of flowers into a vase and be done with it, the Japanese consider the arrangement of flowers an art in itself. Many young girls have at least some training in flower arranging, known as *ikebana.* First popularized among aristocrats during the Heian Period (A.D. 794–1192) and spread to the common people in the 14th to 16th centuries, traditional *ikebana,* in its simplest form, is supposed to represent heaven, man, and earth; it's considered a truly Japanese art without outside influences. As important as the arrangement itself is the vase chosen to display it. Department store galleries sometimes have *ikebana* exhibitions, as do shrines; otherwise, check with the local tourist office.

GARDENS Nothing is left to chance in a Japanese landscape garden: The shapes of hills and trees, the placement of rocks and waterfalls—everything is skillfully arranged in a faithful reproduction of nature. To Westerners, it may seem a bit strange to arrange nature to look like nature; but to Japanese, even nature can be improved upon to make it more pleasing through the best possible use of limited space. Japanese are masters at this, as a visit to any of their famous gardens will testify.

Japanese have been sculpting gardens for more than 1,000 years. At first, gardens were designed for walking and boating, with ponds, artificial islands, and pavilions. As with almost everything else in Japanese life, however, Zen Buddhism exerted an influence, making gardens simpler and attempting to create the illusion of boundless space within a small area. To the Buddhist, a garden was not for merriment but for contemplation—an uncluttered and simple landscape on which to rest the eyes. Japanese gardens often use the principle of "borrowed landscape"—that is, the incorporation of surrounding mountains and landscape into the overall design and impact of the garden.

ETIQUETTE

Much of Japan's system of etiquette and manners stems from its feudal days, when the social hierarchy dictated how a person spoke, sat, bowed, ate, walked, and lived. Failure to comply with the rules would bring severe punishment, even death. Many Japanese have literally lost their heads for committing social blunders.

Today, Japanese still attach much importance to proper behavior, though as a foreigner you can get away with a lot. There are two cardinal sins, however, that you should never commit: Never wear your shoes into a Japanese home, traditional inn, temple, or any room with *tatami,* and never wash with soap inside a communal Japanese bathtub or pull the plug. Except for these two horrors, you will probably be forgiven any other social blunders (such as standing with your arms folded or your hands in your pockets).

That being said, because of increased tourism, some cities have initiated "good manners" projects to educate visitors about Japanese etiquette. Among good manners being stressed are to wait your turn and not jump the queue, to not litter but instead throw your trash in a rubbish bin (trash cans are rare, however, so you might take a cue from the Japanese, who carry plastic sacks to bring all their litter home with them), to honor restaurant reservations (one high-end restaurant in Kyoto told me they have had many no-shows), and to refrain from washing clothes in a public bath (which to me signals it's been done). To see how Kyoto is handling etiquette education, see **https://kyoto.travel/en/akimahen**.

At any rate, if you're invited to a Japanese home, you should know that it's both a rarity and an honor. Most Japanese consider their homes too small and humble for entertaining guests, which is why there are so many restaurants, coffee shops, and bars. If you're invited to a home, don't show up empty-handed. Bring a small gift such as candy, fruit, flowers, alcohol, or perhaps a souvenir from your hometown. And if someone extends you a favor or plays host, be sure to thank him again the next time you see him—even if it's a year later.

BOWING The main form of greeting in Japan is the bow rather than the handshake. Although at first glance it may seem simple enough, the bow—together with its implications—is actually quite complicated. The depth of the bow and the number of seconds devoted to performing it, as well as the total number of bows, depend on who you are, to whom you're bowing, and how he's bowing back. In addition to bowing in greeting, Japanese also bow upon departing and to express gratitude. The proper form for a bow is to bend from the waist with a straight back and to keep your arms at your sides if you're a man or clasped in front of you if you're a woman, but if you're a foreigner, a simple nod of the head is enough. Knowing foreigners shake hands, a Japanese may extend his hand, although he probably won't be able to stop himself from giving a little bow as well. (I've even seen Japanese bow when talking on the telephone.) Although I've occasionally witnessed Japanese businessmen shaking hands among themselves, the practice is still quite rare. Kimono-clad hostesses of a high-end traditional Japanese inn will often kneel on *tatami* and bow to the ground as they send you off on your journey.

VISITING CARD You're a nonentity in Japan if you don't have a visiting card, called a ***meishi.*** Everyone—from housewives to bank presidents—carries *meishi* to give out during introductions. If you're trying to conduct business in Japan, you'll be regarded suspiciously—even as a phony—if you don't have business cards. *Meishi* are very useful business tools for Japanese. Likewise, a *meishi* can be used as an introduction to a third party—a Japanese may give you his *meishi,* scribble something on it, and tell you to present it to his cousin who owns a restaurant in Fukuoka. *Voilà*—the cousin will treat you like a royal guest. As a tourist, you don't have to have business cards, but it certainly doesn't hurt. The card should have your address and occupation on it; you might even consider having your *meishi* made in Japan, with *katakana*

(Japanese syllabic script) written on the reverse side. Needless to say, there's a proper way to present a *meishi.* Turn it so that the other person can read it (that is, upside-down to you), and present it with both hands and a slight bow.

SHOES Nothing is so distasteful to Japanese as the soles of shoes. Therefore, you should take off your shoes before entering a home, a Japanese-style inn, temple, or shrine, and even some museums and restaurants. Usually there are plastic slippers at the entryway for you to slip on, but whenever you encounter *tatami,* you should take off even these slippers—only bare feet or socks are allowed to tread upon *tatami.*

Restrooms present another set of slippers. If you're in a home, Japanese inn, or restaurant where you've removed your shoes, you'll notice another pair of slippers sitting right inside the restroom door. Slip out of the hallway plastic shoes and into the bathroom slippers, and wear these the entire time you're in the restroom. When you're finished, change back into the hallway slippers. If you forget this last changeover, you'll regret it—nothing is as embarrassing as walking into a room wearing toilet slippers and not realizing what you've done until you see the mixed looks of horror and mirth on the faces of Japanese people.

BATHING On my very first trip to Japan, I was certain I would never enter a Japanese bath. I was under the misconception that men and women bathed together, and I couldn't imagine getting into a tub with a group of smiling and bowing Japanese men. I needn't have worried—in almost all circumstances, bathing is gender segregated. There are some exceptions, primarily at outdoor hot-spring spas in the countryside, but the women who go to these are usually grandmothers who couldn't care less. Young Japanese women wouldn't dream of jumping into a tub with a group of male strangers.

Japanese baths are delightful—I'm addicted to them. You'll find them at Japanese-style inns, at *onsen* (hot-spring spas), and at *sento* (neighborhood baths). Sometimes they're elaborate affairs with indoor and outdoor tubs, and sometimes they're nothing more than a tiny tub. Public baths have long been regarded as social centers for Japanese—friends and coworkers will visit hot-spring resorts together; neighbors exchange gossip at the neighborhood bath. Sadly, neighborhood baths have been in great decline over the past decades, as most Japanese now have private baths in their homes. Hot-spring spas, however, remain hugely popular.

In any case, whether large or small, the procedure at all Japanese baths is the same. After completely disrobing in the changing room and putting your clothes in either a locker or a basket, hold a washcloth (provided free or available for sale at the bathhouse) in front of you so that it covers your vital parts and walk into the bathing area. There you'll find plastic or wood basins and stools and faucets along the wall. Sit on the stool in front of a faucet and use the basin (or hand-held faucet if available) to splash water all over you. If there's no hot water from the faucet, it's acceptable to dip your basin into the hot bath, but your washcloth should never touch the tub water. Rinsing yourself thoroughly is not only proper *onsen* manners; it also acclimatizes your body to the bath's hot temperature so you don't suffer a heart attack.

As in a Jacuzzi, everyone uses the same bath water. For that reason, you should never wash yourself in the tub, never put your washcloth into the bath (place it on your head or lay it beside the bath), and never pull the plug when you're done. After your bath is when you scrub your body and wash your hair. I have never seen a group of people wash themselves so thoroughly as the Japanese, from their ears to their toes. All *sento* provide shampoo and body soap, along with interesting products provided free by companies hoping to rope in new customers, but in small public baths you might have to provide your own.

The Japanese are so fond of baths that many take them nightly, especially in winter when a hot bath keeps them toasty warm for hours. At an *onsen,* where hot-spring waters are considered curative, Japanese will bathe both at night and again in the morning, often making several trips between the faucet and the tubs and being careful not to rinse off the curative waters when they're done. With time, you'll probably become addicted, too. ***Note:*** Because tattoos in Japan have long been associated with *yakuza* (Japanese mafia), most public baths do not admit people with tattoos. However, if your tattoo is discreet and you're at, say, a small Japanese inn, you probably won't have any problems.

THE JAPANESE LANGUAGE

No one knows the exact origins of the Japanese language, but we do know it existed only in spoken form until the 6th century. That's when the Japanese borrowed the Chinese pictorial characters, called *kanji,* and used them to develop their own form of written language. Later, two phonetic alphabet systems, *hiragana* and *katakana,* were added to kanji to form the existing Japanese writing system. Thus, Chinese and Japanese use some of the same pictographs, but otherwise there's no similarity between the languages.

As for the spoken language, there are many levels of speech and forms of expression relating to a person's social status and sex. Even nonverbal communication is a vital part of understanding Japanese, because what isn't said is often more important than what is. It's little wonder that St. Francis Xavier, a Jesuit missionary who came to Japan in the 16th century, wrote that Japanese was an invention of the devil designed to thwart the spread of Christianity. And yet, astoundingly, adult literacy in Japan is estimated to be 99%.

It's worth noting that Japanese nouns do not have plural forms; thus, for example, *ryokan,* a Japanese-style inn, can be both singular and plural, as can kimono. Plural sense is indicated by context. In addition, the Japanese custom is to list the family name first followed by the given name, though nowadays Japanese working with international companies increasingly follow the Western custom of listing the family name last. In this guide, I've listed family names first for Japanese born before the Meiji Period (1868) and given names first for people born after that.

JAPANESE english

English-language words are often misspelled, sometimes with wonderful results. Menus can be entertaining, listing dishes like "lice" (instead of rice) or "sandwitches." English is also fashionable in Japanese advertising, appearing on shop signs, posters, shopping bags, and T-shirts. Sometimes, however, you can only guess at the original intent. What, for example, can possibly be the meaning behind TODAY BIRDS, TOMORROW MEN, which appeared below a picture of birds on a shopping bag? I have treasured ashtrays that read THE YOUNG BOY GRASPED HER HEART FIRMLY and LET'S TRIP IN HOKKAIDO. In Okayama, I saw a shop whose name was a stern admonition to customers to GROW UP, while in Gifu you can only surmise at the pleasures to be had at HOTEL JOYBOX. A staff member of the Hokkaido Tourist Association whose business card identified him working for the PROPAGANDA SECTION was probably more truthful than most. And imagine my consternation upon stepping onto a bathroom scale that called itself the BEAUTY-CHECKER. But the best sign I've seen was at Narita Airport many years ago, where each check-in counter displayed a notice about checking in FOR YOUR FRIGHT. I explained the cause of my amusement to the person behind the counter, and when I came back through 2 weeks later, I was almost disappointed to find that all signs had been corrected. That's Japanese efficiency.

Finally, you may find yourself confused because of suffixes attached to Japanese place names. For example, *dori* can mean street, avenue, or road; sometimes it's attached to a street name with a hyphen, while at other times it stands alone. Thus, you may see Chuo-dori, Chuo Dori, or even Chuo-dori Avenue on English-language maps and street signs, but they're all the same street. Likewise, *dera* means "temple" and is often included at the end of the name, as in Kiyomizudera, which may be translated into English as Kiyomizu Temple. *Jo* means "castle," while *ji* at the end of a word means "shrine."

EATING & DRINKING IN JAPAN

Whenever I leave Japan, it's the food I miss the most. Sure, there are sushi bars and other Japanese specialty restaurants in many major cities around the world, but they don't offer nearly the variety available in Japan and often they aren't nearly as good. For just as America has more to offer than hamburgers and steaks and England more than fish and chips, Japan has more than just sushi and *teppanyaki.* For both the gourmet and the uninitiated, Japan is a treasure trove of culinary surprises and a foodie's delight.

Japanese Cuisine

There are more than a dozen different and distinct types of Japanese cuisine, plus countless regional specialties. A good deal of what you eat may be completely new to you as well as completely unidentifiable. Don't worry; often even Japanese don't know what they're eating, so varied and so wide is the range of available edibles. The rule is simply to enjoy, and enjoyment begins even before you raise your chopsticks to your mouth.

To the Japanese, **presentation** of food is as important as the food itself, and dishes are designed to appeal to the palate and to the eye. In contrast to the American way of piling as much food as possible onto a single plate, Japanese traditionally use lots of small plates, each arranged artfully with bite-size morsels of food. After you've seen what can be done with maple leaves, flowers, bits of bamboo, and even pebbles to enhance the appearance of food, your relationship with what you eat may change forever. If there's such a thing as designer cuisine, Japan is its home. No wonder traditional Japanese cuisine is on UNESCO's Intangible Cultural Heritage list.

Below are explanations of some of the most common types of Japanese cuisine. Generally, only one type of cuisine is served in a given restaurant—for example, raw seafood is the specialty in a sushi bar, whereas tempura is featured at a tempura counter. There are of course exceptions to this, especially in regards to raw fish, which is served as an appetizer in many restaurants, and set meals, which contain a variety of dishes. Hotel restaurants may also offer a great variety, and some Japanese drinking establishments (called *izakaya* or *nomiya*) offer a wide range of foods from soups to sushi to skewered pieces of chicken known as *yakitori.*

KAISEKI The king of Japanese cuisine, *kaiseki* is the epitome of delicately and exquisitely arranged food, the ultimate in Japanese aesthetic appeal. It's also among the most expensive meals you can eat, though some restaurants do offer more affordable mini-*kaiseki* courses. In addition, the better Japanese inns serve *kaiseki,* a reason for their high cost. *Kaiseki,* which is not a specific dish but rather a complete meal, is expensive because much time and skill are involved in preparing each of the many dishes, with the ingredients cooked to preserve natural flavors. Even the plates are chosen with great care to enhance the color, texture, and shape of each piece of food.

Kaiseki cuisine is based on the four seasons, with the selection of ingredients and their presentation dependent on the time of the year. In fact, so strongly does a *kaiseki* preparation convey the mood of a particular season, the *kaiseki* gourmet can tell what season it is just by looking at a meal. A *kaiseki* meal is usually a lengthy affair with various dishes appearing in set order. Although meals vary greatly depending upon the region and what's fresh, common dishes include some type of sashimi, tempura, cooked seasonal fish, and bite-size pieces of various vegetables. Because *kaiseki* is always a set meal, there's no problem in ordering. Let your budget be your guide.

KUSHIAGE/KUSHIKATSU *Kushiage* foods (also called *kushikatsu*) are breaded and deep-fried on skewers and include chicken, beef, seafood, and lots of seasonal vegetables like snow peas, green pepper, gingko nuts and lotus root. Their morsels are served with a slice of lemon and usually a specialty sauce. Ordering the set meal is easiest, and what you get is often determined by both the chef and the season.

OKONOMIYAKI *Okonomiyaki,* which originated in Osaka after World War II and literally means "as you like it," is often referred to as Japanese pizza or pancake, to which meat or seafood, shredded cabbage, and vegetables are added, topped with Worcestershire sauce. At some places the cook makes it for you, but at other places it's do-it-yourself at your table. *Yakisoba* (fried Chinese noodles with cabbage) is also usually offered at *okonomiyaki* restaurants, which are always very reasonably priced.

RICE As in other Asian countries, rice has been a Japanese staple for about 2,000 years. In fact, rice is so important to the Japanese diet that *gohan* means both "rice" and "meal." There are no problems here—everyone is familiar with rice. The difference, however, is that in Japan it's quite sticky, making it easier to pick up with chopsticks. Traditionally it was eaten plain, though nowadays trendy restaurants sprinkle rice with black sesame seeds, plum powder, or other seasoning. In the old days, not everyone could afford the expensive white kind, which was grown primarily to pay taxes or rent to the feudal lord; peasants had to make do with a mixture of brown rice, millet, and greens. Restaurants offering organic foods often serve *genmai* (unpolished brown rice).

ROBATAYAKI *Robatayaki* refers to restaurants in which seafood and vegetables are cooked over an open charcoal grill. In days of yore, a *robata* (open fireplace) in the middle of an old Japanese house was the center of activity for cooking, eating, socializing, and keeping warm. Today's *robatayaki* restaurants are therefore like nostalgia trips back into Japan's past and are often decorated in rustic farmhouse style with staff dressed in traditional clothing. There's no special menu in a *robatayaki* restaurant; rather, it includes just about everything eaten in Japan, with the difference being that most of the foods are grilled. Favorites of mine include *ginnan* (gingko nuts), asparagus wrapped in bacon, *piman* (a type of green pepper), mushrooms (various kinds), grilled skewers of beef and chicken, and just about any kind of fish. Because ordering is often a la carte, you'll just have to look and point.

SASHIMI & SUSHI Like rice, seafood is a staple of the Japanese diet. Although it may be served in any number of ways from grilled to boiled, a great deal of it is eaten raw. Sashimi is simply raw seafood, usually served as an appetizer and eaten with soy sauce. If you've never tried it, you might start out with *maguro,* or lean tuna, which doesn't taste fishy at all and is so delicate in texture that it almost melts in your mouth. Sushi, which is raw fish with vinegared rice, comes in many varieties. The best known is *nigiri-zushi:* raw fish, seafood, or vegetables placed on top of vinegared rice with just a touch of wasabi. It's also dipped in soy sauce. Use chopsticks or your fingers to eat sushi; remember you're supposed to eat each piece in one bite—quite a mouthful, but about the only way to keep it from falling apart. Another trick is to turn it upside down when you dip it in the sauce, to keep the rice from crumbling.

Also popular is *maki-zushi,* which consists of seafood, vegetables, or pickles rolled with rice inside a sheet of *nori* seaweed. *Inari-zushi* is vinegared rice and chopped vegetables inside a pouch of fried tofu bean curd.

Typical sushi includes *maguro* (tuna), *hirame* (flounder), *tai* (sea bream), *ika* (squid), *tako* (octopus), *ebi* (shrimp), *anago* (sea eel), and *tamago* (omelet).

Ordering is easy—you usually sit at a counter where you can watch the sushi chefs at work and see all the food in a refrigerated glass case in front of you, with the typical meal starting with sashimi and followed by sushi. If you don't want to order separately, there are always various *seto* (set meals or courses). Pickled ginger is part of any sushi meal.

One way to enjoy sushi without spending a fortune is at a *kaiten* sushi shop, in which plates of sushi circulate on a conveyor belt on the counter—customers reach for the dishes they want and pay for the number of dishes they take.

SHABU-SHABU & SUKIYAKI Until the Meji Restoration beginning in 1868, which brought foreigners to Japan, Japanese could think of nothing as disgusting as eating the flesh of animals (fish was okay). Meat was considered unclean by Buddhists, and consuming it was banned by the emperor way back in the 7th century. It wasn't until Emperor Meiji himself announced his intention to eat meat that Japanese accepted the idea. Today, Japanese are quite skilled in preparing beef dishes.

Sukiyaki is among Japan's best-known dishes. Like fondue, it's cooked at the table and consists of thinly sliced beef cooked in a broth of soy sauce, stock, and sake along with scallions, spinach, mushrooms, tofu, bamboo shoots, and other vegetables. All diners serve themselves from the simmering pot and then dip their morsels into their own bowl of raw egg. You can skip the raw egg if you want (most Westerners do), but it adds to the taste and also cools the food down enough so that it doesn't burn.

Shabu-shabu is also prepared at your table and consists of thinly sliced beef cooked in a broth with vegetables in a kind of Japanese fondue. (It's named for the swishing sound the beef supposedly makes when cooking.) For dipping, there's typically either sesame sauce with diced green onions or a more bitter fish stock sauce.

The main difference between the two dishes is the broth: Whereas in sukiyaki it consists of stock flavored with soy sauce and sake and is slightly sweet, in *shabu-shabu* it's relatively clear and has little taste of its own. The pots used are also different. Restaurants serving sukiyaki usually serve *shabu-shabu* as well, and they're often happy to show you the right way to prepare and eat it.

SHOJIN RYORI *Shojin Ryori* is the ultimate vegetarian meal, created centuries ago to serve the needs of Zen Buddhist priests and pilgrims. Dishes may include *yudofu* (simmered tofu) and an array of local vegetables. Kyoto is the best place to experience this type of cuisine.

SOBA, UDON & RAMEN Japanese love eating noodles, but I suspect at least part of the fascination stems from the way they eat them—they slurp, sucking in the noodles with gravity-defying speed. What's more, slurping noodles is considered proper etiquette; it also helps cool the noodles when they're piping hot. In any case, noodles are among the least expensive dishes in Japan.

There are many different kinds of noodles, with seemingly every region proud of its own special style or kind—some are eaten plain, some in combination with other foods such as shrimp tempura, some served hot, some served cold. *Soba,* made from unbleached buckwheat flour and enjoyed for its nutty flavor and high nutritional value, is eaten hot *(kake-soba)* or cold *(zaru-soba). Udon* is a thick white wheat noodle originally from Osaka, usually served hot. *Somen* is a fine white noodle eaten cold in the summer and dunked in a cold sauce. Establishments serving noodles range from stand-up eateries to more refined noodle restaurants with *tatami* seating.

Although technically considered Chinese fast food, **ramen** in recent years has been elevated from a cheap, late-night snack after bouts of drinking to celebrity status, with everyone weighing in on their own favorite restaurant. Many regions have their own style; chefs cultivate their own secret recipes. But what they have in common is noodles served in a broth that probably simmered for hours. Ramen shops can be found everywhere. In addition to ramen, you can also usually order *yakisoba* (fried noodles) or—my favorite—*gyoza* (fried pork dumplings). What these places lack in atmosphere is made up for in price; they're some of the cheapest places in Japan for a meal.

TEMPURA Today a well-known Japanese food, tempura was actually introduced by the Portuguese in the 16th century. Tempura is fish and vegetables coated in a batter of egg, water, and wheat flour, delicately deep-fried, and served piping hot. To eat it, dip it in a sauce of soy, fish stock, *daikon* (radish), and grated ginger; in some restaurants, only some salt, powdered green tea, or a lemon wedge is provided as an accompaniment. Various tempura specialties may include *nasu* (eggplant), *shiitake* (mushroom), *satsumaimo* (sweet potato), *shishito* (small green pepper), *renkon* (sliced lotus root), *ebi* (shrimp), *ika* (squid), *shisho* (lemon-mint leaf), and various fish. Again, the easiest thing to do is to order the *teishoku* (set meal).

TEPPANYAKI A *teppanyaki* restaurant is a Japanese steakhouse. The chef slices, dices, and cooks your meal of tenderloin or sirloin steak and vegetables on a smooth, hot grill right in front of you—though with much less fanfare than most Japanese restaurants in the U.S. *Teppanyaki* restaurants tend to be expensive, simply because of the price of beef in Japan, with Kobe beef the most prized.

TOFU Originally from China, tofu, or bean curd, is made from soy milk. It has little flavor of its own and is served cold in summer and *yudofu* (boiled) in winter. A by-product of tofu is *yuba,* thin sheets rich in protein.

TONKATSU *Tonkatsu* is Japanese comfort food, made by dredging pork in wheat flour, moistening it with egg and water, dipping it in bread crumbs, and deep-frying it in vegetable oil. Because *tonkatsu* restaurants are inexpensive, they're popular with office workers and families. It's easiest to order the *teishoku,* which usually features either the *hirekatsu* (pork filet) or the *rosukatsu* (pork loin). In any case, *tonkatsu* is served on a bed of shredded cabbage, and one or two different sauces will be at your table, a Worcestershire sauce and perhaps a specialty sauce. If you order the *teishoku,* it will come with rice, miso soup, pickled vegetables, and often free refills. Pork cutlet served on a bowl of rice is *katsudon.*

UNAGI I'll bet that if you eat *unagi* without knowing what it is, you'll find it very tasty—and you'll probably be very surprised to find out you've just eaten eel. Popular as a health food because of its rich protein and high vitamin A content, eel is supposed to help you fight fatigue during hot summer months but is eaten year-round. *Kabayaki* (broiled eel) is prepared by grilling filet strips over a charcoal fire; the eel is repeatedly dipped in a sweetened barbecue soy sauce while cooking. A favorite way to eat broiled eel is on top of rice, in which case it's called *unaju* or *unagi donburi.*

YAKITORI *Yakitori* is chunks of chicken or chicken parts basted in a sweet soy sauce and grilled over a charcoal fire on thin skewers. The cheapest way to dine on yakitori is to order a set course, which will often include various parts of the chicken including the skin, heart, and liver. If this isn't to your taste, you may wish to order a la carte, which is more expensive but gets you exactly what you want. In addition to chicken, other skewered, charcoaled delicacies are usually offered (called *kushi-yaki*). If you're ordering by the stick, you might want to try *sasami* (chicken breast), *tsukune* (chicken meatballs), *piman* (green peppers), *negima* (chicken and leeks), *shiitake* (mushrooms), or *ginnan* (gingko nuts). Places that specialize in yakitori (*yakitori-ya,* often identifiable by a red paper lantern outside the front door) are technically not restaurants but drinking establishments; they usually don't open until 5 or 6pm.

OTHER CUISINES During your travels you might also run into these types of Japanese cuisine: *Kamameshi* is a rice casserole served in individual-size cast-iron pots with different toppings that might include seafood, meat, or vegetables. *Donburi* is also a rice dish, topped with tempura, eggs, and meat such as chicken or pork. *Nabe,* a stew cooked in an earthenware pot at your table, consists of chicken, sliced beef, pork, or seafood; noodles; and vegetables. *Oden* is a broth with fish cakes, tofu, eggs, and vegetables, served with hot mustard. If a restaurant advertises that it specializes in *Kyodo-Ryori,* it serves local specialties for which the region is famous and is often very rustic in decor. See individual city lists for more on regional cuisine.

Drinks

All Japanese restaurants serve complimentary green tea with meals. You might also want to order sake (also known as *nihonshu*), an alcoholic beverage made from rice and served hot or cold. Produced since about the 3rd century, sake varies by region, production method, alcoholic content, color, aroma, and taste. There are more than 1,800 sake brewers in Japan producing about 10,000 varieties. Miyabi is a prized classic sake; other brands are Gekkeikan, Koshinokanbai, Hakutsuru (meaning White Crane), and Ozeki.

Japanese beer is also very popular. The biggest sellers are Kirin, Sapporo, Asahi, and Suntory, with each brand offering a bewildering variety of brews. Microbreweries are also found everywhere in Japan. Businessmen are fond of whiskey, which they usually drink with ice and water (Suntory and Nikka are the two biggest brands). *Shochu,* a clear, distilled spirit usually made from rice but sometimes from wheat, sweet potatoes, barley, or sugar cane, can be consumed straight but is often combined with soda water in a drink called *chuhai.* My personal favorite is *ume-shu,* a plum-flavored *shochu.* But watch out—the stuff can be deadly. Wine, usually available only at restaurants serving Western food, has become popular in recent years, with both domestic and imported brands available. Although cocktail lounges have become trendy in the big cities, most Japanese stick with beer, wine, sake, *shochu,* or whiskey.

Tips on Dining in Japan

UPON ARRIVAL As soon as you're seated in a Japanese restaurant (that is, a restaurant serving Japanese food), you'll be given a wet towel, which will be steaming hot in winter or pleasantly cool in summer. Called an *oshibori,* it's for wiping your hands. In all but the fancy restaurants, men can get away with wiping their faces as well, but women are not supposed to (although some ignore this if it's hot and humid outside). Sadly, many Japanese restaurants now resort to a paper towel wrapped in plastic, which isn't nearly the same. *Oshibori* are usually not provided in Western restaurants in Japan.

ORDERING The biggest problem facing the hungry foreigner in Japan is ordering a meal in a restaurant without an English-language menu. This book alleviates the problem to some extent by recommending sample dishes and giving price ranges; I've also noted which restaurants offer English-language menus.

One aid to simplified ordering is the use of plastic food models in glass display cases either outside or just inside the front door of many restaurants, especially those in tourist areas and department stores. Sushi, tempura, daily specials, spaghetti—they're all there in mouthwatering plastic replicas along with corresponding prices. Simply decide what you want and point it out to staff.

Not all restaurants, however, have plastic display cases, especially the more exclusive or traditional ones. In fact, you'd be missing a lot of Japan's best cuisine if you restrict yourself to eating only at places with displays. If there's no display, English menu, or photographs in the Japanese menu, a simple solution is to order the *teishoku,* or daily special meal (also called "seto," "set course" or simply "course," especially in restaurants serving Western food); these fixed-price meals consist of a main dish and several side dishes, including soup, rice, and Japanese pickles. Although most restaurants have set courses for dinner as well, lunch is the usual time for the *teishoku,* generally from 11 or 11:30am to 1:30 or 2pm.

In any case, once you've decided what you want to eat, flag down a waiter or waitress; they will not hover around your table waiting for you to order but come only when summoned. In most restaurants there are no assigned servers to certain tables; rather, servers are multitaskers, so don't be shy about stopping any who pass by. Finally, unless you're dining in an *izakaya* (a Japanese pub serving food), meals in restaurants are not shared, so you'll want to order at least one dish per person.

EATING & DRINKING ETIQUETTE The first thing you'll be confronted with in a Japanese restaurant is chopsticks (in restaurants serving Western food, knives and forks are provided instead). Chopstick etiquette says that if you're taking something from a communal bowl or tray, you're supposed to turn your chopsticks upside down and use the part that hasn't been in your mouth; after transferring the food to your plate, you turn the chopsticks back to their proper position. The exception is *shabu-shabu* and *sukiyaki*.

You don't use a spoon with Japanese soup. Rather, you'll pick up the bowl and drink from it, using your chopsticks to fish out larger pieces of food. You should also pick up a bowl of rice to eat it. It's considered good taste to slurp with gusto, especially if you're eating hot noodles. Noodle shops in Japan are always well orchestrated with slurps and smacks.

> **Eating on the Move**
>
> It's considered bad manners to walk down the street eating or drinking (except at a festival). You'll notice that if a Japanese buys a drink from a vending machine, he'll stand there, gulp it down, and throw away the container before going on. To the chagrin of their elders, young Japanese sometimes ignore this rule.

As for drinking etiquette, women should hold their glass or cup with both hands, but men do not. The main thing to remember if you're with a group is that you never pour your own glass (bottles of beer are so large that people often share one). The rule is that in turn, one person pours for everyone else in the group, so be sure to hold up your glass when someone is pouring for you. As the night progresses Japanese get sloppy about this rule. If someone wants to pour you a drink and your glass is full, the proper thing to do is to take a few gulps so that he or she can fill your glass. Because each person is continually filling everyone else's glass, you never know exactly how much you've had to drink, which (depending on how you look at it) is either very good or very bad. If you really don't want more to drink, leave your glass full and refuse refills.

PAYING THE BILL If you go out with a group of friends (not as a visiting guest of honor and not with business associates), it's customary to split the dinner bill equally, even if you all ordered different things. Even foreigners living in Japan adopt the practice of splitting the bill; it certainly makes figuring everyone's share easier, especially since there's no tipping in Japan. But it can be hard on frugal diners on a budget. If you're with friends who do wish to pay for only what they ate, tell the cashier you want to pay *"betsu, betsu."*

EXTRA CHARGES & TAXES Japan's consumption tax imposed on goods and services, including restaurant meals, is 8% (it's scheduled to rise to 10% in Oct 2019). Some restaurants include the tax in their menu prices, while others do not (it's usually stated on the menu whether taxes are included). In finer restaurants and nightlife establishments, a 10% to 15% service charge may also be levied (there is no tipping in Japan). You should also be aware of the "table charge" imposed on customers by some bars (especially *nomiya* or izakaya), many cocktail lounges, and, only rarely, restaurants. Included in the table charge is usually a small appetizer—maybe nuts, chips, or a vegetable; for this reason, some locales call it an *otsumami* (also called *otoshi*), or snack charge. The charge is usually between ¥300 and ¥500 per person.

HOURS In larger cities, most restaurants are open from about 11am to 9pm and later. Many close for a few hours in the afternoon (2–5pm), though inexpensive ones are open all day. In big cities like Tokyo or Osaka, try to avoid the lunchtime rush from noon to 1pm. In rural areas, restaurants tend to close early, often by 7:30 or 8pm. Traditional Japanese restaurants hang a *noren* (split curtain) over the front door to signify they're open. Keep in mind that the closing time posted for most restaurants is exactly that—everyone is expected to pay his or her bill and leave. A general rule of thumb is that the last order is taken at least a half-hour before closing time, sometimes an hour or more for *kaiseki* restaurants (staff members will usually alert you that they're taking last orders). To be on the safe side, try to arrive at least an hour before closing time so you have time to relax and enjoy your meal.

How to Eat Without Spending a Fortune

During your first few days in Japan—particularly if you're in Tokyo—money will seem to flow from your pockets like water. In fact, money has a tendency to disappear so quickly that many people become convinced they must have lost some of it somehow. Here are some tips for getting the most for your yen.

BREAKFAST Buffet breakfasts are popular at Japanese hotels and can be an inexpensive way to eat your fill. Otherwise, coffee shops offer what's called "morning service" until 10 or 11am; it generally consists of a cup of coffee, a small salad, a boiled egg, and thick toast. There are also many coffee-shop chains, including Doutour, Pronto, and the ever-expanding Starbucks (1,342 in Japan at last count). Except at most hotel breakfast buffets, there's no such thing as the bottomless cup in Japan.

SET LUNCHES Eat your biggest meal at lunch. Many restaurants serving Japanese food offer a daily set lunch, or *teishoku,* at a fraction of what the set dinners might be, from about 11am to around 2pm. A Japanese *teishoku* will include the main course (such as tempura, grilled fish, or the specialty of the house), soup, pickled vegetables, rice, and tea, while the set menu in a Western-style restaurant (often called a "seto" or *coursu*) usually consists of a main dish, salad, bread, and coffee.

CHEAP EATS Inexpensive restaurants can be found in department stores (often one whole upper floor will be devoted to restaurants, most with plastic-food displays), underground shopping arcades, nightlife districts, and in and around train and subway stations. Hotel restaurants can also be good bargains for inexpensive set lunches or buffets (often called *viking* in Japanese). Plus, buffets always give price breaks for children.

Some of the cheapest establishments for a night out on the town are *yakitori-ya,* izakaya, noodle and ramen shops, coffee shops (which often offer inexpensive pastries and sandwiches), and conveyor-belt sushi restaurants. Restaurants serving *gyudon* (beef bowl) are also cheap, with **Yoshinoya** (www.yoshinoya.com/en/) the largest chain, while **Curry House CoCo ICHIBANYA** (www.ichibanya.co.jp/english/) serves Japanese-style curry rice, including vegetarian and Halal options. Japan also has American fast-food chains, such as McDonald's and KFC, as well as Japanese chains—Freshness Burger, MOS Burger, and First Kitchen, among them. Ethnic restaurants, particularly those serving Indian, Korean, Chinese, Italian, and other cuisines, are plentiful and usually inexpensive.

Street-side stalls, called *yatai,* are also good sources of inexpensive meals. These restaurants-on-wheels sell a variety of foods, including *oden* (fish cakes), *yakitori* (skewered barbecued chicken), and *yakisoba* (fried noodles), as well as sake and beer. They appear largely at night, lighted by a single lantern or a string of lights, and most have a counter with stools as well, protected in winter by a wall of tarp. Sadly, traditional pushcarts are being replaced by motorized vans, which are not nearly as romantic and do not offer seating. You can still find yatai, however, at festivals.

PREPARED FOODS You'll save even more money by avoiding restaurants altogether and buying prepared foods. Some are even complete meals, perfect for picnics in a park or right in your hotel room. Perhaps the best known is the *bento,* or box lunch, commonly sold at train stations, in food sections of department stores, and at counter windows of tiny shops throughout Japan. In fact, the bento served by vendors on some Shinkansen trains and at train stations are an inexpensive way to sample regional cuisine since they often include food typical of the region you're passing through. The basic bento contains a piece of meat (generally fish or chicken), various side dishes, rice, and pickled vegetables. Sushi boxed lunches are also readily available.

My favorite place to shop for prepared foods is department stores. Located in basements, these enormous food and produce sections harken back to Japanese markets of yore, with vendors yelling out their wares and crowds of housewives deciding on the evening's dinner. Different counters specialize in different items—tempura, yakitori, Japanese pickles, cooked fish, sushi (sometimes made by robots!), salads, vegetables, and desserts. Practically the entire spectrum of Japanese cuisine is available, as are counters selling bento box meals. There's nothing like milling with Japanese housewives to make you feel like one of the locals. Though not as colorful, 24-hour convenience and grocery stores also sell packaged foods like sandwiches, cooked foods, and bento.

TIPS ON ACCOMMODATIONS

Accommodations available in Japan range from Japanese-style inns *(ryokan)* to large Western-style hotels, in all price categories. Although you can theoretically travel throughout Japan without making reservations beforehand, it's essential to book in advance if you're visiting during peak travel seasons and is highly recommended at other times (see "When to Go," p. 38, for peak travel times). If you arrive in a town without reservations, most local tourist offices—generally located in or near the main train station—will find accommodations for you at no extra charge. ***Note:*** Most lodgings, especially in popular destinations, raise their rates in peak season and on weekends.

All accommodations levy an 8% consumption tax (10% starting in Oct 2019). Upper-end and some moderately priced hotels also add a 10% to 15% service charge, while expensive *ryokan* will add a 10% to 20% service charge. No service charge is levied at business hotels and inexpensive lodgings for the simple reason that no services are provided. In hot-spring resort areas, an *onsen* (spa) tax of ¥150 is added per night. Tokyo and Kyoto also levy their own local hotel tax (see chapters 4 and 8). Unless otherwise stated, prices in this guide include all consumption taxes and service charges (but not *onsen* or local hotel tax) and range from the cheapest room in low season to the highest-priced deluxe room in peak season.

For bookings, I recommend checking individual hotel websites first to see whether any special rates or packages are available, and then comparing them to Japan's largest travel booking website **www.japanican.com** or other online sites like **www.booking.com**.

Japanese-Style Inns

Although an overnight stay in a *ryokan* can be astoundingly expensive, it's worth the splurge at least once during your stay. Nothing quite conveys the simplicity and beauty—indeed the very atmosphere—of old Japan more than these inns with their gleaming polished wood, *tatami* floors, rice-paper sliding doors, and meticulously pruned gardens. Personalized service by kimono-clad hostesses and exquisitely prepared *kaiseki* meals are the trademarks of such inns, some of which are of ancient vintage. Indeed, staying in one is like taking a trip back in time.

If you want to experience a Japanese-style inn but can't afford the prices of a full-service *ryokan,* a few alternatives are described below. Although they don't offer the same personalized service, beautiful setting, or memorable cuisine, they do offer the chance to sleep on a futon in a simple *tatami* room and, in some cases, eat Japanese meals.

RYOKAN *Ryokan* developed during the Edo Period, when *daimyo* (feudal lords) were required to travel to and from Edo (present-day Tokyo) every 1 or 2 years. The *daimyo* always traveled with a full entourage including members of their family, retainers, and servants. The best *ryokan,* of course, were reserved for the *daimyo* and members of the imperial family. Some of these exist today, passed down from generation to generation.

Traditionally, *ryokan* are small, only one or two stories high, contain about 10 to 30 rooms, and are made of wood with a tile roof. Most guests arrive at their *ryokan* at around 3 or 4pm. The entrance is often through a gate and small courtyard garden; upon entering, you're met by the gate attendant or a bowing woman in a kimono. Take off your shoes, slide on the proffered plastic slippers, and follow your hostess down the long wooden corridors until you reach the sliding door of your room. After taking off your slippers, step into your *tatami* room, almost void of furniture except for a low table in the middle of the room, floor cushions, an antique scroll hanging in a *tokonoma* (alcove), and a simple flower arrangement. Best of all is the view past rice-paper sliding screens of a Japanese landscaped garden with bonsai, stone lanterns, and a meandering pond filled with carp. Notice there's no bed in the room.

Almost immediately, your hostess serves you welcoming hot tea and a sweet at your low table so you can sit there for a while, recuperate from your travels, and appreciate the view, the peace, and the solitude. Next comes your hot bath, either in your own room or in the communal bath. Because many *ryokan* are clustered around *onsen,* many offer the additional luxury of bathing in thermal baths, including outdoor baths. (For bathing, be sure to follow the procedure outlined above under "Etiquette"—soaping and rinsing *before* getting into the tub.) After bathing and soaking away all travel fatigue, aches, and pains, change into your *yukata,* a cotton kimono provided by the *ryokan.* You can wear your *yukata* throughout the *ryokan,* even to its restaurant if there is one (in Western-style hotels, however, never wear a *yukata* outside your room unless you're going to its public bath or it's located in a resort *onsen* setting; take your cue from other guests).

How to Wear Your Yukata

The proper way to wear a *yukata* is to first fold the right side over your body and then wrap over it with the left side on the outside; the opposite is done only when a person has died.

When you return to your room from your bath, you'll find the maid ready to serve your *kaiseki* dinner, an elaborate spread that is often the highlight of a *ryokan* stay. It generally consists of locally grown vegetables, sashimi (raw fish), grilled or baked fish, tempura, and various regional specialties, all spread out on many tiny plates; the seasonal menu is determined by the chef. Admire how each dish is in itself a delicate piece of artwork; it all looks too wonderful to eat, but finally hunger takes over. If you want, you can order sake or beer to accompany your meal (you'll pay extra for drinks).

After your meal, your maid will return to clear away the dishes and to lay out your futon, a two-layered mattress with quilts, on the *tatami* floor. The next morning, the maid will wake you, put away the futon, and serve a breakfast of fish, pickled vegetables, soup, dried seaweed, rice, and other dishes. Feeling rested, well-fed, and pampered, you're then ready to pack your bags and pay your bill. Your hostess sees you off at the front gate, smiling and bowing as you set off for the rest of your travels.

Such is life at a good (read: expensive) *ryokan.* Sadly, the number of upper-class *ryokan* diminishes each year. Unable to compete with more profitable high-rise hotels, many *ryokan* in Japan have closed down, especially in large cities; very few remain in cities like Tokyo and Osaka. If you want to stay in a Japanese inn, it's best to do so in Kyoto, smaller towns like Takayama, or at a hot-spring spa like Hakone.

In addition, although ideally a *ryokan* is an old wooden structure that once served traveling *daimyo* or was perhaps the home of a wealthy merchant, many today—especially those in hot-spring resort areas—are actually modern concrete affairs with as many as 100 or more rooms, and where meals are served in communal dining rooms. What they lack in intimacy and personal service, however, is made up for by cheaper prices and amenities like modern bathing facilities and perhaps outdoor recreational facilities.

Although I heartily recommend you try spending at least 1 night in a *ryokan,* there are a number of disadvantages to this style of accommodations. The most obvious problem is that you may find it uncomfortable sitting on the floor. And because the futon is put away during the day, there's no place to lie down for an afternoon nap or rest, except on the hard, *tatami*-covered floor. In addition, some of the older *ryokan,* though quaint, can be cold in the winter and—though increasingly rare—may have only Japanese-style toilets (see "Toilets," on p. 342). As for breakfast, you might find it difficult to swallow raw egg, rice, and seaweed in the morning. Some *ryokan,* however, offer a Western-style breakfast if you order it the night before, but more often than not the fried or scrambled eggs will arrive cold, leading you to suspect that they were cooked right after you ordered them. Resort *ryokan* with dining halls almost always offer breakfast buffets, however, with both Western and Japanese dishes.

Roller Bag Etiquette

I love my roller bag, but under no circumstances should you roll a bag on *tatami* or on old wooden floors of Japanese inns.

A traditional *ryokan* is also quite rigid in its schedule. You're expected to arrive sometime between 3 and 5pm, take your bath, and then eat at around 6 or 7pm. Breakfast is served early, usually by 8am, and checkout is by 10am. That means you can't sleep in, and because the maid is continually coming in and out, you have a lot less privacy than you would in a hotel.

RATES & RESERVATIONS Rates in a *ryokan* are always per person rather than per room and include breakfast, dinner, and often service and tax. Thus, while rates may seem high, they're actually competitively priced compared to what you'd pay for a hotel room and comparable meals in a restaurant. Although rates can vary from ¥10,000 to an astonishing ¥150,000 per person, the average cost is generally ¥12,000 to ¥25,000. Even within a single *ryokan* the rates can vary greatly, depending on the room you choose, the dinner courses you select, and the number of people in your room. If you're paying the highest rate, you can be certain you're getting the best room with the best view and maybe even a more elaborate meal than lower-paying guests. All the rates for *ryokan* in this book are based on double occupancy; if there are more than two of you in one room, you can generally count on a slightly lower per-person rate; small children who sleep in the same bed as their parents often receive a discount as well. Although most Japanese would never dream of checking into an exclusive *ryokan* solo, lone travelers may be able to secure a room if it's not peak season.

You should always make a **reservation** if you want to stay in a first-class *ryokan* (and even in most medium-priced ones unless it offers buffet meals), because the chef has to shop for and prepare your meals. For more information on *ryokan,* including destinations not covered in this guide, check the websites of the **Japan Ryokan & Hotel Association** (www.ryokan.or.jp), which lists some 1,200 inns and hotels, and **Japanese Guest Houses** (www.japaneseguesthouses.com), with more than 400 member high-end and moderately priced Japanese inns.

MINSHUKU Technically, a *minshuku* is inexpensive Japanese-style lodging in a private home—the Japanese version of a bed-and-breakfast. Usually located in tourist areas like hot springs or ski resorts, rural settings, or small towns, *minshuku* can range from thatched farmhouses and rickety old wooden buildings to modern concrete structures. Because *minshuku* are family-run affairs, there's no personal service, which means you may be expected to lay out your own futon at night, stow it away in the morning, and tidy up your room. Most also do not supply a towel or *yukata,* nor do they generally have rooms with a private bathroom. There is, however, a public bathroom, and meals, usually included in the rates, are served in a communal dining room. Many *minshuku* owners have day jobs, so it's important for guests to be punctual for meals and checkout. Sadly, because of the hands-on time involved, some minshuku owners are finding it easier to convert to a guesthouse, which is cheaper but provides less one-on-one interaction (see below).

Officially, what differentiates a *ryokan* from a *minshuku* is the level of service and corresponding price, but the differences in each category are sometimes large. I've stayed in cheap *ryokan* providing almost no service and in *minshuku* too large to be considered private homes. The average per-person cost for 1 night in a *minshuku,* including two meals, is generally ¥7,000 to ¥10,000 with two meals; most do not accept credit cards. Reservations for *minshuku* should be made directly with the establishment.

Western-Style Accommodations

Western-style lodgings range from luxurious first-class hotels to inexpensive ones catering primarily to Japanese business travelers.

HOTELS Both first-class and mid-priced hotels in Japan are known for excellent service and cleanliness. Japan's first-class hotels can compete with the best in the world, offering exceptional service and wide-ranging facilities, including health clubs and spas, top-class restaurants, and shopping arcades. Unfortunately, health clubs and swimming pools usually cost extra—anywhere from ¥1,050 to an outrageous ¥5,000 per single use. In addition, outdoor pools are open only from about mid-July through August (the school holiday season); many of these also charge a fee.

Almost all hotels in Japan offer a spectrum of rooms at various prices, with room size the overwhelming factor in pricing, though other factors can include bed size, which floor you're on (higher floors are more expensive), and in-room amenities. Rooms with views—whether of the sea or a castle or even of cityscapes—are usually pricier.

Rooms come with such standard features as a minibar or empty fridge you stock yourself, TV, free Wi-Fi, *yukata* or pajamas, a hot-water pot and tea (many now offer also coffee, although you may have to pay extra for it), a hair dryer, and a private bathroom with a tub/shower combination. (Because Japanese are used to soaping down and rinsing off before bathing, it is rare to find tubs without showers; similarly, showers without tubs are also rare in this nation of bathers.) Virtually all hotels also have "Washlet" toilets, combination toilets and spray bidets with a controllable range of speeds and temperatures.

Be sure to give your approximate time of arrival, especially if it's after 6pm, or they might give your room away. Check-in ranges from about 1 or 2pm in first-class hotels to 3 or 4pm for business hotels. Checkout is generally 10am for business hotels and 11am or noon for upper-range hotels. In any case, it's perfectly acceptable to leave luggage with the front desk or bell captain if you arrive early or want to sightsee after checking out.

BUSINESS HOTELS Catering traditionally to Japanese business travelers, a "business hotel" is a no-frills establishment with tiny, sparsely furnished rooms, most of them singles but usually with some twin and maybe double rooms also available (some also offer semi-double-size beds, wider than a single but narrower than a double, for one or two persons). Primarily just places to crash for the night, these rooms usually have everything you need, but in miniature form—minuscule bathroom, tiny bathtub/shower, small bed (or beds), TV, pajamas, free Wi-Fi, empty fridge, and barely enough space to unpack your bags. There are no bellhops, no room service, and sometimes not even a lobby or coffee shop, although usually there are vending machines selling beer, soda, cigarettes, and snacks. The advantages of staying in business hotels are price (starting as low as ¥7,000 for a single) and location—usually near major train and subway stations. Check-in is generally not until 3 or 4pm, and checkout is usually at 10am; you can leave your bags at the front desk.

As for business-hotel chains, I'm partial to **Toyoko Inn** (www.toyoko-inn.com), which boasts locations around Japan and almost always employs

A Double or a Twin?

In Japan, a **twin room** refers to a room with twin beds, and a **double room** refers to one with a double bed or larger (many upper-range hotels also have king- or queen-size beds); most hotels charge more for a twin room, but some charge more for doubles. Because Japanese couples generally prefer twin beds, doubles are often in short supply, especially in business hotels. A **Hollywood twin** means two twin beds pushed together side by side. ***Note:*** For the sake of convenience, the "double" rates for hotels listed in this book refer to two people in one room and include twin, double, and larger beds.

female managers. Other budget and medium-priced chains are **Tokyu REI Hotels,** many with specially designed Ladies Rooms with female-oriented toiletries and amenities (www.tokyuhotelsjapan.com); the **Washington Hotels** and **Hotel Gracery** brands (http://en.washington-hotels.jp/properties); the **Sunroute Hotel Chain** (www.sunroute.jp); **Mitsui Garden Hotels** (www.gardenhotels.co.jp); fast-growing **APA Hotels & Resorts** (www.apahotel.com); and **Super Hotel** (www.superhoteljapan.com/en), with the lowest rates around.

Other Accommodations Alternatives

SHUKUBO These are lodgings in a Buddhist temple, similar to inexpensive *ryokan,* except they're attached to temples and serve vegetarian food. There's usually an early morning service at 6am, which you're welcome—in some *shukubo,* required—to join. Probably the best place to experience life in a temple is at Mount Koya (see chapter 10) or in Kyoto. Prices at shukubo generally range from about ¥10,000 to ¥20,000 per person, including two meals.

GUESTHOUSES Virtually nonexistent more than a decade ago, low-cost guesthouses and private hostels have spread like wildfire in cities around the country, catering primarily to backpackers and travelers who don't mind close quarters. Although they often have a few tiny private rooms with *tatami* or beds for one or two people, sometimes with private bathrooms, the majority are known primarily for their dormitory rooms, with shared bathrooms down the hall. Many have communal kitchens and lounging areas as well. Some are better than others; I've included those that rise above the rest in some of the more expensive cities.

YOUTH HOSTELS Japan has some 230 youth hostels, most of them privately run and operating in locations ranging from temples to concrete blocks. There's no age limit (although children 3 and younger may not be accepted), and most require a youth hostel membership card—but some let foreigners stay without one at no extra charge or for ¥600 extra per night (after 6 nights, you automatically become a YH member). Or buy an International Hostel Card for ¥2,800. Youth hostels average about ¥3,360 per day without meals and can be reserved in advance.

Hostels generally come with quite a few restrictions, however, such as a 9 or 10pm curfew, a lights-out policy shortly thereafter, an early breakfast time, and closed times through the day, generally from about 10am to 3pm. In addition, rooms are usually dormitory-style with bunk beds or futons, though some have rooms for two or more persons. Because youth hostels are often inconveniently located, I have included only two (in Tokyo and Kyoto), but if you plan on staying almost exclusively in hostels, check **www.jyh.or.jp**.

CAPSULE HOTELS Capsule hotels became popular in the 1980s and were used primarily by Japanese businessmen who had spent an evening out drinking and missed the last train home. They've now become more mainstream, with many catering to both male and female tourists. Costing about

¥3,000 to ¥5,000 per person, units are small—no larger than a coffin—and are usually stacked two deep in rows down a corridor; the only thing separating you from your probably inebriated neighbor is a curtain. A cotton kimono and a locker are provided, and bathrooms and toilets are communal. Because they are so economic, some guesthouses (see above) have also gone the capsule route. Offering aviation-themed rooms, newcomer **First Cabin** (https://first-cabin.jp/en/) lies somewhere between business and capsule hotels and has locations in Tokyo, Kyoto (see p. 224), Osaka, and elsewhere.

AIRBNB Home-sharing became legal in Japan in 2017 (though Airbnb was widespread before then) and requires hosts to register with local authorities. Properties range from older traditional homes to apartments to a small room in a shared flat, with ordinances related to neighborhoods and seasonal availability set by individual principalities.

LOVE HOTELS Finally, a word about Japan's so-called "love hotels." Usually found close to entertainment districts and along major highways, such hotels do not provide sexual services themselves; rather, they offer rooms for rent by the hour to couples. You'll know that you've wandered into a love-hotel district when you notice hourly rates posted near the front door, though gaudy structures shaped like ocean liners or castles are also a dead giveaway. Because many have reasonable overnight rates, I have friends who, finding themselves out too late and too far from home, have checked into love hotels, solo.

WHEN TO GO

Weather-wise, the best times to visit western Honshu are spring (Apr to mid-June) and autumn (Sept–Nov). Most of the area lies in a temperate seasonal wind zone similar to that of the East Coast of the United States, which means there are four distinct seasons. Japanese are very proud of their seasons and place much more emphasis on them than people do in the West. Kimono, dishes and bowls used for *kaiseki,* and even *Noh* plays change with the season. Almost all haiku have seasonal references. The cherry blossom signals the beginning of spring, and most festivals are tied to seasonal rites. Even urban dwellers note the seasons; almost as though on cue, businessmen will change virtually overnight from their winter to summer attire.

Summer, which begins in June, is heralded by the rainy season, which lasts from about mid-June to mid-July. Although it doesn't rain every day, it does rain a lot, sometimes quite heavily, making umbrellas imperative. After the rain stops, it turns unbearably hot and uncomfortably humid throughout the country, with the exception of mountaintop resorts such as Hakone and the Japan Alps. You'll be more comfortable in light cottons, though you should bring a light jacket for unexpected cool evenings or air-conditioned rooms. You should also pack sunscreen and a hat (Japanese women are also fond of parasols).

The period from the end of August to September is **typhoon season,** although the majority of storms stay out at sea and generally vent their fury on land only in thunderstorms.

Autumn, lasting through November, is one of the best times to visit Japan, but it's also one of the most crowded seasons. The days are pleasant and slightly cool, and the changing red and scarlet of leaves contrast brilliantly with the deep blue skies. There are many chrysanthemum shows in Japan at this time, popular maple-viewing spots, and many autumn festivals. Bring a warm jacket.

Winter, lasting from December to March, is marked by snow in much of Japan, especially in the mountain ranges, which attracts Asian tourists who don't see snow in their own countries. Many tourists also flock to hot-spring resorts during this time. The climate is generally dry, and on the Pacific coast the skies are often blue. Tokyo doesn't get much snow, though it can be crisp, cold, and wet. Wherever you are, you'd be wise to bring warm clothing throughout the winter months.

Spring arrives in March and April with a magnificent fanfare of plum and cherry blossoms, an exquisite time when all of Japan is ablaze in whites and pinks. The blossoms themselves last only a few days, symbolizing to Japanese the fragile nature of beauty and of life itself. Other flowers blooming through May or June include azaleas and irises. Numerous festivals throughout Japan celebrate the rebirth of nature.

Tokyo's Average Daytime Temperatures & Rainfall

	JAN	FEB	MAR	APR	MAY	JUNE	JULY	AUG	SEPT	OCT	NOV	DEC
TEMP. (°F)	42	45	50	61	69	71	78	81	76	68	57	48
TEMP. (°C)	5	7	10	16	21	22	26	27	24	20	14	9
DAYS OF RAIN	4.3	6.1	8.9	10	9.6	12.1	10	8.2	10.9	8.9	6.4	3.8

BUSY SEASONS Japanese have a passion for travel, and they generally travel at the same time, leading to jam-packed trains and hotels. The worst times to travel are around New Year's, from the end of December to January 4; Golden Week, from April 29 to May 5; and during the Obon Festival, about a week in mid-August. Avoid traveling on these dates at all costs, since all long-distance trains and most accommodations are booked solid and prices are higher. The weekends before and after these holidays are also likely to be crowded or booked. And because Chinese and South Koreans account for most tourists to Japan, you might also want to check their vacation calendars.

Other busy times are during the school summer vacation, from around July 19 or 20 through August, cherry blossom season, and when leaves change in autumn. In addition, you can expect destinations to be packed during major festivals, so if one of these is high on your list, make plans well in advance.

HOLIDAYS National holidays are January 1 (New Year's Day), second Monday in January (Coming-of-Age Day), February 11 (National Foundation Day), March 20 (Vernal Equinox Day), April 29 (Showa Day, after the late Emperor Showa), May 3 (Constitution Memorial Day), May 4 (Greenery Day), May 5 (Children's Day), third Monday in July (Maritime Day), August 11 (Mountain Day); third Monday in September (Respect-for-the-Aged Day), September 23 (Autumn Equinox Day), second Monday in October (Health Sports Day), November 3 (Culture Day; many municipal museums are free), November 23

(Labor Thanksgiving Day), and December 23, 2018 (Emperor Akihito's Birthday; date in 2019 undecided as we go to press; in 2020, new Emperor's birthday will be celebrated Feb 23).

When a national holiday falls on a Sunday, the following Monday becomes a holiday. Although government offices and some businesses are closed on public holidays, most stores and restaurants remain open. The exception is during the New Year's celebration, January 1 through January 3 or 4, when virtually all restaurants, public and private offices, stores, and even ATMs close; during that time, you'll have to dine in hotels.

All museums close for New Year's for 1 to 4 days, but most major museums remain open for the other holidays. If a public holiday falls on a Monday (when most museums are closed), many museums will remain open but will close instead the following day, Tuesday. Note, however, that privately owned museums, such as art museums or special-interest museums, generally close on public holidays. To avoid disappointment, be sure to phone ahead if you plan to visit a museum on a holiday or the day following it.

Western Honshu Calendar of Events

JANUARY

New Year's Day is the most important national holiday in Japan. Because this is a holiday when Japanese are with their families and virtually all businesses, restaurants, museums, and shops close down, it's not a particularly rewarding time for visitors. Best bets are shrines and temples, where Japanese come in their best kimono or dress to pray for health and happiness. January 1.

Dezomeshiki (New Year's Parade of Firemen), Tokyo Big Sight, Odaiba, Tokyo. Agile firemen dressed in Edo Period costumes prove their worth with acrobatic stunts atop tall bamboo ladders in this parade, with fire trucks, helicopters, and emergency drills adding to the excitement. January 6.

Coming-of-Age Day. This national holiday honors young people who have reached the age of 20, when they can vote, drink alcohol, and assume other responsibilities. On this day, they visit shrines throughout the country to pray for their future, with many women dressed in kimono. In Tokyo, the most popular shrine is Meiji Shrine near Harajuku Station. Second Monday in January.

Toka Ebisu Festival, Imamiya Ebisu Shrine, Osaka. Ebisu is considered the patron saint of business and good fortune, so this is the time when businesspeople pray for a successful year. The highlight of the festival is a parade of women dressed in colorful kimono and carried through the streets in palanquins (covered litters). Stalls sell good-luck charms. January 9 to January 11.

Toh-shiya, Kyoto. This traditional Japanese archery contest is held in the back corridor of Japan's longest wooden structure, Sanjusangendo Hall. Sunday closest to January 15.

Yamayaki (Grass Fire Ceremony), Nara. As evening approaches, Wakakusayama Hill is set ablaze and fireworks are displayed. The celebration marks a time more than 1,000 years ago when a dispute over the boundary of two major temples in Nara was settled peacefully. Fourth Saturday in January.

FEBRUARY

Setsubun Mantoro (Lantern Festival), Kasuga Shrine, Nara. A beautiful sight in which more than 3,000 stone and bronze lanterns are lit from 6:30 to 9pm. February 3 and August 14 and 15.

MARCH

Omizutori (Water-Drawing Festival), Todaiji Temple, Nara. This festival includes a solemn evening rite in which young ascetics brandish large burning torches and draw circles of fire. The biggest event takes place on March 13, when water is drawn and offered to Buddhist deities to the accompaniment of ancient Japanese music. March 1 to March 14.

Hinamatsuri (Doll Festival), observed throughout Japan. It's held in honor of young girls to wish them a future of happiness. In homes where there are girls, dolls dressed in ancient costumes representing the emperor, empress, and dignitaries are set up on a tier of shelves along with miniature household articles. Many hotels also display dolls in their lobbies. March 3.

AnimeJapan, Tokyo Big Sight, Odaiba (www.anime-japan.jp). One of the world's largest Japanese animation events draws more than 100 production companies, film agencies, toy and game software companies, publishers, and other *anime*-related companies. Usually third weekend in March.

APRIL

Kanamara Matsuri, Kanayama Shrine, Kawasaki (just outside Tokyo). This festival extols the joys of sex and fertility (and, more recently, raises awareness about AIDS), featuring a parade of giant phalluses, some carried by transvestites. You'll definitely get some unusual photographs here. First Sunday in April.

Kamakura Matsuri, Tsurugaoka Hachimangu Shrine, Kamakura. This festival honors heroes from the past, including Minamoto Yoritomo, who made Kamakura his shogunate capital back in 1192. Highlights include horseback archery (truly spectacular to watch, although fewer and fewer men have the skill), a parade of portable shrines, and sacred dances. Second to third Sunday of April.

Takayama Spring Festival, Takayama. Supposedly dating from the 15th century, this festival is one of Japan's grandest with a dozen huge, gorgeous floats that are wheeled through the village streets. April 14 and 15.

Yayoi Matsuri, Futarasan Shrine, Nikko. Yayoi Matsuri features parades of portable shrines and dance, with the biggest a parade of floats embellished with artificial cherry blossoms and paper lanterns on April 17. April 16 and April 17.

MAY

Takigi Noh Performances, Kofukuji Temple, Nara. These *Noh* plays are presented outdoors after dark under the blaze of torches. Third Friday and Saturday in May.

Kanda Festival, Kanda Myojin Shrine, Tokyo. This festival, which commemorates Tokugawa Ieyasu's famous victory at Sekigahara in 1600, began during the Feudal Period as the only time townspeople could enter the shogun's castle and parade before him. Today this major Tokyo festival features a parade of dozens of portable shrines carried through the district, plus geisha dances and a tea ceremony. Held in odd-numbered years (with a smaller festival held in even years) on the Saturday and Sunday closest to May 15.

Aoi Matsuri (Hollyhock Festival), Shimogamo and Kamigamo Shrines, Kyoto. This is one of Kyoto's biggest events, a colorful parade with 500 participants wearing ancient costumes to commemorate the days when the imperial procession visited the city's shrines. May 15.

Shunki Reitaisai (Grand Spring Festival), Nikko. Commemorating the day in 1617 when Tokugawa Ieyasu's remains were brought to his mausoleum in Nikko, this festival re-creates that drama with more than 1,000 armor-clad people escorting three palanquins through the streets. May 17 and 18.

Sanja Matsuri, Asakusa Shrine, Tokyo. Tokyo's most celebrated festival features about 100 portable shrines carried through the district on the shoulders of men and women in traditional garb. Third Sunday and preceding Friday and Saturday of May.

JUNE

Takigi Noh Performances, Kyoto. Evening performances of *Noh* are presented on an open-air stage at the Heian Shrine. June 1 and 2.

Hyakumangoku Matsuri (One Million Goku Festival), Kanazawa. Celebrating Kanazawa's production of 1 million *goku* of rice (1 *goku* is about 150kg/330 lb.), this extravaganza features folk songs and traditional dancing in the streets, illuminated paper lanterns floating downriver, public tea ceremonies, geisha performances, and—the highlight—a parade that winds through the city in reenactment of Lord Maeda Toshiie's triumphant arrival in Kanazawa on June 14,

1583, with lion dances, ladder-top acrobatics by firemen, and a torch-lit outdoor *Noh* performance. Three days centered on first Saturday in June.

Sanno Festival, Hie Shrine, Tokyo. This Edo Period festival, one of Tokyo's largest, features the usual portable shrines, transported through the busy streets of the Akasaka District. June 6 to June 17.

Otaue Rice-Planting Festival, Sumiyoshi Taisha Shrine, Osaka. In hopes of a successful harvest, young girls in traditional farmers' costumes transplant rice seedlings in the shrine's rice paddy to the sound of traditional music and songs. June 14.

JULY

Gion Matsuri, Kyoto. One of the most famous festivals in Japan, this dates back to the 9th century, when the head priest at Yasaka Shrine organized a procession to ask the gods' assistance in a plague raging in the city. Although celebrations continue throughout the month, the highlight is on the 17th, when more than 30 spectacular wheeled floats wind their way through the city streets to the accompaniment of music and dances. Many visitors plan their trip to Japan around this event. July 17.

Obon Festival, nationwide. This festival commemorates the dead who, according to Buddhist belief, revisit the world during this period. Many Japanese return to their hometowns for religious rites, especially if a family member has recently died. As one Japanese whose grandmother had died a few months before told me, "I have to go back to my hometown—it's my grandmother's first Obon." Mid-July or mid-August, depending on the region.

Tenjin Matsuri, Temmangu Shrine, Osaka. One of Japan's biggest festivals, this dates from the 10th century when the people of Osaka visited Temmangu Shrine to pray for protection against diseases prevalent during the long, hot summer. They would take pieces of paper cut in the form of human beings and, while the Shinto priest said prayers, would rub the paper over themselves in a ritual cleansing. Afterward, the pieces of paper were taken by boat to the mouth of the river and disposed of. Today, events are reenacted with a procession of more than 100 sacred boats making their way downriver, followed by a fireworks display. There's also a parade of some 3,000 people in traditional costume. July 24 and 25.

Kangensai Music Festival, Itsukushima Shrine, Miyajima. There are classical court music and *Bugaku* dancing, and three barges carry portable shrines, priests, and musicians across the bay along with a flotilla of other boats. Late July or early August, according to the lunar calendar.

Hanabi Taikai (Fireworks Display), Tokyo. This is Tokyo's largest summer celebration, and everyone sits on blankets along the banks of the Sumida River near Asakusa to see the show. It's great fun! Last Saturday of July.

AUGUST

Peace Ceremony, Peace Memorial Park, Hiroshima. This ceremony is held annually at 8:15am in memory of those who died in the atomic bomb blast of August 6, 1945. In the evening, thousands of lit lanterns are set adrift on the Ota River in a plea for world peace. August 6.

Daimonji Bonfire, Mount Nyoigadake, Kyoto. A huge bonfire in the shape of the Chinese character *dai*, which means "large," and other motifs are lit near mountain peaks; it's the highlight of the Obon Festival (see July, above). August 16.

SEPTEMBER

Reitaisai (Yabusame), Tsurugaoka Hachimangu Shrine, Kamakura. Archery performed on horseback recalls the days of the samurai, along with classical Japanese dance and a parade of portable shrines. September 16.

OCTOBER

Takayama Matsuri (Autumn Festival), Takayama. As in the festival held here in April, huge floats are paraded through the streets. October 9 and 10.

Doburoku Matsuri, Ogimachi, Shirakawago. This village festival honors unrefined sake, said to represent the spirit of God, with a parade, an evening lion dance, and plenty of eating and drinking. October 14 and 15.

Nikko Toshogu Shrine Festival, Nikko. A parade of warriors in early-17th-century dress are accompanied by spear-carriers, gun-carriers, flag-bearers, Shinto priests, pages, court musicians, and dancers as they escort a sacred portable shrine. October 17.

Jidai Matsuri (Festival of the Ages), Kyoto. Another of Kyoto's grand festivals, this one began in 1894 to commemorate the founding of the city in 794. It features a procession of more than 2,000 people dressed in ancient costumes representing different epochs of Kyoto's 1,200-year history, who march from the Imperial Palace to Heian Shrine. October 22.

NOVEMBER

Daimyo Gyoretsu (Feudal Lord Procession), Yumoto Onsen, Hakone. The old Tokaido Highway, which used to link Kyoto and Tokyo, comes alive again with a faithful reproduction of a feudal lord's procession in the olden days. November 3.

Shichi-go-san (Children's Shrine-Visiting Day), held throughout Japan. Shichi-go-san literally means "seven-five-three" and refers to children of these ages who are dressed in their kimono best and taken to shrines by their elders to express thanks and pray for their future. November 15.

Tori-no-Ichi (Rake Fair), Otori Shrine, Tokyo. This fair in Asakusa (and other Otori shrines throughout Japan) features stalls selling rakes lavishly decorated with paper and cloth, which are thought to bring good luck and fortune. Based on the lunar calendar, the date changes each year. Mid-November.

DECEMBER

Kasuga Wakamiya On-Matsuri, Kasuga Shrine, Nara. This festival features court music with traditional dance and a parade of people dressed as courtiers, retainers, and wrestlers of long ago. December 15 to December 18.

Hagoita-Ichi (Battledore Fair), Sensoji Temple, Tokyo. Popular since Japan's feudal days, this Asakusa festival features decorated paddles of all types and sizes. Most have designs of *kabuki* actors—images created by pasting together padded silk and brocade—and make great souvenirs and gifts. December 17 to December 19.

New Year's Eve. At midnight, temples ring huge bells 108 times to signal the end of the old year and the beginning of the new. Families visit temples and shrines throughout Japan to pray for the coming year. December 31.

SUGGESTED ITINERARIES

3

With its rich culture and stunning scenery, the western half of Honshu has much to offer the curious visitor, not only in and around the major cities like Tokyo and Osaka but in outlying rural regions and villages as well. As the largest of Japan's four major islands and home to most of the country's population, Honshu is where the majority of Japan's important historical events have taken place; you'll find castles, imperial palaces, gardens, temples, shrines, and other attractions linked to the past here, many of them World Heritage Sites. Throw in museums displaying everything from avant-garde art to folk art, shops selling everything from lacquerware to designer wear, and scenery ranging from the rugged Japan Alps to the Seto Inland Sea, and it's little wonder that many travelers to Japan never make it off this central island.

If you want to see *everything* outlined in this book, you should plan on spending a minimum of 2 months in Japan. More likely, your time will be limited to a week or two, so you'll have to be selective. This chapter is designed to help you decide on an itinerary and whether you should buy one of several options for rail passes or even traveling by bus (see chapter 12). If you're lucky enough to be in Japan for several weeks, you can fashion a personalized tour by combining several of these suggested itineraries and adding a town or two from the chapters that follow. But regardless of what itinerary you plan, *Kyoto is a must for first-time visitors.* It served as the nation's capital for some 1,000 years and has more temples, shrines, and historic sights than any other Japanese city.

THE REGIONS IN BRIEF

Separated from China and Korea by the Sea of Japan, Japan stretches in an arc about 2,900km (1,800 miles) long from northeast to southwest, yet it is only 403km (250 miles) wide at its broadest point. Japan consists primarily of four main islands—**Honshu, Hokkaido, Shikoku,** and **Kyushu**—surrounded by more than 6,000 smaller, mostly uninhabited islands and islets.

If you were to superimpose Japan's four main islands onto a map of the United States, they would stretch all the way from Boston to Atlanta. Yet Japan's total landmass is slightly smaller than California in area. As much as 70% of it is mountainous and uninhabitable and another 20% is devoted to agriculture. That means that Japan's 127 million people are concentrated primarily in only 10% of the country's landmass, mostly along Honshu's vast plains surrounding Tokyo and Osaka. In other words, imagine 39% of the U.S. population living in California—primarily in San Diego County—and you get an idea of how crowded Japan is.

Because many of Japan's mountains are volcanic in origin, earthquakes have plagued the country throughout history. In the 20th century, the two most destructive earthquakes were the 1923 Great Kanto Earthquake, which killed more than 100,000 people in the Tokyo area, and the 1995 Great Hanshin Earthquake, which claimed more than 6,000 lives in Kobe. They were followed in 2011 by Japan's largest earthquake in recorded history, the Great East Japan Earthquake, which struck off the northeast Honshu coast and triggered a massive tsunami that contributed to the loss of more than 20,000 lives.

For this island nation—isolated physically from the rest of the world, struck repeatedly through the centuries by earthquakes, tsunamis, fires, and typhoons, and possessed of only limited space for harmonious living—geography and topography have played major roles both in determining its development and in shaping its culture, customs, and arts.

As Japan's largest island, Honshu might be considered the Japanese mainland (its name translates as "Main Province"). It holds 80% of Japan's population, Japan's tallest mountain (Mount Fuji), and 34 of Japan's 47 **prefectures,** which are comparable to the U.S. state or the British county and each with its own capital. The western half of Honshu can be divided into four regions, namely **Kanto** (where the Tokyo metropolitan area is located), **Chubu** (central Honshu), **Kansai** (home to Kyoto and Osaka), and **Chugoku** (the westernmost end of Honshu).

TOKYO & THE KANTO DISTRICT Located in east-central Honshu, this district is characterized by the vast Kanto Plain, the largest flatland in Japan. Although development of the area didn't begin in earnest until the establishment of the shogunate government in Edo (present-day Tokyo) in 1603, Tokyo and surrounding mega-cities like Yokohama comprise the most densely populated region in Japan, if not the world, home to more than 38 million people. There are seven prefectures in Kanto, including Tokyo, the name of both the city (with 9 million inhabitants) and the larger prefecture (with 13 million inhabitants). Although Tokyo is the main tourist draw, worthwhile side trips include Nikko, Kamakura, and Hakone.

KANSAI DISTRICT Also called the Kinki District and encompassing seven prefectures, this is Japan's most historic region. **Nara** and **Kyoto**—two of Japan's ancient capitals—are here, as is Japan's third largest city, **Osaka.** Since the 1994 opening of Kansai International Airport outside Osaka, many foreign visitors opt to bypass Tokyo altogether in favor of Kansai's many historic spots, including **Mount Koya** with its many temples, **Himeji** with what I consider to be Japan's most beautiful castle, Nara with its Great Buddha and temples, and, of course, Kyoto, the former capital for more than 1,000 years, with so many temples, imperial villas, and gardens that it ranks as Japan's foremost tourist destination.

CHUBU DISTRICT The Chubu, or central, District lies between the Kanto and Kansai plains and straddles central Honshu from the Pacific Ocean to the Japan Sea, encompassing nine prefectures. The district features mountain ranges, including the **Japan Alps,** host of the 1998 XVIII Winter Olympics, volcanoes (including **Mount Fuji**), large rivers, and coastal regions on both sides of the island. The quaint mountain villages of **Takayama** and **Shirakawa-go** are rewarding respites from city life. In 2015, Japan's newest bullet train, the Hokuriku Shinkansen, made **Kanazawa,** with its spectacular garden and Edo-era attractions, easily accessible from Tokyo.

CHUGOKU DISTRICT Honshu's southwestern district has five prefectures and is divided by the Chugoku Mountain Range. Industrial giant **Hiroshima** is one of the region's biggest cities and draws many tourists to its Memorial Peak Park, dedicated to victims of the world's first atomic bomb. En route to Hiroshima is **Kurashiki,** a must-see for its photogenic warehouse district, while **Miyajima,** part of the Seto-Naikai (Inland Sea) National Park, is considered one of Japan's most beautiful islands.

WESTERN HONSHU HIGHLIGHTS

This trip, designed for first-timers, takes you to Japan's highlights, from fast-paced Tokyo to the quiet temples of Kyoto, along with a couple of other worthwhile destinations like Hiroshima. Plan on about a week, but if time permits, add destinations from the other two itineraries outlined below or one of the recommended side trips in chapters 6 or 10.

Days 1 & 2: Tokyo ★★★

No one should miss this adrenaline rush of a metropolis; you'll need at least 2 full days to do it justice. Hit the highlights like the **Toyosu Market,** the 45th-floor **observatory** in Shinjuku for its eye-popping views, and the **Tokyo National Museum** with the world's largest collection of Japanese art. Be sure to allow time wandering the diverse neighborhoods, including **Asakusa** with its famous Sensoji Temple and old downtown atmosphere; electrifying **Akihabara** with stores selling everything from cameras to anime figurines; and **Harajuku** with its vibrant teenybopper scene and Oriental Bazaar souvenir shop. Top it off with a stroll through **Kabukicho,** Japan's most notorious nightlife district. See chapters 4 and 5.

Day 3: Hakone ★★★

Take an early train to Hakone Yumoto, gateway to the wonderful **Fuji-Hakone-Izu National Park,** where you can see some of Japan's most

scenic countryside via a circuitous route that includes a three-car mountain train, a funicular, ropeway, and a boat, as well as sights like the wonderful **Hakone Open-Air Museum** and, if you're lucky, the elusive **Mount Fuji.** Be sure to schedule some time for a dip in a hot-spring bath, and spend the night in the historic **Fujiya Hotel** or a Japanese inn. See chapter 6.

Days 4, 5 & 6: Kyoto ★★★

Capital for more than 1,000 years, Kyoto is Japan's number-one must-see. Top historic sites include **Nijo Castle,** former home of the shogun; **Ryoanji Temple** with its famous Zen rock garden; the **Golden Pavilion,** and, with advance planning, the **Katsura Imperial Villa.** Take a self-guided walk through eastern Kyoto, seeing **Sanjusangendo Hall** with its 1,001 wooden statues and **Kiyomizu Temple,** shopping for crafts along the way. Be sure to sample Kyoto's legendary Buddhist vegetarian cuisine, stroll through its famous geisha quarters, and spend at least 1 night in a Japanese-style inn. See chapter 8.

Day 7: Hiroshima ★★

The top destination in Hiroshima is **Peace Memorial Park** with its memorials and museum detailing events surrounding the dropping of the atomic bomb. Within walking distance of the park is also a castle, garden, and art museum, but if you have another day, be sure to include a trip to the nearby island of **Miyajima,** home of a famous shrine and considered one of Japan's most scenic places. See chapter 11.

HIGHLIGHTS OF CHUBU

The completion of the Hokuriku Shinkansen in March 2015 made Kanazawa easily accessible from Tokyo for the first time, cutting the trip between the two cities from 4 hours to about 1½. The destinations I outline here—a former castle town, a mountain village, and an attractive former merchants' town—are a fun alternative to the usual tourist agenda. The circuitous route can begin and end in Tokyo, or it can be added to a trip that continues onward to Kyoto. For more on these towns, see chapter 7.

Days 1 & 2: Kanazawa ★★

A former castle town, Kanazawa is famous for its **Kenrokuen Garden,** considered one of Japan's best landscape gardens and the one I recommend the most. Because of its lofty position, there are no skyscrapers to detract from its gorgeous setting of ponds, streams, and strategically placed trees and rocks. It once served as the outer garden of **Kanazawa Castle,** now Kanazawa Castle Park with the original Ishikawa Gate, reconstructed fortifications built using traditional methods, and a re-created garden. While in Kanazawa be sure to visit other sights related to Japan's feudal era, including its well-preserved former geisha and samurai districts and **Myoryuji Temple** (known as the Ninja Temple).

Day 3: Shirakawa-go ★★

It's a 90-minute bus ride onward to Shirakawa-go, home to the village of **Ogimachi,** part of a World Heritage Site thanks to its thatch-roofed houses. Several farmhouses are open to the public as museums, but your reason for coming here is to actually spend the night in one so you can explore this unique place after the day-trippers have gone. For further relaxation, consider taking a dip in the public hot-spring bath.

Days 4 & 5: Takayama ★★★

An hour's bus ride from Shirakawa-go, Takayama is nestled in the Japan Alps and is often nicknamed "Little Kyoto" because of its picturesque, narrow streets. This old castle town is the perfect place to experience *tatami* living, with accommodations available at various price ranges. A must-see is **Takayama Jinya,** the only regional administrative building from the shogun era still in existence, but I also wouldn't miss the two **merchant homes** open to the public. Other highlights include the **Hirata**

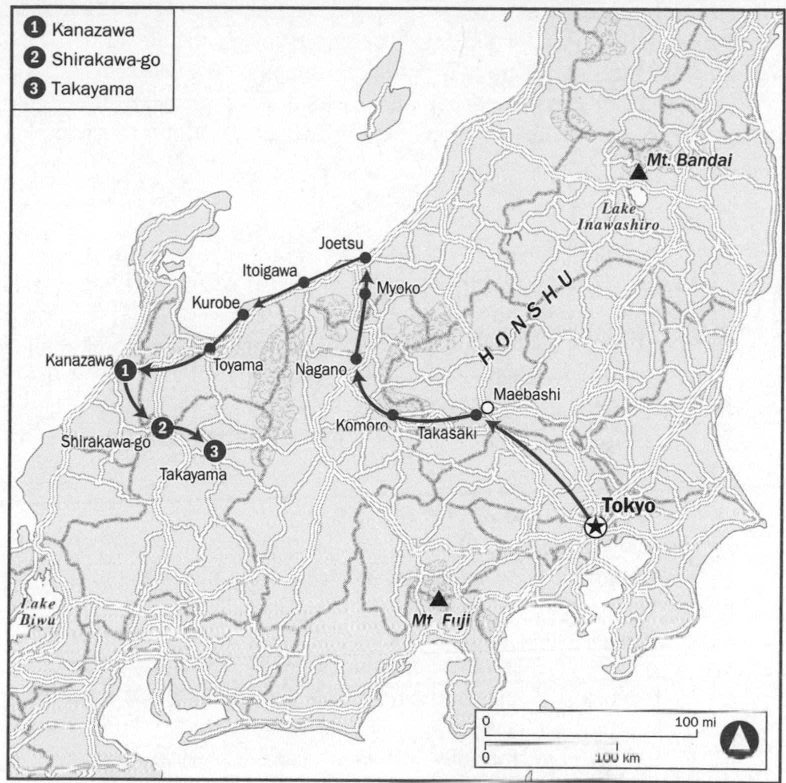

Folk Art Museum, filled with everyday items used during the feudal age, and the quirky **Takayama Showa Museum,** which provides fascinating insights into life in Japan from the 1920s to 1980s. On your second day, the **Miyagawa Morning Market** is a great way to start the morning, followed by explorations through the historic district and a hike along the **Higashiyama Walking Course** on a ridge above town that leads past a dozen temples and shrines. From Takayama you can take a bus back to Tokyo or board a train for Osaka or Kyoto.

WESTERN HONSHU'S WORLD HERITAGE SITES

Japan has 21 cultural and natural properties inscribed on the World Heritage List, 13 of them in west Honshu. It should be noted, however, that many listed sites actually consist of a collection of properties, such as the 17 temples, shrines, and castle that make up the "Historic Monuments of Ancient Kyoto." For that reason, you'd have to be pretty dedicated to visit all the World Heritage

Sites contained in this book. This tour takes in the highlights, excluding Shirakawa-go, already mentioned above; if time is limited, you could also skip Nikko and fly directly into KIX airport and then head to Kyoto. But don't forget to schedule time for kicking back and enjoying the Japan of today, including that most satisfying of experiences, dining on Japanese cuisine. But even that could be considered part of this tour, since *washoku,* traditional Japanese cuisine, was added to UNESCO's Intangible Cultural Heritage list in 2013.

Day 1: Nikko ★★★

About 2 hours north of Tokyo, **Nikko** is famous for its sumptuous mausoleum of Tokugawa Ieyasu, Japan's most famous shogun, set in a forest of majestic cedars. It's part of the "Shrines and Temples of Nikko," which became a World Heritage Site in 1999 and were constructed mostly in the 17th century. To get the most out of your stay, spend the night in the old Nikko Kanaya Hotel or in a Japanese inn with hot-spring baths. See chapter 6.

Days 3, 4 & 5: Kyoto ★★★

En route to Kyoto on the Shinkansen, keep a lookout as you near Shizuoka Station for views of **Mount Fuji,** declared a World Heritage Site in 2013 as a sacred place and the source of artistic inspiration. Otherwise, **Kyoto,** Japan's capital and center of Japanese culture for more than 1,000 years, could be considered the epitome of World Heritage Sites in Japan. Its 16 religious structures and **Nijo Castle,** most built or designed from the 10th to the 17th centuries, include an astounding 189 buildings and 12 gardens. Among the must-sees are Nijo Castle (where the shogun stayed whenever he came to Kyoto), **Ryoanji** with its Zen rock garden, **Kiyomizu Temple, Ginkakuji** (Temple of the Silver Pavilion), and **Kinkakuji** (Temple of the Golden Pavilion). See chapter 8.

Days 6 & 7: Nara ★★★ & Horyuji ★★★

Less than an hour's train ride from Kyoto, **Nara** is even older than Kyoto and served as the nation's capital for 74 years. Although it can be visited in a day's outing, you'll need to spend the night to see all that make up the "Historic Monuments of Ancient Nara" and the "Buddhist Monuments in the Horyuji Area." On the way, stop in Uji to visit **Byodoin Temple,** part of Kyoto's heritage sites and considered one of the best examples of temple architecture from the Heian Period (795–1192); its famed Phoenix Hall graces the back of ¥10 coins. Most of Nara's impressive sights are within expansive **Nara Park,** where deer (considered divine messengers) roam free; foremost here is the **Great Buddha,** housed inside the largest wooden structure in the world (p. 289). In Horyuji are Japan's earliest Buddhist monuments, some of them dating from the 7th century and considered the oldest surviving wooden buildings in the world (p. 290).

Western Honshu's World Heritage Sites

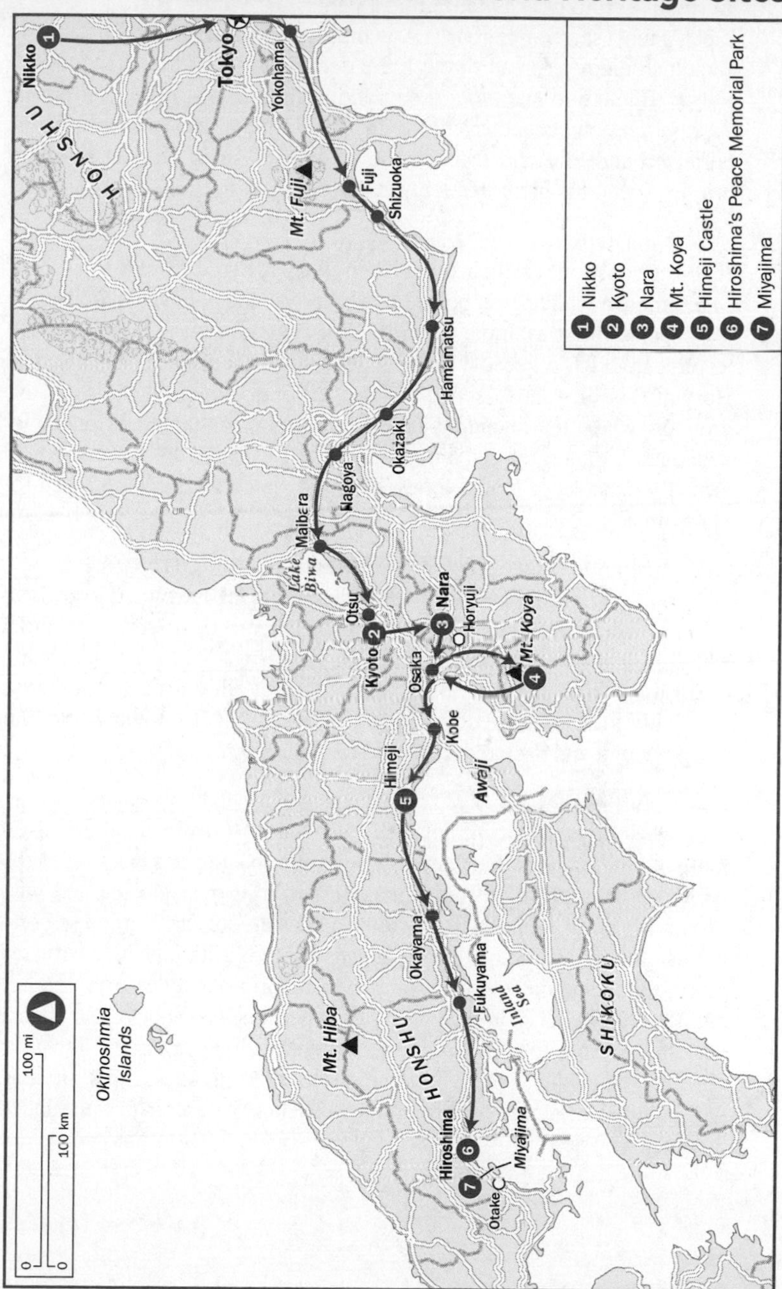

Day 8: Mount Koya ★★★

Accessible from Osaka via train and cable car, **Mount Koya** (p. 293) is Japan's most sacred religious site, achingly beautiful with more than 115 Buddhist temples spread through the dense forests of the Kii Mountain Range. Be sure to take both a day and a nighttime stroll past towering cypress trees and countless tombs and memorial tablets to **Okunoin,** the burial ground of Kobo Daishi, one of Japan's most revered Buddhist priests. Spend the night in a temple, dining on vegetarian food.

Day 9: Himeji Castle ★★★

If you see only one castle in town, **Himeji Castle** (p. 298) is the one. Said to resemble a white heron poised in flight over the plains, it is quite simply Japan's finest example of early-17th-century Japanese castle architecture. In 1993. it became Japan's first World Heritage Site along with Horyuji. You'll want to spend at least 2 hours exploring the extensive grounds, where the ingenious defense mechanisms include a five-story keep, gates, moats, turrets, and maze of passageways that have survived virtually intact since feudal times. Then hop back on the Shinkansen for Hiroshima.

Day 10: Hiroshima's Peace Memorial Park ★★★

Hiroshima is most famous for its **Peace Memorial Park** (p. 316), which contains some 50 statues and memorials and the Peace Memorial Museum, dedicated to those who lost their lives in the atomic bomb explosion. While you'll certainly want to see it all, most eye-catching is the **Genbaku Dome,** the only structure left standing from the World War II destruction and declared a World Heritage Site in 1996.

Day 11: Miyajima ★★★

Most visitors see **Miyajima** on a day trip from Hiroshima, but you'll get more out of this gem of an island, a holy Shinto site since early times, by spending the night. Ikutsukushima Shrine, built over the sea and with Mount Misen rising in the background, does an outstanding job of combining traditional Shinto architecture with nature. Although reconstructed twice, the shrine meticulously preserves its original styles from the late 12th and early 13th centuries. And if time permits, you should also hike or take the cable car up to Mount Misen, where you'll be rewarded with great views of the Inland Sea and hiking paths to religious sites. If it's summer, you might also want to hit Miyajima's beaches. After this treasure-laden itinerary, you deserve it.

TOKYO ESSENTIALS

4

To the uninitiated, **Tokyo ★★★** may seem a whirlwind of traffic and people, so dense and confusing that visitors might think they have landed on another planet. More than 13 million people reside in Greater Tokyo's 2,188 sq. km (845 sq. miles); no matter where you go, you're never alone. After you've been here for a while, Paris, London, and even New York will seem deserted. Perhaps that's why some visitors are disappointed with Tokyo: It has almost nothing of historical importance to match, say, Kyoto. Yet crowds and urban sprawl are what you'll see only if you don't bother to look beneath the surface. So, put any notions of quaint Japan out of your mind and plunge headfirst into the 21st century, because that's what Tokyo is all about.

Even though the city has a fast paced, somewhat zany side, it also has a quieter and often overlooked side that makes the city both lovable and livable. Although formidable at first glance, Tokyo is nothing more than a series of small towns and neighborhoods clustered together, each with its own atmosphere and history. What's more, beneath Tokyo's concrete shell is a thriving cultural life left very much intact. In fact, if you're interested in Japan's performing arts like *kabuki* as well as such diverse activities as sumo, Tokyo is your best bet for offering the most at any one time. It is rich in museums and claims the largest repository of Japanese art in the world. It also gets my vote as the pop-art capital of the world, so if you're into kitsch or *anime* (Japanese animation), you'll be in high heaven. And if you're into style, you'll find Tokyo a mecca for cutting-edge fashion and innovative design.

I love Tokyo. I can't imagine being bored here, even for a minute.

ESSENTIALS

Arriving

BY PLANE

Tokyo has two international airports. **Narita International Airport (NRT;** www.narita-airport.jp; **© 0476/34-8000**), located in Narita about 66km (41 miles) east of Tokyo, is by far the largest and serves the most flights. Closer at just 14km (8.6 miles) is **Haneda Airport**

A LOOK AT THE past

Though today the nation's capital, Tokyo is a relative newcomer to the pages of Japanese history. For centuries it was nothing more than a rather unimportant village called Edo, which means simply "mouth of the estuary." In 1603, Edo was catapulted into the limelight when the new shogun, Tokugawa Ieyasu, made the sleepy village the seat of his government. He expanded Edo Castle, making it the largest and most impressive castle in the land, and surrounded it with an ingenious system of moats that radiated from the castle in a great swirl, giving him easy access to the sea and an upper hand in thwarting enemy attacks.

The town developed quickly, due largely to the shogun's decree requiring all *daimyo* (feudal lords) to permanently leave their families in Edo, a shrewd move to thwart insurrection in the provinces. There were as many as 270 *daimyo* in Japan in the 17th century, all of whom maintained several mansions in Edo, complete with elaborate compounds and expansive gardens. The *daimyo*'s trusted samurai soon accounted for more than half of Edo's population, and the merchant class expanded as well. By 1787 the population had grown to 1.3 million, making Edo—even then—one of the largest cities in the world.

When the Tokugawas were overthrown in 1868, the Japanese emperor was restored to power and moved the capital from Kyoto to Edo, now renamed Tokyo (Eastern Capital). Japan's Feudal Era—and its isolation from the rest of the world—was over. As the capital city, Tokyo was the hardest hit in this new era of modernization, with fashion, architecture, food, and even people imported from the West. West was best, and things Japanese were forgotten or ignored.

It didn't help that Tokyo was almost totally destroyed twice in the first half of the 20th century: In 1923, a massive earthquake measuring 7.9 on the Richter scale destroyed more than a third of the city and claimed some 140,000 lives in Tokyo and Yokohama; disaster struck again in 1945, toward the end of World War II when Allied incendiary bombs laid more than half the city to waste and killed another 100,000 people.

But under Allied occupation, which lasted until 1952, Tokyo quickly rebuilt. By 1964 it showcased as one of Asia's most progressive cities when it hosted the Summer Olympics. Although the 6-minute 2011 Great East Japan Earthquake was the most terrifying most Tokyoites had ever experienced, there was virtually no damage to the city itself. The city is now gearing up for another big moment in its history, the 2020 Summer Olympics.

(**HND;** www.haneda-airport.jp/inter/en/; ✆ **03/5757-8111**), which operates as Tokyo's domestic airport but also has an international terminal.

NARITA AIRPORT There are three terminals (1, 2 and, used mostly by regional low-cost airlines, 3), all with ATMs and counters for money exchange. Change enough money here to last several days—the exchange rate is about the same as in town and the process is speedy. **Tourist Information Centers (TIC)** located in the arrival lobbies of terminals 1 and 2 are open daily 8am to 8pm and offer free maps and pamphlets; staff here can make budget hotel reservations until 7:30pm. If you've purchased a Japan Rail Pass, you can turn in your voucher at the **Japan Railways (JR) Travel Service Center,** located in all terminals and open daily 6:30am to 9:45pm. Other facilities and services at terminals 1 and 2 include post offices, medical clinics, shower rooms, day rooms for napping, beauty salons, children's playrooms, luggage storage and lockers, cellphone rentals, free Wi-Fi, and, in Terminal 2, a capsule hotel (useful if you have a very early flight). You can also have your suitcase delivered to your place of lodging no matter where you're staying in Japan; it costs about ¥1,909 to ¥2,362 per bag in the Tokyo area depending on the weight and size.

By Train The quickest way to reach Tokyo is by train, with several options available. Trains depart directly from the airport's two underground stations, Narita Airport Terminal 1 and Airport Terminal 2-3. The JR **Narita Express (N'EX;** www.jreast.co.jp; ✆ **050/2016-1603**) is the fastest way to reach Tokyo Station, Shinagawa, Shibuya, Shinjuku, or Ikebukuro, with departures approximately twice an hour. The 56-minute trip to Tokyo Station costs ¥3,020 one-way or ¥6,040 round-trip. At Tokyo Station, the train splits, with some cars going to Shibuya, Shinjuku, and, less frequently, Ikebukuro, and other cars going to Shinagawa (cost to these stations: ¥3,190, ¥6,380 round-trip). As this book was going to press, a special **N'EX Tokyo Round Trip Ticket** was being offered to foreign visitors for only ¥4,000. Sold only at Narita Airport, it even allows you to transfer to another JR train line to reach your Tokyo destination; check the website for more information. Otherwise, if you've validated your JR Rail Pass as mentioned above, you can ride the N'EX free.

Another train option, especially if your destination is Ueno, is the privately owned **Keisei Skyliner** (www.keisei.co.jp; ✆ **0570-081-160**), which departs directly from terminals 1 and 2 and travels to Ueno Station in Tokyo in as little as 41 minutes. Trains depart Narita approximately one to three times an hour from about 7:30am to 10:30pm. The fare between Narita Airport and Ueno Station is ¥2,470 one way. Travelers on a budget can take one of Keisei's slower limited express trains to Ueno Station, with fares starting at ¥1,030 for the 80-minute trip. If your destination is Asakusa, Nihombashi, Higashi-Ginza, Shimbashi, or Shinagawa, you can also travel on the Narita Sky Access Line or Keisei Main Line. For details, check the Keisei website or drop by the Keisei ticket counters in the arrival lobbies of terminals 1 and 2.

By Bus The most popular and stress-free way to get from Narita to Tokyo is via the **Airport Limousine Bus** (www.limousinebus.co.jp; ✆ **03/3665-7220**), which picks up passengers and their luggage from just outside the arrival lobbies of Terminals 1 and 2 and delivers them to downtown hotels. This is the best mode of transportation if you have heavy baggage or are staying at one of the 40 or so major hotels served by the bus. Buses depart for the various hotels generally once an hour, but note it can take almost 2 hours to reach a hotel in Shinjuku. Buses also travel to both Tokyo and Shinjuku stations, Haneda Airport, and the **Tokyo City Air Terminal (TCAT)** in downtown Tokyo, with more frequent departures (up to four times an hour in peak times); all are served by public transportation. Even if your hotel is not served by limousine bus, you can still take it to the hotel or station nearest your destination. Check with the staff at the Airport Limousine Bus counter in the

Saving on Transportation

If you plan to travel around Tokyo by public transportation (and who doesn't?), you can save money by purchasing a combination Keisei Skyliner and Tokyo subway ticket, available only at Narita Airport. One-, 2-, and 3-day tickets offering unlimited subway rides are ¥2,800, ¥3,200, and ¥3,500, respectively, for a one-way Skyliner ticket and ¥4,700, ¥5,100, and ¥5,400 with a round-trip Skyliner ticket. Likewise, there are Airport Limousine & Subway Pass combination tickets that include a one-way or round-trip Airport Limousine Bus plus 24-, 48-, or 72-hour unlimited rides on all subways (it doesn't have to be the same day of arrival), with a one-way bus and 24-hour combination ticket costing ¥3,400. This ticket, which I consider very good value, is available at Airport Limousine counters at the airport, TCAT, and Shinjuku Station West Exit in front of Keio Department Store. There are also combination tickets for visitors arriving at Haneda airport. Check websites for more information.

arrival lobbies to ask which bus stops nearest your hotel and its departure time. The fare to most destinations is ¥3,100. Children 6 to 12 are charged half-fare; those 5 and under ride free.

Cheaper buses, the **Access Narita** (www.accessnarita.jp) and the **Tokyo Shuttle** (www.keiseibus.co.jp/inbound/tokyoshuttle/en/), travel from all three terminals at Narita to Tokyo and Ginza for only ¥1,000 one-way (children pay half-fare). Travel time is 95 to 105 minutes, with departures up to three times an hour during peak times. You pay upon boarding with cash for Access Narita, while Tokyo Shuttle tickets are purchased at a Keisei Bus ticket counter.

By Taxi Jumping into a **taxi** is the easiest way to get to Tokyo, but it's also prohibitively expensive—and may not even be the quickest if you happen to hit rush-hour traffic. Taxis have both metered and—probably better—fixed-fare rates, but expect to spend around ¥19,000 to ¥25,000 for a 1½- to 2-hour taxi ride to areas in central Tokyo. Note that highway toll charges and a surcharge applied from 10pm to 5am will cost extra.

HANEDA AIRPORT **Haneda Airport** has both domestic and international terminals (it's officially named Tokyo International Airport, but everyone calls it Haneda). The international terminal has a **Tokyo Tourist Information Center** (on the second floor of the arrival lobby, open daily 24 hr.), currency exchange, free Wi-Fi, luggage storage and delivery, and cellphone rental. But the overriding benefit of Haneda is its central location compared to Narita. Taxi fares from Haneda are more reasonable than from Narita, but you can still expect to pay about ¥7,000 to reach downtown Tokyo.

Like Narita, Haneda Airport is served by the **Airport Limousine Bus,** with service to Shinjuku Station, Tokyo Station, the Tokyo City Air Terminal (TCAT) in downtown Tokyo, and selected hotels in Ginza, Hibiya, Shinjuku, Ikebukuro, Shibuya, Roppongi, and Akasaka. Fares run ¥930 to ¥1,230 for most destinations.

Locals, however, are more likely to take the **monorail** from Haneda 16 minutes to Hamamatsucho Station (fare: ¥490), or the **Keikyu Line** 11 minutes to Shinagawa (fare: ¥410). Both Hamamatsucho and Shinagawa connect to the very useful Yamanote Line, which travels to major stations like Tokyo and Shinjuku.

BY TRAIN

If you're traveling to Tokyo from elsewhere in Japan, you'll most likely arrive via Shinkansen bullet train at Tokyo, Ueno, or Shinagawa stations (avoid Tokyo Station if you can; it's very big and confusing). All are well served by trains (including the useful JR Yamanote Line), subways, and taxis.

BY BUS

Long-distance bus service from Hiroshima, Osaka, Kyoto, and other major cities delivers passengers mostly to Tokyo and Shinjuku stations, both of which are connected to the rest of the city via subway and commuter train, including the JR Yamanote Line, which loops around the city. For more info on long-distance bus service, check the websites www.bus.or.jp, www.jrbuskanto.co.jp, and http://travel.willer.co.jp/endex.php, or go to the individual city descriptions in this guide.

Visitor Information

In addition to those located at both airports (see above), there's another **Tourist Information Center (TIC)** in the heart of Tokyo in the Shin-Tokyo Building, 3–3–1 Marunouchi (www.japantravelinfo.com; © **03/3201-3331;** station: Yurakucho), within walking distance of the Ginza. The TIC staff is courteous and efficient—I cannot recommend them highly enough. In addition to city maps and sightseeing materials, this office (affiliated with the Japan National Tourism Organization) has more information on the rest of Japan than any other tourist office in town, including pamphlets and brochures on major cities and attractions such as Kyoto and Kamakura. Hours are daily 9am to 5pm.

A great source for local information is the **Tokyo Tourist Information Center,** operated by the Tokyo Metropolitan Government and located on the first floor of the Tokyo Metropolitan Government (TMG) Building no. 1, 2–8–1 Nishi-Shinjuku (www.gotokyo.org; © **03/5321-3077;** station: Tochomae or Shinjuku). You'll want to come here anyway for the great views from TMG's free observation floor. The center dispenses pamphlets, its own city map, and the handy **Tokyo Travel Guide** (also available as a free app), with information and detailed maps of various neighborhoods, from Ueno to Roppongi. It's open daily 9:30am to 6:30pm. Other city-run information counters are located at Keisei Ueno Station (© **03/3836-3471**), open daily 9:30am to 6:30pm, and at the Shinjuku Expressway Bus Terminal (© **03/6274-8198**), open daily from 6:30am to 11pm.

Near Tokyo Station, the **TIC TOKYO,** facing the Nihombashi exit of Tokyo Station's north end at 1–8–1 Marunouchi (www.tictokyo.jp; © **03/5220-7055**), dispenses information on traveling in Tokyo and Japan and offers SIM cards and mobile Wi-Fi routers; it's open daily 10am to 7pm. Inside Tokyo

Station at the Marunouchi north exit is the **JR EAST Travel Service Center** (www.jreast.co.jp; ✆ **050/2016-1603**), which provides tourist information as well as train tickets and is open daily from 7:30am to 8:30pm. **Tokyo City i,** in JP Tower next to the Central Post Office, 2–7–2 Marunouchi (http://tokyocity-i.jp; daily 8am–8pm), provides support and information to both international tourists and foreigners conducting business in Japan.

Among the increasing number of neighborhood tourist offices are the **Asakusa Culture Tourist Information Center,** 2–18–9 Kaminarimon (✆ **03/6280-6710;** daily 9:30am–8pm); the **Shibuya Tourist Information Center** in an old train car at the Hachiko exit of Shibuya Station (daily 10am–6pm); and the **Sumida City Tourist Information Office** outside Ryogoku Station (daily 10am–6pm).

Tourist Publications: Of the many free giveaways available at tourist information centers, restaurants, bars, bookstores, hotels, and other establishments where visitors and expats are likely to frequent, the best are the weekly ***Metropolis*** (www.metropolisjapan.com), with features on Tokyo, club listings, and restaurant and movie reviews, and the quarterly ***TimeOut Tokyo*** (www.timeout.jp) which covers so much information, including offbeat destinations, that it's even useful for expats living in Tokyo. Look also for the free ***att.Japan*** (www.att-japan.net) and **WAttention** (www.wattention.com). Local English-language newspapers the ***Japan Times*** and the ***Japan News*** also carry entertainment sections and articles.

City Layout

Your most frustrating moments in Tokyo will probably occur when you find that you're totally lost. Maybe it will be in a subway or train station or on a street somewhere as you search for a museum, restaurant, or bar. At any rate, accept it here and now: You *will* get lost if you are at all adventurous and strike out on your own. It's inevitable. But take comfort in the fact that Japanese get lost, too. And don't forget that most of the hotel and restaurant listings in this book have the number of minutes (in parentheses) it takes to walk there from the nearest station, so you'll at least know the radius from the station to your destination. It's wise, too, to always allow extra time to find your way around.

Tokyo, situated at one end of Tokyo Bay and spreading across the Kanto Plain, still retains some of its Edo Period features. If you look at a map, you'll find a large green oasis in the middle of the city, site of the Imperial Palace and its grounds. Surrounding it is the castle moat; a bit farther out are remnants of another circular moat built by the Tokugawa shogun. The JR Yamanote Line forms another loop around the inner city; most of Tokyo's major hotels, nightlife districts, and attractions are near or inside this oblong loop.

For administrative purposes, Tokyo is broken down into **23 wards,** known as ***ku.*** Its business districts of Marunouchi and Hibiya, for example, are in Chiyoda-ku, while Ginza is part of Chuo-ku (Central Ward). These two ku are the historic hearts of Tokyo, for it was here that the city had its humble beginnings. Greater Tokyo is also Japan's largest prefecture (similar to a state or province), with a population of more than 13 million, and includes 26 cities, five towns, and eight villages in addition to its 23 wards, as well as Pacific islands. For most purposes, however, references to Tokyo in this guide pertain mostly to central Tokyo's 23 wards, home to 9 million residents.

MAIN STREETS & ARTERIES One difficulty in finding your way around Tokyo is that hardly any streets are named. Think about what that means: 9 million people living in a huge metropolis of nameless streets. Granted, major thoroughfares received names after World War II at the insistence of American occupation forces, and more have been labeled or given nicknames since then, but for the most part, Tokyo's address system is based on a complicated number scheme that before GPS must have made the postal worker's job a nightmare. To make matters worse, most streets in Tokyo zigzag—an arrangement apparently left over from olden days, to confuse potential attacking enemies. Now they confuse Tokyoites and visitors alike.

Among Tokyo's most important named streets are **Meiji Dori,** which follows the loop of the Yamanote Line and runs from Minato-ku in the south through Ebisu, Shibuya, Harajuku, Shinjuku, and Ikebukuro in the north; **Yasukuni Dori** and **Shinjuku Dori,** which cut across the heart of the city from Shinjuku to Chiyoda-ku; and **Sotobori Dori, Chuo Dori, Harumi Dori,** and **Showa Dori,** which pass through Ginza. Other major thoroughfares are named after the districts they're in, such as **Roppongi Dori** in Roppongi and **Aoyama Dori** in Aoyama (*dori* means avenue or street, as does *michi*).

Intersections in Tokyo are called a crossing (and more recently a scramble); it seems every district has a famous crossing. **Ginza 4-chome Crossing** is the intersection of Chuo Dori and Harumi Dori. **Roppongi Crossing** is the intersection of Roppongi Dori and Gaien-Higashi Dori. The **Shibuya Scramble** became famous after being featured in the movie *Lost in Translation*.

ADDRESSES Because streets did not have names when Japan's postal system was established, Tokyo has a unique address system. A typical address might read 7–10–1 Ginza, Chuo-ku, which is the address of Hotel Gracery. Chuo-ku is the name of the ward. Wards are further divided into named districts, in this case Ginza. Ginza itself is broken down into *chome* (numbered subsections), the first number in the series, here 7. The second number (10 in the example) refers to a smaller area within the *chome*—usually an entire block, sometimes larger. Thus, houses on one side of the street will usually have a different middle number from houses on the other side. The last number, in this case 1, refers to the actual building.

Addresses are usually, but not always, posted on buildings beside doors, on telephone poles, and at major intersection traffic lights, but sometimes they are written in kanji only. One frustrating trend is that newer buildings omit posting any address whatsoever on their facades, perhaps in the belief that no one understands the address system anyway.

FINDING YOUR WAY AROUND If you're traveling by subway or JR train, the first thing you should do upon exiting your compartment is to look for **yellow signs** posted on every platform that tell you which exit to take for particular buildings, attractions, and *chome*. At Roppongi Station, for example,

Tokyo at a Glance

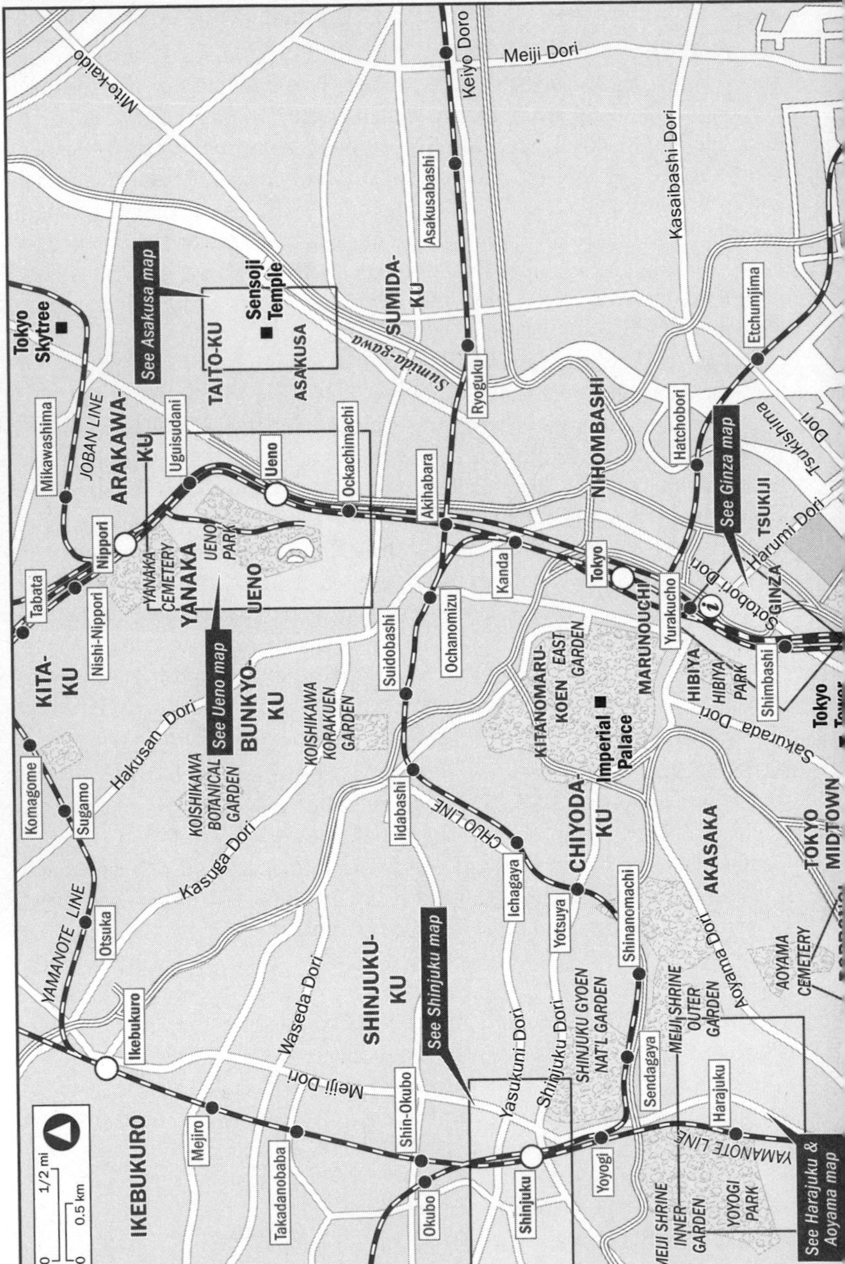

IKEBUKURO
Ikebukuro
Mejiro
Takadanobaba
Shin-Okubo
Okubo
Shinjuku
Yoyogi
Sendagaya
Harajuku
Otsuka
Sugamo
Komagome
Tabata
Nishi-Nippori
Nippori
Mikawashima
Uguisudani
Ueno
Okachimachi
Akihabara
Kanda
Tokyo
Yurakucho
Shimbashi
Suidobashi
Ochanomizu
Iidabashi
Ichagaya
Yotsuya
Shinanomachi
Ryoguku
Asakusabashi
Hatchobori
Etchumjima
YAMANOTE LINE
JOBAN LINE
CHUO LINE
KITA-KU
ARAKAWA-KU
TAITO-KU
ASAKUSA
SUMIDA-KU
YANAKA
YANAKA CEMETERY
UENO
UENO PARK
BUNKYO-KU
KOISHIKAWA BOTANICAL GARDEN
KOISHIKAWA KORAKUEN GARDEN
SHINJUKU-KU
CHIYODA-KU
KITANOMARU-KOEN
EAST GARDEN
Imperial Palace
MARUNOUCHI
NIHOMBASHI
HIBIYA
HIBIYA PARK
GINZA
TSUKIJI
AKASAKA
TOKYO MIDTOWN
AOYAMA CEMETERY
MEIJI SHRINE OUTER GARDEN
MEIJI SHRINE INNER GARDEN
YOYOGI PARK
SHINJUKU GYOEN NAT'L GARDEN
Tokyo Skytree
Sensoji Temple
Tokyo Tower
Sumida-gawa
Mito-kaido
Meiji Dori
Keiyo Doro
Kasaibashi Dori
Hakusan Dori
Kasuga Dori
Waseda Dori
Yasukuni Dori
Shinjuku Dori
Aoyama Dori
Sakurada Dori
Sotobori Dori
Harumi Dori
Tsukishima Dori
See Asakusa map
See Ueno map
See Shinjuku map
See Ginza map
See Harajuku & Aoyama map
0 1/2 mi
0 0.5 km

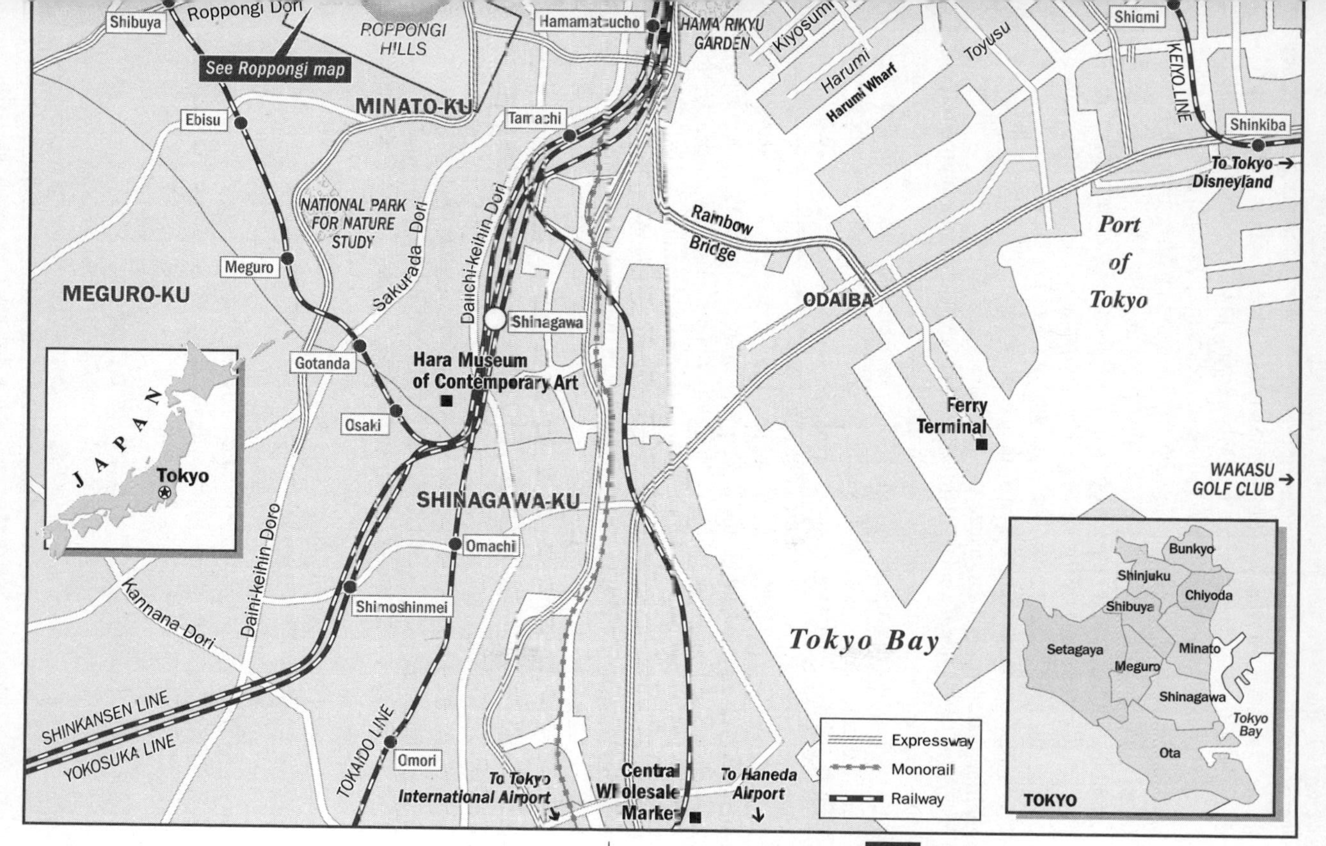
Shibuya
Roppongi Dori
ROPPONGI HILLS
See Roppongi map
Hamamatsucho
HAMA RIKYU GARDEN
Kiyosumi
Harumi
Harumi Wharf
Toyosu
Shiomi
KEIYO LINE
Shinkiba
To Tokyo Disneyland
MINATO-KU
Ebisu
Tamachi
NATIONAL PARK FOR NATURE STUDY
Sakurada Dori
Daiichi-keihin Dori
Rainbow Bridge
Port of Tokyo
Meguro
MEGURO-KU
Shinagawa
ODAIBA
Gotanda
Hara Museum of Contemporary Art
Osaki
Ferry Terminal
JAPAN
Tokyo
WAKASU GOLF CLUB
SHINAGAWA-KU
Omachi
Daini-keihin Doro
Shimoshinmei
Kannana Dori
Tokyo Bay
SHINKANSEN LINE
YOKOSUKA LINE
TOKAIDO LINE
Omori
To Tokyo International Airport
Central Wholesale Market
To Haneda Airport
Expressway
Monorail
Railway
Bunkyo
Shinjuku
Chiyoda
Shibuya
Setagaya
Minato
Meguro
Shinagawa
Tokyo Bay
Ota
TOKYO

you'll find yellow signboards that tell you the exit to take for Roppongi Hills, which will at least get you pointed in the right direction once you emerge from the station. Stations also have maps of the areas either inside the station or at the exit and some even have actual printouts available from the station attendant; these are your best plan of attack when trying to find a particular address.

As you walk around Tokyo, you will also notice **map boards** posted beside sidewalks (look for a white circle with an "i" in the middle) giving a breakdown of the postal number system for that particular neighborhood. The first time I tried to use one, I stopped one Japanese, then another, and asked them to locate a specific address on the map. They both studied the map and pointed out the direction. Both turned out to be wrong. Not very encouraging, but if you learn how to read these maps, they're invaluable. Nowadays, many of them include landmarks translated in English.

Another invaluable source of information is the numerous **police boxes,** called *koban,* located in major neighborhoods and beside major train and subway stations throughout the city. Police officers have area maps and are very helpful (helping lost souls seems to occupy much of their time). You should also never hesitate to ask a Japanese the way, but be sure to ask more than one. You'll be amazed at the conflicting directions you'll receive. Apparently, Japanese would rather hazard a guess than impolitely shrug their shoulders and leave you standing there. The best thing to do is ask directions of several Japanese and then follow the majority opinion. You can also duck into a shop and ask someone where a nearby address is, although in my experience employees do not even know the address of their own store. However, they may have a map of the area.

MAPS Before leaving home, you'll want to download an app of offline maps to help you navigate Tokyo's streets, such as the Tokyo Offline City Map. In addition, the free Tokyo Handy Guide app issued by the Tokyo government has offline maps and lots of tourist information. Once in Tokyo, you might also find it useful to arm yourself with physical maps to understand the big picture. Maps are so much a part of life in Tokyo that they're often included in shop or restaurant advertisements or brochures, on business cards, and even in private party invitations. You can pick up free maps at Tokyo's many tourist information centers (see p. 342 for locations), many of which include a subway map. Hotels sometimes distribute their own maps. Many Metro subway stations also have area maps of surrounding neighborhoods, so don't be shy about asking the attendant. Armed with these maps, you should be able to locate at least the general vicinity of every place mentioned in this book. In short, never pass up a free map.

Tokyo's Neighborhoods in Brief

Taken as a whole, Tokyo seems formidable and unconquerable. It's best, therefore, to think of it as nothing more than a series of villages scrunched together, much like the pieces of a jigsaw puzzle. Holding the pieces together, so to speak, is the **Yamanote Line,** a commuter train loop around central Tokyo that passes through such important stations as Yurakucho, Tokyo, Akihabara, Ueno, Ikebukuro, Shinjuku, Harajuku, Shibuya, and Shinagawa.

Marunouchi Bounded by the Imperial Palace to the west and Tokyo Station (used by about 500,000 people daily) to the east, Marunouchi is one of Tokyo's oldest business districts. On the site of the **Imperial Palace** is where the Tokugawa shogun built his magnificent castle and the center of old Edo; many samurai had mansions here. Remnants of the castle can be seen in the wonderful **East Garden,** open free to the public. Marunouchi has undergone a massive revival since the turn of this century. It's home to the Tourist Information Center, office buildings, swanky hotels, and wide avenues like the fashionable, tree-lined **Marunouchi Naka Dori,** with international boutiques from Armani to Tiffany and famous for its winter illuminations.

Ginza Across the train tracks and to the south of Marunouchi is the Ginza, the swankiest and most expensive **shopping area** in all Japan. When the country opened to foreign trade in the 1860s, after 2 centuries of self-imposed seclusion, it was here that Western imports and adopted Western architecture were first displayed. Today, it's where you'll find the **KabukIza Theatre,** department stores, international name-brand boutiques, exclusive restaurants, hotels, art galleries, and drinking establishments.

Tsukiji Located only two subway stops from Ginza, Tsukiji was born from reclaimed land during the Tokugawa shogunate; its name, in fact, means "reclaimed land." From 1935 to 2018, it was home to the famous **Tsukiji Fish Market,** one of the largest wholesale fish markets in the world, which in 2018 moved 2.5km (1½ miles) away to larger quarters in Toyosu, thus freeing up valuable Tsukiji land for the 2020 Olympics. Near Tsukiji is **Hama Rikyu Garden,** one of Tokyo's most famous gardens.

Akihabara Two stops north of Tokyo Station on the Yamanote Line, Akihabara has long been Japan's foremost shopping destination for electronics and electrical appliances, with hundreds of shops offering a look at the latest in gadgets, including **Yodobashi Camera,** Japan's largest appliance store. More recently, Akihabara has also become a mecca for *otaku* (geek) culture, home of *anime* and *manga* stores and maid cafes. This is a fascinating area for a stroll, even if you don't buy anything.

Asakusa Northeast of central Tokyo, Asakusa and areas to its north served as the pleasure quarters for old Edo. Today it's known throughout Japan as the site of the famous **Sensoji Temple,** one of Tokyo's top and oldest attractions. It also has a wealth of tiny shops selling traditional Japanese crafts. When Tokyoites talk about old *shitamachi* (downtown), they are referring to the traditional homes and tiny narrow streets of the Asakusa and Ueno areas. Every visitor should spend at least half a day here.

Ueno Located just west of Asakusa, on the northern edge of the JR Yamanote Line loop, Ueno is also part of the city's old downtown. Ueno boasts **Ueno Park,** a huge green space comprising a zoo and several acclaimed museums, including the **Tokyo National Museum,** which houses the largest collection of Japanese art and antiquities in the world. Under the train tracks of the JR Yamanote Line loop is the spirited **Ameya Yokocho,** a thriving market for food, clothing, and accessories.

Shinjuku Originating as a post town in 1698 to serve the needs of feudal lords and their retainers traveling between Edo and the provinces, Shinjuku was hardly touched by the 1923 Great Kanto Earthquake, making it an attractive alternative for businesses wishing to relocate following the destruction. Today dozens of skyscrapers, including several hotels, dot the Shinjuku skyline, and with the 1991 opening of the **Tokyo Metropolitan Government Office (TMG;** with a great free observation floor), Shinjuku's transformation into the capital's upstart business district was complete. Separating eastern and western Shinjuku is **Shinjuku Station,** the nation's busiest commuter station, located on the western end of the Yamanote Line loop. Shinjuku is also known for its nightlife, especially in **Kabuki-cho,** one of Japan's most famous—and naughtiest—amusement centers; and in **Shinjuku 2-chome,** Tokyo's premier gay nightlife district. An oasis in the middle of Shinjuku madness is **Shinjuku Gyoen Park,** with a tranquil Japanese garden at its center.

Harajuku The mecca of Tokyo's younger generation, Harajuku swarms throughout the week with teens in search of fashion and fun. **Takeshita Dori** is a narrow pedestrian lane packed elbow to elbow with young people looking for the latest in inexpensive clothing; at its center is the ¥100 discount shop **Daiso.** Harajuku is also home to one of Japan's major attractions, the **Meiji Jingu Shrine,** built in 1920 to deify Emperor and Empress Meiji; **Yoyogi Park,** with its expansive grounds; and the small but delightful **Ukiyo-e Ota Memorial Museum of Art,** with its woodblock prints. Another draw is the **Oriental Bazaar,** Tokyo's best shop for souvenir hunting. Linking Harajuku with Aoyama (below) is **Omotesando Dori,** a fashionable tree-lined avenue flanked by trendy shops, restaurants, and sidewalk cafes, making it a premier promenade for people-watching. The upscale **Omotesando Hills** shopping center on Omotesando Dori stretches from Harajuku to Aoyama.

Aoyama While Harajuku is for Tokyo's teenyboppers, nearby chic Aoyama is its playground for trendsetting yuppies, boasting sophisticated restaurants, pricey boutiques, and more cutting-edge designer-fashion outlets than anywhere else in the city. It's located on the eastern end of **Omotesando Dori** (and an easy walk from Harajuku), centered on Aoyama Dori. Its cultural highlight is the **Nezu Museum**, devoted to items related to the tea ceremony, Chinese bronzes, and more. The **Japan Traditional Crafts Aoyama Square** sells beautifully crafted items made by artisans from around Japan.

Shibuya Located on the southwestern edge of the Yamanote Line loop, Shibuya serves as a vibrant nightlife and shopping area for the young. More subdued than Shinjuku, more down-to-earth than Harajuku, and less cosmopolitan than Roppongi, it's home to more than a dozen department stores specializing in everything from designer clothing to housewares. **Hikarie** is a 34-story complex with shops, restaurants, and a gallery for artists and artisans from around Japan. Don't miss the light change at **Shibuya Scramble,** reportedly Japan's busiest intersection, with its hordes of pedestrians, neon, and five video billboards that have earned it the nickname "Times Square of Tokyo" (and a spot in the movie *Lost in Translation*).

Roppongi Tokyo's best-known nightlife district for young Japanese and foreigners, Roppongi has more bars and nightclubs than any other district outside Shinjuku, as well as a multitude of restaurants serving international cuisines. It's anchored by two sprawling developments: the eye-popping, 11-hectare (28-acre) **Roppongi Hills,** Tokyo's largest urban development, housing 230 shops and restaurants, a first-class hotel, a garden, apartments, offices, a cinema complex, and Tokyo's highest art museum, on the 53rd floor of Mori Tower; and the smaller **Tokyo Midtown,** which boasts Tokyo's tallest building, a luxury hotel, medical center, 130 restaurants and fashion boutiques, apartments, offices, a garden, and the Suntory Museum of Art. Also in Roppongi is the **National Art Center, Tokyo,** focusing on changing exhibitions of modern and contemporary art.

Odaiba Tokyo's newest district was constructed from reclaimed land in Tokyo Bay. Connected to the mainland by the **Rainbow Bridge** (famous for its chameleon colors after nightfall), the Yurikamome Line monorail, the Rinkai Line, and a vehicular harbor tunnel, it's home to hotels, Japan's largest convention space, shopping and amusement complexes, museums, the **Ooedo-Onsen Monogatari** hot-spring baths, and **Megaweb,** a car amusement and exhibition center sponsored by Toyota. It's also one of Tokyo's hottest date spots and offers great views of Tokyo's skyline.

Getting Around Town

For short-term visitors, calculating travel times in Tokyo is tricky business. The first rule of getting around Tokyo: It will always take longer than you think. Taking a taxi is expensive and involves the probability of getting stuck interminably in traffic, with the meter ticking away. Taking the subway is usually more efficient, even though it's harder on your feet and more complicated: Choosing which route to take isn't always clear, and transfers between lines are sometimes quite a hike in themselves. If I'm going from one end of Tokyo to the other by subway, I usually allow anywhere from 30 to 60 minutes, depending on the number of transfers and the walking distance to my final destination. If you don't have to change trains, you can travel from one end of central Tokyo to the other (say, from Shibuya to Ueno) in about 30 minutes or less.

Your best bet for getting around Tokyo is to take the subway or a Japan Railways (JR) commuter train such as the Yamanote Line to the station nearest your destination. From there you can either walk or take a taxi. For all accommodations, restaurants, sights, shops, and nightlife venues listed in this chapter and the next, I've included both the nearest station and, in parentheses, the approximate time it takes to walk from the station to the destination. Unfortunately, Tokyo doesn't offer public transportation late at night (most services stop from around midnight to 4 or 5am), but maybe the 2020 Olympics will spur extended hours.

TIPS ON TAKING PUBLIC TRANSPORTATION Each mode of transportation in Tokyo—**subway** (with two different companies), **JR train** (such as the Yamanote Line), **private rail companies,** and **bus**—has its own fare system and therefore requires a new ticket each time you transfer from one mode of transport to another. It's much more convenient to purchase a **Suica** (www.jreast.co.jp/e/pass/suica), issued by JR East and available at any JR station via ticket vending machine, or a **PASMO** (www.pasmo.co.jp), issued by Tokyo Metro subways and sold from ticket vending machines in subway stations. Both are contactless prepaid **IC** (integrated circuit) cards that automatically deduct fares and can be used on virtually all modes of transportation, including JR trains (excluding the Shinkansen), private railways (such as the Rinkai Line to Odaiba), subways, and buses at a slight discount. They can even be used for purchases at designated vending machines, convenience stores, and fast-food outlets that display the Suica/PASMO sign. Best of all, the cards can be used on various modes of local transportation throughout Japan, whether you're in Kamakura or Kyoto. Note that both cards come with a ¥500 deposit, plus any initial value between ¥1,000 to ¥10,000 that you choose to load. You can then reload them at ticket vending machines as needed. If you don't have enough balance on your card when you reach your destination, simply top off your card at the exit's fare adjustment machine. When you're ready to leave Tokyo, PASMO will refund the deposit and any remaining balance on the card, while Suica will refund the deposit but charge a handling fee of up to ¥220 for any remaining balance (so be sure the card is depleted). Although other options are available, including 1-day cards and metro-only cards, the Suica and the Pasmo are by far my favorites.

That being said, if you think you're going to be traveling a lot by public transportation on any given day, consider purchasing a **Tokyo Combination Ticket (Tokyo Furii Kippu)** for ¥1,590, which allows unlimited travel for 1 day on all subways, JR trains, and Toei buses within Tokyo's 23 wards. It's available at almost all JR and subway stations. There are also 1-day tickets that can be used only on Metro subway lines for ¥600, on all subway lines of both companies for ¥900, or only on JR trains for ¥750. In addition, there are 24-hour, 48-hour, and 72-hour discount tickets just for visitors. See **www.tokyometro.jp/en/ticket/value/travel/index.html** for details.

Note that children 6 to 11 pay half-fare on public transportation in Japan; children 5 and under ride free. Note, too, that all cellphones should be switched to silent mode (called "manner mode" in Japanese) on public conveyances. Finally, avoid taking the subway or JR train during the weekday morning **rush hour,** from 8 to 9am—the stories you've heard about commuters packed like sardines into trains are all true. There are even "platform pushers," men who push people into compartments so that the doors can close. If you want to witness Tokyo at its craziest, go to Shinjuku Station at 8:30am—but get there by taxi unless you want to experience the crowding firsthand. Most lines provide women-only compartments at the end of the train weekdays until 9am.

BY SUBWAY

To get around Tokyo on your own, it's imperative to learn how to ride its subways. Fortunately, the subway system is efficient, modern, clean, and easy to use; in fact, I think it's one of the most user-friendly systems on the planet. And to remove the guessing game regarding which route to take, what it will cost, and the estimated time of the ride, download the free and invaluable **Tokyo Subway Navigation app.** Tokyo subway stations provide free Wi-Fi.

Altogether, some 13 underground subway lines crisscross the city, operated by two companies: **Tokyo Metro** (the bigger of the two, which uses a symbol "M" that is vaguely reminiscent of McDonald's famous arches) and **Toei,** which uses a gingko leaf symbol and operates four lines. Station names are written in English, and each subway line is color-coded and assigned a letter (usually the subway's initial). The Ginza Line, for example, is orange, which means that all its trains and signs are orange, and it's identified by the letter "G." Additionally, each station along each line is assigned a number in chronological order beginning with the first station (Shibuya Station, for example, is G1 because it's the first station on the Ginza Line, while Asakusa Station is G19). Before boarding, however, make sure the train is going in the right direction—signs at each station show both the previous and the next stop, so you can double-check that you're heading in the right direction. Tokyo's newest line, Toei's Oedo Line, makes a zigzag loop around the city and can be useful, but be aware that it's buried deep underground and platforms take a while to reach, despite escalators.

Whereas it used to be a matter of skill to know exactly which train compartment to board if making transfers down the line, diagrams at each station (usually on a pillar at the entrance to each platform) show which end of the train and compartment is most useful for connections. Signs also show exactly how many minutes it takes to reach every destination on that line. Once you're on your way, trains display the next station in English on digital signs above their doors and announce stops in English.

Remember, once you reach your destination, look for the yellow signs on station platforms designating which exit to take for major buildings, museums, and addresses. If you're confused about which exit to take, ask an attendant near the ticket gate. Taking the right exit can make a world of difference, especially in Shinjuku, where there are some 60 station exits.

Because buying individual tickets is a hassle, I suggest buying either a Suica or PASMO prepaid card (see above). Otherwise, vending machines at all subway stations sell tickets; fares begin at ¥170 for the shortest distance and increase according to how far you're traveling. Vending machines give change, even for a ¥10,000 note. **To purchase your ticket,** insert money into the vending machine until the fare buttons light up, and then push the amount for the ticket you want.

Before purchasing your ticket, you first have to figure out your **fare.** Fares are posted on a large subway map above the vending machines, but they're sometimes in Japanese only. Some stations also have a signboard posting fares to other stations. If you still don't know the fare, just buy the cheapest ticket for ¥170. When you reach your destination, look for the **fare adjustment machine;** insert your ticket to find out how much more you owe, or look for a subway employee at the ticket window to tell you how much extra you owe. In any case, be sure to hang onto your ticket, since you must give it up at the end of your journey.

Most subways run from about 5am to midnight, although the times of the first and last trains depend on the line, the station, and whether it's a weekday or a weekend. Schedules are posted in the stations, and throughout most of the day, trains run every 3 to 5 minutes.

For more information on tickets, passes, and subway routes, as well as a detailed subway map, stop by **Metro Information desks** located at Ueno, Ginza, Shinjuku, and Omotesando stations. Or check the website **www.tokyometro.jp**. Information on **Toei Subway** is available at **www.kotsu.metro.tokyo.jp**.

BY TRAIN

In addition to subway lines, commuter trains operated by the **East Japan Railway Company (JR)** run aboveground throughout greater Tokyo. These are also color-coded, with fares beginning at ¥140. Buy your ticket from vending machines just as you would for the subway, but more convenient is the Suica or PASMO. Otherwise, if you think you'll be traveling a lot by JR lines on any given day, the **1-Day Metropolitan District Pass (Tokunai Pass)** allows unlimited travel within Tokyo's 23 wards for ¥750. If you have a validated Japan Rail Pass, you can travel on JR trains for free.

The **Yamanote Line** (green-colored coaches) is the best-known and most convenient JR line. It makes an oblong loop around the city in about an hour, stopping at 29 stations along the way, all of them announced in English and with digital signboards in each compartment (a new station between Shinagawa and Tamachi is scheduled to open in spring 2020). Another convenient JR line is the orange-colored **Chuo Line;** it's an express train that cuts across Tokyo between Shinjuku and Tokyo stations, with a stop at Ochanomizu. The yellow-colored **Sobu Line** runs between Shinjuku and Akihabara and beyond to Ryogoku and Chiba. Other JR lines serve outlying districts for the metropolis's commuting public, including Yokohama and Kamakura. Because the Yamanote, Chuo, and Sobu lines are often not identified by their specific names at major stations, look for signs that say JR LINES.

For more information on JR trains, as well as train travel throughout Japan, stop by the **JR East Travel Service Center** at Tokyo Station's Marunouchi North Exit. Open daily 7:30am to 8:30pm, it also offers free Wi-Fi, hotel reservations, tourist information, currency exchange and luggage delivery and storage. You can also exchange vouchers here for the Japan Rail Pass. Otherwise, for traveling in Tokyo, stop by a **JR East Travel Service Center** at Ueno, Shinjuku, Shibuya, and Ikebukuro stations, call the English-language **JR East Infoline** (✆ **050/2016-1603;** open daily 10am–6pm), or visit the website **www.jreast.co.jp/e**.

In addition to JR, private train companies provide service from Tokyo to outlying areas. **Tobu Railway,** for example, operates trains to Nikko, while **Odakyu Electric Railway** covers the Hakone area. Both offer discount travel passes. For more information, see individual destinations in chapter 6.

BY BUS

Toei buses are not as easy to use as trains or subways unless you know their routes, because only the end destination is written on the bus and many bus drivers don't speak English. However, I find they're more user-friendly than they used to be (buses even offer free Wi-Fi onboard) and are often convenient for short distances (such as traveling between Roppongi and Shibuya). If you're feeling adventurous, board the bus at the front and drop the exact fare (usually ¥210) into the box. If you don't have the exact amount, fare boxes accept coins or bills; your change minus the fare will come out below. Better yet, use a Suica or PASMO (see above) card. A signboard at the front of the bus displays the next stop, usually in English. When you wish to get off, press one of the purple buttons on the railing near the door or the seats. You can pick up an excellent Toei bus map showing all major routes at one of the Tokyo Tourist Information Centers operated by the Tokyo Metropolitan Government (see "Visitor Information," p. 57). The Toei website at **www.kotsu.metro.tokyo.jp** also provides information on routes, timetables, and fares.

In addition to Toei buses, the tourist-oriented **Sky Bus** (www.skybus.jp; ✆ **03/3215-0008**) offers 50-minute double-decker open-top bus tours around the Imperial Palace (¥1,600) and other tourist sites. It also offers hop-on, hop-off buses that travel three routes—Asakusa/Tokyo SkyTree, Odaiba, and Roppongi. These begin and end in Marunouchi near Tokyo Station and cost ¥3,500 for 24 hours. But frankly, taking public transportation is much cheaper.

BY TAXI

Taxis are expensive in Tokyo, unless you're going a short distance. **Fares** start at ¥410 for the first 1.052km (.65 miles) but increase ¥80 for each additional 237m (924 ft.) or 90 seconds of waiting time. There are also smaller, more compact taxis that charge slightly less, but these are fewer in number. Fares are posted on the back of the front passenger seat. If you're like me, you probably won't shop around—you'll gratefully jump into the first taxi that stops. Note that from 10pm to 5am, an extra 20% is added to your fare. Perhaps as an admission of how expensive taxis are, fares can be paid by credit card.

With the exception of some major downtown thoroughfares, you can hail a taxi from any street or go to a taxi stand or a major hotel. A red light above the dashboard shows if a taxi is free to pick up a passenger; a greenish-yellow light indicates that the taxi is occupied. ***Note:*** Be sure to stand clear of the back left door—it swings open automatically. Likewise, it shuts automatically once you're in. Taxi drivers are quite perturbed if you try to maneuver the door yourself. ***Note:*** The law requires that back-seat passengers wear seat belts.

Because many taxi drivers don't speak English, it's best to have your destination written out in Japanese, but even that may not help. Tokyo is so complicated that taxi drivers may not know a certain area, although many now have navigation systems. If you have a landline telephone number for your destination, the driver can locate it by entering it into his GPS.

There are so many taxis cruising Tokyo (about 50,000) that you can hail one easily on most thoroughfares—except when you need it most: when it's raining, or just after 1am on weekends when subways and trains have stopped. To call a taxi for a pickup (which carries a ¥310 surcharge), try **Nihon Kotsu** (www.nihon-kotsu.co.jp; **© 03/5755-2336**) for an English-speaking operator. I have rarely telephoned for a taxi—as in the movies, one usually cruises by just when I raise my hand.

Unlike in many cities around the world, **Uber** (www.uber.com/cities/tokyo) is tightly restricted, isn't widely used, and works in conjunction with high-end private drivers and taxi companies. Expect some changes before the 2020 Olympics, however, including the prospect of driverless taxis.

[Fast FACTS] TOKYO

If you can't find answers to your questions here, check "Fast Facts: Japan," in chapter 12. If you still can't find an answer, call one of the tourist information offices listed above under "Visitor Information." Another good source is the free **Foreign Residents' Advisory Center** (**© 03/5320-7744**), which can answer questions on a wide range of topics concerning daily life in Japan, including legal matters, taxes, traffic accidents, emergency numbers, and even Japanese social customs; it's open Monday to Friday 9:30am to noon and 1 to 5pm. Finally, if you're staying in a first-class hotel, another valuable resource is the concierge or guest-relations desk, where the staff can tell you how to reach your destination, answer general questions, and even make restaurant reservations.

ATMs/Banks **Narita Airport** and **Haneda Airport** have exchange counters for all incoming international flights that offer better exchange rates than what you'd get abroad, as well as ATMs. Change enough money to last several days, since the exchange rate is the same as banks in town. Otherwise, all banks displaying an AUTHORIZED FOREIGN EXCHANGE sign can exchange currency and traveler's checks, with exchange rates usually displayed at the appropriate foreign-exchange counter. More convenient and quicker—but at a slightly less favorable rate—are **Travelex** foreign-exchange kiosks (www.travelex.co.jp), with more than 20 locations across town, including Tokyo Station (**© 03/5220-4311**), next to the JR East Travel Service Center and open daily 7:30am to 8:30pm. Other locations are Roppongi, Ueno, Shinjuku, Shibuya, Asakusa, Shinagawa, and Akihabara, among others. **WORLD CURR€nc¥ $HOP** (www.tokyo-card.co.jp/wcs/wcs-shop-e.php) is a Japanese company offering similar money-exchange services, with counters in the Ginza Core Building, 5–8–20 Ginza (✆ **03/6254-6851;** station: Ginza), open daily 11am to 8pm; in Roppongi Hills, 6–19–1 Roppongi (✆ **03/5413-9722;** station: Roppongi), open Monday to Friday 11am to 7pm and Saturday, Sunday, and holidays noon to 5pm; and in Shinjuku, Shibuya, Ikebukuro, Ueno, Marunouchi, Nihombashi and other locations. For ATMs that accept foreign credit cards, head to any post office or 7-Eleven. I've even seen ATMs operated by 7-Eleven and JP Post in subway stations and other convenient locations. For details on changing or obtaining money, see "Money & Costs," in chapter 12.

Dentists The **Tokyo Clinic Dental Office,** 3–4–30 Shiba-koen, Minato-ku (www.tcdo.jp; ✆ **03/3431-4225**), is near Kamiyacho, Onarimon, Akabanebashi, or Daimon stations and across from Tokyo Tower. Just a 3-minute walk away is the **United Dental Office,** 2–3–8 Azabudai, Minato-ku (http://uniteddentaloffice.com; ✆ **03/5570-4334**). Tokyo Midtown Medical Center (see "Doctors & Hospitals," below) also has a **Dental Clinic** (**03/5413-7912**). All have English-speaking staff.

Doctors & Hospitals Many first-class hotels offer medical facilities or an in-house doctor. Tokyo Metropolitan Government's office for **Hospital Management** (www.byouin.metro.tokyo.jp/english/index.html) can refer you to medical professionals who speak English and has staff who can also explain the health insurance system in Japan; its emergency translation services at ✆ **03/5285-8181** is staffed with translators who can act as go-betweens during treatment if problems arise, available daily 9am to 8pm. Providing similar services is the **AMDA International Medical Information Center** (http://amda-imic.com; ✆ **03/5285-8088**), open Monday to Friday 9am to 5pm. Embassies (see chapter 12) also have lists of English-speaking health professionals.

Otherwise, clinics with English-speaking staff and popular with foreigners living in Tokyo include **Tokyo Midtown Medical Center,** sixth floor of Midtown Tower, 9–7–1 Akasaka, Minato-ku, near Roppongi Station (www.tokyomidtown-mc.jp; ✆ **03/5413-7911**), and **Tokyo Medical & Surgical Clinic** (www.tmsc.jp; ✆ **03/3436-3028**), in the same building as Tokyo Clinic Dental Office, above.

Large hospitals in Japan are open only a limited number of hours (designated hospitals remain open for emergencies, of course, and an ambulance will automatically take you there). Hospitals with English-speaking staff (you can also make appointments to see a doctor) include the **Seibo International Catholic Hospital,** 2–5–1 Naka-Ochiai, Shinjuku-ku, near Mejiro Station on the Yamanote Line (www.seibokai.or.jp; ✆ **03/3951-1111**); **St. Luke's International Hospital (Seiroka Byoin),** 9–1 Akashi-cho, Chuo-ku, near Tsukiji Station on the Hibiya Line (www.luke.or.jp; ✆ **03/5550-7166**); and **Japanese Red Cross Medical Center (Nihon Sekijujisha Iryo Center),** 4–1–22 Hiroo, Shibuya-ku (www.med.jrc.or.jp; ✆ **03/3400-1311**), whose closest subway stations are Roppongi, Hiroo, and Shibuya—from there, you should take a taxi.

Emergencies See "Fast Facts" in chapter 12, p. 333. The Metropolitan Police Department also maintains a telephone counseling service for foreigners at ✆ **03/3501-0110** Monday to Friday from 8:30am to 5:15pm.

Internet & Wi-Fi Access All listed Tokyo accommodations in this chapter provide free use of computers for travelers without a laptop, usually in the lobby or business center, as well as free in-room Wi-Fi. Otherwise, a good place to set up a temporary office is at the sophisticated **Gran Cyber Café Bagus,** on the 12th floor of the Roi Building, 5–5–1 Roppongi (✆ **03/5786-2280;** station: Roppongi). Open 24 hours, it offers individual cubicles with prices that depend on the chair you select: For a seat that reclines, it's ¥296 for 30 minutes. Three- and 4-hour packages are also available, and, unsurprisingly given Tokyo's high taxi and accommodation prices, it even offers a 24-hour package for ¥4,815, as well as—brace yourself—booths for couples. You have to wonder how many people actually work.

As for free Wi-Fi, it's a lot more ubiquitous than it used to be, though from experience I have to say reception can be spotty. All subway stations, JR Yamanote stations, and Toei buses provide free Wi-Fi. In addition, several neighborhoods offer their own free Wi-Fi at key spots, including Ginza, Marunouchi, Ueno, Asakusa, Shibuya, and Akihabara, as well as at most department stores. Many coffee shops, restaurants, and bars offer it to paying customers as well (you may need to ask for the password). Finally, many entities offer free Wi-Fi, most of which require you to sign up. The Tokyo Metropolitan Government, for example, offers **Free Wi-Fi & Tokyo** (www.wifi-tokyo.jp). Go to its website to register and see all the parks, museums, and other places where you can connect. For more on using the Internet and Wi-Fi in Japan, see "Fast Facts" in chapter 12.

Luggage Storage & Delivery Major JR train stations have lockers for luggage, but with the increasing number of tourists, these can be full. **Sagawa** (www.sagawa-exp.co.jp) offers luggage storage and delivery, with offices in Tokyo Station, Tokyo SkyTree, Asakusa, and Shinjuku Expressway Bus Terminal. There's also a baggage storage room near the **JR East Travel Service Center** at the Marunouchi north exit of Tokyo Station (www.tokyostationcity.com/en/information/locker.html; ✆ **03/5221-8123**) open daily 7:30am to 8:30pm.

Mail & Postage Although all post offices (called a *yubinkyoku*) are open Monday to Friday from 9am to 5pm, major post offices located in every ward remain open to 7pm (to mail a package, you'll need to go to one of these). Tokyo's **Central Post Office,** 2-7-2 Marunouchi, Chiyoda-ku (✆ **03/3217-5231;** station: Tokyo or Marunouchi), is open Monday to Friday 9am to 9pm and Saturday and Sunday 9am to 6pm, but it also has a counter open 24 hours for mail and packages. For details on domestic and international postage, see "Fast Facts" in chapter 12 or go to www.post.japanpost.jp.

Newspapers & Magazines In addition to two English-language newspapers published daily in Japan—the ***Japan Times*** (www.japantimes.co.jp), which comes distributed with the *International New York Times,* and the ***Japan News*** (www.the-japan-news.com)—***Metropolis*** (www.metropolisjapan.com) is a free weekly with features on Tokyo, club listings, and restaurant and movie reviews. The quarterly ***TimeOut Tokyo*** (www.timeout.jp) offers more in-depth coverage of the city.

Pharmacies Tokyo has no 24-hour drugstores (*kusuri-ya*), but ubiquitous 24-hour convenience stores such as 7-Eleven, Lawson, and FamilyMart carry things like aspirin. If you're looking for specific pharmaceuticals, a good bet is the **American Pharmacy,** in the basement of the Marunouchi Building, 2-4-1 Marunouchi, Chiyoda-ku (✆ **03/5220-7716;** station: Tokyo or Marunouchi; Mon–Fri 9am–9pm, Sat 10am–9pm, Sun and holidays 10am–8pm), which has many of the same over-the-counter drugs you can find at home (many of them imported from the U.S.) and can fill American prescriptions—but note that you *must first visit a doctor in Japan* before foreign prescriptions can be filled. It's best to bring an ample supply of any prescription medication with you.

Safety According to a 2017 study by *The Economist,* Tokyo is the safest major urban destination in the world. There are, however, precautions you should always take when traveling: Stay alert and be aware of your immediate surroundings. Be especially careful with cameras, purses, and wallets, particularly in crowded subways, department stores, or tourist attractions—pickpocketing has been on the rise. Some Japanese also caution women against walking through parks alone at night.

WHERE TO STAY

Tokyo has no old, grand hotels in the tradition of Hong Kong's Peninsula or Bangkok's Oriental; it has hardly any old hotels, period. But what the city's hotels lack in quaintness or old grandeur is more than made up for by excellent service—for which the Japanese are legendary—as well as cleanliness and efficiency. Be prepared, however, for small rooms. Space is at a premium in Tokyo, so with the exception of Tokyo's expensive hotels, rooms seem to come in only three sizes: small, minuscule, and barely adequate.

Unfortunately, Tokyo also doesn't have many first-class *ryokan,* or Japanese-style inns. You may, therefore, want to wait for your travels around the country to experience a first-rate *ryokan.* Otherwise, there are moderate and inexpensive Japanese-style inns in Tokyo. In fact, if you're traveling on a tight budget, a simple Japanese-style inn is often the cheapest way to go, though don't expect much in the way of service or amenities. In addition, most upper-bracket hotels offer at least a few Japanese-style rooms, with *tatami* mats, a Japanese bathtub (deeper and narrower than the Western version), and a futon. Although these rooms tend to be expensive, they're usually large enough for four people.

Note: Unless otherwise indicated, in-room Wi-Fi is free and units have private bathrooms.

For details on the various types of accommodations, see "Tips on Accommodations" in chapter 2.

TAXES & SERVICE CHARGES Unless otherwise stated, prices for accommodations include taxes (but not the local hotel tax where applicable) and service charge. All hotel rates below include an 8% government tax (slated to rise to 10% in October 2019) unless stated otherwise. An additional local hotel tax will be added to bills that cost more than ¥10,000 per person per night: ¥100 is levied per person per night for rates between ¥10,000 and ¥14,999; rates of ¥15,000 and up are taxed at ¥200. Furthermore, all upper-class hotels and most medium-range hotels add a **service charge** of 10% to 15% (cheaper establishments do not add a service charge, because no service is provided).

Mapping Out Tokyo's Hotels

Once you've chosen a hotel or inn that appeals to you, you can locate it using the following neighborhood maps:

- To locate accommodations in and near **Ginza,** p. 74.
- To locate accommodations in **Asakusa,** p. 81.
- To locate accommodations in **Ueno,** p. 83.
- To locate accommodations in **Shinjuku,** p. 84.
- To locate accommodations in **Harajuku and Aoyama,** p. 88.
- To locate accommodations in **Roppongi,** p. 90.

price CATEGORIES

Expensive	¥32,000 and up
Moderate	¥12,000–¥31,000
Inexpensive	Under ¥12,000

The hotel recommendations below are arranged by geographical location. However, because Tokyo's attractions, restaurants, and nightlife are widely scattered, and because the public transportation system is fast and efficient (I've provided the nearest subway or train stations for each listing), there's no one location in Tokyo that's more convenient than another—and because this is one of the most expensive hotel cities in the world, the overriding factor in selecting accommodations will likely be cost.

Hotels in & Around Ginza

EXPENSIVE

Conrad Tokyo ★★★ Many attributes of this fine, contemporary hotel win me over, starting with the large *sumi-e* (Japanese brush painting) in the lobby by one of my favorite Japanese artists, Toko Shinoda, just one of 23 leading Japanese craftsmen with artwork gracing the hotel. It also has one of the city's largest spa and fitness centers, occupying the entire 29th floor with 10 treatment rooms, a 25m pool (with a *sumi-e* design on the bottom, naturally), and a gym offering aerobics, yoga, and other classes. But it's what's outside the hotel that makes this property special: fantastic views of Tokyo Bay and Odaiba over Hama Riku Garden. Because the cheapest rooms (sized at a very respectable 48 sq. m [516 sq. ft.]) face the city, I think it's worth splurging for bayside rooms, which take full advantage of those panoramic views with couches that extend the entire length of the wall-to-wall window and are great places to relax with the morning newspaper or evening drink. Located a short walk from Ginza and Shiodome, the hotel is surrounded by office buildings housing mostly TV and advertising conglomerates, which perhaps explains why half of Conrad's guests are international travelers, most of them American.

1-9-1 Higashi-Shinbashi, Minato-ku. www.conradhotels.com. ✆ **03/6388-8000.** 290 units. ¥45,000–¥89,000 single or double; ¥57,000–¥118,500 executive room; from ¥119,000 suite. Rates exclude tax and service charge. Station: Shiodome (1 min.) or Shimbashi (7 min.). **Amenities:** 4 restaurants, lounge/bar; concierge; executive-level rooms; free entrance to health club and 25m indoor pool (classes cost ¥3,150); room service; spa; Wi-Fi.

Imperial Hotel ★★★ This is one of Tokyo's oldest and most respected hotels, with a prime location near subway stations, Ginza, Hibiya Park, and Imperial Palace. First opened in 1890 at the request of the imperial family to house foreign visitors, it was rebuilt in 1922 by Frank Lloyd Wright and survived the horrific 1923 earthquake, only to succumb in 1970 to developers in a complete makeover. Wright's legacy lives on in the hotel's Art Deco **Old Imperial Bar** and Wright-inspired designs and furniture in public spaces. Rooms are spread throughout the main building, popular with Japanese because its showers are located outside of tubs (which allows them to bathe in

In & Around Ginza

HOTELS ■
Conrad Hotel Tokyo **5**
Hotel Gracery **8**
Imperial Hotel **1**
Mitsui Garden Hotel Ginza Premier **6**
Park Hotel Tokyo **4**
Remm Hibiya **11**

RESTAURANTS ◆
Andy Shin's Hinomoto **13**
Din Tai Fung **24**
Gonpachi **25**
The Imperial Viking Sal **1**
La Boheme **15, 25**
Maru **17**
Meal Muji **14**
Mugi to Olive **9**
Monsoon **25**
Rangetsu **22**
Shabusen **19**
Ten-ichi **2, 17**
Tsukiji Sushi Sen **20**
Tsunahachi **23**
Yakitori stands **12**
Zest Cantina **25**

NIGHTLIFE ◆
300 Bar **3, 18**
Ginza Sapporo Lion **7**
Kabuki-za **21**
Old Imperial **1**
Tokyo Takarazuka Theater **10**

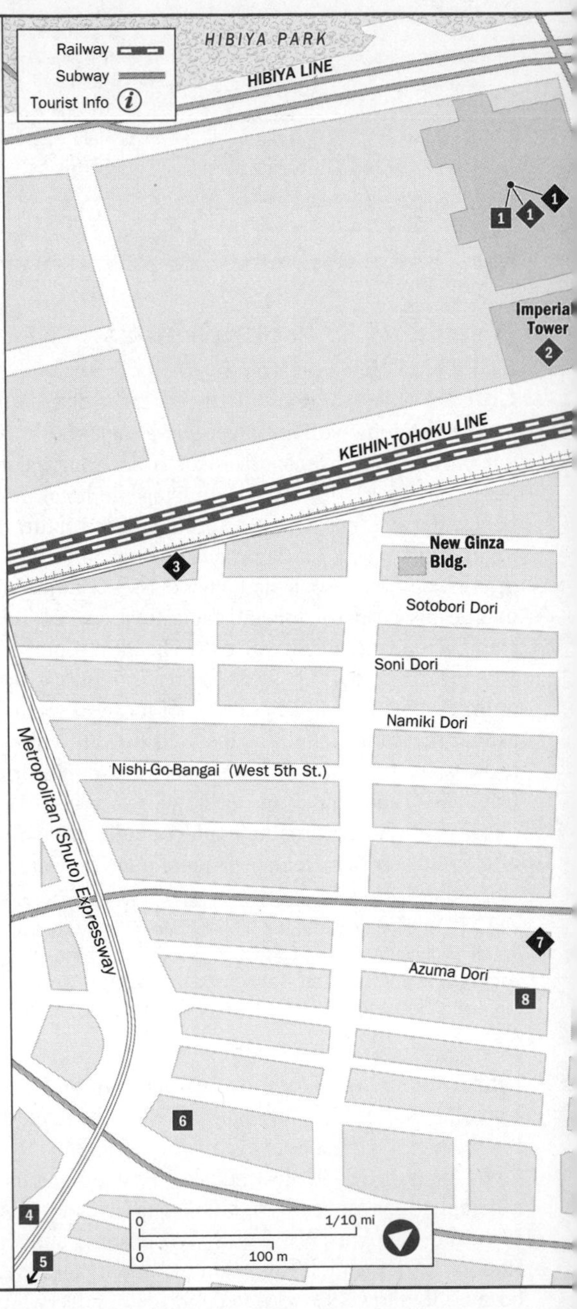

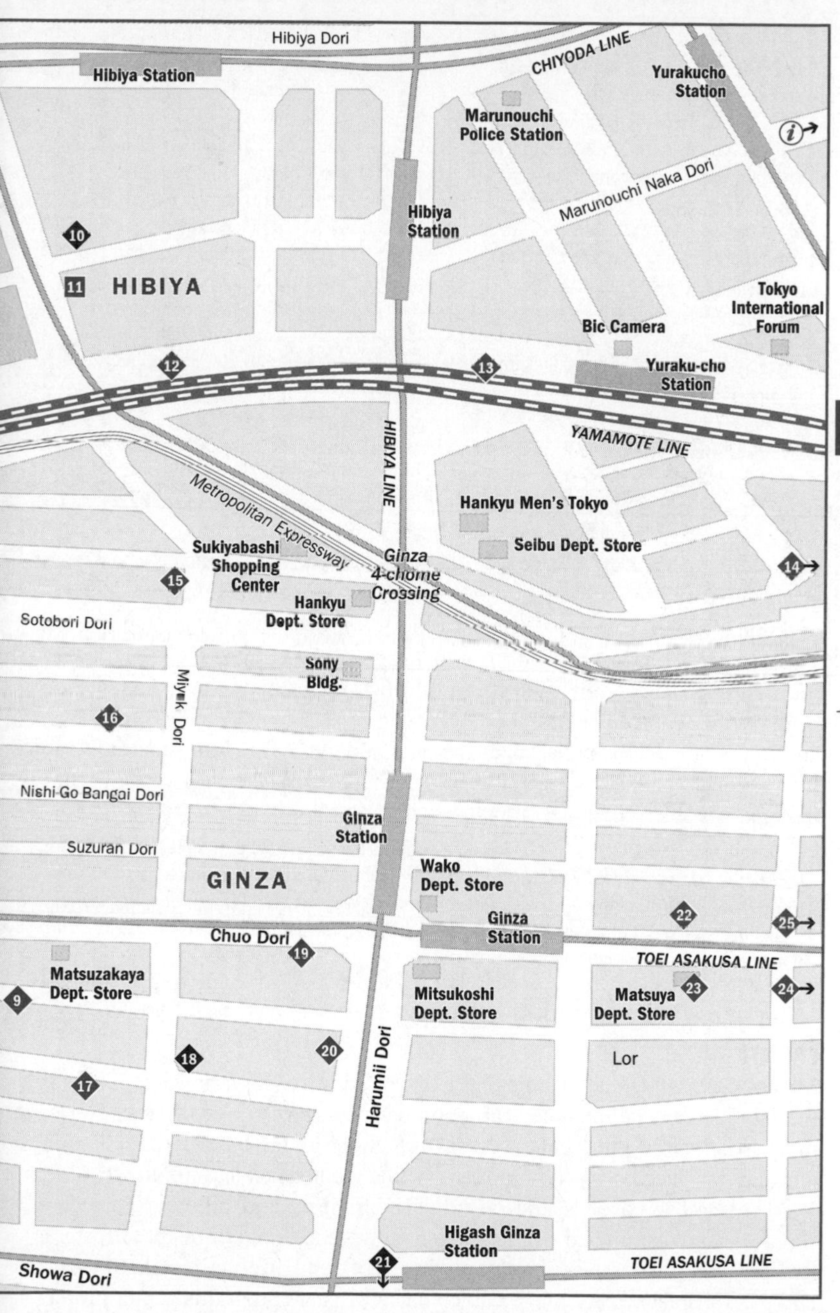

Hibiya Dori
Hibiya Station
CHIYODA LINE
Yurakucho Station
Marunouchi Police Station
Marunouchi Naka Dori
Hibiya Station
10
11
HIBIYA
Tokyo International Forum
Bic Camera
12
13
Yuraku-cho Station
YAMAMOTE LINE
HIBIYA LINE
Metropolitan Expressway
Hankyu Men's Tokyo
Seibu Dept. Store
Sukiyabashi Shopping Center
Ginza 4-chome Crossing
14
15
Hankyu Dept. Store
Sotobori Dori
Sony Bldg.
16
Nishi-Go Bangai Dori
Ginza Station
Suzuran Dori
GINZA
Wako Dept. Store
22
25
Ginza Station
Chuo Dori
19
TOEI ASAKUSA LINE
Matsuzakaya Dept. Store
23
24
9
Mitsukoshi Dept. Store
Matsuya Dept. Store
18
20
Harumii Dori
17
Higash Ginza Station
21
TOEI ASAKUSA LINE
Showa Dori

WHY THE big range IN HOTEL PRICES?

In Tokyo, Kyoto, and other major Japanese cities, nearly all high-end and medium-range hotels offer various categories of rooms at varying rates, with names such as premium, superior, etc., that are based on a variety of factors that may or may not include room size, decor, view, and what floor they're on. Sometimes, rooms can even be fairly identical but still vary in price because of the floor they're on and the views. Because of those many different levels of quality at top-rated and medium-range hotels, there's often a wide range of rates for any given hotel regardless of the season. Check individual hotel websites to see specific room types.

Another factor influencing hotel rates, of course, is an increasingly fluctuating market based on demand. Because of a marked upswing in international tourism the past few years, hotel rates can change wildly from one week to the next, as well as with holidays and seasons such as Chinese New Year, cherry blossom season, and summer vacation. For a hotel with a price range of 30,000 to 60,000 yen, for example, you can expect to pay about 30,000 for the cheapest room (such as a small one on a low floor facing another building) in low season and about 60,000 in high season for a deluxe bigger room with views of a garden or Tokyo Bay. For most of the year, you'll probably pay somewhere in between. Inexpensive accommodations, on the other hand, tend to charge the same rate year-round.

traditional fashion), and in a 31-story tower added in 1983. Although access to the tower, via a second-floor passageway, is a bit cumbersome, and tower rooms are smaller, foreign guests tend to like rooms here because views are better (with a choice of either the Ginza with its sparkling neon or Hibiya Park and Imperial Palace) and it's near the pool and gym. ***Tip:*** Join Imperial Club International—membership is free—and you can use the pool and gym for free and get other hotel discounts.

1-1-1 Uchisaiwaicho, Chiyoda-ku. www.imperialhotel.co.jp/e/tokyo. ✆ **03/3504-1111.** 1,019 units. ¥33,750–¥91,800 single or double; from ¥100,000 suite. Rates exclude service charge. Station: Hibiya (1 min.). **Amenities:** 13 restaurants; 2 bars; lounge; babysitting; children's day-care center for ages 2 weeks to 6 years (fee: ¥5,400 for 2 hr.); concierge; executive-level rooms; exercise room (fee: ¥1,080; free for Imperial Club International members); 20th-floor indoor pool and sauna (fee: ¥1,080; free for Imperial Club International members); room service; tea-ceremony room; post office; Wi-Fi.

MODERATE

Hotel Gracery ★★ Rooms here may be tiny, but high-powered Ginza is literally just outside the door. Targeting business travelers by offering convenient locations in city centers across the country, this business chain stays ahead of the pack with accommodations that are updated and minimally chic, with duvet-covered beds and colorful bed runners and pillows. There are rooms geared just toward women, some with wood floors (thought to foster a feeling of well-being when trod upon barefoot), and offering female toiletries and the Takarazuka Sky Stage cable channel (where programs center on this all-female troupe), as well as doubles and executive-level rooms with massage chairs.

7–10–1 Ginza, Chuo-ku. www.ginza.gracery.com. ✆ **03/6686-1000.** 270 units. ¥11,800–¥24,200 single; ¥13,000–¥28,000 double. Station: Ginza (3 min.) or Shimbashi (7 min.). 1 block east of Chuo Dori, behind Ginza Sapporo Lion. **Amenities:** Restaurant; bar; Wi-Fi.

Mitsui Garden Hotel Ginza Premier ★★★ Mitsui Garden is a chain of business hotels that generally rises above the others in terms of decor and facilities, but this one ranks as one of Mitsui Garden's top properties. Its location is superb for business and leisure travelers alike, on the southern edge of Ginza near Shimbashi. Occupying the upper floors of an office building, it has a 16th-floor lobby that welcomes guests with lots of sofas, a comfy computer corner for travelers without laptops, and floor-to-ceiling windows revealing great views of Tokyo Bay, Hama Rikyu Garden, and Tokyo Tower. Rooms are compact though thoughtfully designed, but their best feature is the panoramic views of Tokyo Tower (the most requested), the Ginza (most beautiful at night), or the bay (note that a new building now obstructs bay views from some rooms, so be sure to request an unobstructed view). Views are even afforded from bathrooms, either through windows that look out past the bedroom toward the city (in the cheaper rooms) or, in View Bath and Premier rooms, from windows right beside the tub that let you take in the vistas as you soak. Although this hotel has lots going for it, the views in this price range really set it apart.

8–13–1 Ginza, Chuo-ku. www.gardenhotels.co.jp/eng. ✆ **03/3543-1131.** 361 units. ¥17,900–¥29,700 single; ¥19,800–¥48,300 double. Station: Shimbasi (5 min.) or Ginza (7 min.). **Amenities:** Restaurant; bar; Wi-Fi.

Park Hotel Tokyo ★★★ Occupying the top 10 floors of a triangular-shaped building it shares with international media organizations (like Kyodo News), this hotel is well located within walking distance of the Ginza and Hama Rikyu Garden. Its lobby, on the 25th floor and decorated with large trees and dark woods in a theme of "nature and health," is bathed in the natural sunlight afforded by a 10-story atrium topped with an opaque ceiling, making the **ART Lounge** a great place for breakfast. The front desk is one of the most dramatic I've seen, backed by nothing but great views of Tokyo Tower and the city. Rooms, simply decorated with original art, also provide views, the best of which can be found on the 30th floor and above facing Hama Rikyu Garden and Tokyo Bay. One of the things I like most about this hotel is its dedication

A Double or a Twin?

For the sake of convenience, the price for two people in a room is listed as a "double" in this book. Japanese hotels, however, differentiate between rooms with a double bed or two twin beds, usually with different prices. Although most hotels charge more for a twin room, sometimes the opposite is true; so be sure to inquire about prices for both. Note, too, that hotels usually have more twin rooms than doubles, for the simple reason that Japanese couples, used to their own futons, traditionally prefer twin beds.

to art, with changing exhibits on lobby walls, and 31 rooms on the 31st floor painted by Japanese artists—like the Bamboo Room with wall murals of greenery or the brightly colored Geisha Goldfish—complete with an art concierge to explain the concept and artist behind each room.

Shiodome Media Tower, 1–7–1 Higashi Shimbashi, Minato-ku. www.parkhoteltokyo.com. ✆ **03/6252-1111.** 269 units. ¥17,400–¥25,000 single; ¥20,135–¥40,000 double. Rates exclude service charge. Station: Shiodome (1 min.) or Shimbashi (8 min.). **Amenities:** 2 restaurants; bar; lounge; concierge; personal-size gym (free, on a reservation basis); room service; spa; Wi-Fi.

remm Hibiya ★ This low-key business hotel slips under the radar of most passersby, despite its prime location across from the Imperial Hotel and just steps away from the Ginza. Its second-floor reception shares space with a branch of Muji Café & Meal, known for its inexpensive salads and healthy dishes and open from 7am for breakfast. Rooms are tiny, but all have the surprising addition of massage chairs, and some single and double rooms facing west even have views of Hibiya Park or palace grounds between buildings; note that single/double rooms, with showers instead of tubs, are actually the same room and are cramped for two people. Glass walls separating bathrooms from living space give the illusion of space (thank goodness there's a blind you can pull down). Although a business hotel, this place also caters to women with a devoted Ladies Floor and the Takarazuka Sky Stage cable channel free of charge, but the extremely popular Takarazuka Kagekidan theater just across the street, with its all-female cast performing musical revues, is what draws its devoted (and overwhelmingly women) fans. There are branches in Akihabara and Roppongi.

1–2–1 Yurakucho, Chiyoda-ku. www.hankyu-hotel.com/hotel/remm/hibiya. ✆ **03/3507-0606.** 225 units. ¥8,800–¥18,500 single; ¥12,600–¥36,000 double. Station: Hibiya (2 min.) or Yurakucho (5 min.). **Amenities:** Restaurant; free Wi-Fi.

Near Tokyo Station

EXPENSIVE

Hoshinoya Tokyo ★★★ Traditional Japanese inns have gone the way of the geisha in Tokyo, and so it was with some fanfare that this ryokan opened its discreet doors in 2016. Hidden among Otemachi's high-rises, it's an oasis of Japanese refinement, apparent the moment you are greeted upon entering by a traditionally clad hostess, who will place your shoes in one of the decorative bamboo boxes that line the corridor like works of art. In fact, you won't wear shoes or slippers at all during your stay (except for your own bathroom slippers), because tatami runs throughout the inn, inviting you to relax and feel at home. Rooms are decorated in a graceful minimalist style, resplendent with natural materials like wood, bamboo, slate-colored papered walls, and shoji covering floor-to-ceiling windows. In keeping with the personalized service that's the trademark of a great ryokan, each of the inn's 14 floors has its own **Ochanoma Lounge,** where guests are invited to relax and enjoy tea, sake, and snacks. But the crowning glory is the top-floor hot-spring bath, a rarity in Tokyo, with water drawn from 1,500m (4,921 ft) from below ground and an open roof, letting you gaze up at passing clouds or maybe even falling snow. It's hard to believe you're in Tokyo.

1-9-2 Otemachi, Chiyoda-ku. https://hoshinoya.com/tokyo/en. ✆ **03/6214-5151.** ¥52,736–¥68,646 single; ¥75,200–¥105,500 double. Rates include breakfast. Station: Otemachi (2 min.) or Tokyo (10 min.). **Amenities:** Restaurant; spa; hot-spring bath; Wi-Fi.

Tokyo Station Hotel ★★ Tokyo Station was built in 1914 in the tradition of Europe's great train stations; the Tokyo Station Hotel opened a year later. Although the station itself has grown crazily over the years, the historic section containing the hotel, which faces Marunouchi with a handsome brick facade, retains its century-old glory. And luckily, the hotel has its own dedicated entrance (as well as direct access to subway and train stations, handy in inclement weather), so it's away from the chaos that reigns in the station and has little foot traffic. As Japan Railway's flagship hotel, it retains many of its original features, including a high-ceilinged lobby lounge, which once served as the first-class waiting lounge, and the original 330-m.-long (1,082-ft.) corridor leading to rooms. Even Hisashi Sugimoto, at the hotel since 1958, is back at the historic **Bar Oak** concocting his signature cocktails. Six different styles of rooms, all with high-vaulted ceilings and expansive windows, are available, from Classic Queens, which are fairly standard and also dark, since they face another building, to Dome Side Rooms, which face a concourse with the spectacularly restored reliefs from the train station's Cupola domed ceiling. With both fine and casual dining and old-world ambience, not to mention easy access to one of the busiest train stations in the world, this is a unique property in Tokyo. Train buffs won't want to stay anywhere else.

Tokyo Station, 1-9-1 Marunouchi, Chiyoda-ku. www.thetokyostationhotel.jp. ✆ **03/5220-1111.** 150 units. ¥33,000–¥46,800 single; ¥38,400–¥61,8000 double. 10% discount for holders of Japan Rail Pass on specific rooms. Station: Tokyo (1 min.). **Amenities:** 7 restaurants; 2 bars; lounge; concierge; small gym (fee: ¥1,000); room service; spa; Wi-Fi.

INEXPENSIVE

Super Hotel Lohas Tokyo-eki Yaesu Chuo-guchi (スーパーホテルＬｏｈａｓ東京駅八重洲中央口) ★ It's a mouthful, but what its name really means is that it's super cheap (by central Tokyo standards) and has a super location only a block east of Tokyo Station. Part of a growing hotel chain that edges competitors out with low prices, it offers small rooms with all the basics, plus pull-down window shades for total darkness, wall-mounted TVs (there's nowhere else to really put them), and humidifier/air purifiers. There's also a ladies' floor that offers the additions of face steamers, makeup mirrors and other amenities in rooms done up in feminine colors. However, with the rest of Tokyo within such easy reach, I'm betting you won't want to spend much quality time in your room, though you might want to take a dip in the large public baths, which feature playful—if slightly weird—seasonal additions, such as lemons added to the water.

2-2-7 Yaesu, Chuo-ku. www.superhoteljapan.com/en/s-hotels/yaesu. ✆ **03/3241-9000.** 325 units. ¥11,500–¥15,000 single; ¥14,000–¥22,500 double. Station: Tokyo (Yaesu Central exit, 3 min.) or Kyobashi (4 min.). **Amenities:** Restaurant; Wi-Fi.

Asakusa

MODERATE

Ryokan Kamogawa ★★ Established in 1948 by the present owner's parents and located just off Nakamise Dori, this inn is small and personable, with a coffee shop and a Japanese-style bath you can lock and use privately (reserve in advance). Its *tatami* rooms, with shoji screens and other traditional touches, sleep up to five persons, making them a good choice for families. Note that only one room (the size of four-and-a-half *tatami* mats; a single *tatami* measures 1m×1.8m) is available at the cheapest rates below, so you're more likely to pay ¥19,800 for a standard room whether you're one or two people. In any case, the small inn is often fully booked, especially in April, October, December, and February, so if you hope to stay here then, book far ahead. Note, too, that the front door is locked at 11:30pm; if you wish to stay out later, be sure to ask for the back-door key. Dinners, served in the coffee shop, start at ¥2,400 but must be ordered in advance.

1–30–10 Asakusa, Taito-ku. www.f-kamogawa.jp. ✆ **03/3843-2681.** 10 units. ¥8,100–¥20,300 single; ¥12,000–¥28,000 double; ¥26,700–¥38,400 triple. Station: Asakusa (3 min.). **Amenities:** Coffee shop; Wi-Fi.

Sadachiyo Sukeroku-no-yado ★★★ This 70-year-old *ryokan* is a rarity in Tokyo and a great find in Asakusa's traditional neighborhood. It has lots of Edo-era touches, from the rickshaw outside the front door to stone and paper lanterns, bamboo screens, and antiques that fill public places. Even the staff wears traditional clothing, and the lounge is typically Japanese with floor seating. Rooms are all *tatami* and have woodblock prints, shoji screens, and other traditional features, with some large enough for a family of six. The cypress-and-granite public baths are a perk, and to really feel like you're living in old Edo (present-day Tokyo), sign up for the Japanese dinner, featuring dishes typical of the times and beginning at ¥5,500 for a 10-dish meal (make dinner reservations when you book your room). The ryokan has a 2am curfew.

2–20–1 Asakusa, Taito-ku. www.sadachiyo.co.jp. ✆ **03/3842-6431.** 20 units. ¥14,100–¥15,100 single; ¥19,600–¥28,800 double. Station: Tawaramachi (8 min.), Asakusa (15 min.), or Tsukuba Express Asakusa (3 min.). **Amenities:** Restaurant; Wi-Fi.

INEXPENSIVE

Book and Bed Tokyo ★★ A library room that doubles as a hostel? It's a bit gimmicky, and yet it works, mainly because it's well-done and the coffin-size sleeping cubbyholes are tucked away among a wall of bookshelves, making guests feel more insulated from their neighbors than the usual capsule hotel. But this is still a hostel, after all, with shared toilets and showers, and only a curtain separates you from the communal living space in the center of the room, where sofas invite guests to read some of the library's 1,500 books, including those in English and guidebooks on Japan. There are three types of sleeping spaces available: 10 "compact" units filled with a single bed, 30 slightly larger standard units with a semi-double-size bed, and six double units with king-size beds, all with reading lamps and electric outlets. At one end of the room is a counter offering breakfast and alcoholic drinks, making sleep a

Asakusa

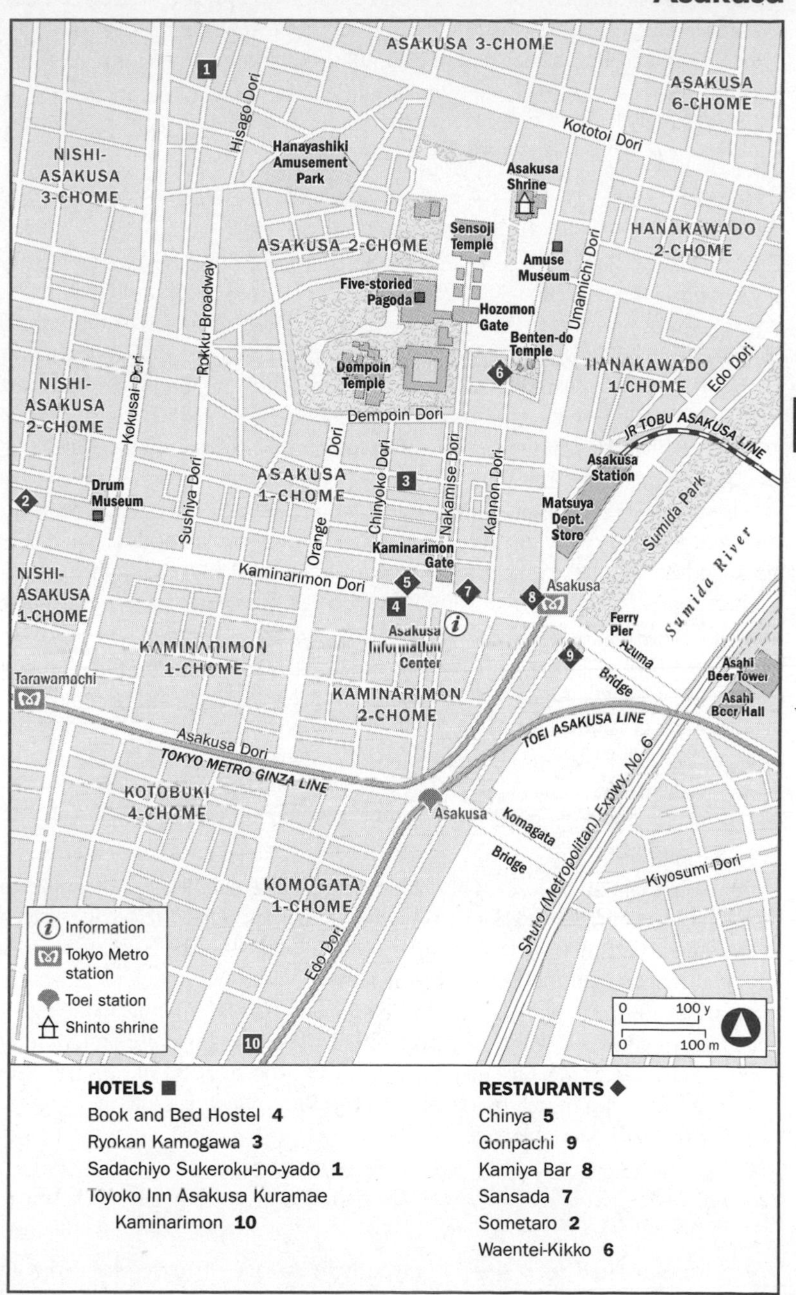
ASAKUSA 3-CHOME
ASAKUSA 6-CHOME
Kototoi Dori
Hisago Dori
NISHI-ASAKUSA 3-CHOME
Hanayashiki Amusement Park
Asakusa Shrine
HANAKAWADO 2-CHOME
Sensoji Temple
ASAKUSA 2-CHOME
Amuse Museum
Umamichi Dori
Rokku Broadway
Five-storied Pagoda
Hozomon Gate
Benten-do Temple
Dompoin Temple
Edo Dori
NISHI-ASAKUSA 2-CHOME
Kokusai Dori
Dempoin Dori
JR TOBU ASAKUSA LINE
Asakusa Station
Drum Museum
Sushiya Dori
ASAKUSA 1-CHOME
Orange Dori
Chinyoko Dori
Nakamise Dori
Kannon Dori
Matsuya Dept. Store
Sumida Park
Sumida River
Kaminarimon Gate
Kaminarimon Dori
NISHI-ASAKUSA 1-CHOME
Asakusa
Ferry Pier
Asakusa Information Center
KAMINARIMON 1-CHOME
Azuma Bridge
Tarawamachi
KAMINARIMON 2-CHOME
Asahi Beer Hall
TOEI ASAKUSA LINE
Asakusa Dori
TOKYO METRO GINZA LINE
Shuto (Metropolitan) Expwy. No. 6
KOTOBUKI 4-CHOME
Asakusa
Komagata Bridge
Kiyosumi Dori
KOMOGATA 1-CHOME
Edo Dori
Information
Tokyo Metro station
Toei station
Shinto shrine
0 100 y
0 100 m
HOTELS
Book and Bed Hostel 4
Ryokan Kamogawa 3
Sadachiyo Sukeroku-no-yado 1
Toyoko Inn Asakusa Kuramae Kaminarimon 10
RESTAURANTS
Chinya 5
Gonpachi 9
Kamiya Bar 8
Sansada 7
Sometaro 2
Waentei-Kikko 6

challenge, perhaps, for those who like to turn in early or get up late. Note that payment can be made only with a credit card or the Suica or PASMO transportation card (no cash). Sensoji Temple is just a few minutes' walk away. Other Book and Bed hostels are in Shinjuku, Ikebukuro, and Kyoto.

2–16–9 Kaminarimon, Taito-ku. http://bookandbedtokyo.com/en/asakusa/index.html. ✆ **03/6231-6893.** 46 units. ¥4,200–¥6,300 single; ¥7,200–¥10,200 double. Station: Asakusa (exit 2, 3 min.). **Amenities:** Bar; Wi-Fi.

Ueno

MODERATE

Hotel Coco Grand ★★★ This hotel is located in the *shitamachi* (old downtown) area of Ueno where commoners once lived, but guests won't sacrifice style or comfort to stay here. Across the street from the south end of Shinobazu Pond and an easy walk from Ueno Park and Ueno's Keisei Station with direct service from Narita Airport, it has an upbeat, boutiquelike atmosphere, with a welcoming gas fireplace in the lobby; a cake shop that draws in Japanese women; public baths; and small but chic rooms, many with views of the pond and decorated in splashes of bright colors. Rooms are mostly small singles, but even the cheapest are snazzy and perfectly fine. There are also doubles and twins, including two Park View Doubles with views of the pond and Zen Twins, which impart an air of traditional Japan with their raised beds on *tatami* and shoji-like window coverings. The best room in the house is the Villa Suite Twin, which feels like an exotic getaway with its private outdoor terrace outfitted with Jacuzzi, sofa, and TV, plus a steam room and bathroom tub big enough for two. The website is only in Japanese, but it does have photos of rooms. There's a public bath and a sauna.

2–12–14 Ueno, Taito-ku. www.cocogrand.co.jp/uenoshinobazu. ✆ **03/5812-1155.** 58 units. ¥9,800–¥16,800 single; ¥16,800–¥36,300 double. Rates include breakfast. Station: Ueno (4 min.). **Amenities:** Cake shop; public baths; Wi-Fi.

INEXPENSIVE

Annex Katsutaro ★★ Old-fashioned Yanaka neighborhood, home to many temples and the Yanaka Ginza shopping street, is part of what makes a stay here special. It's also within a 20-minute walk from Ueno Park with its many museums, and the Keisei Skyliner from Narita Airport stops at nearby Nippori Station. Though the inn itself is a three-story concrete building, it manages to convey a sense of place with its spotless Japanese-style *tatami* rooms and a complimentary map that introduces the area and how to navigate it. It's the sister inn of nearby **Katsutaro Ryokan,** which is older and slightly cheaper but isn't nearly as nice.

3–8–4 Yanaka, Taito-ku. www.katsutaro.com. ✆ **03/3828-2500.** 17 units. ¥6,750–¥8,100 single; ¥12,420–¥16,200 double. Station: Sendagi (2 min.) or Nippori (7 min.). **Amenities:** Rental bikes (¥300/day); Wi-Fi.

Ryokan Sawanoya ★★★ I stayed here on one of my earliest trips to Japan; I'm happy to report that it has only gotten better over the years and remains one of my favorites. A family-run affair since 1949, the smoke-free

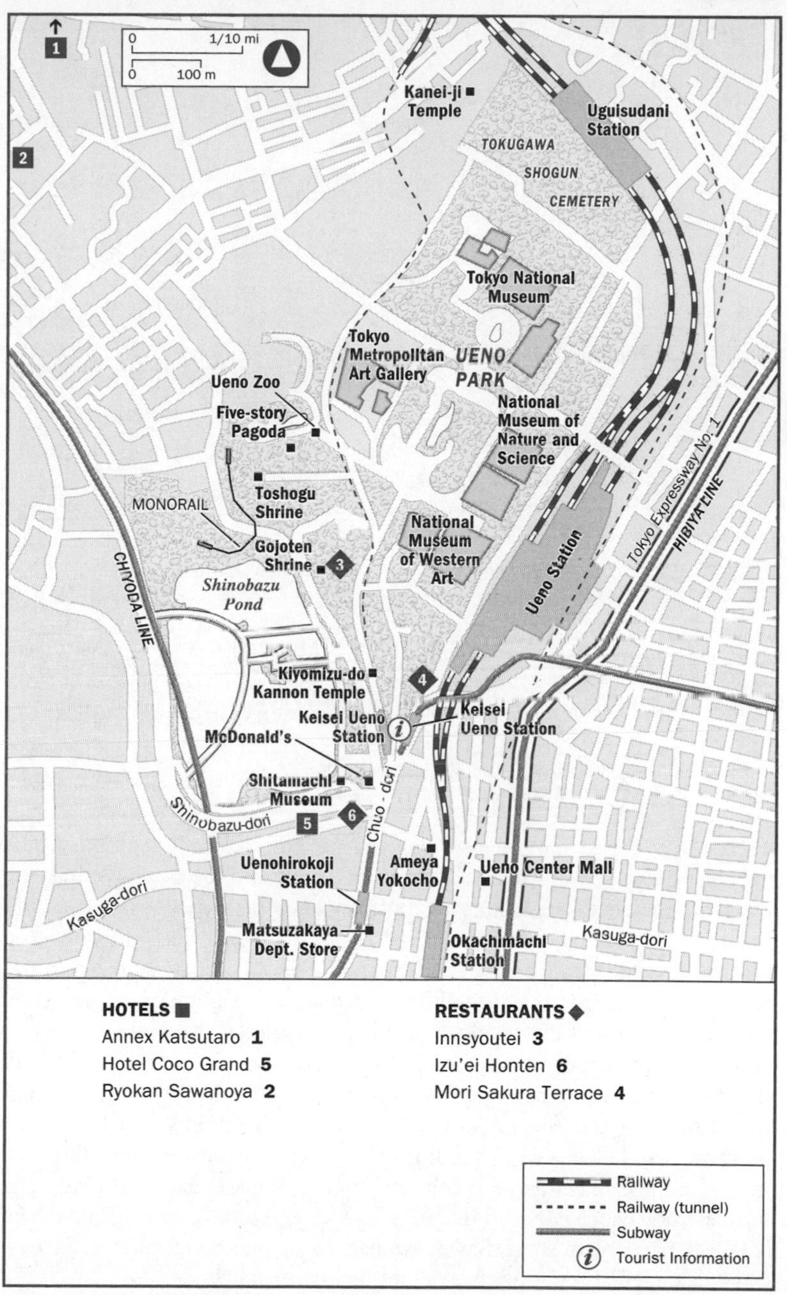

HOTELS ■

Annex Katsutaro **1**

Hotel Coco Grand **5**

Ryokan Sawanoya **2**

RESTAURANTS ◆

Innsyoutei **3**

Izu'ei Honten **6**

Mori Sakura Terrace **4**

Shinjuku

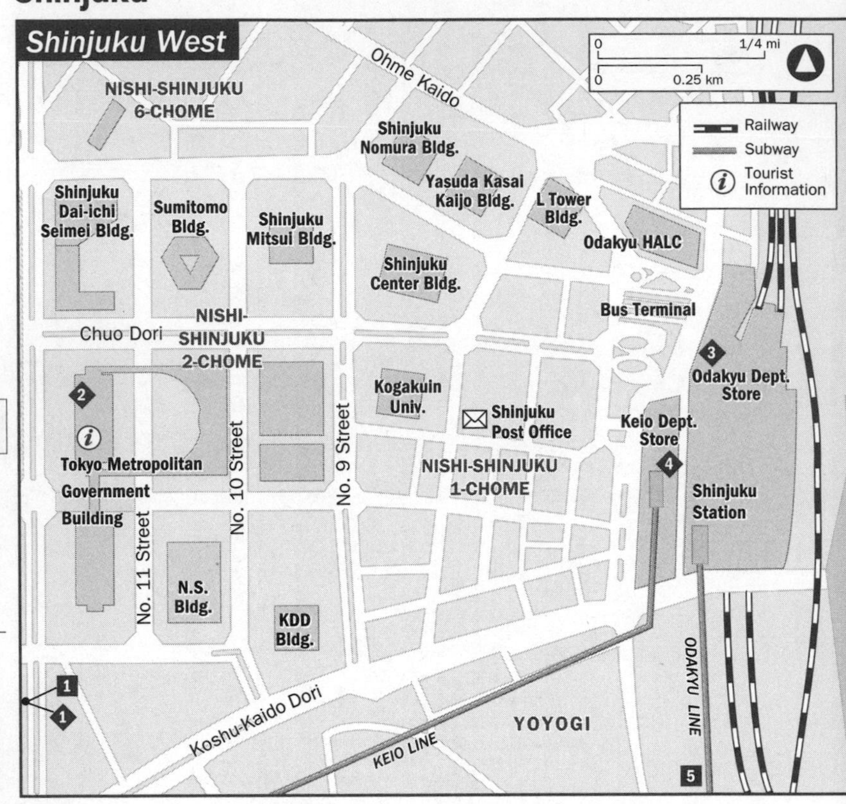

inn is now in the capable hands of the original proprietress' grandson, though the elder Sawa-san still pours his heart and soul into the business and even wrote a book about the history of Sawanoya and his experiences as an innkeeper. Located about a 15-minute walk from Ueno Park and 5 minutes from Nezu Shrine, it's nestled in a residential area known for its *shitamachi* (old downtown) atmosphere and traditional architecture. Upon arrival, guests are given a short tour of the establishment, which includes two baths with views of a garden (which can be locked for privacy) and a nice laundry room with free detergent, before being led to their *tatami* room on the second or third floor (there's no elevator). Guests also receive a hand-drawn map outlining restaurants and other nearby facilities. The large lobby offers free coffee and tea and a huge selection of brochures from throughout Japan. A traditional Japanese lion dance is staged free of charge several times a month, and the inn is LGBT friendly. In short, Sawanoya has a long history of making travelers feel welcome in Tokyo and thus comes highly recommended.

2–3–11 Yanaka, Taito-ku. www.sawanoya.com. ✆ **03/3822-2251.** 12 units (2 with bathroom). ¥5,616 single without bathroom; ¥10,584 double without bathroom, ¥11,664

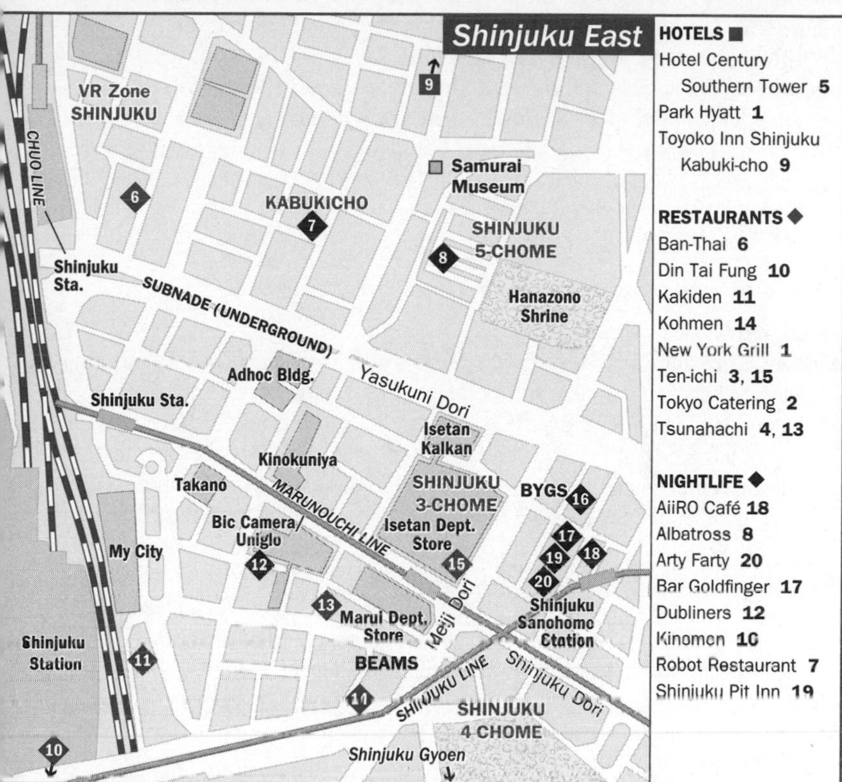

double with bathroom; ¥14,580 triple without bathroom, ¥16,848 triple with bathroom. Closed Dec 29–Jan 3. Station: Nezu (exit 1, 7 min.). **Amenities:** 2 rental bikes (¥300/ day); Wi-Fi.

Shinjuku

EXPENSIVE

Park Hyatt Tokyo ★★★ When the Park Hyatt opened in 1994 as Tokyo's first skyscraper hotel, I knew it was bound for glory the moment I stepped out of the elevator onto the light-drenched 41st floor. No hotel yet offered views as surreal as this; and with its gorgeous layout, high-tech rooms, and polished service (check-in is at one of three sit-down desks), it seemed light-years ahead of the competition. No wonder it starred in the 2003 hit, "Lost in Translation" and has inspired many competitors. Rooms, measuring a minimum of 45 sq. m (480 sq. ft.), have walk-in closets, deep soaking tubs (and separate showers), original pieces of artwork, Japanese-style paper lamps, paneling made from 2,000-year-old wood from Hokkaido, and great views (although east views of Shinjuku's nightlife and the greenery of several parks are the most popular, the west side sometimes has glimpses of Mount

Fuji). I also like the hotel's 2,000-book library, the **New York Grill** with outstanding views and cuisine, the free bikes for exploration of nearby Yoyogi, Chuo, and Shinjuku parks (complete with helmets and bottled water), and the 47th-floor fitness facilities overlooking the city, with free use of a sky-lit lap pool, gym, and studio offering complimentary yoga, aerobics, Pilates, and a relaxing "Good Night Sleep Stretch." I'm ready to move in.

3–7–1–2 Nishi-Shinjuku, Shinjuku-ku. www.tokyo.park.hyatt.com. ✆ **03/5322-1234.** 177 units. ¥65,530–¥137,000 single or double; from ¥130,000 suite. Station: Shinjuku (a 13-min. walk or 5-min. free shuttle ride); Hatsudai, on the Keio Line (7 min.); or Tocho-mae (8 min.). **Amenities:** 3 restaurants; 2 bars; lounge; babysitting; concierge; free entrance to gym and dramatic 20m indoor pool w/great views; room service; free shuttle service to Shinjuku Station up to 3 times an hour; spa; Wi-Fi.

MODERATE

Hotel Century Southern Tower ★★★ Conveniently located amid the skyscrapers of Shinjuku and connected to Takashimaya Shinjuku shopping complex via a footbridge, this superb choice offers smallish rooms with a view, at a fraction of the price of nearby competitors. Luggage carts instead of bellhops and vending machines in place of room service seem like no sacrifice at all when the rewards are mesmerizing panoramas from the 20th-floor lobby lounge and the rooms, which occupy the 22nd to 35th floors and come with skyline maps that help identify landmarks outside your window. The best—and most expensive—rooms (ask for one on a higher floor) face east or south, where views over central Tokyo take on a neon glow at night. Couples might note, however, that doubles are much smaller than twins.

2–2–1 Yoyogi, Shibuya-ku. www.southerntower.co.jp. ✆ **03/5354-0111.** 375 units. ¥17,480–¥19,000 single; ¥25,000–¥37,000 double. Station: Shinjuku (south exit, 3 min.). **Amenities:** 3 restaurants; lounge; Wi-Fi.

INEXPENSIVE

Tokyo Central Youth Hostel ★ This spotless hostel is definitely the best place to stay in its price range—situated on the 18th and 19th floors of a high-rise, it offers fantastic Tokyo views from all its rooms. This location is prime real estate, and no private rooms are offered, so couples who wish to room together with their own private bathroom will likely be happier at low-cost business hotel chains like Toyoko Inn. Here, all beds are dormitory style, with four or more bunk beds to a room. Rooms are very pleasant, with big windows, and each bed has its own curtain for privacy and comes with a locker. There are also two *tatami* rooms sleeping four to six people as well as a tiny communal kitchen. In summer, it's a good idea to reserve about 3 months in advance (reservations can be made a maximum of 3 months in advance). Check-in is from 3pm, the front door is locked at 11pm (lights out at midnight), and checkout is by 10am.

Central Plaza Building, 18th floor, 1–1 Kagura-kashi, Shinjuku-ku. www.jyh.gr.jp/tcyh. ✆ **03/3235-1107.** 158 beds. ¥4,050 adult (¥600 less for youth hostel members), ¥2,910 child. Breakfast ¥700. Station: Iidabashi (take the west exit from the JR station or the B2b subway exit, 2 min.). **Amenities:** Wi-Fi.

Aoyama & Akasaka

EXPENSIVE

The Prince Gallery Tokyo Kioicho ★★★ It's all about the views at this striking hotel, which occupies the top seven floors of a 36-story high-rise in Akasaka. That's apparent the moment you step out of the elevator to behold an eye-catching cocktail bar, framed by undulating glass walls that draw attention to a huge picture window broadcasting Tokyo in all its glory. Rooms, too, capitalize on the views, with day beds spreading the length of wall-to-wall windows. Even bathrooms have views, either via glass walls that look out past the room toward the window (thankfully those glass walls turn opaque with the push of a button) or from window-side tubs in more deluxe rooms. The hotel is also high-tech, with an iPad in each room controlling everything from lighting and temperature to blackout drapes and programmed with information on sightseeing, the weather, flight schedules and more. The indoor lap pool and state-of-the-art gym (free for hotel guests) as well as restaurants also take advantage of Tokyo as a backdrop. Yet it's worth tearing your eyes away from the views to admire the 100 artworks by Japanese artists that grace the hotel's public spaces and more than justify the word "gallery" in the hotel's name. This is a great choice in the heart of the city.

1–2 Kioi-cho, Chiyoda-ku. www.princehotels.com/en/kioicho. ✆ **03/3234-1111.** 250 units. ¥53,600–¥74,850 single; ¥59,400–¥82,000 double; from ¥71,280 club room; from ¥157,900 suite. Station: Akasaka-mitsuke or Nagatacho (1 min.). **Amenities:** 3 restaurants; 2 bars; lounge; concierge; executive-level rooms; exercise room; lap pool; spa; room service; Wi-Fi.

MODERATE

Hotel New Otani ★★ This hotel's most splendid feature is its garden, the best of any Tokyo hotel: more than 400 years old and once the private estate of a feudal lord. Spreading over 4 hectares (10 acres), it contains ponds filled with koi, waterfalls, arched bridges, manicured bushes (the azaleas are striking in spring), stone lanterns, and bamboo groves; it's not unusual to see Japanese in their finest kimono gathered here for family photos. The large outdoor pool, shrouded by greenery, provides more privacy than most hotel pools and is free for members of Otani Club International (membership is free). That's about it, however, when it comes to communing with nature, as this is one of Tokyo's largest hotels (be sure to pick up hotel and garden maps at the concierge—you're going to need them). Its 33 restaurants and 6 bars draw huge crowds of locals, especially the very popular **Garden Lounge,** offering the best garden views. A huge variety of rooms are spread among the main building, built for the 1964 Olympics and offering up-close views of the garden, and the 40-story Garden Tower, with glittering city vistas. Rates are the same regardless of view, so request a room facing the garden. Hotel facilities are so exhaustive, this is like a city within a city; folks who shun crowds may be happier elsewhere.

4–1 Kioi-cho, Chiyoda-ku. www.newotani.co.jp. ✆ **03/3265-1111.** 1,479 units. ¥23,760–¥49,300 single; ¥25,000–¥52,500 double; from ¥50,400 Executive House Zen; from ¥89,250 suite. Station: Akasaka-mitsuke or Nagatacho (3 min.). **Amenities:** 33 restaurants and cafes; 6 bars and lounges; children's day-care center for ages 2 months to 5

Harajuku & Aoyama

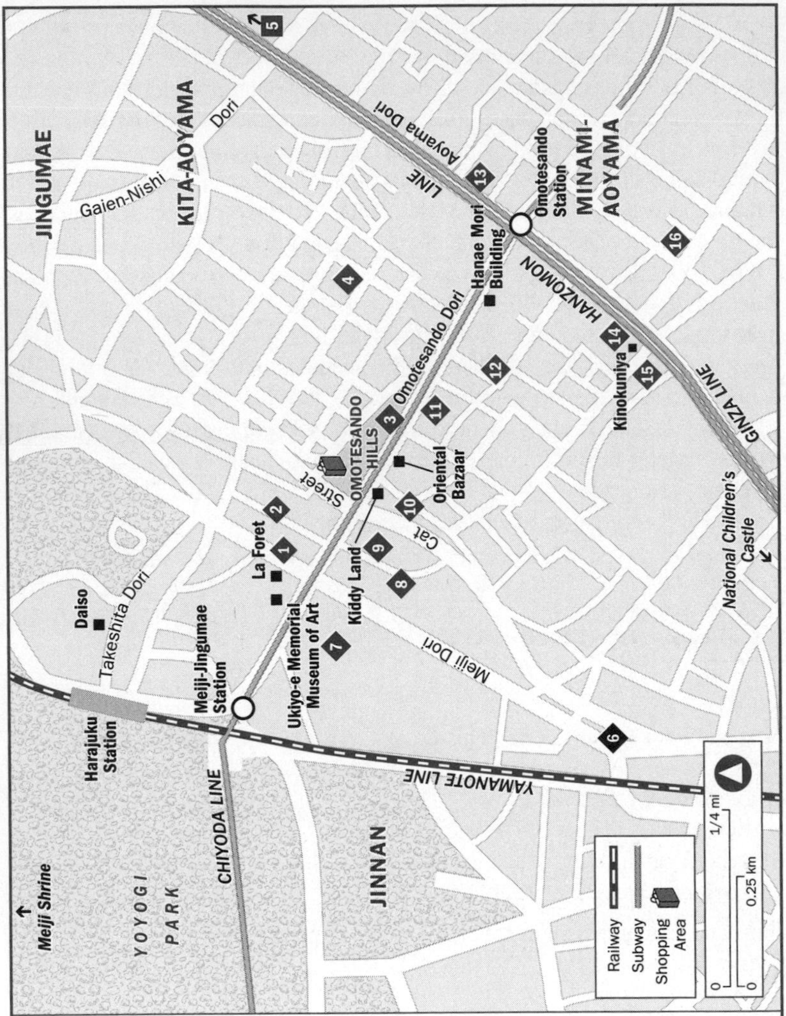

HOTELS ■

Hotel Asia Center of Japan **5**

Tokyu Stay Aoyama Premier **5**

RESTAURANTS ◆

Cicada **16**

Commune 2nd **13**

eatrip restaurant **7**

Harajuku Gyoza Lou **10**

Heirokuzushi **11**

Hiroba **12**

Kohmen **9**

Maisen **4**

Maru **15**

Toriyoshi **2**

Two Rooms Grill/Bar **14**

Venire Venire **1**

Yai Yai **8**

Yasaiya Mei **3**

NIGHTLIFE ◆

Crocodile **6**

Meiji Shrine
YOYOGI PARK
Harajuku Station
Daiso
Takeshita Dori
JINGUMAE
Gaien-Nishi Dori
KITA-AOYAMA
CHIYODA LINE
Meiji-Jingumae Station
La Foret
Ukiyo-e Memorial Museum of Art
Cat Street
OMOTESANDO HILLS
Kiddy Land
Oriental Bazaar
JINNAN
YAMANOTE LINE
Meiji Dori
Omotesando Dori
Hanae Mori Building
Aoyama Dori
HANZOMON LINE
Omotesando Station
MINAMI-AOYAMA
Kinokuniya
GINZA LINE
National Children's Castle
Railway
Subway
Shopping Area
0 1/4 mi
0 0.25 km

years (fee: ¥6,000 for 2 hr.); concierge; executive-level rooms; small exercise room; health club w/indoor pool and spa (fee: ¥5,400; ¥3,240 before 10am); medical and dental clinics; art museum; outdoor pool (fee: ¥2,000; free for Club International members); post office; room service; tea-ceremony room; lighted outdoor tennis courts; Wi-Fi.

Tokyu Stay Aoyama Premier ★★★ Tokyu Stay hotels are designed for business travelers who intend to stay put for a while and want the comforts of home. Rooms come with extra storage space, kitchenettes (including cooking utensils and tableware; the cheapest have microwaves but no stovetop), and even combination washers/dryers. Of the 18 Tokyu Stay hotels in town, the Aoyama Premier is the chain's star property, with a great location near Roppongi and Aoyama, rooms just for ladies, and good city views from its perch atop an office building. Cheaper locations include those in Ikebukuro, Nishi-Shinjuku, Suidobashi, Gotanda, Shibuya, Nihombashi, and Higashi-Ginza. Check the website for details.

2–27–18 Minami-Aoyama, Minato-ku. www.tokyustay.co.jp. ✆ **03/3497-0109.** 170 units. ¥11,760–¥23,100 single; ¥16,900–¥32,400 double. Discounts for stays longer than 6 nights. Station: Gaienmae (exit 1a, 2 min.). **Amenities:** Restaurant; Wi-Fi.

INEXPENSIVE

Hotel Asia Center of Japan (Asia Kaikan) ★★ A great location in central Tokyo, a Japanese restaurant popular with area office workers for its ¥1,500 lunch (including a salad bar and choice of main entree), and reasonable rates for Western-style rooms have made this a favorite domicile for everyone from business travelers and educators to youth groups for decades. Established in 1957 and recently renovated, it has the atmosphere of a college dorm, with tiny, mostly single rooms equipped with the basics: a double-size bed (all beds are extra long), wall-mounted TV, and desk. These are great for one person, but they're also sold for two people at the same price, making for inexpensive (if cramped) quarters. There are only 47 twin rooms (including twins with a sofa that can be turned into an extra bed). Probably my favorite feature of the hotel is that it's in a quiet residential area but only a 15-minute walk to Roppongi or Akasaka, or one station away by subway. Aoyama Dori, lined with shops and restaurants on its way to Omotesando, is just a 5-minute walk away.

8–10–32 Akasaka, Minato-ku. www.asiacenter.or.jp. ✆ **03/3402-6111.** 175 units. ¥9,000–¥16,000 single; ¥9,000–¥24,000 double. Station: Aoyama-Itchome (exit 4, 5 min.) or Nogizaka (exit 3, 5 min.). **Amenities:** Restaurant; Wi-Fi.

Roppongi

MODERATE

APA Hotel Roppongi Ekimae ★ APA hotels have been popping up around Japan like wildfire. Every time I turn around there's a new one in Tokyo, with 55 to date and undoubtedly more on the way. This one, open since 2016, is aimed at both business and leisure travelers, with just eight rooms on its 15 floors. The single and double rooms are equally tiny, while pricier twin rooms give you double the space. Views are confined to other surrounding buildings, but the higher the floor the better. Otherwise, this is your basic no-nonsense hotel, but its location in the heart of Tokyo's nightlife (and

Roppongi

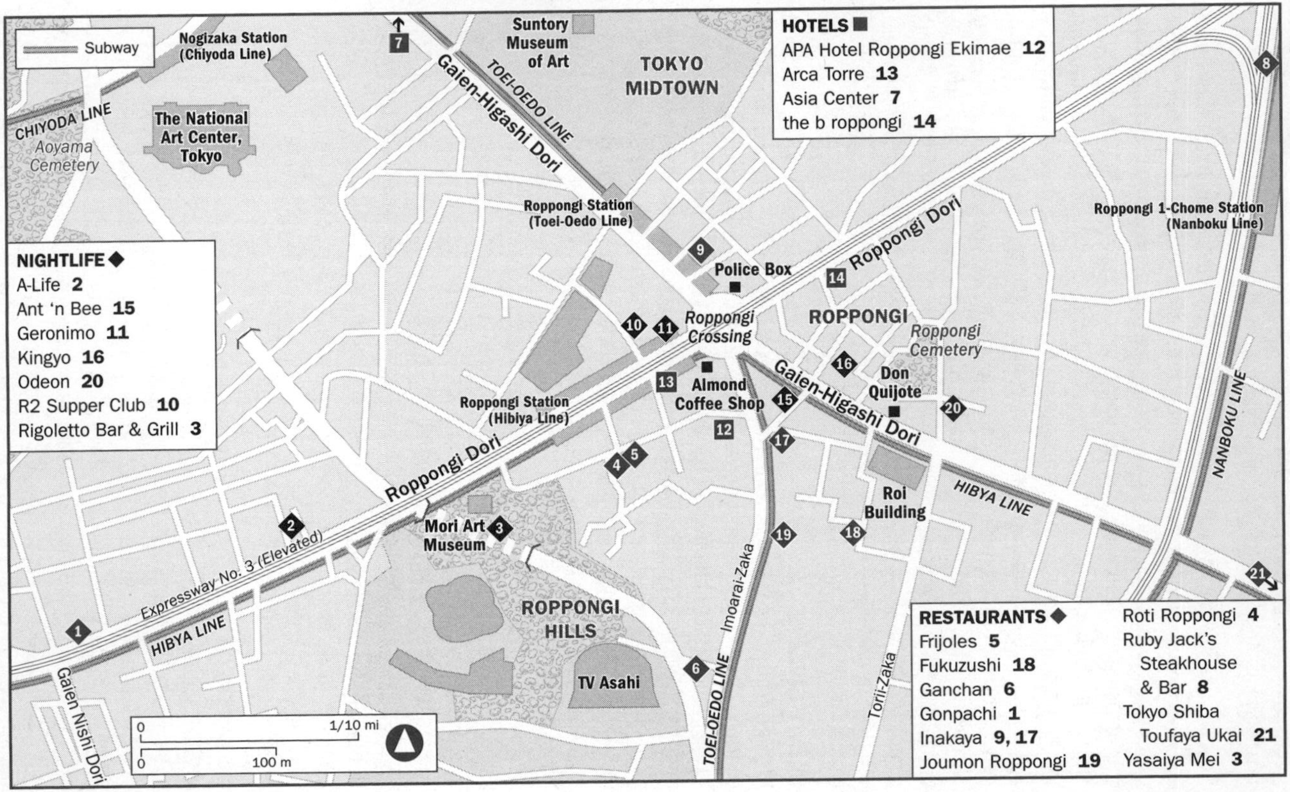

HOTELS ■
APA Hotel Roppongi Ekimae **12**
Arca Torre **13**
Asia Center **7**
the b roppongi **14**

NIGHTLIFE ◆
A-Life **2**
Ant 'n Bee **15**
Geronimo **11**
Kingyo **16**
Odeon **20**
R2 Supper Club **10**
Rigoletto Bar & Grill **3**

RESTAURANTS ◆
Frijoles **5**
Fukuzushi **18**
Ganchan **6**
Gonpachi **1**
Inakaya **9, 17**
Joumon Roppongi **19**
Roti Roppongi **4**
Ruby Jack's Steakhouse & Bar **8**
Tokyo Shiba Toufaya Ukai **21**
Yasaiya Mei **3**

Subway

Nogizaka Station (Chiyoda Line)
The National Art Center, Tokyo
Aoyama Cemetery
CHIYODA LINE
Suntory Museum of Art
TOKYO MIDTOWN
TOEI-OEDO LINE
Gaien-Higashi Dori
Roppongi Station (Toei-Oedo Line)
Police Box
Roppongi Crossing
Roppongi Dori
ROPPONGI
Roppongi Cemetery
Don Quijote
Roppongi 1-Chome Station (Nanboku Line)
NANBOKU LINE
HIBIYA LINE
Roi Building
Torii-Zaka
Imoarai-Zaka
Almond Coffee Shop
Roppongi Station (Hibiya Line)
Mori Art Museum
ROPPONGI HILLS
TV Asahi
Expressway No. 3 (Elevated)
Gaien Nishi Dori
0 — 1/10 mi
0 — 100 m

practically in front of the Roppongi subway station) makes it a very convenient choice.

6–7–8 Roppongi, Minato-ku. www.apahotel.com. ✆ **03/5413-6351.** 125 units. ¥8,000–¥18,000 single; ¥11,850–¥50,000 double. Station: Roppongi (1 min.). **Amenities:** Restaurant/bar; Wi-Fi.

the b roppongi ★★ The b roppongi opened in 2004 as the first of 14 business hotels under the "b" brand. Its quirky name is based on four concepts: a comfortable **b**ed, a good **b**reakfast (which nonetheless costs extra), a **b**alanced life, and a contemporary and relaxed atmosphere for conducting **b**usiness. What this boils down to is a boutique business hotel that is more stylish than most of its genre, with beds that are indeed comfortable and have focused reading lamps. Otherwise, standard and superior rooms are your typical business-hotel tiny size, so travelers yearning for a bit more space might want to splurge on a deluxe room, which offers both more windows and more space. Deluxe Plus rooms have corner locations with even more windows, plus a kitchenette. Facilities are practically nonexistent, unless you count the free coffee in the lobby, but Roppongi's nightlife is just outside the door. Note that the hotel is opening an addition in 2019. Other b hotels in Tokyo are in Ochanomizu, Akasaka, Ikebukuro, Shimbashi, and other locations; check the website.

3–9–8 Roppongi, Minato-ku. www.itheb-hotels.com. ✆ **03/5412-0451.** 76 units. ¥7,350–¥18,300 single; ¥11,250–¥27,000 double. Station: Roppongi (1 min.). **Amenities:** Restaurant/bar; Wi-Fi

INEXPENSIVE

Arca Torre ★ This 10-story business hotel has a great location on Roppongi Dori near Roppongi Crossing, making it popular with business types and tourists on a budget. Its mostly single rooms are small but cheerful, with complimentary bottled water in the otherwise empty fridge; two people can opt to stay in a single room but they'll be happier in a double. Rooms facing the back are quiet but face another building with glazed windows and are rather dark. If you opt for a room facing the front, spring for the more expensive rooms on higher floors above the freeway; your views from the cheaper rooms on lower floors will be of cars and, at certain times of the day, traffic jams.

6–1–23 Roppongi, Minato-ku. www.arktower.co.jp/arcatorre. ✆ **03/3404-5111.** 76 units. ¥9,420–¥13,740 single; ¥10,500–¥18,360 double. Station: Roppongi (1 min.). **Amenities:** Restaurant; bar; Wi-Fi.

Shibuya

EXPENSIVE

Shibuya Excel Hotel Tokyu ★★ If you saw the movie *Lost in Translation,* you might remember a scene of an intersection that's crazy busy with pedestrians walking in all directions when the light turns red. That's Shibuya Scramble, and it's just a stone's throw from this hotel, located across from bustling Shibuya Station and connected by underground passage and a footbridge. (***Tip:*** The footbridge is a good place to photograph Shibuya Scramble.)

Located above Mark City shopping mall, with reception on the fifth floor, it's a business hotel that also appeals to women with its women-only floor accessed by a special key and offering extras like face cream, jewelry boxes, and face steamers. Rooms are on the 7th to 24th floors, with those higher up facing Shinjuku costing more but providing great night views; the 25th-floor French restaurant also has great views along with reasonable prices. There are many dining options near the hotel, including the Center Gai nightlife district, a pedestrian lane lined with restaurants and bars, and the Hikarie complex.

1–12–2 Dogenzaka, Shibuya-ku. www.tokyuhotelsjapan.com. ✆ **03/5457-0109.** 408 units. ¥24,000–¥31,000 single; ¥31,600–¥54,800 double. Station: Shibuya (1 min. by footbridge). **Amenities:** 2 restaurants; lounge; room service; Wi-Fi.

Other Neighborhoods

MODERATE

Shiba Park Hotel ★★ This is a well-respected older hotel, tucked away in a quiet residential area near Shiba Park, Zozoji Temple, and Tokyo Tower (and a sobering 25-min. walk from Roppongi nightlife). Friendly staff and the hotel's low-key atmosphere make it more intimate than the beehive activity of Tokyo's larger hotels, though all bets are off in winter, when it serves as a popular way station for Australians headed for the slopes. The hotel consists of a main building and an annex across the street in back. The main 151 Building is the pricier but better choice, with shoji sliding doors separating rooms from bathrooms and other Japanese touches, while the Annex Building attracts groups and families with its mostly twin rooms and larger units that sleep up to four people. But one of the things that impresses me most is its **Japanese Culture Salon Sakura,** offering daily morning and early afternoon cultural experiences, from calligraphy and origami to the tea ceremony.

1–5–10 Shiba-koen, Minato-ku. www.shibaparkhotel.com. ✆ **03/3433-4141.** 169 units. ¥14,400–¥21,000 single; ¥15,300–¥29,000 double. Station: Onarimon (2 min.), Daimon (4 min.), or Hamamatsucho (8 min.). **Amenities:** 3 restaurants; bar; room service; Wi-Fi.

The Hilltop Hotel (Yama-no-Ue Hotel) ★★ This delightfully old-fashioned, unpretentious (some might say dowdy) relic qualifies as historic in contemporary Tokyo. Built in 1937 and serving as a research institute and then as living quarters for U.S. occupation forces before becoming a hotel in 1954, it remains true to its past, not much different from when it was a favorite retreat of writers like novelist Yukio Mishima. With a distinctive Art Deco facade, the hotel has furnished some of its rooms with such endearing, homey touches as fringed lampshades, doilies, and cherrywood furniture. Some twins even combine a *tatami* area and shoji with beds; the most expensive twin overlooks its own Japanese garden. While not as conveniently located as other tourist hotels, this is a nostalgia-invoking place (don't be surprised if reception staffers remember you by name), hidden on a hill near Meiji University and near restaurants, bookshops, and other student hangouts, which bring lots of young people and liveliness to the area. And though small by Tokyo standards, this hotel has an impressive number of restaurants and bars, due, no doubt, to its popularity among steadfast local fans.

1–1 Surugadai, Kanda, Chiyoda-ku. www.yamanoue-hotel.co.jp. ✆ **03/3293-2311.** 35 units. ¥17,000–¥18,000 single; ¥24,000–¥32,000 double. Rates exclude service charge and taxes. Station: Ochanomizu or Shin-Ochanomizu (8 min.) or Jimbocho (5 min.). **Amenities:** 5 restaurants; 2 bars; room service; Wi-Fi.

INEXPENSIVE

Kimi Ryokan ★★★ This inexpensive Japanese-style inn has long been on the international radar as one of the best in Tokyo for its traditional details and up-to-date conveniences. Flower arrangements (created by English-speaking owner Minato Kisaburo), shoji screens, scrolls of calligraphy and other artwork, a public bath made of cypress, and polished wood-floor corridors where traditional Japanese music plays faintly in the background are complemented by a lounge with cable TV (a good place to meet fellow travelers, who are mostly in their twenties), a kitchen, a Japanese cypress bath you can lock for privacy, an inviting rooftop terrace, and a bulletin board and newsletter providing information on rental apartments and jobs, mostly as English teachers. Guest rooms are all Japanese style and rather small, with the cheapest room (for one or two persons) measuring four-and-a-half *tatami* mats, and the larger rooms (for two or three guests) six mats or eight mats (sleeping up to five persons); bathrooms are shared. Be sure to download the area map on Kimi's website—this place is a bit difficult to find, and note that there's a 2am curfew.

2–36–8 Ikebukuro, Toshima ku. www.kimi-ryokan.jp. ✆ **03/3971-3766.** 38 units (none with private bathroom). ¥5,400 single; ¥8,100–¥9,180 double; ¥12,150–¥14,580 triple. Station: Ikebukuro (west exit; 7 min.). **Amenities.** Wi-Fi.

Shinagawa Tobu Hotel ★★ A step up from the nearby Toyoko Inn (see below) in both style and amenities, this property opened in 2017 with a much snazzier lobby than the usual business hotel, with red ceramic bowls on brown walls serving as artwork and eye-catching red wingback chairs with black pillows, plus an Italian restaurant. Several different types of rooms are available, from the most common tiny economy double with a semi-double bed (okay for one person but challenging for two) to six much larger standard doubles with a true double bed and twins that sleep from two to four people with the addition of extra beds. But the main reason to stay here is its proximity to Shinagawa Station, providing connections to Narita Airport or via the Shinkansen bullet train to the rest of Japan.

4–7–6 Takanawa, Minato-ku. www.shinagawatobuhotel.com. ✆ **03/3447-0111.** 190 units. ¥9,000–¥16,000 single; ¥10,740–¥26,000 double. Station: Shinagawa (5 min.). From JR station's Takanawa (west) exit, cross the street, walk one block and turn left. **Amenities:** Restaurant; Wi-Fi.

Toyoko Inn Tokyo Shinagawa-Eki Takanawaguchi ★ Business hotels were often dingy and dismal before this chain raised the bar a few decades back, offering clean and inexpensive rooms and a slew of freebies that have since become standard, including free Internet, lobby computers guests can use for free, and even free breakfast. Now with more than 250 locations throughout Japan, usually within easy walking distance of stations and noted for having managers that are mostly women, it offers very tiny rooms that are nonetheless equipped with everything guests need. This one is convenient for its location near Shinagawa station, but other Tokyo locations include those in Shinjuku, Ikebukuro, Asakusa, Ueno, Nihombashi, and Akihabara.

4-23-2 Takanawa, Minato-ku, Tokyo 108-0074. www.toyoko-inn.com. ✆ **03/3280-1045.** 180 units. ¥8,100–¥8,424 single; ¥9,720–¥11,880 double. Rates include continental breakfast. Station: Shinagawa (3 min.). From JR station's Takanawa (west) exit, cross the street and turn left. **Amenities:** Wi-Fi.

WHERE TO EAT

From stand-up noodle shops and pizzerias to exclusive *kaiseki* restaurants and sushi bars, Tokyo has more than 80,000 restaurants—which gives you some idea of how fond Japanese are of eating out. In a city where apartments are so small and cramped that entertaining at home is almost unheard of, restaurants serve as places for socializing and wooing business associates—as well as great excuses for drinking a lot of beer, sake, and whiskey.

One of the best deals is the **fixed-price lunch,** usually available from 11am to 2pm. Called a *teishoku* in a Japanese restaurant and a "seto coursu" (or simply "seto" or *coursu*) in restaurants serving Western food, the set lunch lets you dine in style at reasonable prices. If possible, avoid the noon-to-1pm weekday crush when Tokyo's army of office workers floods area restaurants. Because Japanese tend to order fixed-price meals rather than a la carte, set dinners are also usually available (although they're not as cheap as set lunches). All-you-can-eat buffets (called *viking* in Japanese, probably because Japan's first buffet was in a restaurant called Viking in Tokyo's Imperial Hotel), offered by many hotel restaurants, are also bargains for hearty appetites. See p. 30 in chapter 2 for more recommendations on saving money.

Otherwise, so many of Tokyo's good restaurants fall into the moderate category that it's tempting to simply eat your way through the city—and the range of cuisines is so great you could eat something different at each meal. Bargain hunters should note that many of the most colorful, noisy, and popular restaurants fall into the inexpensive category, many offering meals for less than ¥2,000 and lunches for ¥1,000 or less. The city's huge working population heads to these places to catch a quick lunch or to socialize with friends after hours. There are also many excellent but inexpensive French bistros, Italian *trattorie,* and ethnic restaurants, particularly those serving Indian, Chinese, and other Asian cuisines. Finally, see "Entertainment & Nightlife," in chapter 5, for suggestions on inexpensive drinking places that serve food. I also suggest you ask your concierge or hotel manager for recommendations; there's probably a great little place just around the corner.

Note that an 8% consumption tax (scheduled to increase to 10% in October 2019) is added to meals in restaurants. Some restaurants include the tax in their prices; others do not. In any case, menus usually state whether prices include taxes. The prices listed in this book are those taken directly from

Mapping Out Tokyo's Restaurants

You can locate the restaurants reviewed below using the following neighborhood maps:

- To locate restaurants in and around **Ginza,** p. 74.
- To locate restaurants in **Asakusa,** p. 81.
- To locate restaurants in **Ueno,** p. 83.
- To locate restaurants in **Shinjuku,** p. 84.
- To locate restaurants in **Harajuku** and **Aoyama,** p. 88.
- To locate restaurants in **Roppongi,** p. 90.

menus, so be prepared for tax to be added to your meal. In addition, first-class restaurants, as well as hotel restaurants, also add a 10% to 15% service charge to the bill. For information on Japanese food, see "Eating & Drinking in Japan," in chapter 2.

Finally, keep in mind that the **last order** is taken at least 30 minutes before the restaurant's actual closing time, sometimes even an hour before closing at the more exclusive restaurants. I've included some websites only in Japanese, either because they have photos of dishes or maps that will help you find them.

In & Near Ginza

EXPENSIVE

Ten-ichi ★★★ TEMPURA Founded in 1930, this may well be the most famous tempura restaurant in the world, with many foreign dignitaries among its customers over the years. With branches all over Japan, its main shop is here on Namiki Dori, a street blazing with neon in Ginza's nightlife district. But indoors it's all spartan and spare, decorated with blond wood trim, sliding doors, and flower arrangements. Tempura counters on each floor seat no more than 10 customers, who get an intimate view of master chefs going about their work (reservations are recommended for lunch, required for dinner). Ten-ichi is famous for its delicately fried food, with a batter so refined and an oil so light, the flavor of fish, shrimp, scallop, eggplant, sweet potato, and other ingredients is enhanced rather than overwhelmed. The piping-hot morsels can be dipped into a variety of sauces, from the restaurant's own secret recipe to a simple lemon juice with a pinch of salt. Although it's not on the menu, a ¥4,860 lighter lunch of tempura over rice is also usually available. Ten-ichi branches include those nearby in the Imperial Hotel's Tower basement and the Sony Building, as well as locations in department stores, including Seibu in Ikebukuro, Tokyu in Shibuya, Takashimaya in Nihombashi, and Isetan and Odakyu in Shinjuku.

6–6–5 Ginza. www.tenichi.co.jp. ✆ **03/3571-1949.** Set lunches ¥4,860–¥14,17,280; set dinners ¥11,880–¥20,520. Daily 11:30am–9pm (last order). Station: Ginza (3 min.). On Namiki Dori.

The Imperial Viking Sal ★★ INTERNATIONAL All over Japan, the all-you-can-eat buffet is called "Viking" in Japanese, because that's how the Imperial Hotel introduced the concept with the country's very first spread back in 1958, dubbing it a Viking smorgasbord. Today, of course, many hotels offer buffets fit for a true Viking, but this remains one of the most famous and luckily bears no resemblance to what passed for Western food back in the 1950s. In fact, this might well be the priciest buffet in Japan (as with all buffets, prices are discounted for children). More than 40 mostly European dishes make their debut with offerings that change monthly, from roast beef with horseradish to salmon, desserts, and more, with seasonal promotions adding ethnic cuisine from around the world. Live jazz serenades guests some evenings, but if you opt for the more economical lunch, make a reservation and ask for a table overlooking the Ginza or Hibiya Park. Or come for breakfast.

Imperial Hotel, 17th floor, 1–1–1 Uchisaiwai-cho. www.imperialhotel.co.jp. ✆ **03/3539-8187.** Buffet breakfast ¥3,800; buffet lunch Mon–Fri ¥5,500, Sat–Sun and holidays ¥6,000; buffet dinner Mon–Fri ¥8,200, Sat–Sun and holidays ¥8,700. Daily 7am–9:30am and 11:30am–2:30pm; Mon–Fri 5:30–9:30pm; Sat–Sun and holidays 5–9:30pm (last order). Station: Hibiya (1 min.).

MODERATE

Also worth seeking out is **Maru** (p. 105), offering modern interpretations of Japanese food, at 6–12–15 Ginza (✆ **03/5537-7420**).

Rangetsu (らん月) ★ SUKIYAKI/SHABU-SHABU/KAISEKI/BENTO "Orchid moon" is the English translation of Rangetsu, a Ginza restaurant founded in 1947 and still under the same family ownership. It specializes in sukiyaki and shabu-shabu, made with A5-grade Japanese Wagyu beef and cooked at your table. The English-language menu with photos lists many other dishes, too, from yaki shabu-shabu cooked on a grill at your table and crab dishes (like the crab shabu-shabu set meal for ¥10,500) to bento, *kaiseki,* and more. Lunch sets, served until 4pm, are especially good deals, offering steaks, shabu-shabu, bento, and many other combinations. A sake bar in the basement stocks more than 80 varieties from all over Japan, all of which you can also order with your meal no matter which floor you dine on.

> **A Note on Establishments with Japanese Signs**
>
> Many establishments and attractions in Japan do not have signs in Roman (English-language) letters. Those that don't are provided with the Japanese equivalent to help you locate them.

3–5–8 Ginza. www.ginza-rangetsu.com. ✆ **03/3567-1021.** Beef sukiyaki or shabu-shabu set meals from ¥8,000 for dinner, ¥3,500 for lunch; *kaiseki* ¥6,000–¥12,000; bento ¥2,400–¥3,500; set lunches ¥1,950–¥3,900. Daily 11:30am–10pm. Station: Ginza (3 min.). On Chuo Dori, across from the Matsuya department store.

INEXPENSIVE

In addition to the following restaurants, check out **Meal Muji,** 3–8–3 Marunouchi (✆ **03/5208-8241**), a cafeteria on the second floor of the popular minimalist Muji clothing and housewares store, where you can load up on mostly salads and veggies daily from 10am to 9pm. A number of restaurants are also located on the eighth floor of **Matsuya Ginza department store,** serving everything from French and Chinese food to sushi, tempura, noodles, and more. For Chinese dumplings, there's a **Din Tai Fung** at 1–8–19 Ginza (✆ **03/5159-4141**); see p. 103 for a review.

For atmospheric dining, head to an arch beneath the elevated Yamanote railway tracks located about halfway between Harumi Dori and the Imperial Hotel Tower; it has a handful of tiny ***yakitori* stands,** each with a few tables and chairs. These cater to a rather boisterous working-class clientele, mainly men. The atmosphere, unsophisticated and dingy, harks back to prewar Japan, somewhat of an anomaly in otherwise chic Ginza. Stalls are open from about 5pm to midnight Monday through Saturday.

Finally, in the basement of the behemoth that is Tokyo Station, the eight ramen shops along **Koji Ramen Street** offer specialties like Oreshiki Jun's rich pork-stock ramen. There are instructions in English; you decide what you want and then buy a ticket from that shop's vending machine. Note, however, that Ramen Street is very difficult to find. Assuming you do, avoid the mealtime crunch or else get in the queue. The shops are open daily 9:30am to 10:30pm.

Andy's Shin Hinomoto ★★ VARIED JAPANESE This hole-in-the-wall underneath the Yamanote elevated train tracks looks like it's been here since the rubble of post–World War II…because it has. Founded in 1945 when there were cubbyholes like this throughout a bombed-out Tokyo, it is owned by the founder's son-in-law, a Brit named Andy. As tiny as it is, it has an upstairs with an arched ceiling that is only marginally better than the downstairs with the charm of a fallout shelter. Yet this place is packed elbow to elbow every night with office workers, and the only way you might get your foot in the door without a reservation is to come right when it opens. The food, made with seafood and vegetables bought fresh daily at Tsukiji Market, includes tempura, a fish of the day, deep-fried chicken, chili prawns, salads (usually sold out by 8pm), and its signature stuffed *gyoza* chicken wings. Even with fluorescent lighting, soot-blackened walls, and a no-credit-card policy, this throwback is, in the words of Andy, always "insanely busy," and all from word of mouth.

2–4–4 Yurakucho. www.andysfish.com/Shin-Hinomoto. ✆ **03/3214-8021.** Main dishes ¥750–¥1,200. Mon–Sat 5pm–midnight. Station: Yurakucho or Ginza (1 min.). Underneath the Yamanote elevated tracks, across from the Yurakucho Denki Building.

Mugi to Olive ★★★ RAMEN With ramen the hottest food craze, everyone has their favorites. The emphasis of this small, unassuming restaurant, with just two counters, is clearly on food and not decor. It distinguishes itself by combining wheat noodles ("mugi" means wheat) with olive oil. Choose from three soup stocks, made with chicken, clam, or small dried sardines (or order a dish with all three), available with different toppings. There's also the mazesoba, which eschews broth altogether but comes with thick noodles, concentrated sauce, and toppings you mix together. After deciding what you want, buy the corresponding ticket from the vending machine.

6–12–12 Ginza. No phone or website. Ramen ¥880–¥1,180. Mon–Fri 11:30am–10pm; Sat–Sun and holidays 11:30am–9pm. Station: Ginza (exit 3A, 3 min.) or Higashi-Ginza (exit A1, 3 min.). Behind Ginza Six shopping complex; look for "CHINESE NOODLES" sign.

La Boheme ★ ITALIAN The food is passable, but what sets La Boheme apart is that it's open every day until 1am, making it a good bet for a late-night meal. In addition to pizza (like the one topped with shrimp, bacon, mushrooms, bell peppers, and cheese) and pasta (like creamy fettucine served with four kinds of mushrooms), it also offers a few meat dishes, like roasted chicken. La Boheme is actually one of four restaurants under the same ownership and all ensconced under a freeway in a winding dining complex called **G-Zone,** with Southeast Asian fare offered at **Monsoon** (www.monsoon-cafe.jp); burritos, enchiladas, tacos, and other Tex-Mex served at **Zest Cantina** (www.zest-cantina.jp); and Japanese food dished out in **Gonpachi** (p. 111). English-language menus, cheap prices, friendly staff, and late open hours make these restaurants winners. Check the website for other locations around Tokyo.

1–2–3 Ginza. www.boheme.jp. ✆ **03/5524-3616.** Pizza and pasta ¥980–¥1,880; set lunches ¥1,000–¥1,500. Daily 11:30am–1am. Station: Kyobashi (exit 3, 2 min.) or Ginza-Itchome (exit 7, 1 min.). On Chuo Dori, at the northern edge of Ginza.

Shabusen (しゃぶせん) ★★ SHABU-SHABU Ginza Core is a fashion department store near the Ginza 4–chome Crossing (the Harumi Dori–Chuo Dori intersection) and the improbable home of not one, but two very reasonably priced Shabusen restaurants. Although shabu-shabu is usually shared between two or more diners (you cook it yourself in a communal boiling pot at your own table), Shabusen also caters to individuals with one-person portions. The second-floor Shabusen is a bit nicer, with round counters good for lone diners and tables that are perfect for groups, while the second-basement restaurant features U-shaped counters that are a great choice for dining alone or with one other person. I personally love the experience of sitting at the counter—you can watch chefs preparing orders and, with other customers seated in close quarters, it doesn't really feel like you're eating alone. The English-language menu lists both pork and beef shabu-shabu sets, which you cook along with vegetables and eat with a ponzu or sesame dipping sauce.

Core Building, 5–8–20 Ginza. www.zakuro.co.jp/syabusen/index.html. ✆ **03/3572-3806** (2nd basement) or 03/3571-1717 (2nd floor). Set lunches ¥1,500–¥4,000; set dinners ¥2,500–¥5,800. Daily 11am–9pm (last order). Station: Ginza (1 min.). On the east side of Chuo Dori just south of Harumi Dori.

Tsukiji Sushi Sen (築地すし鮮) ★ SUSHI Renovated to provide more privacy between tables and with dimmer lights than its interrogation-room-like predecessor, this second-floor Ginza branch offers fresh sushi at bargain prices, served at a counter or at tables overlooking busy Harumi Dori. Other dishes are also available on the English-language menu, including salads, grilled seafood, and tempura. If you find yourself hungry in Ginza in the dead of night, this all-nighter is a good choice.

5–9–1 Ginza. ✆ **03/5537-2878.** Sushi a la carte (one piece) ¥98–¥398; set lunches ¥999–¥2,980; *nigiri* sets ¥1,980–¥4,800. 24 hr. Station: Higashi Ginza or Ginza (2 min.). From Ginza 4-chome Crossing, on the right side of Harumi Dori in the first block heading toward Showa Dori.

Asakusa

EXPENSIVE

Waentei-Kikko (和えん亭 吉幸) ★★★ KAISEKI/BENTO I can't imagine a better place to cap off a visit to Asakusa than this. Located in a tiny house just a stone's throw from Sensoji Temple, it evokes the atmosphere of a farmhouse with its flagstone entry, wooden rafters, rustic furnishings, and *tatami* seating (with leg wells for those errant appendages). But what sets this place apart are the engaging couple who manage it and the live performances of traditional Japanese music four times daily (at 12:15, 1:30, 6:30, and 8pm), including concerts by Fukui Kodai, the husband of the managing duo and one of Japan's most accomplished Tsugaru shamisen musicians, who plays with the fervor of a rock star. Ordering is easy, as only seasonal set meals that change every month or so are served. Lunch features bento boxes, while *kaiseki* is served for dinner, including *fugu* (blowfish) *kaiseki* if you order it in advance. In short, dining here provides nourishment for both body and soul and is an experience you're likely to remember long after your trip has ended.

2–2–13 Asakusa. www.waentei-kikko.com. ✆ **03/5828-8833.** Bento lunches ¥2,500 and ¥3,500; *kaiseki* dinners ¥6,800–¥13,800. Thurs–Tues 11:30am–1:30pm and 5–8pm (last order). Station: Asakusa (5 min.). Walk on Nakamise Dori toward Sensoji Temple, turning right after the last shop; go past the 2 stone Buddhas, and then turn right again at the tiny Benten-do Temple with the large bell. The restaurant is on the right side of the street across from the playground.

Chinya (ちんや) ★★ SHABU-SHABU/SUKIYAKI Established in 1880 but now ensconced in a seven-story building just steps away from Sensoji Temple, this well-known restaurant has been welcoming foreigners with an English-language menu for decades. Its foyer entrance, next to its own butcher shop (always a good sign), gives no hint as to what lies beyond, but soon there's a man taking your shoes and a kimono-clad hostess leading you upstairs to one of the *tatami*-floored rooms. It has various options for sukiyaki and shabu-shabu set meals and even provides instruction for how to cook at your table, making it a good bet for the sukiyaki/shabu-shabu novice. The set lunch is the best deal, served until 3pm and including an appetizer, pickles, miso soup, rice, dessert, and shabu-shabu or sukiyaki, while dinners require reservations and are much more extensive. These are not quick meals (and at this price you wouldn't expect them to be), so come prepared to relax and enjoy the occasion.

1–3–4 Asakusa. www.chinya.co.jp. ✆ **03/3841-0010.** Set lunches ¥4,300–¥6,300; set dinners ¥7,900–¥13,900. Table charge ¥500 extra per person for lunch, ¥600 for dinner. Mon and Thurs–Fri noon–3pm; Mon and Wed–Fri 4:30–9:30pm; Sat–Sun and holidays 11:30am–9pm (guests should arrive 2 hr. before closing time). Station: Asakusa (1 min.). On Kaminarimon Dori, to the left of the Kaminarimon Gate if you stand facing Asakusa Kannon Temple.

INEXPENSIVE

Copper-colored **Gonpachi** (p. 111), overlooking the Sumida River at 2–1–15 Kaminarimon (✆ **03/5830-3791**) right by the bridge, offers Japanese food.

Kamiya Bar ★ VARIED JAPANESE/WESTERN I'm including this all-purpose restaurant not because it serves great food, but because it's been an Asakusa institution since 1880, attracting a largely working-class and elderly Japanese crowd with a down-home atmosphere that has all but died out in sophisticated Tokyo. Plus, ordering is easy thanks to plastic-food display cases and you have the choice of both Japanese and Western food (the Japanese food is better). For the full immersion, a bar with food on the first floor is famous for its Denki Bran, a concoction of brandy, gin, wine, vermouth, Curacao, and herbs (¥270 for a glass). The second floor serves yoshoku (the Japanese interpretation of Western food), like hamburger steak, crab croquette, spaghetti, fried shrimp, and fried chicken, while the third floor is the place to go for everything from sashimi and udon noodles to yakitori, bento, and tempura, as well as kaiseki lunches and, with advance reservations, dinners. Credit cards are accepted only on the second and third floors.

1–1–1 Asakusa. www.kamiya-bar.com. ✆ **03/3841-5400.** Main dishes ¥550–¥1,540; set lunches ¥850–¥1,200; Japanese set meals ¥1,540–¥3,600; *kaiseki* ¥4,100–¥7,200. Wed–Mon 11:30am–9:30pm (last order; 1st and 3rd floors closed 2–4pm). Station: Asakusa (1 min.). Located on Kaminarimon Dori in a plain, brown-tiled building btw. Kaminarimon Gate and the Sumida River.

Sansada (三定) ★★ TEMPURA Established in 1837 and located right beside Kaminarimon Gate, this simple tempura restaurant specializes in Edo-style tempura, fried in a light sesame oil. On the first floor, seating is either at tables or on *tatami,* while the upstairs is more traditional with *tatami* seating; one room overlooks the temple gate. Run by an army of very able grandmotherly types, the restaurant has an English-language menu with photos of various options, including *tendon* (tempura on rice), noodles with tempura, bento boxes, and full-course meals.

1–2–2 Asakusa. www.tempura-sansada.co.jp. ✆ **03/3841-3400.** *Tendon* ¥1,460–¥2,700; set meals ¥1,700–¥7,680. Daily 11:30am–9:30pm (last order). Station: Asakusa (1 min.). East of Kaminarimon Gate, with entrances beside Kurodaya paper shop and also on Kaminarimon Dori.

Sometaro (染太郎) ★ OKONOMIYAKI This very atmospheric neighborhood restaurant specializes in *okonomiyaki,* a working-class meal that is basically a Japanese pancake filled with beef, pork, and vegetables, and prepared by diners themselves as they sit on *tatami* at low tables inset with griddles. Realizing that some foreigners may be intimidated by having to cook an unfamiliar meal, this restaurant makes the process easier with an English-language menu complete with instructions. The busy but friendly staff can help you get started. *Yakisoba* (fried noodles) with meat or vegetables and other do-it-yourself dishes are also available. This is a fun, convivial way to enjoy a meal, but note that no credit cards are accepted. Before entering the restaurant, be sure to deposit your shoes in the proffered plastic sacks by the door.

2–2–2 Nishi-Asakusa. ✆ **03/3844-9502.** Main dishes ¥800–¥1,300. Daily noon–10pm (last order). Station: Tawaramachi (2 min.) or Asakusa (5 min.). At west end of Kaminarimon Dori, past Kokusai Dori with the corner police station, in 2nd block on right.

Ueno

MODERATE

You'll find a multitude of restaurants in all price categories between JR Ueno Station and Ueno Park in several new buildings, including **Mori Sakura Terrace,** with more than a dozen eateries offering French, Italian, and Chinese fare, as well as noodles, sushi, yakitori, *udon,* and other Japanese foods.

Innsyoutei (韻松亭) ★★★ KAISEKI/BENTO I love the museums and attractions in Ueno Park, but a meal at this traditional restaurant makes the outing even more special. A Tokyo landmark since 1875, it has a simple tearoom with snacks on the ground floor and a restaurant upstairs, where meals are served in private *tatami* rooms or a small dining room overlooking greenery. There's an English-language menu, but let your budget be your guide in choosing a vegetarian, bento, or *kaiseki* set lunch, all of which change with the seasons. Dinner offers more expensive *kaiseki* and chicken sukiyaki. This restaurant is extremely popular with older Japanese women, but reservations are accepted only for four or more, so be prepared to wait in line. During the cherry blossom season, when Ueno Park swarms with sightseers, Innsyoutei limits its menu to only a few set meals complete with flowers to honor the season, but you'll be lucky to get your foot in the door then. Credit cards are not accepted.

In Ueno Park. www.innsyoutei.jp. ✆ **03/3821-8126.** Set lunches ¥1,680–¥6,800; set dinners ¥5,500–¥16,000. Daily 11am–3pm; Mon–Sat 5–9:30pm; Sun 5–8:30pm (last order). Station: JR Ueno (6 min.). Beside the row of orange *torii* leading downhill.

Izu'ei Honten (伊豆栄本店) ★★ EEL This restaurant's history goes back a mere 270 years to the middle of the Edo Period, but you'd never know that from the modern multistoried building that stands here today. The dining rooms are pleasant and overlook Shinobazu Pond, but the star of the show here is grilled eel. The quality of charcoal used to grill the eel is considered paramount, and this restaurant is justly proud of its very own furnace in the mountains of Wakayama Prefecture, said to produce the best charcoal in Japan. An English-language menu with photos will help you select from about 15 different set meals featuring eel, but there's also tempura, bento, and, with advance reservations, *kaiseki.* Not all eel restaurants go to the lengths this one does to assure the quality of its food, so I consider this place a real treat.

2–12–22 Ueno. www.izuei.co.jp. ✆ **03/3831-0954.** Set meals ¥1,750–¥5,400; *kaiseki* ¥6,480–¥16,200. Daily 11am–9:30pm (last order). Station: JR Ueno (3 min.). On Shinobazu Dori, across the street from Shinobazu Pond and the Shitamachi Museum, next to KFC.

Shinjuku

EXPENSIVE

New York Grill ★★★ AMERICAN Stunning views, great steaks and seafood, an artsy vibe, and live jazz wafting in from the adjoining bar all contribute in making a meal at this 52nd-floor venue an experience to remember. Even the short walkway to the dining area is singular, with an all-white open kitchen on the left and a glass wall on the right that gives the illusion of a sheer drop-off—definitely not for the vertigo-challenged. The restaurant backs up its dramatic setting with a menu of grilled and baked dishes using ingredients from around the world, including steaks from various regions of Japan, Australian rack of lamb, and Hokkaido scallops. Its 1,600-bottle cellar features almost exclusively Californian wines, including boutique vintages you won't find anywhere else in Japan. For less formal dining (and where I like to sit when eating solo), counter seats along the open kitchen let you watch chefs in action. Both the set lunch and the weekend and holiday brunches are among the city's best and most sumptuous—and great options for those who don't want to pawn their belongings just to eat dinner here. No matter when you come, reservations are a must. I wouldn't miss it.

Park Hyatt Tokyo, 3–7–1–2 Nishi-Shinjuku. http://restaurants.tokyo.park.hyatt.co.jp/nyg.html. ✆ **03/5323-3458.** Main dishes ¥3,600–¥12,400; set lunch ¥5,500; set dinners ¥11,000–¥20,000; Sat–Sun and holiday brunch ¥7,500. Daily 11:30am–2:30pm and 5:30–10pm. Station: Shinjuku (west exit, 13-min. walk or 5-min. free shuttle ride), Hatsudai on the Keio Line (7 min.), or Tochomae on the Oedo Line (8 min.).

Kakiden (柿伝) ★★ KAISEKI Although it's located on the eighth floor of a rather uninspiring building, Kakiden has a relaxing yet simple teahouse atmosphere, with shoji screens providing privacy between tables and soothing traditional Japanese music playing softly in the background. Sibling restaurant to one in Kyoto founded more than 270 years ago as a catering service for practitioners of the tea ceremony, this *kaiseki* restaurant has been serving set meals that change with the seasons for 40 years, according to what's fresh and available. An English-language menu lists the set meals, but it's probably best to simply pick a meal to fit your budget. Some of the more common dishes here include fish, seasonal vegetables, sashimi, shrimp, and mushrooms, but don't worry if you can't identify everything—I've found that even the Japanese don't always know what they're eating. Set lunches are available until 3pm.

Yasuo Building 8F, 3–37–11 Shinjuku, 8th floor. www.kakiden.com. ✆ **03/3352-5121.** Set lunches ¥4,000–¥7,000; set dinners ¥5,000–¥20,000. Mon–Fri 11am–2pm; Sat–Sun and holidays 11am–3pm; daily 5–8pm (last order). Station: Shinjuku (east exit, 1 min.). Next to Shinjuku Station's east side, north of Flags.

MODERATE

Ban-Thai (バンタイ) ★ THAI One of Tokyo's longest-running Thai restaurants and credited with introducing authentic Thai food to the Japanese, Ban-Thai prepares excellent Thai fare, with 90-plus mouthwatering items on the menu. My favorites are the spicy minced chicken salad, the chicken soup with coconut and lemongrass, the deep-fried flatfish with sweet and spicy topping, and the pad Thai. Note that portions are not large, so if you order several portions and add beer, your tab can really climb. Also, service is indifferent. Still, this place is packed every time I come here. If you don't have a reservation, you can queue and wait, but the line moves fairly quickly.

1–23–14 Kabuki-cho, 3rd floor. www.ban-thai.jp. ✆ **03/3207-0068.** Main dishes ¥1,200–¥1,800; set lunches ¥850–¥1,300 (Mon–Fri only). Mon–Fri 11:30am–3pm and 5–11:45pm; Sat–Sun and holidays 11:30am–11:45pm. Station: Shinjuku (east exit, 7 min.). In the seediest part of Kabuki-cho (don't worry, the interior is nicer than the exterior). From Yasukuni Dori, take the pedestrian street beside 7-Eleven with a red neon archway; it's soon on the left side, above St. James Bar.

INEXPENSIVE

Din Tai Fung ★ CHINESE Tokyo's first branch of Taiwan's most popular dumpling restaurant is so popular, you'll probably have to join the long line of people waiting to get in. Luckily, the line moves fast and you'll soon find yourself dining inside the noisy restaurant or outside on the spacious terrace (unfortunately, sans views). The English-language menu lists various steamed and soup dumplings, including the signature pork dumplings served in piping-hot bamboo steamers, along with dishes like rice cakes and noodle soups. Din Tai Fung started out in 1958 as a retailer selling cooking oil in Taiwan and has been a smashing success across Asia. The Japanese are among its most avid customers, with seven locations in Tokyo alone, including one in Ginza.

Takashimaya Shinjuku, 12th floor, 5–24–2 Sendagaya. http://d.rt-c.co.jp/shinjuku. ✆ **03/5361-1381.** Dim sum ¥238–¥1,361; set lunches ¥1,556–¥1,890. Daily 11am–10pm (last order). Station: Shinjuku (New South Exit, 1 min.). Next to Uniqlo.

Kohmen (光麺) ★ RAMEN I like popping in here mid-afternoon when I missed lunch or as a lifesaver for those very late revelries. Kohmen has branches across the city, including in Ueno, Akihabara, and Harajuku, each with its own decor and opening hours. The English-language menu lists options like thick or thin noodles, various broths (the basic soup is made from stewing pig and chicken bones for up to 12 hr.), and extra toppings like grilled pork. I like the *kagashi-tantanmen* (a creamy sesame soup with noodles, hot chili, and chargrilled marinated pork) so much that I've never tried anything else, which is highly unusual for me. I also can't resist an order of *gyoza.* Bring cash; Kohmen doesn't accept credit cards.

3–32–2 Shinjuku. www.kohmen.com. ✆ **03/5919-1660.** Ramen ¥820–¥1,200. Mon–Thurs 10:30am–2am; Fri–Sat 10:30am–5am; Sun and holidays 10:30am–midnight. Station: Shinjuku or Shinjuku Sanchome (4 min.) Between the stations, south on the side street running west of Beams.

Tokyo Catering ★ VARIED JAPANESE This is probably the cheapest place in town for a meal with a view. Located on the 32nd floor in the north tower of the Tokyo Metropolitan Government Office (TMG), which offers a free observation room on its 45th floor, this cafeteria serves public employees but is open to everyone. Choose your meal—from pork cutlet, fried fish, sushi, tempura, and curry rice to noodles—from the cart laden with displays of daily set meals or the display case, where every item is identified by a number. You then purchase your selections from a vending machine (no credit cards accepted) and take your tickets to the cafeteria window. My last set meal consisted of fish tempura, rice, soup and salad. The cafeteria lacks charm, but if you can get a table by the window, you'll have a good view of Tokyo. Although it's open throughout the weekday, only snacks like ramen are available after 2pm (avoid dining from noon to 1pm, when government employees eat their lunch). There's another staff restaurant on the 32nd floor of the south tower with the same system and hours.

TMG, 32nd floor of North Tower (take the office elevator, not the elevator to the observatory), 2-8-1 Nishi-Shinjuku. ✆ **03/5320-7513.** Set meals ¥590–¥690. Mon–Fri 11:30am–2pm. Closed holidays. Station: Tochomae (1 min.), Shinjuku (10 min.), or Nishi-Shinjuku (5 min.).

Tsunahachi (つな八) ★★ TEMPURA Tsunahachi has been serving tempura since 1923, with this location opened the same year as the Tokyo Olympics, in 1964. Occupying a modest, old-fashioned building east of Shinjuku Station, it's nevertheless Tsunahachi's largest outlet, with both tables and—more fun—counter seating along the open kitchen. Unfortunately, during busy times foreigners tend to be shunted to the second-floor counter, so try to avoid the meal-time rush for a seat on the more atmospheric ground floor. There's an English-language menu, but probably the easiest thing to do is to order one of three set meals, with the cheapest including six pieces of tempura deep-fried in sesame oil, including shrimp, conger eel, seasonal fish, shrimp balls, and vegetables, plus rice, miso soup, and Japanese pickles; if you're still hungry, you can always order a la carte. Branches are located in department stores around town, including Keio in Shinjuku, Matsuya in Ginza, Lumine in Ikebukuro, and Daimaru on the Yaesu side of Tokyo Station.

3-31-8 Shinjuku. www.tunahachi.co.jp. ✆ **03/3352-1012.** Set lunches ¥1,500–¥2,500; tempura set meals ¥2,300–¥8,000. Daily 11am–10pm (last order). Station: Shinjuku Sanchome (2 min.) or Shinjuku (east exit, 5 min.). Off Shinjuku Dori on the side street that runs along the east side of the combination Bic Camera/Uniqlo store.

Harajuku & Aoyama

EXPENSIVE

Two Rooms Grill/Bar ★★★ CONTINENTAL Dress smartly to fit in with the fashion-conscious 40-somethings who gather here for high-powered business lunches and after-work cocktails. The sleek dining room looks like a setting in a black-and-white movie with its white walls and tablecloths, waiters decked out in black with crisp white aprons, and steel and glass architectural details. Bringing the scene to life are warm woods (including tables made of 50,000-year-old swamp kauri timber from New Zealand), jazz playing softly in the background, and an open kitchen briskly turning out orders. But what I love most about this place is the bar, with an outdoor terrace over an infinity pool offering poster-perfect views of the city skyline from comfy sofas. As for the menu, Wagyu beef reigns supreme, though there other yummy choices include the lamb chops or the slow-cooked pork sirloin. Weekday lunches and weekend brunches also come highly recommended (make reservations), but even if you don't dine here, a drink on the outdoor terrace will make Tokyo seem like the most relaxing place in the world. The bar is open until 2am (Sun until 10pm).

AO Building, 5th floor, 3-11-7 Kita-Aoyama. www.tworooms.jp. ✆ **03/3498-0002.** Main dishes ¥2,800–¥9,500; set lunches ¥2,500–¥6,100; set dinners ¥8,500–¥11,000. Daily 11:30am–2:30pm; Mon–Sat 6–10pm; Sun 6–9pm (last order). Station: Omotesando (exit

B2, 1 min.). It's on the right side of Aoyama Dori in the direction of Shibuya, in the striking, trapezoidal AO Building.

MODERATE

Cicada ★★ MEDITERRANEAN Occupying a half-century-old building designed by a well-known architect and tucked away in its own little world, Cicada offers dishes influenced by the sun-drenched countries of southern Europe and northern Africa. For starters, you might choose Iberico chorizo or the manchego platter with membrillo (a Spanish quince snack) and pumpkin seeds, though there's also a wide choice of tapas, like the spicy Moroccan crab cakes. For a main, tempting dishes include grilled jumbo shrimp in tomato, garbanzo, and olive sauce with harissa cream; the lamb tagine with couscous; or one of the many vegetarian options. In addition to its own craft beer, Cicada offers wines from Spain, Italy, Greece, Morocco, and other Mediterranean countries. With its subdued lighting and classy dining areas that include outdoor terraces surrounded by a pool or greenery, this is the perfect spot for a romantic meal. For that reason, note that if you have a child younger than six you'll have to pay extra for a private room. In that case, I'd say go elsewhere.

5–7–28 Minami-Aoyama. www.tysons.jp. ✆ **03/6434-1255.** Main dishes ¥2,000–¥2,800; set lunches ¥1,800–¥3,800 (Mon–Fri only). Daily 11:30am–3pm and 5:30–11pm (last order). Station: Omotesando (exit B1, 1 min.). Behind the Spiral Building; take the first left and then right. It's in a courtyard, past a cafe and bakery.

eatrip restaurant ★★★ VARIED JAPANESE/WESTERN You'd never think you're in the middle of bustling Harajuku when dining here. That's because eatrip is located in a small, free-standing rustic house, not unlike what you might find in the Italian countryside. In addition, it's reached via stairs that take you through a small garden adjacent to a flower shop, looking all the world like a place in which fairies might live. Specializing in locally sourced organic food, it offers constantly changing farm-to-table dishes expertly prepared. A limited a-la-carte menu is served only on the terrace, so you'll probably want to go for one of the set meals with seasonal appetizers and meat, fish, or vegetable of the day, accompanied, perhaps, by organic wine or homemade ginger ale. In any case, make reservations to experience this whimsical place.

6–31–10 Jingumae. http://restaurant-eatrip.com. ✆ **03/3409-4002.** Set meals ¥5,000–¥8,000. Sat 11:30–2pm; Sun 11:30am–3:30pm; Tues–Sat 6–11pm (last order). Station: Meiji-Jingumae (1 min.) or Harajuku (2 min.). Between the two stations, behind Zara.

Maru (圓) ★★ MODERN JAPANESE Reservations are a must at this tiny hideaway off Aoyama Dori, where seating is confined to only a few wooden tables and a long counter stretching along the open kitchen. The English-language menu, which changes to reflect what's in season, offers a tempting roster of choices ranging from classic Kyoto-style *kaiseki* to creative dishes with a contemporary twist. The friendly and hip staff is happy to help narrow down selections based on individual preferences, but one dish you shouldn't pass up is the restaurant's signature *donabe,* rice simmered in a clay pot and served with a choice of toppings. Other main dishes may include Wagyu beef preserved in Kyoto miso or a seasonal vegetable tempura. But for a splurge or for those who can't make up their mind, there are monthly set meals that always include *donabe.* Drinks range from wine to sake and *shochu,* including *awamori,* an Okinawan *shochu* made from Thai rice. There's a branch in Ginza, serving only three set meals for dinner and a ¥1,000 lunch.

5–50–8 Jingumae. www.maru-mayfont.jp. ✆ **03/6418-5572.** Main dishes ¥1,050–¥2,800; set meals ¥5,500–¥7,500. Mon–Fri 6–11pm; Sat 5–11; Sun and holidays 5–10:30pm (last order). Station: Omotesando (3 min.). Walk toward Shibuya on Aoyama Dori and turn right at Muji; it's almost immediately on the right, in a basement.

Yasaiya Mei (やさい家めい) ★★ VARIED JAPANESE If you like veggies, this restaurant is a must, specializing in fresh, seasonal, and mostly organic vegetables (note that because it uses fish stock for many of its dishes and meat dishes, it is not a strictly vegetarian restaurant). Reservations are also a must. Although it offers a few à la carte selections (carrot kimchi, say, or the Mei Special bagna cauda, which comes with a variety of veggies such as eggplant, radish, and asparagus), set meals are the emphasis here. For lunch your meal might include vegetable pressed "sushi" with vegetable tempura and side dishes, while dinner offers sukiyaki and meals like the Vegetable Gozen, which comes with sweet potato soup, bagna cauda, and a slew of vegetables and other dishes. Seating is either at the U-shaped open kitchen or a table—try to snag one beside the large windows overlooking the trees of Omotesando Dori.

Omotesando Hills, 3rd floor, 4–12–10 Jingumae. www.eat-walk.com/en/mei/index.html. ✆ **03/5785-0606.** Set lunches ¥1,290–¥2,090; set dinners ¥4,900–¥4,900. Mon–Sat 11am–10:30pm; Sun 11am–9:30pm (last order). Station: Meiji-Jingumae or Omotesando (4 min.). On Omotesando Dori.

INEXPENSIVE

In addition to the choices below, **Kohmen** (p. 103), 6–2–8 Jingumae (✆ **03/5468-6344**), serves tasty ramen and *gyoza.* Off Aoyama Dori is **Commune 2nd,** 3–13 Minami Aoyama, a plaza with food trucks and carts offering falafel, vegan curries, gourmet French fries, noodles, and more from 11am to 10pm, with indoor heated seating in winter.

Harajuku Gyoza Lou (原宿餃子樓) ★ GYOZA If you like *gyoza* (pork dumplings), you owe yourself a meal here. Hip yet unpretentious, it draws a young crowd with its straightforward menu posted on the wall (an English-language menu is also available). Only one type of *gyoza* is offered, which you can order steamed *(sui-gyoza)* or fried *(yaki-gyoza),* and with or without garlic *(ninniku).* A few side dishes, such as boiled cabbage with vinegar, sprouts with a spicy meat sauce, and rice, are available, as are beer and sake. A U-shaped counter encloses the open kitchen, which diners can watch as they chow down on the very good *gyoza.* There's usually a queue out the door, but this isn't the kind of place people linger, so it's worth the wait. No credit cards accepted.

6–2–4 Jingumae. ✆ **03/3406-4743.** *Gyoza* ¥290 for a plate of 6. Mon–Sat 11:30am–4:30am; Sun and holidays 11:30am–10:30pm (last order). Station: Meiji-Jingumae (3 min.) or Harajuku (5 min.). From the Meiji/Omotesando Dori intersection, walk on Omotesando Dori toward Aoyama and take the 3rd right (just before Kiddy Land); it's at the end of this alley, on the right.

Heirokuzushi (平禄寿司) ★ SUSHI Bright (a bit too bright), clean, and modern, this was the first *kaiten* sushi restaurant I ever saw, one of those fast-food sushi bars where plates of food roll along a conveyor belt on the counter. It's now extremely popular with foreigners from around the world, who help themselves to whatever strikes their fancy, from the usual tuna to more unusual avocado. To figure your bill, the cashier counts the number of plates you took from the conveyor belt: Green plates cost ¥130, for example; blue ones ¥170, and so on; no credit cards are accepted. You can also order takeout, which you might want to eat in nearby Yoyogi Park.

5–8–5 Jingumae. www.g-taste.co.jp/en/brands/heiroku-sushi/. ✆ **03/3498-3968.** Plates of sushi ¥130–¥490. Daily 11am–9pm. Station: Meiji-Jingumae (2 min.) or Omotesando (5 min.). On Omotesando Dori close to Oriental Bazaar.

Hiroba ★★ JAPANESE/VEGETARIAN Located in the basement of the Crayon House, which specializes in Japanese children's books, this natural-food restaurant offers lunch and dinner buffets of organic veggies, fish, brown rice, and other health foods. On Mondays the dinner buffet is completely vegetarian. From 2:40 to 5:30pm, during so-called tea time, it also offers three curry set meals (including a vegetarian option), pizza, and desserts. The dining hall, next to an organic food store, is very simple (it reminds me of a potluck supper in a church basement), but it also offers outdoor seating in a sunken courtyard surrounded by plants, where you can order organic wine. And because of the upstairs bookstore, there are likely to be families here.

Crayon House, 3–8–15 Kita-Aoyama. www.crayonhouse.co.jp/shop/pages/restaurant_en.aspx. ✆ **03/3406-6409.** Lunch buffet ¥1,500; dinner buffet ¥2,700. Mon–Fri 11am–2pm; Sat–Sun 10:30am–2pm; daily 5:30–10pm (last order). Station: Omotesando (2 min.). From the Omotesando/Aoyama Dori intersection, walk on Omotesando Dori toward Harajuku and take first left (btw. Coach and Hugo Boss).

Maisen (まい泉) ★★ TONKATSU Plenty of Tokyoites consider this the best *tonkatsu* (deep-fried breaded pork cutlet) restaurant in Tokyo. In business since 1965, it now has several locations around town, including the basement of Daimaru department store and the Hikarie Building in Shibuya. But this is the main store and the most atmospheric, with a main dining hall ensconced in what was once the dressing room of a pre–World War II public bathhouse, where a tall ceiling and other original architectural details hint at its former life. The English-language menu lists various dishes and set meals, the most famous of which features *tonkatsu* made from black pig from Kagoshima, which has a sweet, more intense flavor than regular pork. *Tonkatsu* comes with finely shredded cabbage and Maisen's own sauce. Lunch specials, available until 4pm, are listed only in Japanese, but photos are provided. A takeout window offers various bento boxes and Maisen products, including its own curry sauce.

4–8–5 Jingumae. www.mai-sen.com. ✆ **03/3470-0071.** Set meals ¥1,730–¥3,960; set lunches ¥990–¥1,300. Daily 11am–10pm (last order). Station: Omotesando A2 exit (4 min.). Heading toward Harajuku on Omotesando Dori, take the first right (an archway here has FITNESS CLUB GOLD'S GYM written on it), then the 1st left and an immediate right. It will be in the next block on the left.

Toriyoshi (鳥良) ★ JAPANESE/INTERNATIONAL This hip, upscale bar is a popular dining spot as well, especially for its chicken specialties such as fried chicken wings and half a fried chicken. The English menu isn't up to date, but it has photos and is a good starting point for ordering ramen, yakitori, salads, kimchi, and other Japanese and Asian pub fare. You'll want to order several dishes tapas style and then share. It's a good place for a convivial meal, but note that there's a ¥399 snack charge per person.

4–28–21 Jingumae. ✆ **03/3470-3901.** Main dishes ¥460–¥988. Mon–Fri 11:30pm–3pm and 5–11pm; Sat–Sun 11:30am–2pm and 4–11pm (last order). Station: Meiji-Jingumae (3 min.). From the Meiji Dori/Omotesando intersection, walk on Omotesando Dori toward Aoyama and take the 1st left; it's down this street on the right side, beside a willow tree.

Venire Venire ★ ITALIAN At Venire Venire, you can see for yourself how inexpensive doesn't necessarily mean drab. This tall-ceilinged trattoria is light and airy, with a large outdoor terrace (open from late Apr to Oct) affording sweeping views over the surrounding rooftops. It offers pizzas and pastas, as well as a handful of main dishes like lamb chops with red wine and a green herb sauce. It has a large selection of Italian wines. This is a popular wedding venue, so call ahead to avoid disappointment, or have an alternative plan.

Y.M. Square, 5th floor; 4–31–10 Jingumae. ✆ **03/5775-5333.** Pizza and pasta ¥1,400–¥1,800; main dishes ¥1,400–¥2,400; set lunches ¥1,000–¥3,800. Mon–Fri 11:30am–3:30pm and 5–11pm; Sat–Sun and holidays 11:30am–4pm and 5–10:30pm. Station: Harajuku (1 min.). On Meiji Dori, just north of Tokyu Plaza and across from La Foret.

Yai Yai (やいやい) ★ OKONOMIYAKI Instead of having to cook your own *okonomiyaki,* all you have to do here is order, whereupon the young staff sets to work cooking your meal on a griddle in front of you. You choose the toppings—such as pork and leek, seafood, and kimchi—to add to the pancakelike base, cabbage, and egg. Fried noodles and *negi-yaki* (flat dough with leeks) are also available, as well as some vegetarian options. The interior is dark and homey, a nice escape from the crowds of Harajuku.

6–8–7 Jingumae. www.opefac.com/yaiyai. ✆ **03/3406-8181.** *Okonomiyaki* or fried noodles ¥880–¥1,490. Mon–Fri 1:30pm–midnight; Sat–Sun and holidays 11:30am–midnight. Station: Meiji-Jingumae (3 min.) or Harajuku (7 min.). From the Meiji Dori/Omotesando intersection, walk on Omotesando Dori toward Aoyama and take the 2nd right; it will be on the left, past TGI Friday's.

Roppongi

Because Roppongi is such a popular nighttime hangout for young Tokyoites and foreigners, it boasts a large number of both Japanese and Western restaurants. To find the location of any of the Roppongi addresses below, stop by the tiny police station on Roppongi Crossing (Roppongi's main intersection of Roppongi Dori and Gaien-Higashi Dori) to study a map of the area or ask for directions. Catty-cornered from the police station, on the other side of the overhead expressway, is the number-one meeting spot in Roppongi, in front of Almond coffee shop. If you're meeting someone, this will likely be the spot.

About a 12-minute walk west of Roppongi (via Roppongi Dori in the direction of Shibuya) is **Nishi Azabu,** with more restaurants and bars. Between

Roppongi Crossing and Nishi Azabu is **Roppongi Hills,** a sprawling urban development with many choices in dining.

EXPENSIVE

Fukuzushi (福鮨) ★★★ SUSHI Tokyo has thousands of sushi restaurants in all price ranges, but this classy spot has proven the test of time with its superb fresh fish and devoted following. Founded in 1917 and now under its fourth generation of owners, it has a courtyard entrance that beckons with lit lanterns and the sound of water, but inside it's all contemporary Tokyo, with pop-out reds contrasted against black furnishings. Because the owner-chef goes to market daily, dishes change regularly and with the seasons. Lunch offers four set meals, from a *nigiri-zushi* course to *anago-jyu* (sea eel on rice), all with side dishes like steamed egg custard or miso soup and dessert. Set dinners feature many more dishes, with the ¥9,000 meal including an appetizer, sashimi and sushi, egg custard, the day's dish (like grilled fish), miso soup, dessert, and coffee. Or tell the chef your budget and preferences and he'll take it from there.

5–7–8 Roppongi. www.roppongifukuzushi.com. ✆ **03/3402-4116.** Set lunches ¥2,500–¥3,500; set dinners ¥7,000–¥15,000. Mon–Sat 11:30am–1:30pm and 6–10pm (last order). Closed holidays. Station: Roppongi (4 min.). From Roppongi Crossing, walk toward Tokyo Tower on Gaien-Higashi Dori, turning right at the first stoplight, left in front of Hard Rock Cafe, and then right.

Inakaya (田舎屋) ★★ ROBATAYAKI Although tourist-oriented and over priced, this restaurant is still great entertainment; the drama of the place alone is worth it. Customers sit at a long, U-shaped counter, on the other side of which are mountains of fresh vegetables, beef, and seafood. And in the middle of all that food, seated in front of a grill, are male chefs—ready to cook whatever you point to in the style of *robatayaki.* Orders are shouted out by your waiter and repeated in unison by the other waiters, resulting in ongoing, excited yelling. Sounds strange, I know, but actually it's a lot of fun. Food offerings may include yellowtail, red snapper, scallops, king crab legs, giant shrimp, steak, meatballs, gingko nuts, potatoes, eggplant, and asparagus, all piled high in wicker baskets and ready for the grill. My main gripe is that unless you keep referring to the menu, the price of individual dishes quickly adds up, with most meals averaging around ¥25,000 to ¥30,000. Come expecting to spend money, and you won't be disappointed. Another branch nearby, at 5–3–4 Roppongi (✆ **03/3408-5040**), is open the same hours.

4–10–11 Roppongi. www.roppongiinakaya.jp. ✆ **03/5775-1012.** Grilled vegetables ¥756–¥2,160; grilled seafood and meats ¥1,890–¥5,400. Daily 5–10:30pm (last order). Station: Roppongi (2 min.). Off Gaien-Higashi Dori on a side street; from Roppongi Crossing, walk on Gaien-Higashi Dori in the direction of Midtown and take the 2nd right.

Ruby Jack's Steakhouse & Bar ★★★ STEAK These people really know their steak. If you wish, they'll give you a primer on the differences among Japanese Wagyu (aged 45 days in the restaurant and the fattiest and, to my mind, most tender), U.S. prime cuts, and Australian grain-fed black Angus. If you really want to go all out, order the teppan-grilled foie gras to go with that grilled steak. Other choices are on the menu, including rack of lamb and fish of the day, but really, why bother? The ciabatta is house-made and oysters make a great starter, and you may want to add the yummy mashed potatoes with garlic chips or the creamed spinach. And what would a good steak be without red wine? This is a very corporate type of place, with tall ceilings and a glass facade overlooking a terrace where you can enjoy drinks and dessert. Lunches add sandwiches and lighter fare, while weekend brunches include breakfast choices.

Ark Hills South Tower, 1–4–5 Roppongi. www.rubyjacks.jp. ✆ **03/5544-8222.** Main dishes ¥3,200–¥8,500; set dinners ¥7,500–¥10,000. Mon–Fri 11am–2:30pm; Sat–Sun and holidays 11am–3pm; Mon–Sat 6–10pm; Sun and holidays 6–9pm (last order). Station: Roppongi (8 min.), Roppongi-Itchome (3 min.), or Tameike-Sanno (5 min.). At the bottom of Roppongi Dori, near ANA InterContinental Tokyo.

Tokyo Shiba Toufuya Ukai ★★★ TOFU This restaurant lies practically in the shadows of Tokyo Tower, but it has such a serene setting and lush gardens that it instantly transports customers to another time and place. Specializing in classic tofu cuisine, the restaurant is spread over several structures that are remakes of traditional architecture, from the *kura* (warehouse) with its thick, white walls and vaulted door to the main building with its heavy beams and foot-thick lacquered pillars (once part of an old farmhouse in Takayama). Surrounding the buildings are exquisite gardens, tended to by three fulltime gardeners and boasting ponds, streams, gnarled pines, stone lanterns, arched bridges, and strolling paths (be sure to walk through the back garden after your meal). The main dining hall overlooks the back garden, but most guests opt for one of the private *tatami* rooms, many also with garden views. It offers only set meals, which change with the seasons and are explained on an English-language menu. The least expensive lunch (available only weekdays) may start with a lotus root cake with sea urchin and deep-fried tofu coated with miso sauce, followed by assorted sashimi, deep-fried simmered tofu with crab, a main dish, tofu boiled in a seasoned soy milk, rice with sweet potato, and dessert. Reservations are a must.

4–4–13 Shibakoen. www.ukai.co.jp. ✆ **03/3436-1028.** Set lunches ¥5,940–¥7,560; set dinners ¥10,800–¥16,200. Mon–Fri 11:45am–3pm and 5pm–10pm; Sat–Sun and holidays 11am–10pm (last order 8pm). Station: Akabanebashi (5 min.). Behind Tokyo Tower.

MODERATE

Joumon Roppongi ★★★ KUSHIYAKI This hipster *kushiyaki* restaurant specializes in seasonal grilled delicacies, like scallops in butter soy sauce or yellowtail in teriyaki sauce, as well as menu items like chicken breast with wasabi, seared Japanese beef, homemade sesame tofu, salads, and noodle dishes. Or, order eight skewers chosen by the chef for ¥1,680. Reservations are required, with seating either at the low counter (best for watching the action of the kitchen) or one of the tables in back.

5–9–17 Roppongi. www.teyandei.com. ✆ **03/3405-2585.** Skewers ¥200–¥250. Main dishes ¥700–¥1,500. Sun–Thurs 5:30–11pm; Fri–Sat 5:30pm–5am. Station: Roppongi (4 min.). From Roppongi Crossing, take the small street going downhill to the left of the Almond coffee shop; it will be on your left, with a somewhat hidden and obscure door.

Roti Roppongi ★★ AMERICAN A casual brasserie with both indoor (nonsmoking) and outdoor seating, Roti counts many expats among its loyal customers, thanks in part to its quiet, tucked-away location just a minute's walk from Roppongi Hills. It offers a fresh take on modern American fare, which includes imported oysters, free-range roasted or grilled chicken (available with green garlic, mushroom, or coconut curry sauce), grilled steaks, a variety of burgers, serious Caesar salads, and many other delectable dishes too numerous to mention. More than 90 bottles of New World, Australian, and New Zealand wines, as well as American craft beers and Belgian microbrews, round out the menu. It's also a great place for the weekend brunch, served until a decent 5pm.

6-6-9 Roppongi. www.roti.jp. ✆ **03/5785-3671.** Main dishes ¥1,400–¥3,200. Daily 11:30am–5pm and 6–10. Station: Roppongi (A1 exit, 1 min.). On a side street that parallels Roppongi Dori, a stone's throw from Roppongi Hills and beside Frijoles.

INEXPENSIVE

Frijoles ★ MEXICAN Next to Roti (above), this casual eatery serves only a few dishes—burritos, tacos, and salads—but it does them extremely well, making this a very popular choice for a quick meal or takeout. Head to the counter and choose your medium (taco, burrito, or salad bowl), your meat (chicken, steak, or seasoned pork; vegetarian also available), toppings (black beans, pinto beans, cheese, etc.), and salsa (from mild to fiery hot), and then head to the small dining area or one of the outdoor tables. Most of the food is prepared on-site, and it shows. Frijoles will remind you of Chipotle, except that here you can also order a margarita.

6-6-9 Roppongi. www.frijoles.jp. ✆ **03/6447-1433.** Main dishes ¥980–¥1,690. Daily 11am–10pm (closed 2nd Sun of every month). Station: Roppongi (A1 exit, 1 min.). On a side street that parallels Roppongi Dori, a stone's throw from Roppongi Hills, beside Roti.

Ganchan (がんちゃん) ★ YAKITORI This is one of my favorite *yakitori-ya.* Small and intimate, with seating along a single counter with room for only a dozen or so people, it has a young and fun-loving staff. Though there's an English-language menu, it's easiest to order the *yakitori seto,* a delicious set course that comes with salad and soup and eight skewers of such items as chicken, beef, meatballs, green peppers, and asparagus rolled with bacon. The ¥600 per-person table charge includes an appetizer.

6-8-23 Roppongi. ✆ **03/3478-0092.** *Yakitori* skewers ¥320–¥750; *yakitori* set course ¥2,700. Mon–Fri 5pm–1:30am; Sat and holidays 5–11:30pm. Station: Roppongi (7 min.). From Roppongi Crossing, take the small street going downhill left of the Almond coffee shop; Ganchan is at the bottom of the hill on the right, just before the stoplight.

Gonpachi ★★ VARIED JAPANESE/YAKITORI Housed in a re-created *kura* (traditional Japanese warehouse) with a high ceiling, three-tiered seating, and a central, open kitchen, this is one of Tokyo's most imaginative inexpensive Japanese restaurants (it's said to have served as the inspiration for the animated restaurant scene in the movie *Kill Bill*). It offers a wide variety of dishes, including *yakitori* (such as duck breast with wasabi), fish (such as miso-glazed black cod), sushi (on the third floor), tempura, and noodles. From the outside, you'd expect this place to be much more exclusive than it is—and you probably *will* be excluded if you fail to make reservations for dinner. Branches include those in the G-Zone, 1–2–3 Ginza, and in Shibuya on the 14th floor of E-Space Tower, 3–6 Maruyama-cho, but they don't match this location's atmosphere.

1–13–11 Nishi Azabu. www.gonpachi.jp. ✆ **03/5771-0170.** *Yakitori* ¥300–¥1,400; main dishes ¥1,580–¥2,980; set lunches ¥1,000–¥3,000 (from ¥2,000 Sat–Sun; set dinners ¥4,500–¥6,000. Daily 11:30am–3:30am. Station: Roppongi (12 min.). From Roppongi Crossing, walk toward Shibuya on Roppongi Dori. It will be on your right, at the corner of Gaien-Nishi Dori.

Shibuya

MODERATE

Legato Sky Lounge ★★★ ITALIAN/FUSION With its dramatic setting and innovative cuisine, you'd expect this restaurant to be much more expensive than it is. After the elevator delivers you to the 15th floor, you might be tempted to stop or come back later for a drink at the tear-shaped bar, open until 3am, where the view takes in the shimmering lights of Shibuya. Then you'll make your entrance down the short flight of steps to the sunken restaurant below, bathed in the warm glow of lanterns hanging from the ceiling and candles on each table, which are spaced widely enough to make this an intimate romantic splurge. The open kitchen turns out a handful of main dishes like steak and roasted lobster, plus a few pasta and pizza choices, including a black truffle pizza with onion, bacon, and cream. The knowledgeable, mostly international staff is happy to make recommendations. The wine list travels the world with bottles in all price ranges, but there's also plenty of bubbly to help celebrate a special occasion. Be sure to call for reservations and weekend hours—weddings and other events often close this venue to the public

E-Space Tower, 15th floor, 3–6 Maruyama-cho. https://legatoskylounge.com. ✆ **03/5784-2121.** Main dishes ¥1,800–¥4,500; set lunches ¥1,300–¥2,800; set dinners ¥3,800–¥5,800. Mon–Fri 11:30am–2pm; daily 5:30–10:30pm (last order). Station: Shibuya (Hachiko exit, 8 min.). From the station, walk straight up Dogenzaka; it will be on the right, just past the *koban* police box.

INEXPENSIVE

In addition to the recommendations here, there's a branch of **Maisen** (p. 107), offering *tonkatsu,* on the sixth floor of Hikarie (✆ **03/3486-2365**). **Gonpachi** (p. 111), on the 14th floor of E-Space Tower, 3–6 Maruyama-cho (✆ **03/5784-2011**), offers Japanese fare at inexpensive prices.

d47 Shokudo ★★ VARIED JAPANESE Since I've traveled to most of Japan's 47 prefectures and grown fond of many regional dishes, I'm excited that I don't have any farther to go than Shibuya to experience many of them. The menu can't offer all prefectural dishes at once, of course, but the staff roams around Japan and continually brings back new recipes for the kitchen. You might, therefore, get to sample Oita Prefecture's famous chicken, *natto* (fermented soybean) with Japanese plum sauce and ginger from Nagano, or Okinawan specialties that are foreign even to Japanese. Beer (like stout beer from Shizuoka) and sake from around Japan are also a treat. If you can, get a seat facing bustling Shibuya Station.

Hikarie, 8th floor, 2–21–1 Shibuya. ✆ **03/6427-2303.** Main dishes ¥600–¥1,000; set meals ¥1,400–¥1,780. Daily 11:30am–2:30pm and 6–10pm (last order). Station: Shibuya (east gate, 1 min.).

Uobei ★ SUSHI Genki Sushi is a wildly successful chain of conveyor-belt sushi restaurants, with branches throughout Japan, China (I first encountered them in Hong Kong), and the U.S. West Coast, but this one takes it up a notch by removing humans from the equation. Not completely, I guess, as a hostess delivers you to your assigned counter seat and there must be an army of cooks back in the kitchen making your order. But then it's just you and your touch screen, available in English and other languages, making this a super-easy place to dine if you don't speak Japanese. Simply place your order of sushi, add side dishes like miso soup or French fries, help yourself to the hot-water spigot and powdered tea, and voila! Your meal comes racing down a conveyor belt and stops right in front of you, with almost all plates costing just ¥108. It's a bit eerie, and you have to wonder, is this the restaurant of the future?

2–29–11 Dogenzaka. www.genkisushi.co.jp/en. ✆ **03/3462-0241.** Main dishes ¥108. Daily 11am–midnight. Station: Shibuya (Hachiko exit, 6 min.). From the station, walk straight up Dogenzaka until you get to Mos Burger (on your right) and then turn right.

Akasaka

MODERATE

Ninja Akasaka ★ VARIED JAPANESE At this themed restaurant, diners enter the secret world of the ninja as soon as they step inside the darkened entrance, where costumed waiters appear out of nowhere to lead the hungry through a labyrinth of twisting passageways to private dining nooks. The English-language menu, written on a scroll, offers a la carte dishes like sweet-and-sour pork, salmon grilled with saikyo miso, roast lamb with Korean flavoring, and various sushi, soups, and salads. But most people go with one of the set dinners like the shabu-shabu course (there are also vegetarian courses). As the meal winds down, on most nights a roaming ninja will drop by to entertain with a variety of magic acts that are darn near impossible to figure out (tipping is up to you). Although I admit Ninja may be corny, the food is good, the intimate dining venues are great for couples and groups, and the staff is beyond reproach. For families with kids, this place is tough to beat (see the website, however, for details and restrictions). Reservations are a must.

Akasaka Tokyu Plaza, 1st floor, 2–14–3 Nagata-cho. www.ninjaakasaka.com. ✆ **03/5157-3936.** Main dishes ¥1,500–¥6,800; set dinners ¥5,700–¥20,000. Mon–Sat 5–10:30pm (last entry); Sun and holidays 5–9:45pm. Station: Akasaka-mitsuke (1 min.). In the candy-cane-striped building, below the Akasaka Excel Tokyu Hotel.

EXPLORING TOKYO

5

Tokyo hasn't fared very well over the centuries. Fires and earthquakes have taken their toll, old buildings have been torn down in the zeal for modernization, and World War II left most of the city in ruins. Save your historical sightseeing, therefore, for places such as Kyoto or Takayama, and consider Tokyo an introduction to the newest of the new in Japan and the showcase of the nation's accomplishments in the arts, technology, fashion, pop art, and design. Tokyo also has more museums than any other city in Japan, as well as a wide range of parks, temples, and shrines. In Tokyo you can explore mammoth department stores, sample unlimited cuisines, walk around unique neighborhoods, revel in kitsch, and take advantage of the glittering nightlife.

When planning your sightseeing itinerary, keep in mind that the city is huge, and it takes time to get from one end to the other. It's best, therefore, to cover Tokyo neighborhood by neighborhood, coordinating sightseeing with dinner and evening plans. Most museums in Tokyo are closed 1 day of the week (usually Mon) and for New Year's (generally the last day or two in Dec and the first 1 to 3 days of Jan). If Monday happens to be a national holiday, most national and municipal museums will remain open but will close Tuesday instead. Some of the privately owned museums, however, are closed on national holidays, as well as for exhibition changes. Call beforehand or check websites to avoid disappointment. Remember, too, that you must enter museums at least 30 minutes before closing time. For a listing of current exhibitions, including those being held at major department stores, consult *Metropolis,* an English-language weekly available in hotels, restaurants, and bars around town as well as online at www.metropolisjapan.com.

CENTRAL TOKYO: GINZA & THE VICINITY OF THE IMPERIAL PALACE

For an overview of Tokyo, see the map in chapter 4, p. 60.

East Garden (Higashi Gyoen) ★★ GARDEN The 21 hectares (52 acres) of the formal Higashi Gyoen—once the main grounds of Edo Castle and located next to the Imperial Palace—are a wonderful respite in the middle of the city. Yet surprisingly, this garden is hardly ever crowded, except when cherry trees, azaleas, and other blossoms are in full bloom or at lunchtime when *bento*-eating office workers fill the benches. **Ninomaru,** my favorite part, is laid out in Japanese style with a pond, stepping stones, and winding paths; it's particularly beautiful when the wisteria, azaleas, irises, and other flowers are at their peak. Near Ninomaru is the **Sannomaru Shozokan,** with free, changing exhibitions of art treasures belonging to the imperial family.

On the highest spot of East Garden is the **Honmaru** (inner citadel), where Tokugawa's main castle once stood, the mightiest in the land. Built in the first half of the 1600s, the massive castle was surrounded by a series of whirling moats and guarded by 29 watchtowers and 38 gates around its 15km (10-mile) perimeter. At its center was Japan's tallest building at the time, the five-story castle keep, soaring 50m (168 ft.) above its foundations and offering an expansive view over Edo. This is where Tokugawa Ieyasu would have taken refuge, had his empire ever been seriously threatened. Although most of the castle was a glimmering white, the keep was black with a gold roof, which must have been quite a sight in old Edo as it towered above the rest of the city. All that remains today of the shogun's castle are a few towers, gates, stone walls, moats, and the stone foundations of the keep.

Free guided tours of the garden and Marunouchi, run by volunteers, are given Saturday 1 to 3pm. Appointments aren't necessary; just show up at the meeting point outside Tokyo Station's Marunouchi Central Exit and look for the sign FREE WALKING TOUR. For details, go to http://tfwt.sharepoint.com.

1–1 Chiyoda, Chiyoda-ku. www.kunaicho.go.jp/e-event/higashigyoen02.html. ✆ **03/3213-1111.** Free admission. Tues–Thurs and Sat–Sun 9am–5pm (to 4:30pm Mar to mid-Apr and Sept–Oct; to 4pm Nov–Feb). You must enter 30 min. before closing. Closed Dec 23 and Dec 28–Jan 3; open other national holidays. Station: Otemachi, Takebashi, or Nijubashi-mae.

The Imperial Palace (Kyokyo) ★ HISTORIC SITE The Imperial Palace, home of the imperial family, is the heart and soul of Tokyo. Built on the very spot where the massive Edo Castle compound used to stand during the days of the Tokugawa shogunate, it became the imperial home upon its completion in 1888 and is the residence of Emperor Akihito, 125th emperor of Japan (who will abdicate in 2019 and be followed by his son, Crown Prince Naruhito). Destroyed during air raids in 1945, the palace was rebuilt in 1968 using the principles of traditional Japanese architecture. But don't expect to

Tokyo Attractions

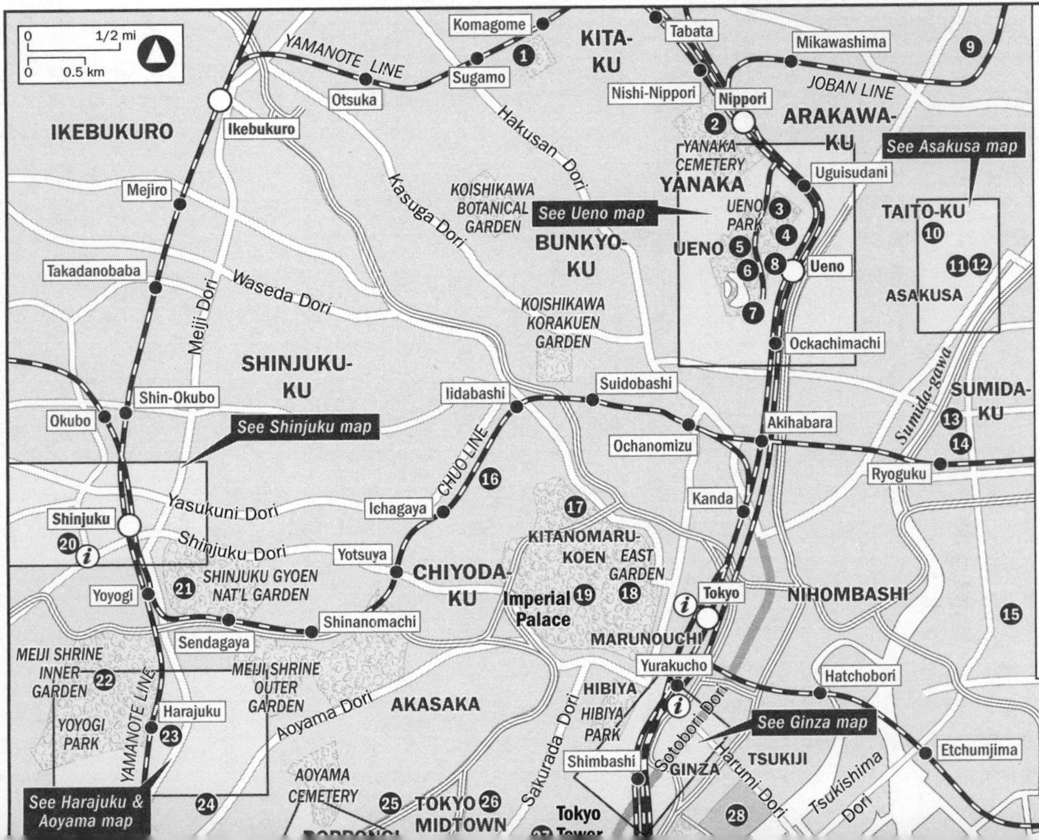

Amuse Museum **12**
Asakura Choso Museum **2**
East Garden **18**
Edo-Tokyo Museum **14**
Fukugawa Edo Museum **15**
Hama Rikyu Garden **30**
Hanayashiki **10**
Imperial Palace **19**
Kokugikan (Sumo Stadium) **13**
Meiji Jingu Shrine **22**
Mori Art Museum **29**
The National Art Center, Tokyo **25**
National Children's Castle **24**
National Museum of Modern Art **17**
National Museum of Nature and Science **4**
National Museum of Western Art **8**
Oedo-Onsen Monogatari **31**
Rikugien Garden **1**
Sensoji Temple **11**
Shinjuku Gyoen **21**
Suntory Museum of Art **26**

Key continues below

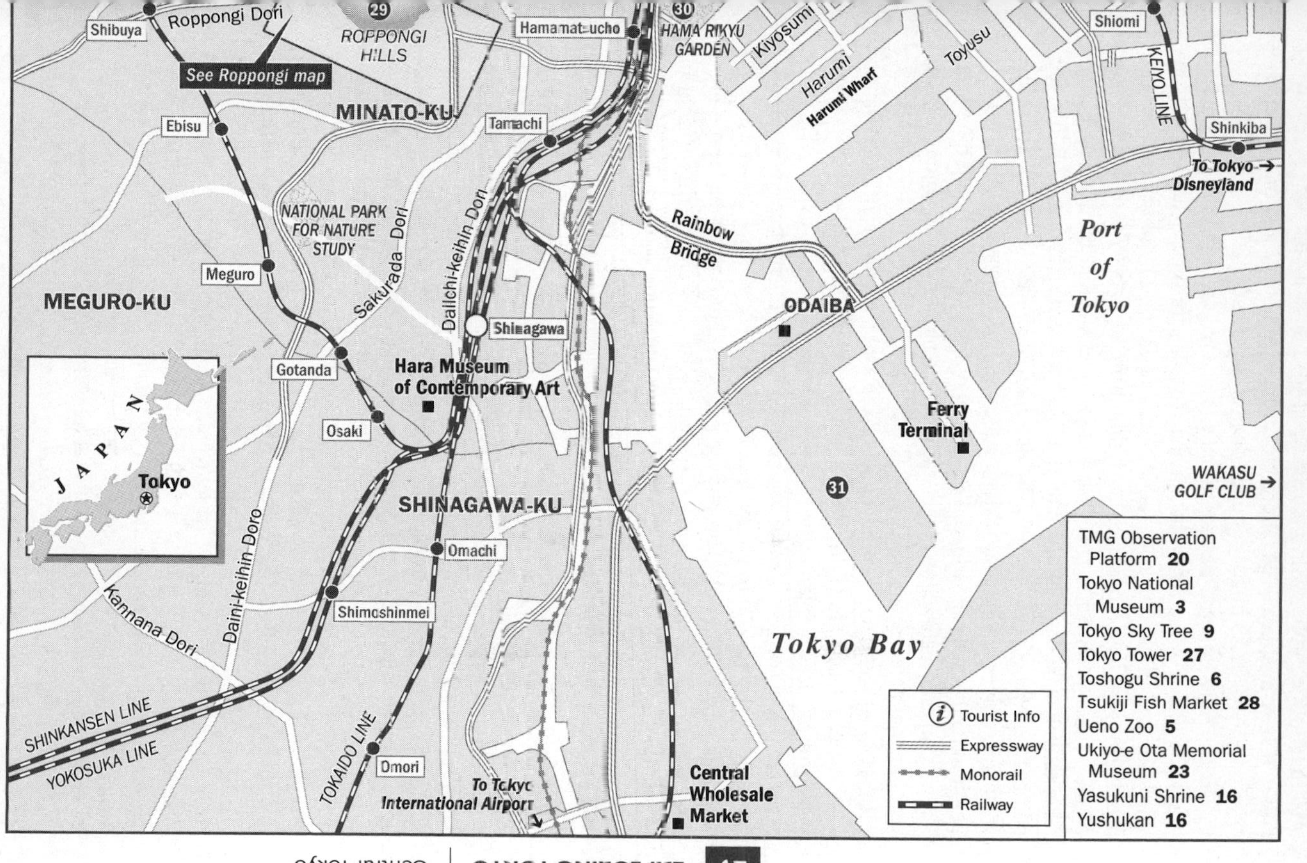
Shibuya
Roppongi Dori
29
ROPPONGI HILLS
See Roppongi map
MINATO-KU
Ebisu
Hamamatsucho
30
HAMA RIKYU GARDEN
Kiyosumi
Harumi
Harumi Wharf
Toyusu
Shiomi
KEIYO LINE
Shinkiba
To Tokyo Disneyland →
Tamachi
NATIONAL PARK FOR NATURE STUDY
Sakurada-Dori
Daiichi-keihin Dori
Rainbow Bridge
Port of Tokyo
Meguro
MEGURO-KU
Shinagawa
ODAIBA
Gotanda
Hara Museum of Contemporary Art
Osaki
Ferry Terminal
JAPAN
Tokyo
WAKASU GOLF CLUB →
31
SHINAGAWA-KU
Omachi
Daini-keihin-Doro
Shimoshinmei
Kannana Dori
Tokyo Bay
SHINKANSEN LINE
YOKOSUKA LINE
TOKAIDO LINE
Omori
To Tokyo International Airport
Central Wholesale Market
Tourist Info
Expressway
Monorail
Railway
TMG Observation Platform 20
Tokyo National Museum 3
Tokyo Sky Tree 9
Tokyo Tower 27
Toshogu Shrine 6
Tsukiji Fish Market 28
Ueno Zoo 5
Ukiyo-e Ota Memorial Museum 23
Yasukuni Shrine 16
Yushukan 16

get a good look at it; most of the palace grounds' 114 hectares (282 acres) are off-limits to the public, with the exception of 2 days a year when the royal family makes an appearance before the throngs: January 2 and on the emperor's birthday (Dec 23 in 2018; undecided for 2019 and 2020).

You can visit Imperial Palace grounds (not any buildings) on free **guided tours** conducted in Japanese and English Tuesday through Saturday at 10am and 1:30pm (1:30pm tour not available July 21–Aug 31), but reservations are mandatory and are accepted up to 1 month in advance. Easiest is to book online, which you must do at least 4 days in advance at the website below. Alternatively, you can make a same-day or advance reservation by calling the number below, but note that only 50 tour participants are accepted. Tours last about 75 minutes and include official buildings, the inner moat, historic fortifications, and Nijubashi Bridge. I recommend this tour only if you have seen Tokyo's other top attractions (and it doesn't come close to the more impressive imperial palace tours in Kyoto).

Otherwise, you'll have to console yourself with a camera shot of the palace from the southeast side of **Nijubashi Bridge,** where the moat and an original palace turret rises above the trees. Most Japanese tourists make brief stops here to pay their respects. The wide moat, lined with cherry trees, is especially beautiful in spring. You might even want to set aside an hour or two strolling or jogging the 5km (3 miles) around the palace and moat. But the most important thing to do in the palace's vicinity is visit its **East Garden (Higashi Gyoen;** see above).

Hibiya Dori Ave. http://sankan.kunaicho.go.jp/english/guide/koukyo.html. ✆ **03/5223-8071.** Station: Nijubashi-mae (1 min.) or Hibiya (5 min.).

National Museum of Modern Art (Tokyo Kokuritsu Kindai Bijutsukan) ★★ MUSEUM This is the place to go for Japan's largest collection of modern Japanese art. The inventory of 13,000 works includes paintings in both Japanese and Western styles, prints, watercolors, drawings, and sculpture, from the end of the Meiji Period to the present time. From that, about 200 are selected for exhibitions that change quarterly, but there are usually works by well-known Japanese artists like Ryusei Kishida, Shiko Munakata, Seiki Kuroda, and Yokoyama Taikan. Works by Western artists like Kokoschka, Van Gogh, Paul Klee, and others are included as examples of artistic styles from the same period. Expect to spend about 1 hour here, more if you spring for the ¥300 audio guide, but you might also want to head over to the nearby Crafts Gallery (it's included in the ticket price). Occupying a disappointingly small part of a Gothic-style 1910 brick building that once served as Imperial Guard headquarters, it holds changing exhibitions of contemporary crafts that can range from pottery and metalwork to glassware and often includes works of living national treasures and great masters.

3 Kitanomaru Koen Park, Chiyoda-ku. www.momat.go.jp. ✆ **03/3214-2561.** Admission ¥500 adults, ¥250 college students, free for children and seniors; special exhibits cost more. Free admission 1st Sun of every month. Tues–Thurs and Sun 10am–5pm; Fri–Sat 10am–8pm. Station: Takebashi (exit 1b, 3 min.).

Yasukuni Shrine ★ SHRINE/MUSEUM Built in 1869 to commemorate Japanese war dead, Yasukuni Shrine is constructed in classic Shinto style, with a huge steel *torii* gate at its entrance. During times of war, soldiers were told that if they died fighting for their country, their spirits would find glory here; even today, it's believed that the spirits of some 2.4 million Japanese war dead are at home here, where they are worshipped as deities. Every August 15, the shrine is thrust into the national spotlight when World War II memorials are held. Visits by prime ministers and other officials have caused national outrage among Japan's Asian neighbors, who think it improper to visit—and thereby condone—a shrine so closely tied to Japan's nationalistic and militaristic past.

If you can, come on a Sunday, when a small flea market for antiques and curios is held at the entrance to the shrine from about 6am to 3pm. But the most important thing to see is the **Yushukan,** a war memorial museum outlining Japan's military history. It chronicles the rise and fall of the samurai, the colonization of Asia by Western powers by the late 1800s, the Sino-Japanese War, the Russo-Japanese War, and World Wars I and II, though explanations in English are rather vague and Japan's military aggression in Asia is barely touched. Still, you could spend a fascinating 90 minutes here gazing on samurai armor, swords, uniforms, tanks, artillery, and a Mitsubishi Zero fighter plane, as well as such thought-provoking displays as a human torpedo (a tiny submarine guided by one occupant and loaded with explosives) and a suicide attack plane. But the most chilling displays are the seemingly endless photographs of war dead, some of them very young teenagers. In stark contrast to the somberness of the museum, temporary exhibits of beautiful *ikebana* (Japanese flower arrangements) and bonsai are often held on the shrine grounds in rows of glass cases. Yasukuni Shrine is also famous for its cherry blossoms.

Yasukuni Shrine, 3–1–1 Kudan-kita, Chiyoda-ku. www.yasukuni.or.jp. ✆ **03/3261-8326.** Free admission to shrine; Yushukan ¥1,000 adults, ¥500 students, ¥300 seniors, junior-high and high-school students, free for children. Shrine daily 24 hr.; Yushukan daily 9am–4:30pm. Station: Kudanshita (5 min.) or Ichigaya or Iidabashi (10 min.). On Yasukuni Dori, northwest of Imperial Palace grounds.

ASAKUSA

On the corner of Kaminarimon Dori and Asakusa Dori (across from the entry gate to Sensoji Temple) is the **Asakusa Culture Tourist Information Center,** open daily 9am to 8pm, where you can get a map of the area and take in views of the temple from the 8th-floor observation floor with a small coffee kiosk. On Saturdays and Sundays, volunteers give free 1-hour tours of Asakusa, departing here at 10:30am and 1:15pm.

Amuse Museum ★★★ MUSEUM This is one of my favorite museums in Tokyo, and while you certainly can amuse yourself here, it's not in a way you might think. Rather, this museum with the curious name has a very serious purpose: to preserve and display items and traditions of Japan's past that might otherwise slip from public view. The perfect example of this is the museum's fascinating collection of *boro,* patchwork clothing originating in

Japan's cold and snowy north, lovingly mended through the years with additional stitching and pieces of cloth and passed down from generation to generation. Although made solely for practical reasons—such as sheets used in childbirth or blankets so large and heavy that the entire family could huddle naked under one as they slept—today *boro* are celebrated as textile art. The fact that they have survived at all is due to the diligence of Chuzaburo Tanaka, a private collector who scoured the hinterlands for *boro,* folk art, and antiques. Japanese director Akira Kurosawa was so impressed with Tanaka's rare *boro* collection that he used some in his movie *Dreams;* one room is dedicated to the movie. In addition to temporary exhibitions, other displays feature antique clocks, teapots, and other everyday household objects. At the **Ukiyo-e Theater,** a 28-minute film teaches us how to see woodblock prints as windows into the past, from clothing worn by fishermen to hairstyles of the Edo Period. On the roof is a viewing deck with great vistas of Sensoji Temple, while on the sixth floor is **Bar Six,** open from 6pm to 2am and offering night views of the illuminated temple. The ground-floor museum shop is also worth browsing for its arts and crafts from all over Japan.

2-34-3 Asakusa, Taito-ku. www.amusemuseum.com. © **03/5806-1181.** Admission ¥1,080 adults, ¥864 university and high-school students, ¥540 children. Tues–Sun 10am–6pm. Station: Asakusa (5 min.). Just east of Sensoji Temple, past Nitemmon Gate.

Hanayashiki ★ AMUSEMENT PARK Opened in 1853 while the shogun still reigned, this small and rather corny amusement park is Japan's oldest. It has a small rollercoaster, a kiddie Ferris wheel, a carousel, a haunted house, a 3-D theater, and other diversions appealing to younger children. New is the Telepathy Walker, a headset device that lets you "see" how Hanayashiki has changed over the years. Note, however, that after paying admission, you must still buy tickets for each ride (except for the Telepathy Walker, which is free but available only to people 12 and older). Tickets are ¥100 each, and most rides require two to four tickets.

2-28-1 Asakusa (northwest of Sensoji Temple), Taito-ku. www.hanayashiki.net. © **03/3842-8780.** Admission ¥1,000 adults, ¥500 children 7–12 and seniors, free for children 6 and under. Daily 10am–6pm (to 5pm in winter). Station: Asakusa (5 min.).

Sensoji Temple ★★★ TEMPLE Also popularly known as Asakusa Kannon, this is Tokyo's oldest and most celebrated temple. Its history dates back to A.D. 628, when, according to popular lore, two brothers fishing in the nearby Sumida River netted the catch of their lives: a tiny golden statue of Kannon, the Buddhist goddess of mercy and happiness, who is empowered with the ability to release humans from all suffering. Sensoji Temple was erected in her honor, and although the statue is housed here, it's never shown to the public. Still, through the centuries, worshipers have flocked here seeking favors of Kannon; and when Sensoji Temple burned down during a 1945 bombing raid, it was rebuilt with donations from the Japanese people. After sunset, the temple and pagoda are illuminated until 11pm.

Entrance to the temple is via colorful Kaminarimon Gate onto lively **Nakamise Dori,** a pedestrian lane leading to the shrine and lined with more than 80 stalls selling souvenirs and traditional Japanese goods. In fact, the whole Asakusa area is one of my favorite neighborhoods, and you can easily spend half a day here. If you're here on a Saturday or Sunday, free 1-hour tours of Sensoji and the neighborhood are led by volunteers at 10:30am and 1:15pm; the meeting place is at the Asakusa Culture Tourist Information Center, across the street from Kaminarimon Gate.

2-3-1 Asakusa, Taito-ku. www.senso-ji.jp. ✆ **03/3842-0181.** Free admission. Daily 6:30am–5pm (from 6am in summer). Station: Asakusa (2 min.).

UENO & VICINITY

Ueno is a hugely popular family destination, making this a priority for those traveling with kids. Among family must-sees are the National Museum of Nature and Science, Shitamachi Museum, and Ueno Park.

Asakura Choso Museum ★★★ HISTORIC HOME This museum is actually a very unique home that once belonged to a famous artist, making it a must if you've never had the opportunity to visit a traditional Japanese house. Of course, this isn't just any house. Designed by sculptor Fumio Asakura (1883–1964) to serve as his residence, studio, and Asakura Sculpture School, it's a delightful combination of both modern and traditional architecture, restored to reflect how it would have looked in 1955. Probably the most enviable feature is the inner courtyard pond, fed by a natural spring and visible from many rooms in the house. There's a library, his airy studio, and tatami rooms, including one for visitors where they could enjoy the rising sun. On the roof is a garden, where Asakura's students tended vegetables to sharpen their senses. And throughout the house are furniture, antiques, hundreds of orchids, and statues of statesmen, women, and cats (Asakura loved cats; he once had as many as 10). An audio guide, available for ¥200 extra, is worth it for the additional information it gives on everything from the books in Asakura's library to his statue "Grave-Keeper." Visitors are asked to take off their shoes and wear socks through the museum.

7-18-10 Yanaka, Taito-ku. www.taitocity.net/zaidan/asakura. ✆ **03/3821-4549.** Tues–Wed and Fri–Sun 9:30am–4:30pm. Station: Nippori (northwest exit, 5 min.).

National Museum of Nature and Science (Kokuritsu Kagaku Hakubutsukan) ★★ MUSEUM Of all of Tokyo's museums, this is the one that would probably delight both kids and parents the most. As Japan's largest science museum, it has an informative section that concentrates just on Japan—making it a good learning tool as well—and lots of imaginative displays and exhibits geared toward youngsters. Of its two sections, a **Global Gallery** covers earth, space, the development of technology, the diversity of life, and the evolution of humans, dinosaurs, and other life forms; and the **Japan Gallery** focuses on the country's natural history. One of my favorite sections is the **Animals of the Earth** hallway filled with incredible taxidermic animals from around the world, including a polar bear, camel, gorilla, tiger, and bear; some of the animals are those that died at nearby Ueno Zoo. Other highlights include dinosaur exhibits; a Japanese mummy from the Edo Period still curled up in a burial jar; Hachiko (stuffed and so famous there's a statue of the dog at Shibuya Station); and re-created wood and marine habitats. **ComPaSS,** a playroom geared toward kids ages 4 to 6, is free but requires a special ticket with a specified time stamp. On the roof are a **sky deck, herb garden,** and seasonal **coffee shop.** This museum is huge, so expect to spend a minimum of 2 hours here, though you'll likely stay longer if you rent the audio guide (¥310), a must since English-language descriptions are disappointingly limited.

Ueno Park, Taito-ku. www.kahaku.go.jp. ✆ **03/5777-8600.** Admission ¥620 adults, free for children and seniors. Sun and Tues–Thurs 9am–5pm; Fri–Sat 9am–8pm. Station: Ueno (5 min.).

Shitamachi Museum (Shitamachi Fuzoku Shiryokan) ★ MUSEUM One of the things I like about this museum is the spirit it conveys of Tokyo's *shitamachi* (old downtown), both in its folksy, down-to-earth presentation and in the friendliness of the people who work here, including volunteers eager to give free tours. *Shitamachi* is where commoners used to live, mainly in the north part of Tokyo around Ueno and Asakusa. But after the 1923 Great Kanto Earthquake and the air raids of World War II, precious little remains. Much of what you see here was donated by people living in the area. The ground floor contains a reconstructed *shitamachi* street as it might have looked around 1920, with a life-size merchant's house, a candy shop, and a small tenement shared by two families. These row tenements were long and narrow, with thin wooden walls separating one from the next and alleyways serving as communal living rooms. On the second floor are displays of cooking utensils, tools, toys, and games, most of which you can pick up and try out yourself, as well as a reconstruction of what was once the entrance to a public bath. Another display describes the 1923 earthquake, which hit at lunchtime when housewives were busy cooking over fires and which destroyed nearly half of Tokyo and killed more than 105,000 people (after the earthquake, up to 500,000 people sought refuge in Ueno Park alone). Since the museum is small, you can tour it in about 20 minutes, but I suggest the free tour as well, when volunteers can explain things you might not notice on your own, like the old-fashioned fly-catcher.

Ueno Park, Taito-ku. www.taitocity.net/zaidan/shitamachi. ✆ **03/3823-7451.** Admission ¥300 adults, ¥100 children. Tues–Sun 9:30am–4:30pm. Station: Ueno (3 min.). Southwest edge of Shinobazu Pond, north of Shinobazu Dori avenue.

The National Museum of Western Art (Kokuritsu Seiyo Bijutsukan) ★★ MUSEUM This is Japan's only national museum of Western art, and how it came to be is just as notable as its collection of sculpture and art from the end of the Middle Ages through the 20th century. Kojiro Matsukata was a wealthy shipbuilder who made frequent trips to Europe to buy art, eventually acquiring about 10,000 works that he intended to show in a Tokyo museum. The Great Depression interrupted those plans and forced him to sell off much of his collection, while those that had been left in a London warehouse perished in a 1939 fire. About 400 works remained, in Paris, but these were sequestrated by the French government during World War II and only returned to Japan in 1951, a year after Matsukata had died. Those works formed the basis of this museum, opened in 1959 in a building designed by Le Corbusier that was declared a UNESCO World Heritage Site in 2016. The museum now includes works by Old Masters like Lucas Cranach the Elder, Rubens, El Greco, Murillo, Tintoretto, and Tiepolo, and by 19th- and 20th-century French painters like Delacroix, Monet (an entire room is devoted to his works alone), Manet, Renoir, Pissarro, Sisley, Courbet, Cézanne, Van Gogh, and Gauguin. The museum's 20th-century works, by Picasso, Max Erst, Miró, Dubuffet, Pollock, and others round out the collection, but also notable is one of the largest Rodin collections in the world, with 50-some sculptures that include "The Kiss," "The Thinker," and, outside the museum's front entrance, "The Gates of Hell." Plan on at least an hour here, unless you also take advantage of one of the special exhibitions—often from prestigious overseas collections—which almost always draw large crowds. Ueno Park, Taito-ku. www.nmwa.go.jp. ✆ **03/3828-5131.** Admission ¥500 adults, ¥250 college students, free for children 17 and under and seniors; special exhibits require separate admission fee. Free admission to permanent collection 2nd and 4th Sat of the month. Tues–Thurs 9:30am–5:30pm, Fri–Sat 9:30am–9pm. Station: Ueno (4 min.).

Tokyo National Museum (Tokyo Kokuritsu Hakubutsukan) ★★★
MUSEUM Quite simply, this is the top museum in Tokyo, if not in all of Japan. It has the largest collection of Japanese art in the world, making it the single best place to see a vast variety of Japanese antiques and art, including lacquerware, metalwork, pottery, old kimono, samurai armor, swords, scrolls, screens, *ukiyo-e* (woodblock prints), calligraphy, textiles, and ceramics. And that's just the main building **(Japanese Gallery).** Other galleries display Japanese archaeological finds, priceless treasures from Nara, art from other Asian countries, and frequent special exhibitions. As Japan's oldest museum, founded in 1872 and moved to Ueno Park in 1882, it has amassed an inventory of more than 113,000 objects, with about 3,000 items on display at any one time, which means that there's something new to see every time you visit. Schedule a morning or afternoon to visit. Barring that, concentrate on the 24 exhibition rooms of the Japanese Gallery, which you can see in 1 or 2 hours, depending on your interest. I also recommend browsing the museum shop, with its reproductions of museum masterpieces and traditional crafts by contemporary artists, including jewelry and miniature fans.

If time allows, I also highly recommend a tour of the **Gallery of Horyuji Treasures (Horyuji Homotsukan),** which displays priceless Buddhist treasures from the Horyuji Temple in Nara, founded by Prince Shotoku in A.D. 607. Although it seems incongruous that antiquities should find a home in a building as starkly modern as this, low lighting and spacious displays allow the bronze Buddhist statues, ceremonial Gigaku masks used in ritual dances, lacquerware, textiles, and paintings to shine.

The **Asian Gallery (Toyokan)** is the place to see art and archaeological artifacts from surrounding Asian regions, including China, Korea, Southeast and Central Asia, India, and Egypt. Chinese art, including jade, paintings, calligraphy, and ceramics—makes up the largest part of the collection, a reflection of China's tremendous influence on Japanese art, architecture, and religion. Although exhibitions change, items on display might include Buddhas from

China and Gandhara, embroidered wall hangings and cloth from India, Iranian and Turkish carpets, Thai and Vietnamese ceramics, and Egyptian relics.

The **Heiseikan Gallery** houses archaeological finds of ancient Japan, including pottery and Haniwa clay burial figurines of the Jomon Period (10,000 B.C.–1000 B.C.) and ornamental, keyhole-shaped tombs from the Yayoi Period (400 B.C.–A.D. 200). The **Hyokeikan,** built in 1909 to honor the wedding of Emperor Taisho, has occasional special exhibitions.

Ueno Park, Taito-ku. www.tnm.jp. ✆ **03/3822-1111.** Admission ¥620 adults, ¥410 college students, free for seniors and children. Special exhibits cost more. Tues–Thurs 9:30am–5pm; Fri–Sat 9:30–9pm. Station: Ueno (10 min.).

Toshogu Shrine ★ SHRINE Come here to pay respects to the man who made Edo (present-day Tokyo) the seat of his government and thus elevated the small village to the most important city in the country. Erected in 1651, it's dedicated to Tokugawa Ieyasu, founder of the Tokugawa shogunate. Like Toshogu Shrine in Nikko, it was built by Ieyasu's grandson, Iemitsu, and boasts some of the same richly carved, ornate design favored by the Tokugawas, especially the Chinese-style main gate. Remarkably, it survived the civil war of 1868, the Great Kanto Earthquake of 1923, and even World War II. The pathway to the shrine is lined with massive stone lanterns, as well as 50 copper lanterns donated by *daimyo* from all over Japan, while the grounds themselves are shrouded by a 600-year-old camphor tree. Paying admission allows a closer look at the shrine's magnificent carvings. At the counter to the left you can buy good-luck charms that will supposedly bring you fortune, happiness, and other earthly desires. On a more somber note, a flame on shrine grounds, lit from flames burning in both Hiroshima and Nagasaki, appeals for world peace.

Ueno Park, Taito-ku. www.uenotoshogu.com. ✆ **03/3822-3455.** Free admission to shrine grounds; admission to inner compound ¥500 adults, ¥200 children. Daily 9am–4:30pm Oct–Feb; 9am–5:30pm March–Sept. Station: Ueno (4 min.).

Ueno Zoo ★ ZOO Founded in 1882, Japan's oldest zoo is small by today's standards but remains one of the most well-known zoos in Japan, with more than 3,000 animals in residence. Its most celebrated residents are Ri Ri and Shin Shin, two pandas on loan from a wildlife sanctuary in China's Sichuan province, and their baby panda, Xiang Xiang, born in 2017 (because of their popularity, admission to see them is granted on a first come, first served basis beginning at 9:30am). A vivarium houses amphibians, fish, and reptiles, from snakes to crocodiles. Also of note is the five-story pagoda dating from the Edo era, along with a teahouse built 350 years ago to receive the shogun when visiting nearby Toshogu Shrine. Shinobazu Pond, on the southwest end of the zoo, serves as a sanctuary for wild cormorants and other birds. Personally, I can't help but feel sorry for some of the animals in their small spaces, but children will enjoy the Japanese macaques, polar and Hokkaido brown bears, California sea lions, penguins, gorillas, giraffes, zebras, elephants, hippos, deer, and tigers. Expect to spend a minimum of 2 hours here.

Ueno Park, Taito-ku. www.tokyo-zoo.net/english. ✆ **03/3828-5171.** Admission ¥600 adults, ¥300 seniors, ¥200 children 13–15, free for children 12 and under. Tues–Sun 9:30am–5pm (enter by 4pm). Closed some holidays. Station: Ueno (4 min.).

SHINJUKU

Samurai Museum ★ MUSEUM For a crash course on everything a warrior samurai wore and used in battle, this is the place to go. One-hour guided tours, departing about every 15 minutes and conducted in English, visit various rooms of the museum, with explanations on helmets, masks, armor, swords, matchlocks, and more. You'll learn about the samurai fighting spirit and code of honor; the different types of swords (like the sword made specifically to slash a horse's legs to bring it down); heavy armor that it took at least 20 minutes just to put it on; and samurai sons, who started training at age 5 and were ready to join battlefields by the time they reached 15. Included in the tour are samurai gear and kimono you can try on for photographs with your own camera. I find admission fees rather high, but there's no question this museum is popular.

2-25-6 Kabukicho, Shinjuku-ku. http://samuraimuseum.jp. ✆ **03/6457-6411.** Admission ¥1,800 adults, ¥800 children. Daily 10:30am–9pm. Station: JR Shinjuku (8 min.) or Higashi-Shinjuku (6 min.).

Shinjuku Gyoen ★★ PARK/GARDEN Formerly the private estate of a feudal lord and then of the imperial family, this is considered one of the most important parks of the Meiji Era. This place amazes me every time I come here. It's wonderful for strolling because of the variety of its planted gardens; styles range from French and English to Japanese traditional. The park's 58 hectares (143 acres) make it one of the city's largest, and each bend in the pathway brings something completely different. Ponds and sculpted bushes give way to a promenade lined with sycamores that opens onto a rose garden. Cherry blossoms, azaleas, chrysanthemums, and other flowers provide splashes of color from spring through autumn. The Japanese garden, buried in the center, is exquisite; if you have time only for a quick look at traditional landscaping, you won't be disappointed here. Wide, grassy expanses are popular for picnics and playing, and a greenhouse is filled with tropical plants. You could easily spend a half-day of leisure here, but it's also good for a quick fix of rejuvenation.

11 Naitocho, Shinjuku-ku. www.env.go.jp/garden/shinjukugyoen/english/index.html. ✆ **03/3350-0151.** Admission ¥200 adults, ¥50 children. Tues–Sun 9am–4:30pm. Station: Shinjuku Gyoen-mae (5 min.) or Sendagaya (5 min.).

VR Zone Shinjuku ★★★ AMUSEMENT PARK Virtual reality games are big in Tokyo, and this VR game center is one of the largest. It offers about a dozen games, including Dragon Quest, Mario Kart, and games that pit you against dinosaurs, test your fear of heights, and even let you demonstrate your fishing skills. Because of its popularity, your best bet is to purchase tickets in advance, either through the website or its mobile app, but you may still have to wait in line for each game unless you come on a weekday morning. Check the website for ticket options, game descriptions, and suggestions.

1-29-1 Kabuki-cho, Shinjuku-ku. https://vrzone-pic.com/en/. ✆ **03/3200-8076.** Admission including 4 games ¥4,400. Daily 10am–10pm. Station: Shinjuku (10 min.). Take the east exit, turn left and keep left; it's past Shinjuku Prince Hotel and Seibu-Shinjuku Station.

Tokyo Metropolitan Government Office (TMG) ★★★ OBSERVATION DECK Tokyo's city hall—designed by one of Japan's best-known architects, Kenzo Tange—comprises three buildings—**TMG no. 1, TMG no. 2,** and the **Metropolitan Assembly Building.** Together they contain everything from Tokyo's Disaster Prevention Center to the governor's office. Most important for visitors is TMG no. 1, the tall building to the north, which offers the best free view of Tokyo. This 48-story, 240m (787-ft.) structure, among the tallest buildings in Shinjuku, boasts two observatories on the 45th floors of both its north and south towers. Both observatories offer the same spectacular views but have different open hours and closed days (check the website)—on clear winter days you can even see Mount Fuji. Note that the North Tower has a **Hakuhinkan Toy Park,** with fun souvenirs, but a cafe annoyingly takes up the entire east side of the observatory; for that reason, I prefer the South Tower during the day (it usually closes at 5:30pm). At night, however, the North Tower cafe becomes a bar, with great views. In expensive Tokyo, this is one of the city's best bargains, and kids love it. On the first floor is a **Tokyo Tourist Information Center,** open daily 9:30m to 6:30pm, where you can pick up maps and brochures; this is also the meeting point for inexpensive city tours (see "Organized Tours," below).

2-8-1 Nishi-Shinjuku. www.metro.tokyo.jp/english/offices/observat.html. ✆ **03/5321-1111.** Free admission. Daily 9:30am–11pm (South Tower usually closes at 5:30pm). Station: Tochomae (1 min.), Shinjuku (10 min.), or Nishi-Shinjuku (5 min.).

HARAJUKU & AOYAMA

Meiji Jingu Shrine ★★ SHRINE This is Tokyo's most venerable Shinto shrine, opened in 1920 in honor of Emperor and Empress Meiji, who were instrumental in opening Japan to the outside world about 150 years ago. Japan's two largest *torii* (the traditional entry gate of a shrine), built of cypress more than 1,700 years old, give dramatic entrance to the grounds, once the estate of a *daimyo.* The shaded pathway is lined with trees, shrubs, and dense woods, making it an incredible sanctuary in the middle of the city. In late May/June, the **Iris Garden** is in spectacular bloom, but its location in the Inner Garden makes it also a good respite from crowds during the rest of the year (admission ¥500). About a 10-minute walk from the first *torii,* the shrine is a fine example of dignified and refined Shinto architecture. It's made of plain Japanese cypress and topped with green-copper roofs. It's not unusual to see a Shinto wedding procession here. Meiji Jingu Shrine is also the place to be on New Year's Eve, when more than 2 million people crowd onto the grounds to usher in the new year.

Meiji Shrine Inner Garden, 1–1 Kamizono-cho, Yoyogi, Shibuya-ku. www.meijijingu.or.jp. ✆ **03/3379-5511.** Free admission. Daily sunrise to sunset (about 6:40am–4pm in Dec, 5am–6:30pm in June). Station: Harajuku or Meiji-Jingumae (1 min.).

Ukiyo-e Ota Memorial Museum of Art (Ota Kinen Bijutsukan) ★ MUSEUM Harajuku is teenybopper heaven, so it comes as something of a surprise to find this small but delightful museum tucked away on a side street. It specializes in *ukiyo-e* (woodblock prints), collected by the late Seizo Ota over a period of more than 50 years in an attempt to preserve this uniquely Japanese art form. Although the collection contains 12,000 prints, fewer than 100 are displayed at any one time, in thematic exhibitions that change monthly. You can tour it in about 30 minutes, and be sure to pop in to the small basement shop with its *furoshiki* (traditional wrapping cloth), handkerchiefs, and other items (it has a separate basement entrance for those not visiting the museum).

1–10–10 Jingumae, Shibuya-ku. www.ukiyoe-ota-muse.jp. © **03/3403-0880.** Admission ¥700–¥1,000 adults, ¥500–¥700 high-school and college students, free–¥200 children; price depends on the exhibit. Tues–Sun 10:30am–5:30pm (enter by 5pm). Closed the last few days of each month for exhibition changes. Station: Harajuku (2 min.) or Meiji-Jingumae (exit 5, 1 min.). Near the Omotesando Dori and Meiji Dori intersection, behind La Forêt.

ROPPONGI

Mori Art Museum (Mori Bijutsukan) ★★★ MUSEUM/OBSERVATION DECK This is one of Tokyo's top museums, not only because its exhibits are always topnotch, but also because it's the highest museum in the city. Fifty-three stories high, in fact, providing unparalleled panoramas in virtually all directions. But if that's not high enough, you have the option of going all the way to the top, to the open-air rooftop **Sky Deck,** for ¥500 extra. As for the art, exhibits change four times a year for innovative shows from both new and established artists, with past shows covering everything from contemporary African art to the largest Warhol exhibition ever presented in Japan. The art space is gorgeous, too, with 6m-tall (20-ft.) ceilings and controlled natural lighting. Most shows give access to a free audio guide. You'll want to spend at least 90 minutes here.

Roppongi Hills Mori Tower, 6-10-1 Roppongi, Minato-ku. www.mori.art.museum/eng/index.html. © **03/5777-8600.** Admission varies according to the exhibit but averages ¥1,800 adults, ¥1,200 high-school and college students, and ¥600 children. Wed–Mon 10am–10pm; Tues 10am–5pm. Station: Roppongi (Roppongi Hills exit, 1 min.) or Azabu Juban (5 min.).

The National Art Center, Tokyo ★★ MUSEUM This museum has one of Japan's largest exhibition spaces, yet it doesn't even have a permanent collection of its own. Rather, it serves as the canvas for Japanese artists' associations, shows organized by its own curators, and joint exhibitions in cooperation with other art institutions and even mass-media corporations. As such, its shows are both eclectic and impressive, with past exhibitions including a retrospective of Japanese government-sponsored art exhibitions from the last century; a powerful display of masks, religious idols, and other objects from around the world from Japan's National Museum of Ethnology; and Impressionist works from Paris's Musée d'Orsay. In other words, you never know what you might see; there are also smaller galleries showing the works of regional and national artists. Many people drop by just to dine in the museum's **Brasserie Paul Bocuse Le Musée** or browse the expansive museum shop (you can enter both without paying admission). Of the three museums in the Art Triangle Roppongi, which includes the nearby Mori Art Museum and Suntory Museum of Art, this is by far the sexiest, with a seductive undulating facade that would entice me to visit even without knowing what's inside.

7–22–2 Roppongi, Minato-ku. www.nact.jp. ✆ **03/5777-8600.** Admission varies, but top shows are ¥1,000–¥1,600 adults, ¥500–¥1,200 college students, free–¥800 high-school students, free for children. Sun–Mon and Wed–Thurs 10am–6pm; Fri–Sat 10am–8pm. Station: Nogizakai (exit 6, 1 min.) or Roppongi (exit 4A or 7, 5 min.).

Suntory Museum of Art (Suntory Bijutsukan) ★★ ART MUSEUM This private museum (part of the same corporation that brews beer and other alcoholic beverages) boasts a collection of 3,000 Japanese antiques and arts and crafts, including lacquerware, ceramics, paintings, glassware, *Noh* costumes, kimono, ornamental hairpins, scrolls, teaware, and other items, which it displays in themed exhibitions, along with visiting collections. An audio guide, when available, costs ¥500 extra. Although modern in design, the museum incorporates such traditional Japanese materials as wood and paper in darkened rooms to create a soothing, inviting atmosphere. That's in keeping with its basic philosophy and mission: to make us see ancient art in a renewed way, to bridge the differences of time, place and culture.

Tokyo Midtown, 9–7–4 Akasaka, Minato-ku. www.suntory.com/sma. ✆ **03/3479-8600.** Admission varies, averaging ¥1,300 adults, ¥1,000 high-school and college students, free for children. Sun–Mon and Wed–Thurs 10am–6pm; Fri–Sat 10am–8pm. Station: Roppongi (2 min.) or Nogizaka (exit 3, 3 min.).

Tokyo Tower ★ OBSERVATION DECK Japan's most famous observation tower was built in 1958 and modeled after the slightly smaller Eiffel Tower in Paris. Lit up at night, this 330m (1,083-ft.) tower, a relay station for TV and radio stations, is a familiar and beloved landmark in the Tokyo cityscape; but with the construction of skyscrapers over the past few decades (including the TMG Observatory and Sky Tree), it has lost some of its appeal as an observation platform and seems more like a relic from the 1950s. With its tacky souvenir shops selling everything from T-shirts to key chains and small aquarium, this place is about as kitsch as kitsch can be. If you have kids, you might also consider visiting the **Tokyo One Piece Tower** theme park (https://onepiecetower.tokyo/?lang=en), where you can spend about 3 hours seeing a movie on an "omnidirectional" 360-degree screen and a live show, try your hand at various challenges and games, and peruse One Piece comic books at its cafe. As for the tower, it has two observatories: the Main Deck, at 149m (489 ft.), and the Top Deck, at 250m (825 ft.), the latter recently renovated and, regrettably, accessible only with advance reservations at high admission prices. The best time of year for viewing is said to be during Golden Week at the beginning of May. With many Tokyoites gone from the city and most factories and businesses closed down, the air at this time is thought to be the cleanest and clearest.

4–2 Shiba Koen, Minato-ku. www.tokyotower.co.jp. ✆ **03/3433-5111.** Admission to both observatories ¥2,800 adults, ¥1,800 primary and junior-high students, ¥1,200 children. Main Deck ¥900, ¥500, and ¥400, respectively. Daily 9am–11pm. Station: Onarimon or Kamiyacho (6 min.).

ODAIBA

Ooedo-Onsen Monogatari ★★ SPA For a unique bathing experience, nothing beats a 3- or 4-hour respite at this re-created Edo-era bathhouse village, which taps mineral-rich hot-spring waters 1,380m (4,528 ft.) below ground to supply its various baths. After changing into a *yukata* (cotton kimono, with a choice of nine patterns) and depositing your belongings in a locker (your key is bar-coded, so there's no need to carry any money), you'll stroll past souvenir shops and restaurants on your way to massage rooms, sand baths (extra fee charged), and *onsen* (hot-spring baths) complete with outdoor baths, Jacuzzi, steam baths, foot baths, and saunas. Because it can be quite crowded on weekends, try to come on a weekday. Also, signs in English are virtually nonexistent, so observe gender before entering bathing areas (hint: Women's baths usually have pink or red curtains, men's blue), though there is an English pamphlet with a map and instructions for proper bathing etiquette. Finally, because tattoos are associated with the Japanese mafia, people with tattoos are prohibited here, as they are in virtually all public baths in Japan.

2–57 Aomi, Odaiba. www.ooedoonsen.jp. Ⓒ **03/5500-1126.** Admission ¥2,828 adults, ¥1,600 children 4 to 12; reduced prices weekdays and after 6pm (for adults only). Daily 11am–9am the next day. Station: Telecom Center Station (2 min.).

OTHER NEIGHBORHOODS

Edo-Tokyo Museum (Edo-Tokyo Hakubutsukan) ★★★ MUSEUM Tokyo's history is riveting, making this museum's job easy as it vividly portrays the history, art, culture, architecture, and disasters of Tokyo from its founding in 1590—when the first shogun, Tokugawa Ieyasu, chose it as the seat of his government—to the 1964 Tokyo Olympics. Displays begin on the sixth floor, where you'll begin your journey through the centuries with a walk over a replica Nihombashi Bridge, once the starting point for all roads leading out of Edo (old Tokyo). Displays of the Edo Period (1603–1868) center on the lives of the shogun, merchants, craftsmen, and townspeople, and though descriptions are mostly in Japanese, no explanations are necessary for the replica *kabuki* theater, models of Edo and a feudal lord's mansion, maps, photographs, portable festival floats, and a life-size replica row-house tenement, measuring only 10 sq. m (108 sq. ft.), where most of Edo's commoners lived. Other displays relay the events of the Meiji Restoration and Japan's opening to the rest of the world; the Great Kanto Earthquake of 1923 killed more than 100,000 people; the bombing raids of World War II that destroyed much of the city (although I must add that Japan's role as aggressor is disappointingly glossed over); and Tokyo today. It takes a good 2 hours to see the museum, but you will enhance your visit with a free audio guide or museum tour offered by volunteers daily from 10am to 3pm (last tour). Tours last from 1 to 2 hours, depending on your interest, and are good for gaining an

SPECTATOR sports

Baseball Japanese are so crazy about baseball, you'd think they invented the game. Actually, it was introduced to Japan by the United States way back in 1873. Today, it's as popular among Japanese as it is among Americans. Even the annual high-school playoffs keep everyone glued to the TV set. As with other imports, the Japanese have added their own modifications, including cheerleaders and enthusiastic fan clubs, making the game practically a cultural experience. Several American players have proven very popular with local fans; there's also been a reverse exodus of top Japanese players defecting to American teams.

Japan has two professional leagues, the Central and the Pacific, which play from April to October and meet in the Japan Series. In Tokyo, the home teams are the **Yomiuri Giants,** who play at Tokyo Dome (www.tokyo-dome.co.jp; ✆ **03/5800-9999;** station: Korakuen or Suidobashi), and the **Yakult Swallows,** who play at Meiji Jingu Stadium (www.yakult-swallows.co.jp; ✆ **03/3404-8999;** station: Gaienmae). Good English-language websites that explain and follow Japanese baseball are http://japanese-baseball.com and www.japanball.com.

Except for Giants games, which often sell out, you can usually get tickets at the ballpark before the game. Otherwise, advance tickets can be purchased through each team's website, at convenience stores like Lawson, or at **Ticket Pia** locations around town (ask your hotel for the one nearest you). But probably the easiest method for obtaining tickets is through the website **www.japanballtickets.com;** tickets must be ordered at least 4 days in advance and can even be delivered to your hotel. Prices for Tokyo Dome, all for reserved seating, range from ¥1,700 in the outfield to ¥6,200 for seats behind home plate—but the Giants are so popular that tickets are sometimes hard to come by. Tickets for Jingu Stadium range from ¥1,600 for an unreserved seat in the outfield to ¥4,600 for seats behind home plate.

Sumo Sumo matches are held in Tokyo at the **Kokugikan,** 1–3–28 Yokoami, Sumida-ku (www.sumo.or.jp; ✆ **03/3622-1100;** station: Ryogoku, then a 1-min. walk). Matches are held in January, May, and September for 15 consecutive days, beginning at around 9:30am and lasting until 6pm; the top wrestlers compete after 3:30pm. The best seats are ringside box seats, but they're often snapped up by companies or the friends and families of sumo wrestlers. Usually available are balcony arena seats, which can be purchased at Ticket Pia locations around town or through the websites http://sumo.pia.jp/en or www.japanballtickets.com. You can also purchase tickets directly at the Kokugikan ticket office beginning at 9am every morning of the tournament. Prices range from ¥2,200 for an unreserved seat (sold only on the day of the event at the stadium, with about 400 seats available); reserved seats start at ¥3,800.

If you can't make it to a match, watching on TV is almost as good. Tournaments in Tokyo, as well as those that take place annually in Osaka, Nagoya, and Fukuoka, are broadcast on the NHK channel from 4 to 6pm daily while tournaments are taking place. For more information on sumo, see p. 17.

understanding for displays that are only in Japanese, but you'll probably still want to take time seeing the museum on your own.

1–4–1 Yokoami, Sumida-ku. www.edo-tokyo-museum.or.jp. ✆ **03/3626-9974.** Admission ¥600 adults, ¥480 college students, ¥300 seniors and junior-high/high-school students, free for younger children. Tues–Sun 9:30am–5:30pm (Sat to 7:30pm). Station: Ryogoku on the JR Sobu Line (west exit, 3 min.) and Oedo Line (exit A4, 1 min.).

Fukagawa Edo Museum (Fukagawa Edo Shiryokan) ★ MUSEUM There's no better place than this to ignite children's imagination of what old Edo might have looked like in the 19th century. Even for adults without children, this museum is fun. Ensconced in the museum's hangarlike building is a life-size reproduction of a prosperous Fukugawa neighborhood, with 11 full-scale replicas of Japanese homes, inns, a watchtower, and shops selling vegetables, rice, and fish—most of which are open so you can explore and actually touch the items inside. The attention to details is delightful, like the dog relieving itself on a pole, the cat sleeping on a roof, and the voice of a vendor selling his wares. And like a real village, it even changes with the seasons, with the clap of thunder during summer storms and cherry blossoms in spring. Finally, every 45 minutes or so, the village goes through a day's cycle, beginning with the rising of the sun and roosters crowing in the morning to sunset at night. Just don't confuse this museum with the Edo-Tokyo Museum, which covers the history of the city.

1–3–28 Shirakawa, Koto-ku. www.kcf.or.jp/fukagawa ✆ **03/3630-8625.** Admission ¥400 adults, ¥50 children. Daily 9:30am–5pm. Closed 2nd and 4th Monday of every month. Station: Kiyosumi-Shirakawa (3 min.).

Hama Rikyu Garden PARK/GARDEN Considered by some to be the best garden in Tokyo (but marred, in my opinion, by Shiodome skyscrapers that detract from its charm; there ought to be a law), this urban oasis has origins stretching back 300 years, when it served as a retreat for a former feudal lord and as duck-hunting and falconry grounds for the Tokugawa shogun. In 1871, possession of the garden passed to the Imperial family, which used it to entertain such visiting dignitaries as Gen. Ulysses S. Grant. Come here to see how the upper classes enjoyed themselves during the Edo Period; to gain a better understanding, pick up the park's free audio guide. The garden contains an inner tidal pool, spanned by three bridges draped with wisteria (views from the south end of the garden are the most picturesque). The garden also has a refuge for ducks, herons, and migratory birds; a promenade along the bay lined with pine trees; a 300-year-old pine; moon-viewing pavilions; and teahouses (powdered green tea and a sweet for ¥510). Plan on at least an hour's stroll to see everything, but the best reason for coming here is to board a ferry from the garden's pier bound for Asakusa, with departures every 30 minutes between 10:25am and 4:45pm; the fare is ¥740 one-way.

1–1 Hamarikyuteien, Chuo-ku. www.tokyo-park.or.jp. ✆ **03/3541-0200.** Admission ¥300 adults, ¥150 seniors, free for children 12 and under. Daily 9am–5pm. Station: Shiodome (exit 5, 5 min.) or Tsukiji-shjjo (7 min.).

Rikugien Garden ★★★ GARDEN Though not as centrally located nor as easy to reach as Tokyo's other famous gardens, this one is a must for fans of traditional Japanese gardens and is probably my favorite. It was created in 1702 by a trusted confidante of the shogun, who began as a page and rose to the highest rank as a feudal lord. During the Meiji Era, the founder of Mitsubishi took it over for his second residence and later donated it to the city. What I like most about the garden is that it's dominated by a pond in its center, complete with islands and islets, viewing hills, and strolling paths around its perimeter, providing enchanting views. The garden is especially famous for its changing maple leaves in autumn. Since it takes some effort to reach, you'll probably want to enjoy at least an hour here.

6–16–3 Hon-Komagome, Bunkyo-ku. www.tokyo-park.or.jp. ✆ **03/3941-2222.** Admission ¥300 adults, ¥150 seniors, free for children 12 and under. Daily 9am–5pm. Station: Komagome (8 min.) or Sengoku (10 min.).

Tokyo Disneyland & Tokyo DisneySea ★★★ THEME PARK Virtually a carbon copy of Disneyland in California, Tokyo Disneyland includes popular rides like Jungle Cruise, Pirates of the Caribbean, and Space Mountain. Other hot attractions include **Toontown,** a wacky theme park where Mickey and other Disney characters work and play, and **Star Tours,** a 3D thrill adventure created by Disney and George Lucas.

Adjacent to Disneyland, the **DisneySea** theme park is based on ocean legends and myths. It offers seven distinct "ports of call," including the futuristic Port Discovery marina with its Nemo & Friends SeaRider theater, which takes you on a pretend journey under the sea; the Lost River Delta with its Indiana Jones Adventure; Mermaid Lagoon, based on the film *The Little Mermaid;* the Arabian Coast, with its Sinbad's Seven Voyages boat ride; Mysterious Island with its 20,000 Leagues Under the Sea; and the American Waterfront with its Tower of Terror. Because DisneySea is unique to Tokyo, I personally think this is the one to see; its installations are a class act. On the other hand, if you have very young kids in tow, you'll probably find more for them to do at Disneyland.

1–1 Maihama, Urayasu-shi, Chiba. www.tokyodisneyresort.jp. ✆ **0570/00-8632.** 1-day passport to either Disneyland or DisneySea, including entrance to and use of all attractions, ¥7,400 adults, ¥6,700 seniors, ¥6,400 children 12–17, ¥4,800 children 4–11, free for children 3 and under. Daily 8 or 9am to 10pm, with slightly shorter hours in winter. Station: Maihama, on the JR Keiyo Line from Tokyo Station (1 min.).

Tokyo SkyTree ★★ OBSERVATION DECK I used to think Tokyo Tower was expensive (p. 128), but then the world's tallest free-standing telecommunications tower (documented by Guinness World Records) took over as Japan's tallest structure, with sky-high admissions to boot. Opened in 2012 to handle digital broadcasting and cellphone transmission, the 634m (2,080-ft.) tower contains two observatories, one at 350m (1,150 ft.) and the highest at 450m (1,476 ft.). Yet despite the steep price and potentially long queues, I have to say I found identifying Tokyo's landmarks from such a lofty vantage challengingly fun, with plenty of 360-degree viewing areas that make the hour or so you spend here go quickly. For those less familiar with the capital's iconic buildings, high-tech touch panels let you zoom in on the cityscape. Other diversions include a **cafe** in the first observatory and **Sky Restaurant 634** (http://restaurant.tokyo-skytree.jp/english; reservations required), offering Japanese/French fusion cuisine with what is certainly Tokyo's most expansive views. At the tower's base is **Solamachi,** a complex with 300 more shops and restaurants, including a Pokémon Center. To beat the long lines, go early on a weekday or head to the fourth-floor Fast SkyTree Ticket counter, open only to international visitors, though you'll pay extra for the privilege. If you're in Tokyo only a couple days, I'd spend my time elsewhere. But for people who have been here, done that, this makes for an entertaining new destination. In any case, visible from many areas of Tokyo, SkyTree makes Tokyo Tower seem downright diminutive.

1-1-2 Oshiage, Sumida-ku. www.tokyo-skytree.jp. ✆ **0570/55-0634.** Admission to lower observatory ¥2,060 adults, ¥1,540 children 12–17, ¥930 children 6–11, ¥620 children 4–5; to top observatory an extra ¥1,030, ¥820, ¥510, and ¥310, respectively. Fast SkyTree Ticket ¥3,000 for lower observatory, ¥1,500 for children 4–11; combo ticket for both observatories ¥4,000 and ¥2,000, respectively. Daily 8am–10pm. Station: Oshiage (exit B3, 2 min.), Tokyo SkyTree (2 min.), or Asakusa (15 min.).

Toyosu Fish Market ★★★ MARKET Iconic Tsukiji Market, which served as Japan's largest fish and produce market since 1935, closed on October 6, 2018, reopening as Toyosu Market just 4 days later. That's some feat, considering that this is one of the largest wholesale fish markets in the world, handling about 2,000 tons daily of seafood consumed in and around Tokyo. Whereas Tsukiji used to allow visitors to roam freely around its tuna auction site and wholesale stalls, over the years an increasing number of visitors forced ever more restrictions. To deal with its celebrity status, Toyosu Market prohibits visitors from its wholesale floor altogether, restricting them to observation platforms from which to view the action. And there's a lot going on, with men in black rubber boots rushing wheelbarrows and forklifts through the aisles, hawkers shouting, and knives chopping and slicing. Like at Tsukiji, Toyosu has restaurants serving the freshest sushi you'll ever taste along with shops, but it also offers displays relating to the market and a rooftop garden with views of the waterfront. Its prime location makes it integral to development for the 2020 Olympics. Remaining is Tsukiji's **Outer Market *(Jogai),*** where you can wander rows of retail shops and stalls selling seafood, dried fish and, seaweed, knives, and cooking utensils.

Toyosu. ✆ **03/3542-1111.** Free admission. Open hours not established at press time. Station: Shijo-mae (2 min.).

ORGANIZED TOURS

With the help of this book and good online maps, you should be able to visit Tokyo's attractions easily on your own. Should you be pressed for time, however, you might consider taking a group tour of Tokyo and its environs offered by the **Japan Travel Bureau (JTB;** www.japanican.com/en/tour; ✆ **03/3865-5718**). Day tours may include Tokyo Tower, the Imperial Palace and Ginza districts, Asakusa Sensoji Temple, Meiji Jingu Shrine, and a harbor or river cruise. Specialized tours take in Tsukiji's Outer Market or neighborhoods like Akihabara, as well as cultural-themed tours that allow participants to experience such activities as the tea ceremony, making sushi, or dressing up in a kimono. Be warned, however, that these itineraries are very tourist-oriented, do not allow much time for exploration, and are more expensive than touring Tokyo on your own. Prices average ¥12,000 for a full-day tour (children pay half-fare). Tours are easily booked through most hotels and travel agencies like JTB. Although its offerings are not nearly as extensive, **Japan Gray Line** (www.jgl.co.jp/inbound/index.htm; (✆ **03/3595-5939**) also offers a morning, afternoon, and full-day tour.

The 13 tours offered by the **Tokyo Metropolitan Government** concentrate on specific areas or themes, such as Japanese gardens, Asakusa, or the tea ceremony. What I like most about these tours is that they are more personable than those above, with a maximum tour-group size of only 5 persons. Lasting 2 to 6 hours, they are conducted mostly on foot or utilize public transportation and vary in price from free (a walking tour of Shinjuku and the food floor of Isetan department store) to ¥5,200 for a trip to Mt. Takao outside the city, plus transportation and admission costs of the volunteer guides. Prices may be cheaper for some tours if there's more than one participant. Tours depart from the Tokyo Tourist Information Center in the TMG Building No. 1 in Shinjuku (the same building as the free observatory; see p. 126) at 10am and/or 1pm Monday to Friday (excluding public holidays; the Mt. Takao tour departs at noon). Preregistration 3 days in advance of the tour is required, and a minimum of one participant must be at least 20 years old. For details, contact the tourist office (see p. 126, earlier in this chapter) or book online at **www.gotokyo.org/en/guide-services**.

Volunteer guides are also on hand at the **Ueno Green Salon** in Ueno Park every Wednesday, Friday, and Sunday for free 90-minute walking tours departing at 10:30am and 1:30pm; and at the **Asakusa Culture Tourist Information Center** every Saturday and Sunday for 1-hour tours departing at 10:30am and 1:15pm. No registration is required, but you should arrive 10 minutes beforehand. For more information, call ✆ **03/6280-6710.**

Free guided tours lasting up to 4 hours are also offered through **www.tokyofreeguide.com**, staffed by volunteers ranging from students and housewives to retirees and businesspeople. You're expected to pay for the guide's entrance to museums, meals, and transportation fees if applicable, but you get to choose what you'd like to see; because many of these volunteers work, weekends are the best days to book a tour.

One tour I especially like is the **Tokyo Cruise** boat trip on the Sumida River between Hama Rikyu Garden and Asakusa. Commentary on the 45-minute trip is in both Japanese and English (be sure to pick up the English-language leaflet, too). You'll get descriptions of the 14 bridges you pass along the way and views of Tokyo you'd otherwise miss, including riverside promenades, high-rise apartments, and artwork. Boats depart Hama Rikyu Garden every 30 minutes between 10:25am and 4:45pm, with the fare to Asakusa costing ¥740 one-way. Other cruise routes include those between Hinode Pier (closest station: Hinode, about a 1-min. walk) and Asakusa (fare: ¥780); and between Asakusa and Odaiba Seaside Park (closest stations: Yurikamome Daiba or Tokyo Teleport stations; fare: ¥1,560). For details, contact the **Tokyo Cruise Ship Co.** (www.suijobus.co.jp; ✆ **0120-977311**). Another option is the new amphibious bus called **Tokyo no Kaba** (http://en.kaba-bus.com/tokyo; ✆ **03/3455-2211**), which departs from Aqua City (station: Yurikamome Daiba) and tours Odaiba and

Tokyo Bay. Departing eight times a day from April to September daily except Wednesday, it costs ¥3,500 adults and ¥1,700 children (¥500 for infants).

You can also see Tokyo by bike by joining one of four guided **Tokyo Bicycle Tours** (www.tokyobicycletours.com; © **080/3209-9666**). The 4-hour ride, costing ¥5,000 per person, takes in Shibuya, Yoyogi Park, Meiji Jingu Shrine, Harajuku, and Aoyama. See the website for more information.

Finally, for personalized, one-on-one tours of Tokyo, contact **Jun's Tokyo Discovery Tours,** managed by Tokyoite Junko Matsuda, which offers tailored sightseeing trips to Tsukiji, Asakusa, Imperial Palace, Harajuku, Aoyama, Shibuya, Shinjuku, and Yanaka, as well as shopping and personalized trips designed to fit your interests. Tours utilize public transportation and are especially useful if you wish to meet shopkeepers and the locals, want to learn more about what you're seeing, or are timid about finding your way on public transportation (if you wish, you'll be met at your hotel). The cost is ¥22,000 for a half-day (4 hr.) for up to four adults or a family. Reserve tours at least 3 days in advance (1 week preferred) by e-mail (junkomatsuda1022@gmail.com), stating the desired tour date and what you'd like to see; messages can also be left at © **090/7734-0079** (if you're calling from abroad, drop the initial 0).

SHOPPING

It won't take you long to become convinced that shopping is the number-one pastime in Tokyo. Women, men, couples, and even entire families go on buying expeditions in their free time, making Sunday the most crowded shopping day of the week. Even those on a budget can shop; 100-Yen discount stores are virtually everywhere.

The Shopping Scene

BEST BUYS Tokyo is the country's showcase for everything from the latest in camera, computer, or music equipment to original woodblock prints, anime products, and designer fashions. Traditional Japanese crafts and souvenirs that make good buys include toys (both traditional and the latest in technical wizardry), kites, Japanese dolls, carp banners, swords, lacquerware, bamboo baskets, *ikebana* (flower-arranging) accessories, ceramics, pottery, iron teakettles, chopsticks, fans, masks, knives, scissors, sake, incense, and silk and cotton kimono. And you don't have to spend a fortune: You can pick up handmade Japanese paper *(washi)* products, such as lanterns, boxes, stationery, and other souvenirs, for a fraction of what they cost in import shops in the United States. In Harajuku, stores sell the latest fashion craze at cheap prices, and I can't even count the number of pairs of fun, casual shoes I've bought for a song. Reproductions of famous woodblock prints make great inexpensive gifts, and most items—from pearls to electronic video and audio equipment and even food—can be bought tax-free if you spend over a certain amount in one store (see "Taxes," below).

GREAT SHOPPING AREAS Another enjoyable aspect of shopping in Tokyo is that specific areas are often devoted to certain goods. **Asakusa**

(station: Asakusa) is the place to go for Japanese souvenirs from fans to T-shirts, while **Akihabara** (station: Akihabara) is packed with shops selling the latest in electronics and anime-related items. **Ginza** (station: Ginza) is the chic address for high-end international designer brands and art galleries. **Aoyama** (station: Omotesando) boasts the city's largest concentration of Japanese designer-clothing stores and an ever-increasing number of international names on Omotesando Dori, while nearby **Harajuku** (stations: Harajuku or Meiji-Jingu-mae) and **Shibuya** (station: Shibuya) are the places to go for youthful, fun, and inexpensive fashions.

The best place to shop for items related to cooking and serving is **Kappabashi-dougugai Dori** (www.kappabashi.or.jp; station: Tawaramachi), popularly known as Kappabashi; this is Japan's largest wholesale area for cookware, but most stores sell to individual shoppers as well. The approximately 150 specialty stores here sell everything a restaurant needs, including sukiyaki pots, woks, lunch boxes, pots and pans, aprons, knives, china, lacquerware, rice cookers, plastic food (the kind you see in restaurant display cases), *noren* (Japanese curtains), and disposable wooden chopsticks in bulk. Stores are closed on Sunday.

TAXES An 8% consumption tax (scheduled to rise to 10% in October 2019) is included in the price of marked goods, but all major department stores and tourist shops will refund the tax to foreign visitors if the total purchases in 1 day in any one store amount to more than ¥5,000 (excluding tax) for general items like household goods, clothing, and accessories, as well as for consumables like foods, beverages, and cosmetics, provided you don't consume them in Japan. Note, however, that stores generally charge a service fee equivalent to 1.1% of your total tax-free purchases, and you must present your passport. For more information, see "Fast Facts" in chapter 12.

Shopping from A to Z

ANIME & MANGA

Although **Akihabara** has long boasted Japan's largest concentration of electronics shops, in the past decade it has also gained a reputation as *the* place to shop for manga (Japanese comic books and graphic novels) and items related to anime (Japanese animation) and cosplay (costume play), as well as for its maid cafes. One of the best anime/manga chain stores in Japan is **Mandarake,** which first opened in 1987 as a secondhand shop for manga. Its shop in Akihabara, about 4 minutes from JR Akihabara Station at 3–11–2 Soto-Kanda (www.mandarake.co.jp; ✆ **03/3252-7007**), offers eight floors of both new and secondhand goods, including pop and vintage figurines, video games, manga, and posters (some products are definitely X-rated; even the website is an eye-opener). A branch in Shibuya lies deep underground beneath Shibuya BEAM on Inokashira Dori, 31–2 Udagawacho (✆ **03/3477-0777;** station: Shibuya). Serious shoppers, however, will want to make a pilgrimage to **Nakano Broadway Mall** at 5–52–15 Nakano (www.nbw.jp/#!/en; ✆ **03/3388-7004**), a 5-minute walk from the north exit of Nakano Station and known throughout the country as *otaku* (geek) heaven for its slew of cubbyhole-size shops dedicated to both new and retro pop goods from Japan and overseas, including software, games, manga, figures, and anime and cosplay fare. Having gotten its start here, Mandarake is the biggest player, and the biggest in the world, with 30 different departments spread throughout the mall, each specializing in particular products, from manga and cosplay clothing to CDs of anime songs and figurines (✆ **03/3228-0007**). All Mandarake stores are open daily from noon to 8pm.

Back in Akihabara, **Radio Kaikan,** just outside the Denkigai exit of JR Akihabara Station at 1–15–16 Soto-Kanda (www.akihabara-radiokaikan.co.jp; ✆ **03/6450-8272**), offers 10 floors of anime-related goods, including figurines, trading cards, manga (including X-rated comics), capsule toys, dolls and doll clothing (for adults, not kids), posters, DVDs, and other items from 10am to 8pm daily. **Animate Akiba Girls Station,** off Chuo Dori around the corner from Edion at 1–2–13 Soto Kanda (www.animate.co.jp/shop/akibags; ✆ **03/3526-3977**), is unique for catering almost exclusively to female fans. It's also worth popping into **Don Quijote** (p. 145), on the main drag of Chuo Dori. It has to be seen to appreciate its jumble of everyday goods too numerous to mention, including maid costumes and even an @home maid cafe (I don't even want to get into why these are so popular) on the fifth floor. If **maid cafes** are why you're here, however, there are more **@home Cafés** in the nearby Mitsuwa Building, 1–11–4 Soto-Kanda (www.cafe-athome.com), with maid cafes on the 4th, 5th, 6th, and 7th floors and open Monday to Friday 11:30am to 10pm and Saturday and Sunday 10:30am to 10pm. It costs ¥700 to get in (discounts for students and children) and you must order a minimum of ¥570 in food or drink. Frankly, I find maid cafes more cheesy than titillating, but you might still want to have your picture taken with a maid at an extra cost.

ANTIQUES & CURIOS

In recent years, it has become a buyer-beware market in Japan, with fake antiques produced in China infiltrating the Japanese market. You shouldn't have any problems with the reputable dealers listed here, but if you're buying an expensive piece, be sure to ask whether it comes with papers of authenticity.

In addition to the listings here, Tokyo's outdoor **flea markets** (see later in this section) are also good places to browse.

Antique Mall Ginza ★★★ Japanese, European, and some American antiques, collectibles, and odds and ends crowd two floors of Tokyo's largest antiques mall, where you could spend an hour or more browsing among furniture, jewelry, watches, porcelain, pottery, dolls, *netsuke,* fans, scrolls, glassware, kimono, folk art, and more. Open daily 11am to 7pm. 1–13–1 Ginza, Chuo-ku. www.antiques-jp.com. ✆ **03/3535-2115.** Station: Ginza-Itchome, Kyobashi, or Takaracho (3 min.). Btw. Chuo Dori and Showa Dori.

Ginza Antiques ★ While not nearly as extensive as the Antique Mall Ginza (see above), the half-dozen or so stalls here on the second floor of the Ginza 5 Building (located under an expressway) offer a variety of high-end antiques, including porcelain, furniture, dolls, swords, kimono, and other treasures from Japan and Europe, interspersed with stalls selling crafts, clothing, and jewelry. Open daily 10 or 11am to 7 or 8pm (some stalls closed on Sun). 5–1 Ginza, Chuo-ku. © **03/5572-5559.** Station: Ginza (exit C1, 1 min.) or JR Yurakucho (2 min.). On Harumi Dori, across from the Hankyu Men's Tokyo department store.

CRAFTS & TRADITIONAL JAPANESE PRODUCTS

If you want to shop for traditional Japanese folk crafts in a festival-like atmosphere, nothing beats **Nakamise Dori** (station: Asakusa), a pedestrian lane leading to Sensoji Temple in Asakusa. It's lined with stall after stall selling souvenirs galore, from hairpins worn by geisha to T-shirts, fans, umbrellas, toy swords, and dolls. Most are open daily from 10am to 6pm; some may close 1 day a week. The side streets surrounding Nakamise Dori, including Demboin Dori and a covered pedestrian lane stretching from both sides of Nakamise Dori, are also good bets.

Another good place to search for traditional crafts are **flea markets,** as well as **department stores,** which usually have sections devoted to ceramics, pottery, bambooware, flower-arranging accessories, and kimono.

BEAMS ★★ Showcasing hip domestic Japanese brands, this six-story flagship store sells pottery, glassware and other handicrafts as well as fashionable clothing and accessories, often with a pop-art emphasis. The inventory changes regularly and sometimes highlights a specific region in Japan, like Okinawa or Hokkaido. Open daily 11am to 8pm. 3–32–6 Shinjuku. www.beams.co.jp/global/shop/j. © **03/5368-7300.** Station: Shinjuku Sanchome (2 min.) or Shinjuku (east exit, 5 min.).

Japan Traditional Crafts Aoyama Square (Zenkoku Dentoteki Kogeihina) ★★★ Established to promote the country's artisans, this beautiful shop is a great introduction to both traditional and contemporary Japanese design, with explanations in English about the products and where they're from. It sells top-quality crafts from all over Japan on a rotating basis, so there are always new items on hand. Crafts may include woodblock prints, lacquerware, ceramics, textiles, paper products, calligraphy brushes, fans, metalwork, knives, furniture, and sometimes even stone lanterns or Buddhist family altars (many items are also sold online). Be sure to look in the sliding drawers along the wall—these hold prints and other works of art. Prices are high, but rightfully so. Craftsmen are sometimes on hand, demonstrating their techniques. Open daily 11am to 7pm. 8–1–22 Akasaka, Minato-ku. www.kougeihin.jp. © **03/5787-1301.** Station: Aoyama-Itchome (exit 4 north, 5 min.). On Aoyama Dori, between the Akasaka Post Office and the Canadian embassy.

Oriental Bazaar ★★ If you have time for only one souvenir shop in Tokyo, this should be it. It's the city's best-known and largest souvenir/crafts store, selling products at reasonable prices on three floors. Souvenir and gift items include cotton *yukata,* kimono (new and used), woodblock prints, jewelry boxes, fans, chopsticks, incense, Imari chinaware, sake sets, Japanese dolls, pearls, books on Japan, and antique furniture. This store will also send purchases home for you (via airmail, although it also works with a shipping company should you purchase furniture) and even accepts U.S. dollars and euro. Open Friday to Wednesday 10am to 7pm. 5–9–13 Jingumae, Shibuya-ku. www.orientalbazaar.co.jp. ✆ **03/3400-3933.** Station: Meiji-Jingumae (3 min.), Harajuku (4 min.), or Omotesando (5 min.). On Omotesando Dori in Harajuku; look for its shrine-like facade of orange and green.

DEPARTMENT STORES

Japanese department stores are institutions in themselves. Usually enormous, well designed, and chock-full of merchandise, they have about everything you can imagine, including museums and art galleries, travel agencies, restaurants, grocery markets, and, on the rooftop, playgrounds, greenhouses, and even shrines. You could easily spend an entire day in a department store—eating, attending cultural exhibitions, planning your next vacation, exchanging money, and, well, shopping.

One of the most wonderful aspects of the Japanese department store is the **courteous service.** If you arrive at a store as its doors open at 10 or 10:30am, you'll witness a daily rite: Lined up at the entrance are staff members who bow in welcome. Some Japanese shoppers arrive just before opening time so as not to miss this favorite ritual. Sales clerks are everywhere, ready to help you. In some stores, you don't even have to go to the cash register once you've made your choice; just hand over the product, along with your money, to the sales clerk, who will return with your change, your purchase neatly wrapped, and an *"Arigato gozaimashita"* ("Thank you very much"). Many department stores will also ship your purchases home for you, send them to your hotel, or hold them until you're ready to leave the store. A day spent in a Japanese department store could spoil you for the rest of your life.

Most department stores include **boutiques** by famous Japanese and international fashion designers, like Issey Miyake, Rei Kawakubo (creator of Comme des Garçons), Tsumori Chisato, Vivienne Westwood, Armani, and Paul Smith, as well as departments devoted to the kimono. Near the **kimono department** may also be the section of **traditional crafts,** including *ikebana* vases, pottery, and lacquerware. Many famous **restaurants** maintain branches in department stores, but not to be missed is the basement (nicknamed a *depa-chika,* which is a combination of *depa*—from department store—and *chika,* meaning basement), where you'll find one or two levels devoted to **foodstuffs:** fresh fish, produce, green tea, sake, prepared snacks and dinners, and delectable pastries. There are often free samples of food; if you're hungry, walking through the food department could do nicely for a snack.

To find out what's where, stop by the store's information booth located on the ground floor near the front entrance and ask for the floor-by-floor English-language pamphlet. Be sure, too, to ask about **sales** on the promotional floor—you never know what bargains you may chance upon. Department stores also have **tax-free counters** where you can get an immediate cash refund on taxes paid for items totaling more than a specific amount (see p. 340, in chapter 12), so make sure you bring your passport. They usually also have ATMs that accept overseas credit cards, foreign currency-exchange machines, and free Wi-Fi.

Isetan ★★★ With a history stretching some 130 years, Isetan is a favorite among foreigners visiting and living in Tokyo. Part of the Isetan-Mitsukoshi conglomerate, it has a good line of conservative work clothes, as well as contemporary and fashionable styles, including designer goods (Issey Miyake, Yohji Yamamoto, Comme des Garçons, Marc Jacobs, Junya Watanabe, and Tsumori Chisato), as well as a great kimono section along with all the traditional accessories (*obi,* shoes, purses). The tax-free counter is on the 6th floor. On the seventh floor are branches of well-known restaurants offering grilled eel, tonkatsu, sushi, and Western food, including **Ten-ichi,** specializing in tempura (p. 95). Its basement food hall is legendary, the dessert and massive chocolate sections an especially illuminating commentary on Japan's obsession with food. In its efforts to woo male shoppers, a nine-floor annex behind the main building caters entirely to men (it even has a golf school on the roof). Open daily 10:30am to 8pm. 3–14–1 Shinjuku, Shinjuku-ku. http://isetan.mistore.jp/store/shinjuku/foreign_customer_service/index.html. ✆ **03/3352-1111.** Station: Shinjuku Sanchome (1 min.) or Shinjuku (east exit, 6 min.). On Shinjuku Dori, east of Shinjuku Station.

Matsuya Ginza ★★★ This is one of my favorite department stores in Tokyo; if I were buying a wedding gift, Matsuya, in business 145 years, is one of the first places I'd look. It has a good selection of Japanese folk crafts, kitchenware, and kimono, and beautifully designed contemporary housewares, in addition to the usual designer apparel ("queen" sizes are on the sixth floor). I always make a point of stopping by the seventh floor's Design Collection, which displays examples of fine design from around the world selected by the Japan Design Committee, from the Alessi teapot to Braun razors. Two basement floors are devoted to food. Also in the basement is the tax-free counter (Isetan refunds the entire 8% and does not charge a service fee), where there's also free Wi-Fi and currency-exchange machines. Open daily 10am to 8pm. A branch is in Asakusa at 1–41–1 Hanakawado (✆ **03/3842-1111;** daily 10am–8pm). 3–6–1 Ginza, Chuo-ku. www.matsuya.com. ✆ **03/3567-1211.** Station: Ginza (2 min.). On Chuo Dori, just a long block north of Ginza 4–chome Crossing.

Mitsukoshi ★★★ This Nihombashi department store is one of Japan's oldest and grandest, founded in 1673 by the Mitsui family as a kimono store. In 1683, it became the first store in the world to deal only in cash sales; it was also one of the first stores in Japan to display goods on shelves rather than have merchants fetch bolts of cloth for each customer, as was the custom of the time. Today, housed in a building dating from 1935, it remains one of Tokyo's loveliest department stores, with a beautiful and stately Renaissance-style facade and an entrance guarded by two bronze lions, replicas of the lions in Trafalgar Square. The store carries many name-brand boutiques, from Chanel to Ferragamo. Its kimono, by the way, are still hot items. The tax-free counter is in the annex. Open daily 10:30am to 7:30pm. Another branch, located at Ginza 4–chome Crossing (✆ **03/3562-1111;** open daily 10am–8pm), is popular with young shoppers. 1–4–1 Nihombashi Muromachi, Chuo-ku. http://mitsukoshi.mistore.jp/store/nihombashi/fcs/english/index.html. ✆ **03/3241-3311.** Station: Mitsukoshimae (1 min.).

Takashimaya ★★★ This department store has always provided stiff competition for Mitsukoshi, with a history just as long. It was founded as a kimono shop in Kyoto during the Edo Period and opened in Tokyo in 1933. Today it's one of the city's most attractive department stores, with a Renaissance-style building and gloved elevator operators whisking customers to eight floors of shopping and dining. Naturally, it features boutiques by such famous designers as Chanel, Louis Vuitton, Gucci, Miyake, and more. Its sale of used kimono draws huge crowds. Its tax-refund counter is on the second floor. Open daily 10:30am to 7:30pm. A branch, **Takashimaya Shinjuku,** 5–24–2 Sendaygaya, Shinjuku (✆ **03/53610111;** open daily 10am–8pm; station: Shinjuku), boasts 14 floors of clothing and restaurants (lower floors target affluent seniors, while upper floors appeal to younger shoppers and families; petite and "queen-size" clothing is on the sixth floor); here, too, is **Tokyu Hands,** with everything imaginable for the home hobbyist (p. 146), and **Kinokuniya** bookstore, with English-language books on the sixth floor. 2–4–1 Nihombashi (on Chuo Dori Ave.), Chuo-ku. www.takashimaya.co.jp/tokyo/store_information/index.html. ✆ **03/3211-4111.** Station: Nihombashi (1 min.) or JR Tokyo Station (Yaesu north exit, 5 min.).

ELECTRONICS

Several areas around town are known for their electronics stores, especially just west of **Shinjuku Station,** where Yodobashi dominates with several shops devoted to electronics. The largest concentration of electronics and electrical-appliance shops in Japan, however, is in an area of Tokyo called **Akihabara,** also known simply as Akiba and centered on Chuo Dori (station: Akihabara). This is a must-see simply for its sheer size, with hundreds of multilevel stores, shops, and stalls. Even if you don't buy anything, it's great fun walking around. Most stores and stalls are open-fronted and painted in eye-catching colors. Salespeople yell out their wares, trying to get customers to look at cellphones, computers, digital cameras, TVs, calculators, watches, and rice cookers. This is the best place to see the latest models of everything electronic; it's an educational experience in itself.

If you intend to buy, however, it pays to do some comparison shopping before you leave home so that you can spot a deal when you see one, as you can probably find these products just as cheaply, or even more cheaply, at home. On the other hand, you may be able to pick up something that's unavailable back home. Make sure, too, that whatever you purchase is made for export—that is, with instructions in English, an international warranty, and the proper electrical connectors. All the larger stores have duty-free floors where products are made for export. Most shops are open daily from about 10am to 8pm or later.

Bic Camera ★★ This chain electronics store has about 40 shops in Japan, including its main shop in Ikebukuro, several locations in Shinjuku, Akihabara, and Shibuya. But this eight-floor store in Yurakucho is the largest, offering not only single-lens reflex, large and medium format, and digital cameras (plus all the accessories, including that all-important selfie extender), but also computers, cellphones, camcorders, watches, eyeglasses, luggage, toys, home appliances, sporting goods, and much more. Note, however, that it caters primarily to Japanese; English-speaking sales clerks are scarce, and export models are limited. Ask for the English-language brochure, and, if you're buying sensitive equipment, make sure it will work outside Japan and comes with English-language instructions. Open daily 10am to 10pm. 1–11–1 Yurakucho, Chiyoda-ku. www.biccamera.co.jp. ✆ **03/5221-1112.** Station: Yurakucho (1 min.), Hibiya (exit D4, 3 min.), Ginza (6 min.).

Yodobashi Akiba ★★★ This is Akihabara's largest store, offering a staggering number of electronic-related goods such as phones, cameras, computers, printers, TVs, microwaves, vacuum cleaners, hair dryers, and more. But it also offers a slew of other leisure-related items as well, including bicycles, games, luggage, and watches. Plus, it has 30 restaurants on the eighth floor. Yodobashi is found also in west Shinjuku, with a main shop and many branches specializing in various goods like watches or games. Open daily 9:30am to 10pm. 1-1 Hanaoka-cho, Chiyoda-ku. www.yodobashi-akiba.com. ✆ **03/5209-1010.** Station: Akihabara (1 min.). Just east of JR Akihabara Station.

FASHION

The **department stores** listed earlier are good places to check out the latest trends. For international designers, chic boutiques abound in **Ginza** and neighboring **Marunouchi.** Otherwise, **Harajuku** and **Shibuya** are the places to go for hundreds of small shops selling inexpensive designer knockoffs, as well as fashion department stores—multistoried buildings filled with concessions of various designers and labels, like Shibuya 109 selling clothing and accessories and packed with teenagers.

Ginza Six ★★ The 13-story Ginza Six shopping complex houses 241 high-end international boutiques, restaurants, a basement food floor, and even a Noh theater and rooftop shrine and garden (offices occupy floors seven through 12). Occupying what was once the full-block footprint of Matsuzakaya department store, this place is huge and seems especially popular with busloads of Chinese tourists with deep pockets. Open daily 10:30am to 8:30pm. 6–10–1 Ginza. https://ginza6.tokyo. ✆ **03/6891-3390.** Station: Ginza (2 min.). 1 block from Ginza 4–chome Crossing on Chuo Dori in the direction of Shimbashi.

La Forêt ★★★ This is not only the largest store in Harajuku but also one of the most fashionable, appealing mostly to teenage and 20-something shoppers. Young and upcoming Japanese designers are here as well as established names, in boutiques spread on several floors. In addition to men's and women's fashions there are also shops selling jewelry, shoes, handbags, and other accessories. There's so much to see—from pink frilly dresses to Goth—you can easily kill a few hours here. Note, however, that not all shops offer tax-free shopping, and since each shop is its own entity, you can't combine purchases to qualify for the tax refund. Open daily 11am to 9pm. 1–11–6 Jingumae, Shibuya-ku. www.laforet.ne.jp. ✆ **03/3475-0411.** Station: Meiji-Jingumae (1 min.) or Harajuku (4 min.). On Meiji Dori, just off Harajuku's main intersection of Omotesando Dori and Meiji Dori.

Uniqlo ★★ Having seemingly taken the world by storm, with stores in the U.S., UK, Australia, Germany, Russia, and throughout Asia, Uniqlo specializes in inexpensive, basic clothing (think: the Japanese version of Gap) and has 40-some outlets in Tokyo alone. This is its flagship store, 12 stories offering clothing for the whole family. Connected to Uniqlo in the back is the boutique **Dover Street Market,** with six small floors offering men's and women's fashions by Comme des Garçons, Miu Miu, Junya Watanabe, and other designers. Open daily 11am to 9pm. 6–9–5 Ginza, Chuo-ku. www.uniqlo.com/jp. ✆ **03/6252-5161.** Station: Ginza (2 min.). On Chuo Dori.

Designer Boutiques

Ginza is home to international designer names, including Prada, Ferragamo, Cartier, Chanel, Christian Dior, and Louis Vuitton. Nearby, on Marunouchi Naka Dori, are outlets for Hermes, Tiffany & Co., Armani, and Issey Miyake, among others.

For top Japanese designers, the blocks between Omotesando Crossing and the Nezu Museum in **Aoyama** (station: Omotesando, 2 min.) are the Rodeo Drive of Japan. Even if you can't afford the steep prices, a stroll is de rigueur for clothes hounds and anyone interested in design. Most shops are open daily from 11am to 8pm. **Issey Miyake** (www.isseymiyake.com; (✆ **03/3423-1408**), on the left side as you walk from Aoyama Dori, offers two floors of cool, spacious displays of Miyake's interestingly structured and colorful designs for men and women. His very popular **Pleats Please** line is next door (✆ **03/5772-7750**). Across the street is **Comme des Garçons** (www.comme-des-garcons.com; (✆ **03/3406-3951**), Rei Kawakubo's showcase for her daring—and constantly evolving—men's and women's designs (even her shop is constantly evolving). The goddess of Japanese fashion and one of the few females in the business when she started, Kawakubo has remained on the cutting edge of design for more than 4 decades. Farther down the street on the right is **Yohji Yamamoto** (www.yohjiyamamoto.co.jp; ✆ **03/3409-6006**), where Yamamoto's unique, classically wearable clothes are sparingly hung, flaunting the avant-garde interior space. Of the many non-Japanese designers to have invaded this trendy neighborhood, including **Alexander McQueen** and **Stella McCartney,** none stands out as much as **Prada** (✆ **03/6418-0400**), a bubble of convex/concave windows on the right side of the street.

Kimono

Chicago, on Omotesando Dori at 6–31–21 Jingumai in Harajuku (www.chicago.co.jp; ✆ **03/3409-5017;** station: Meiji-Jingumae or Harajuku), stocks hundreds of affordable used kimono, cotton *yukata* (casual kimono), and *obi* (sashes) back in the far left corner of the basement shop, past the used American clothes. It's so successful it has opened nearby branches, including a nicer and larger one practically next door. All are open daily from 11am to 8pm. The nearby **Oriental Bazaar** (p. 138) also has a decent selection of new and used kimono at affordable prices, including elaborate wedding kimono.

In addition, department stores sell new kimono, notably **Takashimaya** and **Mitsukoshi** in Nihombashi and **Isetan** in Shinjuku. They also hold sales for rental wedding kimono. **Flea markets** are also good for used kimono and *yukata.*

MARKETS

Flea markets are good places to shop for antiques and delightful junk. You can pick up secondhand kimono at very reasonable prices (usually around ¥1,000 or less), as well as kitchenware, vases, cast-iron teapots, small chests, woodblock prints, dolls, household items, and odds and ends. (Don't expect to find any good buys in furniture.) Bargaining is expected. Note that since most markets are outdoors, they tend to be canceled if it rains.

Hanazono Shrine ★, 5–17–3 Shinjuku (✆ **03/3200-3093**), near the Yasukuni Dori/Meiji Dori intersection east of Shinjuku Station (Shinjuku Sanchome Station, 4 min.), has a small flea market every Sunday from about 8am to 2pm (except in May and Nov, due to festivals). Lots of wooden dolls, hair pins, obi sashes and kimono, woodblock prints and more.

Nogi Shrine ★, a 1-minute walk from Nogizaka Station at 8–11–27 Akasaka (✆ **03/3478-3001**), has an antiques flea market from 9am to dusk the fourth Sunday of each month except January and February. It has a lovely setting; the shrine commemorates General Nogi and his wife, both of whom committed suicide on September 13, 1912, to follow the Meiji emperor into the afterlife. Their simple home and stable are on shrine grounds.

Yasukuni Shrine ★★, a 4-minute walk from Kudanshita Station at 3–1–1 Kudanshita (✆ **03/3261-8326**), holds a flea market every Sunday from 6am to about 3pm on the long walkway to this very famous shrine (see p. 119 for information on the shrine and its military museum).

Oedo Antique Market ★★★, beside Yurakucho Station in the courtyard of the Tokyo International Forum, 3–5–1 Marunouchi (www.antique-market.jp; ✆ **03/6407-6011**), claims to be the largest outdoor antiques market in Japan, with about 250 vendors (it has also taken away vendors from Tokyo's other flea markets). Held the first and third Sunday of the month (check the website, as dates can change) from 9am to 4pm, it features Western antiques (at highly inflated prices), as well as Japanese glassware, furniture, lacquerware, hair ornaments, folk toys, ceramics, furniture, kimono, woodblock prints, and odds and ends. If you hit only one flea market, this should be it. It also stages an occasional flea market in Yoyogi Park, with about 180 vendors selling antiques and crafts.

Ameya Yokocho ★★ (also referred to as Ameyoko, Ameyokocho, or Ameyacho; www.ameyoko.net) is the closest thing Tokyo has to a permanent flea market. Occupying a long but narrow area near Ueno Park that runs underneath the elevated tracks of the JR Yamanote Line between Ueno and Okachimachi stations, it has stall after stall selling vegetables and discounted items ranging from cosmetics and handbags to tennis shoes, watches, and casual clothes. The scene retains something of the *shitamachi* spirit of old Tokyo. Although housewives have been coming here for years, young Japanese are also finding it a good bargain spot for youthful fashions and accessories like baseball caps. Hours are usually daily from 10am to 7pm (some shops close Wed); early evening is the most crowded time. Don't even think of coming here on a holiday—it's a standstill pedestrian traffic jam.

VARIETY STORES

The **department stores** listed earlier also sell home furnishings, including bedding, kitchenware, lighting, and decor.

Daiso ★★ The largest chain of 100-Yen shops in Japan (comparable to dollar stores in the U.S.), with more than 3,000 locations in the country and abroad, this four-story shop is also one of the better discount stores, offering mostly its own brand goods, purchased directly from manufacturers (many of which are in China). Items, priced mostly at ¥100 or multiples thereof, include kitchenware, tableware, cosmetics, office supplies, candy, and other household goods and daily necessities, making it a good place to shop for cheap souvenirs such as chopsticks, plastic lunchboxes, and *ikebana* (flower arranging) accessories. This place is so popular, there's usually a long queue at checkout. It adjoins **Bic Camera,** a discount electronics store. Open daily 10am to 9pm. 1–19–24 Jingumae, Shibuya-ku. www.daisoglobal.com. ✆ **03/5775-9641.** Station: Harajuku (north exit, 3 min.) or Meiji-Jingumae (4 min.). On Takeshita Dori, about midway down.

Don Quijote (ドン・キホーテ) ★ Teenagers don't seem to mind the jumble of everyday goods offered here, but I find the narrow aisles so packed that it makes me feel claustrophobic. It offers household goods and gadgets, kitchen appliances, plastic lunchboxes, PEZ dispensers, sporting goods, electronics, clothing, cosmetics, toiletries, party items, Hello Kitty character goods, food, alcohol, and much, much more, including cosplay fare such as maid costumes (a perennial favorite). It's hard to come up with anything Don Quijote *doesn't* sell, but strangely, I never find anything I'm compelled to buy. You might, however, want to check out the **@home Maid Café** on the 5th floor, the games arcade on the 7th floor, or **Color Yellow** nail salon on the ground floor, where staff decorate your nails with anime characters or any design of your choosing. It's open daily from 9am to 5am. Known for its discounted prices and late hours, Don Quijote has more than 30 branches in the Tokyo area, including ones on Yasukuni Dori at 1–16–5 Kabuki-cho (✆ **03/5291-9211;** station: Shinjuku) and in Roppongi, on the left side of Gaien-Higashi Dori if walking from Roppongi Crossing toward Tokyo Tower, at 3–14–10 Roppongi (✆ **03/5786-0811;** station: Roppongi), both open a mind-boggling 24 hours. 4–3–3 Soto-Kanda, Chiyoka-ku. www.donki.com. ✆ **03/5298-5411.** Station: Akihabara (3 min.). On Chuo Dori.

Loft Loft is Seibu's store for the young homeowner, including tableware (chopsticks, *bento* boxes, sake cups, and so forth, on the third floor), cookware, glassware, bathroom accessories, bed linens, office supplies, mobile phone accessories, watches, cosmetics (the choice in face masks alone is bewildering), stationery, games, and more. Don't miss the fifth-floor variety goods department with character items, wind-up toys, party goods, including some weird costumes and small plastic female figurines designed to hang from the side of a glass, and gag gifts. Open daily 10am to 9pm. 21–1 Udagawacho, Shibuya-ku. ✆ **03/3462-3807.** Station: Shibuya (Hachiko exit, 4 min.). Behind Seibu B.

Muji ★★★ Muji was founded in 1980 as a backlash to conspicuous consumption prevalent in bubble-era Japan. Today, with shops around the world, it's known for its minimalist yet hip cotton clothing in basic colors, as well as well-designed housewares at affordable prices, many of them made from recycled materials at affordable prices. Futon, bed linens, kitchen appliances, tableware, storage units, furniture (think rattan and unbleached woods), clothing, cosmetics, and other practical goods are offered at more than 280 locations in Japan, but this is its main store. A **Muji Meal** upstairs offers inexpensive and healthy meals; there's a **Loft** (see above) in the same building. Muji has even expanded into hotels, with one in the works for Ginza slated to open in 2019. Open daily 10am to 9pm. 3–8–3 Marunouchi, Chiyoda-ku. www.muji.com. ✆ **03/5208-8241.** Station: Yurakucho (2 min.) or Ginza (4 min.).

Tokyu Hands ★★★ Billing itself the "Creative Life Store," Tokyu Hands, part of the Tokyu chain, is a huge department store for the serious homeowner and hobbyist, with everything from travel accessories (like padded eye masks), *noren* (doorway curtains), beauty products (including wigs), chopsticks, suitcases, miniature Shinkansen models, pet accessories, and kitchen knives, to equipment and materials for do-it-yourselfers and hobbyists, like paper for repairing shoji. If there's a practical Japanese product you've decided you can't live without (lunchbox? bathroom slippers? hanging laundry rack?), this is a good place to look. Open daily 10am to 9pm. You'll also find Tokyu Hands at 1–28–10 Higashi Ikebukuro beside the Sunshine City Building (✆ **03/3980-6111;** station: Higashi Ikebukuro or Ikebukuro) and in the Takashimaya Shinjuku complex (✆ **03/5361-3111;** station: Shinjuku). 12–18 Udagawacho, Shibuya-ku. www.tokyu-hands.co.jp/en/index.html. ✆ **03/5489-5111.** Station: Shibuya (Hachiko exit, 6 min.). At the top of Inokashira Dori.

ENTERTAINMENT & NIGHTLIFE

By day, Tokyo's sprawl can make it seem monotonous and colorless. Come dusk, however, Tokyo comes into its own. The drabness fades, the city blossoms into a profusion of giant neon lights and billboards, and its streets fill with millions of overworked Japanese out to have a good time. If you ask me, Tokyo at night is one of the craziest cities in the world, a city that never gives up and never sleeps. Entertainment districts are as crowded at 3am as they are at 10pm, with many establishments open until the first subways start running after 5am. Whether it's jazz, gay bars, dance clubs, or mania that you're searching for, Tokyo has it all.

GETTING TO KNOW THE SCENE Tokyo has several nightlife districts spread throughout the city, each with its own atmosphere, price range, and clientele. Most famous are probably **Ginza, Kabuki-cho** in Shinjuku, and **Roppongi.** Before visiting any of these locales suggested below, be sure to just walk around one of these neighborhoods and absorb the atmosphere. The streets will be crowded, the neon lights will be overwhelming, and you never know what you might discover on your own.

The most popular nightlife spots are **drinking establishments,** where the vast majority of Japan's office workers, college students, and expats go for an evening out. These places include Western-style bars as well as Japanese-style watering holes, called *nomi-ya* (literally "drinking place") or *izakaya,* a Japanese-style pub serving food. *Yakitori-ya,* restaurant-bars that serve *yakitori* and other snacks, are included in this group. Dancing and live-music venues are also popular with young Tokyoites. At the low end of the spectrum are Tokyo's topless bars, strip shows, massage parlors, and porn shops, with the largest concentration in Shinjuku's **Kabuki-cho District.**

A chic and expensive shopping area by day, **Ginza** transforms itself into a dazzling entertainment district of restaurants, bars, and first-grade hostess bars at night. It's the most sophisticated of Tokyo's nightlife districts and can also be one of the most expensive. However, because Ginza has great restaurants and several hotels, I've included some reasonably priced recommendations for a drink if you happen to find yourself here after dinner. The cheapest way to absorb the atmosphere in Ginza is simply to wander about, particularly around **Namiki Dori** and its side streets.

In **Shinjuku,** northeast of Shinjuku Station, is **Kabuki-cho,** which undoubtedly has the craziest nightlife in all of Tokyo: block after block of strip joints, massage parlors, pornography shops, peep shows, love hotels, bars, restaurants, and, as the night wears on, drunk revelers. A world of its own, it's sleazy, chaotic, crowded, vibrant, and fairly safe. Despite its name, Shinjuku's primary night spot has nothing to do with *kabuki,* though at one time, there was a plan to bring some culture to the area by introducing a *kabuki* theater. The plan never materialized, but the name stuck. Although Kabuki-cho used to be the domain of businessmen out on the town, nowadays young Japanese, including college-age men and women, have claimed parts of it as their own, adding inexpensive eating and drinking venues to the mix. It has also become very popular with visiting tourists.

The best thing to do in Shinjuku is simply walk about. In the glow of neon light, you'll pass everything from smoke-filled restaurants to hawkers trying to get you to step inside so they can part you from your money. If you're looking for strip joints, topless or bottomless coffee shops, peep shows, or porn, I leave you to your own devices, but you certainly won't have any problems finding them. Just be sure you know what you're getting into; your bill may end up much higher than you bargained for.

A word of **warning** for women traveling alone: Forgo the experience of strolling around Kabuki-cho. The streets are crowded and therefore safe, but you may not feel comfortable with so many inebriated men stumbling around. If there are two of you, however, go for it. I took my mother to Kabuki-cho for a spin around the neon, and we escaped relatively unscathed. You're also fine walking alone to any of my recommended restaurants.

About a 5-minute walk east of Kabuki-cho, just west of Hanazono Shrine, is a smaller district called **Golden Gai.** It's a warren of tiny alleyways leading past even tinier bars, each consisting of just a counter and a few chairs.

Although many thought Golden Gai would succumb to land-hungry developers in the 1980s, the economic recession brought a stay of execution, and now Golden Gai has experienced a revival, with more than 200 tiny drinking dens lining the tiny streets. Still, it occupies such expensive land that I fear for the life of this tiny enclave, one of Tokyo's most fascinating.

A 5-minute walk farther east is **Shinjuku Ni-chome** (pronounced "knee-chomay"). With 300-some bars, lounges, dance clubs, and shops, it's the largest gay-bar district in Japan, if not all of Asia. Its lively street scene of mostly gays and some straights of all ages (but mostly young) make this one of Tokyo's most vibrant nightlife districts. It's here that I was once taken to a host bar featuring young men in crotchless pants. The clientele included both gay men and groups of young, giggling office girls. It has since closed down, but Shinjuku is riddled with other spots bordering on the absurd.

To Tokyo's younger crowd, **Roppongi** is one of the city's most fashionable places to hang out. It's also a favorite with the foreign community, including models, business types, English-language teachers, and tourists staying in Roppongi's posh hotels. Some Tokyoites complain that Roppongi is too crowded, too crass, and too commercialized (and has too many foreigners). However, for the casual visitor, Roppongi offers an excellent opportunity to see what's new and hot in the capital city. It's also easy to navigate because nightlife activity is so concentrated. There is one huge **caveat,** however: Roppongi's concentration of foreigners has also attracted the unscrupulous, with reports of spiked drinks and patrons passing out, only to awaken hours later to find credit cards missing or fraudulently charged for huge amounts. In other words, never leave drinks unattended, and you're best off following the buddy system. Otherwise, consider signing up for a guided **Roppongi pub crawl** (see p. 155).

The center of Roppongi is **Roppongi Crossing** (the intersection of Roppongi Dori and Gaien-Higashi Dori), at the corner of which sits the Almond Coffee Shop with its pink flags and decor. The shop has mediocre coffee and desserts at inflated prices, but the sidewalk in front is the number-one meeting spot in Roppongi.

If you need directions, there's a conveniently located *koban* (police box) catty-corner from the Almond Coffee Shop and next to a bank. It has a big map of the Roppongi area showing the address system, and someone is always there to help.

EXTRA CHARGES & TAXES One more thing you should be aware of is the **"table charge"** imposed on customers at some bars (especially *nomiya*) and many cocktail lounges—usually between ¥300 and ¥500 per person. Included in the table charge is usually a small snack—maybe nuts, chips, or a vegetable; for this reason, some locales call it an *otsumami,* or snack charge. Some establishments levy a table charge only after a certain time in the evening; others may add it only if you don't order food. If you're not sure and it matters to you, ask before you order anything. Remember, too, that there's an 8% consumption tax (scheduled to rise to 10% in October 2019), though some menus already include it in their prices. Some higher-end establishments,

Finding Out What's On

Keep an eye out for *Metropolis* (www.metropolisjapan.com), a free weekly that carries sections covering concerts, theaters, and events and is available at bars, restaurants, and other venues around town. You should also check to see what's going on at www.timeout.jp.

In addition, the *Japan Times* and *Daily Yomiuri* have entertainment sections. For an online rundown of what's happening at Tokyo's hundreds of venues, live houses, and clubs weekly, go to www.tokyogigguide.com.

especially nightclubs, hostess bars, and dance clubs, will also add a service charge ranging anywhere from 10% to 20%.

GETTING TICKETS If you're staying in a higher-end hotel, the concierge or guest-relations manager can usually get tickets for you. Otherwise, head to the theater or hall itself. An easier way is to go through one of many ticket services, such as **Ticket PIA;** ask your hotel concierge for the one nearest you. Lawson and FamilyMart convenience stores also sell tickets to many events from kiosks, but instructions are in Japanese only.

The Performing Arts

For descriptions of Japanese traditional performance arts such as *kabuki* and *Noh,* see "Japanese Arts in a Nutshell," in chapter 2. In addition to the listings below, Tokyo also has occasional shows of more avant-garde or lesser-known performance art productions, including highly stylized Butoh dance performances and percussion demonstrations by Kodo drummers and other Japanese drum groups. See publications listed above for complete listings.

Kabukiza Theatre ★★★ Kabukiza Theatre, an easy walk from Ginza, is Japan's largest and most famous *kabuki* theater. It has been rebuilt several times since making its debut in 1889, with the most recent version, completed in 2013 and adding a 29-story tower, thankfully preserving its eye-catching Momoyama-style facade (influenced by 16th-century castle architecture). Like all *kabuki* theaters, its stage includes a revolving circle in its center, a platform that can be lowered below the floor level so that actors magically appear and disappear to dramatic effect, and a runway that extends into the audience. In the lobby, stalls sell *bento* lunch boxes and souvenirs (you're welcome to eat at your seat during intermission).

On the fifth floor is a roof garden and the **Kabukiza Gallery,** where you can get a close look at *kabuki* costumes, stage props, old posters, and such daily from 10am to 5:30pm; admission here is ¥600 for adults, ¥500 for children. It's a fun way to spend 20 minutes, especially if you aren't able to see a live a performance (the museum shows kabuki videos).

There are *kabuki* productions most months of the year, with each production running from about the first or third of each month for 25 days. Generally, each production consists of two shows, with matinees staged from about 11 or 11:30am to 4pm and evening shows starting at around 4:30. Of course, you won't be able to understand what the actors are saying, but *kabuki* plays, all written before the 20th century, have plots that are easy to follow, with love, duty, and revenge popular themes. Furthermore, because *kabuki* developed as a form of entertainment for commoners in feudal Japan, it doesn't have any of the highbrow seriousness attached to, say, *Noh,* which was popular among the aristocracy. In fact, one of the things I most love about *kabuki* is the level of spectator engagement, with fans shouting out approval during particularly good performances. And of course, one of the most interesting things about *kabuki* is that all roles are played by men, even the female ones.

Mapping Out Tokyo's Nightlife

Once you've chosen a nightlife spot that appeals to you, you can locate it using the following neighborhood maps:

- To locate bars and clubs in **Ginza,** p. 74.
- To locate bars and clubs in **Shinjuku,** p. 84.
- To locate bars and clubs in **Roppongi,** p. 90.

Luckily, English-language translation tablets (¥1,000) provide information about the plot, music, actors, and other aspects of *kabuki* so you can follow what's going on. Tickets can be purchased at the box office in Basement Level 2 from 10am to 6pm and from automatic ticket dispensers. You can also make advance reservations by phone (✆ **03/6745-0888**) or online.

Because programs often run about 4 hours, you might want to buy tickets for only part of a production. Or, if you think one act *(makumi)* is enough and you don't mind being up in the balcony (on the fourth floor, a bit far from the stage), you can save money by buying single-act tickets. A single act lasts about 30 minutes to 2 hours. These tickets, sold to the left of the main entrance (no credit cards accepted), go on sale just before each act and are available on a first-come, first-served basis. Everyone in your party must be present and stand in line (that is, no substitutions and no one holding your place). Note that only 96 seats are available, with another 60 spaces for standing room only. You'll be assigned a number and allowed into the auditorium accordingly. There are no assigned seats, but by your place in line they'll be able to tell you whether you're standing or sitting. If you wish, you can buy tickets for consecutive acts as well. English-language tablets here for one act cost ¥500, plus a refundable deposit. 4–12–15 Ginza, Chuo-ku. www.kabukiweb.net/theatres/kabukiza. ✆ **03/3545-6800;** ✆ 03 6745-0888 for reservations. Regular tickets ¥4,000–¥20,000, depending on the program and seat location; single-act tickets ¥800–¥2,000, depending on time of day and length of show. Station: Higashi-Ginza (1 min.).

Kingyo ★★ For unique, casual entertainment, nothing beats an evening at an entertainment nightclub, featuring fast-paced dancing in intimate venues. Although the emcee may speak Japanese only, no translation is necessary for the stage productions, which center on easy-to-understand themes or include humorous antics. Kingyo is one of Tokyo's oldest show nightclubs (since 1994, with management recently passed down to the second generation). It stages one of the most high-energy, visually charged 1-hour shows I've seen—nonstop action of ascending and receding stages and stairs, fast-paced choreography, elaborate costumes, and loud music. In addition to female dancers, there are also male dancers assuming female parts, just like in *kabuki* (and I swear, it's difficult to tell the difference). Some of the acts center on traditional Japanese themes with traditional dress and kimono (a perennial favorite is a well-known song from Okinawa), but there are also satires and social commentaries. It's great fun, and you'll admire the cast not only for their talent but for their quick costume changes. Shows are Tuesday to Sunday at 7:30 (doors open at 6pm) and 10pm (doors open at 9pm). Reservations are recommended. 3–14–17 Roppongi, Minato-ku. www.kingyo.co.jp/en. ✆ **03/3478-3000.** Cover ¥3,500, plus a minimum of 1 drink and 1 food item; or admission packages including set meal and drinks starting at ¥6,000. Station: Roppongi (4 min.). From Roppongi Crossing, walk toward Tokyo Tower on Gaien-Higashi Dori and take the second left; it's on the right.

National Noh Theatre (Kokuritsu Nogakudo) ★★ *Noh* is performed at a number of locations in Tokyo, but this is the most famous stage. Opened in 1983, it's dedicated to presenting classical *Noh* and *kyogen,* with about three to five performances monthly, many of which have English subtitles. Tickets are often sold out in advance, but about 30 tickets are held back to be sold on the day of the performance. In addition, privately sponsored *Noh* performances are also held here, for which the admission varies. See www.theatrenohgaku.org for information on *Noh* performances being staged throughout Japan. 4–18–1 Sendagaya, Shibuya-ku. www.ntj.jac.go.jp. ✆ **03/3432-1331** or 3230-3000 for reservations. Tickets ¥2,700–¥4,900. Station: Sendagaya or Kokuritsu Kyogijo (5 min.).

Robot Restaurant ★★ I can hardly think about this bizarre place without cracking up; it's definitely one of those only-in-Japan experiences. Although it calls itself a restaurant, you are not coming here for the rather ordinary and optional *bento* box. You're here for the 1-hour show that includes larger-than-life-size robots (controlled mostly by remote control), loud music, flashing lights, and scantily clad women in a fast-paced revue that will have you laughing at the absurdity of it all and in awe of the robots. Is it cheesy? Yes, and delightfully so. But this sensory overload is also expensive, so while I am thoroughly glad I've seen it, I probably wouldn't go twice—unless, of course, I just had to bring a friend new to Japan. Shows are staged three or four times daily from 4pm (but get there earlier to experience its over-the-top lurid lounge), and reservations are recommended. 1–7–1 Kabuki-cho, Shinjuku-ku. www.shinjuku-robot.com. ✆ **03/3200-5500.** Cover ¥8,000; bento meal ¥1,000 extra. Station: Shinjuku (5 min.). From Yasukuni Dori, take the street with the blue archway and a FamilyMart on the corner.

Tokyo Takarazuka Theater (Tokyo Takarazuka Kagekidan) ★★ This world-famous, all-female troupe stages elaborate musical revues with dancing, singing, and gorgeous costumes. Performances range from Japanese versions of Broadway hits to original Japanese works based on local legends. The first Takarazuka troupe, formed in 1914 at a resort near Osaka, gained instant notoriety because all its performers were women, in contrast to the all-male *kabuki.* When I went to see this troupe perform, I was surprised to find that the audience also consisted almost exclusively of women; indeed, the troupe, all unmarried, has an almost cultlike following. Posters outside the box office show what's on and what's coming. Performances, accompanied by live music and with story synopses available in English, are scheduled throughout the year. Tickets are available at the box office, online or through **Ticket Pia.** Same-day tickets, sold on a first-come, first-served basis, cost ¥2,500 for a seat and ¥1,500 for standing room only. Tokyo Takarazuka Gekkjo, 1–1–3 Yurakucho, Chiyoda-ku. www.kageki.hankyu.co.jp/english. ✆ **03/5251-2001.** Cover ¥3,500–¥12,000. Station: Hibiya (1 min.). Down the street from the Imperial Hotel.

Live Music Clubs

The live-music scene exploded in the 1990s and is now located throughout the metropolis. In addition to the dedicated venues below, which represent only the tip of the iceberg, be sure to check out http://metropolis.co.jp and www.tokyogigguide.com for more suggestions.

Crocodile ★★ Crocodile has spoken to generations of young Japanese with its casual rock-n-roll vibe and eclectic schedule of live bands offering everything from rock and blues to jazz-fusion, reggae, soul, experimental, salsa, and country. It's a good place to check out what people are listening to and mingle with a mostly Japanese crowd, except on the last Friday of every month, when the **Tokyo Comedy Store** (www.tokyocomedy.com) provides more than 2 hours of comedy and improv in English starting at 8pm for ¥1,500. The club has a good, laidback atmosphere; although it's a not a dance club per se, no one will mind if you just can't help yourself. Open daily 6pm to 2am; performances start around 7 or 8pm. 6–18–8 Jingumae, Shibuya-ku. www.crocodile-live.jp. ✆ **03/3499-5205.** Cover generally ¥2,500–¥3,500, more for big acts. Station: Meiji-Jingumae or Shibuya (10 min.). On Meiji Dori halfway btw. Harajuku and Shibuya.

Liquidroom ★★★ Once a scruffy place in Shinjuku, this venue shot to stardom after relocating to this cavernous space with a fantastic sound system in Ebisu. It's well known for its concerts (bands often use it as a launching pad for world tours), DJs, and other stage events most nights of the week. Otherwise, if you just want to chill, there's a **Time Out Café & Diner** on the second floor, open from 11:30am Monday to Friday and from 1pm on weekends, offering free Wi-Fi and a menu that includes salads and burgers. Liquidroom opens around 6 or 7pm, with performances 1 hour later. 3–16–6 Higashi, Shibuya-ku. www.liquidroom.net. ✆ **03/5464-0800.** Cover generally ¥3,500–¥6,000, depending on the event. Station: Ebisu (3 min.). Take the west exit, cross Komazawa Dori and turn right, and then turn left at Meiji Dori; it will be almost immediately on your left.

The Ruby Room ★★★ I've seen living rooms larger than this second-floor venue, home to local acts, open-mic Tuesdays, house and techno DJs, and other events, from poetry readings to comedy shows. The crowd depends on the music, but because there's no room to move, people dance where they are. The band is close, close, close—any closer and you'd be in the drummer's lap. In any case, the energy in this place is great, making it one of my favorite live-music venues. Open daily from 7pm or later, depending on the event (some concerts start at midnight), until 5am. 2-25-17 Dogenzaka, Shibuya-ku. www.rubyroomtokyo.com. © **03/3780-3022.** Cover ¥1,000–¥2,000 most nights, including 1 drink; Tues open mike ¥1,500, including 2 drinks. Station: Shibuya (Hachiko exit, 4 min.). Walk on Dogenzaka past the round 109 building and take the 1st right at Mos Burger; keep to the left at the Y intersection.

Shinjuku Pit Inn ★★★ Musicians from Japan and abroad have been playing their hearts out at this famed institution since 2001. It's still one of the best clubs in town for jazz, fusion, or blues, nothing fancy but dedicated to the music (it even has a recording studio). There are two programs daily, with up-and-coming bands performing at 2:30pm and more established groups taking the stage in the evening, around 7:30 or 8pm, making it a great place to stop for a bit of music in the middle of the day. It's *the* place for serious jazz fans interested in seeing firsthand the level of talent in Japan. 2–12–4 Shinjuku, Shinjuku-ku. www.pit-inn.com. © **03/3354-2024.** Cover, including 1 drink, ¥1,300 for the 2:30pm show (¥2,500 Sat–Sun and holidays); ¥3,000 and up for the evening shows. Station: Shinjuku Sanchome (3 min.). Northeast of the Shinjuku Dori/Meiji Dori intersection.

What the Dickens! ★★ This laid-back expat bar is kind of a dive, but it's been much-loved for almost 20 years as a great place to kick back and hear free live music nightly. Bands play everything from rock to reggae, jazz, blues, folk, and even Dixieland jazz, with live music from 8:30 to 11:30pm. It has British beer on tap, as well as a menu of steak pie, fish and chips, and other pub fare, with happy hour Monday to Saturday 5 to 7pm. Hours are Tuesday to Thursday 5pm to 1am, Friday and Saturday 5pm to 2am, and Sunday 5pm to midnight. 1–13–3 Ebisu Nishi, Shibuya-ku. 4th floor of the Roob Building. www.whatthedickens.jp. © **03/3780-2099.** Station: Ebisu (west exit, 3 min.). On the other side of Komazawa Dori street, take the small street beside St. Marc Café; it's at the end of the 2nd block on the left, on the corner.

Bars & Dance Clubs

GINZA

Ginza Sapporo Lion ★ Yebisu and Sapporo beer are the draw at this large beer hall, a Ginza institution since 1934 and popular with older Japanese for its vaulted mock Gothic ceiling, wall murals, colored mosaic tiles, and German decor. It's also a big hit with Chinese tourists, probably because tour buses drop them off out front and it's located next to Laox duty-free store. A display of plastic foods and an English-language menu offer snacks ranging from *yakitori* and tempura to Vienna sausage and spaghetti. Hours are Monday to Saturday from 11:30am to 11pm, Sunday and holidays 11:30am to 10:30pm. 7–9–20 Ginza. © **03/3571-2590.** Station: Ginza (3 min.). On Chuo Dori, next to Laox.

Old Imperial Bar ★★ This clubby bar is a Tokyo institution, the only place in the Imperial Hotel that Frank Lloyd Wright's legacy as architect of the former 1923 Imperial lives on. It has a subdued atmosphere, with dim lighting, comfy chairs, and reproduction Wright furniture, as well as Wright originals like the small desk at the entrance, standing lamp in the corner, the mural, and the Art Deco terra-cotta wall behind the bar. To pay tribute to Wright, order the bar's original Mount Fuji, a cocktail with dry gin, lemon juice, pineapple juice, egg white, and maraschino cherry, first served in 1924. This is a quiet escape from busy Tokyo, but it's also good for a lunchtime sandwich if you're in the area. Hours are daily 11:30am to midnight. Imperial Hotel, 1–1–1 Uchisaiwai-cho. www.imperialhotel.co.jp. ✆ **03/3539-8088.** Station: Hibiya (1 min.).

300 Bar ★ You don't want to come here when you're drop-dead tired, because there are no seats in this standing bar. But you do come because it's cheap, with all food and most drink items priced at only ¥300 plus tax, the same price as when it opened 25 years ago. It's a good place for a quick drink or as an early spot to meet up with friends in the Ginza, since by 10pm there can be a line of mostly young Japanese queued up at the door. It's self-service, and upon entry you're required to purchase a minimum of two tickets (at ¥324 each) if you're a woman, three if you're male, which can be redeemed for any drink or food item from the 100-plus menu listing everything from the excellent mojito made with the bar's own herbs to a Cuban sandwich. Open daily noon to 2am (4am Fri and Sat). Two other branches, at 8–3–12 Ginza and 1–2–14 Yurakucho, also open from noon. 5–9–11 Ginza. www.300bar.com. ✆ **03/3572-6300.** Station: Ginza (2 min.). On a side street southeast of the Ginza 4–chome Crossing called Ginza Mihara Dori.

SHINJUKU

Albatross ★★ I've been a Golden Gai regular for more than 30 years and have seen its metamorphosis from a mysterious hidden enclave accessible only to Japanese customers to a boarded-up place on the brink of extinction to the thriving hotspot it is today. The 170 or so miniature establishments packed into Goruden Gai attract a healthy mix of Japanese and foreigners, young and old, straight and gay, and it's fun to just walk around and see where the night takes you. For a recommendation, however, Albatross has been around for a while, with a mostly young clientele and an eclectic decor that ranges from chandeliers to a deer head. You'll have to squeeze in to find a seat, either at the counter or up the narrow stairs to one of two Lilliputian levels above. Once settled, you'll find it has a very welcoming vibe. There's a ¥500 snack charge per person. Open daily 7pm to 5am. 1–1–7 Kabuki-cho. www.alba-s.com ✆ **03/3203-3699.** Station: Shinjuku Sanchome (7 min.). In Goruden Gai, on 5th St. (Gobangai).

Dubliners' Irish Pub ★ Attracting expats and locals alike—mostly in their 30s and 40s—this chain Irish bar has a happening happy hour from 3 to 7pm weekdays (noon–3pm Sat and Sun). The menu lists such perennial favorites as fish & chips, shepherd's pie, and beef and Guinness stew. Free live Irish music is staged twice a month. Check website for a schedule and addresses of other Dubliners' in Ikebukuro, Akasaka, Shibuya, and Shinagawa. Open Monday to Friday 3 to 11:30pm, Saturday noon to 11:30pm, Sunday noon to 11pm. 3–28–9 Shinjuku. www.dubliners.jp ✆ **03/3352-6606.** Station: Shinjuku (east exit, 3 min.). In east Shinjuku, behind Bic Camera/Uniqlo complex to the southwest, above Sapporo Lion.

ROPPONGI

By yourself but still want to hit the town? Or maybe with friends but don't know where to go? Join the **Tokyo Pub Crawl** (www.tokyopubcrawl.com; ✆ **070/1326-1423**), which is like a party every Friday and Saturday night when up to 100 people visit three bars and a club in Roppongi. The cost is ¥2,900 for men and ¥2,000 for women (which includes a shot at each venue); the website has discounts, signup, and details. Interestingly, some 30% attendees are Japanese (many of whom come weekly), making for a diverse international crowd. Lots of fun.

A-Life ★★★ Roppongi's biggest and most sophisticated dance club, with three stories offering small and large dance floors plus bar and lounge areas so that you can alternate between action and relaxation. It targets 30-somethings (men under 23 and women under 20 are not allowed), and scruffy dressers will probably be rejected unless that scruffiness looks hip. Open Monday to Saturday 9pm to 4:30am. 1–7–2 Nishi Azabu. www.e-alife.net. ✆ **03/3408-1111.** Cover, including 2 drinks, ¥2,000 men and ¥1,000 women weekdays (free until 11pm), Fri/Sat ¥4,000 men and ¥2,500 women (discounts until 11pm). Station: Roppongi (exit 2, 5 min.). On Roppongi Dori's right side walking from Roppongi Crossing toward Shibuya, past Roppongi Hills.

Ant 'n Bee ★★ Not sure what ants and bees have to do with beer, but this secret hideaway offers a cozy, laidback vibe and about 20 Japanese craft beers on tap, making it a great place to sample national brews, from wheat to stout. Limited but decent food (like buffalo wings and fish and chips), a friendly staff, and free Wi-Fi make this a good place to hang out in Roppongi, away from all the hype. Open daily 5pm to 6am. 5–1–5 Roppongi. http://antnbee.favy.jp. ✆ **03/3478-1250.** Station: Roppongi (1 min.). From Roppongi Crossing, on right side of Gaien-Higashi Dori in the direction of Tokyo Tower (look for the sign; this basement bar is easy to miss).

Geronimo Shot Bar ★ This is such a tiny place, it is darn near impossible to elbow your way to the bar or avoid conversation with the people around you. That's because it's a party scene most nights of the week, fueled, no doubt, by the 40 or so different shots available (the Russian Quaalude is quite a production). If you hear the drum, it means someone has bought a shot for everyone in the bar (it happens more than you'd think). Drink 15 shots in 1 night and you get a free T-shirt and your name immortalized on the Shot Hall of Fame. If I even tried, management would probably see fit to establish a secondary Wall of Shame. Maybe that's why people seem to either love or hate this place. There must be more of the former than the latter, because this shot bar has been in business 25 years and attracts many regulars, including expats. Happy hour is daily until 9pm. Open Monday to Friday 6pm to 5am, Saturday and Sunday 7pm to 4am. 7–14–10 Roppongi. www.geronimoshotbar.com. ✆ **03/3478-7449.** Station: Roppongi (1 min.). On Roppongi Crossing, across from Almond Coffee Shop.

Odeon ★ A small dance floor, good house music, a reasonably priced cover charge and open hours way past dawn draw a young international crowd. Arrive before midnight to take advantage of happy hour, when all drinks are ¥500. Open daily 8pm to 9am. 3–15–23 Roppongi (3rd floor). http://odeon-bar.com. ✆ **03/-3478-4555.** Cover ¥1,000 including 1 drink (some events cost more). Station: Roppongi (4 min.). From Roppongi Crossing, walk three blocks toward Tokyo Tower and turn left.

Rigoletto Bar & Grill ★★ It's standing room only for the young professionals who crowd this swanky yet reasonably priced bar in Roppongi Hills, especially on Friday nights when it buzzes with disco music. The bar overlooks the restaurant, which offers upscale Spanish/Italian bar food (pizza, pasta, and main dishes like shrimp paella). Note, however, that the bar allows smoking after 5pm, a real turnoff for some diners, and because this is considered an adult venue, children are allowed only on weekdays from 1 to 6pm. Open Monday to Thursday 11am to 2am, Friday and Saturday 11am to 4am, Sunday and holidays 11am to 11pm. Roppongi Hills, 5th floor of West Walk, 6–10–1 Roppongi. www.huge.co.jp/restaurant/rigoletto/roppongi. ✆ **03/6438-0071.** Cover for dining tables ¥300 after 5pm, 10% extra at the bar after 10pm. Station: Roppongi (Roppongi Hills exit, 3 min.).

R2 Supper Club ★★★ The owners of this lounge decided that Roppongi needed a sophisticated hangout for expats with money, and it must be working, because R2 can be crazy full from 10pm onward, with the targeted corporate types packing the place. In a dark interior where a huge bar is center stage, it offers mojitos (like yuzu mojito), martinis, cocktails, and margaritas. It gets kudos for promoting mostly local up-and-coming Japanese (and some international) DJs nightly, usually jazz paired with live instruments. Open daily at 4pm, closing at 4am Monday to Thursday, 5am Friday and Saturday, and midnight Sunday. 7–14–23 Roppongi. www.r2sc.jp. ✆ **03/6447-0002.** Station: Roppongi (2 min.). From Roppongi Crossing, walk on Gaien-Higashi Dori toward Tokyo Midtown and take the first left.

SHIBUYA

Kurand Sake Market ★ Sample from about 100 different kinds of sake from small breweries all over Japan. It costs ¥500 for a small glass, but all-you-can drink options include beer, with 30 minutes of drinking costing ¥1,000, 90 minutes ¥2,000, and unlimited minutes ¥3,000 plus tax (the entire table must order these options). You're even allowed to bring your own food. It's a small place, so reservations are encouraged. Branches are located all over town. 2–9–10 Shibuya (3rd floor). https://kurand.jp/en. ✆ **03/6455-0277.** Station: Shibuya (Hachiko exit, 5 min.). On the left side of Dogenzaka, across from Royal Host.

Gay & Lesbian Bars

Shinjuku Ni-chome (pronounced "knee-chomay"), southeast of the Yasukuni-Gyoen Dori intersection (station: Shinjuku Sanchome), is Tokyo's gay and lesbian quarter, with a lively street scene and countless establishments catering to a variety of age groups and preferences. The following are good starting points, but you'll find a lot more in the immediate area by networking and exploring on your own.

AiiRO Café ★★ Where to start in Ni-chome? This is a good bet, right on Ni-chome's main drag, Naka-dori, and with an open facade that overflows with both gays and straights (but mostly gays) extending past the sidewalk to the street most nights. It's a good place to gain bearings, check out the people parading past, and connect with the friendly crowd. A few drinks here, and you'll probably have a list of several places you want to hit next, but the bar's website also gives excellent pointers. Open Monday to Thursday 6pm to 2am, Friday and Saturday 6pm to 5am, and Sunday 6pm to midnight. 2–18–1 Shinjuku. http://aliving.net/aiirocafe. ✆ **03/6273-0740.** Station: Shinjuku Sanchome (4 min.). On the street behind Bygs, to the right, with a red torii gate at its entrance.

Arty Farty ★★★ One of Ni-chome's larger gay bars is also one of the best places to dance, thanks to a good sound system and music ranging from house to hip hop. On the first Saturday of the month, the nightly party turns into a major event; the ¥1,500 cover for this includes two drinks. Although Arty Farty used to be strictly males only, it threw open its doors to all when it moved to this location across from the legendary **Pit Inn** jazz house (p. 153). A fun climax to a pub crawl in Shinjuku. Open 8pm to 5am daily. 2–11–7 Shinjuku. www.arty-farty.net. ✆ **03/5362-9720.** Station: Shinjuku Sanchome (3 min.). Northeast of the Shinjuku Dori/Meiji Dori intersection.

Bar Goldfinger ★ This small women-only bar offers free popcorn and karaoke, though it does let in a mixed LGBT crowd every night except Saturdays. Happy hour is from 6 to 8pm, but it's a happy, friendly place any time. Open Sunday, Monday, Wednesday, and Thursday from 6pm to 2am, Friday and Saturday 6pm to 4am. 2–12–11 Shinjuku. www.goldfingerparty.com. ✆ **03/6383-4649.** Station: Shinjuku Sanchome (4 min.).

Kinsmen ★★ This long-standing second-floor gay bar welcomes customers of all persuasions. It's a pleasant oasis, small and civilized. Hours are Sunday and Tuesday to Thursday 8pm to 1am, Friday and Saturday 8pm to 3am. 2–18–5 Shinjuku. http://kinsmen2.sakura.ne.jp. ✆ **03/3354-4949.** Station: Shinjuku Sanchome (3 min.). On the street behind BYGS, on the left.

6 SIDE TRIPS FROM TOKYO

If your stay in Tokyo is long enough, consider taking an excursion or two. **Kamakura** and **Nikko** rank as two of the most important historical sites in Japan, renowned for temples and shrines that relate to former shogun (military dictators). For an overnight stay, I heartily recommend **Hakone,** famous for its hot-spring spas, spectacular scenery, and unique modes of transportation that include travel by ropeway and boat; you might even see Mt. Fuji on the way.

Your main problem will be deciding where to go. If you take only one day trip, I would probably choose Kamakura, especially if you're unable to include the ancient capitals of Kyoto and Nara in your travels. If you're going to Kyoto and Nara, however, I would probably go to Nikko, but note that it's a much longer journey. As for Hakone, it can be enjoyed as a side trip from Tokyo or seen en route to other destinations like Kyoto.

KAMAKURA, ANCIENT CAPITAL ★★★

51km (32 miles) S of Tokyo

Kamakura is a delightful hamlet with no fewer than 65 Buddhist temples and 19 Shinto shrines spread throughout the town and surrounding wooded hills. Most of these were built centuries ago, when a warrior named Minamoto Yoritomo seized political power and established his shogunate government in Kamakura back in 1192. Wanting to set up his seat of government as far away as possible from what he considered to be the corrupt imperial court in Kyoto, Yoritomo selected Kamakura because it was easy to defend. The town is enclosed on three sides by wooded hills and on the fourth by the sea—a setting that lends a dramatic background to its many temples and shrines.

Although Kamakura remained the military and political center of the nation for a century and a half, the Minamoto clan was in power only a short time. After Yoritomo's death, both of his sons were assassinated, one after the other, after taking up military rule. Power then passed to the family of Yoritomo's widow, the Hojo clan, which ruled until 1333, when the emperor in Kyoto sent troops to

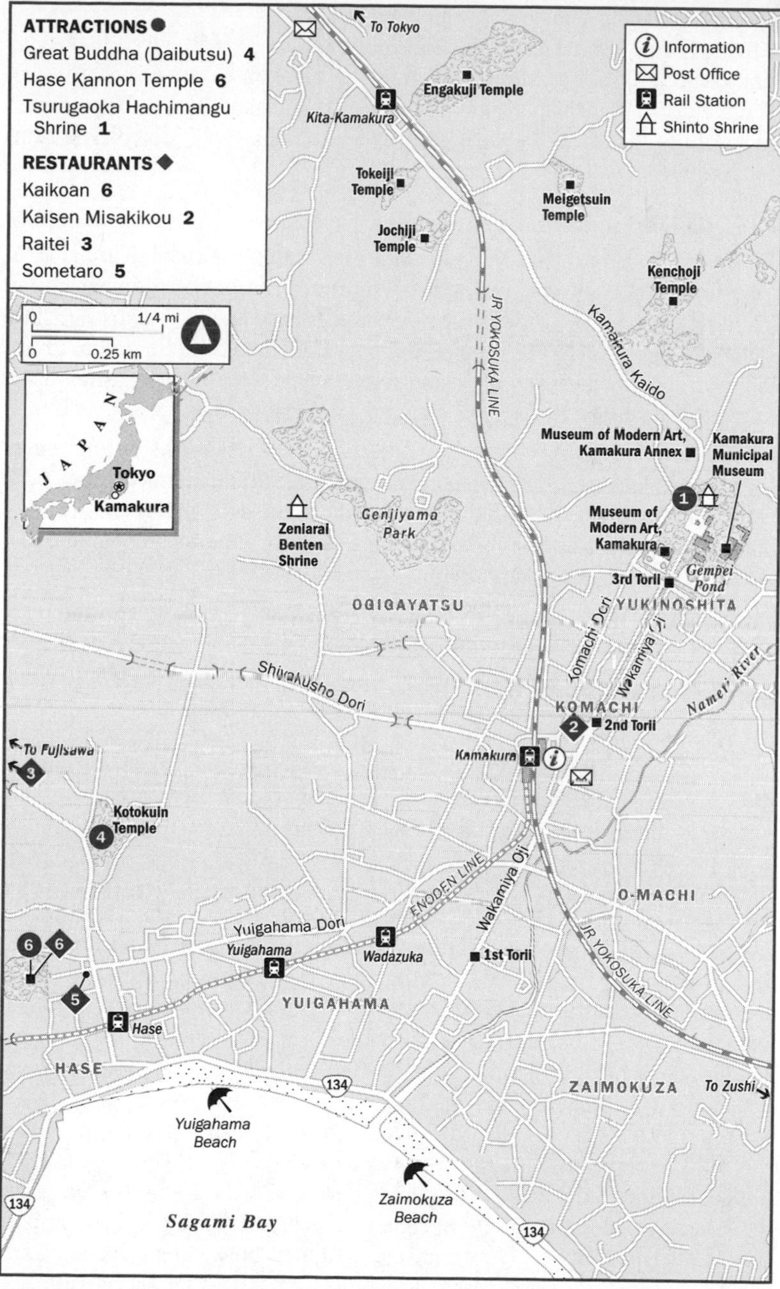
ATTRACTIONS
Great Buddha (Daibutsu) 4
Hase Kannon Temple 6
Tsurugaoka Hachimangu Shrine 1
RESTAURANTS
Kaikoan 6
Kaisen Misakikou 2
Raitei 3
Sometaro 5
0 1/4 mi
0 0.25 km
JAPAN
Tokyo
Kamakura
Information
Post Office
Rail Station
Shinto Shrine
To Tokyo
Engakuji Temple
Kita-Kamakura
Tokeiji Temple
Jochiji Temple
Meigetsuin Temple
Kenchoji Temple
Kamakura Kaido
JR YOKOSUKA LINE
Museum of Modern Art, Kamakura Annex
Kamakura Municipal Museum
Museum of Modern Art, Kamakura
Genjiyama Park
Zeniarai Benten Shrine
3rd Torii
Gempei Pond
OGIGAYATSU
YUKINOSHITA
Komachi Dori
Wakamiya Oji
Shiyakusho Dori
Nameri River
KOMACHI
2nd Torii
To Fujisawa
Kamakura
Kotokuin Temple
ENODEN LINE
Wakamiya Oji
O-MACHI
Yuigahama Dori
Yuigahama
Wadazuka
1st Torii
JR YOKOSUKA LINE
YUIGAHAMA
Hase
HASE
134
ZAIMOKUZA
To Zushi
Yuigahama Beach
Zaimokuza Beach
134
Sagami Bay
134

crush the shogunate government. Unable to stop the invaders, 800 soldiers retired to the Hojo family temple at Toshoji, where they disemboweled themselves in ritualistic suicide known as *seppuku.*

Today Kamakura is a thriving seaside resort (pop. 173,000), with old wooden homes, temples, shrines, and wooded hills—a pleasant 1-day trip from Tokyo. (There's also a beach in Kamakura called Yuigahama Beach, but I find it unappealing; it's often strewn with litter and unbelievably crowded in summer. Skip it.)

Essentials

GETTING THERE The **JR Yokosuka Line** bound for Zushi, Kurihama, or Yokosuka departs several times an hour from Shinagawa, Shimbashi, and Tokyo JR stations. The trip takes 1 hour from Tokyo Station and costs ¥920 to Kamakura Station. The JR Shonan-Shinjuku Line runs from Shinjuku, Ebisu, Shibuya, or Ikebukuro for the same price. Suica (see "Getting Around" in chapter 4) and Japan Rail Passes can be used for both lines.

VISITOR INFORMATION In Kamakura, a **tourist information center** (www.city.kamakura.kanagawa.jp/visitkamakura/en/index.html; ✆ **0467/22-3350**) is inside Kamakura Station to the right of the east (main) exit. Pick up a map here and get directions to the village's most important sights and restaurants. It's open daily 9am to 7pm.

ORIENTATION & GETTING AROUND Kamakura's major sights are clustered in two areas: **Kamakura Station,** the town's downtown, with souvenir shops and restaurants spread along Komachi Dori and Wakamiya Oji on the way to Tsurugaoka Hachimangu Shrine; and **Hase,** with the Great Buddha and Hase Kannon Temple. You can travel between Kamakura Station and Hase Station in 5 minutes via the **Enoden Line,** a wonderful small train, or you can walk the distance in about 20 minutes. Destinations are also easily reached by buses from Kamakura Station.

Exploring Kamakura

AROUND KAMAKURA STATION About a 12-minute walk from Kamakura Station, **Tsurugaoka Hachimangu Shrine** ★★★ (www.tsurugaoka-hachimangu.jp; ✆ **0467/22-0315**) is the spiritual heart of Kamakura and one of its most popular attractions. It was built by Yoritomo and dedicated to Hachiman, the Shinto god of war who served as a protector of the warrior class and the clan deity of the Minamoto family. The pathway to the shrine is along Wakamiya Oji, a cherry-tree-lined pedestrian lane that was constructed by Yoritomo in the 1190s so that his oldest son's first visit to the family shrine could be accomplished in style with an elaborate procession. The lane stretches from the shrine all the way to Yuigahama Beach, with three massive *torii* gates set at intervals along the route to signal the approach to the shrine. On both sides of the pathway are souvenir and antiques shops selling lacquerware, pottery, and folk art. (I suggest returning to Kamakura Station via Komachi Dori, a pedestrian shopping lane that parallels Wakamiya Oji to the west.)

At the bottom of the 62 stairs to the vermilion-colored shrine is the massive trunk of a 1,000-year-old gingko tree that was sadly uprooted during a 2010 storm, but offshoots are making a comeback. It was at this site that Yoritomo's second son was ambushed and murdered in 1219; his head was never found. Such stories of murder and betrayal were common in feudal Japan. Fearful that his charismatic brother had designs on the shogunate, Yoritomo banished him and ordered him killed. Rather than face capture, the brother committed *seppuku.* When the brother's mistress gave birth to a boy, the baby was promptly killed. Today, the lotus ponds, arched bridge, and bright vermillion sheen of the shrine give little clue to such violent history.

At the top of the stairs is the shrine with its small museum (admission ¥200). You can also get your fortune told in English for ¥100 by shaking out a bamboo stick with a number on it and giving it to the attendant, or buy a charm to assure good luck in health, driving a car, business, or other ventures. Shrine grounds, free to the public, are open daily 6am to 8:30pm.

AROUND HASE STATION To get to these next attractions, you can take any bus departing from platform no. 1 or 6 from in front of Kamakura Station and getting off at the Daibutsuen-mae stop. Or, for a more romantic adventure, you can go by the **Enoden Line,** a tiny train that putt-putts its way seemingly through backyards on its way from Kamakura Station to Hase and beyond. Since it's mostly only one track, trains have to take turns going in either direction. I suggest that you take the bus from Kamakura Station directly to the Great Buddha, backtrack to Hase Shrine, and then take the Enoden train back to Kamakura Station.

Probably Kamakura's most famous attraction is the **Great Buddha ★★★** (www.kotoku-in.jp; ✆ **0467/22-0703**), called the Daibutsu in Japanese and located at **Kotokuin Temple.** Eleven meters (36 ft.) high and weighing 93 tons, it's the third-largest bronze image in Japan. The second-largest Buddha is in Nara and the largest (erected in the 1990s) is near Ushiku Station outside Tokyo, but in my opinion the Kamakura Daibutsu is much more impressive. For one thing, the Kamakura Buddha sits outside against a dramatic backdrop of wooded hills. Cast in 1252, the Kamakura Buddha was indeed once housed in a temple like the Nara Buddha, but a huge tidal wave destroyed the wooden structure—and the statue has sat under sun, snow, and stars ever since. I also prefer the face of the Kamakura Buddha; I find it more inspiring and divine, as though with its half-closed eyes and calm, serene face it's above the worries of the world. It seems to represent the plane above human suffering, the point at which birth and death, joy and sadness, merge and become one. It's open daily from 8am to 5:30pm (to 5pm Oct–Mar). Admission is ¥200 for adults and ¥150 for children. If you want, you can pay an extra ¥20 to go inside the statue—it's hollow—but there's usually a line and I find it claustrophobic.

About a 10-minute walk from the Daibutsu is **Hase Kannon Temple (Hasedera) ★★★** (www.hasedera.jp; ✆ **0467/22-6300**), located on a hill with sweeping views of the sea and a picturesque setting around a pond and flowering trees and bushes. This is the home of an 11-headed gilt statue of Kannon, the goddess of mercy, housed in the Kannon-do (Kannon Hall). More than 9m (30 ft.) high and the tallest wooden image in Japan, it was made in the 8th century from a single piece of camphor wood. Note how each face has a different expression, representing the Kannon's compassion for various kinds of human suffering. The legend surrounding this Kannon is quite remarkable. Supposedly, two wooden images were made from the wood of a huge camphor tree. One of the images was kept in Hase, not far from Nara, while the second was given a short ceremony and then tossed into the sea to find a home of its own. The image drifted about 483km (300 miles) eastward and washed up on shore but was thrown back in again when all who touched it became ill or incurred bad luck. Fifteen years after being cast to sea, the image finally reached Kamakura, sending out rays of light. This was interpreted as a good omen, and Hase Kannon Temple was erected at its present site. Also in the Kannon-do is a museum with religious treasures from the Kamakura, Heian, Muromachi, and Edo periods.

Another golden statue housed here is of **Amida,** a Buddha who promised rebirth in the Pure Land to the West to all who chanted his name. It was created by order of Yoritomo Minamoto upon his 42nd birthday, considered an unlucky year for men. You'll find it housed in the Amida-do (Amida Hall) beside the Kannon-do to the right. **Benten-kutsu Cave** contains many stone images, including one of Benzaiten (seated, with a lute and a money box in front). A sea goddess and patroness of music, art, and good fortune, she is the only female of Japan's Seven Lucky Gods. **Prospect Road** is a 10-minute hiking path featuring flowers in bloom and panoramic views.

As you climb the steps to the Kannon-do, you'll encounter statues of a different sort. All around you will be likenesses of **Jizo,** the guardian deity of children. Although parents originally came to Hase Temple to set up statues to represent their children in hopes the deity would protect and watch over them, through the years the purpose of the Jizo statues changed. Now they represent miscarried, stillborn, or aborted infants. The hundreds or so you see here will remain only a year before being burned or buried to make way for others. Some of the statues are fitted with hand-knitted caps, bibs, and sweaters; the effect is quite chilling.

Hase Temple is open daily 8am to 5:30pm (to 5pm Oct–Feb); admission is ¥300 for adults, ¥100 for children.

Where to Eat

Hase Temple's **Kaikoan,** with views of Yuigahama Beach, offers *udon,* spaghetti, curry, and Buddhist vegetarian dishes daily from 10am to 3pm.

Kaisen Misakikou (海鮮三崎港) ★ SUSHI Located just past the red *torii* gate that marks the entrance to the Komachi Dori pedestrian lane (catty-corner from Kamakura Station to the left), this is a simple *kaiten* (conveyor belt) sushi restaurant. The color of the plates indicates the price, with red plates ¥110, bright blue ones ¥180, white ones ¥250 and dark blue ones ¥300.

You can also order from the menu with photos of each dish (many people do just to assure freshness); help yourself to the tea dispensed at the counter.

1–7–1 Komachi. ✆ **0467/22-6228.** Plates of 2 pieces of sushi ¥110–¥580. Daily 11am–9:30pm (last order). Station: Kamakura (2 min.). On Komachi Dori, almost immediately to the right after passing under the red *torii;* look for its red sign and pictures of sushi.

Raitei (擂亭) ★★★ NOODLES/BENTO Though it's a bit inconveniently located, this is the absolute winner for a meal in Kamakura. Visiting Raitei is as much fun as visiting the city's temples and shrines. The restaurant is situated in the hills on the edge of Kamakura, surrounded by verdant countryside, and the wonder is that it serves inexpensive *soba* (Japanese noodles) and *bento* lunch boxes, as well as priestly *kaiseki* feasts. After paying an entry fee of ¥500, which counts toward the price of your meal, follow the stone steps to the right of the traditional house to the back entry, where you'll be given an English-language menu offering a soba lunchbox with tempura and side dishes and a more expensive *bento* with seasonal dishes (the Japanese menu also lists individual dishes of soba with tempura, yam, etc.). If you make a reservation for *kaiseki* (which requires a minimum of two people), you'll dine upstairs in your own private room in a refined traditional setting with great views. The house, once owned by a wealthy landowner, was moved to this site in 1929. Be sure to take the 20-minute looping path through the garden, past a bamboo grove, Buddhist stone images, and a miniature shrine; in fine weather, you can even see Mt. Fuji.

Takasago. www.raitei.com. ✆ **0467/32-5656.** Noodles ¥950–¥1,650; *bento* ¥3,780; *soba* set meal ¥2,700; *kaiseki* from ¥7,020. Daily 11am–sundown (about 7pm in summer). Closed last week of July. Bus: 4 from platform no. 6 at Kamakura Station or Daibutsuen-mae to Takasago stop, then straight ahead on the left (or a 15-min. taxi ride).

Sometaro (染太郎) ★ OKONOMIYAKI Located near the approach to Hase Temple, this small, second-floor restaurant offers do-it-yourself *okonomiyaki* (a kind of Japanese pancake; cooking instructions are available in English) stuffed with cabbage, bean sprouts, and a choice of a main ingredient like beef, pork, or shrimp. It also serves *yakisoba* (fried noodles) and *teppanyaki* (grilled steak, seafood, or vegetables), all from an English-language menu. No credit cards are accepted.

3–12–11 Hase. ✆ **0467/22-8694.** Main dishes ¥900. Thurs–Tues 11:30am–9pm (last order). Station: Hase (2 min.). On the slope leading to the entrance of Hase Temple, at the beginning on the left side.

SHOGUN COUNTRY: NIKKO ★★★

150km (93 miles) N of Tokyo

James Clavell's novel *Shogun* was fictional, but it was based on the life and times of Tokugawa Ieyasu, the powerful shogun of the 1600s who quashed all rebellions and unified Japan under his leadership. Tokugawa established such a military stronghold that his heirs continued to rule Japan for the next 250 years without serious challenge, making him one of the most important figures in Japanese history.

If you'd like to join the millions of Japanese who through the centuries have paid homage to this great leader, head north of Tokyo to Nikko, where **Toshogu Shrine ★★★** was constructed in his honor in the 17th century and where Tokugawa's remains were entombed in a mausoleum. Nikko means "sunlight"—an apt description of the way the sun's rays play upon this sumptuous shrine of wood and gold leaf. In fact, nothing else in Japan matches Toshogu Shrine for its opulence. Nearby is another mausoleum containing Tokugawa's grandson, as well as a temple, a shrine, and a garden. Surrounding the sacred grounds, known collectively as Nikko Sannai and designated a World Heritage Site by UNESCO in 1999, are thousands of majestic cedar trees in the 80,000-hectare (200,000-acre) **Nikko National Park ★★**. Another worthwhile sight is the **Nikko Tamozawa Imperial Villa ★★**, built in 1899.

I've included recommendations for an overnight stay. Otherwise, you can see Nikko in a very full day. Plan on 4 to 5 hours for round-trip transportation, 2½ hours to see Toshogu Shrine and vicinity, and 1 hour to see the imperial villa.

Essentials

GETTING THERE The fastest and most luxurious way to get to Nikko is on the Tobu Line's Limited Express **Spacia,** which departs every hour or more frequently from Tobu's Asakusa Station and offers free onboard Wi-Fi. The cost is ¥2,700 one-way for the 1-hour-and-50-minute trip. All seats are reserved, which means you are guaranteed a seat; if you're traveling on a holiday or a summer weekend, you may wish to purchase and reserve your ticket in advance. Otherwise, you can also reach Nikko on Tobu's slower **rapid train** from Asakusa, which costs ¥1,360 one-way and takes 2 hours and 10 minutes to 2½ hours depending on the train, with departures every hour or so until 10:40am and every 2 hours after that. There are no reserved seats, which means you might have to stand if trains are crowded. Make sure to board cars 5 and 6 at the back of the train, as train cars are separated at Shimo-Imaichi Station.

To save yourself the hassle of buying individual tickets, consider purchasing Tobu's 2-Day Nikko Pass, which provides round-trip train travel between Asakusa and Nikko via rapid train, unlimited bus travel in Nikko, and other discounts listed on its website. Cost of the pass, valid for 2 days, is ¥2,670 for adults and ¥1,340 for children; you can upgrade to the Limited Express Spacia for an extra charge. You can purchase the pass online at www.tobu.co.jp/foreign if you buy it at least 3 days before your trip, or at the **Tobu Sightseeing Service Center** at Tobu Asakusa Station (✆ **03/3841-2871**), open daily 7:20am to 7pm.

If you have a Japan Rail Pass, take the Tohoku Shinkansen bullet train from Tokyo Station to Utsunomiya (leaving every 20–40 min.; the trip takes about 50 min.), where you then change for the JR train to Nikko (45 min., with departures every hour or less).

VISITOR INFORMATION The **Tobu Sightseeing Service Center** (see above) stocks pamphlets on train schedules and sightseeing. In Nikko, you'll find the Tobu and JR stations located almost side by side in the village's downtown area. Inside Tobu Station is the **Nikko Tobu Station tourist information counter,** open daily 8:30am to 5pm, with staff who can give you a map, answer

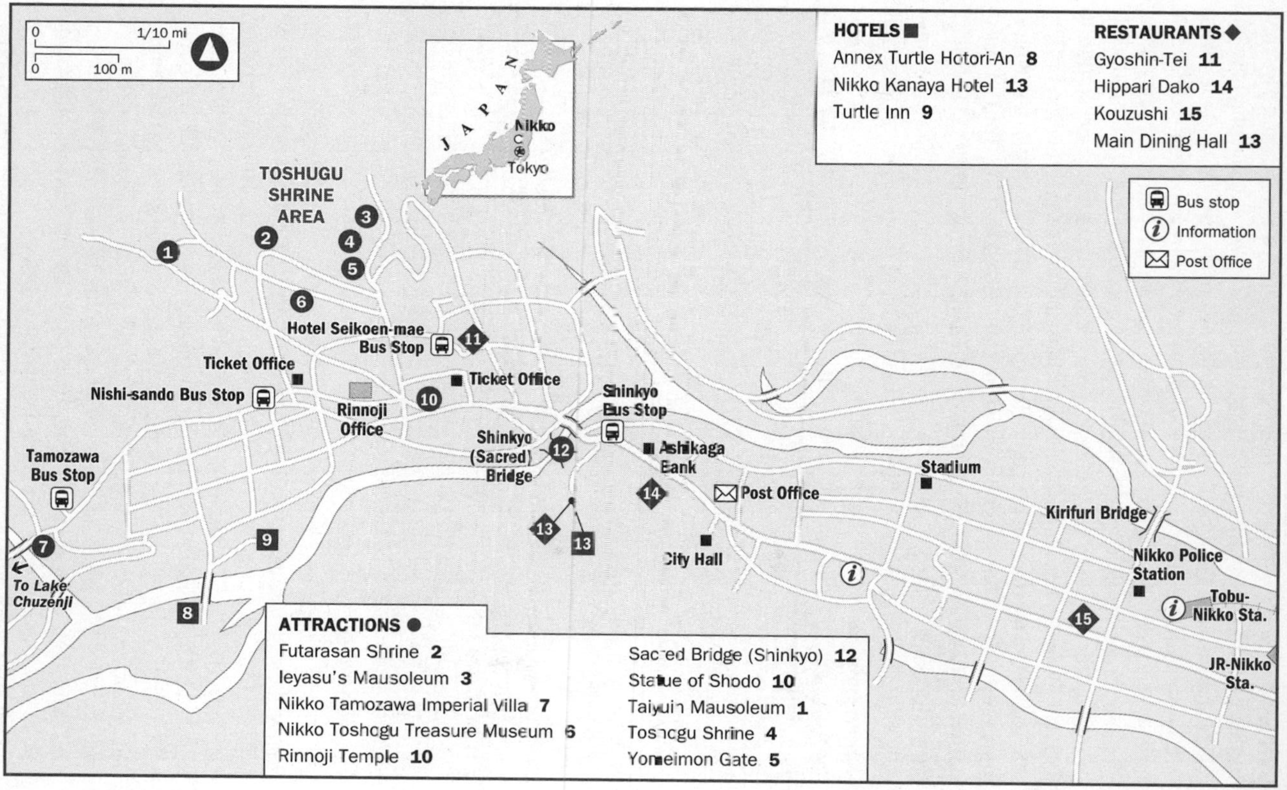

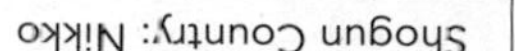

0 1/10 mi
0 100 m

JAPAN
Nikko
Tokyo

HOTELS ■
Annex Turtle Hotori-An **8**
Nikko Kanaya Hotel **13**
Turtle Inn **9**

RESTAURANTS ◆
Gyoshin-Tei **11**
Hippari Dako **14**
Kouzushi **15**
Main Dining Hall **13**

Bus stop
Information
Post Office

TOSHUGU SHRINE AREA
Hotel Seikoen-mae Bus Stop
Ticket Office
Nishi-sando Bus Stop
Rinnoji Office
Ticket Office
Shinkyo Bus Stop
Shinkyo (Sacred) Bridge
Ashikaga Bank
Post Office
City Hall
Stadium
Kirifuri Bridge
Nikko Police Station
Tobu-Nikko Sta.
JR-Nikko Sta.
Tamozawa Bus Stop
To Lake Chuzenji

ATTRACTIONS ●
Futarasan Shrine **2**
Ieyasu's Mausoleum **3**
Nikko Tamozawa Imperial Villa **7**
Nikko Toshogu Treasure Museum **6**
Rinnoji Temple **10**
Sacred Bridge (Shinkyo) **12**
Statue of Shodo **10**
Taiyuin Mausoleum **1**
Toshogu Shrine **4**
Yomeimon Gate **5**

basic questions, and point you in the right direction. If you arrive before noon, you can also leave your luggage here for delivery by 4pm to a limited list of area hotels and *ryokan* for ¥500 per bag. Next to the information counter in Tobu Station is the **Tourist Center** (daily 8:20am–5pm), where you can purchase bus tickets and entrance fees for Toshogu Shrine. You can also make reservations here for some 50 member hotels and *ryokan* for ¥540 per room; if you decide not to take a recommended room, however, you will be charged a ¥1,080 fee.

Another tourist office, the **Nikko Kyodo Center Tourist Information,** is located on the left side of the main road leading from the train station to Toshogu Shrine. It has English-speaking staff and lots of information in English, including information on public hot springs and hiking trails. Open daily from 9am to 5pm. For more information, call the **Nikko City Tourist Association** (**© 0288/22-1525**) or go to http://nikko-travel.jp/english.

GETTING AROUND Nikko Sannai with its Toshogu Shrine and other sights is on the edge of town, but you can walk there from the JR or Tobu train stations in about half an hour, passing souvenir shops and restaurants along the way. Head straight out the main exit, pass the bus stands, and then turn right. English-language signs point the way throughout town. Keep walking on this main road (you'll pass the Nikko Kyodo Center Tourist Information about halfway down on the left side) until you come to a T-intersection with a vermilion-colored bridge spanning a river to the left (about a 15-min. walk from the train stations). The stone steps opposite lead up the hill into the woods and to Toshogu Shrine in 15 minutes.

You can also travel to Nikko's attractions by bus. The World Heritage Bus travels from both the JR station (platform 1B) and Tobu station (platform 2B) to Shodo Shonin zo mae (near Rinnoji Temple; see below) for ¥310, or ¥500 for a day pass. There are also a confusing number of other passes, as well as regular buses that you can take to Shinkyo (a 7-min. ride; fare: ¥290), Omotesando (a 9-min. ride; fare: ¥290) and Tamozawa Imperial Villa (a 12-min. ride; fare: ¥300). Digital signboards at the front of buses announce stops in English. Still, I almost always walk.

Exploring Nikko

The first indication that you're nearing Nikko Sannai is the vermilion-painted **Sacred Bridge (Shinkyo)** arching over the rushing Daiyagawa River. It was built in 1636 for visiting shogun and their emissaries. Across the road from the Sacred Bridge, steps lead uphill into a forest of cedar where, after a 5-minute walk, you'll see a statue of **Shodo** (also spelled Shoto), a priest who founded Nikko 1,200 years ago when mountains were revered as gods. In the centuries that followed, Nikko became one of Japan's greatest mountain Buddhist retreats, with 500 subtemples spread through the area. Behind Shodo is the first major temple, Rinnoji Temple, with the other shrines and mausoleums spread past it underneath the verdant canopy of trees.

Toshogu Shrine and the other sights in Nikko Sannai are open daily from 8am to 5pm April through October (to 4pm the rest of the year); you must enter at least 30 minutes before closing time.

RINNOJI TEMPLE ★ This temple (✆ **0288/54-0531**) was founded by the priest Shodo in the 8th century, long before the Toshogu clan came onto the scene. Here you can visit **Sanbutsudo Hall,** a large building that enshrines three 8.4m-high (28-ft.) gold-plated wooden images of Buddha, considered the "gods of Nikko"; today people pray here for world peace. Admission is ¥400 adults, ¥200 children. (***Note:*** Sanbutsudo is undergoing restoration until 2021, but you can still see inside.) A combination ticket for both Rinnoji and Taiyuin Mausoleum (see below) is ¥900 and ¥400, respectively. Perhaps the best thing to see at Rinnoji Temple is **Shoyo-en Garden** (opposite Sanbutsudo Hall), which costs ¥300 extra for adults and ¥100 for children. Completed in 1815 and typical of Japanese landscaped gardens of the Edo Period, this small strolling garden provides a different vista with each turn of the path, making it seem much larger than it is. Your ticket to the garden also gains entrance to a small treasure house, where relics are displayed. The nearest bus stop is Shodo Shonin zo mae.

TOSHOGU SHRINE ★★★ The most important and famous structure in Nikko is Toshogu Shrine (✆ **0288/54-0560**). When Ieyasu died in 1616 at the age of 75, his wish was to be enshrined in Nikko so that he could serve as a guardian against evil demons, who were thought to come from the north, and thereby ensure the safety and long reign of the Tokugawa regime. Although Ieyasu requested a small shrine, Tokugawa's grandson (and third Tokugawa shogun), Tokugawa Iemitsu, replaced the modest 1616 shrine with this grand complex as an act of devotion. It seems that no expense was too great in creating the monument: It took some 4.5 million artisans and other workers 1½ years to erect a group of buildings more elaborate and gorgeous than any other Japanese temple or shrine. Rich in colors and carvings, Toshogu Shrine is gilded with 2.4 million sheets of gold leaf (they could cover an area of almost 2.4 ha/6 acres). The mausoleum was completed in 1636, almost 20 years after Ieyasu's death, and was most certainly meant to impress anyone who saw it as a demonstration of the Tokugawa shogunate's wealth and power. The shrine is set in a grove of magnificent ancient **Japanese cedars** planted over a 20-year period during the 1600s by a feudal lord named Matsudaira Masatsuna. Some 13,000 of the original trees still stand, adding a sense of dignity to the mausoleum and shrine.

You enter Toshogu Shrine via a flight of stairs that passes under a huge stone *torii* gateway, one of the largest in Japan. On your left is a five-story, 35m-high (115-ft.) **pagoda.** Although normally found only at temples, this pagoda is just one example of how Buddhism and Shintoism are combined at Toshogu Shrine. After climbing a second flight of stairs, turn left and you'll see the **Sacred Stable,** which houses a sacred white horse. Horses have long been dedicated to Shinto gods and are kept at shrines. Shrines also kept monkeys as well, since they were thought to protect horses from disease; look for the three monkeys carved above the stable door, fixed in the poses of "see no evil, hear no evil, speak no evil." Across from the stable is **Kami-Jinko,** famous for its carving by Kano Tanyu, who painted the images of the two elephants (under the eaves) after reading about them but without seeing what they actually looked like.

The central showpiece of Nikko is **Yomeimon Gate,** popularly known as the Twilight Gate, implying that it could take you all day (until twilight) to see everything carved on it. Painted in red, blue, and green, and gilded and lacquered, this gate is carved with more than 500 flowers, dragons, birds, and other animals. It's almost too much to take in at once and is very un-Japanese in its opulence, having more in common with Chinese architecture than with the usual austerity of most Japanese shrines.

Be sure to enter the shrine's main sanctuary, **Hai-den,** comprising three halls: One was reserved for the imperial family, one for the shogun, and one (the central hall) for conducting ceremonies. You can buy good-luck charms here that will guard against such misfortunes as traffic accidents, or that will ensure good health, success in business, easy childbirth, or other achievements in daily life. To the right of the main hall is the entrance to **Tokugawa Ieyasu's mausoleum,** where there's a carving of a sleeping cat above the door, dating from the Edo Period and famous today as a symbol of Nikko (you'll find many reproductions in area souvenir shops). Beyond that are 200 stone steps leading past cedars to Tokugawa's tomb. After the riotous colors of the shrine, the tomb seems surprisingly simple.

On the way out you'll pass **Yakushido,** famous for the dragon painting on the ceiling. A monk gives a brief explanation (in Japanese) and demonstrates how two sticks struck together produce an echo that supposedly resonates like a bell. Twelve statues here represent the Chinese zodiac calendar.

Admission to Toshogu Shrine is ¥1,300 for adults and ¥450 for children.

FUTARASAN SHRINE ★ Directly to the west of Toshogu Shrine is Futarasan Shrine (✆ **0288/54-0535**), one of the oldest buildings in the district (ca. 1617), which has a pleasant garden and is dedicated to the gods of mountains surrounding Nikko. The miniature shrines here are dedicated to the god of fortune, god of happiness, god of trees, god of water, and god of good marriages. On the shrine's grounds is the so-called **ghost lantern,** enclosed in a small vermilion-colored wooden structure. According to legend, it used to come alive at night and sweep around Nikko in the form of a ghost. It apparently scared one guard so much that he struck it with his sword 70 times; the marks are still visible on the lamp's rim. Entrance is ¥200 for adults, ¥100 for children.

TAIYUIN MAUSOLEUM ★★ Past Futarasan Shrine is **Taiyuin Mausoleum (✆ 0288/53-1567)**, the final resting place of Iemitsu, the third Tokugawa shogun (look for his statue). Completed in 1653, it's not nearly as large as Toshogu Shrine, but it's ornate and serenely elegant nevertheless. To show respect for the first shogun, Taiyuin's buildings face Toshogu Shrine. Tourists usually bypass this shrine, making it a pleasant last stop on your tour of Nikko Sannai. If you didn't buy a combination ticket with Rinnoji Temple, admission here is ¥550 for adults, ¥250 for children. The nearest bus stop is Taiyun Temple-Futarasan Shrine.

NIKKO TAMOZAWA IMPERIAL VILLA (TAMOZAWA GOYOUTEI KINEN KOEN) ★★★ If you haven't seen the Imperial villas of Kyoto (which require advance planning), this villa, at 8–27 Honcho (✆ **0288/53-6767**), is a great alternative. It's not as old, having been built in 1899 for Prince Yoshihito (who later became the Taisho emperor), and so painstakingly restored that it looks brand-new. It is the largest wooden Imperial villa of its era, with 106 rooms, 37 of which are open to the public. In addition, the central core of the villa is actually much older, constructed in 1632 by a feudal lord and brought to Nikko from Edo (present-day Tokyo). Altogether, three emperors and three princes used the villa between 1899 and 1947. A self-guided tour of the villa provides insight into traditional Japanese architectural methods—from its 11 layers of paper-plastered walls to its nail-less wood framing—as well as the lifestyle of Japan's aristocracy. If you have time, an audio guide (¥200) covers 20 stops along the way in about an hour. Be sure to also see the small outdoor garden. Admission is ¥510 for adults, ¥250 for children. Open Wednesday to Monday 9am to 5pm (to 4:30pm Nov–Mar). You must enter by 4pm. It's about a 20-minute walk from Nikko Sannai, or take the bus to Tamozawa stop.

Where to Eat

In addition to rainbow trout, Nikko is famous for *yuba,* a high-protein soy by-product formed by boiling soy milk, which causes a thin film to rise to the liquid's surface. Thought to have originated in Kyoto, it was popular among monks training at Rinnoji Temple for its nutrition, meatlike protein, and light weight for carrying on mountain retreats. Only priests and members of the imperial family were allowed to consume it until the Meiji Period. Now you can enjoy it, too, at many restaurants in Nikko. Another popular dish is *Mizu-yokan,* a traditional sweet made from the Azuki bean.

Gyoshin-Tei (堯心亭) ★★★ VEGETARIAN/KAISEKI This lovely Japanese restaurant, with a simple tatami room and a view of pines, moss, and bonsai, serves two kinds of set meals—*kaiseki* and Buddhist vegetarian cuisine (Shojin Ryori)—both of which change monthly and include the local soy specialty, *yuba.* Another restaurant in the parklike setting under the same management is **Meiji-no-Yakata.** Occupying a stone house built more than 110 years ago as the private retreat of an American businessman and little changed since then, it serves Western food such as grilled rainbow trout, veal cutlet, and steak, as well as multi-course meals starting at ¥4,000. It's open daily from 11am (11:30am in winter) to 7:30pm (last order). The drawback to these restaurants: They're harder to find than my other recommendations, but only a 4-minute walk northeast of Rinnoji Temple, on the other side of a parking lot.

2339–1 Sannai. ✆ **0288/53-3751.** Vegetarian/*kaiseki* meals ¥3,800–¥5,500; set lunch ¥3,000. Fri–Wed 11am–7pm (from 11:30am in winter). A 25-min. walk from Nikko Tobu Station, or the World Heritage Bus to the Hotel Seikoen stop.

Hippari Dako (ひっぱり凧) ★ VARIED JAPANESE This tiny, three-table establishment offers a limited selection of noodle dishes, including ramen and stir-fried noodles with vegetables, as well as *yakitori* (skewered barbecued chicken), *gyoza* (dumplings), and vegetarian dishes that include *yuba.* There's an English-language menu complete with photos, and the walls and ceiling are covered with business cards and messages left by travelers from around the world. Cash only.

1011 Kami-Hatsuishi. ✆ **0288/53-2933.** Main dishes average ¥1,000. Mon–Sat noon–5pm and 6:30–9pm. A 15-min. walk from the station, on the left side of the main street leading to Nikko Sannai, 1 min. before the Sacred Bridge; or by bus to the Shinkyo stop.

Kouzushi (晃寿司) SUSHI/YUBA Although it looks so new it might have opened yesterday, this restaurant has been serving its own secret recipe for *yuba* for generations, with ordering made easy by an English menu complete with pictures. Although a dish of delicious *yuba* is just ¥650 and you can order any number of sushi and sashimi platters, I recommend the special set for ¥2,800 that includes *yuba,* sushi, sashimi, soup, and seasonal dishes. It's easy to find, on Nikko's main street not far from the station.

9–1 Matsubara-cho. ✆ **0288/54-0752.** Set meals ¥1,200–¥2,800. Daily 11am–9pm (last order). Closed occasionally Wed or Thurs. A 3-min. walk from the station, on the right side of the main street.

Main Dining Hall ★★★ CONTINENTAL Even if you don't spend the night here, the Kanaya Hotel's quaint dining hall with its colorful wood-carved pillars is a great place for lunch. I suggest Nikko's specialty: locally caught rainbow trout available three ways. I always order mine cooked Kanaya style—covered with soy sauce, sugar, and sake, grilled, and served whole. The best bargain is the set lunch, available until 3pm, which comes with soup, salad, a main dish (such as veal cutlet cordon bleu), bread or rice, and dessert. Steak, lobster, chicken, and other Western fare are also listed on the English-language menu. At the entrance is a table where original table-ware, silver teapots, and other items from long ago are displayed; in any other country, they'd surely be locked behind glass. In another nod to the past, a chime announces when the restaurant opens for dinner.

Nikko Kanaya Hotel, 1300 Kami-Hatsuishi. ✆ **0288/54-0001.** Main dishes ¥2,970–¥12,474; set lunches ¥3,600–¥10,800; set dinner ¥11,340. Daily 11:30am–2:30pm and 6–8pm (last order). A 20-min. walk from Nikko Tobu Station; or by bus to the Shinkyo stop.

Where to Stay

If it's peak season (mid-March through Golden Week, Aug, Oct–Nov.) or a weekend, it's best to reserve a room in advance.

Annex Turtle Hotori-An ★★ Owned by the friendly family that runs Turtle Inn (below), this is one of my favorite places to stay in Nikko. One dip in the hot-spring bath overlooking the Daiyagawa River (which you can lock for privacy) will tell you why; at night, you're lulled to sleep by the sound of the rushing waters. A simple but spotless modern structure (all nonsmoking), it's located in a nice rural setting on a quiet street with a few other houses; an adjoining park and playground make it an excellent choice for families. All rooms except one are Japanese style. The plentiful Western-style breakfast costs ¥1,000 in the pleasant living area/dining room. For dinner, you can go to the nearby Turtle Inn (available only Sat; reservations should be made the day before). There's also a communal refrigerator where you can store food.

8–28 Takumi-cho. www.turtle-nikko.com. ✆ **0288/53-3663.** 11 units. ¥6,500–¥6,900 single; ¥12,600–¥14,800 double. Bus: From Nikko Station to the Sogo Kaikan-mae stop, a 7-min. ride; then a 10-min. walk. **Amenities:** Wi-Fi.

Nikko Kanaya Hotel ★★★ Founded in 1873 as Nikko's first hotel (until then, visitors stayed in area temples), this distinguished-looking place on a hill above the Sacred Bridge combines the rustic heartiness of a European country lodge with elements of old Japan. The present complex, built in spurts over the past 145-some years, has a rambling, delightfully old-fashioned atmosphere that fuses Western architecture with Japanese craftsmanship. Through the decades it has played host to a number of VIPs, from Charles Lindbergh to Indira Gandhi to Shirley MacLaine; Frank Lloyd Wright left a sketch for the bar fireplace, which was later built to his design. Even if you don't stay here, you might want to drop by for lunch and gaze at the old photos lining the hallways. Pathways lead to the Daiyagawa River and several short hiking trails. All rooms are Western-style twins, with the differences in price based on room size, view (river view is best), and facilities. Some 10 rooms have been updated, but I prefer the older, simpler rooms because they have more character; some have antiques and claw-foot tubs. The best (and priciest) room is the annex corner room in the 80-year-old wing where the emperor once stayed.

1300 Kami-Hatsuishi. www.kanayahotel.co.jp. ✆ **0288/54-0001.** 70 units. ¥17,820–¥60,000 single or double. Bus: From Nikko Tobu Station to the Shinkyo stop, a 5-min. ride. On foot: 17 min. from Nikko Tobu Station. **Amenities:** 2 restaurants, including the Main Dining Hall (see review); cafe; bar; small outdoor heated pool (mid-July to Aug only); outdoor skating rink (Dec–Feb, free for guests, including shoes); shuttle bus from Tobu Nikko Station 3–4 times a day; Wi-Fi.

Turtle Inn ★ This excellent, nonsmoking pension is within walking distance of Nikko Sannai in a newer two-story house (recently painted a bright orange) on a quiet side street beside the Daiyagawa River. The friendly owner, Mr. Fukuda, speaks English and is helpful in planning a sightseeing itinerary. Rooms are bright and cheerful in both Japanese and Western styles; the five tatami rooms are without private bathroom, but there are hot-spring baths. Excellent Japanese dinners served Saturdays only on local Mashiko pottery are available for ¥2,000 if you order a day in advance, as are Western breakfasts for ¥1,000.

2–16 Takumi-cho. www.turtle-nikko.com. ✆ **0288/53-3168.** 10 units (3 with bathroom). ¥4,750–¥6,000 single without bathroom, ¥5,800–¥6,200 single with bathroom; ¥9,200–¥10,400 double without bathroom, ¥9,900–¥11,700 double with bathroom. Bus: From Nikko Station to the Sogo Kaikan-mae stop, a 7-min. ride; then a 5-min. walk. **Amenities:** Wi-Fi.

HAKONE ★★★

97km (60 miles) SW of Tokyo

Part of **Fuji-Hakone-Izu National Park,** Hakone is one of the closest and most popular weekend destinations for residents of Tokyo. Beautiful Hakone has about everything a vacationer could wish for: hot-spring resorts, mountains, lakes, breathtaking views of Mount Fuji when the weather is clear (mostly in cooler months), and interesting historical sites. Although you can conceivably tour Hakone on a day trip if you leave very early in the morning and limit your sightseeing to a few key attractions, adding an overnight stay or two—either roundtrip from Tokyo or as a stopover between Tokyo and Kyoto, coupled with a soak in a hot-spring tub—is much more rewarding. If you can, travel on a weekday, when modes of transportation are likely to be less crowded. Some hotels offer cheaper weekday rates in the off season.

Essentials

GETTING THERE & GETTING AROUND Getting to and around Hakone is half the fun! An easy loop tour you can follow through Hakone includes various forms of unique transportation: Starting out by train from Tokyo, you switch to a three-car mountain railway that zigzags up the mountain, then change to a cable car, and then to a smaller ropeway, and end your trip with a boat ride across Lake Ashi, stopping to see major attractions along the way. From Lake Ashi (that is, from the villages of Togendai, Hakone-machi, or Moto-Hakone), you then take a bus to Odawara Station (an hour's ride), where you board the train back to Tokyo. Buses also connect all the recommendations listed below, which is useful if you wish to complete part of your sightseeing the first day before going to your hotel for the evening. A bus also runs directly between Togendai and Shinjuku in about 2¼ hours.

The most economical and by far easiest way to travel is Odakyu Railway's **Hakone Free Pass,** which, despite its name, isn't free but does give you a round-trip ticket on the express train from Shinjuku Station to Odawara or Hakone-Yumoto and includes all modes of transportation in Hakone listed above and described below. The pass lets you avoid the hassle of buying individual tickets and gives nominal discounts on most Hakone attractions. A 2-day pass costs ¥5,140 and a 3-day pass is ¥5,640. Children pay ¥1,500 and ¥1,750, respectively.

The trip from Shinjuku to Odawara via Odakyu Express takes 100 minutes, with departures two to four times an hour. In Odawara, you then transfer to another train for a 15-minute trip to Hakone-Yumoto. If time is of the essence or if you want to ensure a seat during peak season, reserve a seat on the faster and more luxurious **Odakyu Romance Car,** which offers free onboard Wi-Fi; it travels from Shinjuku all the way to Hakone-Yumoto in 85 minutes, and costs an extra ¥890 one-way with a Hakone Pass.

If you have a **Japan Rail Pass,** you should take the Shinkansen bullet train first to Odawara (not all bullet trains stop here, so make sure yours does). From there, you can buy a 2-day Hakone Free Pass for ¥4,000 or a 3-day Pass for ¥4,500. Children pay ¥1,000 and ¥1,250, respectively. This is also a good option if you are traveling onward to, say, Kyoto.

All passes described above can be purchased at any station of the Odakyu Railway, including Shinjuku, Odawara, and Hakone-Yumoto. In Tokyo, the **Odakyu Sightseeing Service Center,** located on the ground floor near the

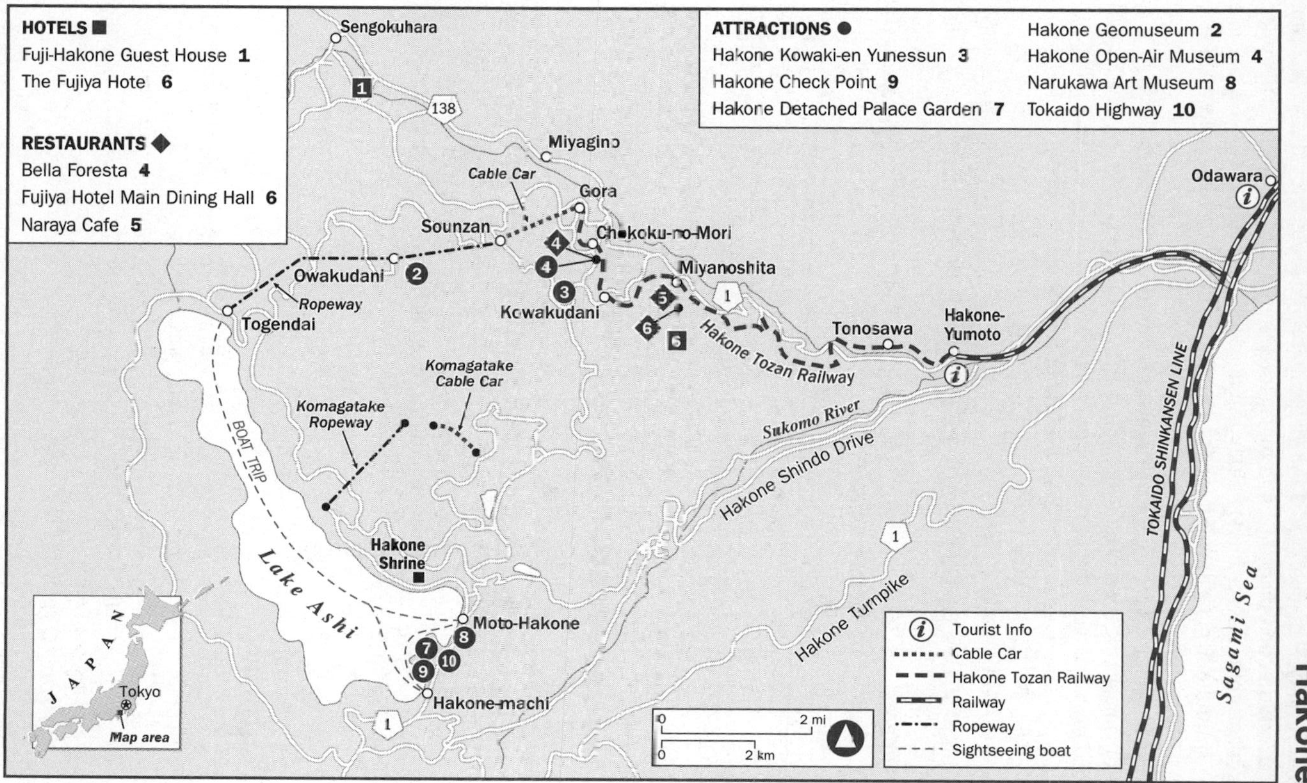
HOTELS ■
Fuji-Hakone Guest House 1
The Fujiya Hote 6
RESTAURANTS ◆
Bella Foresta 4
Fujiya Hotel Main Dining Hall 6
Naraya Cafe 5
ATTRACTIONS ●
Hakone Kowaki-en Yunessun 3
Hakone Check Point 9
Hakone Detached Palace Garden 7
Hakone Geomuseum 2
Hakone Open-Air Museum 4
Narukawa Art Museum 8
Tokaido Highway 10
Sengokuhara
138
Miyagino
Cable Car
Gora
Sounzan
Chokoku-no-Mori
Miyanoshita
Owakudani
Ropeway
Togendai
Kowakudani
1
Tonosawa
Hakone-Yumoto
Hakone Tozan Railway
Odawara
Komagatake Cable Car
Komagatake Ropeway
BOAT TRIP
Sukomo River
Hakone Shindo Drive
TOKAIDO SHINKANSEN LINE
Hakone Shrine
Lake Ashi
Moto-Hakone
Hakone-machi
Hakone Turnpike
Sagami Sea
JAPAN
Tokyo
Map area
0
2 mi
2 km
Tourist Info
Cable Car
Hakone Tozan Railway
Railway
Ropeway
Sightseeing boat

west exit of Odakyu Shinjuku Station (www.odakyu.jp/english; (© **03/5321-7887;** daily 8am–6pm), sells the Hakone Free Pass and provides sightseeing information and maps in English. Next to the Service Center is a Travelex counter for changing money and a luggage storage facility.

In addition to the different modes of transportation described below, Hakone has a very efficient bus network (included in the Free Pass), with lines conveniently identified by a letter that is also on the front of the bus. The Togendai (T) Line is the most useful, traveling between Togendai and Odawara and making stops near the three accommodations recommended below. Pick up the excellent route map for **Hakone Tozan Bus** (www.hakone-tozanbus.co.jp; © **0465-35-1271**) at the Odawara or Yumoto tourist office.

VISITOR INFORMATION In addition to the Odakyu Sightseeing Service Center, there's the **Odawara Tourist Office** (© **0465-22-2339;** daily 9am–5pm) inside Odawara Station and the **Yumoto Tourist Office** (© **0460/85-5700;** daily 8:30am–4:30pm) inside Hakone-Yumoto Station. You can make hotel and *ryokan* reservations here. Information on Hakone is also available at www.hakone.or.jp.

LUGGAGE If you plan to return to Tokyo, I suggest you leave your luggage in storage at your Tokyo hotel or in Shinjuku Station and travel to Hakone with only an overnight bag. If you're heading onward to, say, Kyoto, you can leave your bags at Odawara Station's **Yamato Luggage** (© **080/7776-3514;** open daily 9am–8pm) for ¥500 per piece per day; or you can have it sent to your Hakone hotel if you deliver it by 12:30pm (around ¥1,350). I find luggage service better at Hakone-Yumoto Station, however, because it's smaller and cheaper. You'll find its **Left Luggage** check-in counter outside the ticket gate and up the escalator, open daily 8am to 10pm (storing a large bag costs ¥510 per day). Or, if you deliver your bags to the **Hakone Baggage Service** (© **0460/86-4140**), located just ahead after getting off the train at Hakone-Yumoto Station, between 8:30am and 12:30pm, it will transport your bags to your Hakone accommodations by 3pm. The next day, it can also pick up your bags at your hotel by 10am and deliver them to Hakone-Yumoto Station by 1pm, where they will keep them until 7pm. This service costs ¥800 to ¥1,100 per bag, depending on size and weight; a ¥100 discount is provided for holders of the Hakone Free Pass.

Exploring Hakone

If you plan on spending only a day in Hakone, you should leave Tokyo very early in the morning and plan on seeing only a few key attractions. I recommend the **Hakone Open-Air Museum** and **Owakudani.** Keep in mind that it takes about 5 hours to travel the loop from Odawara and that the ropeway and sightseeing boat, as well as museums, close around 5pm.

But if you're spending the night—and I strongly urge that you do—you can arrange your itinerary in a more leisurely fashion and devote more time to Hakone's attractions. You may wish to travel only as far as your hotel the first day, stopping at sights along the way. The next day you could continue with the rest of the circuit through Hakone. Or, head straight to your accommodation in the afternoon and then do your sightseeing the next day. Finally, if it's a clear day and there's a chance Mt. Fuji is visible, you might want to do the following tour in reverse to make sure you get to Hakone-machi in the morning—clouds sometimes cloak the mountain by afternoon.

SCENIC RAILWAY TO GORA Regardless of whether you travel via the Odakyu Romance Car or the ordinary Odakyu express, you'll end up at Hakone-Yumoto Station. Here you'll transfer to the **Hakone Tozan Railway** (www.hakone-tozan.co.jp; ✆ **0465-32-6823**), in operation since 1919. This delightful mountain-climbing, three-car electric train winds its way through forests and over streams and ravines as it travels upward to Gora, making several switchbacks along the way. The entire trip from Hakone Yumoto Station to Gora takes only 40 minutes, but the ride through the mountains is beautiful—it's my favorite part of the whole journey. The railway, which runs every 15 to 20 minutes (less frequently 8–11pm), makes about a half-dozen stops before reaching Gora, including **Tonosawa** and **Miyanoshita,** two hot-spring spa resorts with a number of old *ryokan* and hotels. Some of the *ryokan* date back several centuries, to the days when they were on the main thoroughfare to Edo, called the old Tokaido Highway. Miyanoshita is the best place for lunch. See "Where to Eat" and "Where to Stay," later.

For relaxing hot-spring bathing en route, visit **Hakone Kowaki-en Yunessun ★★** (www.yunessun.com; ✆ **0460/82-4126**). To reach it, disembark from the Hakone Tozan Railway at Kowakudani and take a 15-minute taxi or bus ride (bus stop: Kowaki-en). This self-described "Hot Springs Amusement Park" offers both indoor and outdoor family baths, which means you wear your bathing suit. In addition to indoor Turkish, Roman, and salt baths, there's also a children's play area with slides and a large outdoor area with a variety of small baths, including those mixed with healthy minerals and—I am not making this up—coffee, green tea, sake, or wine. For more traditional bathing, there's the **Mori No Yu,** with both indoor and outdoor baths separated for men and women (you don't wear your suit here). As with most public bathhouses, people with tattoos are not allowed. Most people stay 2 to 3 hours. Admission to Yunessun is ¥2,900 for adults and ¥1,600 for children. Admission to Mori No Yu is ¥1,900 and ¥1,200, respectively. Admission to both is ¥4100 and ¥2,100 (¥3,200 and ¥1,600 if you have a Hakone Free Pass). Upon admission, you'll be given a towel, robe, and wristband to pay for drinks and extras (rental suits are available), so you can leave all valuables in your assigned locker. Yunessun is open daily 9am to 7pm; Mori No Yu is open daily 11am to 8pm.

The most important stop on the Hakone Tozan Railway is the next-to-the-last one, Chokoku-no-Mori, where you'll find the famous **Hakone Open-Air Museum (Chokoku-no-Mori Bijutsukan) ★★★** (www.hakone-oam.or.jp; ✆ **0460/82-1161**), a minute's walk from the station. With the possible exception of views of Mount Fuji, this museum is, in my opinion, Hakone's number-one attraction. Using nature as a dramatic backdrop, it showcases sculpture primarily of the 20th century in a spectacular setting of glens, formal gardens, ponds, streams, and meadows. Some 400 sculptures are on display, both outdoors and in several buildings, with works by Carl Milles, Manzu Giacomo, Jean Dubuffet, Willem de Kooning, Barbara Hepworth, Taro Okamoto, and Joan Miró, and more than 25 pieces by Henry Moore, shown on a rotating basis. Several installations geared toward children allow them to climb and play. The Picasso Pavilion contains works by Picasso from pastels to ceramics, one of the world's largest collections. I could spend all day here; barring that, count on a visit of at least 2 hours. Be sure to stop off at the "foot *onsen,*" where you can immerse your tired feet in soothing, hot-spring water. The museum is open daily 9am to 5pm; admission is ¥1,600 adults, ¥1,200 university and high-school students, and ¥800 children (children free on Sat). Your Hakone Free Pass gives you a ¥200 discount.

BY CABLE CAR (FUNICULAR) TO SOUNZAN & ROPEWAY TO TOGENDAI Hakone Tozan cable cars leave Gora every 20 minutes or so and arrive 10 minutes later at the end station of Sounzan, making several stops along the way as they travel steeply uphill. From Sounzan, you board the **Hakone Ropeway** (www.hakoneropeway.co.jp) with gondolas for an 8-minute ride to **Owakudani ★**, the ropeway's highest point. You'll have to change gondolas here for the final stretch into Togendai, so you might as well stay for the views, including those of Mt. Fuji in winter. Owakudani means "Great Boiling Valley," and you'll soon understand how it got its name when you see (and smell) the sulfurous steam escaping from fissures in the rock, testament to the volcanic activity still present here (if you want to learn more, spend ¥100 to visit the small **Hakone Geomuseum** (www.hakone-geomuseum.jp; **✆ 0460-83-8140;** daily 9am–4pm). Most Japanese commemorate the trip by buying boiled eggs cooked here in the boiling waters. The ropeway continues another 16 minutes to Togendai, which lies beside Lake Ashi, known as Ashinoko in Japanese. Note that the ropeway stops running at around 5pm in summer and 4:15pm in winter.

ACROSS LAKE ASHI BY BOAT From Togendai you can take a **Hakone Sightseeing Cruise** (www.hakone-kankosen.co.jp; **✆ 0460-83-7722**) across Lake Ashi, which was formed by a volcanic eruption some 3,000 years ago. Believe it or not, the boats plying the waters are replicas of a man-of-war pirate ship. It takes about a half-hour to cross the lake to Hakone-machi (also called Hakonemachi-ko; *machi* means city and *ko* means lake) and Moto-Hakone, two resort towns right next to each other on the southern edge of the lake. This end of the lake affords the best view of Mount Fuji, one often depicted in tourist publications (mornings in cooler months offer the best chance to see this elusive beauty). Boats are in operation year-round, though they run less frequently in winter and not at all in stormy weather; the last boat departs around 5pm from the end of March to the end of November. If you miss it, buses connect Togendai with Odawara and Shinjuku.

After the boat ride, if you're heading back to Tokyo, buses depart for Hakone-Yumoto and Odawara near the boat piers in both Hakone-machi and

Moto-Hakone. Otherwise, for more sightseeing, get off the boat in Hakone-machi, turn left, and walk about 5 minutes along the town's main road, following the signs and turning left to **Hakone Check Point (Hakone Sekisho) ★★** (http://hakonesekisyo.jp; ✆ **0460/83-6635**), on a road lined with souvenir shops. This is a reconstructed checkpoint, originally built in 1619 and used until 1869 as one of many along the famous Tokaido Highway, which connected Edo (present-day Tokyo) with Kyoto. In feudal days, local lords, called *daimyo,* were required to spend alternate years in Edo; their wives were kept in Edo as virtual hostages to discourage the lords from planning rebellions while in their homelands. This was one of 53 checkpoints in Japan that guarded against the transport of guns, spies, and female travelers trying to flee Edo. Passes were necessary for travel, and although it was possible to sneak around it, male violators who were caught were promptly executed, while women suffered the indignity of having their heads shaven and then being given away to anyone who wanted them. Inside the reconstructed guardhouse, which was rebuilt on the site of the original checkpoint using traditional carpenter tools and architectural techniques of the Edo Period, you'll see life-size models reenacting scenes inside a checkpoint. Other reconstructions include soldiers' quarters, gates, stables, and a hilltop lookout. A small exhibition hall has displays relating to the Edo Period, including woodblock prints and photos of the old checkpoint and items used for travel, including a tiny abacus and an even smaller case holding grooming supplies. Open daily from 9am to 5pm (to 4:30pm Dec–Feb); admission is ¥500 for adults and ¥250 for children. Your Hakone Free Pass gives a ¥100 discount. It shouldn't take more than 20 minutes to see everything.

Just beyond the Hakone Check Point's exhibition hall, at the big parking lot with the traditional gate, is the **Hakone Detached Palace Garden (Onshi-Hakone-Koen) ★**, which lies on a small promontory on Lake Ashi and has spectacular views of the lake and, in clear weather, Mount Fuji. Originally part of an Imperial summer villa built in 1886 but destroyed by earthquake, the well-kept garden is free and open to the public and is a great place for wandering.

Just a 5-minute walk away is the neighboring resort town, **Moto-Hakone,** but you'll want to get there by crossing the highway for a shaded footpath lined with ancient and mighty cedars, once part of the old **Tokaido Highway.** During the Edo Period, more than 400 cedars were planted along this important road, which today stretches 2.5km (1½ miles) along the curve of Lake Ashi. Upon entering Moto-Hakone, up the hill to the right when you reach the orange *torii* gate, **Narukawa Art Museum ★★** (www.narukawamuseum.co.jp; ✆ **0460/83-6828**) offers both art and sweeping scenic views (look for the escalators to help you reach it). It specializes in modern works of the *Nihonga* style of painting, developed during the Heian Period (794–1185) and sparser than Western paintings (which tend to fill in backgrounds and every inch of canvas). Large paintings and screens by contemporary *Nihonga* artists are on display, from well-known artists to younger up-and-comers. I wouldn't miss it; views of Lake Ashi and Mount Fuji, especially from its tea lounge, are a bonus. Open daily 9am to 5pm; admission is ¥1,300 adults, ¥900 high-school and university students, and ¥600 children. The Hakone Free Pass gives a ¥200 discount.

WHEN YOU'RE DONE SIGHTSEEING FOR THE DAY Buses depart for Hakone-Yumoto and Odawara from both Hakone-machi and Moto-Hakone two to four times an hour. Be sure to check the time of the last departure; generally it's around 8pm, but this can change with the season and the day of the week. The trip from Moto-Hakone takes approximately 30 minutes to Hakone Yumoto and 50 minutes to Odawara, where you can catch the Odakyu train back to Shinjuku or the Shinkansen bullet train onward toward Kyoto.

Where to Stay & Eat

Most accommodations cost more during peak travel times like Golden Week, school holidays, New Year's, weekends and national holidays, and during cherry blossom season in spring and the changing of the leaves in autumn.

For casual dining, the Hakone Open-Air Museum has a pleasant restaurant, **Bella Foresta ★**, overlooking the park's fantastic scenery and offering a buffet lunch of mostly Western fare daily from 11am to 3pm for ¥1,980. There are also informal restaurants at the **Owakudani** Ropeway Station and **Togendai** boat cruise building, both with scenic views and serving curry rice and other fare for less than ¥1,400.

But my favorite place for a meal is the **Fujiya ★★★**, located in Hakone's grandest, oldest hotel (see "The Fujiya Hotel," below), serving French food and offering impressive views of the Hakone hills. This main dining hall, dating from 1930, is bright and cheerful, with a high, intricately detailed ceiling, large windows with Japanese screens, a wooden floor, and white tablecloths. Oddly enough, it's famous for its curry, but other options include rainbow trout, sirloin steak, and set lunches. Afterward, be sure to tour the landscaped garden, because that's one of the reasons you're here. ***Note:*** The Fujiya Hotel is scheduled for renovation, with an expected reopening in early 2020; check the hotel website for an update.

Otherwise, just minutes' walk from Miyanoshita Station, the cute **Naraya Café ★** (**✆ 0460/82-1259**) feels like a mountain lodge. It offers coffee, tea, beer, desserts, and a limited selection of pizzas, hot dogs, and soups, but my favorite part is the outdoor terrace complete with a table over a footbath so you can soak your feet while you eat. It's open 10:30am to 6pm (to 5pm Dec–Feb); closed Wednesday and the fourth Thursday of every month.

Fuji-Hakone Guest House ★★ It's not on the circuitous route detailed above, but this family-owned Japanese inn has been welcoming foreign guests since 1984 and offers inexpensive, spotlessly clean lodging in tatami rooms, all nonsmoking, in two buildings located side by side. Situated in tranquil surroundings set back from a tree-shaded road, it's run by a couple who speak good English and go out of their way to provide sightseeing information, bus schedules, and a map marked with area restaurants and attractions, including many art museums. In fact, if you stay here, you may well be tempted to stay

2 nights. Four hot-spring baths can be reserved for private use, including an outdoor bath (extra ¥500 charge). The best rooms are in the annex, with room no. 6 facing woods and a stream and room no. 7 big enough for three or four people. If this inn is full, the Takahashi family also owns the **Moto-Hakone Guest House,** across Lake Ashi.

912 Sengokuhara, Hakone. www.fujihakone.com. ✆ **0460/84-6577.** 15 units (none with private bathroom). ¥5,000–¥6,000 single; ¥10,000–¥12,000 double; ¥15,000–¥18,000 triple. Rates exclude taxes. Peak season and Sat–Sun ¥1,080–¥2,160 extra. Minimum 2-night stay preferred. Western buffet breakfast ¥810 extra. Bus: Hakone Tozan T (included in the Hakone Free Pass) from Togendai (10 min.) or from Odawara Station (50 min.) to the Senkyoro-mae stop (announced in English), and then a 1-min. walk (there are also direct buses from Shinjuku and Haneda airport). **Amenities:** Hot-spring bath; Wi-Fi.

The Fujiya Hotel ★★★ The Fujiya, established in 1878, is quite simply the grandest, most majestic old hotel in Hakone; indeed, it might be the loveliest historic hotel in Japan. (***Note:*** The Fujiya is closed for renovations to upgrade its earthquake reinforcements, with an expected reopening in early 2020; check website for updates.) I love this hotel for its comfortably old-fashioned atmosphere, including such Asian touches as a Japanese-style roof and long wooden corridors with photographs of famous guests, from Einstein to Eisenhower. A landscaped garden out back, with a waterfall, pond, greenhouse, outdoor pool, and stunning views over the valley, is great for strolls and meditation. There's also an indoor thermal pool and public hot-spring baths (hot-spring water is piped in to each guest's bathroom). Even if you don't stay here, come for a meal or tea. There are five separate buildings, all different and added on at various times in the hotel's long history, but management has been meticulous in retaining its historic traditions. Rooms are old-fashioned and spacious with high ceilings and antique furnishings. The most expensive rooms are the largest, but my favorites are those in the Flower Palace—it's got an architectural style reminiscent of a Japanese temple and seems unchanged since its 1936 construction.

359 Miyanoshita, Hakone. www.fujiyahotel.jp. ✆ **0460/82-2211.** 146 units. Check website for rates. Station: Miyanoshita (Hakone Tozan Railway; 5 min.). Bus: From Odawara, Hakone-Yumoto, Moto-Hakone, Hakone-Machi or Togendai to Miyanoshita Onsen stop (1 min.). **Amenities:** 3 restaurants; lounge; bar; hot-spring baths; Jacuzzi; indoor/outdoor pools; room service; sauna; Wi-Fi.

HIGHLIGHTS OF CHUBU

7

The terrain of the Chubu (central) region of Honshu varies dramatically, from rugged coastline to volcanic mountain ranges, including the **Japan Alps National Park (Chubu Sangaku Kokuritsu Koen).** With the exception of Japan's tallest peak, Mount Fuji, all of Japan's loftiest mountains are in Chubu. Some villages nestled in the Japan Alps retain much of their traditional architecture, especially in **Takayama** and **Shirakawa-go,** providing a unique look at mountain life both past and present. The former castle town of **Kanazawa** boasts one of Japan's most spectacular gardens and Edo-era attractions. See chapter 3 for a suggested itinerary for these three towns.

KANAZAWA, RENOWNED FOR ITS GARDEN & CRAFTS ★★

622km (386 miles) W of Tokyo; 224km (140 miles) NE of Kyoto

Near the northwest coast of Honshu on the Sea of Japan, Kanazawa is the gateway to the rugged, sea-swept Noto Peninsula. It was the second-largest city (after Kyoto) to escape bombing during World War II, and some of the old city has been left intact, including a district of former samurai mansions, old geisha quarters, temple towns, Edo-era canals, and tiny narrow streets that run crookedly without rhyme or reason (apparently to confuse any enemies foolish enough to attack). Kanazawa is most famous for its **Kenrokuen Garden,** one of the most celebrated gardens in all of Japan (and one of my favorites). It's the main reason people come here, though several fine museums are also worth the visit. Kanazawa is also renowned for its crafts dating from the shogun era.

Kanazawa first gained notoriety about 500 years ago, when a militant Buddhist sect joined with peasant rebels to overthrow the feudal lord and establish its own autonomous government, an event unprecedented in Japanese history. The independent republic survived almost 100 years before it was attacked by an army commanded by Oda Nobunaga, who was trying to unite Japan at a time when civil wars wracked the nation. Kanazawa was subsequently

Kanazawa

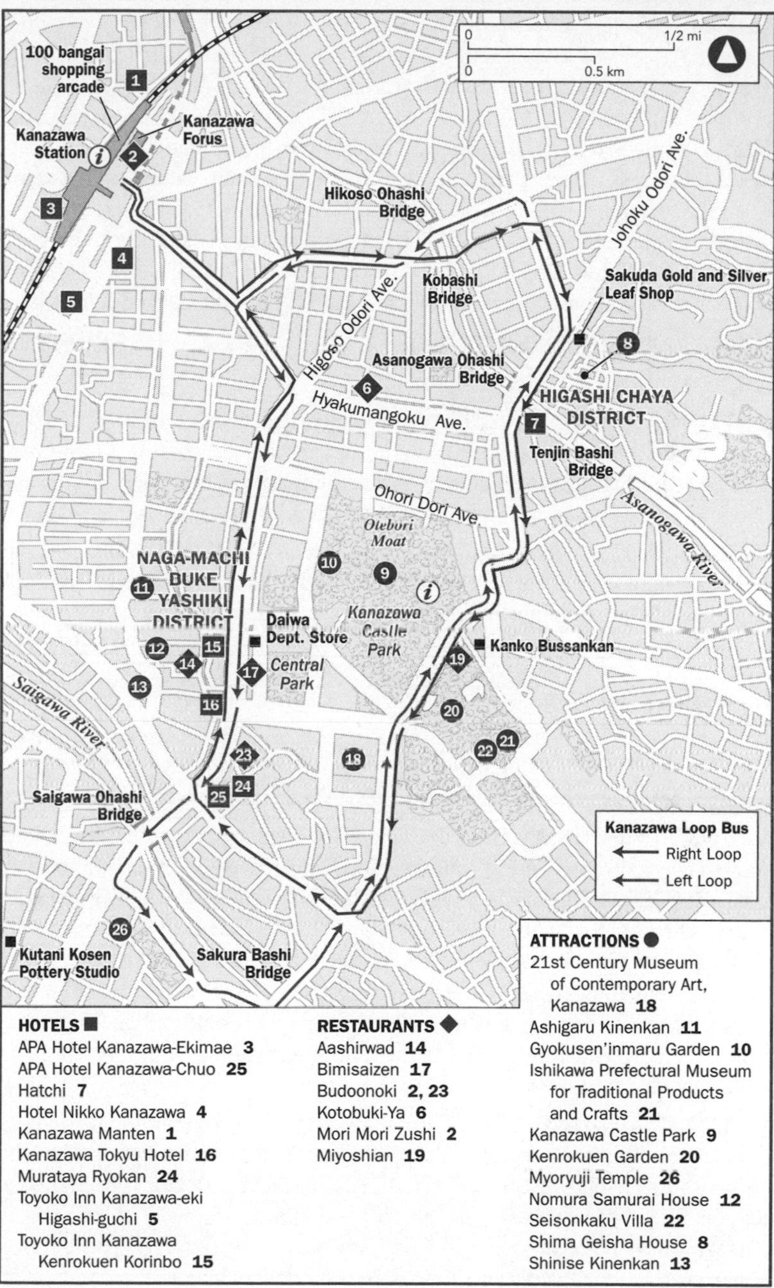
0 1/2 mi
0 0.5 km
100 bangai shopping arcade
Kanazawa Station
Kanazawa Forus
Hikoso Ohashi Bridge
Johoku Odori Ave.
Kobashi Bridge
Higoso Odori Ave.
Sakuda Gold and Silver Leaf Shop
Asanogawa Ohashi Bridge
Hyakumangoku Ave.
HIGASHI CHAYA DISTRICT
Tenjin Bashi Bridge
Ohori Dori Ave.
Asanogawa River
Oteburi Moat
NAGA-MACHI BUKE YASHIKI DISTRICT
Daiwa Dept. Store
Kanazawa Castle Park
Central Park
Kanko Bussankan
Saigawa River
Saigawa Ohashi Bridge
Kanazawa Loop Bus
Right Loop
Left Loop
Kutani Kosen Pottery Studio
Sakura Bashi Bridge
HOTELS
APA Hotel Kanazawa-Ekimae 3
APA Hotel Kanazawa-Chuo 25
Hatchi 7
Hotel Nikko Kanazawa 4
Kanazawa Manten 1
Kanazawa Tokyu Hotel 16
Murataya Ryokan 24
Toyoko Inn Kanazawa-eki Higashi-guchi 5
Toyoko Inn Kanazawa Kenrokuen Korinbo 15
RESTAURANTS
Aashirwad 14
Bimisaizen 17
Budoonoki 2, 23
Kotobuki-Ya 6
Mori Mori Zushi 2
Miyoshian 19
ATTRACTIONS
21st Century Museum of Contemporary Art, Kanazawa 18
Ashigaru Kinenkan 11
Gyokusen'inmaru Garden 10
Ishikawa Prefectural Museum for Traditional Products and Crafts 21
Kanazawa Castle Park 9
Kenrokuen Garden 20
Myoryuji Temple 26
Nomura Samurai House 12
Seisonkaku Villa 22
Shima Geisha House 8
Shinise Kinenkan 13

granted to one of Nobunaga's retainers, Maeda Toshiie, who built a castle and transformed the small community into a thriving castle town. The Maeda clan continued to rule over Kanazawa for the next 300 years, amassing wealth in land and rice and encouraging development of the arts. Throughout the Tokugawa shogunate, the Maedas remained the second-most powerful family in Japan and controlled the largest domain in the country. The arts of Kutani ware, Yuzen silk dyeing, lacquerware, and *Noh* theater flourished—and enjoy popularity in Kanazawa even today. In 2009 it was named Japan's first UNESCO Creative City of Crafts and Folk Art. Japan's fourth-largest city at the end of the Feudal Era, Kanazawa is today capital of Ishikawa Prefecture, with a population of 465,000. It gets 160 rainy days a year, inspiring a local proverb you'd be wise to heed: "Even if you forget your packed lunch, don't forget your umbrella."

Essentials

GETTING THERE **By Train** The **Hokuriku Shinkansen** from Tokyo takes about 2½ hours and costs ¥14,120 for an unreserved seat. From Osaka (via Kyoto), direct **JR trains** depart once or twice an hour; the ride takes 2 hours and 45 minutes and costs ¥7,130 for an unreserved seat.

By Bus **JR Highway** (www.jrbuskanto.co.jp; ✆ **03/3844-1950**) and **Willer Express** (http://willerxpress.com; ✆ **050/5805-0383**) buses offer multiple departures from Shinjuku, Tokyo, and Shibuya stations, with prices dependent on the month, day of the week, and, in the case of Willer, even the type of seat chosen. Both companies also run daytime and overnight buses between Osaka and Kanazawa. **Nohi** buses (www.nouhibus.co.jp; ✆ **0577/32-1688**) and **Hokutetsu** buses (www.highwaybus.com; ✆ **076/237-8004**) connect Kanazawa with Takayama (with a stop in Shirakawa-go) six times a day; reservations are required for most trips and the fare is ¥3,390 for the 2¼-hour trip.

VISITOR INFORMATION In Kanazawa Station near the Kenrokuen (east) Gate exit, the **Tourist Information Center** (www.kanazawa-tourism.com; ✆ **076/232-3993**), open daily 8:30am to 8pm (with English-speaking staff on hand 9:30am–7pm), can book hotel rooms and distributes maps, bus schedules, brochures, and the useful *Eye on Kanazawa* with tips on sightseeing. Adjacent counters sell 1-day bus passes (see below) and provide luggage delivery service to city hotels for ¥600 if dropped off before 3pm. The tourist office even offers umbrellas and rubber boots you can use during your stay in Kanazawa for free.

GETTING AROUND Kanazawa's attractions spread south and southeast from the station's Kenrokuen Gate exit. Katamachi and adjacent Korinbo, 3km (2 miles) southeast of the station, is Kanazawa's downtown. Sights are too far-flung to see everything on foot, so the easiest way to get around Kanazawa is by **bus.** Although there are many city buses departing from Kanazawa Station, dedicated tourist buses service major attractions, with departures every 15 to 20 minutes from about 8:30am to 6:48pm. The **Kanazawa Loop Bus,** departing from platform 7, makes a circular route in both directions to all the tourist sights (stops are announced in English). The **Kenrokuen Shuttle,** departing from platform 6, makes a shorter run to sights around Kenrokuen Garden. A single ride costs ¥200, and a 1-day pass, which also allows rides on city buses but must be purchased in advance, costs ¥500. Alternatively, if you have a Japan Rail Pass, you can ride for free on JR buses, which depart up to three times hourly from platform 4 and also go to major sights. Pick up maps and schedules at the tourist office.

[Fast FACTS] KANAZAWA

ATM/Mail The **Kanazawa Central Post Office,** 1–1 Sanja (✆ **076/224-3822**), is open Monday to Friday 9am to 9pm, but a counter remains open until midnight for mail. Its ATMs are open 12:05am to 11:55pm Monday through Saturday and 12:05am to 9pm on Sunday.

Wi-Fi/Internet Kanazawa offers free Wi-Fi in Kanazawa Station and various places around town, including shopping centers, museums, Kenrokuen Garden, and more; a map distributed by the tourist office shows locations.

Where to Stay

Keep in mind that some accommodations charge higher rates on Saturday and nights before public holidays. You'll also pay more during peak season—New Year's, Golden Week (Apr 29–May 5), and mid-July through mid-November. Low season is generally January through March.

Directions are from Kanazawa Station; minutes in parentheses indicate the walking time required from the bus stop.

EXPENSIVE

Hotel Nikko Kanazawa ★★★ Rising 30 stories high, Kanazawa's tallest building was designed by a Japanese-French team, who succeeded in giving it a boutique-hotel ambience despite its size. The lobby exudes a French Colonial drawing-room atmosphere, with groups of sofas and armchairs spread throughout for more intimacy and outfitted with Asian decorative art ranging from ginger jars to Japanese lacquered boxes. The English-speaking concierge staff receives high marks, and its location in front of Kanazawa Station connected by underground passageway can't be beat for convenience. The spacious rooms, from the 17th to 28th floors, reflect Kanazawa's craft heritage, with accents of Yuzen cloth, ceramics, and artwork trimmed with gold leaf created by local artisans. Twin rooms, which are larger, cost more than rooms with a double bed. On the highest floors are Luxe Rooms, which offer great views of either mountains or the Japan Sea in the distance.

2–15–1 Hon-machi. www.hnkanazawa.jp. ✆ **076/234-1111.** 254 units. ¥16,834–¥48,114 single or double. Station: Kanazawa (east exit, 1 min.). **Amenities:** 5 restaurants; 2 bars; 1 lounge; concierge; access to next-door health club and spa w/indoor pool (fee: ¥2,000); room service; Wi-Fi.

Kanazawa Tokyu Hotel ★★ This has been one of Kanazawa's most respected hotels for more than 30 years. It has a convenient downtown location surrounded by shops and restaurants, just minutes from the Naga-machi Samurai district and within walking distance of Kenrokuen Garden and Myoryuji Temple. Its design is contemporary Japanese, reflected in a lobby simply decorated in gold and black with splashes of red. Rooms are comfortably spacious, with local touches like Kutani pottery coffee cups or pine silhouettes stenciled on the walls.

2-1-1 Korinbo. www.kanazawa-h.tokyuhotels.co.jp. ✆ **076/231-2411.** 232 units. ¥8,940–¥30,888 single; ¥16,700–¥51,00 double. Loop Bus: Korinbo (1 min.). **Amenities:** 2 restaurants; bar; lounge; concierge; room service; Wi-Fi.

MODERATE

APA Hotel Kanazawa-Ekimae ★ Although a business hotel, this place does have a special feature that sets it apart: large public baths complete with sauna and open-air bath, free to hotel guests. Other pluses include a convenient location just steps from Kanazawa Station (but on the opposite side from where buses depart); bold use of bright colors—a welcome relief from the usual bland white of most business hotels—and a **Seattle's Best Coffee.** If you're not a fan of public baths, you might choose to stay elsewhere—rooms here are so minuscule that if you open your luggage you may have to leap to reach your bed (there are no closets). Double rooms, which have only one reading light beside the bed, are about right for one person, and twins provide barely enough room for two people to move about.

If you'd rather stay in the heart of the city, APA has three downtown hotels, including **APA Hotel Kanazawa-Chuo,** 1–5–24 Katamachi (✆ **076/235-2111**), which offers similar-size rooms at similar rates and a Seattle's Best Coffee, but the water tapped for its indoor and rooftop outdoor baths comes from hot springs.

1–9–28 Hirooka. www.apahotel.com. ✆ **076/231-8111.** 456 units. ¥5,900–¥19,900 single; ¥8,000–¥23,900 double. Station: Kanazawa (west exit, 1 min.). **Amenities:** 2 restaurants; bar; sauna; Wi-Fi.

Kanazawa Manten ★ A small fountain outside the entrance, a front desk backed by trees, jazz playing in the hotel restaurant, indoor/outdoor hot-spring baths, and attentive service all conspire to make this business hotel (located on the opposite side of the station from where the buses depart) seem more expensive than it is. Alas, the mostly single rooms (there are 141 twin rooms and 42 doubles) are no different or larger than those of any other business hotel, though window panels can be closed for complete darkness. Also, it has ladies' rooms with face steamers and women's toiletries. Couples might want to opt for twin rooms, which are larger than doubles but also more expensive. Ask for a room on a higher floor; those facing the station give views of trains coming and going. In short, cramped quarters reinforce the business-hotel status, but the lobby and baths make you feel grand.

1–6–1 Kita-yasue. www.manten-hotel.com. ✆ **076/265-0100.** 509 units. ¥6,000–¥8,900 single; ¥8,800–¥15,000 double. Prices exclude tax. Station: Kanazawa (west exit, 4 min.). Turn right out of the station and continue walking alongside the station, past the car park. **Amenities:** Restaurant; hot-spring baths w/Jacuzzi, sauna; Wi-Fi.

INEXPENSIVE

In addition to the recommendations here, Kanazawa has two **Toyoko Inns** (www.toyoko-inn.com), **Toyoko Inn Kanazawa-eki Higashi-guchi,** just a

4-minute walk from the east exit of Kanazawa Station, and **Toyoko Inn Kanazawa Kenrokuen Korinbo,** in the heart of the city.

Hatchi ★★ This is one of the best new hostels in Kanazawa. In addition to dormitory cubicles with curtains that can be closed for privacy (one dormitory room is for women only), it also has private rooms. Located near the Higashi Chaya former geisha district, it has a welcoming cafe/bar on its ground floor, local artwork in public places (like the Kutani pottery lampshades), a lounge, and a shared kitchen. Private rooms with sinks but no bathroom sleep up to three people, either on bunk beds or a double-size loft bed plus a sofa bed. The best room in the house is Japanese style with a private bathroom.

3–18 Hashiba. www.thesharehotels.com/hatchi. ✆ **076/256-1100.** 9 units (1 with private bathroom), 20 dormitory beds. ¥8,900–¥17,100 double; ¥2,755 dormitory bed. Loop Bus: Hashiba-cho (1 min.). **Amenities:** Cafe/bar; Wi-Fi.

Murataya Ryokan ★★ This Japanese-style inn, owned by generations of the friendly and caring Murata family for almost 70 years, is in the heart of Kanazawa, just off the Katamachi and Tatemachi shopping streets and within walking distance of Kenrokuen and Naga-machi Samurai district. Although the two-story structure is rather uninteresting from the outside, inside it's comfortable and pleasant, with a tiny courtyard moss garden containing a stone lantern; note the old-fashioned 60-plus-year-old telephone in the reception used to connect Murataya with the outside world. All rooms are clean and Japanese style with *tatami,* with extra long futon for tall foreigners. Note that there's no elevator, but two rooms on the ground floor come with a view of the garden. In addition to laundry facilities, a plus is the inn's own map of the Katamachi area, showing the locations of banks, post offices, stores, and restaurants.

1–5–2 Katamachi. www.murataya-ryokan.com. ✆ **076/263-0455.** 11 units (none with private bathroom). ¥5,700 single; ¥11,400 double. Loop Bus: Katamachi (3 min.). Take the small pedestrian lane on the left side of the APA Hotel (*not* the APA Villa) and then turn right. **Amenities:** Wi-Fi.

Where to Eat

Kanazawa's local specialties, known collectively as ***Kaga Ryori,*** consist of seafood such as tiny shrimp and winter crabs, as well as freshwater fish, duck, and mountain vegetables. Popular in winter is *jibuni,* a duck-and-vegetable stew.

All directions are from Kanazawa Station.

AROUND KANAZAWA STATION

Forus, a shopping center located next to Kanazawa Station (look for *Aeon* on its facade), has a slew of restaurants on its sixth floor, including Mori Mori Zushi and Budoonoki (see reviews below), as well as those serving noodles, *tonkatsu, okonomiyaki,* and Indian and Chinese fare. Most are open daily from 11am to 11pm.

Mori Mori Zushi (もりもり寿し) ★ SUSHI This hugely popular conveyor-belt sushi restaurant has colored plates, each signifying a specific price, but a touch panel at each seat with photos (as well as daily specials) lets you order what you want if it doesn't float past. There are spigots for hot water at the counter; serve yourself and add powdered tea. A more colorful branch at Omi-cho Market (✆ **076/262-7477**) is open daily 10am to 9pm.

Forus, 6th floor, 3–1 Horikawashinmachi. ✆ **076/265-3510.** Sushi platters ¥120–¥480. Daily 11am–9:30pm (last order). Station: Kanazawa (east exit, 1 min.). Turn left out of the station.

AROUND KENROKUEN GARDEN

Miyoshian (三芳庵) ★★ KAGA KAISEKI A great place to try the local *Kaga* cuisine right in Kenrokuen Garden, this century-old restaurant consists of two separate wooden buildings, the best of which is a traditional room extending over a large pond. This is where you'll probably dine, seated on *tatami* with a view of a waterfall and an ancient pond with giant carp swimming in the murky waters. Only set meals of *Kaga* cuisine are served, all featuring *jibuni.* The more expensive the meal, the more dishes it adds. The ¥1,500 *yugao* meal includes soup, *jibuni,* sashimi, a seasonal dish such as eel on rice, and pickles. The ¥3,000 *chakaisekifu* meal adds such dishes as salmon, crab, tofu, and various small delicacies. Lunch is served from 11am to 2:30pm, but you can also come just for green tea and sweets for ¥700. By the way, another hut, Uchihashitei, which extends over Kasumigaike Pond, also sells a set meal with *jibuni* for ¥2,800.

Kenrokuen Garden, 1–11 Kenrokumachi. ✆ **076/221-0127.** *Kaga teishoku* ¥1,500–¥3,000. Thurs–Tues 10am–4pm. Loop Bus or Kenrokuen Shuttle: Kenrokuen Garden (5 min.). In front of the park's Renchimon Gate.

KATAMACHI

Radiating around the downtown Katamachi and Korinbo shopping areas are lots of restaurants and drinking establishments.

Bimisaizen (美味彩膳) ★ TONKATSU/UDON NOODLES Easy to find in Daiwa department store and convenient for people who wish to dine in the middle in the afternoon, this casual eatery combines cuisine from two restaurants: *udon* from Tsuruhan and *tonkatsu* from Tazamura. In addition to a display case showing options, it also has an English menu. I opted for a set meal that included pork, shrimp, and cheese *tonkatsu,* which arrived crispy and flakey. But the best thing about dining here? The view over Central Park, with the woods of Castle Park rising beyond (avoid the noon rush, however).

Daiwa department store, 8th floor. 1-1-1 Korinbo. ✆ **076/222-0236.** Set meals ¥1,029¥1,600. Daily 11am–10pm. Loop Bus or Kenrokuen Shuttle: Korinbo (1 min.). In front of the bus stop.

Budoonoki ★ ITALIAN An informal eatery with a high ceiling and an open facade plus a few outdoor tables facing a courtyard, this pleasant restaurant offers a half-dozen pizzas, pastas (like crab pasta with garlic and leeks), and rice omelets (omelets filled with rice are popular in Japan); make it a meal by adding a salad and a drink. The weekday lunch specials are written only in

Japanese, so ask for a translation. A branch on the sixth floor of Forus next to Kanazawa Station (✆ **076/265-3521**) is open daily 11am to 11pm.

1–3–21 Katamachi. ✆ **076/232-7878.** Main dishes ¥1,080–¥1,380; weekday set lunches ¥980–¥1,280. Daily 11am–9:30pm (last order). Closed irregularly. Loop Bus: Katamachi (2 min.). In a small alley off Katamachi St. called Prego.

NAGA-MACHI SAMURAI DISTRICT

Aashirwad ★★ INDIAN/NEPALESE/VEGETARIAN You'll be met by a very welcoming Nepalese woman at this small but warm two-story restaurant. There's a lot to choose from, including tandoori chicken, *aloo sadeko* (a Nepalese potato dish made with spicy oil, black sesame, and coriander), various curries, and the restaurant's signature deep-fried eggplants stuffed with potatoes. Cash only.

1–4–59 Naga-machi. ✆ **076/231-262-2170.** Main dishes ¥900–¥1,300; set dinners ¥2,000–¥2,900; set lunches ¥850–¥1,000. Tues–Sun 11:30am–2:30pm and 5:30–9:30pm (last order). Loop Bus: Korinbo (3 min.). Take the side street that runs along the right side of the Tokyu Hotel, then turn right and walk beside the canal. It will be straight ahead, on the left.

ELSEWHERE

Kotobuki-Ya (壽屋) ★★★ VEGETARIAN Specializing in *shojin ryori kaiseki* meals (Buddhist vegetarian cooking), Kotobuki-ya occupies a beautiful 170-year-old merchant's house with an airy, two-story entryway. Various rooms were added in the Taisho (1912–26) and Showa (1926–89) eras. Dining here, on beautiful lacquer and pottery tableware while seated at tables or on *tatami* in your own private room, is a wonderful experience—not surprisingly, they get many fine reviews. Although the *kaiseki* served is generally vegetarian, meals with fish are also available. For lunch, you can also dine in a communal room for ¥2,800 on a *donburi teishoku* featuring a rice dish topped with fish and fish eggs, plus sashimi and dessert; or splurge on vegetarian or fish *kaiseki* starting at ¥4,500. Reservations should be made by 4:30pm for dinner, 1 day in advance on weekends.

2–4–13 Owari-cho. ✆ **076/231-6245.** Set lunches ¥2,800–¥5,500; *kaiseki* dinners ¥8,000–¥25,000. Daily 11:30am–1:30pm and 5:30–7pm (last order). Loop Bus or Kenrokuen Shuttle: Musashigatsuji (3 min.). North of Hyakumangoku Dori, on a side street with small parking lot.

Exploring Kanazawa

Much of Kanazawa's charm lies in its atmospheric old neighborhoods. The best way to explore various parts of the city is via your own two feet, so be sure to wear good walking shoes. One suggested itinerary for tackling the city's sights is to take the Loop Bus to the Higashi Chaya district, then another Loop bus onward to Kanazawa Castle Park and Kenrokuen, and then walk the 15 minutes to the Naga-machi Samurai district, stopping at Seisonkaku villa, the 21st Century Museum of Contemporary Art, and other sights along the way. Directional English-language signs to major sights are posted throughout the city. If you apply between 2 weeks and 2 months in advance, you can request a Goodwill Guide to show you the city; the service is free, but you are responsible for the guide's entrance fees, transportation, and lunch. For details, go to http://kggn.sakura.ne.jp/index_e.html.

AROUND KENROKUEN GARDEN

The sights here are listed in the order you reach them on foot from Kenrokuen. See Kanazawa Castle Park *before* entering Kenrokuen.

Kanazawa Castle Park ★ PARK/GARDEN At one time, Kanazawa possessed an impressive castle belonging to the powerful Maeda clan for 14 generations, but it was destroyed by fire several times, most recently in 1881. The only remaining original structure, Ishikawamon Gate, visible from the northwest corner of Kenrokuen and reached via a bridge over a busy thoroughfare, is big and grand—giving you some sense of the magnitude of the original Maeda castle. Remarkably, the roof tiles are made of lead, in case emergency dictated they be melted down for musket balls. The area just beyond the gate is **Kanazawa Castle Park,** where several castle fortifications have been reconstructed using traditional Japanese construction techniques, including Kahokumon Gate and two watchtowers linked by an incredibly long arsenal that doubled as a protective wall. Skip these empty buildings, however, if time is of the essence. What impresses me most is the expansiveness of the grounds, the various stone masonry techniques for the castle's many walls, and **Gyokusen'inmaru Garden,** originally constructed in 1634 and re-created in 2015 based on excavations, drawings, and literature. Goodwill Guides are at hand at the garden's rest house and near Ishikawamon Gate daily from 9:30am to 3:30pm for free tours of the park.

Kenroku-machi. www.pref.ishikawa.jp/siro-niwa/kanazawajou/e/index.html. ✆ **076/234-3800.** Free admission to Castle Park, the garden, and Kahokumon; watchtowers/storehouse ¥310 adults, ¥100 children. Park Mar to mid-Oct daily 7am–6pm, mid-Oct to Feb daily 8am–5pm; watchtowers/storehouse daily 9am–4:30pm. Loop Bus or Kenrokuen Shuttle: Kenrokuen Garden (5 min.).

Kenrokuen Garden ★★★ PARK/GARDEN Kanazawa's main attraction, the 10-hectare (25-acre) **Kenrokuen Garden,** once served as Kanazawa Castle's outer garden. The largest of what are considered to be the three best landscape gardens in Japan—the other two are Kairakuen Garden in Mito and Korakuen Garden in Okayama—it's considered by some to be the grandest. Its name can be translated as "a refined garden incorporating six attributes": spaciousness, careful arrangement, seclusion, antiquity, elaborate use of water, and scenic charm. Ponds, trees, winding streams, rocks, mounds, and footpaths are combined so aesthetically that the effect is spellbinding. Best of all, unlike most other gardens in Japan, there are no surrounding skyscrapers to detract from splendid views, making this one of my personal favorites.

Altogether, it took about 150 years to complete the garden. The fifth Maeda lord started construction in the 1670s, and successive lords added to it according to their individual tastes. The garden as you now see it was finished by the 13th Maeda lord in 1837; only after the Meiji Restoration was it opened to the public, in 1874. Several historic structures are worth seeking out, including the **Yugaotei tea-ceremony house** dating from 1774 and, most important,

Seisonkaku Villa (see below). Plan on 1½ hours of blissful wanderings. ***Tip:*** You may want to arrive early in the morning or near the end of the day, as Kenrokuen Garden is a favorite destination of tour groups, led by flag-carrying guides who explain everything in detail—through loudspeakers.

1–4 Kenroku-machi. www.pref.ishikawa.jp/siro-niwa/kenrokuen. ✆ **076/234-3800.** Admission ¥310 adults, free for seniors, ¥100 children. Mar to mid-Oct daily 7am–6pm; mid-Oct to Feb daily 8am–5pm. Loop Bus or Kenrokuen Shuttle: Kenrokuen Garden (3 min.).

Ishikawa Prefectural Museum for Traditional Products and Crafts (Ishikawa Kenritsu Dento Sangyo Kogeikan) ★★ MUSEUM If I had time to visit only one museum in Kanazawa, this would be my choice. It's the best place in town to view 36 different handcrafted items for which Ishikawa Prefecture has long been famous (the Maeda lords promoted crafts over warfare). You'll learn about the famous Kutani pottery, first produced under the patronage of the Maeda clan in the 1600s and known for its hues of green, red, purple, navy blue, and yellow, as well as Kaga Yuzen dyeing and hand-painting on silk, Kanazawa lacquerware (which uses raised lacquer painting), paulownia woodcrafts, metalwork, family Buddhist altars, Kanazawa gold leaf, *taiko* drums, *koto* and *shamisen* stringed instruments, lion masks, fishing lures (using feathers of wild birds), folk toys, *washi* (Japanese paper), umbrellas, and even fireworks. Plan on 1 hour to appreciate everything, and don't miss the museum shop.

1–1 Kenroku-machi. www.ishikawa-densankan.jp. ✆ **076/262-2020.** Admission ¥260 adults, ¥200 seniors, ¥100 children. Daily 9am–5pm (closed 3rd Thurs of every month Apr–Nov and every Thurs Dec–Mar). Loop Bus: Hirosaka (6 min.); Kenrokuen Shuttle: Seisonkaku-mae (1 min). Next to Seisonkaku Villa; you can also enter the museum directly from Kenrokuen.

Seisonkaku Villa (成巽閣) ★★★ HISTORIC HOME Just outside the Kodatsuno (southeast) exit of Kenrokuen Garden is this must-see villa, built in 1863 by the 13th Maeda lord as a retirement home for his widowed mother. Elegant and graceful, it has a distinctly feminine atmosphere with delicately carved, brightly painted wood transoms and *shoji* wainscoting painted with seashells, butterflies, flowers, and other motifs. The first-floor bedroom is decorated with tortoises painted on its *shoji* wainscoting; tortoises were associated with long life, and it must have worked—the mother lived to be 84. Upstairs, rooms are painted in brilliant colors of blue, red, and purple. Expect to linger about 20 minutes here, but unfortunately you can only photograph the inner garden.

1–2 Kenroku-machi. www.seisonkaku.com. ✆ **076/221-0580.** Admission ¥700 adults, ¥300 junior-high and high-school students, ¥250 children. Thurs–Tues 9am–5pm. Loop Bus: Hirosaka (5 min.); Kenrokuen Shuttle: Seisonkaku-mae (1 min.). Next to the Ishikawa Prefectural Museum for Traditional Products and Crafts.

21st Century Museum of Contemporary Art, Kanazawa ★★ MUSEUM In a word, this museum is fun. Its mission is to revitalize the arts in Kanazawa, bring the community together, and attract young visitors. Centrally located between Kenrokuen and the Katamachi shopping district, it's ensconced in a striking circular building that has no front or back, allowing visitors to explore it from all directions (and, from time to time, get lost). Galleries, which range from bright spaces with sunlight pouring through glass ceilings to darkened rooms with no natural light, display a collection that concentrates on works of the past 35 years, particularly from Japanese artists born after 1965, along with contemporary works from around the world shown in changing exhibitions. My favorite: Leandro Erlich's outdoor "swimming pool" topped with a roof of glass and shallow water; look in, and you might see people who, having entered through a subterranean tunnel, look like they're walking underwater. James Turrell's *Blue Planet Sky Room* is a white courtyard open to the sky, making heaven appear like a work of art. Note that galleries may be temporarily closed for exhibition changes.

1–2–1 Hirosaka. www.kanazawa21.jp. ✆ **076/220-2800.** Admission ¥360 adults, ¥280 seniors and university students, free for children 17 and under. Special exhibits (which sometimes take over most of the museum) ¥1,000, ¥800, and ¥400 respectively. Sun and Tues–Thurs 10am–6pm; Fri–Sat 10am–8pm. Loop Bus and Kenrokuen Shuttle: Hirosaka-21st Century Museum (2 min.).

NAGA-MACHI SAMURAI (BUKE YASHIKI) DISTRICT

About a 15-minute walk west of Kenrokuen Garden and just a couple minutes' walk west of Kanazawa's downtown Katamachi/Korinbo shopping district, the Naga-machi Samurai District is basically a few streets lined with beautiful wooden homes hidden behind gold-colored mud walls (higher-ranked samurai had higher walls; the lowest rank had only hedges) and bordered by canals left over from the Edo Period. An unhurried stroll in the neighborhood will give you an idea of what a feudal castle town might have looked like, though on a much-reduced scale. Lord Maeda had as many as 8,000 samurai retainers, who in turn had their own retainers, making the samurai population here very large indeed. To see how those in the lowest military class lived, stop by the **Kanazawa Ashigaru Kinenkan (金沢市足軽資料館),** consisting of two modest homes: the Shimizu house and the Takanishi house, both occupied until the 1990s and open free to the public daily 9:30am to 5pm. In addition, the **Kanazawa Shinise Kinenkan** (✆ **076/220-2524;** daily 9:30am–5pm), a former Chinese pharmacy established in 1579, displays the old store and family residence and, upstairs, Kanazawa crafts and products from some 60 local stores; admission here is well worth the ¥100.

To reach the Naga-machi Samurai District from Katamachi, take the side street to the right of the Tokyu Hotel.

Nomura Samurai House (Buke Yashiki Ato Nomura Ke; 武家屋敷跡野村家) ★ HISTORIC HOME Stop 20 minutes here to see how higher-ranking samurai lived back in the Edo Period. Occupied by 11 generations of the Nomura family for 400 years, this traditional Japanese home boasts a drawing room made of Japanese cypress, with elaborate designs in rosewood and *shoji* screens painted with landscapes, and a tea-ceremony room upstairs (*matcha* tea costs ¥300 extra). Rooms overlook a small, charming garden with a miniature waterfall, a winding stream, huge carp, a 400-year-old bayberry tree, and stone lanterns (many people come just for the garden). Personal effects of the Nomura family and objects from the Edo Period are on display, including a samurai outfit, swords, lacquerware, the family altar, and a box for bush warblers (deliberately dark so the birds would sing).

1–3–32 Naga-machi. © **076/221-3553.** Admission ¥550 adults, ¥400 high-school students, ¥250 children. Apr–Sept daily 8:30am–5:30pm; Oct–Mar daily 8:30am–4:30pm. Loop Bus: Korinbo (5 min.). Take the side street to the right of Hotel Tokyu, turn right at the T, and then turn left.

OTHER SIGHTS

Higashi Chaya District Approximately 50 geisha practice their trade in three old entertainment quarters in Kanazawa, including this one. A walk here reveals rather solemn-looking, wood-slatted facades of geisha houses dating from the 1820s, where men of means have long come to be entertained with music, dancing, songs, the tea ceremony, poem recitals, and other pleasure pursuits. Geisha still perform at seven houses in the Higashi Chaya District, but most of the other former geisha homes have been turned into shops, inns, and restaurants. For an inside peek at the geisha world, visit the 200-year-old **Shima Geisha House (志摩)** ★, 1–13–21 Higashiyama (© **076/252-5675;** daily 9am–6pm), a former tearoom where geisha performed. Inside, you'll find rooms that were allotted to personal use, as well as to performing, along with displays of ordinary artifacts—from hair ornaments, pipes, and game boards to cooking utensils. Architectural details worth noting include several stairways (so that customers could come and go without being seen); a small Shinto shrine at the entrance to the home; a more elaborate family Buddhist altar in a place of honor in a front room; the gleaming wood-lacquered surfaces of furniture; and cloisonné door pulls on sliding doors. Admission is ¥500 for adults, ¥300 for children; you can also enjoy tea in the peaceful new addition facing a garden, which, depending on the accompanying sweet, costs ¥500 to ¥700. Plan on 15 minutes to tour the house. To reach it, take the Loop Bus to the Hashiba-cho stop.

Myoryuji Temple (妙立寺) ★★ TEMPLE Popularly known as Ninja-dera (Temple of the Secret Agents) because of its secret chambers, hidden stairways, and trick doors, Myoryuji Temple was built by the Maeda clan for family prayer in 1643. It looks small from the outside, just two stories high to comply with height restrictions during the Edo Period. Inside, four stories are evident, but even this is false: Three more levels are concealed. The fortress-like structure contains an amazing 29 stairways and a labyrinth of corridors, along with such trick devices as pitfalls to trap unsuspecting intruders, slatted stairs where lances could stab at passing legs, escape hatches, secret stairways, and a four-mat *seppuku* ritual suicide chamber that could be opened only from the outside—one more example of how deep paranoia ran in the Edo era. Although rumor has it that a tunnel once connected the temple to the castle to serve as an escape route for the feudal lord in case of attack, a river running between them makes it unlikely. Unfortunately, photography is not allowed, except for a shoji-covered stairway, which allowed light penetration so guards hidden underneath could stab intruders' legs.

You must phone ahead for a reservation; chances are good that you'll be able to see it the same day you call. To ensure that you don't get lost (which would be quite easy because of all the trick doors), you must join a guided tour, which last 30 to 40 minutes. Unfortunately, tours are in Japanese only, but an English-language booklet with photos lets you follow along, and demonstrations of the various trick devices are fairly self-explanatory. To reach it, take the Loop Bus to Hirokoji, and arrive at least 10 minutes before the start of your tour.

1–2–12 Nomachi. www.myoryuji.jp. ✆ **076/241-0888.** Tours ¥1,000 adults, ¥700 children (children 5 and younger not admitted). Tours daily 9am–4:30pm (to 4pm in winter).

Shopping

Kanazawa's most famous products are **Kutani pottery,** with its bright five-color overglaze patterns, and hand-painted **Yuzen silk.** Kanazawa also produces *maki-e* lacquerware, sweets, toys, wooden products, and almost all of Japan's gold leaf. For convenient shopping for these and other souvenirs, including food products, there's the **100 bangai shopping arcade** right in Kanazawa Station, open daily 8:30am to 7pm.

For department stores like Daiwa, boutiques, and contemporary shops, visit downtown **Katamachi** and the pedestrian **Tatemachi shopping street** with its many youth-oriented shops, hair salons, and cafes. **Omi-cho Market,** just off Hyakumangoku Dori between Kanazawa Station and downtown, was established 300 years ago as the "kitchen of Kanazawa" and today is a vibrant city market with more than 170 stalls selling seafood, vegetables, fruit, and prepared foods—like grilled eel—you can eat on the go. There are also restaurants up on the second floor. It's open Monday to Saturday from 10am to 6pm (some shops open also on Sun).

Ishikawa Prefectural Products Center (Kanko Bussankan) ★ Located just north of Kenrokuen Garden, this place is good for one-stop shopping of all the products Ishikawa Prefecture is famous for. The ground floor sells crafts ranging from lacquerware and pottery to glassware, as well as foodstuffs like confectionary and sake, while the second floor offers drop-in craft classes (no reservations necessary; small fee charged) and a sushi restaurant. Open daily 9am to 6pm April to October, Wednesday to Monday 10am to 5pm November to March (upstairs closes at 4pm). 2–20 Kenroku-machi. ✆ **076/222-7788.** Loop Bus or Kenrokuen Shuttle: Kenrokuen Garden. On Hyakumangoku Dori.

Sakuda (さくだ) ★ Thinking about wallpapering a room in gold leaf? Then you'll want to pay a visit to Sakuda, located in a modern building in the Higashi Chaya District. (As much as 98% of Japan's entire national output of gold leaf is produced in Kanazawa.) You can watch artisans pounding the gold leaf and spreading it until it's paper-thin and translucent; it's the equivalent of pounding a ¥10 coin into the size of a *tatami* mat. But most people come here to shop for gold-leafed vases, boxes, chopsticks, bowls, trays, screens, furniture, and—this being Japan—golf balls and iPhone covers. You can even buy gold flakes to add to your coffee or sake or gold-laden skincare products. Don't miss the second-floor bathrooms; the women's room is done entirely in gold leaf, the men's in platinum. The staff serves complimentary tea spiked with gold leaf to visitors. Open daily 9am to 6pm. 1–3–27 Higashiyama. www.goldleaf-sakuda.jp. ✆ **076/251-6777.** Loop Bus: Hashiba-cho (4 min.).

RURAL SHIRAKAWA-GO & OGIMACHI ★★

555km (347 miles) NW of Tokyo; 77km (48 miles) S of Kanazawa; 47km (29 miles) NE of Takayama

With its thatched-roof farmhouses, paddies trimmed with flowerbeds, roaring river, and pine-covered mountains rising on all sides, **Shirakawa-go** is one of the most picturesque regions in Japan. Unfortunately, it also has more than its fair share of tour buses (especially in May, Aug, Sept, and Oct, and during the wintry snowy months, which attracts many Asians), with an astounding 1.8 million visitors annually. While I miss the days when Shirakawa-go, accessible only by car or bus, was off the beaten path for most foreign tourists, I think there's still a magic to this rural region in Gifu Prefecture. If you can, spend the night. Most tourists are day-trippers, which means you have the village pretty much to yourself by late afternoon.

Although Shirakawa-go stretches about 39km (24 miles) beside the Shokawa River and covers 229 sq. km (88 sq. miles), mountains and forest account for 95% of the region, and Shirakawa-go's 1,700 residents and cultivated land are squeezed into a valley averaging less than 3km (2 miles) in width. Thus, land in Shirakawa-go for growing rice and other crops has always been scarce and valuable. Farmhouses were built large enough to hold extended families, with as many as several dozen people living under one roof. Because there wasn't enough land available for young couples to marry and build houses of their own, only the eldest son was allowed to marry; the other children were required to spend their lives living with their parents and helping with the farming. But even though younger children weren't allowed to marry, a man was allowed to choose a young woman, visit her in her parents' home, and father her children. The children then remained with the mother's family, becoming valuable members of the labor force.

Before the roads came to Shirakawa-go, winter always meant complete isolation as snow 2m (6 ft.) deep blanketed the entire region. *Irori* (open-hearth fireplaces) in the middle of a communal room were used for cooking, warmth, and light during the long winter months. The family lived, therefore, on the ground floor, while upper floors were used for silk cultivation and storage of utensils. Because of the heavy snowfall, thatched roofs were constructed at steep angles, known as *gassho-zukuri* in reference to the fact that the tops of the roofs look like hands joined in prayer. The steep angle also allowed rain to run off quickly, and the thatch (Japanese pampas grass) dried quickly in the sun, preventing decay. Remarkably, the massive homes were constructed without nails; rather, sturdy ropes held the framework together and helped withstand earthquakes. Because there were no chimneys, smoke from the *irori* simply rose into the levels above, helping to ward off insects in the thatch and keep the ropes taut.

Today, Shirakawa-go has about 114 thatched farmhouses, barns, and sheds, most of them built around 200 to 300 years ago. The thatched roofs are about .6m (2 ft.) thick and last some 40 years. The old roofs are replaced in Shirakawa-go every April, when one to four roofs are changed on successive weekends. The entire process involves about 200 or more people, who can replace one roof in a couple of days.

Shirakawa-go's inhabitants live in several small villages. Of these, **Ogimachi ★★★**, declared a UNESCO World Cultural and Natural Heritage site in 1995 and often referred to as Shirakawa, boasts the greatest concentration of thatched-roof buildings. With just 600 residents, it's a delightful hamlet of narrow lanes winding past thatched-roof farmhouses, which stand like island sentinels surrounded by paddies. Many of the farmhouses have been turned into *minshuku,* souvenir shops, restaurants, and museums, including an **open-air museum** that depicts life in the region before roads opened it to the rest of the world.

Essentials

GETTING THERE Two bus companies serve Shirakawa-go: **Hokutetsu Bus** (www.hokutetsu.co.jp; ✆ **076/234-0123**) based in Kanazawa and **Nohi Bus** (www.nouhibus.co.jp; ✆ **0577/32-1688**) in Takayama. Hokutetsu requires reservations, which you can do on the spot if there's room, but which you should do as soon as possible in high season. Nohi is first-come, first-served to Ogimachi but requires reservations if the bus is continuing to Kanazawa. From Takayama Station, it takes 50 minutes and costs ¥2,470, with about 15 departures daily. From Kanazawa Station, make a reservation for one of 10 daily buses, with the fare costing ¥1,850 for the 1½-hour trip. Note that weather can cancel bus service. In any case, buses deliver you to the center of Ogimachi, with a nearby luggage storage room (¥600 and up per bag) if you're moving on.

VISITOR INFORMATION A **tourist office** (www.shirakawa-go.org; ✆ **05769/6-1013;** daily 8:30am–5pm) is located next to the bus parking lot. You can pick up an English-language map and reserve a room in a *minshuku* if you have not already done so.

GETTING AROUND Your own two feet can do it best. It takes about 15 minutes to **walk** from one end of the village to the other; English-language signs direct you to the various attractions.

Seeing the Sights in & Around Ogimachi

In addition to an open-air museum, several old farmhouses in Ogimachi are open to the public. ***Note:*** Because Ogimachi is so small, no addresses are given below. The village has basically one main street and some side streets.

Gassho Zukuri Minka-en ★★★ MUSEUM To see how rural people lived in centuries past, visit Shirakawa-go's top attraction, an open-air

A View of Ogimachi

For an overview (and the best vantage point for photos) of the entire village, walk 20 minutes along the gently sloping road that leads from the north side of Ogimachi to the **Shiroyama Viewing Point ★★** (in winter, you have to take a shuttle bus, ¥200 each way). There's a souvenir shop/restaurant here, but the best thing to do is to turn left at the crest of the hill and walk to the hill's westernmost point (toward the river), where there are some secluded benches. From here, you'll have a marvelous view of the entire valley, made even more picturesque because all the thatched houses face north and south so that sun hitting the roofs melts snow more quickly. If you're thirsty or hungry, head to the restaurant (also with an outdoor viewing point) to buy a drink or a snack and then take it with you to the lookout.

museum with 25 *gassho-zukuri* houses and sheds that were relocated mostly from Kazura village and restored here. Filled with the tools of everyday life and displays ranging from silk production to straw clothing, the buildings are picturesquely situated around ponds, paddies, flowerbeds, and streams, a photographer's dream. Artisans are occasionally on hand making traditional crafts. A couple of the structures show DVDs, including one that depicts rural life more than 50 years ago in Kazura, abandoned in 1967; another shows *gassho-zukuri* construction and re-thatching. Plan on 1½ hours.

✆ **05769/6-1231.** Admission ¥600 adults, ¥400 children 7–15. Mar–Nov daily 8:40am–5pm; Dec–Feb 9am–4pm (closed Thurs Dec–Mar; if Thurs is a holiday, it remains open but closes Wed instead). Across the river via the Deai Bashi Bridge, next to where tour buses park.

Nagase Ke (長瀬家) ★★ HISTORIC FARMHOUSE Of several homes open to the public, this is my favorite. Built in 1890 using centuries-old cypress and chestnut, the Nagase house is the largest home here, once housing 44 people (three generations of the Nagase family still live here). The enormous cross beam is 18m (59 ft.) long, and the height of the five-story house is more than 17m (55 ft.) high. A 15-minute video shows the 2001 re-thatching in which 500 people took part, including 40 women involved just in cooking meals for the workers. Because Nagase ancestors were personal doctors of the powerful Maeda lords from the Kanazawa region, the house displays gifts from the Maedas as well as medical tools. Like other homes, it contains a family altar, this one 500 years old and adjoined to the house so it could be quickly removed in case of fire. Upstairs is a mezzanine where 17 laborers lived, while the next level displays tools used for everything from threshing rice and making rope to weaving cloth; in this remote area, almost everything people used was handmade. The fourth floor, where silk production once took place, contains tools related to the business, including flat trays where the silkworms were bred.

✆ **05769/6-1047.** Admission ¥300 adults, ¥150 children. Daily 9am–5pm. Occasionally closed. Just north of the main street.

Where to Stay & Eat

Because huge extended families living under one roof are a thing of the past, some residents of Ogimachi have turned their *gassho-zukuri* homes into *minshuku.* Staying in one gives you the unique chance to lodge in a thatched farmhouse with a family that might consist of grandparents, parents, and children. English is often limited to the basics of "bath," "breakfast," and "dinner," but smiles go a long way. Most likely, the family will drag out their photo album with pictures of winter snowfall and the momentous occasion when the thatched roof was repaired. Be sure to take both an evening and early morning stroll.

Most *minshuku* are small, with about four to nine *tatami* rooms open to guests. Rooms are basic without bathroom or toilet, and you may be expected to roll out your own futon. Privacy may be limited—only a flimsy sliding partition may separate you from the guest next door. All recommended *minshuku* below are in thatch-roofed homes; rates include breakfast and dinner (add ¥500 in winter for heating charges), and none accept credit cards or have private bathrooms. Check-in is at 3pm; checkout is 9am. The tourist office can make a reservation for you at these or any others around town.

Although all *minshuku* have public baths, I like soaking in the town's only hot-spring indoor and outdoor baths, at **Shirakawa-go no Yu** (白川郷の温泉; **© 05769/6-0026**), across the street from the bus stop. Open daily from 7am to 9:30pm, it charges ¥700 for adults and ¥300 for children, but ask your *minshuku* for a ¥200 discount coupon.

Juemon (十右エ門) ★★ Juemon is a favorite among foreigners traveling in Japan. This attractive *minshuku,* in a 300-year-old farmhouse, has a stone-ringed pond with flowering shrubs and a couple of benches where you can enjoy the view. In addition, there's an *irori* in the dining room; don't be surprised if the outgoing 80-something Mrs. Sakai, who runs this place along with her son, serenades you during dinner with a *shamisen* and folk songs.

1653 Ogimachi. **© 05769/6-1053.** 4 units (none with bathroom). ¥10,000–¥11,000 per person. A 15-min. walk from the bus stop, on the south edge of Ogimachi.

Koemon (幸エ門) ★★★ This is my top choice for accommodations. It's now run and managed by fifth- and sixth-generation innkeepers of the 200-year-old farmhouse, which became a *minshuku* almost 50 years ago but has been modernized with a heated floor, automatic sensor lights, and even dimmer switches to enhance the mood around the *irori* fireplace, where you'll have your meals and watch a video during dinner showing the re-thatching of the farmhouse. Rooms are spotless, with the best one facing a pond. If you have heavy luggage, you'll be happy to know that this one is closest to the bus terminal. Reservations are accepted only by fax (see the website).

456 Ogimachi. www.shirakawago-kataribe.com/koemon.html. **© 05769/6-1446.** 4 units (none with bathroom). ¥9,000 per person. A 10-min. walk from the bus stop, via Nishi Dori.

Ochudo (落人) Because *minshuku* provide dinner and breakfast, all you'll probably need is lunch. With its small front porch overlooking a paddy and welcoming old-fashioned interior in a thatched house, this tea and coffee shop with soothing music makes for a relaxing place for a snack or light meal. It's owned by charming Miyako-san (whose husband is from the Nagase family; see above), who lets you choose your own cup for tea or coffee and offers a yummy daily beef curry that strays from the usual (with, for example, asparagus). Order it with the sweet red bean soup. No credit cards accepted.

✆ **090/5458-0418.** Set meal ¥1,300. Daily 11am–5pm (to 6pm in summer if there are customers). In the middle of Shirakawa Mura, near the Kanda House.

Shimizu (志みづ) On the edge of town, mercifully far from the tourist crowds and souvenir shops, this small *minshuku* in a 200-year-old thatched house surrounded by a pastoral setting is a good choice for travelers who desire more privacy than that afforded living with a family, as the owner, who speaks some English, lives in the house next door. There's a communal room with an *irori,* where you can serve yourself coffee and tea and where meals are served. Although you can stay here without opting for meals, note that dinner options in the village are minimal.

2613 Ogimachi. www.shimizu-inn.com. ✆ **05769/6-1914.** 3 units (none with bathroom). ¥9,200 per person with meals; ¥6,300 per person without meals. A 15-min. walk from the bus stop, on the south edge of Ogimachi.

HIDA TAKAYAMA, LITTLE KYOTO OF THE MOUNTAINS ★★★

533km (331 miles) NW of Tokyo; 165km (103 miles) NE of Nagoya

Located in the Hida Mountains (part of the Japan Alps National Park) in Gifu Prefecture, **Hida Takayama** is surrounded by 3,000m (10,000 ft.) peaks, making the train or bus ride here breathtaking. The town, situated along a river on a wide plateau with a population of about 90,000, was founded in the 16th century by Lord Kanamori, who selected the site because of the impregnable position afforded by the surrounding mountains. Modeled after Kyoto but also with strong ties to Edo (Tokyo), Takayama borrowed from both cultural centers in developing its own architecture, food, and crafts, all well-preserved today thanks to centuries of isolation. With a rich supply of timber from surrounding forests, its carpenters were legendary, creating not only beautifully crafted traditional merchants' homes in Takayama but also the Imperial Palace and temples in Kyoto.

Today, Takayama boasts a delightful and elegant historic district, called **Sanmachi,** with homes of classical design typical of 18th-century Hida. The streets are narrow and clean and are flanked on both sides by tiny canals of running water, which in centuries past were useful for fire prevention, washing clothes, and dumping winter snow, but which now give the town its distinct character. Rising from the canals are one- and two-story homes and shops of gleaming dark wood with overhanging roofs; latticed windows and slats of wood play games of light and shadow in the white of the sunshine. In the doorways of many shops, curtains flutter in the breeze.

With its quaint old character, great shopping (including a lively city market), and museums, Takayama is a town that invites exploration. As you walk down the streets, you'll also notice huge cedar balls hanging from the eaves in front of several shops, indicating one of Takayama's six sake breweries, most of them small affairs. Go inside, sample the sake, and watch the men stirring rice in large vats. There are also a surprising number of museums, most housed in traditional homes and filled with historical relics and antiques from Takayama's past.

Essentials

GETTING THERE **By Train** The easiest way to reach Takayama is by direct train from Nagoya (which is on the Shinkansen line), with departures approximately every hour for the 2½-hour trip that costs ¥5,510 for an unreserved seat. There's also one early-morning train that departs Osaka and Kyoto directly for Takayama.

By Bus **Nohi buses** (www.nouhibus.co.jp; ✆ **03/5376-2222**) depart Tokyo's Shinjuku Station six to eight times daily, arriving in Takayama 5½ hours later and costing ¥6,690; they depart Osaka (with a stop in Kyoto) four times daily and cost ¥4,700 for the 5-hour trip. From Kanazawa, **Nohi** (✆ **0577/32-1688**) and **Hokutetsu** buses (www.highwaybus.com; ✆ **076/237-8004**) serve Takayama (with a stop in Shirakawa-go) six times a day; reservations are required for most trips and the fare is ¥3,390 for the 2¼-hour trip.

VISITOR INFORMATION The **Takayama Tourist Information Office** (www.hida.jp; ✆ **0577/32-5328;** daily 8:30am–7pm, to 5:30pm Dec–Mar) is just outside the main (east) exit of Takayama Station. You can pick up an English-language map of the town showing the location of all museums and attractions. A small **tourist counter** on Sanno-machi street is open daily 8:30am to 6:30pm.

GETTING AROUND Takayama is one of Japan's easiest towns to navigate. Most of its attractions lie east of the train station in the historic Sanmachi district and are easily reached from the station in about 10 to 15 minutes **on foot.** Throughout the town are English-language signs pointing directions to the many attractions; they're even embedded in sidewalks and streets. A tourist shuttle, called **Machinami Bus,** makes a loop in both directions through the old town, but it travels only once an hour in each direction; you're better off exploring by foot.

That being said, you'll need to take the other shuttle, the **Sarubobo Bus,** to reach Hida Folk Village and Hida Takayama Museum of Art. It departs from in front of the train station twice an hour daily from 9am to 4:40pm and costs ¥210 per ride. Pick up the schedule and route at the tourist office.

Alternatively, lots of shops and hotels rent **bicycles,** with most charging ¥1,200 for the day. Closest to the station is **Ikehata Shouten,** located just past the Nohi Bus Station (✆ **0577/32-0847**); they'll also store your luggage here if lockers are full, at ¥500 per bag per day. As for bike riding, note that

Takayama

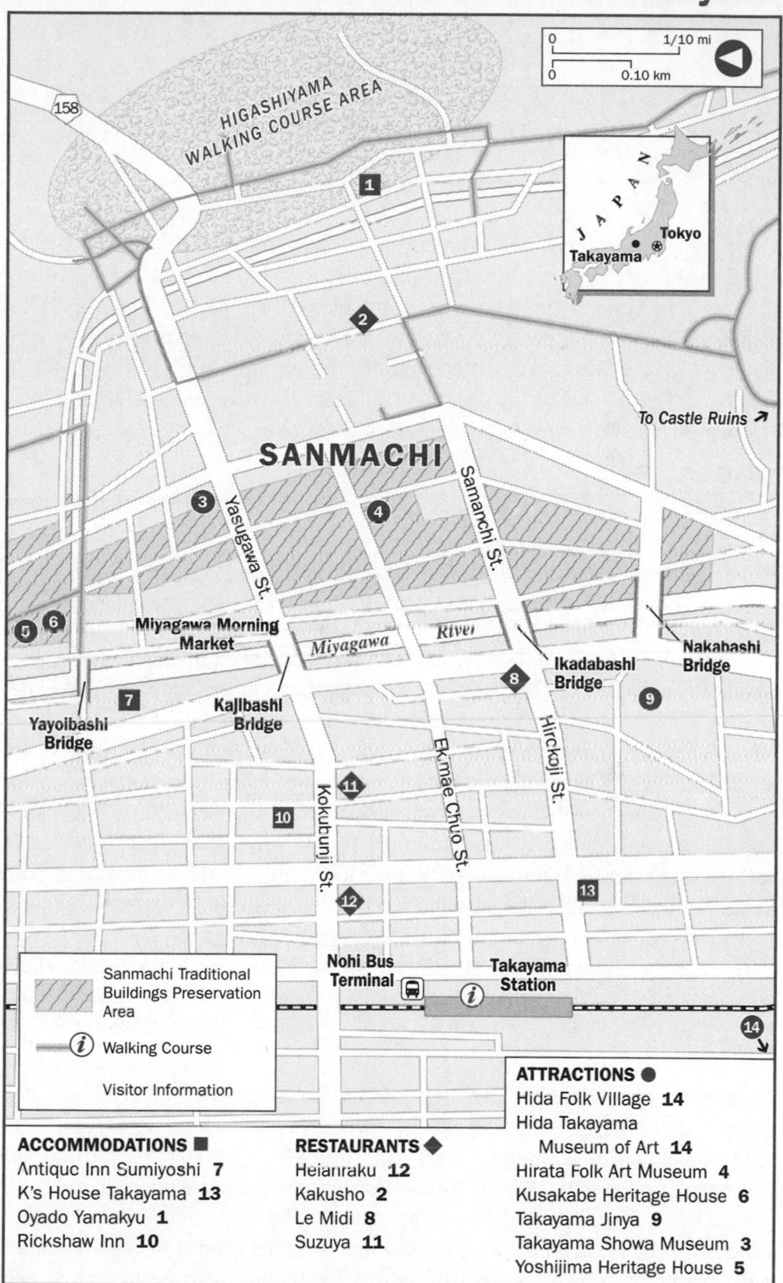
0
1/10 mi
0
0.10 km
158
HIGASHIYAMA WALKING COURSE AREA
JAPAN
Tokyo
Takayama
To Castle Ruins
SANMACHI
Yasugawa St.
Samanchi St.
Miyagawa Morning Market
Miyagawa River
Ikadabashi Bridge
Nakabashi Bridge
Kajibashi Bridge
Yayoibashi Bridge
Hirokoji St.
Ekimae Chuo St.
Kokubunji St.
Nohi Bus Terminal
Takayama Station
Sanmachi Traditional Buildings Preservation Area
Walking Course
Visitor Information
ACCOMMODATIONS
Antique Inn Sumiyoshi 7
K's House Takayama 13
Oyado Yamakyu 1
Rickshaw Inn 10
RESTAURANTS
Heianraku 12
Kakusho 2
Le Midi 8
Suzuya 11
ATTRACTIONS
Hida Folk Village 14
Hida Takayama Museum of Art 14
Hirata Folk Art Museum 4
Kusakabe Heritage House 6
Takayama Jinya 9
Takayama Showa Museum 3
Yoshijima Heritage House 5

Takayama's old town has narrow streets and it's straight up a very long hill to Hida Folk Village and Hida Takayama Museum of Art.

WI-FI ACCESS **iCafe,** located in Takayama Station (✆ **0577-62-8180;** daily 7:30am–7pm), offers free Wi-Fi, recharging of batteries, luggage storage, and same-day baggage delivery to hotels if you arrive before noon. Otherwise, free Wi-Fi is available through much of the old town at selected spots for up to 1 week.

Where to Stay

There are as many *minshuku* and *ryokan* in Takayama as hotels, making it the perfect place to stay in a traditional inn. In fact, staying in a *tatami* room and sleeping on a futon is the best way to immerse yourself in the life of this small community. You should be aware that on weekends and in peak season—April through Golden Week, August (especially during mid-Aug Obon), October, and New Year's—prices are at their highest. They're even higher during Takayama's festivals, in mid-April and mid-October.

MODERATE

Antique Inn Sumiyoshi (寿美よし) ★★★ This calls itself a *ryokan,* but its size and homey atmosphere and the family that runs it make it seem more like a *minshuku.* Built more than 100 years ago by a well-known local carpenter to house a silkworm industry (and then operating as a pawnshop), it opened in 1950 as a *ryokan* and hasn't changed much since then. An open-hearth fireplace, samurai armor, and antiques and folk toys fill the reception area, where you are invited to have tea or coffee. On the second floor is my favorite feature: an outdoor deck facing the river, across which is the morning market. *Tatami* rooms are comfortable and old-fashioned, many with painted screens and antiques; request one facing the river. Minami-san, the man running the *ryokan,* is a fifth-generation innkeeper and speaks English. In addition to Japanese and vegetarian dinners (order when making reservations), both Japanese and Western breakfasts are available. Meals are served in your room. No credit cards are accepted.

4–21 Honmachi. www.sumiyoshi-ryokan.com. ✆ **0577/32-0228.** 8 units (1 with bathroom; 2 with sink/toilet). ¥6,000–¥12,000 per person. Rates exclude tax. Dinner ¥3,000 extra; breakfast ¥1,000 extra. Station: Takayama (10 min. northeast). Across from historic Sanmachi on the Miyagawa River, near the Yayoibashi Bridge. **Amenities:** Wi-Fi (most rooms).

Oyado Yamakyu ★★ This spotless *minshuku,* open since 1972, has a reputation of offering the best meals in town in its price range, served in a communal dining room. Although it's a bit far from the station—about a 20-minute walk or a 5-minute taxi ride (there are also eight free shuttle buses daily)—it's located in a quiet residential area adjacent to the Higashiyama Walking Course, which takes in Takayama's many temples and shrines, and is only a 10-minute walk or short bike ride to the historic district. Its hallways boast a good collection of folk art, antique clocks, and glassware; eaves above all guest-room doors give it a "village" atmosphere. In the mornings, free coffee is available from the small lobby lounge, where you have a view of a small courtyard garden. As with most *minshuku,* the Japanese-style rooms—nicely done with natural woods and artwork—are without private bathrooms, but the communal baths are large and include tiny outdoor tubs, one ceramic and one wood; there's also a private shower room you can lock.

58 Tenshoji-machi. www.takayama-yamakyu.com ✆ **0577/32-3756.** 18 units (all with toilet and sink only). ¥8,000–¥9,000. Rates exclude tax but include 2 meals. Station: Takayama (20 min.). **Amenities:** Rental bikes (¥500 per day, free for guests staying 3 days); free shuttle from the station; Wi-Fi.

INEXPENSIVE

K's House Takayama ★★ This is a backpacker's guesthouse with class. The inviting lobby lounge, exuding a bohemian peacefulness with comfy sofas and beanbag chairs, fosters camaraderie among its mostly international guests, as does the spotless, fully equipped kitchen. Information on local sights and activities is posted everywhere. In addition to dormitory rooms (for women-only or mixed sexes), it also offers five very tiny singles, as well as five twins (all with bunk beds) and nine doubles that also include deluxe rooms with one-*tatami* sitting areas, all with *shoji*-like screens. Rare for guesthouses, all rooms have private bathroom.

4–51–1 Tenmancho. http://kshouse.jp. ✆ **0577/34-4110.** 26 ¥4,500–¥7,200 single; ¥7,500–¥13,800 double; ¥2,900–¥3,200 dormitory. Station: Takayama (3 min.). Walk straight out of the station, cross the road, turn right and then left just before Spa Hotel Alpina. **Amenities:** Rental bikes (¥ 1,000 per day), Wi-Fi.

Rickshaw Inn ★★★ In a modern house (but without an elevator) in a central location, Rickshaw Inn (entirely nonsmoking) is welcoming, thanks in no small part to the friendly owner Eiko-san, a Takayama native who lived in the United States and speaks flawless English. A spacious communal living room—with sofas, TV, and newspapers—is a good place to relax with fellow guests. No dinner is served, but staff can recommend restaurants (ask for the inn's map) and is knowledgeable about museums, crafts, and Takayama's history. There's also a closet-size communal kitchen. Japanese- and Western-style rooms, with sinks or bathrooms, feature Asian artwork and batik shades to block out light. There are also two suites: Sakura, which sleeps up to six people, and Bamboo, accommodating up to four with a kitchenette.

54 Suehiro-cho. www.rickshawinn.com. ✆ **0577/32-2890.** 11 units (8 with bathroom). ¥4,200–¥6,000 single without bathroom; ¥8,000–¥11,000 double without bathroom, ¥11,900–¥14,600 double with bathroom. Suite from ¥18,000 triple; ¥21,000 quad. Rates exclude tax. Station: Takayama (6 min. east), just off Kokubunji St. to the left (look for the archway over the street with a clock). **Amenities:** Wi-Fi.

Where to Eat

You should try Takayama's local specialties while you're here (they may well be served at your *ryokan* or *minshuku*). The best-known is *hoba miso,* soybean paste mixed with dried scallions, ginger, and mushrooms and cooked on a dry magnolia leaf at your table above a small clay burner. *Sansai* are mountain vegetables, including edible ferns and other wild plants; and *ayu* is a small river fish, grilled with soy sauce or salt. Other dishes include Takayama's own style of *soba* (buckwheat noodles), *mitarashi-dango* (grilled rice balls with soy sauce), and Hida beef.

EXPENSIVE

Kakusho (角正) ★★★ VEGETARIAN For a big splurge, dine at Kakusho, established 250 years ago and under the helm of the 12th-generation head chef. It offers local vegetarian fare called *shojin ryori,* typically served at Buddhist temples. Situated on the slope of a hill in the eastern part of the city, a 5-minute walk from Sanmachi, this delightful restaurant serves meals either in small, private *tatami* rooms dating from the Edo Period or in a larger room from the Meiji Period that can be opened to the elements on three sides, all of which overlook a dreamy, mossy garden enclosed by a clay wall. The least expensive meals consist of various mountain vegetables, mushrooms, nuts, tofu, and other dishes, with more dishes added for more expensive meals (tax and service charge will be added to prices below). Reservations are required.

2–98 Babacho. ✆ **0577/32-0174.** *Kaiseki shojin ryori* ¥10,000–¥20,000; set lunches ¥5,500–¥10,000. Daily 11:30am–2pm and 5–8pm (last order). Irregular closing days. Station: Takayama (15 min.). To the left of Sanmachi St., past the Takayama Museum of History and Art.

MODERATE

Le Midi ★★ FRENCH This tiny, two-level restaurant with red-and-white-checkered curtains and black wood trim imparts a European flair and delivers delicious food. The owner-chef worked in France after training at a Japanese culinary school. Its specialty is Hida beef, served French style as sirloin, filet, or beef cheek simmered 6 hours in red wine. Even the humble hamburger steak, served on potatoes and with green beans, is quite a presentation. Other dishes include Hida pork, fish of the day, and duck breast. This restaurant is so successful, it has expanded across the street at Le Midi-i, which also serves Hida beef along with Italian food.

2–85 Honmachi. www.le-midi.jp. ✆ **0577/36-6386.** Main courses ¥2,400–¥6,800; set lunches ¥1,800–¥4,800; set dinners ¥4,800–¥12,000. Fri–Wed 11:30am–3pm and 6–9pm (last order). Station: Takayama (9 min.). On Honmachi near Ikadabashi Bridge.

Suzuya (寿々や) ★ LOCAL SPECIALTIES Darkly lit with traditional Takayama country decor, this restaurant specializing in Takayama cuisine has been a mainstay for decades. There's an English-language menu complete with photographs and explanations of each dish, including such local specialties as mountain vegetables, *hoba miso* (including a vegetarian option), and Hida beef, as well as *shabu-shabu, sukiyaki,* and deep-fried breaded shrimp and pork. But Hida beef is what the restaurant is known for.

24 Hanakawa-machi. ✆ **0577/32-2484.** Set meals ¥1,200–¥6,700. Daily 11am–2pm and 5–8pm (last order). Closed irregularly. Station: Takayama (6 min.). Just off Kokubunji St. to the right, halfway btw. the station and the Miyagawa River.

INEXPENSIVE

Heianraku ★★★ RAMEN/CHINESE/VEGETARIAN It's the second-generation owner and his wife (who live upstairs) that make this welcoming restaurant a delight. In business since 1963, it has an English menu with questions regarding what you can and cannot eat so that the owners can steer you toward dishes that are gluten-free, vegetarian, vegan, or Buddhist. The specialty of the house is Hida Miso ramen, but other dishes include gyoza, stir-fried noodles, deep-fried chicken, meatballs in a sweet-and-sour sauce, and tofu options, like the tofu teriyaki. This place is tiny, with just one counter for eight lucky diners and two tables, making reservations (which you can do on Facebook) a must. No credit cards accepted.

6-7-2 Tenmancho. ✆ **0577/32-3078.** Main dishes ¥800–¥1,300. Wed–Mon 11:30am–1pm and 5–8pm. Station: Takayama (4 min.). On Kokubunji Dori. Turn left out of the station and right onto Kokubunji; it will be on the right.

Exploring Takayama

Takayama's main attraction is its historic center of traditional homes and businesses in a district called **Sanmachi.** Be sure to allow time to wander around. In addition to museums, there are shops selling antiques, souvenirs, and Takayama specialties, including sake, yew woodcarvings, beautiful cypress furniture, and a unique lacquerware called *shunkei-nuri.*

Be sure, too, to visit the **Miyagawa Morning Market ★★**, which stretches on the east bank of the Miyagawa River between Kajibashi and Yayoibashi bridges. Held every morning from 7am (6am in summer) to noon, it's very picturesque, with cloth-covered stalls selling fresh produce, flowers, pickled vegetables, street food, and locally made crafts. A smaller morning market is held in front of Takayama Jinya.

If you have even more free time, consider the **Higashiyama Walking Course ★★**, which leads past a string of 12 temples and a couple of shrines nestled on a wooded hill on the east edge of town in an area called Higashiyama Teramachi. It also leads to Shiroyama Park, site of the Kanamori clan castle until it was torn down in 1695 by order of the Tokugawa shogunate; parts of its stone foundations still remain. The hiking course stretches 5.5km (3 miles) end to end; there are English-language signs, but be sure to get the map provided by the tourist office. If you get lost, consider it part of the fun.

Hida Folk Village (Hida no Sato) ★★ MUSEUM This is an open-air museum of more than 30 old thatched and shingled farmhouses, sheds, and buildings, many of which were brought here from other parts of the region to illustrate how farmers and artisans used to live in the Hida Mountain range. The entire village is picturesque, with swans swimming in the central pond, green moss growing on the thatched roofs, and flowers blooming in season. Some of the houses have *gassho-zukuri*-style roofs, built steeply to withstand the region's heavy snowfalls. All the structures, which range from 100 to 500 years old, are open to the public and filled with furniture, old spindles and looms, utensils for cooking and dining, instruments used in the silk industry, farm tools, sleds, and straw boots and snow capes for winter. Some even have smoldering fires in the *irori* fire pits. Be sure to ask for the free 20-minute English-language audio guide at the entrance, which describes the social life and architecture of the region. Workshops set up in one corner of the village grounds demonstrate Takayama's well-known woodcarving, weaving, and other cottage industries. You can also try your hand at baking rice crackers or painting Hida pottery or other crafts for a small fee (available daily except Thursday; no reservations necessary). You'll want to spend about 1½ hours at the village, but if you're heading to Shirakawa-go, skip it; there's a similar, more accessible open-air museum there.

1-590 Kamiokamoto-choi. www.hidanosato-tpo.jp. © **0577/34-4711.** Admission ¥700 adults, ¥200 children. Daily 8:30am–5pm. Bus: Sarubobo Bus to Hida-no-Sato. Station: Takayama (30-min. walk southwest).

Hida Takayama Museum of Art (Hida Takayama Bijutsukan) ★★ MUSEUM Serious glass lovers will not want to miss this museum with its collection of mostly European Art Nouveau and Art Deco glassware, including works by Tiffany, Lalique, and Gallé, as well as some contemporary works by glassmakers like Fujita Kyohei and Dale Chihuly. Several rooms are furnished in decorative and applied arts by masters such as Louis Majorelle, Mackintosh, and Vienna's Secessionist artists. Don't miss the museum shop with its Japanese and imported glassware and crafts; I also like the Mackintosh-inspired tearoom with outdoor terrace seating. Plan on spending about 45 minutes here.

1–124–1 Kamiokamoto-cho. www.htm-museum.co.jp. © **0577/35-3535.** Admission ¥1,300 adults, ¥1,000 university and high-school students, ¥800 junior-high age and younger. Daily 9am–5pm (closed irregular days mid-Jan to mid-Mar). Bus: Sarubobo Bus to Hida Takayama Museum of Art (only 8 buses daily). Station: Takayama (20-min. southwest).

Hirata Folk Art Museum (Hirata Kinen-kan) ★★ MUSEUM Takayama's most varied and extensive collection of folk art vividly conveys what life was like during the Edo Period by displaying household utensils, crafts, and fine arts found in a typical middle-class home; the house itself, built in 1897 in traditional style with a sunken hearth and both living and working quarters, belonged to a candle-maker. Storerooms *(kura)* in the back date to 1780. Items are identified in English, though detailed explanations are unfortunately lacking. On display are folk toys, coin boxes, mirrors, toiletry sets, *geta* sandals, spectacles, hair adornments, *shunkei* lacquerware, and paper and kerosene lamps; my favorite is the room outfitted with items used for travel, including guide maps, portable abacuses, compasses, a traveling pillow, a folding lantern, and even a folding hat. You'll probably spend 20 minutes here, but note that stairs are steep.

Ichino-machi St., 39 Kaminino-machi. © **0577/33-1354.** Admission ¥300 adults, ¥150 junior-high age and younger. Daily 9am–5pm. Station: Takayama (10 min.).

Merchants' Houses ★★★ HISTORIC HOMES In contrast to other castle towns during the Edo Period, Takayama was under the direct control of the Tokugawa government rather than a feudal lord, which meant its homes were built and owned by merchants and commoners rather than the samurai class that dominated other Japanese cities. Located side by side in the historic center and both toured easily in less than 30 minutes, **Yoshijima-ke** or Yoshijima Heritage House (✆ **0577/32-0038**) and **Kusakabe Heritage House** (www.kusakabe-mingeikan.com; ✆ **0577/32-0072**) are merchants' mansions that once belonged to two of the richest families in Takayama.

With its exposed attic, heavy crossbeams, sunken open-hearth fireplace, and sliding doors, Yoshijima House is a masterpiece of geometric design. It was built in 1907 as both the home and factory of the Yoshijima family, well-to-do brewers of sake. Notice how the beams and details of the home gleam, a state attained through decades of polishing as each generation of women did their share in bringing the wood to a luster. Yoshijima-ke is also famous for its lattices, typical of Takayama yet showing an elegance influenced by Kyoto. Its walls serve as an art gallery for the lithographs of female artist Shinoda Toko, one of my favorite Japanese artists (and a distant relative of present owner Yoshijima Tadao, who also uses the house for his other passion, jazz, heard softly in the back gallery).

Kusakabe Mingei-kan, built in 1879 for a merchant dealing in silk, lamp oil, and finance, is more refined and imposing. Its architectural style is considered unique to Hida but has many characteristics common during the Edo Period, including a two-story warehouse at the back of the house with open beams and an earthen floor—now filled with folk art and other items, plus artwork by Shoji Hamada and Kanjiro Kawai. On display, too, are personal items such as a lacquered pillow box that could be filled with incense to perfume the hair and imports from other countries, handed down through the generations. If you have time for only one house, this one has more to see; free green tea is served in the courtyard.

North end of Nino-machi St., Oshinmachi. Admission to either house ¥500 adults, ¥300 junior high and younger. Mar–Nov daily 9am–5pm; Dec–Feb Wed–Mon 9am–4:30pm (Kusakabe House closes 30 min. earlier). Station: Takayama (20 min.).

Takayama Jinya ★★★ GOVERNMENT BUILDING I highly recommend a visit to this centuries-old government house to anyone interested in Japanese history. The building served as the Tokugawa government's administrative building for 177 years (1692–1868). Of some 60 local government offices that were once spread throughout Japan, this is the only one still in existence. Resembling a miniature palace with its outer wall and an imposing entrance gate, the sprawling complex consists of both original buildings and reconstructions. In addition to administrative offices, chambers, and courts, the complex contained living quarters, a huge kitchen, an interrogation room for criminals with torture devices, a tearoom, and a 400-year-old rice granary, the oldest and biggest in Japan, where rice collected from farmers as a form of taxation was stored. Making visits here especially educational are free guided tours in English, which last about 30 to 40 minutes and provide fascinating insight into administrative life of yore.

1–5 Hachi-ken-machi. ✆ **0577/32-0643.** Admission ¥430 adults, free high-school age and younger. Mar–Oct daily 8:45am–5pm (to 6pm Aug); Nov–Feb daily 8:45am–4:30pm. Station: Takayama (10 min.).

Takayama Showa Museum (昭和館) ★★★ MUSEUM If you're a history or a kitsch buff, this eclectic museum is packed to the rafters with items used in daily life during the Showa era (Showa refers to the reign of Emperor Hirohito, 1926–89), including tiny family cars from the 1960s, posters, shop signs, bikes, typewriters, washing machines, rice cookers, clocks, TVs, cameras, and much more, most of it arranged in themed rooms. You can step inside a toy shop, photo studio, doctor's office, barbershop, appliance store (it's fun to see what was considered high-tech back then), schoolroom, beauty salon, a typical living room, and even a movie theater showing news and movies from the 1960s and 1970s, all providing a unique perspective on how much Japan has changed in just a few short decades (you'll probably find yourself wishing more from the Showa era remained). There are even old pachinko games you can play. After spending about 30 minutes in what was clearly a labor of love for the collector, be sure to take a look at the small museum shop selling replica tin toys and candies of yesteryear.

6 Shimoichino-machi. http://takayama-showakan.com. ✆ **0577/33-7836.** Admission ¥800 adults, ¥500 junior/high school students, ¥300 children. Daily 9am–6pm. Station: Takayama (10 min.); just off Kokubunji Dori.

KYOTO

If you go to only one place in all of Japan, **Kyoto ★★★** should be it. Not only is it the most historically significant town in the nation, this former capital was also the only major Japanese city spared the bombs of World War II. It's filled with temples, shrines, imperial palaces, gardens, and *machiya* (traditional wooden houses). But what makes it exceptional are the scenes from daily life. Spend a few days exploring the city's back streets and neighborhoods, and you'll probably agree that Kyoto is Japan's most romantic city.

Home to the Imperial court for 1,000 years, Kyoto boasts the nation's greatest concentration of craft artisans, whose works are displayed in museums and shops dealing in textiles, dyed fabrics, pottery, bambooware, cutlery, fans, metalwork, umbrellas, and other goods. Kyoto is also famous for its own style of *kaiseki,* which blends ceremonial court cuisine with Zen vegetarian food. No fewer than 17 heritage sites in Kyoto Prefecture comprise UNESCO's Historic Monuments of Ancient Kyoto, including Kiyomizu Temple, Kinkakuji, Ginkakuji, Ryoanji Temple, and Nijo Castle, but there are also offbeat attractions like the Kyoto International Manga Museum and a small but vibrant nightlife. And as you explore the back streets, especially in Gion, you might even glimpse a geisha, decked out in all her finery.

ESSENTIALS

Getting There

BY PLANE

Kyoto is served by two airports, **Kansai International Airport (KIX;** www.kansai-airport.or.jp/en) outside Osaka for international and domestic flights and **Itami Airport** (www.osaka-airport.co.jp/en/) for domestic flights.

KANSAI INTERNATIONAL AIRPORT **By Train** The **JR Kansai-Airport Express Haruka** has direct service every 30 to 60 minutes to Kyoto Station. The trip takes approximately 80 minutes and costs ¥3,370 for a reserved seat (recommended during busy departure times or peak season) and ¥2,850 for a nonreserved seat, or you can ride free with your JR Rail Pass. A cheaper, though slower and less convenient, alternative is the JR Kanku Kaisoku, which departs every 30 minutes or so from Kansai Airport and arrives in Kyoto 1 hour and 50 minutes later, with a change at Osaka Station. It costs ¥1,880.

By Bus If you have lots of luggage, consider taking the **Kansai Airport Limousine Bus** (www.kate.co.jp; ✆ **072/461-1374**) from Kansai Airport; buses depart every hour or less for the 1¾-hour trip to Kyoto Station and cost ¥2,550. More convenient but costlier are **shared-ride vans,** operated by local taxi companies **MK** (www.mktaxi-japan.com; ✆ **075/778-5489**) and **Yasaka** (www.yasaka.jp; ✆ **075/803-4800**), which deliver passengers to any hotel or home in Kyoto for ¥4,200, including one suitcase (a second suitcase costs ¥1,000); make reservations 2 days in advance.

BY TRAIN

Kyoto is a major stop on the Shinkansen bullet train; trip time from **Tokyo** is about 2½ hours, with the fare for a nonreserved seat ¥13,080 one-way. Kyoto is only 15 minutes from Shin-Osaka, but you may find it more convenient to take the JR Tokaido Line, which connects Kyoto directly with Osaka Station in 30 minutes. From **Kobe,** you can reach Kyoto from Sannomiya and Motomachi stations on the Tokaido Line in 50 minutes. The strikingly modern **Kyoto Station,** which is like a city in itself with tourist offices, restaurants, a hotel, a department store, a shopping arcade, a theater, and stage events, is connected to the rest of the city by subway and bus.

BY BUS

Lots of long-distance buses travel between Tokyo and Kyoto; reservations are necessary and prices depend on the bus, the type of seat selected, time of day, and season. **JR Highway buses** (www.jrbuskanto.co.jp; ✆ **03/3844-1950**) depart day and night from Tokyo Station's Yaesu South Exit (some make a stop also in Shinjuku), arriving at Kyoto Station 8 hours later and costing ¥3,500 to ¥14,000. Tickets can be purchased at any major JR station or a travel agency like JTB. **Willer Express buses** (http://willerexpress.com; ✆ **050/5805-0383**) depart Tokyo, Shinjuku, and Ikebukuro stations nightly, arriving at Kyoto Station the next morning. Fares are ¥3,200 to ¥11,100.

Visitor Information

The **Kyoto Tourist Information Center** (www.kyoto.travel; ✆ **075/343-0548;** daily 8:30am–7pm), in the central passageway on the second floor of Kyoto Station near Isetan department store, has city and bus maps, as well as many brochures. Other Kyoto Tourist Information Centers are located in central Kyoto on Kawaramachi Dori, open daily 11am to 6:30pm, and in the Kyoto Handicraft Center (p. 260), open daily 10am to 7pm. For information on the wider Kansai area, the Kansai Tourist Information Center Kyoto (www.tic-kansai.jp; ✆ **075/341-0280;** daily 10am–6pm) is located across from Kyoto Station in Kyoto Tower.

PUBLICATIONS A monthly tabloid distributed free at hotels and restaurants is the ***Kyoto Visitor's Guide*** (www.kyotoguide.com), with maps, a calendar of events, and information on sightseeing and shopping (it's available at the Kyoto Tourist Information Center, too, but you have to ask for it). ***Kansai Scene*** (www.kansaiscene.com) is a monthly giveaway with information on nightlife, festivals, and other events in Osaka, Kobe, Kyoto and Nara. The booklet ***Explorer Kyoto*** has excellent maps.

City Layout

Most of Kyoto's attractions and hotels are north of Kyoto Station (take the Central exit), spreading like a fan toward the northeast and northwest. The **northern and eastern edges** of the city contain the most famous temples. The heart of the city is in **central Kyoto (Nakagyo-ku ward),** which boasts the largest concentration of restaurants, shops, and bars and which radiates outward from the intersection of Kawaramachi Dori and Shijo Dori. It includes a narrow street called Pontocho, a nightlife mecca that runs along the western bank of the Kamo River. Across the Kamo River to the east is the ancient geisha district of Gion.

FINDING AN ADDRESS Kyoto's streets are laid out in a grid pattern with named streets (a rarity in Japan) and an unofficial address system used by locals that's actually quite easy to understand once you get to know the directional terms (official postal addresses are less useful and not even used by some establishments, although some use both). The major streets north of Kyoto Station that run east-west are numbered; for example, *shi* means four and *dori* means avenue, so Shijo Dori means "Fourth Avenue." *Agaru* equates to "to the north," *sagaru* to "to the south," *nishi-iru* means "to the west," and *higashi-iru* means "to the east." Thus, an address that reads Shijo-agaru, Teramachi Higashi-iru means "north of Fourth Avenue, east of Teramachi."

On non-numbered streets, addresses generally indicate cross streets. Take the restaurant Kushi Kura, for example: Its address is Takakura Dori, Oike-agaru, which tells you it's just north of Oike Dori on Takakura Dori. Complete addresses include the ward, or *ku,* such as Higashiyama-ku.

Kyoto's Neighborhoods in Brief

The following are Kyoto's main tourist areas; to locate them, see the "Kyoto" maps on p. 215, 219, and 240.

Around Kyoto Station The southern ward of **Shimogyo-ku,** which stretches from Kyoto Station north to Shijo Dori Avenue, caters to tourists with its cluster of hotels and to commuters with its shops and restaurants. Kyoto Station, which caused quite a controversy when it opened in 1997 because of its size, height, and futuristic appearance, is now this area's top attraction. One of Japan's largest (and to me most beautiful) station buildings, it's very contemporary, with soaring glass atriums, space-age chimes, loads of shops and restaurants, and dramatic public spaces, including a series of escalators and stairs leading to a rooftop plaza. I see more tourists photographing Kyoto Station than any other modern building in town.

Central Kyoto Nakagyo-ku, the central part of Kyoto west of the Kamo River and north of Shimogyo-ku, is home to city hall and embraces Kyoto's main shopping and nightlife districts, with most of the action on **Kawaramachi Dori** and **Shijo Dori** and **Teramachi** and **Shin-kyogoku** covered shopping arcades. Most of Kyoto's legendary craft stores are located here, along with numerous hotels, restaurants, and bars. Home also to **Nijo Castle,** Nakagyo-ku has a number of exclusive *ryokan* tucked away in delightful neighborhoods typical of old Kyoto. But downtown is changing fast, as Kyoto's younger generation lays claim to new shopping and entertainment complexes, such as the **Kyoto International Manga Museum,** housed in a former elementary school. Nakagyo-ku is one of the most desirable places to stay in terms of convenience and atmosphere.

Pontocho, a narrow lane that parallels the Kamo River's western bank just a stone's throw from the Kawaramachi-Shijo Dori intersection, is Kyoto's most famous street for nightlife. It's lined with bars and restaurants that boast outdoor verandas extending over the Kamo River in summer. Paralleling Pontocho to the east is **Kiyamachi,** a narrow lane beside a canal lined with bars and restaurants and bustling with nighttime revelers.

Eastern Kyoto Eastern Kyoto is a great area for walking, shopping, and sightseeing. East of the Kamo River, the wards of **Higashiyama-ku** and **Sakyo-ku** boast a number of the city's most famous temples and shrines, as well as restaurants specializing in Kyoto cuisine and Buddhist vegetarian dishes, and shops selling local pottery and other crafts. **Gion,** Kyoto's most famous geisha entertainment district, is part of Higashiyama-ku. Customers are entertained in traditional wooden geisha houses that are not open to the public (you can only gain entry through introductions provided by someone who is already a customer)—but the area makes for a fascinating stroll.

Northern Kyoto Embracing the **Kita-ku, Kamigyo-ku,** and **Ukyo-ku** wards, northern Kyoto is primarily residential but contains a number of Kyoto's top sights, including the Kyoto Imperial Palace, Kinkakuji (Temple of the Golden Pavilion), and Ryoanji Temple, site of Kyoto's most famous Zen rock garden.

GETTING AROUND

Kyoto is Japan's most visitor-friendly city, with lots of English-language signs and an easy-to-navigate transportation system. Kyoto's subway and bus networks are especially efficient and quite easy to use. For more information, stop by the **Bus and Subway Information kiosk** in front of Kyoto Station to the right of the bus platforms (✆ **075/371-4474;** daily 7:30am–7:30pm) or check schedules and routes online at www.arukumachikyoto.jp and www.city.kyoto.lg.jp/kotsu.

BY SUBWAY Kyoto has two subway lines, with stops announced in English. The older **Karasuma Line** runs north and south, from Takeda in the south to Kokusai Kaikan in the north, with stops at Kyoto Station, central Kyoto, and Imadegawa Station (convenient for visiting the Imperial Palace). The **Tozai Line** runs in a curve from east to west and is convenient for visiting Nijo Castle and Higashiyama-ku. The two lines intersect in central Kyoto at Karasuma Oike Station (if you find station names cumbersome, go by their numbers; Karasuma Oike, for example, is both K08 on the Karasuma Line and T13 on the Tozai Line). Fares start at ¥210 (children pay half-fare) and service runs from about 5:30am to 11:30pm. In addition to subways, the private Keihan Railway runs north-south along the Kamo River on the east side of town and is convenient to Gion and some hotels. Although buses usually get you closer to where you want to go, in central Kyoto I sometimes opt for the subway even if I have to walk a bit, simply to avoid hassling with crowded buses and their unknown stops.

BY BUS The most direct way to get to most of Kyoto's attractions in eastern or northern Kyoto is by bus. Buses depart from Kyoto Station's Central

Discount Passes

Instead of purchasing individual tickets, you can save time with the a prepaid **ICOCA** card (Tokyo's IC cards Suica and Pasmo also work in Kyoto; see p. 65 in chapter 4 for a description of IC cards and how they work). However, if you think you'll be doing a lot of sightseeing in 1 or 2 days, it may pay to buy a pass. A **city-bus all-day pass** costs ¥600. **Passes for both buses and subways** cost ¥900 for 1 day or ¥1,700 for 2 days and are available at subway stations or the Bus and Subway Information counter at Kyoto Station.

(north/Karasuma) Exit, with platforms clearly marked in English listing destinations. Both the Kyoto Tourist Information Center (see "Visitor Information," above) and the Bus and Subway Information counter give out excellent maps showing major bus routes. Some of the buses loop around the city, while others go back and forth between two destinations. Most convenient for sightseeing is Raku bus no. 100, which makes a run every 10 minutes from Kyoto Station to major attractions in east Kyoto, including the Kyoto National Museum, Gojo-zaka (the approach to Kiyomizu Temple), Gion, Heian Shrine, Nanzenji, and Ginkakuji. Raku bus no. 101 departs Kyoto Station for Nijo Castle and Kinkakuji. Unfortunately, at Kyoto Station there are often long queues of foreigners waiting to board these two buses. Hello, people! Many other city buses travel similar routes, so consult your bus map and see if there's an alternative way to reach your destination.

The fare for traveling in central Kyoto is ¥230 for a single ride (¥120 for children). Although buses have been boarded at the rear entrance and paid upon exiting the front door for more than 40 years, a dramatic increase in foreign visitors (some with very large suitcases) has prompted the city to gradually switch to a front entry, where you pay upon boarding, and a rear exit. For a while, you may therefore encounter both systems. If you don't have the exact fare, a fare box can make change for coins and ¥1,000 notes. If the bus is traveling a **long distance** out to the suburbs, you might find a ticket machine right beside the door—take the ticket and hold onto it. It has a number on it and will tell the bus driver when you got on and how much you owe. You can see for yourself how much you owe by looking for your number on a lighted panel at the front of the bus; the longer you ride, the higher the fare. Digital signboards on buses announce each stop in English.

For journeys farther afield, there are regional passes available only to foreign tourists that provide travel throughout the Kansai area (including Osaka, Kyoto, Kobe, Nara, and Himeji) and some even as far away as Hiroshima or Kanazawa. For more information, see p. 330 in chapter 12.

BY TAXI Taxis in Kyoto come in two different sizes with only slightly different fares. Small ones are ¥590 for the first 1.7km (a little more than 1 mile), and large ones are ¥610. Taxis can be waved down or, in the city center, boarded at marked taxi stands or at hotels. **MK Taxi** (www.mktaxi-japan.com; © **075/778-4141**) also offers individualized English-language guided tours.

BY BICYCLE A popular way to get around Kyoto is by bike, made easy because the city has few hills and most streets are named (the ride along the Kamo River is especially wonderful). In peak season, you might even be faster on a bike than a bus. You do have to be on guard for vehicular and pedestrian traffic, and in central Kyoto it's illegal to leave your bike parked on the street (ask the rental company for a map of bike parking lots; bikes left outside a designated bicycle parking area are removed and you'll be fined ¥2,300, plus the cost to return it to the owner). **Kyoto Cycling Tour Project,** a 3-minute walk from the Central (north) Exit of Kyoto Station (turn left upon exiting the station and walk past the post office and APA Hotel; www.kctp.net; ✆ **075/354-3636;** daily 9am–6pm), rents bikes starting at ¥1,000 a day, including a city cycling map. It has additional rental terminals at Nijo Castle and Kinkakuji Temple and offers guided cycling tours as well.

[FastFACTS] KYOTO

In addition to the information here, see "Fast Facts: Japan" in chapter 12. You can also make inquiries at the Kyoto Tourist Information Center (see "Visitor Information," above).

ATMS/Banks In addition to banks all over town, places to exchange money after banks close are large department stores like Isetan (which also has a currency-exchange machine on the second floor), Takashimaya, and Daimaru. You can also exchange money in Kyoto Station at one of two **Travelex** counters: one at the Central Exit (✆ **075/354-9181;** daily 10:30am–7pm) and the other in the central pedestrian passage across from the tourist office, in the Nippon Travel Agency (✆ **075/351-5613;** Mon–Fri 10am–3pm and 4–8pm; Sat–Sun and holidays 10am–2pm and 3–6pm). When changing money, be sure to bring your passport. The most convenient ATMs accepting foreign credit cards are at post offices (like the Kyoto Central Post Office next to Kyoto Station; see "Mail," below) or at one of many 7-Eleven convenience stores in Kyoto.

Climate Kyoto is generally hotter and more humid than Tokyo in summer and colder than Tokyo in winter. For more information, see "When to Go," in chapter 2.

Dentists, Doctors & Hospitals Most hospitals are not equipped to handle emergencies 24 hours a day, but a system has been set up in which hospitals handle emergencies on a rotating basis. **Kyoto University Hospital (Kyoto Daigaku Byoin),** Shogoin Kawahara-cho, Sakyo-ku (www.kuhp.kyoto-u.ac.jp/english; ✆ **075/751-3111**) has English-speaking doctors. For less urgent care, **Sakabe International Clinic,** Gokomachi, Nijo-sagaru, Nakagyo-ku (www.sakabeclinic.com; ✆ **075/231-1624**), also has English-speaking staff, as does **Nakai Dental Office,** 724-1 Yohoji-mae-cho, Teramachi Nijo-agaru, Nakagyo-ku (www.ndo-kyoto.jp; ✆ **075/252-1020**).

Electricity In both Kyoto and Nara it's 100 volts, 60 cycles, almost the same as in the U.S. (110 volts, 60 cycles); your two-pronged appliances should work, but they'll run a little slowly (there are no three-pronged plugs in Japan, so if you brought your laptop, you'll need a plug adapter; many hotels will let you use one for free).

Internet & Wi-Fi Access Kyoto City offers 24 hours of free Wi-Fi, with hotspots located all over town, including Kyoto Station, bus stops, and subway stations; for more information, go to http://kanko.city.kyoto.lg.jp/wifi/en. Many restaurants and stores also offer free Wi-Fi, while hotels offer both Wi-Fi and guest computers for free. Otherwise, **Media Café Popeye** is located just north of Shijo Dori and east of Teramachi (✆ **075/257-5512**) and is open 24 hours. It charges

¥440 for 1 hour, with discounts for additional hours. The Kyoto Tourist Information Center has a couple of coin-operated computers costing ¥100 for 10 minutes.

Luggage Storage & Delivery **Kyoto Station** has lockers for storing luggage beginning at ¥300 for 24 hours, including lockers large enough for big suitcases (¥600) on its south (Shinkansen) side. However, these can fill up during peak season, in which case head to the basement's **Crosta** check-in baggage room (✆ **075/352-5437;** open daily 8am–8pm), where you can store luggage for ¥700 per bag. You can also drop off bags here by 2pm for delivery to most hotels in town; this service costs ¥1,000 per bag and is great if you want to sightsee before check-in.

Mail The **Kyoto Central Post Office,** located just west of Kyoto Station's Central (north) Exit (✆ **075/365-2471**), is open Monday to Friday 9am to 9pm, Saturday 9am to 7pm, and Sunday and holidays 9am to 7pm. You can mail packages bound for international destinations here. To the south of the Central Post Office's main entrance is a counter offering 24-hour postal service. There are also ATMs here, where you can obtain currency Monday to Saturday from 5 minutes past midnight to 11:55pm, Sundays and holidays 5 minutes past midnight to 9pm.

WHERE TO STAY

Kyoto has a wide variety of accommodations, from luxurious, high-end hotels with full facilities to cookie-cutter business hotels and hostels. But if you've never stayed in a *ryokan,* Kyoto is one of the best places to do so. With the exception of hot-spring resorts, Kyoto has more choices of *ryokan* in all price categories than any other city in Japan. Small, traditionally made of wood, and often situated in delightfully quaint neighborhoods, these *ryokan* can enrich your stay in Kyoto by putting you in direct touch with the city's traditional past. Although the prices at upper- and mid-priced *ryokan* may seem prohibitive at first glance, the per-person charge includes two meals and usually tax and service charge (the per-person rates throughout this book are for double occupancy; rates are higher for single occupancy and less for three or more people). These meals are feasts, not unlike *kaiseki* meals you'd receive at a top restaurant where they could easily cost ¥10,000. *Ryokan* in the budget category, on the other hand, usually don't serve meals unless stated otherwise and often charge per room rather than per person, but they do provide the futon experience.

Accommodations are expensive in Kyoto, about on par with Tokyo and sometimes even higher. Because Kyoto is a big tourist destination, be sure to make reservations in advance, particularly in spring when flowers bloom, in autumn (Oct–Nov) for the changing of the leaves, during summer vacation from mid-July through August, and during major festivals (see "Calendar of Events," in chapter 2). With the exception of inexpensive lodgings, most accommodations raise their rates during these times, sometimes shockingly so: A hotel that may charge ¥30,000 to ¥40,000 for a double during most of the year, for example, may charge ¥60,000 or more in high season, with some accommodations requiring a minimum two-night stay. In the off-season (mid-Dec, after New Year's to the beginning of Mar, and June), however, that double might go for as little as ¥18,000. I've arranged the accommodations recommended below, therefore, based on average rates for a double, with "Expensive" usually costing more than ¥30,000; "Moderate" ranging from

¥12,000 to ¥30,000; and "Inexpensive" priced at less than ¥12,000. Keep in mind, however, that a modestly priced hotel could very well be in the expensive category in peak season and in the inexpensive category in February. Furthermore, the wide range of prices I've given for each accommodation runs the spectrum from the cheapest room in off-season to its most expensive room in peak season. Inexpensive accommodations, on the other hand, tend to have the same rates all year.

> **A Note on Directions**
>
> For all hotel and restaurant listings below, directions provided are from Kyoto Station unless otherwise indicated. Numbers in parentheses after stations and bus stops refer to the time it takes to reach your destination **on foot** after alighting from public conveyance.

In recent years, many Kyoto accommodations have become entirely nonsmoking. And because Kyoto is relatively small and has such good bus and subway systems, no matter where you stay you won't be too far away from the heart of the city. Most lodgings are concentrated around Kyoto Station (Shimogyo-ku Ward), in central Kyoto not far from the Kawaramachi-Shijo Dori intersection (Nakagyo-ku Ward), and east of the Kamo River (in the Higashiyama-ku and Sakyo-ku wards).

Some properties have shuttle buses to Kyoto Station's south entrance, convenient for train service but not for city buses, which depart from the north side.

TAXES & SERVICE CHARGES All accommodations levy an 8% consumption tax on room rates (due to rise to 10% in Oct 2019), while mid- and upper-range ones also add a 10% to 15% service fee; in *ryokan,* the service charge can be as high as 20%. Unless noted otherwise, all rates below include consumption tax and service charge. ***Note:*** In October 2018, Kyoto began levying its own accommodations tax. Per person, per night, it is ¥200 for rooms costing less than ¥20,000 a night, ¥500 for rooms costing ¥20,000 to ¥50,000, and ¥1,000 for rates ¥50,000 and more. The prices below are *without* this new local tax.

Around Kyoto Station

EXPENSIVE

Hotel Kanra Kyoto ★★★ The Kanra's corporate-looking facade gives little clue that you are about to enter one of Kyoto's coolest properties, artfully designed and with a decidedly hip vibe. Reception is low-key and relaxing, with sit-down desks for check-in. Rooms, with a miniature moss garden at each entryway, are behind lattice doors in a modern rendition of a *machiya* (merchant house). Even the smallest rooms have plenty of space and oodles of design sense, including wood or black granite floors, raised platform beds, *hinoki* (cedar) soaking tubs (and separate showers), and Japanese-style areas with *tatami* and modular furniture.

190 Kitamachi, Karasuma Dori Rokujo-sagaru, Shimogyo-ku. www.hotelkanra.jp. ✆ **075/344-3815.** 68 units. ¥30,000–¥49,400 single or double. Subway: Gojo (exit 8, 1 min.); Kyoto Station (Karasuma exit, 8 min.). On Karasuma Dori. **Amenities:** 2 restaurants; lounge/bar; room service; spa; Wi-Fi.

Around Kyoto Station

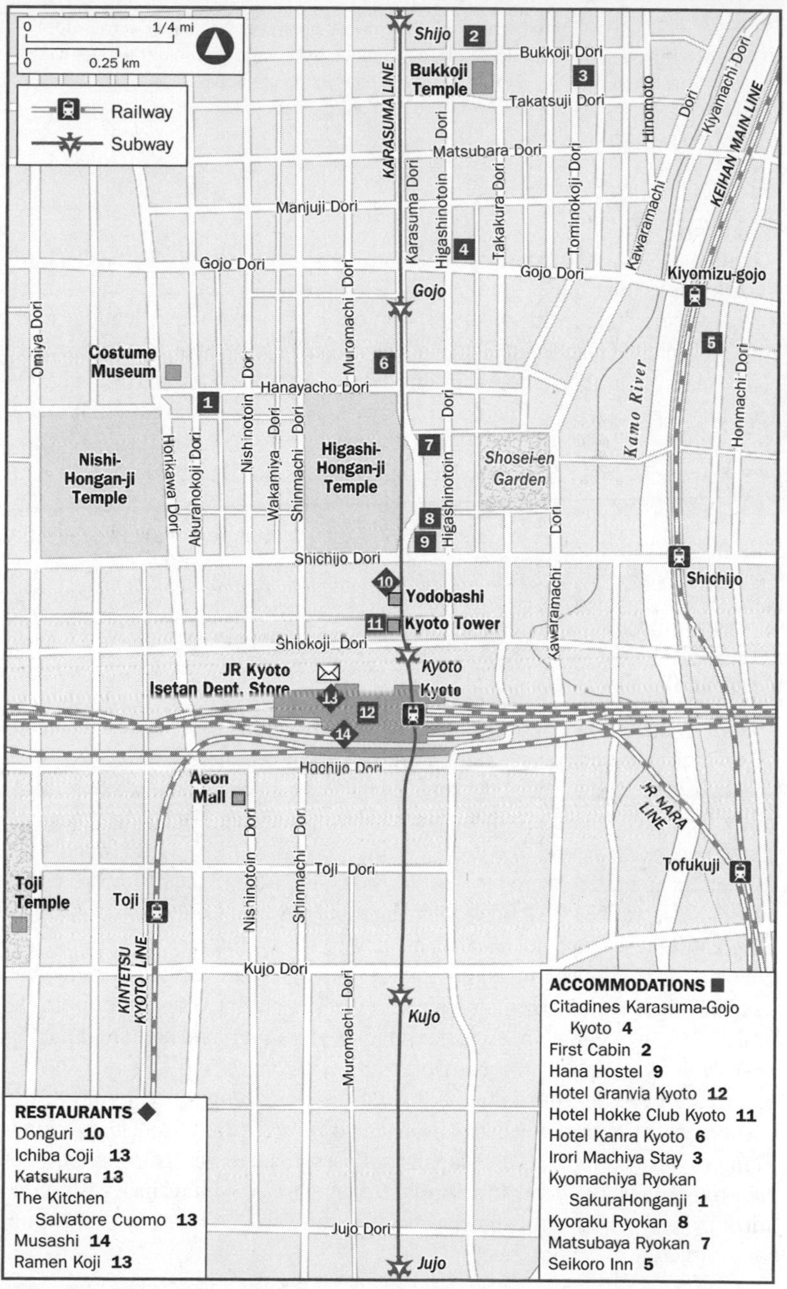

ACCOMMODATIONS ■

Citadines Karasuma-Gojo Kyoto **4**
First Cabin **2**
Hana Hostel **9**
Hotel Granvia Kyoto **12**
Hotel Hokke Club Kyoto **11**
Hotel Kanra Kyoto **6**
Irori Machiya Stay **3**
Kyomachiya Ryokan SakuraHonganji **1**
Kyoraku Ryokan **8**
Matsubaya Ryokan **7**
Seikoro Inn **5**

RESTAURANTS ◆

Donguri **10**
Ichiba Coji **13**
Katsukura **13**
The Kitchen Salvatore Cuomo **13**
Musashi **14**
Ramen Koji **13**

Why the Big Range in Hotel Rates?

Upper- and medium-range hotels in Tokyo, Kyoto, and many other Japanese cities usually charge rates that can vary widely depending on the season and the type of room selected. The hotel prices provided in this guide, therefore, range from what you might expect to pay for the cheapest room in low season to a deluxe room in high season.

MODERATE

Citadines Karasuma-Gojo Kyoto ★★ The Kyoto branch of this "apart-hotel" (apartment hotel) chain is a great choice, evident the moment you enter the stone pathway lined with hanging *washi* paper leading to the mood-lit lobby. Contemporary rooms are actually mini-apartments, complete with small galley kitchens (including range, sink, toaster, microwave, tableware, and more), and available in various configurations, from studios with double or twin beds to premier studios with king-size beds (some premiers even have balconies). Some studio doubles have sofas that can double as beds, along with a sliding door that can make each sleeping area more private. Studios don't have much storage space, however, so for longer stays you might opt for the apartment with a separate bedroom.

432 Matsuya-cho, Gojo Dori Karasuma Higashi-iru, Shimogyo-ku. www.citadines.com. ✆ **075/352-8900.** 124 units. ¥14,850–¥34,450 single or double. Monthly rates available. Subway: Gojo (exit 1, 1 min.). On Gojo Dori, 1½ blocks east of Karasuma Dori. **Amenities:** Wi-Fi.

Hotel Granvia Kyoto ★★★ You can't beat this hotel for convenience, since it's located in Kyoto Station and is only a minute's walk to buses and subways serving the rest of the city. Luckily, the lobby is on the second floor, away from the station's foot traffic, though it can still hum with the hotel's many guests. As part of the hotel's inclusive policy, it is LGBT-friendly and also offers amenities geared toward Muslims, including Halal menus available without reservations and, on request, a prayer mat and Qibla direction sign in all guest rooms. The hotel also has a list of privately guided tour options, from shopping for antiques to walking and cycling tours; it even offers a gay wedding package, with a ceremony at a temple. The cheapest standard rooms are small, have unexciting views of the station's glass roof, and are rather dark, so you might want to spend a bit more for a standard facing outside. The best rooms are large deluxe rooms (with Club Floor privileges) facing north with great views of Kyoto. Because Granvia is owned by the West Japan Railway Company, if you have a valid Japan Rail pass you can get a discount off certain rooms; ask the hotel for details. In any case, if you're in Kyoto only a night or two, this is a convenient choice, but it can't compete with the ambience of hotels in central Kyoto.

JR Kyoto Station, Central Exit, Karasuma Dori Shiokoji-sagaru, Shimogyo-ku. www.granviakyoto.com. ✆ **075/344-8888.** 537 units. ¥16,960–¥41,200 single or double. Granvia Deluxe Club Floors ¥29,200–¥58,200 single or double. **Amenities:** 8 restaurants; bar;

lounge; concierge; executive-level rooms; health club w/indoor pool, fitness gym, and sauna (fee: ¥1,080; only guests 21 and older allowed); room service; Wi-Fi.

Hotel Hokke Club Kyoto ★ Popular with tourists thanks to its great location just opposite Kyoto Station, this chain hotel with a friendly staff first opened about 100 years ago and provides clean, pleasantly decorated Western-style rooms. Reception is up on the second floor, where a rack displays English-language brochures for sightseeing in Kyoto. Singles are tiny with no closets, while doubles are larger with bigger desks and closets, but all have glazed windows because they face another building. Twins seem downright roomy in comparison, with sofas that can serve as sleepers and windows facing the back. The best room is a corner twin facing the front, with views of Kyoto Station (although light sleepers may be distracted by train noise) and Japanese-style bathrooms with separate shower and tub areas.

Kyoto Eki-mae, Shomen Chuoguchi, Karasuma, Shimogyo-ku. www.hokke.co.jp. ✆ **075/361-1251.** 180 units. ¥9,000–¥14,080 single; ¥9,000–¥28,080 double. Across from Kyoto Station's Central exit. **Amenities:** 2 restaurants; Wi-Fi.

Kyomachiya Ryokan Sakura Honganji ★★ Opened in 2009, the smoke-free Sakura has a traditional facade of a *machiya* (merchant's house) but is comfortably contemporary inside. A long slab of wood in the lobby serves as a table, where guests gather for breakfast or conversation. Stone corridors lead to Western-style rooms with twin beds and Japanese decor and Japanese-style *tatami* rooms (with instructions for laying out your own futon). The best tatami room opens onto a garden with its own wooden veranda, and another room is in the style of a tea ceremony room. It's located in an interesting neighborhood of shops selling Buddhist prayer articles; the friendly staff hands out a great bilingual map of local sights and restaurants. An annex, opened in 2015 near central Kyoto, offers similar Japanese- and Western-style rooms at slightly higher prices.

228 Butsuguyacho, Aburanokoji Hanayacho-sagaru, Shimogyo-ku. www.kyoto-ryokan-sakura.com. ✆ **075/343-3500.** 30 units. ¥12,500–¥21,000 double. A 15-min. walk from Kyoto Station's Central (north) exit; turn left on Shiokoji Dori and right after passing the small parking lot onto Aburanokoji Dori (1 block before Horikawa Dori). **Amenities:** Wi-Fi.

Kyoraku Ryokan ★★ Near the Matsubaya (see below), this pleasant and spotlessly clean property offers nicely decorated rooms, some of which look over an inner courtyard garden. Though the English-speaking son is a

A Double or a Twin?

For the sake of convenience, the price for two people in a room is listed as a "double" in this book. Japanese hotels, however, differentiate between rooms with a double bed or two twin beds, usually with different prices. Most hotels charge more for a twin room, but sometimes the opposite is true; if you're looking for a bargain, therefore, be sure to inquire about prices for both. Note, too, that hotels usually have more twin rooms than doubles, for the simple reason that Japanese couples, used to their own futon, traditionally prefer twin beds.

fourth-generation innkeeper, the building housing this *ryokan* was rebuilt in 2007 and has the bonus of an elevator and coin-op laundry machines. Rooms, which include one Western-style room with private bathroom, are simple, with screened windows that open. Note that the women's public bath can be used privately but the men's is communal. ***Note:*** Rooms must be vacated during cleaning time (10am–3pm), and the *ryokan* locks its doors at 11pm.

231 Kogawa-cho, Shichijo-agaru, Akezu-dori, Shimogyo-ku. www.ryokankyoraku.jp. ✆ **075/371-1260.** 13 units (8 with bathroom). ¥6,200–¥7,980 single without bathroom, ¥7,980–¥8,930 single with bathroom; ¥14,400–¥15,960 double without bathroom, ¥15,980–¥18,000 double with bathroom. A 7-min. walk north of Kyoto Station's Central exit; walk north on Karasuma Dori, turn right on Shichijo Dori, and then left. **Amenities:** Wi-Fi.

INEXPENSIVE

Hana Hostel ★★ This is a hostel but with a difference. In addition to four dormitory-style rooms (including one just for women), there are also 14 Japanese-style rooms sleeping one to three people, most with their own bathrooms. This place is spotless, with a large and comfy communal kitchen for cooking and socializing and free coffee and tea. And it has a good location near Kyoto Station.

229 Kogawa-cho, Shichijo-agaru, Akezu-dori, Shimogyo-ku. http://hanahostel.com. ✆ **075/371-3577.** 14 units (11 with bathroom), 4 dorm rooms. ¥3,900–¥5,540 single with or without bathroom; ¥5,200–¥7,650 double without bathroom, ¥5,450–¥8,650 double with bathroom; ¥2,500–¥3,100 dormitory bed. A 7-min. walk north of Kyoto Station's Central exit; walk north on Karasuma Dori, turn right on Shichijo Dori, and then left. **Amenities:** Rental bikes (¥500 per day); Wi-Fi.

Matsubaya Ryokan ★★ The Hayashi family has managed this inn, just east of Higashi Honganji Temple, since the late Edo Period; it's now under ownership of the fifth Hayashi generation. Long an old wooden *ryokan* with character, in 2008 it was torn down and enlarged, though some architectural details were salvaged. In any case, on the ground floor is a courtyard garden and lounge that's a good place to connect with other travelers or converse with the owners about sightseeing in Kyoto. Nearby is a company that rents bicycles. Rooms are mostly Japanese style, with the best overlooking the garden. Also good bets are five Western-style rooms on the fifth floor with kitchenettes and tiny balconies. For families, a combination suite is big enough for six people, with beds and futon along with two bathrooms.

Higashinotoin Nishi, Kamijuzuyamachi Dori, Shimogyo-ku. www.matsubayainn.com. ✆ **075/351-3727.** 32 units (30 with bathroom). ¥4,600–¥8,800 single without bathroom, ¥7,200–¥10,300 single with bathroom; ¥8,600–¥15,600 double without bathroom, ¥11,800–¥18,000 double with bathroom. A 10-min. walk north of Kyoto Station's Central exit; walk north on Karasuma Dori and take the 3rd right after passing Shichijo Dori. **Amenities:** Wi-Fi.

Central Kyoto

EXPENSIVE

Hiiragiya Ryokan ★★★ This exquisite *ryokan* is as fine an example of a traditional inn as you'll find in Japan. Built in 1818 and nestled in the heart

0 1/4 mi
0 0.25 km
Marutamachi Dori
Marutamachi
Takeyamachi Dori
Ebisugawa D.
Nijo Dori
Oshikoji Dori
Oike Dori
Aneyakoji Dori
Sanjo Dori
Rokkaku Dori
Takoyakushi Dori
Nishikikoji Dori
Shijo Dori
Ayanokoji Dori
Bukkoji Dori
Takatsuji Dori
Matsubara Dori
Gojo Dori
Gojo
Nishinotoin Dori
Wakamiya Dori
Shinmachi Dori
Muromachi Dori
KYOTO MUNICIPAL SUBWAY KARASUMA LINE
Karasuma Dori
Kurumayacho Dori
Higashinotoin Dori
Ainomachi Dori
Takakura Dori
Sakaimachi Dori
Tominokoji Dori
Fuyacho Dori
Gokomachi Dori
Teramachi Dori
Kawaramachi Dori
Kamo River
Jingumarutamachi
Karasuma Oike
TOZAI LINE
City Hall
Kyoto Shiyakusho-mae
The Museum of Kyoto
Koromonodana Dori
Ryogaemachi Dori
Yanaginobanba Dori
Pontocho Dori
Nawate Dori
Sanjo Keihan
Sanjo
Karasuma
Kawaramachi
Takashimaya Dept. Store
Gion-shijo
Shijo
Bukkoji Temple
KARASUMA LINE
Hinomoto
Kiyamachi Dori
KEIHAN MAIN LINE
Kawaramachi
Railway
Subway
HOTELS ■
APA Hotel Kyoto Gion Excellent 37
First Cabin 26
Hiiragiya Ryokan 6
Hotel Gimmond 5
Hotel Gracery 15
Hotel Gran M's Kyoto 8
Hotel Monterey Kyoto 10
Hotel Mystays Kyoto Shijo 24
Irori Machiya Stay 27
Kyoto Okura Hotel 7
Nishiyama Ryokan 3
The Palace Side Hotel 1
Piece Hostel Sanjo 12
The Royal Park Kyoto Sanjo 17
The Screen 2
Sumiya 13
NIGHTLIFE ◆
Ace Café 19
Atlantis 36
Gion Corner 39
Hello Dolly 35
Le Club Jazz 14
Live Spot RAG 19
Pig & Whistle 21
Ran Kyoto 34
Rub-A-Dub 22
Spring Valley Brewery 29
RESTAURANTS ◆
Ashoka 32
Bio-Tei 9
Ganko Sushi 20
Gontaro 31
Ichiba Coji 30
Ippudo 25
Kushi Kura 4
Misoguigawa 23
Musashi 16
Orizzonte (Okura hotel) 7
Pizza Salvatore Cuomo & Grill 18
Savory 11
Second House 28
Tagoto 33
Tohkasaikan 38

of old Kyoto, it has all the quintessential design characteristics of an old inn, making artful use of wood, bamboo, screens, and stones in its simple yet elegant *tatami* rooms, decorated with art and antiques and many with garden views and cypress baths. Even modern conveniences are cleverly hidden, like the lacquered remote controls for the lights and curtains, shaped like a gourd and invented by the innkeeper's ancestor. A 2006 wing added seven rooms, elegantly simple in that Zen-like Japanese sensibility of style. Dinners, served in your room in true *ryokan* fashion, are multi-course *kaiseki* feasts, with Western-style breakfasts available on request. No wonder Hiiragiya has played host to writers, artists, politicians, and even members of the imperial family over the decades. Its level of service and hospitality is intuitive and about as perfect as it gets, honed over the years and now under the watchful and caring eye of Ms. Nishimura, the inn's seventh-generation innkeeper.

277 Nakahakusancho, Fuyacho Anekoji-agaru, Nakagyo-ku. www.hiiragiya.co.jp. ✆ **075/221-1136.** 24 units. ¥35,000–¥90,000 per person, excluding tax. Rates include 2 meals. Located on the corner of Fuyacho and Oike sts. Subway: Kyoto Shiyakusho-mae (4 min.) or Karasuma-Oike (7 min.). Bus: 4, 17, or 205 to Kyoto Shiyakusho-mae (5 min.). **Amenities:** Wi-Fi.

Irori Machiya Stay ★★★ Downtown Kyoto used to have many *machiya,* traditional Japanese homes, but time and urban development have wrought the demise of many of them. Luckily, there's a push to preserve these traditional buildings before they disappear altogether. Irori Machiya Stay offers 14 traditional homes in central Kyoto, most built about a century ago and offering visitors the rare chance to experience living in one. Decorated with folding screens, *andon* floor lamps, *tansu* chests, hanging scrolls, ceramics, baths made of cypress, cedar, or stone, and other Japanese details, they also offer such modern conveniences as a fridge, microwave, and Wi-Fi but do not have a TV, phone, or full kitchen (because of fire hazards). Houses vary in size, with the smallest good for two people and the largest accommodating up to nine. Ishifudono-cho, the smallest house, is located on a quiet alleyway and overlooks a tiny garden, but because the bedroom is up a steep flight of stairs (and the bathroom is downstairs), it's best for nimble travelers. Especially nice is Izumiya-cho (sleeping six)—it's located on Kiyamachi Dori and has a view of the Kamo River from the rooms and its own deck, as does the larger Minoya-cho, which sleeps eight. Check in is at the company's address (given below) or at your *machiya.* It's a great choice for travelers who do not need the constant services of an on-site concierge (although staff is always available if you need them) and want more privacy than that afforded by a *ryokan.*

Irori Corporation (office), 144–6 Sujiya-cho, Tominokoji Takatsuji Agaru, Shimogyo-ku. www.kyoto-machiya.com. ✆ **075/352-0211.** 11 houses. ¥28,000–¥52,000 double, depending on season. Subway: Shijo Karasuma (10 min.). Bus: 5 or 26 to Karasuma Matsubara, or 4, 17, or 205 to Kawaramachi Matsubara (6 min.). **Amenities:** Concierge; Wi-Fi.

Kyoto Okura Hotel ★★ This is one of Kyoto's oldest hotels, with a history dating back to 1888. You can't tell that by looking at it, however, as it underwent a complete reconstruction in 1994 that turned it into a 17-story hotel. In a nod to its earlier life, the hotel designed its lobby after the original 1920s ballroom, but rooms, which wrap around a central atrium, are thoroughly modern. The city's tallest building, it offers great views from top-floor restaurants and from more expensive rooms on upper floors, with panoramas of the Kamo River and the hills of Higashiyama rising beyond the city. In addition to restaurants inside the hotel, the hotel also manages **Awata Sanso,** offering *kaiseki* in a traditional Japanese house. Unfortunately, the hotel's fitness facility is a members' club, so access is limited and it's off-limits to those younger than 18. Note, too, that the cheapest double is actually a single room with a semi-double-size bed (bigger than a twin bed but not quite full-size), but it's an option for people who want to stay in this great central location for a cheaper price. Otherwise, standard rooms are on lower floors, while the best views are from superior rooms facing east.

537-4 Ichinofunairi-cho, Kawaramachi-Oike, Nakagyo-ku. http://okura.kyotohotel.co.jp. ✆ **075/211-5111.** 323 units. ¥16,700–¥26,136 single; ¥18,600–¥59,400 double; from ¥55,800 executive double. Subway: Kyoto Shiyakusho-mae (1 min., below the hotel). Bus: 4, 17, or 205 to Shiyakusho-mae (2 min.). **Amenities:** 8 restaurants; bar; lounge; children's day-care center (¥5,400 for 2 hr.); concierge; executive-level rooms; indoor pool w/Jacuzzi and sauna (fee: ¥2,160 7–10am, ¥3,250 other times, including use of gym); room service; Wi-Fi.

Sumiya ★★★ Like Hiiragiya (above) on the same street, the 100-year-old Sumiya has a great location in a typical Kyoto neighborhood just a few minutes' walk from bustling downtown. Offering excellent service amid simple yet elegant surroundings, including wooden corridors that wrap around courtyard gardens and several tearooms (a tea ceremony is performed after dinner on the 7th and 17th of each month), it has a variety of rooms, most with wooden tubs and some with wonderful views of tiny private gardens with outdoor benches and platforms for sitting. The oldest rooms employ a striking variety of different woods (note the Edo-era designs on the sliding doors), while rooms in a 1968 addition may have sliding screen doors that open onto a private garden. Elaborate meals are served in your room and feature Kyoto *kaiseki* cuisine that can last 2 hours or more (request ahead for special dietary needs); Western breakfasts are also available.

433 Shirakabecho, Sanjo-sagaru, Fuyacho, Nakagyo-ku. www2.odn.ne.jp/sumiya. ✆ **075/221-2188.** 20 units. ¥35,000–¥65,000 per person, including 2 meals but excluding tax. Subway: Kyoto Shiyakusho-mae (6 min.) or Karasuma-Oike (10 min.). Bus: 4, 5, 17, or 205 to Kawaramachi Sanjo (3 min.). On Fuyacho Dori just south of Sanjo St. **Amenities:** Tea ceremony (fee: ¥3,000); Wi-Fi.

The Screen ★★ If you prefer small hotels and contemporary design, consider staying at this strikingly modern yet inviting hotel, complete with traditional touches that make it seem like a hybrid between a traditional *ryokan* and a boutique hotel. At check-in, guests are treated to Ippodo tea (its shop is just down the street; see p. 259) and a local sweet. Each of its 13 rooms, by 13 different international designers, has its own style, but all have Jacuzzi tubs and a shower cabin. Two Japanese-style rooms, for example, have futon on raised *tatami* platforms along with black lacquered furniture, while another has a playful forest motif and another yet is lined with sheer white curtains. Its location between the Imperial Palace and downtown, on a street lined with craft and antiques stores, is another plus, and I also like the seasonal rooftop terrace. There aren't many cool hotels like this in Japan, and after stays in unimaginative rooms, you might find this a worthy splurge.

640–1 Shimogoryomae-cho, Nakagyo-ku. www.screen-hotel.jp. ✆ **075/252-1113.** 13 units. ¥22,000–¥55,000 single or double. Subway: Karasuma Marutamachi (7 min.). Bus: 4, 17, or 205 to Kawaramachi Marutamachi (7 min.). Just south of Marutamachi Dori, on Teramachi Dori. **Amenities:** Restaurant; lounge; room service; spa; Wi-Fi.

MODERATE

Hotel Gimmond ★ This small hotel on Oike Dori was built almost 45 years ago but is undergoing a much-needed gradual overhaul until March 2019 that will hopefully bring it up to speed (and probably raise its rates). Though the hotel calls itself a tourist hotel and offers mainly twins, its lack of services and facilities place it squarely in the category of business hotel. Simple rooms are soundproof and have sliding blackout panels behind the curtains, but I still think those that face away from Oike Dori are quieter. All doubles and some twins face the back; ask for one on a higher floor. Deluxe twin rooms, with a sofa that can be made into a bed, are decent sized for the price, while the cheapest rooms are quite small.

Takakura, Oike Dori, Nakagyo-ku. www.gimmond.co.jp. ✆ **075/221-4111.** 140 units. ¥6,500–¥10,800 single; ¥7,400–¥17,600 double. Subway: Karasuma-Oike (2 min.). On Oike Dori west of Takakura Dori. **Amenities:** 2 restaurants; Wi-Fi.

Hotel Gracery Kyoto Sanjo ★★ What I like most about this business/tourist hotel is that it's located smack-dab just off the Teramachi covered shopping arcade, right in the thick of downtown. Rooms are thoughtfully laid out, with the sink, toilet, and separate shower/tub areas all with their own space, making it convenient for two people to get ready at the same time. It's divided into two towers, each with its own check-in counter: the North Tower, with only double rooms, and the South Tower, with only twins, though some twins have a sofa bed and can sleep three. Rooms are surprisingly quiet, despite the hotel's central location.

420 Sakuranocho, Teramachi Higashi-iru Rokkaku Dori, Nakagyo-ku. http://kyoto.gracery.com/. ✆ **075/222-1111.** 225 units. ¥10,000–¥28,280 single; ¥12,000–¥28,280 double. Subway: Kyoto Shiyakusho-mae (5 min.) Bus: 4, 5, 104, or 205 to Kawaramachi Sanjo (2 min.). Just east of Teramachi covered arcade, on Rokkaku Dori. **Amenities:** Wi-Fi.

Hotel Gran M's Kyoto ★ This hotel occupies a former hotel's older brick building, but it's been completely renovated and updated. The lobby, bathed in white with splashes of earth-toned colors and lots of space, has a hidden entrance near the Kawaramachi-Shijo Dori intersection, very centrally located. Because the cheapest singles face an inner courtyard and are fairly dark, it may be worthwhile to dish out extra yen for a brighter room (two people can book it for the cheapest double price, but with its semi-double-size bed, it's pretty cramped). My favorite rooms overlook a quiet temple and Buddhist cemetery—a fitting view in a town that boasts so many religious structures. Among the six

Japanese-style rooms, two combination rooms have both beds and a tatami area and sleep up to eight people. In short, this is a good choice if you like to be in the thick of things and are willing to sacrifice space and facilities to be there.

Kawaramachi, Sango-agaru, Nakagyo-ku. http://granms.jp. © **075/241-2000.** 130 units. ¥5,600–¥11,800 single; ¥5,700–¥35,340 double. Subway: Kyoto Shiyakusho-mae (2 min.). Bus: 4, 5, 17, or 205 to Kawaramachi Sanjo (1 min.). Just off Kawaramachi Dori not far from Sanjo Dori; entrance is on a side street called Aneyakoji Dori. **Amenities:** Wi-Fi.

Hotel Monterey Kyoto ★★ The Monterey hotel chain is known for its old-world designs, but always with some connection to the city it's located in. Monterey Kyoto, occupying a former bank, centers on the Arts & Crafts style of Edinburgh—Kyoto and the Scottish capital are sister cities. The dark and subdued lobby plays up its part with marbled flooring, bookcases, and period European artwork. Rooms, on the other hand, are remarkably bold, most with striped wallpaper in navy blue or crimson red, all with an eye to the largely Japanese female travelers this chain attracts. Great views across the city from the top-floor spa make the entrance fee for the sauna and indoor-outdoor hot-spring baths well worth it; both utilize thermal waters obtained by drilling more than 1,000m (3,300 ft.) below ground. By paying extra (¥1,080 for 30 min.), women also have access to the ladies-only **Bedrock Bath,** where hot stones are thought to help draw out impurities while you lie on them.

604 Manjuya-cho, Karasuma Dori, Sanjo-sagaru, Nakagyo-ku. www.hotelmonterey.co.jp/kyoto. © **075/251-7111.** 327 units. ¥11,300–¥23,900 single; ¥13,600–¥49,400 double. Subway: Karasuma Oike (exit 6, 3 min.). Just south of Sanjo Dori on Karasuma Dori. **Amenities:** 2 restaurants; concierge; spa (fee: ¥1,770); Wi-Fi.

Hotel Mystays Kyoto Shijo ★ This tourist/business hotel is a step ahead of its older competitors, offering a contemporary lobby (on the second floor) decorated with traditional crafts and serving coffee and tea from a machine, plus stylish rooms with modern furnishings (like red lounge chairs in its single and double rooms) and black-and-white photos of Kyoto on the walls. Nagomi twin rooms, with their bamboo floors and low bed, have a traditional Japanese atmosphere, while rooms on the top floors have good city views. Rates fluctuate wildly depending on the season, but you can usually get a good deal. On the down side, it's a bit of a walk, about 15 minutes, from the downtown action.

52 Kasaboko-cho, Aburanokoji Higashi-iru, Shijo Dori, Shimogyo-ku. www.mystays.com/hotel-mystays-kyoto-shijo-kyoto. © **075/283-3939.** 224 units. ¥12,000–¥33,000 single; ¥12,000–¥38,400 double. Subway: Shijo (6 min.). Bus: 26 to Shijo Nishinotoin (2 min.). On the north side of Shijo Dori, just west of Nishitoin and across from Oaks Hotel. **Amenities:** Restaurant; Wi-Fi.

The Royal Park Hotel Kyoto Sanjo ★★★ Close to sightseeing, shopping, nightlife, and transportation, this hotel is stylish, comfy, and up to date, with a hidden (some might say *too* hidden) entryway down a dramatic, darkened corridor leading to a similarly subdued lobby, with spotlights trained on artwork behind the desk and statues arranged on shelves. Rooms are fairly standard and small, though deluxe rooms provide more space and have bathrooms with separate showers and soaking tubs. All have custom-designed mattresses and playful artwork of rabbits jumping over the moon or other motifs that add a dash of color. Rooms and public spaces are nonsmoking, including the bar (a rarity in Japan).

Kawaramachi Higashi-iru, Sango Dori, Nakagyo-ku. www.the-royalpark.jp. ✆ **075/241-1111.** 172 units. ¥9,500–¥24,500 single; ¥14,000–¥34,000 double. Subway: Kyoto Shiyakusho-mae (3 min.). On Sanjo Dori just east of Kawaramachi, on the north side. **Amenities:** Restaurant; bar; concierge; Wi-Fi.

INEXPENSIVE

First Cabin Kyoto Karasuma ★ I can't imagine anyone who enjoys sleeping on a plane, but those who do might want to check in for a similar experience here. A step up from capsule hotels, First Cabin offers 77 "cabins" for men and 44 for women, all nonsmoking and designed for single use (no doubles here) and available in two sizes. A Business Class Cabin is just a smidgen larger than the bed, with the rest of the space taken up by a nightstand with a small locker for valuables. That translates to absolutely no floor space; smaller people might be able to dress standing on the bed, but taller people will have to get creative. In addition, the only storage space for luggage is underneath the low bed, so if yours doesn't fit you might find yourself sleeping with that as well. If that's too cozy for comfort, spring for a First Class Cabin, which offers a bit of floor space. All cabins have wall-mounted TVs and door screens that close for privacy (there's no lock). I also recommend picking up a free pair of earplugs from the front desk, because you're going to need them. Breakfast, beer, and other drinks and snacks are available in the lounge; there's a women's lounge on the dedicated ladies' floor. In short, these rooms are the smallest I've ever seen, but I'd kill to get one on a real plane. First Cabin is so successful, it has opened another one right on Kawaramachi Dori near Sanjo.

Takanoha Square Building, 4th floor, 331 Kamiyanagimachi, Bokkuji Dori, Karasuma Higashi-iru. www.first-cabin.jp. ✆ **075/361-1113.** 121 units (none with private bathroom). ¥4,600 business-class single; ¥5,600 first-class single. East of Karasuma Dori, across from Bokkuji Temple. Subway: Shijo (2 min.). **Amenities:** Lounge; Wi-Fi.

Nishiyama Ryokan ★★★ This family-owned inn, open since 1975 and with third-generation, English-speaking innkeeper brothers, has a great location just a few minutes' walk from downtown. Although the building itself is nondescript, inside it strives for a traditional atmosphere, with a small courtyard garden visible just beyond the lobby, a public bath with a view of the garden's waterfall, and mostly Japanese-style *tatami* rooms (there are also three Western-style twins). *Kaiseki* dinners costing ¥8,000 are available with reservations made at least 3 days in advance; breakfasts are ¥2,000. It even presents a free tea ceremony in the lobby most mornings, with other cultural events like calligraphy, Japanese lessons, sake tasting, origami, or koto performances most nights of the week. The only downside, perhaps, is that its moderate rates attract school groups, but a youthful clientele seems hardly a deterrent for Japanese-style lodgings in this price range in the heart of Kyoto.

Gokomachi, Nijo-sagaru, Nakagyo-ku. www.ryokan-kyoto.com. ✆ **075/222-1166.** 30 units (26 with bathroom, 4 with toilet only). ¥10,000–¥16,000 single; ¥14,000–¥40,000 double. Subway: Shiyakusho-mae (3 min.). Bus: 4, 17, or 205 to Shiyakusho-mae (3 min.). 2 blocks northwest of City Hall. **Amenities:** Wi-Fi.

The Palace Side Hotel ★★ Savvy, budget-conscious travelers have been flocking to this modest hotel with its contemporary lobby and cafe since 1968. Although its location just west of the Imperial Palace is not as convenient as my other inexpensive recommendations in central Kyoto, it's near a subway line, and the palace's expansive parklike grounds are popular with joggers. It keeps rates down by offering bare-boned small rooms with the basics of fridge, desks too small for any serious work, and aging tiled bathrooms. The most expensive twins and doubles have kitchenettes with a hotplate and microwave, making them good for longer stays, but there's also a communal kitchen. Some rooms face the greenery of the palace, but they're also noisier, thanks to busy Karasuma Dori. Probably the most impressive things about the hotel are the artwork in most rooms created over the years by artists who have stayed here, free Japanese lessons offered once or twice a week, and occasional mini-concerts held in the lobby.

Karasuma Shimodachiuri-agaru, Kamigyo-ku. www.palacesidehotel.co.jp. ✆ **075/415-8887.** 116 units. ¥5,300–¥10,200 single; ¥7,700–¥12,000 double. Discounts for stays longer than 2 nights. Subway: Marutamachi (exit 2, 3 min.). **Amenities:** Restaurant; Thai massage room; rental bikes (free 1st hour, then ¥800 for 12 hr.); Wi-Fi.

Piece Hostel Sanjo ★★ Opened in 2015, this spotless hostel is a good example of how far budget accommodations have come in Japan. Converted from a former ryokan, it has a contemporary yet traditional facade, with big chunks of rock lining a long entryway. The communal kitchen is huge, allowing several people to cook at once, and overlooks a dining area that includes a small outdoor terrace. In addition to four dormitory rooms sleeping four to 10 people (including two just for women), it has single, twin, and double rooms without private bathrooms, plus a family room for up to six people and double rooms with private bathrooms. This local brand has big aspirations, with two properties, 22 Pieces and Piece Hostel Kyoto, located near Kyoto Station and a third, across the street from Piece Hostel Sanjo, slated to open in summer 2019 with rooms all having private bathroom.

531 Asakura-cho, Nakagyo-ku. www.piecehostel.com/sanjo/en. ✆ **075/746-3688.** 50 units, 28 dormitory beds. ¥4,500–¥5,500 single without bathroom; ¥6,800–¥9,600 double without bathroom; ¥9,000–¥12,500 double with bathroom. Subway: Karasuma Oike (10 min). Marutamachi (exit 2, 3 min.). On Tominokoji Dori, south of Sanjo. **Amenities:** Cafe; rental bikes (¥500–¥600 per day); Wi-Fi.

Eastern Kyoto

EXPENSIVE

Hyatt Regency Kyoto ★★★ I love this hotel for its location (across the street from the Kyoto National Museum, next to Sanjusangendo Hall, and within walking distance of Kiyomizu Temple) and its spa, which boasts more Asian treatments than any other hotel spa in Japan, including acupuncture, moxibustion, and shiatsu. The lobby is stunning, with a modern take on traditional latticework covering the walls and ceiling. Rooms, too, are topnotch, combining Japanese aesthetics (kimono-fabric-covered headboards and elegant teaware) with modern amenities. For travelers looking to splurge, eight deluxe rooms have *tatami* areas plus Japanese-style tubs placed next to balconies, with views of the garden or the National Museum. I also like the hotel restaurants (including **Touzan** for Japanese and **Sette** for Italian), which use organic vegetables from the hotel garden, maintained by hotel staff.

644–2 Sanjusangendo-mawari, Higashiyama-ku. http://kyoto.regency.hyatt.com. ✆ **075/541-1234.** 187 units. ¥35,000–¥98,850 single or double. Bus: 100, 106, 206, or 208 to Hakubutsukan Sanjusangendo (1 min.). **Amenities:** 3 restaurants; bar; concierge; gym (free for hotel guests); room service; spa with yoga classes; Wi-Fi.

The Westin Miyako Kyoto ★★★ The Miyako opened in 1890 but has gone through many changes since Douglas Fairbanks, Queen Elizabeth II, and other well-known travelers stayed here (the present hotel dates from 1992). What I like most about the Miyako is its hilltop setting, sprawling over more than 6.4 hectares (16 acres) and boasting a Japanese garden. It has a satellite office at Kyoto Station, where you can drop off luggage for delivery to the hotel (¥300 per bag) while you go off sightseeing, but a free shuttle bus can also take you directly to the hotel. For families, there's a playroom equipped with a slide and toys for young children and both indoor and outdoor pools. A city zoo, Heian Shrine, and Nanzenji Temple are within walking distance. A variety of Western-style rooms are available, the best with huge terraces overlooking the valley. For a *ryokan* experience, the Kasui-en annex, built in 1959 next to the hotel, offers 20 Japanese-style rooms complete with cypress baths and views of the garden. In any case, this is one of Japan's best-known hotels; you can't go wrong staying here.

1 Awadaguchi Kacho-cho, Keage, Sanjo, Higashiyama-ku. www.miyakohotels.ne.jp. ✆ **075/771-7111.** 300 units. ¥20,500-¥59,400 single or double; from ¥65,800 Executive Club floor; ¥45,360 double in Kasui-en. Free shuttle every 30 min. from Kyoto Station's Hachijo exit (9am–9pm). Subway: Keage (2 min.). **Amenities:** 5 restaurants; lounge; bar; babysitting; concierge; executive-level rooms; fitness center w/gym, 20m (66-ft.) indoor pool, and shallow outdoor pool (fee: ¥525; free for executive-level guests); room service; sundecks (available also for viewing the full moon); Wi-Fi.

MODERATE

APA Hotel Kyoto Gion Excellent ★ The overwhelming reason to stay at this nearly 50-year-old property, one of the oldest in this fast-growing chain, is its superb location in Gion, within easy walking distance to downtown, the Pontocho and Kiyamachi nightlife districts, and Higashiyama-ku's many temples and sights. Other perks are the Starbucks on the ground floor and a rooftop beer garden open in summer. Otherwise, rooms are updated but tiny. The single rooms are among the smallest I've ever seen, and yet couples on a budget can attempt to squeeze into one—though with no room to unpack and no closet, they'll probably have to store luggage in the shower. Most rooms are twins (there are only 15 doubles), and they, too, are rather small. There are no views, but my recommendation is to ask for a room on a higher floor facing west, with floor-to-ceiling windows overlooking the tiled roofs of

Gion. If off-season rates are on par with the lower spectrum given below, I'd consider this place a bargain. Otherwise, three other APA properties, all within walking distance of Kyoto Station, are often cheaper.

555 Gionmachi-minamigawa, Gion, Higashiyama-ku. www.apahotel.com. ✆ **075/551-2111.** 154 units. ¥7,000–¥26,000 single; ¥10,000–¥36,000 double. Bus: 100 or 206 to Gion (2 min.). On Shijo Dori, west of Yasaka Shrine. **Amenities:** Restaurant; bar; summer beer garden; Starbucks; Wi-Fi.

Seikoro Ryokan ★★★ This *ryokan* just east of the Kamo River was established in 1831, with the present building dating from about 115 years ago. After passing through a traditional front gate and small courtyard, you'll find yourself in one of the most charming entryways I've seen in Kyoto, which adjoins a cozy parlor replete with an eclectic mix of Japanese and Western antiques. Rooms, occupying the older main building and an annex built just before the 1964 Olympics, are comfortable and decorated with antiques and have wooden bathtubs. Rooms in the main building consist of old and renovated *tatami* rooms, most with sliding doors and *shoji* screens that open onto the garden. Those in the annex, including three combination rooms with beds and tatami areas, only provide views over the surrounding rooftops. The nice public bath boasts a tub made of 400-year-old hinoki cypress, making it one of the inn's most treasured possessions. The English-speaking, seventh-generation innkeeper doesn't mind if you take your meals elsewhere in the off-season, especially if you're here for a while. The staff is warm and welcoming and will prepare Western breakfasts on request. If you wish, you can dress up in an elaborate 12-layer kimono (a 30-min. process) for ¥3,000 so you can take pictures.

Tonyamachi Dori, Gojo-sagaru, Higashiyama-ku. http://ryokan.asia/seikoro/. ✆ **075/561-0771.** 20 units. ¥19,800–¥30,875 per person without meals; ¥32,000–¥60,000 per person including 2 meals. Bus: 4, 17, or 205 to Kawaramachi Gojo and then a 5-min. walk; cross the bridge over the Kamo River and after Kawabata Dori take the 1st right. Keihan Electric Railway: Gojo Station (2 min.). **Amenities:** Wi-Fi.

Northern & Western Kyoto

INEXPENSIVE

Kyoto Utano Youth Hostel ★★★ This could well be the most attractive youth hostel I've ever seen, located amid greenery in northwest Kyoto and with an airy, lodgelike atmosphere that makes it seem more like a family resort. It stages free events most nights, from flute or guitar concerts to learning how to make Japanese sweets, plus traditional experiences that cost extra, such as trying on a Japanese kimono for ¥3,500. Rackets and balls are provided free for use on the tennis court. Otherwise, there's no denying that this is a youth hostel with its 11:30pm curfew, public baths and showers, and simple rooms that include four twins, eight triples, and dormitory rooms with bunk beds sleeping four to six people. Japanese-style *tatami* rooms sleep five or six. There's a communal kitchen if you don't opt for breakfast or dinner, and rates are the same whether you're a hostel member or not.

29 Nakayama-cho, Uzumasa Ukyo-ku. www.yh-kyoto.or.jp/utano. ✆ **075/462-2288.** 40 units (none with private bathroom). ¥8,220 double; ¥3,390 dormitory bed. Bus: Take

bus 26 40 min. to Youth Hostel Mae (1 min.). **Amenities:** Bicycles (1 hr. free; ¥500 all day); tennis court; Wi-Fi.

Rakucho ★★★ This accommodation isn't as conveniently situated as most of the other inns listed above, but that shouldn't stop anyone from staying in this well-kept 80-year-old *ryokan,* managed by English-speaking Kimiko Urade and her son Katsunori, both very kind. All but one of the spotless *tatami* rooms, decorated with such traditional touches as scrolls, have views of a small, peaceful garden. Entrance to the *ryokan* is through a well-tended tiny courtyard filled with plants. The kitchenette has two communal refrigerators, a toaster, microwave, and free instant coffee and tea, and laundry facilities are on-site.

67 Higashihangi-cho, Shimogamo, Sakyo-ku. www.rakucho-ryokan.com. ✆ **075/721-2174.** 11 units (none with private bathroom). ¥5,300 single; ¥8,400–¥9,240 double; ¥12,600 triple. Subway: Kitaoji Station (10 min.); walk east on Kitaoji Dori and turn left at the 5th traffic light. Bus: 205 to Furitsudaigaku-mae (2 min. to the north). **Amenities:** Wi-Fi.

Shunko-In Temple and Guesthouse ★★★ For a different kind of experience, consider staying at this Buddhist temple in west Kyoto, established in 1590 and serving as a sub-temple of Myoshinji Temple with its expansive grounds. Although the Japanese-style rooms are rather basic and located in a nondescript building (with the great name of "Cave of Enlightened Dragon"), perks include a communal kitchen offering free coffee and tea, free use of bicycles, and, best of all, the chance to join 90-minute Zen meditation classes offered most mornings (non-guests also welcome). Costing ¥2,500, they're led by head priest Rev. Taka Kawakami, who speaks flawless English and is the fifth generation of his family to have presided over the temple the past 150 years. After making suggestions on how to incorporate Zen Buddhism into daily life, he leads two 15-minute meditation sessions and then gives a tour of the strikingly beautiful 18th-century temple, gardens, and art treasures. No meals are served, but guests are given a hand-drawn map showing nearby restaurants. And in case you're interested, the temple also offers Buddhist weddings in English, regardless of sexual orientation.

42 Myoshinji-Cho, Hanazono, Ukyo-ku. www.shunkoin.com. ✆ **075/462-5488.** 8 units. ¥7,500 single; ¥13,000 double. Prices exclude tax. Student discount available. Station: Hanazono on the JR Sagano Line (6 min.). Bus: 26 to Myoshim-ji Kitamon stop (3 min.). **Amenities:** Bicycles (free); Wi-Fi.

WHERE TO EAT

Kyoto cuisine, known as ***Kyo-ryori,*** is linked to Kyoto's long history and to seasonal foods produced in the surrounding region. Among the various types of Kyo-ryori available, most famous are the vegetarian dishes, which were created to serve the needs of Zen Buddhist priests and pilgrims making the rounds of Kyoto's many temples. Called *shojin ryori,* these vegetarian set meals may include *yudofu* (blocks of tofu simmered in a pot at your table and served with dipping sauce), filmy sheets of *yuba* (soy milk curd), and an array of local vegetables. Kyoto is also renowned for its own style of *kaiseki* called *Kyo-kaiseki,* originally conceived as a meal to be taken before the tea ceremony but eventually becoming an elaborate feast enjoyed by the capital's nobility with a blend of ceremonial court cuisine, Zen vegetarian food, and simple tea-ceremony dishes. You'll typically need a reservation for *kaiseki* (Kyoto's better *ryokan* also serve *kaiseki* as the evening meal). Simpler restaurants specialize in *obanzai,* home-style Kyoto cooking using traditional seasonal ingredients. For more on *kaiseki* and other Japanese cuisines, see "Tips on Dining in Japan," beginning on p. 28 in chapter 2.

Remember: Last orders are taken 30 to 60 minutes before the restaurant's actual closing time, even earlier for *kaiseki* restaurants. Bus information to each restaurant is from Kyoto Station.

Around Kyoto Station

In addition to the restaurants listed here, a good place to browse for dining is **Kyoto Station,** which houses dozens of restaurants in underground arcades, at major exits, and in Isetan department store, which has more than 20 outlets alone, mostly on the 10th and 11th floors, including the **Kitchen Salvatore Cuomo.** A cheap standout is **Ramen Koji (拉麺小路),** where nine of the best ramen shops from around the country are assembled on the 10th floor of Isetan (© **075/361-4401**). Dishes, most priced less than ¥1,000, run from miso ramen (ramen in miso broth) from Sapporo to so-thick-it's-almost-creamy *tonkotsu* (pork broth) from Hakata (Fukuoka). After choosing what you want, buy a ticket from vending machines outside each shop (English-speaking staff is usually on hand to help) and then line up in that restaurant's queue. Ramen Koji is open daily from 11am to 10pm. Another inexpensive option is the conveyor-belt sushi shop **Musashi** (p. 234), located in Kyoto Station in the Asty Road concourse on the station's south side.

INEXPENSIVE

Donguri (どんぐり) ★★ OKONOMIYAKI/YAKISOBA I don't care for pancakes, but I'll eat the Japanese version even for dinner. Called *okonomiyaki* and filled with your favorite meat and vegetables, it's the number-one choice in this lively basement restaurant. In their black outfits and black kerchiefs, the young staff is decked out like hip ninjas. The touch-screen English-language menu at your table presents about 20 possibilities, from the "standard" with ground beef, pork, and squid to the "Italian" with bacon, cheese, and corn, flavored with sweet or spicy sauce and served on a *teppan* (steel plate) built into your table. *Yakisoba* (fried noodles) are also available, along with side dishes like *gyoza* and tofu steak. Because it's open mostly for dinner, it's a popular drinking place as well, with beer, sake, *shochu,* and other drinks livening things up as the evening wears on.

Karasuma Shichijo-sagaru, Nishigawa. www.kyoto-donguri.co.jp. © **075/361-5777.** Dishes ¥736–¥1,080. Mon–Sat 5pm–1am; Sun 11:30am–11:30am. Station: Kyoto (5 min.). On Karasuma Dori's west side, a half-block north of Yodobashi and just south of Shichijo Dori.

Ichiba Coji (市場小路) ★ VARIED JAPANESE/INTERNATIONAL Isetan department store is connected to Kyoto Station, making it convenient for meals near the station. On the ninth floor, with great views north over the city from window-side seats (make reservations for these), is this combination restaurant/beer hall offering food that pairs well with its extensive list of locally brewed beer and sake. Many dishes are listed on an English-language menu and rendered in plastic for the food display case. The dinner menu includes the likes of salads, homemade tofu wrapped in yuba, noodle dishes (including a seafood pad Thai), sashimi, beef dishes, and small dishes that are like tapas. A drink option of all the beer, wine, sake, and other drinks you care to quaff within 90 minutes costs an extra ¥1,620. The set lunches provide several choices for the main dish, such as grilled chicken or rice bowl with egg omelet. A downtown branch is in the Teramachi covered shopping arcade in the basement of the Withyou Building (© **075/252-2008**).

A Note on Japanese Characters

Many hotels, restaurants, attractions, and other establishments in Japan do not have signs giving their names in Roman (English-language) letters. Where they don't, we've given the Japanese script here, next to the restaurant name.

10th floor, Isetan department store, Kyoto Station. © **075/365-3388.** Main dishes ¥500–¥1,200; set lunches ¥1,500–¥2,500. Daily 11am–10pm (last order). Above Kyoto Station.

Katsukura ★ TONKATSU *Tonkatsu* (breaded pork cutlet) is inexpensive comfort food in Japan. This restaurant, on the top floor of the Isetan department store at Kyoto Station, has both a display case of popular dishes and an English-language menu to help you choose your meal. Set meals are the way to go, with combinations like tonkatsu plus crab cream croquette or prawn cutlet, plus barley rice, miso soup, cabbage, and pickled vegetables (like most tonkatsu restaurants, you get free refills of rice, cabbage, soup, and vegetables). At your table will be a mortar and pestle for sesame seeds that you can grind up and add to your tonkatsu sauce. But what really sets this place apart from tonkatsu restaurants across Japan is that because it's in Kyoto, it also offers *yuba* (thin sheets of soy bean curd), such as the *yuba*-rolled seasonal vegetable cutlet, making it also good for vegetarians.

Isetan department store, The Cube, 11th floor, JR Kyoto Station. www.katsukura.jp/en/index.html. © **075/365-8666.** Set meals ¥1,280–¥2,980. Daily 11am–9:15pm (last order).

Central Kyoto

The heart of Kyoto's shopping, dining, and nightlife district is in Nakagyo-ku, especially on Kawaramachi and Shijo Dori and along the many side streets. In summer, restaurants on the west bank of the Kamo River erect large wooden outdoor platforms that extend over the water and offer open-air dining.

EXPENSIVE

Misoguigawa (禊川) ★★★ FRENCH KAISEKI This is one of my favorite restaurants of all time thanks to an idyllic location on the Kamo River, its historic ambience, its innovative cuisine, and the welcoming personality of master-chef/owner Teruo Inoue, who created his own take on fusion cuisine long before it became fashionable. Trained by a three-star Michelin chef, Inoue is a genius at blending classic French cuisine with Japanese ingredients, creating a style best described as French *kaiseki.* Served on Kyoto tableware, his dishes are works of art, beautifully arranged to please both the eye and the palate. Open since 1981, Misoguigawa occupies a century-old former teahouse on Pontocho that once belonged to a geisha. It has several dining options: private *tatami* rooms (with leg wells for comfort); a casual counter, open only for dinner and offering a-la-carte dishes and the opportunity to watch the chef at work; and, my favorite, an outdoor summer veranda extending over the Kamo River.

Three set dinners and three lunch sets are available, but chef Inoue always asks about allergies and preferences and makes changes accordingly. One of the delights of dining here is the English-speaking staff, with explanations of each dish as it's presented. Mr. Inoue travels to France every year to buy wine directly from the Bourgogne region and commission chocolate from a Parisian chocolatier. Note that a 10% service charge is added to meals taken on the veranda, while a 15% service charge is added to meals in private *tatami* rooms (the casual a-la-carte counter, where dishes cost ¥1,400–¥4,200, doesn't add a service charge). Reservations are required and must be made at least 3 days in advance; lunch requires a minimum of six people. In any case, dining here could well be the culinary highlight of your trip.

Sanjo-sagaru, Pontocho. www.misogui.jp. ✆ **075/221-2270.** Set lunches ¥7,000–¥13,000; set dinners ¥15,000–¥30,000 (prices exclude tax and service charge). Mon–Tues and Thurs–Sat 11:30am–1:30pm and 5:30–8:30pm (last order). Bus: 4, 5, 17, or 205 to Kawaramachi Sanjo (5 min.); on Pontocho, north of the playground.

MODERATE

Ashoka ★ INDIAN One of Kyoto's most popular and longest-running Indian restaurants, in business more than 35 years, this pleasant venue serves vegetarian and meat curries prepared by Indian chefs, including mutton, chicken, fish, vegetable, and shrimp selections, as well as tandoori and Halal dishes. On weekdays, it offers an even cheaper vegetable set lunch than given below, only ¥900.

Kikusui Building, 3rd floor, Teramachi Dori. www.ashoka-jp.com. ✆ **075/241-1318.** Main dishes ¥1,500–¥2,400; set lunches ¥1,200–¥1,800; set dinners ¥2,800–¥6,000. Daily 11am–3pm and 5–9pm (last order). Bus: 4, 5, 17, or 205 to Shijo Kawaramachi (1 min.). On the north side of Shijo Dori, to the right at entrance of the Teramachi covered shopping arcade.

Ganko Sushi (がんこ寿司) ★ SUSHI/VARIED JAPANESE This popular, lively sushi chain got its start in 1963 in Osaka but can now be found throughout the Kansai area and Tokyo. Although its specialty is sushi, with seafood sourced directly from fishermen, it also offers plenty of à la carte alternatives for people who don't like fish, including tempura, grilled eel, French fries, tofu, and crab dishes on an English-language menu with photos. This branch has several floors for dining, with the ground floor offering a long sushi counter (sit here if you want to order sushi à la carte) and tables divided by screens for privacy.

Kawaramachi-Sanjo, Higashi-iru. www.gankofood.co.jp/en. ✆ **075/255-1128.** Set meals ¥1,382–¥3,758. Daily 11am–10:30pm (last order). Subway: Kyoto Shiyakusho-mae (4 min.). Bus: 4, 5, 17, or 205 to Kawaramachi Sanjo (2 min.). On Sanjo Dori, just west of the Kamo River (look for its logo of a face with glasses and a bandanna).

Kushi Kura (串くら) ★★ YAKITORI This restaurant has a great atmosphere, in a century-old warehouse where heavy beams and dark polished wood contrast with whitewashed walls. Seating is at the counter where you can watch the chefs, at tables, or on *tatami.* It specializes in grilled chicken using top-grade charcoal, served *yakitori*-style on skewers. The English-language menu, with photos, lists other possibilities as well, along with set meals and a variety of individual meat and vegetable skewers you order à la carte. The least expensive set dinner includes an appetizer, raw veggies with a dipping sauce, and six skewers that include chicken breast, Kyoto-style wheat gluten, chicken and leeks, ground chicken, and small sweet green peppers, although most diners prefer to select their own meals to get exactly what they want. Try the locally made Fushimi sake.

584 Hiiragi-cho. www.kushikura.jp. ✆ **075/213-2211.** Set lunches ¥980–¥3,800; set dinners ¥2,900–¥6,000. Daily 11:30am–2pm and 5–9:40pm (last order). Subway: Karasuma-Oike (2 min.). Just north of Oike Dori on Takakura Dori.

Orizzonte ★★ INTERNATIONAL A buffet restaurant by day and a cocktail lounge at night, this 17th-floor venue offers expansive views of eastern Kyoto and the Higashiyama mountain range. Its mostly Western fare ranges from salads and seafood to casseroles and dim sum (dumplings). If you come for drinks, be aware that there's a ¥324 cover charge from 8:30pm.

Kyoto Hotel Okura, 537-4 Ichinofunairi-cho, Kawaramachi-Oike. http://okura.kyotohotel.co.jp. ✆ **075/254-2534.** Buffet breakfast ¥2,700; buffet lunch ¥3,300; buffet dinner ¥4,500. Daily 6–10am, 11:30am–2:30pm, and 5:30–8pm. Subway: Kyoto Shiyakusho-mae (1 min., below the hotel). Bus: 4, 17, or 205 to Shiyakusho-mae (2 min.).

Savory ★★★ INTERNATIONAL This light-enfused eatery, on the third floor above an upscale grocery, has a glass facade overlooking its very own rooftop garden, planted with rows of lettuce, kale, spring onions, and other veggies that may well end up in your meal. The food is delicious but a bit hard to categorize, a mix of Spanish, Californian, Japanese, and other national favorites and ingredients. Red snapper, duck, Hokkaido venison, and Japanese stew are some items listed on the menu, along with tapas like stuffed mushrooms, steamed chicken with sesame, and paella.

Yaoichi Honkan, 3rd floor, 220 Sanmonji. www.kyotoyaoichihonkan.com/restaurant02.html. ✆ **075/223-2320.** Main dishes ¥1,800–¥2,100; set lunches ¥2,000–¥3,800; set dinner ¥2,800. Thurs–Tues 11:30–3pm and 5:30–9:30pm. Subway: Shijo (4 min.). Bus: 5 or 101 to Shijo Karasuma (4 min.). On Higashinotoin Dori, north of Rokkaku Dori.

Tagoto **(田ごと)** ★★ KYO-RYORI/KAISEKI/BENTO/SOBA Open since 1868 and nestled just off bustling Shijo Dori in an inner courtyard complete with a koi pond, this updated, modestly decorated restaurant offers a variety of Japanese dishes. Its English-language menu offers several choices, including *soba* noodles starting at ¥800 and Kyoto specialties like *yuba* set meals for ¥3,700. Set meals, however, like the *bento* box, are the way to go. For a splurge, seasonal *kaiseki* meals start at ¥7,000. With its convenient yet buffered location, in the heart of downtown, this is a good choice for high-quality meals at reasonable prices.

Shijo-Kawaramachi, Nishi-iru, Kitagawa. www.kyoto-tagoto.co.jp. ✆ **075/221-1811.** Set lunches ¥1,800–¥3,500; set meals ¥3,150–¥12,000. Daily 11am–8:30pm. Bus: 4, 5, 17, or 205 to Shijo Kawaramachi (1 min.). The entrance is on the north side of Shijo Dori just west of Kawaramachi (look for a narrow passageway to the back courtyard).

INEXPENSIVE

In addition to the choices here, a branch of **Ichiba Coji** (p. 230) in the Teramachi covered shopping arcade (on the west side about halfway down, just north of Nishiki Dori) has a hip, modern decor and serves pub food that goes well with beer, sake, and spirits.

Aburiya ★★ GRILLED BEEF This *yakiniku* restaurant offers an all-you-can-eat set meal, with the star of the show consisting of various cuts of Japanese beef, which you cook at your own table. Although there's an à la carte menu, most people opt for one of the all-you-can-eat courses, one with 48 items from which to choose and the other 95 items. They include salads and side dishes and one dessert; discounts are offered for people in their 50s, 60s, and 70s and older, as well as for kids. If you want, you can also have the all-you-can-drink option for ¥980 that includes alcoholic beverages (sorry, no senior discounts for that). Both come with a 2-hour time limit (last order is at the 90-minute mark), and your entire party must order it.

Shijo Kawaramachi Building, 7th floor, 305 Junpu-cho. ✆ **075/344-4929.** All-you-can eat ¥3,080 and ¥3,580. Daily 5–10:30pm (last order). Bus: 4, 5, 17, or 205 to Shijo Kawaramachi (1 min.). On the east side of Kawaramachi Dori, just south of Shijo Dori.

Bio-Tei **(びお亭)** ★★★ VEGETARIAN/HEALTH FOOD An army of capable women slicing and dicing and cooking up aromatic dishes in the open kitchen make a meal here seem like you've been invited right into their home. The dining room is very casual, with seating at heavy wooden tables made from Japanese cypress that you'll likely share with other diners during peak times, and food served on tableware from local kilns. Using organic, preservative-free ingredients, it offers only one thing for lunch: a tasty *teishoku* (daily fixed-price meal) that comes with *genmae* (brown rice), miso soup, pickles, and a choice of a main dish that changes daily and includes vegan and vegetarian options (on the day I dined, it was curry-based tofu stew with potatoes and carrots). Dinner offers set meals and à la carte selections from an English-language menu that might include tea-simmered chicken with mustard and fresh greens, salmon salad, and deep-fried tofu. In short, for a vegetarian or health-food fix, this unassuming and cozy place hits the spot, but be sure to bring cash because no credit cards are accepted. As befits a health-food restaurant, smoking is not allowed.

Sanjo Dori Higashinotoin. ✆ **075/255-0086.** Lunch *teishoku* ¥870; set dinner ¥1,490; dinner main courses ¥750–¥1,200. Tues–Fri 11:30am–2pm; Tues–Wed and Fri–Sat 5–8:30pm (last order). Closed holidays. Subway: Karasuma-Oike (exit 5, 3 min.). On the southwest corner of Sanjo-Higashinotoin intersection (catty-corner from the post office), on the 2nd floor up a tightly wound spiral staircase.

Gontaro (権太呂) ★★ NOODLES This shop has been serving its own handmade noodles for a mere 100-plus years. A multilevel place with a modern yet traditional interior, kimono-clad staff, and English-language menu, it offers various noodle dishes of either *soba* (buckwheat) or *udon* (a thicker wheat noodle) with such toppings as tempura, as well as *nabe* (udon boiled in broth with seafood, chicken, and vegetables). Those with insatiable appetites can have it all with the Okimari set meal (¥6,000), which comes with *nabe,* tempura, barbecue chicken, and noodles. There are two other branches, in northern Kyoto (✆ **075/463-1039**), between Ryoanji and Kinkakuji temples, and near Heian Shrine (✆ **075/751-7880**).

Fuyacho Dori, Shijo-agaru. http://gontaro.co.jp. ✆ **075/221-5810.** Noodles ¥1,000–¥1,600; *nabe* ¥4,300 per person. Thurs–Tues 11am–8pm. Bus: 4, 5, 17, or 205 to Shijo Kawaramachi (5 min.). On the west side of Fuyacho Dori just north of Shijo Dori; look for lacquered lanterns, a tiny shrine out front, and a lone pine tree.

Ippudo (一風堂) ★ RAMEN This chain opened its first restaurant in Fukuoka in 1985 and has since spread to hundreds of locations in Japan and abroad. But while ramen might be eaten around the world, no one eats it with as much gusto as the Japanese. To fully enjoy the flavors of ramen, which at Ippudo means a broth made from three types of pork bones simmered for 18 hours, it's imperative to slurp the noodles, which also helps cool the ramen so you don't burn yourself (waiting until it cools diminishes the aroma and flavor). The thin ramen noodles served here come with a variety of choices, like Ippudo Karaka with a spicy miso topping (you get to choose the level of spiciness), plus extra toppings like scallions or pork for ¥80 to ¥200. On your table is also pickled ginger, spicy sprouts, and do-it-yourself sesame grinders and garlic presses. I can't resist the *gyoza* (fried pork dumplings), so my favorite meal is the weekday lunch, which lets you add them for only ¥100 extra. Ippudo has a contemporary setting, with both tables and counters where you can watch the cooks in action in the open kitchen.

653-1 Higashitoin Bandoyacho. www.ippudo.com. ✆ **075/213-8800.** Ramen ¥790–¥1,100; set lunch (weekdays only) ¥890–¥1,280; set meals ¥1,440–¥1,500. Mon–Sat 11am–3am; Sun and holidays 11am–2am. Subway: Shijo (3 min.). On Nishiki-Koji Dori, west of the food market and Higashitoin Dori.

Musashi (むさし) ★ SUSHI Purists might think it's sacrilege to eat sushi from a conveyor belt, but for the rest of us it's one of the cheapest ways to eat sushi. (Besides, sushi in Japan is almost always better than what passes for sushi in many other places in the world, even in conveyor-belt restaurants, because the standard is so high.) Plates of sushi slowly swing by via a conveyor on the counter, so all you have to do is reach out and take whatever you wish. It's quick, there's no menu or ordering to deal with, and plates are priced at ¥146 to ¥346, with usually two pieces of sushi per plate. If you're really in a hurry, takeout sushi is sold from the restaurant's sidewalk kiosk. And if you want takeout when departing Kyoto, a branch is in Kyoto Station.

440 Ebisucho. www.sushinomusashi.com. ✆ **075/222-0634.** ¥146–¥346 per plate. Daily 11am–10pm. Bus: 4, 5, 17, or 205 to Kawaramachi Sanjo (1 min.). On the northwest corner of the Kawaramachi-Sanjo intersection.

Pizza Salvatore Cuomo & Grill ★★ ITALIAN Instead of the usual Japanese greeting of *irashaimase!* when you walk into this restaurant, here you'll get a *buona sera!* And if it is indeed a fine evening and you're dying for pizza, there's no better place to be than here, with its very cool setting alongside the Kiyamachi canal. Seating is either outdoors or indoors where a wall of glass faces the canal. The emphasis here is clearly on pizza, with more than a half-dozen varieties available in two different sizes (hearty appetites will find even the small one ample, but daintier diners might want to share). Salads, pasta, and a few meat entrees like chicken or spareribs round out the menu, along with the requisite Italian desserts and wines, but the real bargain is the lunch buffet with appetizers, salads, pizzas, pastas, and desserts on offer.

90 Nakajima-cho, Kawaramachi Sanjo-Higashiiru. www.salvatore.jp/restaurant/kyoto/index.html. ✆ **075/212-4965.** Small pizzas ¥1,470–¥2,200; lunch buffet ¥1,200 Mon–Fri, ¥1,400 Sat–Sun. Daily 11:30am–3pm and 5–11pm. Subway: Kyoto Shiyakushomae (3 min.). Bus: 4, 5, 17, or 205 to Kawaramachi Sanjo (2 min.). On the west side of Kiyamachi canal, on Sanjo Dori.

Second House ★ PASTA Occupying a former *machiya* (merchant's house) with tall ceilings, a large nonsmoking section, and a young staff, this casual restaurant (no credit cards accepted) is part of a local chain offering a variety of Western and Asian pasta dishes, such as spaghetti with eggplant, tomato, and bacon or pasta with pork and *kimchi* (Korean-style spicy cabbage). The English-language menu also offers homemade cakes and pastries. The restaurant is up on the second floor, with rustic furnishings and a view of a park, while a cake shop is on the ground floor.

283 Misayamacho. ✆ **075/241-2323.** Pasta ¥880–¥1,260; pasta set lunch ¥1,000 Mon–Fri, ¥1,260 Sat–Sun. Daily 11am–10pm (last order). Subway: Shijo (3 min.). Bus: 5 or 101 to Shijo Karasuma (3 min.). On Higashinotoin, north of Takoyakushi, across from a small park with a playground.

Tohkasaikan ★ BEIJING CHINESE This Beijing-style Chinese restaurant popular with families started life as a Western restaurant. The old building features an ancient, manually operated elevator from the U.S. (Japan's oldest, installed in 1924), lots of wood paneling, high ceilings, old-fashioned decor, and a friendly staff. From May to mid-September, you can sit outside on a wooden veranda over the Kamo River, one of the cheapest places along the river to do so. If it's winter or raining, consider sitting in the fourth- or fifth-floor dining rooms, which have nice views of the city. The best views, however, are from the rooftop garden (open weekends in summer only), where you can order mugs of beer and dine on dishes from the English-language menu listing sweet-and-sour pork, fried shrimp with chili sauce, and chicken with red pepper. I've had better Chinese food, but the atmosphere is great and reminiscent of another era.

Nishizume, Shijo Ohashi. © **075/221-1147.** Main dishes ¥1,200–¥2,500; set meals from ¥5,000 (2-person minimum, reservations required). Daily 11:30am–9pm (last order). Bus: 4, 5, 17, or 205 to Shijo Kawaramachi (2 min.). A large stone building on Shijo Dori, on the west end of the bridge spanning the Kamo River.

Eastern Kyoto

EXPENSIVE

Hyotei (瓢亭) ★★★ KAISEKI/BENTO This is one of Kyoto's oldest and most famous restaurants, opened around 400 years ago as a teahouse to serve pilgrims on their way to Nanzenji Temple. It specializes in *kyo-kaiseki,* a multi-course meal that originated with the tea ceremony but has evolved into Kyoto's special cuisine. The setting is rustic and lovely, with individual teahouses, the oldest of which is 400 years old, spread around a beautiful garden with a pond. Kimono-clad women deliver your *kaiseki* meal to your private *tatami* room, much as they have been doing for centuries. The cuisine, the dishes they're served on, the outdoor scenery, and the gracious service all conspire to create the ultimate traditional Japanese experience.

For travelers who find the prices of *kaiseki* prohibitive, adjoining the main *kaiseki* restaurant is a modern annex *(bekkan)* to the left with its own separate entrance. It specializes in *shokado bento* (lunch boxes), which also change with the seasons and are served in a communal dining room with views of a garden, though the experience doesn't match that in the main restaurant.

In addition to set meals, there are also seasonal options. In July and August, a special breakfast called *asagayu* is available in the main restaurant from 8 to 10am for ¥6,000; in the annex, it's available mid-March through November 8 to 11am for ¥4,500. From December to mid-March, the main restaurant offers the seasonal *uzuragayu* meal from 11am to 2pm for ¥12,100, while the annex offers it from 8 to 11am for ¥4,500. No matter where or when you dine, a boiled egg, served to Hyotei's guests since its founding and one of its specialties, will be part of your meal. Note that reservations are required, and because of recent no-shows, must be made by your hotel and secured with a credit card. Note, too, that you should dress respectfully (no T-shirts, shorts, or sandals), and only children older than 10 are allowed. If you want a time machine to old Kyoto, you can't get any closer than this.

35 Kusakawa-cho, Nanzenji. http://hyotei.co.jp/en/. © **075/771-4116.** *Kaiseki* lunches from ¥23,000, dinners from ¥27,000; *shokado bento* ¥5,400. *Kaiseki* daily 11am–7:30pm (closed 2nd and 4th Tues of each month); *shokado bento* daily noon–4pm. Subway: Keage (5 min.). Bus: 5 or 100 to Dobutsuen-mae (7 min.). West of Shirakawa Dori Murin-an; look for a plain facade hidden behind a bamboo fence with a sign shaped like a gourd.

MODERATE

Junsei (順正) ★★ TOFU/KAISEKI/BENTO This well-known tofu restaurant near Nanzenji has been open since 1961, but its extensive garden and thatched-roof main building are remnants from the days when the location served as a medical school established in 1839 during the shogun era. It attracts tourists and tour groups, but everything runs with smooth Japanese efficiency. As soon as you arrive you'll be given an English-language menu and asked what you'd like to eat, because that determines where you'll be seated in the restaurant's various buildings. If you order the house specialty—one of the *yudofu* set meals that includes tofu simmered in an earthen pot, vegetable tempura, grilled skewers of tofu, and an assortment of other dishes—you'll probably be led to an older building near the front of the property filled with antiques and overlooking the garden. Other set meals offer *yuba* (like the *yuba kaiseki* for ¥6,170) and shabu-shabu.

Another location, **Kiyomizu Junsei Okabeya** (✆ **075/541-7111**), is just off Kiyomizu-zaka, the main slope leading to Kiyomizu Temple. Housed in a grand, 1914 former villa with high ceilings, wainscoting, and stained-glass windows, it offers set tofu meals priced ¥2,160 to ¥5,400 and is open daily 10:30am to 5pm (last order); closed irregularly.

Nanzenjimon-mae, Sakyo-ku. www.to-fu.co.jp. ✆ **075/761-2311.** Yudofu meals ¥3,090–¥4,110; shabu-shabu ¥8,230; *kaiseki* ¥8,230–¥15,430. Daily 11am–8pm (last order). Subway: Keage (5 min.). Bus: 5 to Nanzenji-Eikando-michi (7 min.). East of Shirakawa Dori on the road to Nanzenji Temple, north side.

Okutan (奥丹) ★★★ TOFU/VEGETARIAN If you love tofu or simply want a quintessential Kyoto meal in a wonderful setting, Okutan, open since 1635 and Japan's oldest tofu restaurant, should be high on your list. Located near Nanzenji Temple and originally serving Buddhist monks, today the rustic, thatched-roof restaurant offers just one thing, making ordering easy: *yudofu* (a tofu set meal). Although it changes slightly with the seasons, it comes with a pot of tofu boiled at your table, *dengaku* (baked tofu on a stick), vegetable tempura, *goma-dofu* (a sesame dish), grated yam soup, and pickled vegetables. But in my opinion, it's the atmosphere that makes a meal here extra special. The restaurant has a pond and garden, and in fine weather you can sit outside on cushioned platforms. Otherwise you'll dine in rustic *tatami* rooms. Women wearing traditional rural clothing bring your food, making the atmosphere seem like you're dining somewhere in the countryside a long time ago. Note that reservations are accepted only for groups of six or more people, so you may have to stand in line in peak season. Cash only.

86–30 Fukuchi-cho, Nanzenji. ✆ **075/771-8709.** Yudofu set meal ¥3,240. Fri and Mon–Wed 11am–3:45pm; Sat–Sun and holidays 11am–4:15pm (last order, but it closes earlier if it runs out). Bus: 5 to Nanzenji-Eikando-michi (6 min.). Just north of Nanzenji Temple's main gate (the Sanmon Gate).

The Sodoh ★★★ ITALIAN Temples, Japanese restaurants, and boutiques have long been the draws of Higashiyama-ku, so it comes as somewhat of a pleasant surprise to find an Italian restaurant—especially one of this caliber and in this setting—in their midst. It occupies a 1929 villa that once served as residence, studio, and garden of Seiho Takeuchi, whose family owned a restaurant in nearby Arashiyama and who was a well-known master of the sparse *nihonga* style of painting. With a somewhat rustic yet refined atmosphere and dining rooms overlooking the dense garden, the restaurant serves reasonably priced weekday lunches that change according to what›s fresh and in season. My ¥2,800 lunch, which came with an appetizer, sweet-potato soup, carbonara pasta with bacon and spinach, a choice of six main dishes (I had the grilled chicken cacciatore), dessert, and coffee, was plenty enough for me. Dinner offers set meals and a few à la carte choices like pappardelle with beef ragout and savory cabbage. Take a stroll around the garden after your meal. Understandably, this is a popular venue for weddings and private parties, so be sure to call ahead to make sure they're open.

366 Yasaka Kami-machi, Yasakadori Shimokawara Higashi-iru. www.thesodoh.com. ✆ **075/541-3331.** A la carte dishes (available only for dinner) ¥1,600–¥2,400; set lunches ¥1,500 (available only weekdays)–¥5,500; set dinners ¥4,000–¥9,000. Bus: 206 to Higashiyama Yasui (3 min.). Catty-corner from Ryozen Kannon Temple.

Western Kyoto

A branch of **Gontaro,** serving noodles, at Hinomiyashiki-cho 26 (✆ **075/463-1039;** closed Wed), has the same English-language menu as its main shop (p. 234). It's located about halfway down the street that runs between Ryoanji and Kinkakuji, on the west side; look for the red paper lantern.

INEXPENSIVE

Seigen-in ★★ TOFU/VEGETARIAN If you're visiting Ryoanji Temple in northeastern Kyoto, there's no lovelier setting for a meal than this traditional restaurant, which calls itself the Ryoanji Seven Herb Tofu Restaurant in honor of its signature dish, *yudofu,* boiled tofu and vegetables topped with seven herbs. You can order it by itself, or as a set meal of *shojin ryori* (Buddhist vegetarian) with side dishes (no credit cards accepted; there's an English

Home-Style Cooking Class

So you've eaten your way around town and now want to cook your own Japanese food. Taro Saeki, who once cooked the meals at a *minshuku* (family-style inn), now teaches home-style cooking at his **Haru Cooking Class** (www.kyoto-cooking-class.com; ✆ **090/4284-7176**). Classes take place in his home in English (he used to live in the U.S.), and his wife and young daughters are often on hand to help. After instruction in the basics of soy sauce, miso, and other common ingredients, you'll have hands-on kitchen time, and within a few hours you'll be eating your creations from the beef, chicken, or vegetarian menu. Classes cost ¥5,900 for a vegetarian meal and ¥7,900 to ¥10,900 per person for the Kobe beef meal. Take bus No. 4 or 205 to Shin-Aoibashi bus stop in northeast Kyoto, and Taro will meet you. Some participants say this experience is the highlight of their trip. Also offering cooking lessons is **Cooking Sun** (www.cooking-sun.com; ✆ **075/746-5094**).

menu). Entrance to the restaurant, situated beside the Kyoyoike Pond on temple grounds, is along a small path that takes you past a stream, a small pond, a grove of maple and pine, and moss-covered grounds, which are also what you see as you dine seated on *tatami.* You'll know you're getting close to the restaurant when you hear the *thonk* of a bamboo trough fed by a stream, which fills and hits against stone as it empties.

Ryoanji Temple. ✆ **075/462-4742.** Yudofu ¥1,500; yudofu vegetarian set meal ¥3,300. Daily 10am–4:30pm (last order). Bus: 59 from Shijo Kawaramachi to Ryoanji-mae (2 min.), or 50 to Ritsumeikan Daigaku-mae (4 min.).

EXPLORING KYOTO

As Japan's seventh-largest city with a population of almost 1.5 million people, Kyoto hasn't escaped the afflictions of the modern age. In fact, if you arrive in Kyoto by train, your first reaction is likely to be great disappointment. There's Kyoto Tower looming in the foreground like some misplaced spaceship. Kyoto Station itself is strikingly modern and unabashedly high tech, looking as though it was airlifted straight from Tokyo. Modern buildings and hotels surround the station on all sides, making Kyoto look like any other Japanese town.

Once you escape to Kyoto's old neighborhoods, however, you'll find yourself in an entirely different place. Kyoto boasts an astonishing 2,000 temples and shrines and 20% of Japan's National Treasures. Because there are so many worthwhile sights, you must plan your itinerary carefully. Even the most avid sightseer can become jaded after days of visiting yet another temple or shrine, no matter how beautiful or peaceful, so be sure to temper your visits to cultural and historical sites with time spent simply walking around. Kyoto is a city best seen on foot; take time to explore small alleyways and artisan shops, pausing from time to time to soak in the beauty and atmosphere. If you spend your days in Kyoto racing around in a taxi or a bus from one temple to another, the essence of this ancient capital and its charm may literally pass you by.

"Light Up": Kyoto Illuminated

When the cherry blossoms spring forth or leaves change color, many Kyoto temples (like Kiyomizu) are open at night, their buildings and gardens dramatically lit. It's a great way to see these wondrous spaces, literally in a different light. Ask the tourist office or concierge at your hotel for a list of temples offering "light up."

Before setting out, be sure to stop by **Kyoto City Tourist Information** at Kyoto Station to get a detailed map of the city, a bus map, and the Kyoto's Visitor Guide plus *Explorer Kyoto* (both of which also contain maps).

Keep in mind, too, that you must enter Kyoto's museums, shrines, and temples at least a half-hour before closing time. Listings in this section and those that follow give numbers not only for buses departing from Kyoto Station but from elsewhere as well.

What to See in Kyoto

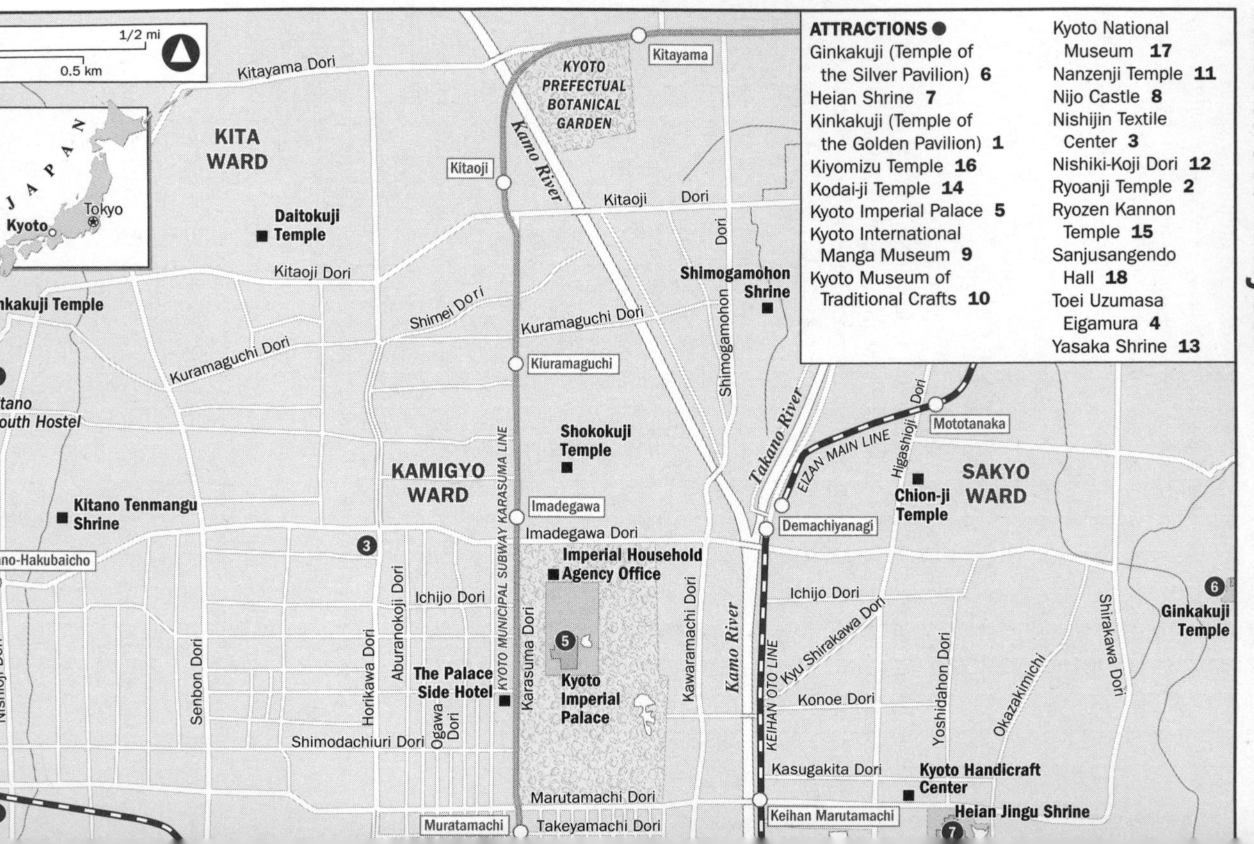

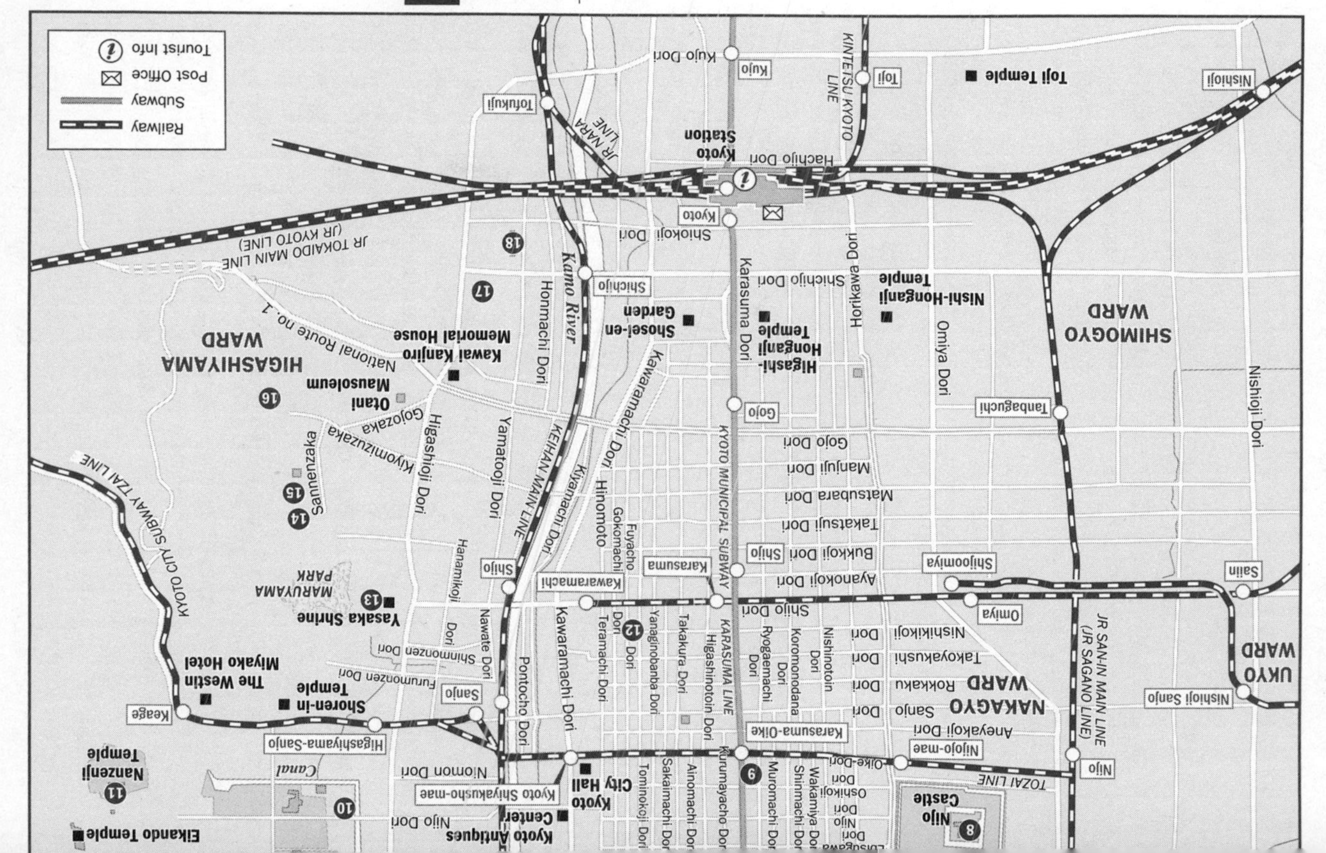
Railway
Subway
Post Office
Tourist Info
Eikando Temple
Nanzenji Temple
Keage
KYOTO CITY SUBWAY TZAI LINE
The Westin Miyako Hotel
Shoren-in Temple
Higashiyama-Sanjo
Canal
Yasaka Shrine
MARUYAMA PARK
Sannenzaka
HIGASHIYAMA WARD
Otani Mausoleum
Kiyomizuzaka
Gojozaka
National Route no. 1
JR TOKAIDO MAIN LINE (JR KYOTO LINE)
Kawai Kanjiro Memorial House
Kyoto Antiques Center
Kyoto Shiyakusho-mae
Nijo Dori
Niomon Dori
Furumonzen Dori
Shinmonzen Dori
Sanjo
Hanamikoji Dori
Nawate Dori
Higashioji Dori
Yamatooji Dori
Shijo
Pontocho Dori
KEIHAN MAIN LINE
Kawaramachi Dori
Kiyamachi Dori
Honmachi Dori
Kamo River
Tofukuji
JR NARA LINE
Kyoto City Hall
Kawaramachi
Teramachi Dori
Hinomoto
Gokomachi Dori
Fuyacho Dori
Kawaramachi Dori
Shosei-en Garden
Shichijo
Tominokoji Dori
Sakaimachi Dori
Yanaginobanba Dori
Ainomachi Dori
Takakura Dori
Karasuma
Higashinotoin Dori
Shiokoji Dori
Kyoto
Kurumayacho Dori
KARASUMA LINE
KYOTO MUNICIPAL SUBWAY
Karasuma Dori
Kyoto Station
Kujo Dori
Karasuma-Oike
Gojo
Muromachi Dori
Ryogaemachi Dori
Koromonodana Dori
Shinmachi Dori
Wakamiya Dori
Nishinotoin Dori
Shijo Dori
Ayanokoji Dori
Bukkoji Dori
Takatsuji Dori
Matsubara Dori
Manjuji Dori
Gojo Dori
Higashi-Honganji Temple
Shichijo Dori
Hachijo Dori
Kujo
Oshikoji Dori
Nijo Dori
Oike-Dori
Horikawa Dori
KINTETSU KYOTO LINE
Nijo Castle
Nijojo-mae
Aneyakoji Dori
Sanjo Dori
Rokkaku Dori
Takoyakushi Dori
Nishikikoji Dori
Shijoomiya
Nishi-Honganji Temple
Toji
Omiya Dori
NAKAGYO WARD
TOZAI LINE
Omiya
Tanbaguchi
Toji Temple
Nijo
JR SAN-IN MAIN LINE (JR SAGANO LINE)
SHIMOGYO WARD
Nishioji Sanjo
Saiin
Nishioji
UKYO WARD
Nishioji Dori

Central Kyoto

Although much of downtown Kyoto has been taken over by the 21st century, it still has wonderful old neighborhoods with *machiya* (traditional townhouses) and historic treasures. My favorite thing to do is to simply explore the backstreets, especially those contained within the square of Shijo, Kawaramachi, Oike, and Karasuma streets. If you've never been to a street market in Japan, say, take a stroll down Nishiki-Koji Dori for a fascinating look at the fish-and-produce Nishiki Food Market in the heart of town.

Kyoto Imperial Palace (Kyoto Gosho) ★★ PALACE This is where the imperial family lived from 1331 until 1868, when they moved to Tokyo. The palace was destroyed several times by fire but was always rebuilt in its original style; the present buildings date from 1855. Modestly furnished with delicate decorations, the palace shows the restful designs of the peaceful Heian Period, and the emperor's private garden is a study in grace. Although you used to be able to enter palace grounds only on 1-hour guided tours, you can now stroll the grounds on your own. But to better understand court life

A Look at the Past

Kyoto served as Japan's capital for more than 1,000 years, from 794 to the Meiji Restoration in 1868. Originally known as Heian-kyo, it was laid out in a grid pattern borrowed from the Chinese with streets running north, south, east, and west. Its first few hundred years—from about A.D. 800 to the 12th century—were perhaps its grandest, a time when culture blossomed and court nobility led luxurious and splendid lives dotted with poetry-composing parties and moon-gazing events. Buddhism flourished and temples were built. A number of learning institutions were set up for the sons and daughters of aristocratic families, and scholars were versed in both Japanese and Chinese.

Toward the end of the Heian Period, military clans began clashing as the samurai class grew more powerful, resulting in a series of civil wars that eventually pushed Japan into the Feudal Era of military government, which lasted nearly 680 years—until 1868. The first shogun to rise to power was Minamoto Yoritomo, who set up his shogunate government in Kamakura. With the downfall of the Kamakura government in 1336, however, Kyoto once again became the seat of power, home to both the imperial family and the shogun. The beginning of this era, known as the Muromachi and Azuchi-Momoyama periods, was marked by extravagant prosperity and luxury, expressed in such splendid shogun villas as Kyoto's Gold Pavilion and Silver Pavilion. Lacquerware, landscape paintings, and the art of metal engraving came into their own. Zen Buddhism was the rage, giving rise to such temples as the Ryoanji rock garden. And, despite civil wars that rocked the nation in the 15th and 16th centuries and destroyed much of Kyoto, culture flourished. During these turbulent times, *Noh* drama, the tea ceremony, flower arranging, and landscape gardening gradually took form.

Emerging as the victor in the civil wars, Tokugawa Ieyasu established himself as shogun and set up his military rule in Edo (presently Tokyo) far to the east. For the next 250 years, Kyoto remained the capital in name only, and in 1868 (which marked the downfall of the shogunate and the restoration of the emperor to power), the capital was officially moved from Kyoto to Tokyo.

and palace architecture, consider joining the free, 50-minute guided tour in English, conducted at 10am or 2pm. In any case, you are not allowed to enter any of the buildings.

Kyotogyoen-nai, Karasuma-Imadegawa. http://sankan.kunaicho.go.jp/english. ✆ **075/211-1215.** Free admission. Tues–Sun 9am–5pm (to 4:30pm Sept and Mar, to 4pm Oct–Feb). Subway: Imadegawa (5 min.). Bus: 59, 102, 201, or 203 to Karasuma Imadegawa (5 min.). Seishomon Gate, on Karasuma Dori south of Imadegawa Dori.

Kyoto International Manga Museum ★ MUSEUM If you think *manga* (Japanese comics, or graphic novels) are just for kids, you'll come away with a whole different perspective after touring the largest *manga* museum in the world. With more than 300,000 items in its collection, it not only serves as a research facility for the study of *manga*'s history and cultural influence but also strives to preserve *manga* in all its forms, including early and contemporary Japanese works, foreign *manga,* animation, and other related images. Most visitors, however, come because of its changing exhibitions, with about 50,000 items on display at any one time. Occupying a former primary school built in 1869, its various rooms include a children's library with *manga* and picture books, an archive illustrating the long history of Japanese *manga,* a display describing the process of making *manga,* an exhibit dedicated to the building's former life as an elementary school, and, perhaps most amazing of all, a Wall of Manga with shelves containing thousands of *manga.* On weekends, you can even see *manga* artists at work, and on select days several times a week you can have your portrait drawn by an artist (¥1,000 for one person or ¥2,000 for two). Of course, while display descriptions are in English, unless you can read Japanese you'll mostly be looking at pictures rather than taking full advantage of what this place offers. But that shouldn't be a deterrent for enjoying this unique art form. In addition to a cafe, there's also a museum shop selling *manga* (including *manga* translated into English), figurines, notepads, and other items.

452 Kinbuki-cho, Karasuma Oike. www.kyotomm.jp. ✆ **075/254-7414.** Admission ¥800 adults, ¥300 junior-high and high-school students, ¥100 children. Thurs–Tues 10am–6pm. Subway: Karasuma-Oike (1 min.). Bus: 15, 51, 61, 62, 63 or 65 to Karasuma Oike (1 min.) On Karasuma Dori, north of Oike.

Nijo Castle (Nijojo) ★★★ CASTLE The Tokugawa shogun's Kyoto home stands in stark contrast to most of Japan's other remaining castles, which were constructed purely for defense. Built by the first Tokugawa shogun, Ieyasu, in 1603, Nijo Castle, a UNESCO World Heritage Site, is considered the quintessence of Momoyama architecture, built almost entirely of Japanese cypress and boasting delicate transom woodcarvings and paintings by the Kano School on sliding doors. Unfortunately, no interior photos are allowed.

The main building, **Ninomaru Palace,** has 33 rooms, some 800 *tatami* mats, and an understated elegance, especially compared with castles being built in Europe at the same time. All the sliding doors on the outside walls of the castle can be removed in summer, permitting breezes to sweep through the

Cultural Immersion

If you're interested in learning firsthand about the tea ceremony, flower arranging, origami, Japanese calligraphy, Japanese cooking, and other cultural pursuits, you can do so with the help of the members of the **Women's Association of Kyoto (WAK Japan;** www.wakjapan.com; ✆ **075/212-9993**). Courses run 55 minutes to 1½ hours and range from ¥4,104 per person for the tea ceremony to ¥6,372 for flower arranging (reservations for one person are more expensive). They're held at Wakwak-kan, an old *machiya* at 761 Tenshucho (subway: Karasuma Oike, exit 7, 5 min.). You can also opt for lessons in a private home, but these are more expensive.

building. Typical for Japan at the time, rooms were unfurnished, with futon stored in closets during the day.

One of the castle's most intriguing features is its so-called **nightingale floors.** To protect the shogun from real or imagined enemies, the castle was protected by a moat, stone walls, and these special floorboards in the castle corridors, which creaked when trod upon. The nightingale floors were supplemented by hidden alcoves for bodyguards. Furthermore, only female attendants were allowed in the shogun's private living quarters. Astoundingly, considering the expense of its construction, no shogun visited the castle between 1634, when the third Tokugawa shogun Iemitsu stayed here, and 1867, when the 15th and last Tokugawa shogun Yoshinobu came to announce the restoration of imperial rule.

Outside the castle is the **Ninomaru Garden,** designed by the renowned gardener Kobori Enshu and famous in its own right, with two other gardens added in 1895 and 1965. For ¥100 extra, you can also visit the castle's **Anniversary Gallery,** with original screens, murals, and paintings from the castle. Plan on spending 1½ hours here, especially if you pay ¥500 extra for an audio guide, recommended because it describes the significance of what you're seeing. Or, for ¥2,000, join a 90-minute guided tour in English offered daily at 10am and 12:30pm.

541 Nijojo-cho. www2.city.kyoto.lg.jp/bunshi/nijojo/english/index.html. ✆ **075/841-0096.** Admission ¥600 adults, ¥350 junior-high and high-school students, ¥200 children. Daily 8:45am–5pm (last entry 4pm). Closed Tues Dec–Jan and July–Aug. Subway: Nijojo-mae Station (1 min.). Bus: 9, 12, 50, or 101 to Nijojo-mae (1 min.). Corner of Horikawa Dori and Nijo Dori.

Nishijin Textile Center (Nishijin-Ori Kaikan) ★★ MUSEUM Kyoto's Nishijin weavers, whose history can be traced back to Kyoto's earliest years, were famous for richly decorative textiles, made into clothing worn by the imperial family, Buddhist monks, and Shinto priests. During the Edo Period (1603–1867), an estimated 7,000 looms were crammed into 160 city blocks comprising the Nishijin District. Unsurprisingly, the district suffered a terrible blow when the capital was moved to Tokyo, but the industry bounced back by adopting Western weaving technology and equipment, which allowed them to produce inexpensive machine-woven clothing alongside luxurious hand-woven fabrics. Today, Nishijin remains one of the country's largest districts for hand weaving. This commemorative museum is located on the very spot where merchants once gathered to bid for textiles sold at auction.

On display are silkworms and descriptions of how they produce silk, old and modern Nishijin fabrics, and looms, with frequent demonstrations of handlooms using the Jacquard system of perforated cards for weaving. A shop sells Nishijin products and fabrics, including kimono, sashes, purses, and more. But my favorite thing to do here is to attend one of the museum's free 10-minute kimono fashion shows held six times daily (10:30am–4pm), showcasing kimono that change with the seasons. If you have 40 minutes to spare, you can also weave your own table mat for ¥2,000; if you have 3 hours and make a reservation, you can weave your own scarf for ¥5,800. Reservations are also required if you'd like to dress up as a *maiko* (geisha apprentice), *geiko* (professional entertainer), or lady of the Imperial court in a 12-layer kimono. These, along with an ancient ceremonial court dress for men, cost ¥13,000, including hair styling, makeup, and photo. You can also try on a simpler everyday kimono for ¥3,000, and even wander around Kyoto in it until 5pm for an extra fee. I'm surprised by how popular this has become, especially among young visitors from other Asian countries.

414 Tatemonzen-cho, Kamikyho-ku. www.nishijin.or.jp. ✆ **075/451-9231.** Free admission. Daily 9am–6pm (to 5pm Nov–Feb). Subway: Imadegawa (8 min.). Bus: 9, 12, 59, 101, 102, 201, or 203 to Horikawa Imadegawa (2 min.). On Horikawa Dori just south of Imadegawa Dori.

Eastern Kyoto

The eastern part of Kyoto, embracing the area of Higashiyama-ku with its Kiyomizu Temple and stretching up all the way to the Temple of the Silver Pavilion (Ginkakuji Temple), is probably the richest in terms of culture and charm. Although temples and gardens are the primary attractions, Higashiyama-ku also boasts several fine museums, forested hills and running streams, great shopping opportunities, and some of Kyoto's oldest and finest restaurants. To make the most of your visit, follow my recommended stroll later in this chapter, which will lead you to the region's best attractions, as well as to lesser-known sights that are worth seeing if you have the time.

Walk in Kyoto, Talk in English

For a personalized English-language tour that takes in temples and shrines, a former geisha area, and Kyoto backstreets before ending near Kiyomizu Temple, join **Walk in Kyoto Talk in English** (www.waraido.com/walking/index.html), conducted rain or shine each Monday, Wednesday, and Friday from 10am to 3pm March through November. Tours start in front of Kyoto Station and cost ¥2,000 for adults, ¥1,000 for 13- to 15-year-olds, and free for children. No reservations are required; pick up the brochure at the tourist office or look online for information. The same company also conducts night tours of **Gion** (p. 263).

Ginkakuji (Temple of the Silver Pavilion) ★★ TEMPLE Ginkakuji, considered one of the more beautiful structures in Kyoto, was built in 1482 as a retirement villa for Shogun Ashikaga Yoshimasa, who intended to coat the structure with silver in imitation of the Golden Pavilion built by his grandfather. He died before this could be accomplished, however, so the Silver Pavilion is not silver at all but remains a simple, two-story wood structure enshrining the goddess of mercy and Jizo, the guardian god of children. The entire complex is designed for enjoyment of the tea ceremony, moon viewing, and other aesthetic pursuits. Note the sand mound in the garden, shaped to resemble Mount Fuji, and the sand raked in the shape of waves, created to enhance the views during a full moon. It's easy to imagine the splendor, formality, and grandeur of the life of Japan's upper class as you wander the grounds and climb the hillside path to its lookout point. In fact, although the temple is worth seeing, for me this place is all about its garden.

2 Ginkakuji-cho. ✆ **075/771-5725.** Admission ¥500 adults, ¥300 junior-high and elementary students, younger children free. Mar–Nov daily 8:30am–5:30pm; Dec–Feb daily 9am–4:30pm. Bus: 5, 17, 102, 203, or 204 to Ginkakuji-michi (10 min.); or 32 or 100 to Ginkakuji-mae (5 min.).

Heian Shrine ★★★ SHRINE Although it dates only from 1895, Kyoto's most famous Shinto shrine was built in commemoration of the 1,100th anniversary of the founding of Kyoto and is a replica of the first Imperial Palace, though on a less grand scale. It deifies two of Japan's emperors: Emperor Kammu, 50th emperor of Japan, who founded Heian-kyo in 794; and Emperor Komei, the 121st ruler of Japan, who ruled from 1831 to 1866. Although the orange, green, and white structure is interesting for its Heian-Era architectural style, the most important thing to see here is the 33,000-sq.-m (8-acre) **Shinen Garden,** the entrance to which is on your left as you face the main hall. Typical of gardens constructed during the Meiji Era and appearing in the movie *Lost in Translation,* it's famous for its weeping cherry trees in spring, its irises and water lilies in summer, and the changing maple leaves in the fall, all beautifully arranged around a central pond. Don't miss it.

Nishi Tennocho, Okazaki. www.heianjingu.or.jp. ✆ **075/761-0221.** Free admission to grounds; Shinen Garden ¥600 adults, ¥300 children. Garden mid-Mar to Sept daily 8:30am–5:30pm (to 4:30pm Nov–Feb; to 5pm Mar 1–14 and Oct). Subway: Higashiyama (10 min.). Bus: 5, 32, 46, or 100 to Okazaki Koen Bijitsukan Heian Jingu-mae (5 min.). Look for the shrine's large orange *torii.*

Kiyomizu Temple (Kiyomizudera) ★★★ TEMPLE This is Higashiyama-ku's most famous temple, known throughout Japan for the grand views afforded from its main hall. Founded in 778 and rebuilt in 1633 by the third Tokugawa shogun, Iemitsu, the temple occupies an exalted spot on Mount Otowa, its main hall constructed over a cliff and featuring a large wooden veranda supported by 139 massive pillars, each 15m (49 ft.) high. The main hall (undergoing renovation until 2020, but you can still enter) is dedicated to the goddess of mercy and compassion, but most visitors come for the magnificence of its height and view, which are so well-known to Japanese that the idiom "jumping from the veranda of Kiyomizu Temple" means that they're about to undertake some particularly bold or daring adventure. Kiyomizu's grounds are particularly spectacular (and crowded) in spring during cherry-blossom season and in fall when the maple leaves turn.

Also worth checking out are the three-story pagoda and Otowa Falls (known for the purity of its water; *kiyomizu* translates as "pure water"), but don't spite the gods by neglecting to visit **Jishu Shrine** (✆ **075/541-2097**), a vermilion-hued Shinto shrine behind Kiyomizu's main hall that has long been considered the dwelling place of the god of love and matchmaking. Be sure to take the ultimate test: On the shrine's grounds are two "love fortune-telling" stones placed 9m (30 ft.) apart; if you're able to walk from one to the other with your eyes closed, your desires for love will be granted.

1–294 Kiyomizu. www.kiyomizudera.or.jp. ✆ **075/551-1234.** Admission ¥400 adults, ¥200 children 7–15, children 6 and under free. Daily 6am–6pm (until 6:30pm in summer; special evening hours several times a year). Jishu Shrine daily 9am–5pm. Bus: 86, 100, 106, 110, 202, 206, or 207 to Gojo-zaka (10 min.).

Kodai-ji Temple ★★ TEMPLE Located between Kiyomizu Temple and Yasaka Shrine, this temple was founded in 1605 by Toyotomi Hideyoshi's widow, popularly referred to as Nene, to commemorate her husband and pacify his spirit. Shogun Tokugawa Ieyasu, who served under Toyotomi before becoming shogun, financed its construction. It contains lovely gardens laid out by Kobori Enshu and Nene's grave (the Otama-ya), as well as teahouses designed by Sen no Rikyu, a famous 16th-century tea master. A memorial hall enshrines wooden images of Hideyoshi and Nene. Nene, by the way, became a Buddhist nun after her husband's death, as was the custom of noblewomen at the time. The one-room **Kodaiji Sho Museum,** across the street from the temple and included in the admission price, contains artifacts relating to Nene and the temple, but skip it if your time is limited.

526 Shimogawara-cho. www.kodaiji.com. ✆ **075/561-9966.** Admission ¥600 adults, ¥250 children 17 and under. Daily 9am–5:30pm. Bus: 86, 202, 206, or 207 to Higashiyama Yasui (5 min.).

Kyoto Museum of Traditional Crafts (Fureaikan) ★★★ MUSEUM Near Heian Shrine is this excellent museum dedicated to the more than 70 crafts that flourished during Kyoto's long reign as the imperial capital. Displays and videos demonstrate the step-by-step production of crafts, from stone lanterns and fishing rods to textiles, paper fans, umbrellas, boxwood combs, lacquerware, Buddhist altars, *Noh* masks, musical instruments, and more. The displays are fascinating, the crafts beautiful, and explanations are in English, making even a 30-minute stop here well worth the effort. Artisans demonstrate their skills most days except Mondays and Thursdays, while *geiko* (what geisha are called in Kyoto) and *maiko* (geisha apprentices) perform traditional dance on selected Sundays (check website for times). If you make reservations 2 weeks in advance, you can apply traditional *Yuzen* dyeing techniques to a placemat (¥1,400), T-shirt (¥2,000), or other item for a personalized souvenir. Be sure to browse the museum crafts store.

9–1 Seishoji-cho, Okazaki. https://kmtc.jp/en/. ✆ **075/762-2670.** Free admission. Daily 9am–5pm. Subway: Higashiyama (7 min.). Bus: 5, 32, 46, or 100 to Okazaki Koen Bijitsukan Heian Jingu-mae (5 min.), or 201, 202, 203, or 206 to Higashiyama-Nijo/ Okazakikoenguchi. In basement of the Miyako Messe (International Exhibition Hall; look for bright orange installation outside).

Kyoto National Museum (Kokuritsu Hakubutsukan) ★★ MUSEUM Housed in an imposing French baroque–style building constructed in 1897 expressly for the collection, as well as in a new wing completed in 2014, this museum displays stone and bronze Buddhist and Shinto sculpture, paintings, ceramics from the Nara through Edo periods, textiles, lacquerware, swords and other metalworks, archaeological relics (like 6th-c. *Haniwa* clay figures excavated from burial mounds), and much more, displayed on a rotating basis from the vast collection. The museum is especially famous for its artifacts from the Heian Period (794–1192) and ancient sutras. Many of the treasures were once in Kyoto's temples, shrines, and imperial palaces, while others—like Chinese sculpture or paintings—were imported to Japan at different times during its history. Plan on staying about an hour, more if you pay ¥500 extra for the audio guide, which describes about 30 items in detail. If you've seen the larger Tokyo National Museum, you may want to skip this one if your time in Kyoto is short, though special exhibitions concentrating on a specific period or genre draw huge crowds.

527 Chaya-machi (across the street from Sanjusangendo Hall). www.kyohaku.go.jp. ✆ **075/ 525-2473.** Admission ¥520 adults, ¥260 university students, free for children. Admission may increase during special exhibitions. Tues–Sun 9:30am–5pm (to 8pm for special exhibits). Bus: 86, 88, 100, 106, 110, 206, or 208 to Hakubutsukan Sanjusangendo-mae (1 min.).

Nanzenji Temple ★★ TEMPLE This Rinzai Zen temple with its massive front gate is set amid a grove of spruce and maple. One of Kyoto's best-known Zen temples, it was founded in 1291, though the present buildings date from the latter part of the 16th century during the Momoyama Period. Attached to the main hall is a Zen rock garden attributed to Kobori Enshu; it's sometimes called "Young Tigers Crossing the Water" because of the shape of one of the rocks, but the association is a bit of a stretch for me. In the building behind the main hall is a sliding door with a famous painting by Kano Tanyu of a tiger drinking water in a bamboo grove. Spread throughout the temple precincts are a dozen other lesser temples and buildings worth exploring if you have the time, including Nanzen-in with its moss, ponds, natural waterfall, and rock garden, which was built before Nanzenji Temple and served as the emperor's vacation house whenever he visited the grounds. There's so much to see, in fact, including an old aqueduct from the Meiji Period, you'll probably wish you had more time (allow at least 1 hour).

Nanzenji-Fukuchi-cho. www.nanzenji.com. ✆ **075/771-0365.** Admission ¥500 adults, ¥400 high-school students, ¥250 children; Nanzen-in ¥300, ¥250, and ¥150 extra, respectively. Daily 8:40am–5pm (to 4:30pm Dec–Feb). Bus: 5 to Nanzenji, Eikando-michi (3 min.).

Sanjusangendo Hall ★★★ TEMPLE Originally founded as Rengeoin Temple in 1164 and rebuilt in 1266, Sanjusangendo Hall has one of the most visually stunning sights I've seen in a Japanese temple: 1,001 wooden statues of the thousand-handed Kannon. Row upon row, these life-size figures, carved from Japanese cypress in the 12th and 13th centuries, make an impressive sight; in the middle is a large seated Kannon carved in 1254 by Tankei, a famous sculptor from the Kamakura Period, when he was 82 years old. Don't expect to actually see a thousand arms on each statue; there are only 40, the idea being that each hand has the power to save 25 worlds. In front of the 1,001 Kannon are a row of 28 guardian deities; not only are they all National Treasures, but it's rare to find a whole set like this one still intact. To accommodate all the statues, the hall stretches nearly 120m (400 ft.), making it the longest wooden building in Japan (no cameras or video allowed inside). Its length was too hard to ignore—archery competitions have been held for centuries in the corridor behind the statues; standing here, you can see how difficult it might be to hit a piece of sacred cloth attached to the wall at the opposite end. The greatest record was set in 1686, when a competitor fired off 13,053 arrows for 24 hours nonstop, hitting the target 8,133 times.

Shichijo Dori. ✆ **075/525-0033.** Admission ¥600 adults, ¥400 junior-high and high-school students, ¥300 children. Apr to mid-Nov daily 8am–5pm; mid-Nov to Mar daily 9am–4pm. Bus: 86, 88, 100, 106, 110, 206, or 208 to Hakubutsukan Sanjusangendo-mae (1 min.).

Western Kyoto

Two of Kyoto's most famous sights are northwest of downtown Kyoto.

Kinkakuji (Temple of the Golden Pavilion) ★★★ TEMPLE One of Kyoto's best-known (and crowded) attractions—and the inspiration for the Temple of the Silver Pavilion (see above)—Kinkakuji was constructed in the 1390s as a retirement villa for Shogun Ashikaga Yoshimitsu. It features a three-story pavilion covered in gold leaf with a roof topped by a bronze phoenix. The first floor is built in the style of a Heian court noble, the second in the martial style of samurai, and the third in Zen Buddhist style. Apparently, the retired shogun lived in shameless luxury while the rest of the nation suffered from famine, earthquakes, and plague. If you come on a clear day (best is late afternoon), the Golden Pavilion shimmers against a blue sky, its reflection captured in the waters of a calm pond. This pavilion is not the original, however; in 1950, a disturbed student monk burned Kinkakuji to the ground (the story is told by author Mishima Yukio in his famous novel *The Temple of the Golden Pavilion*). The temple was rebuilt in 1955 and in 1987 was recovered in gold leaf that was five times thicker than the original coating: You almost need sunglasses. Be sure to explore the surrounding **park** with its moss-covered grounds and teahouses.

1 Kinkakuji-cho. ✆ **075/461-0013.** Admission ¥400 adults, ¥300 children. Daily 9am–5pm. Bus: 12 or 59 to Kinkakuji-mae (1 min.) or 101, 102, 204, or 205 to Kinkakuji-michi (3 min.).

Ryoanji Temple ★★★ TEMPLE About a 20-minute walk (or short ride on bus no. 59) southwest of the Golden Pavilion is Ryoanji—home to what is probably the most famous **Zen rock garden** in all of Japan—laid out at the end of the 15th century during the Muromachi Period. Fifteen rocks set in waves of raked white pebbles are surrounded on three sides by a clay wall and on the fourth by a wooden veranda, in an area that measures about 25m (80 ft.) long and 10m (30 ft.) wide. Sit down and contemplate what the artist was trying to communicate. The interpretation of the rocks is up to the individual. (Mountains above the clouds? Islands in the ocean?) My only objection to this peaceful place is that, unfortunately, it's not always peaceful—a loudspeaker on occasion extols the virtue of the garden, destroying any chance for peaceful meditation. If you get here early enough, you may be able to escape both the crowds and the noise.

After visiting the rock garden, be sure to take a walk around the temple grounds. There's a 1,000-year-old **pond,** on the rim of which sits a beautiful little restaurant, **Seigenin-in,** with *tatami* rooms and screens, where you can eat *yudofu* and enjoy the view. A nice **landscape garden** has moss so inviting you'll wish you could lie down and take a nap.

13 Ryoanji-Goryo-shita-machi. www.ryoanji.jp. ✆ **075/463-2216.** Admission ¥500 adults, ¥300 children. Mar–Nov daily 8am–5pm; Dec–Feb daily 8:30am–4:30pm. Bus: 59 to Ryoanji-mae (2 min.); or 12 or 50 to Ritsumeikan Daigaku-mae (6 min.).

Toei Kyoto Studio Park (Toei Uzumasa Eigamura) ★★ AMUSEMENT PARK If your kids are ready to mutiny because of yet another temple, get on their good side by visiting this studio park, owned by one of Japan's three major film companies and where many samurai flicks and TV shows are made. Don't expect the high-tech, polished glitz of American theme parks—rather, this is a working studio where more than 200 TV and movie productions are filmed each year. Indoor and outdoor movie sets re-create the mood, setting, and atmosphere of feudal and turn-of-the-20th-century Japan, complete with photogenic period "villages" lined with samurai houses and old-time shops. Stagehands carry around props, hammers, and saws, and rework sets. You may even see a famous star walking around dressed in samurai garb or come upon a scene being filmed.

Otherwise, there are many tourist-oriented attractions, including a 20-minute ninja show three times daily (it's in Japanese, but the action is easy to grasp), street performers, an anime museum featuring objects from Toei's films, an indoor playground, and a game arcade. Unfortunately, it costs extra (usually ¥500 each) to enjoy some of the attractions most likely to appeal to older children, including the mazelike Ninja Mystery House, which requires figuring out trap doors and other tricks in order to "escape"; a Ninja training house; a haunted house; and a Trick Art Museum that contains optical illusions that encourage visitors to ham it up and become part of the action (like fighting serpents or bullfighting). You can also pay extra to dress up like a geisha, ninja, or samurai at the **Costume Photo Shop** for that lasting memento, or get the full treatment of wigs, makeup, and costume, after which you can stroll around the studio park for an hour (in fine weather only; ¥8,500 and up). Come here only if you have a lot of time (you'll probably need a minimum of 2 hr. here), are a cinema buff, or have youngsters in tow.

10 Higashi-Hachigaokacho, Uzumasa, Ukyo-ku. www.toei-eigamura.com. ✆ **075/864-7716.** Admission ¥2,200 adults, ¥1,300 junior-high and high-school students, ¥1,100 children. Daily 9am–5pm (9:30am–4:30pm weekdays Dec–Feb; 9:30am–5pm weekends Dec–Feb; 9am–6pm weekends Mar–Sept and daily Aug). Closed periodically for maintenance. Train: JR line to Uzumasa (5 min.) or Randen Kitano Line to Randen Satseishomae (2 min.). Bus: 91 or 93 to Uzumasa Eigamuramae; 11, 72, 73, 74, 75, 76 or 85 to Uzumasa Koryuji-mae; or 75 to Eigamura-michi.

IMPERIAL VILLAS & TEMPLES WITHIN EASY REACH OF KYOTO

If this is your first visit to Kyoto and you're here for only a couple days, you should concentrate on seeing sights in Kyoto itself. If, however, this is your second trip to Kyoto, you're here for an extended period of time, or you have a passion for traditional Japanese architecture or gardens, a number of worthwhile attractions lie in the immediate region surrounding Kyoto. Foremost on my list is **Katsura Imperial Villa.**

Note: The Katsura Imperial Villa and **Shugakuin Imperial Villa** require advance permission to visit. To see the Katsura Imperial Villa or Shugakuin Imperial Villa, which are free, the easiest way to apply for permission is online in English at **http://sankan.kunaicho.go.jp** at least 4 days before your intended visit. It's best to apply earlier, however; applications are accepted up to 3 months in advance. Alternatively, you can go in person to the **Imperial Household Agency Office** (✆ **075/211-1215;** no English is spoken and no reservations are accepted by phone, but you can have a Japanese speaker call to see whether space is available), located on the northwest grounds of the **Kyoto Imperial Palace** near Inui Gomon Gate, a 5-minute walk from Imadegawa subway station. It's open Monday through Friday from 8:45am to 5pm. Here you'll be able to apply for a tour the next day if there's room, but again, the earlier you book (up to 3 months) the better chance you'll have. If you haven't done the above, in a last-ditch effort you can also head directly to Katsura or Shugakuin imperial villas for a same-day application, where a limited number of tickets for tours that afternoon is distributed on a first-come, first-served basis starting at 11am (you'll want to get there much earlier). Obviously, this could turn into an all-day proposition, so you're best off making advance reservations.

Regardless of how you apply, everyone must present their passports, and **participants must be at least 18 years old. Tours,** which take place Tuesday through Sunday, are given at Katsura Imperial Villa at 9am, 10am, 11am, 1:30pm, 2:30pm, and 3:30pm; and at Shugakuin Imperial Villa at 9am, 10am, 11am, 1:30pm, and 3pm. Tours are conducted in Japanese only, but there are videos and a free handheld audio guide in English.

KATSURA IMPERIAL VILLA ★★★ A 20-minute walk from Katsura Station on the Hankyu railway line, or a 30-minute bus ride from Kyoto Station (take bus no. 33 to the Katsura Rikyu-mae stop) and then an 8-minute walk, this villa is considered the jewel of traditional Japanese architecture and landscape gardening. It was built between 1620 and 1624 by Prince Toshihito, brother of the emperor, with construction continued by Toshihito's son. The garden, markedly influenced by Kobori Enshu, Japan's most famous garden designer, is a "stroll garden" in which each turn of the path brings an entirely new view.

The first thing you notice upon entering Katsura is its simplicity—the buildings were all made of natural materials, and careful attention was paid to the slopes of the roofs and to the grain, texture, and color of the various woods. In addition, every garden detail was carefully planned, down to the stones used in the path, the way the trees twist, and how scenes are reflected in the water. A pavilion for moon viewing, a hall for imperial visits, a teahouse, and other buildings are situated around a pond; as you walk along the pathway, you're treated to views that literally change with each step you take. Islets, stone lanterns, scenes representing seashores, mountains, and hamlets, manicured trees, and bridges of stone, earth, or wood that arch gracefully over the water: Everything is perfectly balanced—no matter where you stand, the view is complete and in harmony. Little wonder the Katsura Imperial Villa has influenced architecture not only in Japan but around the world. Sadly, tours are much too hurried (only 1 hr.).

SHUGAKUIN IMPERIAL VILLA ★★ Northeast of Kyoto, about a 40-minute bus ride from Kyoto Station (take bus no. 5 from Kyoto Station to the Shugakuin Rikyu-michi bus stop) and then a 15-minute walk, this villa was built in the mid-1600s as a retirement retreat for Emperor Go-Mizunoo, who came to the throne at age 15 and suddenly abdicated 18 years later to become a monk, passing the throne to his daughter in 1629. Amazingly, though the villa was just 2 hours from the Imperial Palace, the emperor came here only on day trips; he never once spent the night. The 53-hectare (133-acre) grounds, among Kyoto's largest, are situated at the foot of Mount Hiei and are famous for the principle known as "borrowed landscape," in which the surrounding landscape is incorporated into the overall design. Grounds are divided into three levels (only two of which have compelling features): The **upper garden,** with its lake, islands, and waterfalls, is the most extensive of the three, offering grand views of the surrounding countryside from its hillside pavilion. The **middle garden,** built as a residence for the emperor's daughter, contains a villa with the famous "Shelves of Mist"; in keeping with the Japanese penchant for ranking the best three of everything, this is considered one of the three most beautiful shelves in Japan. The gardens are more spacious and natural than most Japanese-style gardens, which are often small and contrived. Tours, which take 1 hour and 15 minutes and cover about 3km (2 miles) of hilly grounds, allow ample time for photography.

FUSHIMI–INARI SHRINE ★★★ Just a 2-minute walk from the JR Inari Station (which is just two stops by local commuter train from Kyoto Station),

Fushimi-Inari Shrine (http://inari.jp/en/; ✆ **075/641-7331**) is one of Japan's most celebrated Shinto shrines and one of Kyoto's most visually memorable sights. Founded in 711, it's dedicated to the goddess of rice (rice was collected as taxes during the shogun era) and has therefore long been popular with merchants, who come here to pray for prosperity. The 4km (2½-mile) pathway behind the shrine is lined with more than 10,000 red *torii,* presented by worshipers through the ages and by Japanese businesses. There are also stone foxes, which are considered messengers of the gods, usually with a key to the rice granary hanging from their mouths. It's a glorious, almost surreal, walk as you wind through the woods and the tunnel of vermilion-colored *torii* gates and gradually climb a hill, for a good view of Kyoto. At several places along the path are small shops where you can dine on a bowl of noodles or other refreshment. Admission is free, and the grounds never close. The most popular times to visit are the first day of each month and New Year's, but I prefer weekdays when almost no one is there.

Note: Fushimi-Inari Shrine is on the same JR line that continues to Nara. If you plan on spending the night in Nara, you could easily take in these two attractions on the way. Note, however, that the express train to Nara does not stop at JR Inari Station; for that you'll have to take a local train.

A STROLL THROUGH HIGASHIYAMA-KU

START:	**Kyoto National Museum on Shichijo Dori a couple of blocks east of the Kamo River; to get there, walk 20 minutes from Kyoto Station or take bus no. 86, 88, 100, 106, 110, 206, or 208 to Hakubutsukan Sanjusangendo-mae.**
FINISH:	**Gion.**
TIME:	**Allow approximately 5 hours, including stops for shopping and museums.**
BEST TIMES:	**Weekdays, when temples and shops aren't as crowded.**
WORST TIMES:	**Monday, when museums are closed.**

A stroll through Higashiyama-ku will take you to Kiyomizu Temple, one of Kyoto's most famous sights, and other worthwhile attractions like Sanjusangendo Hall. It will also take you through some of Kyoto's most charming neighborhoods, with plenty of shopping opportunities en route.

Start your stroll at:

1 Kyoto National Museum (Kokuritsu Hakubutsukan)

In 1889, the Meiji government, fearful that Japan's cultural objects were going the way of the samurai with the increasing import of Western ways and products, established three national museums—one in Tokyo, one in Nara, and this one in Kyoto, which serves as a repository for art objects and treasures that once belonged to Kyoto's temples and royal court. In addition, special exhibitions are mounted three to four times a year.

Across the street is the:

2 Sanjusangendo Hall

This hall dates from 1266 and is only about 15m (50 ft.) wide, but stretches almost 120m (400 ft.), making it Japan's longest wooden building. It's not the building itself that impresses but what it contains—1,001 life-size images of the thousand-handed Kannon. Seeing so many of them—row upon row of gold figures, glowing in the dark hall—is stunning. In the middle is a 3.3m-tall (11-ft.) seated figure of Kannon carved in 1254. At the back of the hall is a 117m (384-ft.) archery range where a competition is held every January 15. (See "Exploring Kyoto," earlier in this chapter, for more on this and other major sights described in this stroll.)

East of Sanjusangendo Hall (toward the wooded hills) are Higashioji Dori and a stoplight; take a left here and walk about 5 minutes until you come to the second stoplight, at a small intersection with a Lawson convenience store. Turn left here, take the first right down a narrow street, and to your right you'll soon see:

3 Kawai Kanjiro's House

Kawai Kanjiro's House, Gojo-zaka (© **075/561-3585**), is the former home and studio of one of Japan's most well-known potters, Kawai Kanjiro (1890–1966). Inspired at a young age by Bernard Leach and one of the cofounders of the Japan Folk Crafts Museum in Tokyo, this versatile man made much of the furniture in this lovely home, a traditional Japanese house with an indoor open-pit fireplace and gleaming woodwork. Pottery, folkcraft, personal effects, and his outdoor clay kiln, built on a slope in the traditional Japanese method, are on display, but this museum is worth seeing for the 1930s house alone, especially if you haven't seen the interiors of many traditional Japanese homes. Admission is ¥900 for adults, ¥500 for students, and ¥300 for children. It's open Tuesday to Sunday 10am to 5pm.

Take a right out of the museum, walk to the busy road with the overpass, and turn right. When you get to the big intersection, look catty-corner across the intersection to the left and you'll see a slope leading uphill between two big stone lanterns. This marks the entrance to the:

4 Otani Mausoleum

It serves as a major mausoleum for members of Shinshu Buddhism (a Japanese religious sect). In addition to a memorial hall dedicated to victims of World War II, it holds many memorial services for deceased Shin Buddhists from throughout Japan.

After passing the second two-story wooden gate, you should turn left and then right for:

5 Toribeyama

Since ancient times it has served as a cremation site and burial ground, with more than 15,000 tombs spread along the slopes.

Follow the pathway uphill, with the cemetery to your right and a succession of temples on your left, for about 10 minutes to the top, where you should then turn left and

Walking Tour: Higashiyama-ku

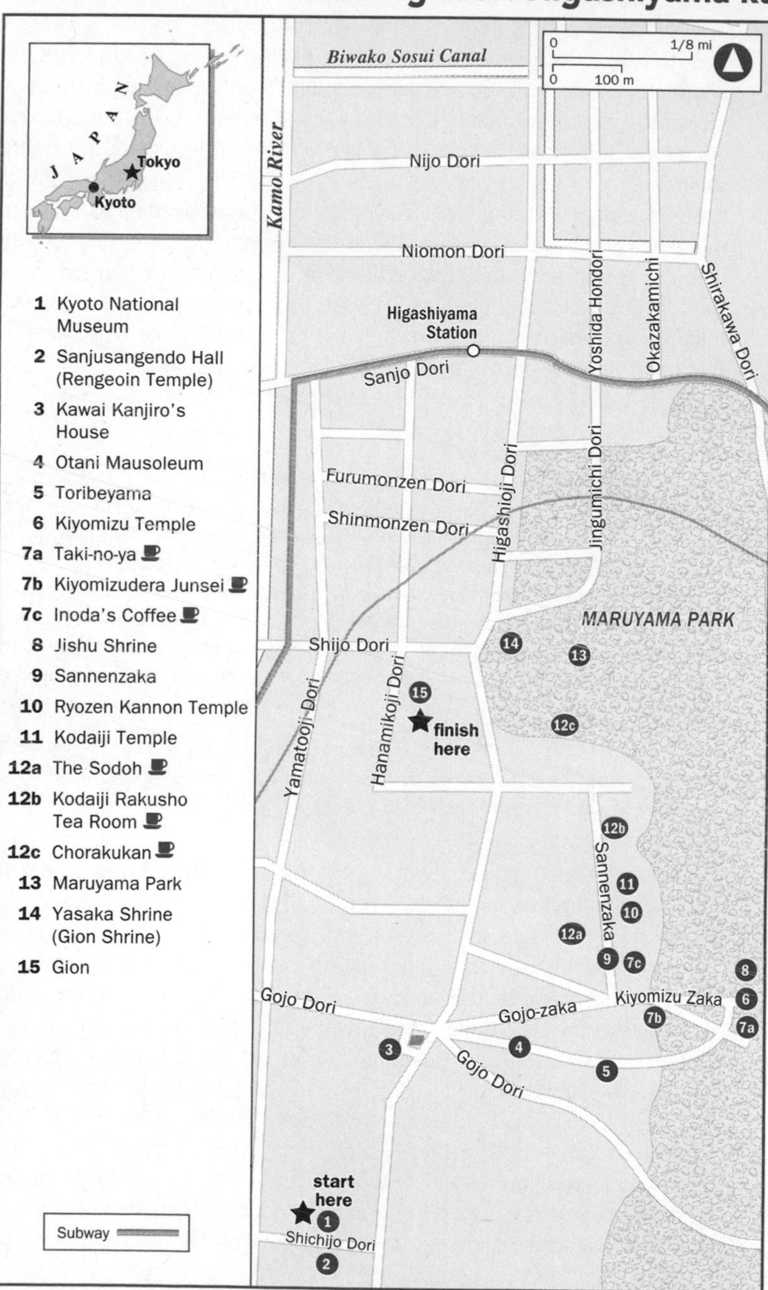

follow the painted white arrow with a wheelchair symbol in the street to the vermilion-colored tower gate, which marks the entrance to:

6 Kiyomizu Temple

This temple is the star attraction of this stroll. First founded in 798 and rebuilt in 1633 by the third Tokugawa shogun, Iemitsu, the temple occupies an exalted spot. The main hall (under wraps for renovation until 2020 but open for visitors) is built over a cliff and features a large wooden veranda supported by 139 pillars, each 15m (50 ft.) high. Take in the view of Kyoto from its deck, but to fully appreciate the grandeur of the main hall with its pillars and dark wood, walk to the three-story pagoda, which offers the best view of the main hall, built without the use of a single nail. From the pagoda, descend the stone steps to Otowa Falls, where you'll see Japanese lined up to drink from the refreshing spring water. Kiyomizu's name, in fact, translates as "pure water" and it's supposedly good for health. From here you'll also have the best view of the temple's impressive pillars.

7 Temple Dining

On the grounds of Kiyomizu Temple, just beside Otowa Falls, is **Taki-no-ya** (✆ **075/561-5117**), an open-air pavilion where you can sit on *tatami* and enjoy *yudofu,* noodles, a beer, or flavored shaved ice from the English-language menu. This is a great place to stop; if you're lucky to be here in autumn, the fiery reds of the maple trees will set the countryside around you aflame. It's open Friday through Wednesday 10am to 5pm. For something more substantial, wait until after your temple visit to dine on tofu at **Kiyomizudera Junsei,** located off Kiyomizu-zaka. On Sannenzaka (see below), keep your eyes peeled for **Inoda's Coffee** (✆ **075/532-5700**), where you'll have views of a Japanese-style garden along with pastries, sandwiches, and coffee. It's open daily 9am to 5pm.

Before departing Kiyomizu Temple, be sure to make a stop at the vermilion-colored Shinto shrine located behind the temple's main hall:

8 Jishu Shrine

This shrine is regarded as a dwelling place of the deity of love and match-making. Throughout the grounds are English-language signs describing the shrine's good-luck stations; for once, you're not left in the dark about the purpose of the various statues and memorials and what Japanese are doing as they make their rounds. It's very enriching. You can buy good-luck charms for everything from a happy marriage to easy delivery of a child to success in passing an examination. On the shrine's grounds are two stones placed about 9m (30 ft.) apart—if you're able to walk from one stone to the other with your eyes closed, you're supposedly guaranteed success in your love life. It sure doesn't hurt to try. There's also a place where you can write down your troubles on a piece of paper and then submerge it in a bucket of water for ¥200, which supposedly will cause both the paper and your troubles to dissolve. If you failed the rock test, you might make a point of stopping here.

From Kiyomizu Temple, retrace your steps to the vermilion-colored entry tower gate you passed earlier. From here, on a downhill slope called Kiyomizu-zaka, you'll pass shop after shop selling sweets, tea, pottery, fans, ties, hats, souvenirs, and curios. If you go crazy shopping here, remember that you're going to have to carry whatever you buy. After a couple of small shrines nestled in among the shops, you'll come to a split in the road and a small shrine on the right shaded by trees. Just beside this shrine are stone steps leading downhill (north) to a stone-cobbled street called:

9 Sannenzaka

The slope leads past lovely antiques stores, upscale craft shops, and restaurants and winds through neighborhoods of wooden buildings reminiscent of old Kyoto. Keep your eyes peeled for downhill stairs to the right leading to Kodaiji and Ninen-zaka; after you take these, the street will wind a bit as it goes downhill and eventually end at a T intersection. (The Sodoh restaurant, described below, is here to the left.) Take the stairs opposite the road and look to the right for:

10 Ryozen Kannon Temple

This temple (www.ryozen-kwannon.jp; ✆ **075/561-2205**) has a 24m-high (80-ft.) white statue dedicated to unknown soldiers who died in World War II. Memorial services are conducted four times daily at a shrine that contains tablets memorializing the 2 million Japanese who perished during the war. A Memorial Hall commemorates the more than 48,000 foreign soldiers who died on Japanese territory. Open daily from 8:40am to 4:20pm; admission is ¥300, so you may only want to take a peek at the statue.

Just past Ryozen Kannon Temple, across the parking lot, is:

11 Kodaiji Temple

This temple was founded by the widow Nene in commemoration of her husband, Toyotomi Hideyoshi, who succeeded in unifying Japan at the end of the 16th century. In addition to teahouses and a memorial hall containing wooden images of the couple, there's a beautiful garden designed by master gardener Kobori Enshu. Don't miss it (a one-room museum is included in admission, but skip it if time is of the essence).

Exit Kodai-ji Temple via the main steps leading downhill and turn right, continuing north.

12 Temple Dining

At the end of Sannenzaka, to the left, is the **Sodoh,** an Italian restaurant located in a rustic 1929 villa (p. 237). Past Kodai-ji Temple and just before the street ends at a pagoda with a crane on top, keep your eyes peeled for a teahouse on your right with a garden, which you can glimpse from the street through a gate. The **Kodaiji Rakusho Tea Room (洛匠),** 516 Washiochiyo (✆ **075/561-6892**), is a lovely place and one of my favorite tearooms in Kyoto. It has a 100-year-old miniature garden with a pond that's home to some of the largest and most colorful carp I've ever seen, some of which are 20 years old and winners of many medals. Sit at a table or in the back *tatami* room and enjoy *matcha* (frothed, powdered green tea), *warabi mochi* (cubes of a jellylike dessert coated in toasted soy flour), and, in summer, *somen* (finely spun cold noodles), or, in winter, hot red bean soup with chestnut. If you're a gardener, you'll probably want to give up the hobby after you've seen what's possible but rarely achieved. Open from 9:30am to 6pm; closed 1 day a week but, unfortunately, not a fixed day. For coffee, sandwiches, dessert, or a bountiful afternoon tea (¥4,000, available noon to 6pm), just inside Maruyama Park to the left, there's an ornate **cafe** in **Chorakukan** (✆ **075/561-0001**) a brick-and-stone Meiji-Era building; it's open daily from 11am to 7:30pm.

Continuing on your stroll north, turn right at the pagoda with the crane and then take an immediate left, which marks the beginning of:

13 Maruyama Park

An unkempt field of shrubs and weeds was designated a public park in 1886, and now this is one of Kyoto's most popular outdoor respites, filled with ponds, pigeons, and gardens. In spring, it's a popular spot for viewing cherry blossoms; to the left after you enter the park is one of the oldest, most famous cherry trees in Kyoto.

Also farther west is:

14 Yasaka Shrine

Yasaka Shrine is also known as Gion Shrine because of its proximity to the Gion District. The present buildings date from 1654; the stone *torii* (gates) on the south side are considered among the largest in Japan. But the reason most people come here is one of practicality—the shrine is dedicated to the gods of health and prosperity, two universal concerns. This shrine, free to the public and open 24 hours, is packed during the Gion Festival and on New Year's Eve.

Exit Yasaka Shrine to the west; this brings you to a busy street called Higashioji. Cross and continue walking west on busy Shijo Dori until you reach Hanamikoji Dori on your left. This is:

15 Gion

One of Japan's most famous nightlife districts, Gion is centered primarily on Hanamikoji Dori, which translates as "Narrow Street for Flower Viewing." This is one of Kyoto's long-standing geisha districts, an enclave of discreet, traditional, and almost solemn-looking wooden homes that reveal nothing of the gaiety inside—drinking, conversation, and business dealings with dancing, singing, and music provided by geisha and their apprentices, called *maiko.* If it's early evening, you might glimpse one of these women as she small-steps her way in *geta* (a traditional wooden shoe) to an evening appointment, elaborately made up and wearing a beautiful kimono. **Gion Corner** on Hanamikoji Dori, offers performances of dance, puppetry, and other traditional arts nightly, or join a guided night tour of Gion; see "Kyoto After Dark," later in this chapter, for details.

Winding Down

If all this sightseeing and shopping have made you thirsty, there are many restaurants and bars to the west across the Kamo River, on Pontocho, and near Shijo and Kawaramachi streets. See "Where to Dine in Kyoto" and "Kyoto After Dark" in this chapter for many suggestions in this area.

SHOPPING

As the nation's capital for more than 1,000 years, Kyoto spawned a number of crafts and exquisite art forms that catered to the elaborate tastes of the imperial court and the upper classes. Kyoto today is still renowned for its **crafts,** including Nishijin textiles, Yuzen-dyed fabrics, Kyo pottery (pottery fired in Kyoto), fans, dolls, cutlery, gold-leaf work, umbrellas, paper lanterns, bamboo crafts, combs, *Noh* masks, cloisonné, and lacquerware.

GREAT SHOPPING AREAS The majority of Kyoto's tiny specialty shops are in central Kyoto's downtown. The rectangular grid formed by **Kawaramachi Dori, Shijo Dori, Nijo Dori,** and **Teramachi Dori** includes two covered shopping arcades and specialized shops selling lacquerware, combs and hairpins, knives and swords, tea and tea-ceremony implements, and more—including, of course, clothing and accessories for customers of all ages. Here, too, is the **Nishiki Food Market** (see below, under "Markets").

For antiques, woodblock prints, and art galleries, head toward the high-end **Shinmonzen Dori** and **Furumonzen Dori** in Gion, which parallel Shijo Dori to the north on the east side of the Kamo River, as well as **Teramachi Dori** north of Oike, home also of Kyoto Antiques Center. You'll find pottery and souvenir shops in abundance on the roads leading to Kiyomizu Temple, particularly the hill known as **Chawan-zaka** (Teacup Slope).

For clothing, accessories, and modern goods, **department stores** are good bets. They're conveniently located in central Kyoto near the Shijo-Kawaramachi intersection and Kyoto Station. Near Kyoto Station are also two large **shopping malls** selling everything from clothing and shoes to stationery and local souvenirs: an underground mall beneath the station and **Aeon** southwest of the station across Hachijo Dori. **Kyoto-Yodobashi,** on Karasuma Dori a block north of Kyoto Tower, contains the Yodobashi Camera electronics store, fashion boutiques, and restaurants.

Crafts & Specialty Shops

Aritsugu (有次) ★★ The fact that this family-owned business is located at the Nishiki Food Market is appropriate, as it sells hand-wrought knives and other handmade cooking implements, including sushi knives, bamboo steamers, pots, pans, and cookware used in the preparation of traditional Kyoto cuisine, as well as *ikebana* scissors. In business for more than 450 years, the shop counts the city's top chefs among its customers despite its diminutive size; look for its display cases of knives. Open daily 9am to 5:30pm. Nishiki-Koji Dori, Gokomachi Nishi-iru, Nakagyo-ku. ✆ **075/221-1091.** Subway: Shijo (8 min.). Bus: 4, 5, 10, 11, 12, 17, 32, 46, 59, 62, 63, 64, 65, 66, 67, 104, 201, 203, 207, or 205 to Shijo Kawaramachi (5 min.). 1 block north of Shijo Dori on the north side of Nishiki-Koji Dori, west of Gokomachi.

Ippodo (一保堂) ★★ In business since 1717, this famous shop is a good place not only to buy high-quality Japanese green teas but to learn more about them. Pick up the shop's English-language brochure, which explains the

Shopping for Secondhand Kimono

Flea markets, especially the one at Toji Temple (see "Markets," below), are good stomping grounds for inexpensive used kimono. I also like **Kikuya,** tucked away in a residential neighborhood on Manjuji Dori, east of Sakaimachi (✆ **075/351-0033;** Mon–Sat 9am–7pm), on the second floor of a nondescript building. Its three rooms are packed with used kimono (both antique and modern), *haori* (short kimono-like jackets, traditionally worn by men), *obi* (kimono sashes often worn as scarves), and kimono accessories for both adults and kids. Another good place is **Chicago,** a thrift shop about halfway down the Teramachi covered shopping arcade (✆ **075/212-5391;** daily 11am–8pm). Its entire second floor is devoted to used kimono (including wedding kimono), *obi, jinbei* (men's pajamas), and *yukata* (cotton sleeping kimono).

different varieties, from *matcha* to *sencha* to *genmaicha,* or sample them at the shop's hands-on tearoom, **Kaboku,** where you can experience brewing techniques for the tea of your choice. In a nod to modern times, Ippodo also sells teabags. Open daily 9am to 6pm (Kaboku open daily 10am–5:30pm). Teramachi Dori, north of Nijo, Nakagyo-ku. www.ippodo-tea.co.jp. ✆ **075/211-3421.** Subway: Kyoto Shiyakusho-mae (5 min.). Bus: 4, 10, 17, 32, 59, 104, or 205 (5 min.).

Kyoto Antiques Center ★ Teramachi is known for its antiques and specialty shops. This store, with about 20 vendors, is the largest. Offering both Western and Japanese antiques and curios, it's a fun place to browse for jewelry, lacquerware, pottery, and dolls. Wednesday to Monday 10:30am to 7pm; closed third Monday of each month. East side of Teramachi, north of Nijo Dori, Nakagyo-ku. ✆ **075/222-0793.** Bus: 4, 10, 17, 32, 59, 104, and 205 to Kyoto Shiyakushomae (7 min.).

Kyoto Handicraft Center ★★★ For one-stop shopping for Japanese souvenirs and crafts, your best bet is the city's largest craft, gift, and souvenir center, in business more than 80 years and founded by the present owner's grandfather. Its two buildings offer pearls, woodblock prints, lacquerware, pottery, dolls, kimono, paper products, ornamental swords, samurai armor, iron teapots, fans, wind chimes, chopsticks, cloisonné, lunch boxes, incense, Nishijin textile goods, sake and sake cup sets, green tea, food items, *furoshiki* (cloth used for wrapping gifts), T-shirts, and refrigerator magnets—and that's just for starters. In addition to a tourist office (where you can also exchange money) and a kimono rental service, it provides workspace for artisans producing their various crafts, including woodblock printing and the production of damascene. You can also try your own hand at nine different craft activities, including woodblock prints, cloisonné, damascene, and more, with English instruction provided. No reservations are necessary, but plan on at least an hour. Lessons run ¥1,950 to ¥4,100 and are a great way for older children to get creative while you shop. The **Kakoh** buffet restaurant is open for lunch from 11:30am to 2:30pm (last order), with a variety of Japanese and Western dishes for only ¥1,500 adults, ¥800 children. Open daily 10am to 7pm. 17 Shogoin Entomi-cho,

Sakyo-ku. www.kyotohandicraftcenter.com. © **075/761-8001.** Bus: 93, 201, 202, 203, 204, or 206 to Kumano-jinja-mae (1 min.). On Marutamachi Dori, north of Heian Shrine.

Yojiya (よーじや) ★ Kyoto is famous for its *aburatorigami,* face-blotting paper long used by geisha and *maiko.* Founded in 1904, this cosmetic shop sells a variety of aburatorigami, which I find very useful for gently removing excess skin oil on hot, humid days. It also sells other beauty products, like *yuzu-tsuyaya,* a citron-scented lip balm. It has outlets all over Kyoto, as well as at Japan's major international airports, but this is its main shop. Daily 11am to 7pm. Shinkyogoku Kayukoji, Nakagyo-ku. © **075/221-4626.** Subway: Kawaramachi (5 min.). Bus: 4, 5, 10, 11, 12, 17, 32, 46, 59, 62, 63, 64, 65, 66, 67, 104, 201, 203, 207, or 205 to Shijo Kawaramachi (2 min.). On Kayukoji Lane, northwest of the Shijo-Kawaramachi intersection. From Shijo Dori, walk north on Shinkyogoku covered shopping arcade and take the first right.

Department Stores

Department stores are good places to shop for Japanese items and souvenirs, including pottery, lacquerware, and kimono as well as clothing, foodstuffs, and everyday items.

JR Kyoto Isetan, located in Kyoto Station (http://kyoto.wjr-isetan.co.jp; © **075/352-1111;** daily 10am–8pm), is Kyoto's most fashionable department store, specializing in women's imported and domestic clothing.

In central Kyoto, **Daimaru,** on Shijo Dori west of Takakura (www.daimaru.co.jp/kyoto; © **075/211-8111;** daily 10am–8pm), is Kyoto's largest department store, with everything from clothing to electronic goods spread over nine floors (and branches of well-known restaurants on the 8th floor). Nearby are **Marui,** on the southeast corner of the Shijo-Kawaramachi intersection (© **075/257-0101;** daily 10:30am–8:30pm), aimed at young shoppers with nine floors of fashion, housewares, and restaurants; and **Takashimaya,** across the street at the southwest corner of the Shijo-Kawaramachi intersection (www.takashimaya.co.jp/kyoto; © **075/221-8811;** daily 10am–8pm), one of Japan's oldest and most respected department stores with a good selection of traditional crafts. **Tokyu Hands** (http://kyoto.tokyu-hands.co.jp/en/index.html; © **075/254-3109;** daily 10am–8:30pm), on Shijo Dori east of Karasuma Dori, sells tools and gadgets for hobbyists, as well as kitchenware, beauty goods, and other items.

Markets

On the 21st of each month, a flea market is held at **Toji Temple** (www.toji.or.jp/en/index.html; © **075/691-3325**), about a 15-minute walk southwest of Kyoto Station. Japan's largest flea market, it's also one of the oldest; its history stretches back more than 700 years, when pilgrims began flocking to Toji Temple to pay their respects to Kobo Daishi, who founded the Shingon sect of Buddhism. Today, Toji Temple, a World Heritage Site, is still a center for the Shingon sect, and its market (popularly known as Kobo-san) is a colorful affair with booths selling Japanese antiques, old kimono, ethnic goods, flowers, bonsai, dried foods, fish, vegetables, crafts, odds and ends, and many other items. Worshipers come to pray before a statue of Kobo Daishi and to have their wishes written on wooden slats by temple calligraphers. Even if you don't buy anything, the festive atmosphere of the market and booths makes a trip memorable. The largest Kobo-san markets take place in December and January. All markets at Toji are held from about 8am to 4pm. A smaller market, devoted entirely to Japanese antiques, is held at Toji Temple on the first Sunday of each month.

Commemorating the scholar and poet Sugawara Michizane, the **Tenjin-san market** held at **Kitano Tenmangu Shrine** (**© 075/461-0005**) the 25th of every month is a large market offering a little bit of everything—antiques, used clothing, ceramics, food—in a beautiful setting, especially in spring when plum trees are in bloom. It's open from 8am to dusk, but go as early as you can. Kitano Shrine is on Imadegawa Dori between Nishi-oji and Senbon; take bus no. 10, 50, 101, 102, and 203 to the Kitano Tenmangu-mae stop.

Unlike the other temple markets, the **Chion-ji market** (**© 075/691-3325**), held the 15th of each month from 9am to 4pm, is devoted to handmade goods and crafts, including pottery and clothing. To reach it, take bus no. 17, 102, 201, 203, or 206 to Hyakumanben at the Higashioji and Imadegawa intersection; **Chion-ji Temple** is just to the northeast.

Although you many not buy anything to take home with you, a stroll through the **Nishiki Food Market** is worthwhile just for the atmosphere. With a 400-plus-year history, this covered shopping arcade in the heart of downtown Kyoto on Nishiki-Koji Dori (one block north of Shijo Dori) has approximately 135 open-fronted shops and stalls selling fish, seasonal produce (like chestnuts in autumn), flowers, eggs, pickled vegetables, teas, confectionary, fruit, kitchenware, and—to cash in on an increasing number of foreign visitors—crafts, souvenirs, and street food like grilled salmon, skewered chicken and sashimi. This is where locals, as well as the city's finest restaurants and inns, buy their food. It's open from the early hours to about 6pm; some shops close on either Wednesday or Sunday.

ENTERTAINMENT & NIGHTLIFE

Nothing beats a fine summer evening spent strolling the streets of Kyoto. From the geisha district of Gion to the bars and restaurants lining Pontocho, Kyoto is utterly charming and romantic at night. Begin with a walk along the banks of the Kamo River—it's a favorite place for young couples in love. In summer, restaurants stretching north and south of Shijo Dori along the river erect outdoor wooden platforms on stilts over the water.

There are many annual events and dances, including Miyako Odori dances in April and Gion Odori dances in November featuring *geiko* and *maiko* (geisha and apprentice geisha) dressed in elaborate costume; and *kabuki* at the Minamiza Theater in December.

To find out what's happening during your stay, ask the tourist office for the ***Kyoto Visitor's Guide*** or check online at www.kyotoguide.com and www.kansaiscene.com.

The Major Nightlife Districts

GION

Of Kyoto's five geisha districts, Gion is the most famous. A small neighborhood of plain wooden buildings in Higashiyama-ku on the eastern side of the Kamo River, Gion doesn't look anything like what you've probably come to expect from an urban Japanese nightlife district. There's little neon in sight, and the atmosphere is almost austere and solemn, as though its raison d'être were infinitely more important and sacred than mere entertainment. Gion is a shrine to Kyoto's past, an era when geisha numbered in the thousands.

Contrary to popular Western misconceptions, geisha are not prostitutes. Rather, they're trained experts in conversation and the traditional arts of music and dance (*geiko,* as they're usually referred to in Kyoto, translates as "art professional"). Their primary role is to make men feel like kings when they're in the soothing enclave of the geisha house. There are now a mere 250 geisha in Kyoto and fewer than 70 in Gion; after all, in today's high-tech world, few women are willing to undergo the years of rigorous training necessary to learn how to conduct the tea ceremony, to play the *shamisen* (a three-stringed instrument), and perform ancient court dances. *Maiko* are not allowed to have cellphones.

Gion is about a 5-minute walk from the Shijo-Kawaramachi intersection; to reach it, walk east on Shijo Dori and take a right on Hanamikoji Dori. Its narrow streets are great for strolling; a good time to take a walk through the neighborhood is around dusk, when geisha are on their way to their evening appointments. Perhaps you'll see one—or a *maiko* (a young woman training to be a geisha)—clattering in her high *geta* (wooden shoes). She'll be dressed in a brilliant kimono, her face a chalky white, and her hair adorned with hairpins and ornaments. From geisha houses, music and laughter lilt from behind paper screens, sounding all the more inviting because you can't enter. Don't take it personally; not even Japanese venture inside without the proper introductions. An increasing number of bars and restaurants in Gion are open to outsiders, however; it's not hard to imagine that in another 100 years, Gion will look no different from many other nightlife districts. ***Note:*** Unfortunately, hordes of visitors now descend upon Gion, hoping to photograph geisha and maiko. Please exercise restraint, don't get in their way, and don't try to coerce them into taking photographs with you.

If you want to find out more about geisha and *maiko,* consider joining a guided **Gion Night Tour** lasting 1 hour and 40 minutes and offered Monday, Wednesday, and Friday at 6pm March to November and 5pm December to February. Costing ¥1,000, the walking tour leads past entertainment and boardinghouses and describes what life is like for *maiko* as she prepares to become a *geiko.* Reservations are not required. The day after I took this tour, I saw three young women at Yasaka Shrine and was able to identify right away by the way they dressed that they were *maiko* rather than geisha. On the other hand, all those women you see everywhere in Kyoto dressed in kimono, especially in Higashiyama-ku, are not Japanese but rather Asian tourists in rental kimono. For more on the Gion Night Tour, pick up a brochure at the tourist office or go to www.waraido.com/walking/gion.html.

Gion Corner ★★ After strolling around Gion, pay a visit to Gion Corner, which introduces Japan's ancient cultural arts. Short demonstrations and performances of the tea ceremony, Japanese flower arranging, *koto* (Japanese harp) music, *gagaku* (ancient court music and dance), *kyogen* (*Noh* comic plays), *kyomai* (Kyoto-style dance) performed by *maiko,* and *bunraku* (puppetry) follow in quick succession and are described in detail in an English-language program. The shows cater to tourists, and none of the individual performances can match a full-scale production of the real thing, but this is a quick and convenient introduction. Before or after the show, visit the Maiko Gallery with its small display of *maiko* hairstyles and accessories. Performances are nightly at 6pm and 7pm mid-March through November (no performances July 16 and Aug 16); only Friday, Saturday, Sunday, and holidays December through early March. Reservations are not necessary, but arrive early or purchase in advance at most hotels or Gion Corner box office. No credit cards are accepted. Yasaka Hall, 570–2 Minamigawa, Gion. www.kyoto-gion-corner.com. ✆ **075/561-1119.** Tickets ¥3,150 adults, ¥2,200 high-school and university students, ¥1,900 children. Bus: 12, 46, 86, 100, 106, 201, 203, 206, or 207 to Gion (6 min.). Located on Hanamikoji Dori south of Shijo Dori.

PONTOCHO & KIYAMACHI

Pontocho is a narrow alley that parallels the Kamo River's western bank, stretching from Shijo Dori north to Sanjo Dori. Once riddled with geisha houses and other members-only establishments, it's now lined with bars, clubs, restaurants, and hostess bars. Pontocho makes for a fun walk as you watch Japanese and visitors from around the world enjoying themselves.

Kyoto's liveliest nightlife district, with bar after bar, is along **Kiyamachi,** another small street that parallels Pontocho just to the west and runs beside a small canal.

The Live Music Scene

Hello Dolly ★★ Among the bars and restaurants on Pontocho is this dark and narrow jazz club overlooking the Kamo River. Open since 1939 but with a retro look more reminiscent of the 1950s, with velvet-upholstered chairs and old album covers in the front window, it offers live jazz Fridays and Saturdays by Japanese musicians, with three sets at 8, 9:30, and 11pm. During the rest of the week it plays classic jazz recordings. In any case, this is a very civilized and old-school place in fast-changing Pontocho. Open daily 6pm (7pm Mon) to 1:30am (to 12:20am Sun). Pontocho. http://hellodolly.hannnari.com. ✆ **075/241-1728.** Cover Fri–Sat ¥1,000 for 2 hr., half-price subsequent hours, plus ¥900 per person table charge. No charge Sun–Thurs. Bus: 4, 5, 10, 11, 12, 17, 32, 46, 59, 62, 63, 64, 65, 66, 67, 104, 201, 203, 207, or 205 to Shijo Kawaramachi (4 min.). East (river) side of Pontocho.

Le Club Jazz ★★ For serious jazz fans, this has been the real deal for more than 20 years, with musicians from around Japan performing on a simple stage six nights a week. It's in a contemporary concrete building on Sanjo

Dori, but its upstairs entrance can be hard to find. The website is in Japanese only, but you can at least get an idea of cover fee. Open Tuesday to Sunday 7pm to 11pm, with matinees some weekends. Arimoto Building, 2nd floor, Sanjo Dori Gokomachi. http://web.kyoto-inet.or.jp/people/ktsin. ✆ **075/211-5800.** Live music cover ¥2,000–¥3,000, including 1 or 2 drinks. Subway: Kyoto Shiyakusho-mae (3 min.). Bus: 4, 5, 10, 11, 17, 32, 59, 62, 63, 64, 65, 66, 67, 104 or 205 to Kawaramachi Sanjo (4 min.). On northwest corner of Sanjo Dori and Gokomachi.

Live Spot RAG ★★★ This is one of Kyoto's oldest live clubs, established in 1981 and still pulling in the college-age crowd with mostly Japanese bands that play jazz but also rock, acoustic, and fusion. It's an intimate and popular place and can fill up fast, so try to buy tickets in advance (you also get a slight discount with advance purchases); students also often get discounts. Live music is from 7:30 to 10:30, after which it winds down to become a mellow bar, so you might just want to drop in for a drink. Open nightly from 6pm to 1am. Empire Building, 5th floor, Kiyamachi Dori, Sanjo Agaru. www.ragnet.co.jp. ✆ **075/241-0446.** Live music cover ¥1,800–¥3,000 for most performances, plus 2-drink/dish minimum. Subway: Kyoto Shiyakusho-mae (3 min.). Bus: 4, 5, 10, 11, 17, 32, 59, 62, 63, 64, 65, 66, 67, 104 or 205 to Kawaramachi Sanjo (2 min.). On the east side of Kiyamachi with its narrow canal, north of Sanjo Dori.

Ran Kyoto ★★ This small theater presents up-close performances by a handful of enthusiastic, traditionally clad musicians singing and playing drums (including a taiko drum), the three-stringed *samisen,* the 13-string *koto* (sometimes referred to as a Japanese harp), and piano. The repertoire ranges from traditional Japanese tunes to contemporary music and folk songs from Hokkaido to Okinawa, played with an infectious passion. Snacks and alcoholic drinks are available, and afterwards you can have your photo taken with the band. A rewarding way to spend 70 minutes; these guys rock. Performances Monday, Wednesday, and Friday at 6 and 8pm. 583-2 Nakanocho. www.rankyoto.com. ✆ **075/253-0150.** Admission ¥4,500 (¥4,000 online in advance). Bus: 4, 5, 10, 11, 12, 17, 32, 46, 59, 62, 63, 64, 65, 66, 67, 104, 201, 203, 207, or 205 to Shijo Kawaramachi. From Shijo Dori, walk north on Shinkyogoku covered shopping arcade and take the second right (it's beside Ninja Kyoto).

The Bar Scene

Ace Cafe ★★ In the same building as RAG (above), this 10th-floor bar has a concrete floor and ceiling, giving it a slight industrial look. But with windows on three sides, it's the view that's the draw, along with reasonable prices for cocktails and snacks. Open daily 6pm to 1 (to 3am Sat). Empire Building, 10th floor, Kiyamachi Dori, Sanjo Agaru. www.ace-cafe.com. ✆ **075/241-0009.** Kyoto Shiyakusho-mae (3 min.). Bus: 4, 5, 10, 11, 17, 32, 59, 62, 63, 64, 65, 66, 67, 104 or 205 to Kawaramachi Sanjo (2 min.). On the east side of Kiyamachi with its narrow canal, north of Sanjo Dori.

Atlantis ★ Located on Pontocho's east (river) side not far from Shijo Dori, this cocktail lounge is recommended mostly for its outside deck overlooking the Kamo River. Otherwise, it's a small, pleasant bar, where you might try one of its signature drinks, such as its orange liqueur and tonic with a green-tea flavor, but it also stocks scotch, bourbon, rum, and brandy for lots of options. It levies a ¥1,000 cover charge, but only when it's busy. Open daily 6pm to 2am (the outdoor deck closes at 11pm). 161 Matsumoto-Cho. www.atlantis.net.co.jp. ✆ **075/241-1621.** Bus: 4, 5, 10, 11, 12, 17, 32, 46, 59, 59, 62, 63, 64, 65, 66, 67, 104, 201, 203, 207, or 205 to Shijo Kawaramachi (4 min.).

Pig & Whistle ★★★ Several generations of Japanese locals, expats, and foreign travelers have visited this English-style pub, a Kyoto mainstay since 1985 where you can play darts, stand at the bar, or sit at a table with your mum. It attracts a mostly older crowd early in the evening followed by younger patrons later in the night, who come for its 12 different beers on tap, 60 single-malt whiskies, free Wi-Fi, foosball table, TVs showing sports from around the world, bar food ranging from fish and chips to minced meat pie, and happy hour daily to 7pm. There's a smoking and a nonsmoking section. Open daily 5pm to 1am (to 2am Fri–Sun). Shobi Building, 2nd floor, 115 Ohashi-cho, Ohashi, Higashi Iru, Sanjo Dori. www.pigandwhistle.beer. ✆ **075/761-6022.** Subway: Sanjo Keihan (2 min.). Bus: 5, 10, 11, 12, 16, 17, 59, 62, 63, 64, 65, 66, 67, 86, or 104 to Sanjo Keihan-mae (2 min.). East of the Kamo River, on the north side of Sanjo Dori.

Rub-a-Dub ★ This tiny basement bar, with a thatch rook over the counter to give it a laid-back, island vibe, has been Kyoto's premier reggae spot for more than 30 years. It plays all genres of Jamaican music, with DJs most weekend nights from 11pm and no cover. Open Sunday to Thursday 7pm to 2am, Friday 7pm to 4am, and Saturday 7pm to 5am. Tsujita Bldg., 115 Ishiya-cho. ✆ **075/256-3122.** Bus: 4, 5, 10, 11, 17, 32, 59, 62, 63, 64, 65, 66, 67, 104, or 205 to Kawaramachi Sanjo (4 min.). On Kiyamachi Dori's east side, south of Sanjo Dori.

Spring Valley Brewery ★★★ Its own craft beer, as well as brews from other small Japanese breweries, is the forte of this relative newcomer, open since 2017. Ensconced in a renovated *machiya,* it's big also on farm-to-table dishes, like the tabbouleh with chicken, black quinoa, and herbs, but and also serves dishes like smoked lamb, grilled fish with miso, craft pizzas, and rice and noodles. The set lunches, ranging in price from ¥800 to ¥1,300, are intriguing, with past choices including a Kyoto-raised smoked mocha pork and sauerkraut and a tomato-stewed Hyogo chicken with anchovy-flavored mashed potatoes. I'm not sure why, but no children younger than 7 are allowed after 5pm. Open daily 11am to 11pm. Takamiya-cho 287-2. www.springvalleybrewery.jp2. ✆ **075/231-4960.** Subway: Shijo (7 min.) or Kawaramachi (5 min). Bus: 5, 11, 12, 17, 32, 46, 201, 203, or 207 to Shijo Takakura (5 min.). On Tominokoji Dori, just north of Niski-Koji Dori.

OSAKA

Although its history stretches back almost 1,500 years, Osaka first gained prominence when Hideyoshi Toyotomi, the most powerful lord in the land, built Japan's most magnificent castle here in the 16th century. To develop resources for his castle town, he persuaded merchants from other parts of the nation to resettle in Osaka. During the Edo Period, the city became an important distribution center as feudal lords from the surrounding region sent their rice to merchants in Osaka, who in turn sent the rice onward to Edo (present-day Tokyo) and other cities. As the merchants prospered, the town grew, and such arts as *kabuki* and *bunraku* flourished. With money and leisure to spare, the merchants also developed a refined taste for food.

Today, with the legacy of the city's commercial beginnings still present, Osaka is the mover and shaker of the Kansai region, known for its international and progressive business and high-tech industries. Capital of Osaka Prefecture and with a population of about 2.6 million, it's the third-most populated city in Japan (after Tokyo and Yokohama). Osakans are usually characterized as being outgoing and clever at money affairs. (One Osakan greeting is "Are you making any money?") It's also known for its food, castle, port, underground shopping arcades, and *bunraku* puppet theater. It boasts Japan's oldest state temple and tallest skyscraper, one of the nation's best aquariums, and the first Universal Studios outside the United States. Because of its international airport, it also serves as a gateway to the rest of Japan. Indeed, some travelers base themselves in Osaka, taking side trips to Kyoto, Nara, Kobe, Himeji, and Mount Koya.

ESSENTIALS

Getting There

BY PLANE Constructed on a huge manmade island 5km (3 miles) off the mainland in Osaka Bay and almost 50km (30 miles) from the center of Osaka, **Kansai International Airport** (**KIX;** www.kansai-airport.or.jp; © **072/455-2500**) receives both international and domestic flights, and, like the city itself, is traveler-friendly. Signs are clear and abundant, and facilities and services—which range from restaurants and shops to a **tourist information center** (see below), **post office, ATMs** that accept foreign credit cards, a

Osaka

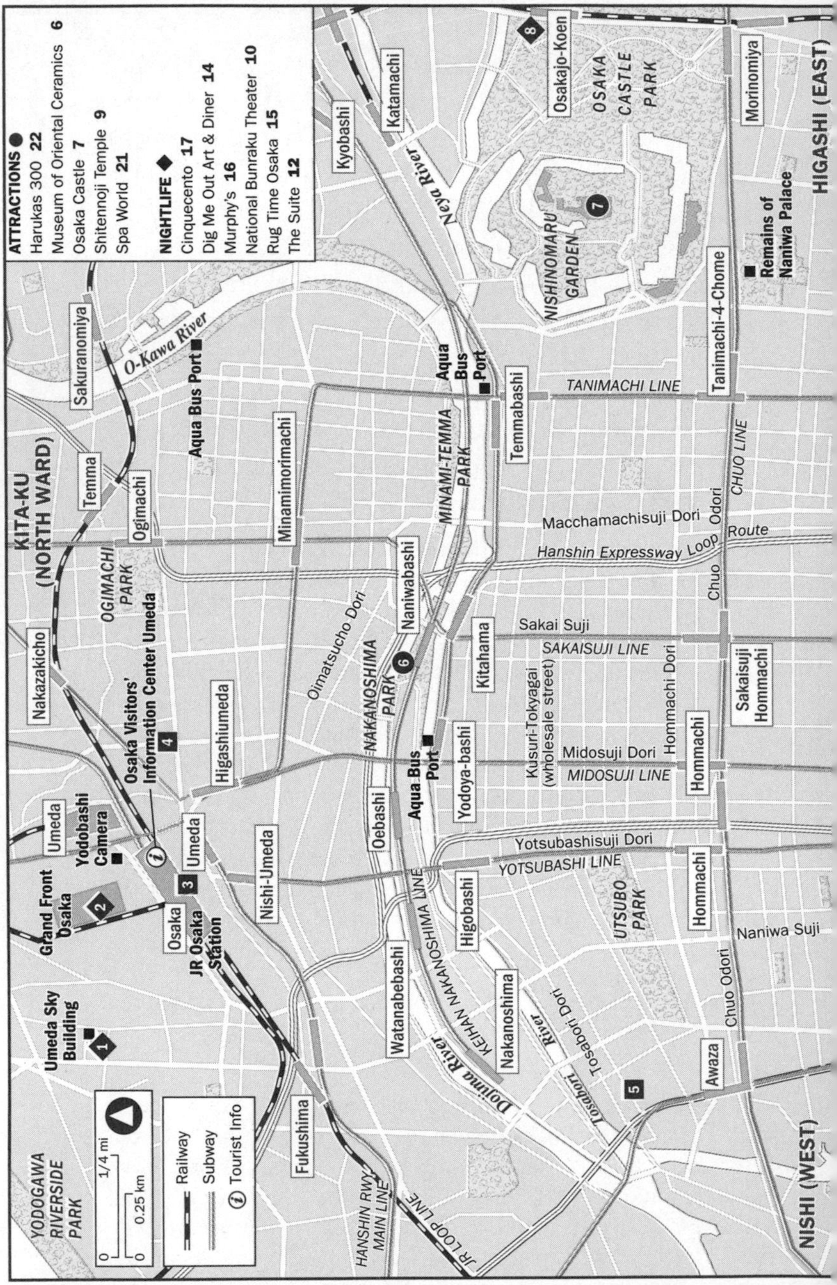

ATTRACTIONS ●
Harukas 300 **22**
Museum of Oriental Ceramics **6**
Osaka Castle **7**
Shitennoji Temple **9**
Spa World **21**

NIGHTLIFE ◆
Cinquecento **17**
Dig Me Out Art & Diner **14**
Murphy's **16**
National Bunraku Theater **10**
Rug Time Osaka **15**
The Suite **12**

0 1/4 mi
0 0.25 km

Railway
Subway
Tourist Info

KITA-KU (NORTH WARD)
HIGASHI (EAST)
NISHI (WEST)
YODOGAWA RIVERSIDE PARK
Umeda Sky Building
Grand Front Osaka
Yodobashi Camera
Osaka Visitors' Information Center Umeda
JR Osaka Station
Osaka
Umeda
Nishi-Umeda
Higashiumeda
Nakazakicho
Temma
Ogimachi
OGIMACHI PARK
Sakuranomiya
O-Kawa River
Aqua Bus Port
Minamimorimachi
Oimatsucho Dori
NAKANOSHIMA PARK
Naniwabashi
MINAMI-TEMMA PARK
Temmabashi
Kyobashi
Katamachi
Neya River
Osakajo-Koen
OSAKA CASTLE PARK
NISHINOMARU GARDEN
Tanimachi-4-Chome
Remains of Naniwa Palace
Morinomiya
TANIMACHI LINE
CHUO LINE
Macchamachisuji Dori
Hanshin Expressway Loop Route
Chuo Odori
Sakai Suji
SAKAISUJI LINE
Kitahama
Kusuri-Tokyagai (wholesale street)
Hommachi Dori
Sakaisuji Hommachi
Midosuji Dori
MIDOSUJI LINE
Hommachi
Yodoya-bashi
Oebashi
Yotsubashisuji Dori
YOTSUBASHI LINE
UTSUBO PARK
Naniwa Suji
Higobashi
KEIHAN NAKANOSHIMA LINE
Watanabebashi
Nakanoshima
Dojima River
Tosabori River
Tosabori Dori
Awaza
Fukushima
HANSHIN RWY MAIN LINE
JR LOOP LINE

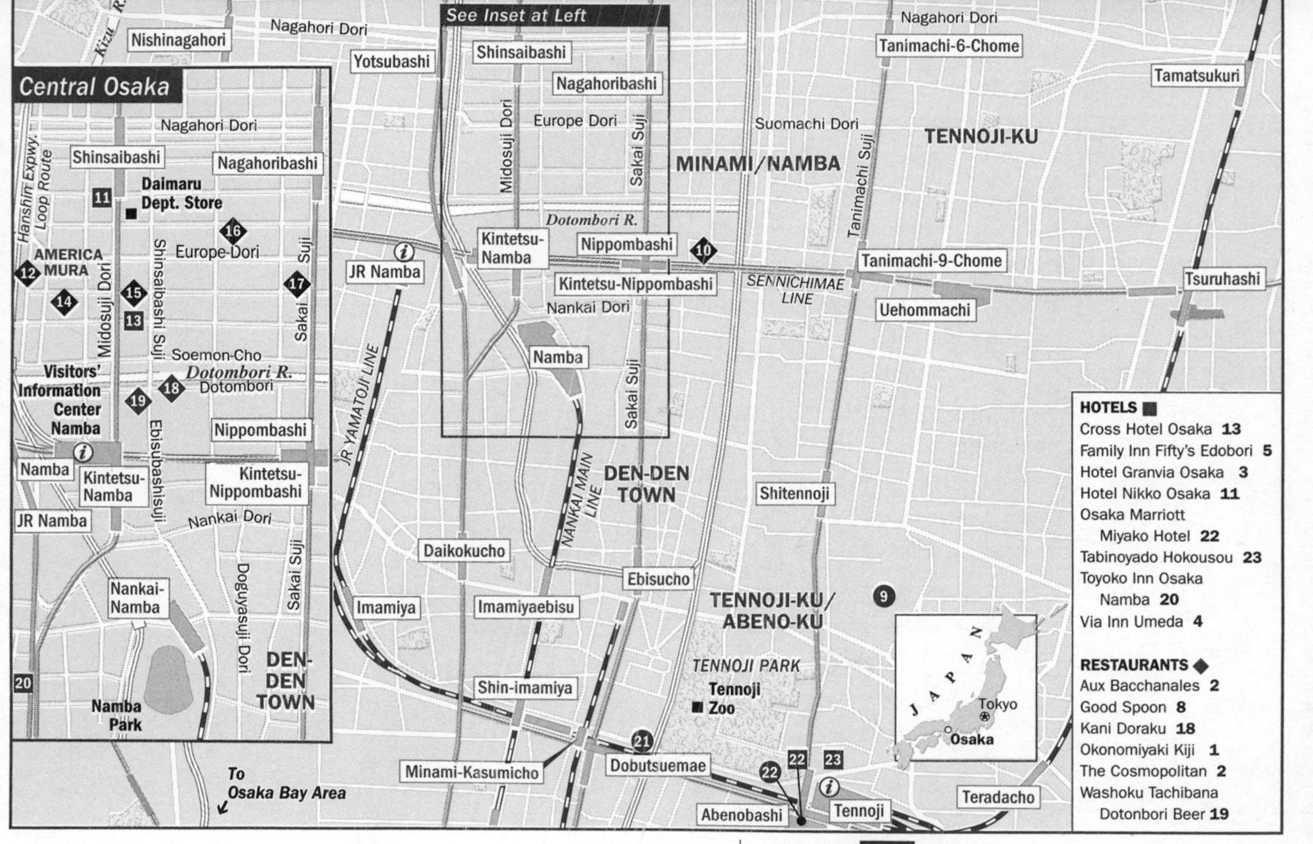
Central Osaka
See Inset at Left
HOTELS
Cross Hotel Osaka 13
Family Inn Fifty's Edobori 5
Hotel Granvia Osaka 3
Hotel Nikko Osaka 11
Osaka Marriott Miyako Hotel 22
Tabinoyado Hokousou 23
Toyoko Inn Osaka Namba 20
Via Inn Umeda 4
RESTAURANTS
Aux Bacchanales 2
Good Spoon 8
Kani Doraku 18
Okonomiyaki Kiji 1
The Cosmopolitan 2
Washoku Tachibana Dotonbori Beer 19
Nishinagahori
Nagahori Dori
Yotsubashi
Shinsaibashi
Nagahoribashi
Europe Dori
Midosuji Dori
Sakai Suji
Suomachi Dori
Tanimachi-6-Chome
Tamatsukuri
TENNOJI-KU
MINAMI/NAMBA
Tanimachi Suji
Dotombori R.
Kintetsu-Namba
Nippombashi
Kintetsu-Nippombashi
Tanimachi-9-Chome
Tsuruhashi
SENNICHIMAE LINE
Uehommachi
Nankai Dori
Namba
JR Namba
JR YAMATOJI LINE
NANKAI MAIN LINE
DEN-DEN TOWN
Shitennoji
Daikokucho
Ebisucho
Imamiya
Imamiyaebisu
TENNOJI-KU/ABENO-KU
TENNOJI PARK
Tennoji Zoo
Shin-imamiya
Minami-Kasumicho
Dobutsuemae
Abenobashi
Tennoji
Teradacho
JAPAN
Tokyo
Osaka
Kizu R.
Hanshin Expwy. Loop Route
AMERICA MURA
Daimaru Dept. Store
Shinsaibashi Suji
Europe-Dori
Soemon-Cho
Dotombori
Visitors' Information Center Namba
Ebisubashisuji
Doguyasuji Dori
Nankai-Namba
Namba Park
To Osaka Bay Area

children's play area in the international departure area, doctor and dental clinics, **cellphone** rental counters, computer stations providing Internet access (¥100 for 10 min.), and free **Wi-Fi**—are seemingly endless.

Getting from KIX to Osaka Taxis are prohibitively expensive: Expect to spend ¥18,200 to ¥20,000 for an hour's cab ride to the city center. Easiest if you have luggage is the **Kansai Airport Transportation Enterprise** (www.kate.co.jp; ✆ **072/461-1374**), which provides bus service to major stations and some hotels in Osaka, as well as to Kyoto, Kobe, Nara, and Himeji. Fares to Osaka average ¥1,550; purchase tickets at counters in the arrival lobby. The same company also offers more frequent service from KIX to the Osaka City Air Terminal (OCAT), located in the heart of Osaka next to JR Namba Station and serving as a major bus terminal for express buses to cities throughout Japan; buses depart KIX every 30 minutes for the 50-minute ride and cost ¥1,050.

You can also take the **train** into Osaka. The **JR Airport Express Haruka** (www.westjr.co.jp; ✆ **0570/00-2486**), which travels to Tennoji and Shin-Osaka stations (but not Osaka Station) before continuing to Kyoto, departs about twice an hour; the fare to Shin-Osaka is ¥2,330 for the 50-minute trip. Slower is the **JR Rapid Service (JR Kanku Kaisoku),** which travels from the airport to Tennoji and Osaka stations, with the 70-minute trip to Osaka Station costing ¥1,190. If you have a **Japan Rail Pass,** you can ride these trains for free after exchanging your voucher at the Kansai Airport (rail) Station on the third floor, open daily 5:30am to 11pm.

Across from the JR trains in the same station at the airport is the private **Nankai Line** (www.howto-osaka.com; ✆ **06/6643-1005**), whose sleek **rapi:t** (pronounced "rapito") train reaches Namba Nankai Station in 38 minutes. There are usually two trains an hour, and ordinary reserved seats cost ¥1,430, though discounts are often available if purchased in advance online, including tickets that bundle airport transfer with local transportation. If you're on a budget, you can also take an ordinary **Nankai Express Line** for ¥920 and reach Namba in 47 minutes.

BY TRAIN Osaka is 2½ to 3 hours from Tokyo and about 80 minutes to almost 3 hours from Hiroshima, depending on the Shinkansen bullet train, with the fare from Tokyo costing ¥13,620 for an unreserved seat. All Shinkansen bullet trains arrive at **Shin-Osaka Station** at the city's northern edge. Take the **Midosuji** subway line from Shin-Osaka Station to Osaka Station (the subway station here is called **Umeda Station**), Namba, Tennoji, and other points south.

JR trains also make runs between Shin-Osaka and Osaka stations. If you haven't turned in your voucher for your **Japan Rail Pass** yet, you can do so at either Osaka Station or Shin-Osaka Station daily from 5:30am to 11pm.

If you're arriving in Osaka from Kobe or Kyoto, the commuter lines, which will deliver you directly to Osaka Station in the heart of the city, are more convenient than the Shinkansen, which will deposit you at out-of-the-way Shin-Osaka Station.

Take note that Osaka Station is huge; in fact, the entire complex is called **Osaka Station City** (https://osakastationcity.com), with department stores, restaurants, and more. Stop by the **Osaka Station City Information Counter** (daily

10am–8pm) on the third floor to pick up a leaflet. On the first floor near the Tourist Information Osaka counter (see below), you can store luggage for ¥800 per day with **Sagawa Express** luggage service (✆ **06/6442-7271;** daily 8am–8pm), or have it delivered to an area hotel for ¥1,815 if you give it up by 11am.

BY BUS **JR "Dream" night buses** depart from both Tokyo Station's Yaesu South exit and Shinjuku Station's Express Bus Terminal several times nightly (including buses just for women), arriving at Osaka Station about 8 or 9 hours later and costing ¥4,900 to ¥14,000, depending on the season, bus and seat. There are also **JR day buses** from Tokyo and Shinjuku stations to Osaka Station. Tickets for most buses can be bought at any major JR station, JR bus terminal, or travel agency. For information, check the website www.jrbus-kanto.co.jp, or call ✆ **03/3844-1950** for inquiries or (✆ **03/3844-0489** for reservations.). **Willer Express** (http://willerexpress.com; ✆ **050/5805-0383**) operates buses departing Tokyo and Shinjuku stations several times nightly, arriving at Osaka Station the next morning. The cost of these range from ¥4,500 to ¥12,500, depending on the date and type of seat (reclining seats cost more); student and senior discounts are available.

Visitor Information

At KIX Airport, the **Kansai Tourist Information Center** (✆ **072/456-6160;** daily 7am–10pm) is in the International Arrivals Lobby of Terminal 1. The multilingual staff dispenses general travel information about Japan and maps and brochures of the Kansai area, including Kyoto and Kobe, and can make hotel reservations. There's also a Tourist Information Center in Terminal 2 (✆ **072/456-8630;** daily 11:30am–7:30pm).

In Osaka, the **Tourist Information Osaka** (✆ **06/6345-2189;** daily 7am–11pm) is on the first floor of Osaka Station's central ticket gates. The downtown **Tourist Information Namba** (✆ **06/6631-9100;** daily 9am–8pm) is located in Nankai Namba Station across from Takashimaya Department Store.

To find out what's going on in Osaka, ***Kansai Scene*** (www.kansaiscene.com) is a free bilingual monthly magazine with articles, reviews, listings, and information on the Kansai area. Information on Osaka city is also available on the Web at **www.osaka-info.jp**, while **www.kansai.gr.jp** gives information on the Kansai region.

City Layout

Osaka is divided into various wards, or *ku,* the most important of which for visitors are **Kita-ku** (North Ward), which encompasses the area around Osaka and Umeda stations; and **Chuo-ku** (Central Ward), where you'll find Osaka Castle and Namba, the heart of the city. Some city maps divide Osaka by location, with Kita (North) around Osaka Station and Minami (South) encompassing Namba and Shinsaibashi. Shin-Osaka Station, three subway stations north of Osaka (Umeda) Station, is a tourist wasteland with a scattering of hotels.

AROUND OSAKA STATION **Kita** embraces the area around Osaka and Umeda stations and includes many of the city's top hotels, office and entertainment complexes (like Grand Front Osaka), lots of restaurants, Nakanoshima with its park and museums, and several shopping complexes, mostly underground. Its maze of buildings and streets, however, make it frustrating to navigate, even for Japanese.

AROUND OSAKA CASTLE Osaka Castle, which lies to the east, is the historic center of the city and is surrounded by a huge park.

MINAMI/NAMBA Four subway stops south of Umeda Station is Namba (also referred to as **Minami,** or South Osaka), with a cluster of stations serving subways, JR trains, and Kintetsu and Nankai lines, all of which are connected to one another via underground passageways. This is the heart of the city, bustling with the spirit of old Osaka, where you'll find more hotels, Osaka's liveliest eating and entertainment district centered on a narrow street called **Dotombori** (also written Dotonbori), the **National Bunraku Theatre,** and major shopping areas such as the enclosed pedestrian street **Shinsaibashi-Suji,** underground arcades, and **America-Mura** (check out the unique streetlamps!), with imported goods from America. Farther south is **Dogayasuji,** famous for cooking supplies; and **Den Den Town,** Osaka's electronics and *anime* district. Connecting Kita-ku with Namba is Osaka's main street, **Midosuji Dori,** a wide boulevard lined with gingko trees and international name-brand shops.

AROUND TENNOJI/ABENO At the south end of the JR Loop Line is **Tennoji-ku,** which was once a thriving temple town with **Shitennoji Temple** at its center. In addition to a park with a zoo, it boasts **Spa World,** one of Japan's biggest and most luxurious public bathhouses. In neighboring **Abeno-ku** is **Abeno Harukas,** which opened in 2013 as Japan's tallest building, with an observatory, Japan's largest department store, a luxury hotel, shops, and restaurants.

OSAKA BAY & PORT West of the city, Osaka's well-developed waterfront offers a quick getaway for Osakans wishing to escape urban life. In addition to its domestic and international ferry terminals, Osaka Bay is where you will find **Universal Studios Japan,** one of Japan's major draws, and the excellent **Osaka Aquarium.**

Getting Around

Despite its size, I find Osaka easy to navigate, thanks to lots of English-language signs and information. The exception is Osaka Station, used for JR trains, and adjoining Umeda Station, used by subway lines and private railway lines Hankyu and Hanshin. Underground passages and shopping arcades complicate navigation; there's no escaping—you will get lost.

When exploring by foot, it helps to know that most roads running east and west end in *"dori"* (street), while roads running north and south end in *"suji,"* meaning "avenue."

BY SUBWAY & PRIVATE RAILWAY The **Osaka Municipal Transportation Bureau** (www.osakametro.co.jp/; ✆ **06/6582-1400**) operates Osaka's user-friendly subway network. All lines are color-coded and identified with a letter ("M" for the Midosuji line); stations are assigned a number in addition to English signage (M20 for Namba Station's Midosuji's stop); and in-car announcements are in English. Lines run from about 5am to midnight. Of the eight lines, the

TRANSPORTATION passes

If you think you'll be traveling a lot by subway on a given day, consider purchasing a **1-Day Enjoy Eco Card** for ¥800 (¥600 weekends and holidays), which allows unlimited rides on subways and buses all day and offers slight discounts (usually ¥100) to 30 attractions, including Osaka Castle, Shitennoji Temple, and Spa World. The **Osaka Amazing Pass** costs ¥2,500 for 1 day and allows unlimited rides on subways, city buses, and private railways in Osaka plus free entrance to 30-some attractions (none of these passes include Osaka Aquarium or Universal Studios). A 2-day Osaka Amazing Pass costs ¥3,300 but doesn't include private railways. Note that JR trains are not included in any of these passes, and you'd have to be fairly manic to get your money's worth. Passes are available at subway stations and tourist information offices. For information on the Amazing Pass, go to www.osp.osaka-info.jp/en/.

For trips outside Osaka, the **Kansai Thru Pass** (**Surutto Kansai;** www.surutto.com) allows foreigners (you must show your passport) to ride subways, private railways (no JR trains), and buses throughout Kansai, including Osaka, Kyoto, Kobe, Nara, Himeji, and Mount Koya, for 2 or 3 days (¥4,000 and ¥5,200, respectively) and they don't have to be consecutive days, plus you get slight discounts to tourist sights. JR West Passes allow travel on JR trains that cover a wider area. For more information on regional passes, see p. 330 in chapter 12.

red **Midosuji Line** is the most important one for visitors; it passes through Shin-Osaka Station and on to Umeda (the subway station next to Osaka Station), Shinsaibashi, Namba, and Tennoji. Fares begin at ¥180 and increase according to the distance traveled. More convenient, however, are prepaid ICOCA cards, which prevent having to buy an individual ticket each time. Various cards are available, all of which include a ¥500 deposit that can be refunded when you turn in the card, minus an annoying ¥220 handling fee. Note that if you already have an ICOCA, such as a Suica from Tokyo, you can use it in Osaka, too. Although there are also city buses, I find it more convenient to travel by subway.

BY JR TRAIN A Japan Railways train called the **JR Loop Line** passes through Osaka Station and makes a loop around the central part of the city (similar to the Yamanote Line in Tokyo); take it to visit Osaka Castle. Fares begin at ¥120, but you can ride free with a valid Japan Rail Pass. For trips outside Osaka, JR-West has several passes, with a **1-day Kansai Area Pass** offering unlimited rides to and around Osaka, Kyoto, Nara, Himeji, and Kobe for ¥2,300 (¥2,200 if booked online in advance at www.westjr.co.jp/global/en/ticket/pass/kansai/). Two-, 3- and 4-day Kansai Area Passes are also available.

[FastFACTS] OSAKA

ATMS/Banks In addition to banks, **Travelex** counters exchange money in Osaka Station on the first floor next to Tourist Information Osaka (daily 8am–8pm); in Grand Front Osaka near Osaka Station (daily 11am–7:30pm); and Namba Walk downtown (daily 10am–9pm). Otherwise, ATMs that accept foreign cards are located in all 7-Eleven stores and post offices.

Internet & Wi-Fi Access **Osaka Free Wi-Fi** (http://ofw-oer.com/en/) offers 1 hour of free Wi-Fi connection (but you can log on as often as you wish) at 5,000 locations in town, including subway stations, tourist offices, and sightseeing facilities. If you need to use a computer, in Namba there's a **Gran Cyber Cafe** in the Cuiadore Building at 1–7–19 Dotombori (✆ **06/6484-2660**), open 24 hours and charging ¥100 for 30 minutes.

WHERE TO STAY

Many hotels are clustered around Osaka Station, but Namba in the city's downtown offers more interesting surroundings. The Tennoji/Abeno area is also emerging as a vibrant place to stay. The prices below reflect demand and can vary markedly; note too, that many hotels charge more on Saturday and nights before a holiday.

Around Osaka Station

EXPENSIVE

Hotel Granvia Osaka ★★ You can't get any closer to Osaka Station than this hotel, with discounts for holders of Japan Rail Passes making it even more attractive for train travelers. But there are prices to pay: a ground-floor lobby that's hard to find in the maze that is Osaka Station, and elevators that are crowded with the hungry masses on their way to the hotel's many 19th-floor restaurants. Rooms, on floors 21 to 27, offer many choices, with top-floor Granvia Floor club rooms providing the best views, through large windows. Families might like one of the 20 huge "Corner Family" rooms (a steep ¥55,000 or more) with two sinks and a toilet separate from the bathroom. Those in search of R&R might find relaxation in the 24th-floor Freja rooms, designed with unique Scandinavian furnishings and aromatherapy amenities. Note, however, that standard rooms are tiny, some of which face an inner courtyard and are dark (some people, however, prefer these—they tend to be quieter).

3–1–1 Umeda, Kita-ku. www.granvia-osaka.jp. ✆ **06/6344-1235.** 716 units. ¥13,080–¥33,600 single; ¥17,600–¥65,300 double. Granvia Floor ¥24,300–¥77,220 single or double. Discounts available for holders of Japan Rail Pass. Station: Osaka or Umeda (1 min.; above the station). **Amenities:** 6 restaurants; 2 bars; 2 lounges; executive-level rooms; room service; Wi-Fi.

MODERATE

Via Inn Umeda ★★ Opened in 2017, this business hotel affiliated with the JR group of hotels offers a great location near Osaka Station, a sleek lobby with slate-gray walls and overstuffed chairs and sofas, and comfortable rooms done up in beige with purple pillows and bedrunners. Rooms are mostly

A NOTE ON directions

For all the attractions, accommodations, and restaurants listed below, I've included the nearest subway or JR station followed by the walking time (in parentheses) to the establishment once you reach the indicated station.

singles and twins, but I especially like the doubles, which are all corner rooms with two windows and a loveseat. In addition to the usual in-room amenities like shampoo and tea, a basket next to the elevator offers additional packets of coffee and other items, allowing you to take as much as you want. Another plus is the door off the lobby providing direct access to a 7-Eleven.

1–20 Komatsubaracho, Kita-ku. www.viainn.com/en/umeda/. ✆ **06/6314-5489.** 217 units. ¥7,800–¥15,000 single; ¥10,800–¥25,800 double. Station: Osaka (5 min.) or Higashi-Umeda (3 min.). Take the covered Hankyu Higashi pedestrian street that runs east from Hankyu department to the overhead highway and turn right. **Amenities:** Wi-Fi.

INEXPENSIVE

There are 20 **Toyoko Inn** hotels in Osaka, including those near Osaka and Shin-Osaka stations and in Namba and Tennoji. See **www.toyoko-inn.com.**

Family Inn Fifty's Osaka ★ This motel-like facility, south of Nakanoshima island, offers low prices and no-nonsense small but clean rooms, identically outfitted with double bed, twin or sofa bed for a third person, retro photo in keeping with its 1950s theme, wall-mounted TV, and tiled bathroom (but no closet). Because there are no single rooms, solo travelers pay the same rate as two people. Check-in is automated, but humans behind the front desk can help with the process. The catch is that it's a bit of a chore to reach from Osaka Station, though there is a bus; and because the inn is across a footbridge south of the Rihga Royal Hotel's back parking lot, some travelers have been known to use the luxury hotel's shuttle bus. Once you're settled in, you'll find its location fine.

2–6–18 Edobori, Nishi-ku. www.fiftys.com. ✆ **06/6225-2636.** 85 units. ¥7,540–¥18,000 single or double. Rates include continental breakfast. Station: Nakanoshima (exit 2, 5 min.); walk around the conference center Grand Cube, cross Tosabori-bashi bridge and busy Tosabori Dori, and take the next left. Bus: 88 to Tosabori 2-chome (1 min.) **Amenities:** Wi-Fi.

Minami

EXPENSIVE

Hotel Nikko Osaka ★★ A white monolith soaring 32 stories above ground, the Nikko has a great location atop a subway station right on Osaka's most fashionable boulevard, Midosuji Dori, making its lobby lounge a popular spot for locals meeting friends. In fact, location is mainly what you're paying for here. There is no health club, and guests are mostly Asian tourists looking for a central place to stay. Rooms, on the 10th to 30th floors, have a pleasing, clean, modern design, especially superior and premium rooms on the 20th to 30th floors with their contemporary flair, sofas that extend the length of the room below picture windows, and large bathrooms. Because there are no high buildings to obstruct views, city panoramas are a plus, except from standard rooms on lower floors. In short, this is a good choice if you want to be in the midst of Osaka's shopping and nightlife.

1–3–3 Nishi-Shinsaibashi, Chuo-ku. www.hno.co.jp/english. ✆ **06/6244-1111.** 603 units. ¥19,200–¥54,700 single; ¥20,320–¥66,800. Station: Shinsaibashi (exit 8 underneath the hotel, 1 min.). **Amenities:** 5 restaurants; 2 bars; 2 lounges; access to 2 health clubs (fee: ¥1,080); room service; Wi-Fi.

MODERATE

Cross Hotel Osaka ★★★ A big red X outside the door marks the spot of this style-conscious hotel on Midosuji Dori. That might come in handy for night owls, since Dotombori, Osaka's main nightlife district, is just a minute's walk away. Rooms are rather large, marking its status as a leisure hotel, with top floors home to so-called "Cross Rooms" and lower levels occupied by less expensive Comfort Rooms. I find Comfort rooms perfectly fine, with twins slightly larger than doubles but both with roomy bathrooms with separate tub and shower areas. There are also rooms with connecting doors, as well as rooms that sleep three or four people. There are no desks, however, a sign that no one staying here plans on working.

2-5-15 Shinsaibashi, Chuo-ku. www.crosshotel.com/osaka/. ✆ **06/6213-8281.** 204 units. ¥15,000–¥34,000 single or double. Station: Namba (3 min.). On Midosuji Dori. **Amenities:** 2 restaurants; bar; Wi-Fi.

Around Tennoji/Abeno

EXPENSIVE

Osaka Marriott Miyako Hotel ★★★ Located in Japan's tallest building, this hotel is so strikingly different from any other I've seen in Japan, I thought I'd landed at the wrong place when I walked into the 19th-floor lobby soon after its 2014 opening. With a soaring 7m-high (23-ft.) ceiling and floor-to-ceiling windows on three sides revealing sweeping views of Osaka, and with the front desk tucked discretely in a far corner, it seems more like a continuum of the 58th-floor Harukas 300 observatory (p. 280) than a hotel. Yet it's also a world apart, with a chic lounge and popular buffet restaurant off to one side of the lobby, far from the madding crowds. For even more eye-popping panoramas, there's **Restaurant ZK** on the 57th floor, serving *teppanyaki* and a variety of food. Rooms, on the 38th to 55th floors, offer many possibilities, though all have a wall of glass providing outstanding views of the city (my favorite view is north at night toward a glittering downtown). Deluxe rooms have views even from the bathroom, but probably best are corner kings, offering views in two directions and from windowside tubs. Many rooms also have a round table and comfortable desk chair right beside the window, great for making those working vacations hardly seem like work at all. Clearly, vast views are the emphasis here, though the hotel's exuberantly contemporary decor ensures guests stay rooted to earth.

1-1-32 Abeno-suji, Abeno-ku. www.miyakohotels.ne.jp. ✆ **06/6628-6111.** 360 units. ¥26,700–¥65,300 single or double. Club room from ¥55,400. Station: Tennoji or Osaka Abenobashi (1 min.). **Amenities:** 2 restaurants; bar; lounge; concierge; gym; room service; Wi-Fi.

INEXPENSIVE

Tabinoyado Hokousou (旅ł の宿葆晃荘) ★★★ This family-owned ryokan (now in its fourth generation of innkeepers) is a gem. The 130-year-old traditional Japanese home has many charming features, including a breakfast room with a soaring ceiling and heavy wooden beams; even the big bouquet of fake flowers by the front door has class. Rooms, with both Japanese- and

Western-style available, vary in style and size, with the best, 10-tatami-mat room sleeping up to five people and overlooking a small garden. It has a great location, within walking distance of Shitennoji Temple and Spa World and with direct access to Kansai airport, Osaka and Shin-Osaka Stations, Osaka Castle, and Nara. Finally, the family that's been running the inn for 60-plus years is warm and welcoming. No credit cards are accepted.

14–16 Horikoshi-cho, Tennoji-ku. www.hokousou.com. ✆ **06/6771-7242.** 13 units (none with private bathroom). ¥5,250–¥6,300 single; ¥8,900–¥12,600 double. Station: Tennoji (north exit, 1 min.). Walk north from Tennoji JR Station on Tanimachi-suji Street, and after passing FamilyMart, turn right at the tiny side street (there's a sign for the inn here); it's immediately on the right, down a small pathway (look for the big stone lantern at the front door).

WHERE TO EAT

There's a saying among Japanese that whereas a Kyotoite will spend his last yen on a fine kimono, an Osakan will spend it on food, not surprising given Osaka's historic role as a distribution center for rice and produce, earning it the nickname of the "nation's kitchen." You don't have to spend a lot of money, however, to enjoy good food. Local specialties include ***Oshi-zushi*** (pressed square-shaped sushi), ***udon*** noodles with white soy sauce, ***omurice*** (a rice omelet topped with ketchup), ***takoyaki*** (wheat-flour dumplings with octopus), and Naniwa black beef.

Osaka is probably best known, however, for ***okonomiyaki,*** which literally means "as you like it." Its origins date from about 1700, when a type of thin flour pancake cooked on a hot plate and filled with miso paste was served during Buddhist ceremonies. It wasn't until the 20th century that it became popular, primarily during food shortages, and gradually, other ingredients such as pork, egg, and cabbage were added. Today, Osaka is riddled with inexpensive *okonomiyaki* restaurants—more than 4,000 of them.

Around Osaka Station

In addition to the choices here, there are a multitude of possibilities in and around Osaka Station, including the 8th floor of Yodobashi-Umeda on the station's north side, where more than 30 restaurants offer pizza, pasta, sushi, dim sum, *udon,* ramen, *shabu-shabu, omurice, tonkatsu,* and more.

EXPENSIVE

The Cosmopolitan ★★★ CONTINENTAL With its dramatic, high-ceilinged dining room, island bar, and outdoor terrace, this restaurant can serve many purposes, whether it's for cocktails and appetizers or a romantic splurge. For dinner, you might start with the Cosmo Caesar, which has a serious dose of Parmesan and is almost a meal in itself. Entrees are heavy on seafood and steaks, like the teppan-grilled lobster and Wagyu beef cheek braised in red wine. Friendly service makes dining here a pleasure. Ask for a table outdoors in fine weather.

Grand Front Osaka, 9th floor, Ofukacho. http://thecosmopolitan.jp/en/. ✆ **06/6147-7700.** Main dishes ¥2,700–¥5,300; set lunch ¥5,000; set dinners ¥5,000–¥8,000. Daily 11am–10am (last order; 9pm on Sun). Station: JR Osaka or Umeda (1 min.). Inside the first building you see exiting from Osaka Station.

MODERATE

Aux Bacchanales ★★ FRENCH This casual brasserie offers sidewalk seating shaded by zelkova trees and specials written in French and Japanese on a blackboard. My set lunch of coq au vin, served with crusty French bread (to sop up the very good sauce), mashed potatoes, green beans, and salad, was enough to qualify as the main meal of the day, but equally satisfying selections include quiche, fish of the day, and croque monsieur. Dinner is more substantial, with choices from terrine de canard to roast lamb.

Grand Front Osaka (south building), Ofukacho. ✆ **06/6359-2722.** Main dishes ¥750–¥2,630; set lunches ¥1,550–¥2,500 (from ¥1,050 on weekdays); set dinner ¥2,980. Daily 9am–11pm. Station: JR Osaka or Umeda (1 min.). Just north of JR Station, on the ground floor of the south building, facing the north building.

INEXPENSIVE

Okonomiyaki Kiji (お好み焼きじ) ★ OKONOMIYAKI Takimikoji Village is a fun place for a meal. It's a re-created Showa-Era 1920s and 1930s Japanese village, filled with period relics ranging from a post office to a police box and a miniature shrine, complete with music of the era. There are also about a dozen small restaurants here, including those serving ramen, *soba, shabu-shabu,* sushi, tempura, and this one, offering what some Osakans swear is the best *okonomiyaki* in town. Customer photos and *meishi* (business cards) that paper the walls and ceiling are testament to customer appreciation. No credit cards are accepted.

Umeda Sky Building basement, 1–1–90 Oyodo-naka. www.takimikoji.jp/shop/kiji. ✆ **06/6440-5970.** *Okonomiyaki* ¥650–¥950. Fri–Wed 11:30am–9:30pm (last order). Station: JR Osaka or Umeda (Central North exit of JR Osaka Station, 8 min.). Keep left of Grand Front Osaka (south building) to the first intersection, turn left, and take the underpass.

Minami

Dotombori (or Dotonbori), a narrow pedestrian lane just off Midosuji Dori that flanks the south bank of the Dotombori River Walk, is the center of Osaka's most famous nightlife district, with lots of restaurants and bars.

EXPENSIVE

Kani Doraku (かに道楽) ★★ CRAB Specializing in *kani* (crab), this restaurant is difficult to miss: It has a huge model crab on its facade, waving its legs and claws. Part of a chain originating in Osaka 50-some years ago, this is the main shop of dozens of branches in Japan, including two others just down the street. The English-language menu lists crab sukiyaki and other dishes, but it's easiest to simply order a set meal. My ¥2,500 lunch came with boiled crab with sweet vinegar, steamed egg custard with crab, crab croquette, crab sushi, and clear soup. There are several floors for dining, all with kimono-clad waitresses and some with tables offering a view of the canal. This place is very popular, but instead of forcing customers to wait in line, they're assigned a specific dining time when they can come back. Otherwise, avoid peak times if you can (lunch is served until 4pm).

1–6–18 Dotonbori. www.douraku.co.jp. ✆ **06/6211-8975.** Set lunches ¥2,500–¥5,000; set dinners ¥5,300–¥9,800. Daily 11am–10pm (last order). Station: Namba (exit 14, 2 min.). On Dotombori beside the Ebisu-bashi Bridge.

MODERATE

Washoku Tachibana & Dotonbori Beer ★★ VARIED JAPANESE Whether you're sightseeing in Dotombori or here for *kabuki,* this restaurant, in the basement of the Shochikuza Theater, is a good pick. A microbrewery that makes its own Doutonbori brand beer on-site (¥490 for a glass of light or dark beer; you can see the tanks from the dining hall), Tachibana offers a variety of dishes, including those with tofu (only in Japan!). There's no English-language menu, but photographs allow you to choose dishes like tofu cream cheese with crackers, tempura, or sashimi. Otherwise, set meals are probably the best way to go. My ¥2,500 set meal (available all day) included tofu, tempura, sashimi, egg custard, miso soup, rice, and pickled vegetables; shabu-shabu is also available. Famous *kabuki* actors dine here, but how can you recognize them without their makeup?

Osaka Shochikuza Theater, 2nd basement, 1–9–19 Dotonbori. ✆ **06/6212-6074.** Set lunches ¥990–¥2,500; set dinners ¥2,000–¥6,480. Daily 11:30am–10pm (last order). Station: Namba (exit 14, 2 min.). On Dotombori near the bridge; look for its improbable side entrance to the left and then take 2 escalators to the second basement.

Near Osaka Castle

MODERATE

Good Spoon ★★ GRILLED MEATS You used to be pretty much out of luck if you were hungry after touring the extensive grounds of Osaka Castle, which I guess is the reason the Jo-Terrace Osaka (https://en.jo-terrace.jp/) dining complex came to be. Good Spoon's lunch menu offers burgers, eggs Benedict, salads, and lunch sets, while dinner entrees are heavy on grilled meats, which range from tandoori chicken to grilled salmon. It also has pizza and pasta and a good selection of craft beers. You'll find it on the second floor, with an outdoor terrace and a view of the castle. In addition to Good Spoon, other restaurants here serve pizzas, ramen, *okonomiyaki,* crepes, and French and Italian fare.

Jo-Terrace Osaka, Osaka Castle Park Grounds, 3–1 Osakajo, Chuo-ku. ✆ **06/6450-6780.** Main dishes ¥1,180–¥2,880; set lunches ¥1,280–¥2,980. Daily 11am–10pm (last order). Station: Osakajo Koen (2 min.).

EXPLORING OSAKA

Near Osaka Station

Museum of Oriental Ceramics (Toyotoji Bijutsukan) ★★★ MUSEUM About a 15-minute walk south of Osaka Station, on Nakanoshima Island between the Dojima and Tosabori rivers, this is my favorite museum in Osaka. Indeed, its 6,000-piece collection of Chinese, Korean, and Japanese ceramics—of which 400 are on display at any one time on a rotating basis—ranks as one of the finest in the world. Built specifically for the collection and featuring shock-absorbent platforms to protect its fragile wares, the museum does a superb job showcasing the exquisite pieces as the masterpieces they truly are, in darkened rooms that utilize natural light and computerized natural-light simulation. Korean celadon, Chinese ceramics from the Eastern Han, Song and Ming dynasties, Chinese snuff bottles, Aritaware from the Edo Period, Imari ware that once graced European palaces, and works by Hamada Shoji are just some of the items that might be on display. Even if you've never given ceramics more than a passing glance, you're likely to come away with a heightened sense of appreciation. You'll want to spend up to an hour here.

1–1–26 Nakanoshima. www.moco.or.jp. ✆ **06/6223-0055.** Admission ¥500–¥600 adults, ¥300–¥400 high-school and university students, free for children. Tues–Sun 9:30am–5pm. Closed during exhibition changes. Station: Naniwabashi on the Keihan Nakanoshima Line (exit 1, 1 min.) or Yodoyabashi (exit 1, 5 min.).

AROUND OSAKA CASTLE

Osaka Castle (Osaka-jo) ★★★ CASTLE First built in the 1580s on the order of Toyotomi Hideyoshi, Osaka Castle was the largest castle in Japan, a magnificent structure used by Toyotomi as a military stronghold from which to wage war against rebellious feudal lords in far-flung provinces. By the time he died in 1598, Toyotomi had accomplished what no man had done before: crushed his enemies and unified all of Japan under his command. After Toyotomi's death, Tokugawa Ieyasu seized power and established his shogunate government in Edo. But Toyotomi's heirs had ideas of their own: Considering Osaka Castle impregnable, they plotted to overthrow Tokugawa. In 1615, Tokugawa sent 155,000 soldiers to Osaka, where they not only annihilated the 55,000 Toyotomi insurrectionists but also destroyed Osaka Castle. The Tokugawas rebuilt the castle in 1629, but the main tower was destroyed by lightning 36 years later, and the rest burned in 1868 as the shogunate made their last stand against imperial forces in what later became known as the Meiji Restoration.

The present Osaka Castle, surrounded by an expansive park famous for its cherry trees and stone-walled moats, dates from 1931 and was extensively renovated in 1997. Built of ferroconcrete, it's not as massive as the original but is still one of Japan's most famous and impressive castles, with its massive stone walls, black and gold-leaf trim, and copper roof. Its eight-story *donjon* (keep) rises 39m (130 ft.), with a top-floor observatory offering bird's-eye views of the city. The rest of the *donjon* houses a high-tech museum that uses videos, holograms, models, replicas, and artifacts to describe the life and times of Toyotomi Hideyoshi and the history of the castle—be sure to pick up the free audio guide, as some explanations are in Japanese only. But there's plenty to see as well, including a magnificent folding screen with meticulously painted scenes of the intense fighting that took place between the Toyotomi and Tokugawa forces; samurai armor and gear; a full-scale reproduction of Toyotomi's Gold Tea Room; and a model of Osaka Castle during the Toyotomi Era. For ¥300 you can dress up in period clothing, including some awe-inspiring samurai helmets. Plan on 45 minutes here.

1–1 Osakajo, Chuo-ku. www.osakacastle.net. ✆ **06/6941-3044.** Admission ¥600 adults, free for children 15 and under. Daily 9am–5pm. Station: Osakajo Koen on the JR Loop Line or Morinomiya (15 min.); or Temmabashi or Osaka Business Park (10 min.).

AROUND TENNOJI/ABENO

Harukas 300 ★ OBSERVATION DECK Sunlight bathes this 300m-high (990 ft.) glass-walled observatory in Japan's tallest building (if it's raining or foggy, spend your time elsewhere). Not as memorable as Tokyo SkyTree (p. 132) but also not as expensive, the observatory on floors 58, 59, and 60 are a good place to get some perspective on sprawling Osaka. If you squint you may be able to pick out Osaka Castle or the bay, and on clear days you can see even farther. Because there isn't much to do here besides gawk at the 360-degree views, stop for a snack at the observatory's 58th-floor cafe. There's also a free public outdoor terrace down on the building's 16th floor, with views north toward to the city, but it doesn't compare to those from the observatory. Other diversions in Abeno Harukas include restaurants, shops, and Japan's largest department store.

Abeno Harukas (ticket counter on 2nd floor), 1–1–43 Abeno-suji. www.abenoharukas-300.jp. © **06/6621-0300.** Admission ¥1,500 adults, ¥1,200 children 12–17, ¥700 children 6–11, ¥500 children 4–5. Daily 9am–10pm. Tennoji or Osaka Abenobashi (1 min.).

Shitennoji Temple ★ TEMPLE Founded some 1,400 years ago as the first—and therefore oldest—officially established temple in Japan, Shitennoji Temple is the spiritual heart of Osaka. It was constructed in 593 by Prince Shotoku, who is credited with introducing Buddhism to Japan and remains a revered, popular figure even today. However, like most wooden structures in Japan, the temple's buildings have been destroyed repeatedly through the centuries by fire and war, including the 1615 Tokugawa raid on Osaka Castle and World War II. And through the centuries, the buildings have been faithfully reconstructed exactly as they were in the 6th century, with the Central Precinct (*Garan*) consisting of the Inner Gate, the five-story Buddhist Pagoda, the Main Hall with its statue of Prince Shotoku as the Buddha of Infinite Mercy, and the Lecture Hall all on a north-south axis. Be sure, too, to wander the temple's Gokuraku-Jodo Teien, a restored Japanese landscape garden first laid out during the Tokugawa regime. Buddhists believe that if you follow the path between the two streams representing greed and anger, you will symbolically reach Paradise, a place of sublime beauty, tranquility, and peace. A **flea market** is held on the temple grounds on the 21st and 22nd of each month.

1–11–18 Shitennoji, Tennoji-ku. © **06/6771-0066.** Admission to either Garan or garden, ¥300 adults, ¥200 students and children. Daily 8:30am–4:30pm Apr–Sept, 8:30–4pm Oct–Mar. Station: Shitennoji-mae Yuhigaoka (exit 4, 5 min.); or JR Tennoji (north exit, 10 min.).

Spa World ★★ SPA This is one of the most ambitious bathhouses I've ever seen. Accommodating up to 5,000 people, it draws upon hot springs 890m (2,970 ft.) below the earth's surface. On its roof, in a large, hangarlike room, a covered swimming complex for families includes a kiddies' pool, two large water slides (¥500 extra), a kids' amusement pool with aquatic activities, and an outdoor sunning terrace with a small pool and a Jacuzzi overlooking retro Tsutenkaku Tower. You wear your swim suits here (rental suits available). For a more grown-up experience, two *onsen* are divided into themed, geographical bathing zones, which are rotated between the sexes (no suits allowed). The Asian Zone, for example, has Persian- and Bali-themed baths, as well as a Japanese cypress bath and an outdoor Japanese bath; while the European Zone features baths that evoke the cultures of ancient Rome and Greece. If you ask me, however, they are all mostly just baths. By paying extra (¥800 weekdays,

¥1,000 Sat–Sun and holidays), you can also use six themed saunas. Spa World also has a gym (included in admission price), a kids' playroom, and restaurants, plus treatment rooms that cost extra—and even a hotel. If you're timid about visiting a public bath, this one will convert you. But sorry, people with tattoos—associated with the Japanese mafia—aren't allowed.

3-4-24 Ebisu-higashi, Naniwa-ku. www.spaworld.co.jp/english. ✆ **06/6631-0001.** Admission weekdays: ¥2,400 adults, ¥1,300 children for 3 hr.; ¥2,700 adults, ¥1,500 children for all day. Weekends: ¥2,700 adults, ¥1,500 children for 3 hr.; ¥3,000 adults, ¥1,700 children for all day. *Onsen* daily 10am–8:45am the next morning; top floor Mon–Fri 10am–7pm, Sat–Sun 10am–10pm. Station: Shin-Imamiya or Dobutsuenmae (2 min.).

OSAKA BAY AREA

Osaka Aquarium (Kaiyukan) ★★★ AQUARIUM Of Japan's many aquariums, this one is among the best. It's constructed around the theme "Ring of Fire," which refers to the volcanic perimeter encircling the Pacific Ocean. Visits begin through a tunnel filled with reef fish and small sharks, followed by an escalator ride to the eighth floor. From there you pass through 15 different habitats, ranging from arctic to tropical as you follow a spiraling corridor back to the ground floor, starting with the daylight world—a Japanese forest—above the ocean's surface and proceeding past the Aleutian Islands, Monterey Bay, South American rainforests, Antarctica, the Great Barrier Reef, and other ecosystems as you travel to the depths of the ocean floor. The walls of the aquarium tank are constructed of huge acrylic glass sheets, making you feel as if you're immersed in the ocean; piped-in classical music transforms swimming fish into performances of aquatic choreography. You'll see 30,000 specimens representing 620 species; stars of the show include whale sharks (the largest fish in captivity), Antarctic penguins, the odd-looking ocean sunfish (with the circumference of a truck tire but as flat as a pancake), and the Japan giant spider crab with its incredible 3m (9¾-ft.) span. English-spoken audio/visual guides are ¥500 extra. Allow about 1½ hours to tour the aquarium, avoiding weekends, but with so many tourists now visiting Japan, it can be packed almost any day of the week.

1-1-10 Kaigan-dori, Minato-ku. www.kaiyukan.com. ✆ **06/6576-5501.** Admission ¥2,300 adults, ¥2,000 seniors, ¥1,200 children 7–15, ¥600 children 4–6. Daily 10am–8pm. Closed 4 days a year in Jan/Feb for maintenance. Station: Osakako (5 min.).

Mutineers Need Not Apply

The quickest and most scenic way to travel between Osaka Aquarium and Universal Studios is via the ***Captain Line*** shuttle boat (www.mmjp.or.jp/Capt-Line/; ✆ **06/6573-8222**) with its all-female crew, which departs every 30 to 60 minutes and charges ¥700 for the 10-minute ride (children ride for half-price). ***Tip:*** A combination ticket for the boat and aquarium shaves ¥300 off the adult price.

Universal Studios Japan ★★★ THEME PARK Following the tradition of Universal's Hollywood and Orlando theme parks, this park takes guests on a fantasy trip through the world of American blockbuster movies, with thrill rides, live entertainment, shows, back-lot streets, restaurants, shops, and other attractions based on actual movies. Board a boat for a harrowing encounter with a great white straight out of JAWS®, escape a T-Rex as you roller-coaster your way through Jurassic Park—The Ride®, dream your way through the mega-coaster Hollywood Dream—The Ride, fly and leap at high speed among sky-scrapers in the Amazing Adventures of SpiderMan—The Ride 4K3D, and see, feel, and smell Shrek's 4D Adventure™ (4-D in movie lingo means there are smells and other sensations). Universal Wonderland features rides and attractions (think Snoopy, Sesame Street, and Hello Kitty) for the wee ones. Waterworld™ is an action-packed stunt show in a dramatic setting, but the most popular attraction is the Wizarding World of Harry Potter™, which re-creates Hogsmeade village. Inside Hogwarts Castle is the motion-simulation ride Harry Potter and the Forbidden Journey, which is so convincing I felt like I was flying with Harry and participating in a Quidditch game, making it hands down the best ride I've ever experienced (height restrictions apply). Plan for an entire day here, but note that it is immensely popular: Avoid weekends, arrive early, and splurge on one of three Universal Express Passes, which allow priority entry into designated rides. Alternatively, choose the "single" line for lone riders, which may get you into attractions up to three times quicker than regular lines.

2–1–33 Sakurajima, Konohana. www.usj.co.jp/e. ✆ **06/6465-4005.** Studio Pass to all attractions ¥7,900 adults, ¥7100 seniors, ¥5,400 children 4–11. Hours vary according to season; generally daily 10am–6pm in winter, 9am–9pm in summer. Station: JR Universal City (5 min.).

SHOPPING

Osaka is famous in Japan for shopping, in no small part because of the discerning nature of the Osakans themselves. Osaka, after all, developed as a commercial town of merchants—and who knows merchandise better than the merchants themselves?

Osaka ranks as one of the world's leading cities in underground shopping arcades. Enter the vast underground arcades in Umeda (where the JR, Hanshin, subway, and Hankyu train lines intersect), with names like **Whity Umeda** and **Diamor Osaka,** and you may never emerge in this lifetime. Downtown, **Crysta Nagahori** is one of the most attractive underground malls in Japan, with a glass atrium ceiling and 100 shops.

There are plenty of aboveground options as well. Tenjinbashisuji is said to be Japan's longest shopping street, stretching 2.6km/1.6 miles and lined with some 800 shops and restaurants. **Midosuji Dori,** a wide boulevard with gingko trees running north and south in the heart of the city, is Osaka's calling card for name-brand international boutiques, but here, too, is the lovely old **Daimaru** department store, with newer annexes on both sides. Just to the east is **Shinsaibashi-suji,** a covered promenade with many long established shops, some dating back to the Edo Period, others new like the **Daiso** ¥100 shop. On the other side of Midosuji Dori is **America-Mura,** a popular spot for young Japanese shopping for American secondhand clothing and other fashions at inflated prices. Teens also flock to **Marui 0101,** a seven-story department store on the corner of Shinsaibashi-suji and Nankai Dori, and to **HEP FIVE,** a huge shopping complex near Umeda Station with a Joypolis amusement arcade and a Ferris wheel on top. At JR Osaka Station are two LUCUA, Daimaru, and flagship **Hankyu** department stores, plus **Yodobashi,** with computers, cameras, toys, bikes, luggage, and more. But the granddaddy department store of them all is **Kintetsu Abeno Harukas** near Tennoji Station, boasting more floor space than any other department store in Japan.

One of the most fun places to shop—or simply browse—is at one of many famous shopping areas specializing in specific goods. In the heart of the city, just east of Sakaisuji Avenue near Nipponbashi Station, is **Kuromon Ichiba,** a covered street where professional chefs shop for seafood, fruit, vegetables, pickles, and other edibles, and tourists munch on grilled scallops, tempura, sushi, and street food. To the south, a few blocks east of Nankai Namba Station, is **Sennichimae Doguya-suji,** a covered shopping lane with about 45 open-fronted shops selling pots, pans, dishes, chopsticks, kitchen knives, aprons, plastic food, and any other implement you need to prepare and serve Japanese food, at very inexpensive prices.

Just south of that is Nipponbashi's **Den Den Town,** stretching along Sakaisuji Avenue and its side streets (station: Ebisucho). This is Osaka's electronics shopping mecca (*Den* is short for "electric"), similar to Tokyo's Akihabara and also experiencing a surge in popularity thanks to shops also specializing in *manga, anime,* and costumes. Stop by the **Nipponbashi Information Center,** just north of Ebisucho Station on Sakaisuji (✆ **06/6655-1717;** daily 11–7pm) for an English map of the area listing approximately 500 stores. Another fun neighborhood is **Matsuyamachi-suji** (station: Matsuyamachi), a shop-lined street offering toys, dolls, *anime* figures, and seasonal party decorations.

Of Osaka's many shopping complexes, worth noting is **Rinkan Premium Outlets** near KIX airport (www.premiumoutlets.co.jp/en/rinku/; station: Rinku Town), one of the largest outlet malls in Japan and offering some 150 shops and even shuttle bus service from the airport (fare: ¥200).

ENTERTAINMENT & NIGHTLIFE

Performing Arts

BUNRAKU The **National Bunraku Theater,** 1–12–10 Nipponbashi, Chuo-ku (www.ntj.jac.go.jp; ✆ **06/6212-2531**), was completed in 1984 as the only theater in Japan dedicated to Japanese traditional puppet theater. Productions are staged five times a year, with most productions running for about 3 weeks. Prices range from about ¥2,500 to ¥6,000. English-language programs are available. The theater is located just east of Namba and Dotombori, a 1-minute walk from exit 7 of Nipponbashi Station.

LIVE MUSIC **Rug Time Osaka,** on Midosuji Dori on the fourth floor of the Across Building, 2–6–14 Shinsaibashi Suji, Minami-ku (www.rugtime-osaka.com; ✆ **06/6214-5306;** station: Namba or Shinsaibashi), is an intimate venue offering a wide range of live jazz bands in two nightly sets beginning at 7:30pm, with cover charges averaging ¥2,500 to ¥3,000. It's open Monday to Saturday 5pm to 2am, Sunday and holidays 5pm to midnight.

The Bar Scene

Osaka's liveliest—and most economical—nightlife district radiates from a narrow pedestrian lane called **Dotombori** (or Dotonbori), which flanks the south bank of the Dotombori Canal. It's lined with restaurants and drinking establishments, making it good for a lively evening stroll even if you don't wish to stop anywhere.

Cinquecento ★★ This bar with a U-shaped counter is a cut above the rest with its welcoming staff and decent bar food, not to mention that all food and drink are priced at only ¥500. Of note is the red Wall of Shame, where gold plaques identify those crazy enough to have consumed 100 shots in one month. Monday to Saturday 8am to 5am; Sunday and holidays 8pm to 3am. Matsumiya Building, 2–1–10 Higashi-Shinsaibashi. ✆ **06/6213-6788.** Station: Nigahoribashi or Nipponbashi (5 min.). Just off Sakaisuji Ave., 1 block south of Suomachi/Europa Dori.

Dig Me Out Art & Diner ★★ In the heart of America-Mura, this casual, friendly bar offers occasional live music, changing art exhibitions, free Wi-Fi, and inexpensive snacks (and a good set lunch for ¥980), making it a fine place to relax and hang out. It's open 11:30am to 11pm Sunday to Friday and noon to 11pm on Saturday. 2–9–32 Nishi-shinsaibashi. http://digmeoutcafe.com. ✆ **06/6213-1007.** Station: Yotsubashi (5 min.) or Shinsaibashi (7 min.). Below the Arrow Hotel.

Murphy's ★★ Of Osaka's several Irish pubs, this is probably the most popular (and my favorite), open 25 years and drawing a mixed crowd of both Japanese and foreigners. It offers live music Saturday nights, free Wi Fi, and TVs broadcasting major sporting events. Fish and chips or one of the Aussie pies are reasonable and surprisingly good, but you can also make a meal of the Guinness or Kilkenny Ale. Sunday and Tuesday through Thursday 5pm to 3am; Friday to Saturday 5pm to about 5am. 1–5–2 Shinsaibashi-suji. www.murphysosaka.com. ✆ **06/6245-3757.** Station: Nagahoribashi or Shinsaibashi (4 min.). One block east of Shinsaibashi-suji covered arcade, behind Daimaru South department store and next to a post office.

The Suite ★★★ Decorated like a 1920s hotel suite, complete with American antiques, sofas, plush chairs, and subdued lighting from a chandelier and lamps, this classy, self-titled "New York Style Bar & Lounge" is a relaxing place to end the day, especially on Friday to Sunday evenings when live music ranges from vocals with piano to soft jazz (music charge: ¥850). Among its most popular signature cocktails, most priced at ¥1,000, is the Lychee Martini, made with Acai berry vodka, cranberry, and lychee liqueur, and the Cotton Candy, with vodka, cranberry and pineapple juice, and Grenadine. Open Wednesday through Sunday 7pm to 1am. 2–18–18 Nishi-Shinsaibashi. www.thesuitejapan.com. ✆ **06/6282-7742.** Station: Yotsubashi (5 min.) or Shinsaibashi (7 min.). In America Mura, across from Dormy Inn Shinsaibashi.

SIDE TRIPS FROM KYOTO & OSAKA

Using Kyoto or Osaka as a base, there are several destinations worth a day's trip or more. Foremost is **Nara,** which predates even Kyoto as the nation's capital and is full of gems that comprise the Historic Monuments of Ancient Nara World Heritage Site. Other World Heritage Sites are **Mount Koya,** a Buddhist mountain retreat offering temple accommodations, and Japan's most beautiful castle in **Himeji.** For information on regional rail passes, see p. 330 in chapter 12.

NARA, ANCIENT CAPITAL ★★★

42km (26 miles) S of Kyoto; 48km (30 miles) east of Osaka

In early Japanese history, the nation's capital was moved to a new site each time a new emperor came to the throne. In 710, however, the first permanent Japanese capital was set up at **Nara.** Not that it turned out to be so permanent: After only 74 years, the capital was moved first to Nagaoka and shortly thereafter to Kyoto, where it remained for more than 1,000 years. What's important about those 74 years, however, is that they witnessed the birth of Japan's arts, crafts, and literature, as Nara imported everything from religion to art and architecture from China. Even the city was laid out in a rectangular grid pattern, modeled after Chinese concepts. It was during the Nara Period that Japan's first historical account, first mythological chronicle, and first poetry anthology (with 4,173 poems) were written. Buddhism flourished, and Nara grew as the political and cultural center of the land with temples, shrines, pagodas, and palaces.

Japanese flock to Nara because it gives them the feeling that they're communing with ancestors. Foreigners come here because Nara offers a glimpse of Japan's past. Remarkably enough, many of Nara's historic buildings and temples remain intact, and long ago someone had enough foresight to enclose many of these historical structures in the quiet and peaceful confines of a large and spacious park, which has the added attraction of free-roaming deer. Farther afield is Horyuji, home to some of Japan's most historically significant religious architecture and the world's oldest buildings.

Although you can see Nara's highlights in a day's trip, I've included a couple of lodging choices in case you wish to explore it more leisurely.

Essentials

GETTING THERE From Kyoto Station, Nara is easily reached on two lines: the JR Nara Line and the private Kintetsu Limited Express. If you have a Japan Rail Pass, you'll probably want to take the commuter **JR Nara Rapid (Kaisoku) Line,** which departs about four times an hour and takes 43 to 57 minutes depending on the train; if you don't have a pass, the trip costs ¥710 one-way. If speed or luxury is of the utmost importance, the deluxe **Kintetsu Special Limited Express** whisks you to Nara in 35 minutes, guarantees you a seat (all seats are reserved), costs ¥1,130, and departs every 30 minutes (advance purchase suggested in peak season). A slower **Kintetsu ordinary express** takes 50 minutes and costs ¥620.

From Osaka, it takes 30 to 50 minutes, depending on the train and station. The **Kintetsu Nara Line,** from Namba Station, takes 40 minutes and costs ¥560. The **JR Yamatoji Rapid Line** from Osaka Station takes 50 minutes and costs ¥800.

VISITOR INFORMATION Tourist information offices at **JR Nara Station** and **Kintetsu Nara Station** are both open daily 9am to 9pm and dispense brochures, a list of free Wi-Fi spots around town, and maps with details on getting around by foot and bus. At JR Station, the **Tourist Information Center** is just outside the JR Station, to the left in the attractive former JR station; it offers luggage storage for ¥600 a bag. In between both JR and Kintetsu stations, on Sanjo Dori about a 5-minute walk from either, is the main **Nara City Tourist Information Center,** also open daily 9am to 9pm. For more info, call ✆ **0742/22-3900** or go to **www.naraexplorer.jp**, **https://narashikanko.or.jp/en/**, and **www.visitnara.jp**.

GETTING AROUND If you take the Kintetsu Line, you'll arrive at **Kintetsu Nara Station;** if you take the JR train, you'll arrive at **JR Nara Station.** Both stations are in Nara's small downtown, with Sanjo Dori serving as the main shopping street and running from JR Nara Station to Nara Park and its attractions. Kintetsu Station is closer, about a 5-minute walk to the entrance of the park, while the JR Station is about a 15-minute walk to the park. Keep in mind,

Your Own Personal Guide

Nara has many volunteer guides (from students and housewives to retirees), who will happily show you the town's sights in exchange for the chance to practice their English. There's no charge, but you pay your own admission and are requested to cover the guide's transportation expenses to meet you (guides do not have to pay admission to attractions); I suggest you also pay for the guide's lunch. Although guides are sometimes waiting at tourist offices, 3-day advance reservations are advised at one of the following organizations: **YMCA Goodwill Guides** (✆ **0742/45-5920** or e-mail at eggnaraymca@hotmail.com), **Nara Guide Club** (✆ **0742/43-2938**), or **Nara SGG Club** (✆ **0742/22-5595**).

however, that Nara Park is quite large and its attractions far-flung; it takes about 20 minutes to walk from Kintetsu Nara Station to Todaiji Temple and another 20 minutes to Kasuga Taisha Shrine. Otherwise, buses no. 70 and 97 travel from both stations all the way to Kasuga Shrine. There's also a Loop Line bus, with no. 2 going clockwise and no. 1 going counter-clockwise, running every 10 minutes and circling past both JR and Kintetsu train stations, Kofukiji and Todaiji temples, and the Naramachi historic district. I, however, usually walk.

IF YOU'RE HEADING TO HORYUJI To visit the Horyuji Temple area (see below), the cheapest and fastest way is on the JR Yamatoji Rapid Line, which travels between Osaka Station and JR Nara Station. Departures from either station are every 10 to 15 minutes, taking 38 minutes from Osaka (fare: ¥640) or 13 from Nara (fare: ¥220). From there, you can either walk to the temple area in about 20 minutes or take bus no. 72 (maps are available at the small tourist office in Horyuji Station). Alternatively, bus no. 97 is an excursion line that runs between Kasuga Taisha Shrine and Horyuji, passing Todaiji Temple and both train stations on the way, but it takes about an hour and costs ¥760 one-way (a day pass costs ¥1,000), with departures once an hour. If you're coming from Osaka, it makes sense to stop by Horyuji on the way to Nara. Otherwise, consider spending the night.

Exploring Nara

The best way to enjoy Nara is to arrive early in the morning before the first tour buses start pulling in. If your time is limited, the most important attractions to see are **Todaiji Temple, Kasuga Taisha Shrine,** and **Kofukuji Temple,** all part of the World Heritage Site and which you can tour in about 3 or 4 hours. If you have more time, add **Horyuji Temple.** Or, take a stroll south of downtown and Nara Park through **Naramachi,** the historic part of town, boasting many *machiya* (traditional wooden residences). Although a reproduction, the free **Koshi-no-ie (© 0742/23-4820;** Tues–Sun 9am–5pm) displays common *machiya* features, such as high windows operated by pulleys and an ingenious entrance; ask the tourist office for a Naramachi map.

AROUND NARA PARK

With its ponds, grassy lawns, trees, and temples, Nara Park covers about 520 hectares (1,300 acres) and is home to more than 1,200 deer, which are considered divine messengers and are therefore allowed to roam freely through the park. The deer are generally quite friendly; throughout the park you can buy "deer crackers," which all but the shyest fawns will usually snatch right out of your hand. All the below listings are within Nara Park, in the order you'll reach them walking east from the stations.

Kofukuji Temple ★★ Established in 710, this was the family temple of the Fujiwaras, the second-most powerful clan after the imperial family from the 8th to 12th centuries. There were once as many as 175 buildings on the Kofukuji Temple grounds, giving it significant religious and political power up until the 16th century; through centuries of civil wars and fires, however, most of the structures were destroyed. Only a handful of buildings remain, but even these were rebuilt after the 13th century.

The **five-story pagoda,** first erected in 730, burned down five times. The present pagoda dates from 1426 and is an exact replica of the original; at 50m (164 ft.) tall, it's the second-tallest pagoda in Japan (the tallest is at Toji Temple in Kyoto). The **Eastern Golden Hall (Tokondo)** was originally constructed in 726 by Emperor Shomu to speed the recovery of the ailing Empress Gensho. Rebuilt in 1415, it houses several priceless images, including a bronze statue of Yakushi Nyorai (the healing Buddha) installed by Emperor Shomu on behalf of his sick aunt; a 12th-century wooden bodhisattva of wisdom, long worshiped by scholar monks and today by pupils hoping to pass university entrance exams; and the 12 Heavenly Guards, wooden reliefs carved in the 12th century. The **Central Golden Hall,** reopened in 2018 after 18 years of renovation, is considered the most important building in the complex.

But the best thing to see is the **Treasure House (Kokuhokan),** which displays works of art originally contained in the temple buildings, many of them National Treasures. Most famous are the standing 8th-century Ashura statue and a bronze head of Yakushi Nyorai. But my favorites are the six 12th-century carved wooden statues representing priests of the Kamakura Period with fascinating facial features that render them strikingly human.

Nara Park. www.kohfukuji.com. ✆ **0742/22-7755.** Admission to Treasure House ¥900 adults, ¥700 junior-high and high-school students, ¥350 elementary-school students; Eastern Golden Hall ¥300 adults, ¥200 junior-high and high-school students, ¥100 elementary-school student. Combination tickets available. Daily 9am–5pm.

Todaiji Temple ★★★ Nara's premier attraction is Todaiji Temple and its **Great Buddha (Daibutsu),** Japan's second-largest bronze Buddha. When Emperor Shomu ordered construction of both the temple and Daibutsu in the mid-700s, he intended to make Todaiji the headquarters of all Buddhist temples in the land. As part of his plans for a Buddhist utopia, he commissioned work for this Daibutsu, a remarkable work of art that took eight castings. At a height of more than 15m (50 ft.), the Daibutsu is made of 437 tons of bronze, 286 pounds of pure gold, 165 pounds of mercury, and 7 tons of vegetable wax. Thanks to Japan's frequent natural calamities, however, the Buddha of today isn't quite what it used to be. In 855, in what must have been a whopper of an earthquake, the statue lost its head. It was repaired in 861, but alas, the huge wooden building housing the Buddha, the **Daibutsuden,** was burned twice during wars, melting the Buddha's head. The present head dates from 1692. As for the Daibutsuden, it was also destroyed several times through the centuries; the present structure dates from 1709. Measuring 48m (160 ft.) tall, 57m (187 ft.) long, and 50m (165 ft.) wide, it's the largest wooden structure in the world—but is only two-thirds its original size. My architect sister, just completing a year's trip around the world with her family, declared the Daibutsuden among the most magnificent buildings she had ever seen.

Be sure to circle around the Great Buddha to take it in from all angles. Behind the statue is a model of how the Daibutsuden used to look, flanked by two massive pagodas. Behind the Great Buddha to the right is a huge wooden column with a small hole in it near the ground. According to popular belief, if you can manage to crawl through this opening, you'll be sure to reach enlightenment (seemingly a snap for children). You can also get your English-language fortune for ¥200 by shaking a bamboo canister until a wooden stick with a number comes out; the number corresponds to a piece of paper. Mine told me that though I will win, it will be of no use; an illness will be serious, and the person for whom I am waiting will not come. And the monk who gave me the fortune said mine was a good one! The **Todaiji Museum** displays the temple's priceless Buddhist statues and other artworks.

Nara Park. ✆ **0742/22-5511.** Admission ¥600 adults, ¥300 children. Combination ticket with Todaiji Museum ¥1,000 and ¥400, respectively. Nov–Mar daily 8am–5pm; Apr–Oct daily 7:30am–5:30pm (museum opens at 9:30am).

Kasuga Taisha Shrine ★★ A stroll through the park brings you to one of my favorite Shinto shrines in the Kyoto area. Originally the tutelary shrine of the powerful Fujiwara family, it was founded in 768 and, according to Shinto concepts of purity, was torn down and rebuilt every 20 years in its original form (the last time it was torn down and rebuilt was in 2015–16). As virtually all empresses hailed from the Fujiwara family, the shrine enjoyed a privileged status with the imperial family. Nestled in the midst of verdant woods (the Kasugayama Primeval Forest rising behind it has been protected since the 9th c.), it's a shrine of vermilion-colored pillars and an astounding 3,000 stone and bronze lanterns. The most spectacular time to visit is mid-August or the beginning of February, when all 3,000 lanterns are lit. Although admission to the shrine's outer grounds is free, admission is charged for the inner cloister, the **Man'yo Botanical Garden,** preserving about 300 varieties of native Japanese plants and famous for its wisteria (it's located to the left on the approach to the shrine), and to the **Kasuga Taisha Museum,** displaying costumes, swords, and armor in exhibitions that change four times a year. Fork out the extra yen only if you have time and the interest.

Nara Park. www.kasugataisha.or.jp. ✆ **0742/22-7788.** Inner cloister ¥500; Man'yo garden ¥500 adults, ¥250 children; museum ¥500 adults, ¥300 junior- and senior-high students, ¥200 children. Grounds daily 6am–6pm Apr–Sept, 6:30am–5pm Oct–Mar; inner cloister daily 8:30am–4pm (periodically closed); botanical garden daily 9am–5pm (to 4:30pm Dec–Feb); museum daily 10am–5pm.

The Horyuji Temple Area ★★★

Founded in 607 by Prince Shotoku as the center for Buddhism in Japan, **Horyuji Temple** (www.horyuji.or.jp; ✆ **0745/75-2555**) is one of Japan's most significant gems for historic architecture, art, and religion. It was from here that Buddhism blossomed and spread throughout the land. Today about 45 buildings remain in the complex, some dating from the end of the 7th century and comprising what are thought to be the oldest wooden structures in the world. Although they are the main reason to come here, it's the atmosphere of the compound itself that I love—serene, ancient, and a fitting tribute to Prince Shotoku, founder of Buddhism in Japan and much revered still today. Little wonder Horyuji was selected as one of Japan's first UNESCO World Heritage Sites, in 1993 (for details on reaching Horyuji, see "Essentials," above).

At the western end of the grounds is the two-story, 17m-high (58-ft.) ***kondo,*** or main hall, considered to be the oldest building at Horyuji Temple, erected sometime between the 6th and 8th centuries. It contains Buddhas commemorating Prince Shotoku's parents, protected by Japan's oldest set of four heavenly guardians (from the late 7th or early 8th c.). Next to the main hall is Japan's oldest **five-story pagoda,** dating from the foundation of the temple and cleverly built to withstand earthquakes; it contains four scenes from the life of Buddha around its base. The **Gallery of Temple Treasures** contains statues, tabernacles, and other works of art from the 7th and 8th centuries, many of them National Treasures. On the eastern precincts of Horyuji Temple is the octagonal **Yumedono Hall,** or the Hall of Visions, built in 739 as a sanctuary to pray for the repose of Prince Shotoku.

Admission to these Horyuji treasures costs ¥1,500 adults, ¥750 children. The grounds are open daily from 8am to 5pm (to 4:30pm Nov 4–Feb 21).

Just behind Yumedono is **Chuguji Temple** (**中宮寺; © 0745/75-2106**), once part of a large nunnery built for members of the imperial family. It contains two outstanding National Treasures: the graceful wooden statue of **Nyoirin Kannon Bosatsu,** dating from the 7th century and noted for its compassionate expression and serene smile reminiscent of Leonardo da Vinci's *Mona Lisa;* and the **Tenjukoku Mandala,** the oldest piece of embroidery in Japan, originally about 5m (16 ft.) long and created by Shotoku's consort and her female companions after Shotoku's death at the age of 48. It shows scenes from the Land of Heavenly Longevity, where only those with good karma are invited by the Buddha in the afterlife and where Shotoku surely resides. Only a replica of the fragile embroidery is now on display. Open daily from 9am to 4:30pm (to 4pm Oct–Mar 20); admission is ¥600 for adults, ¥450 for 13- to 15-year-olds, ¥300 for children.

Where to Stay & Eat

Harishin (はり新) ★★★ BENTO Many tourists never see Naramachi, a lovely area of old Nara with narrow lanes and traditional wooden homes and shops. This restaurant, with a wood-slat facade and an entrance through a tiny courtyard, occupies a 200-year-old house of ocher-colored walls, where dining is on *tatami* with a view of a garden. For lunch, only one seasonal bento is served, the creation of chef-owner Nakagawa-san. My recent bento included an aperitif persimmon wine, sesame-flavored tofu, soup, rice, pickled vegetables, tempura, an ancient cheese first made in Nara in the 7th century (Nara is considered the birthplace of Japanese cheese), and exquisitely prepared, bite-size morsels of shrimp, chicken, fish, mushroom, and potato. *Kaiseki* is available for dinner (make reservations at least 1 day in advance).

15 Nakashinya-cho. **© 0742/22-2669.** Bento ¥2,980; kaiseki ¥4,000–¥6,000. Tues–Sun 11:30am–2:30pm and 6–8pm (last order); closed Tues if Mon is a national holiday. A 5-min. walk south of Sarusawa-ike Pond, on the road that leads south from the west edge of the pond, on the right.

Nara Hotel ★★★ This historic hotel, with a staff eager to please, is reason enough to spend the night in Nara. Spreading like a palace atop a hill on the south edge of Nara Park, it was built in 1909 as a Western-style hotel to accommodate foreigners pouring into the country. But it has many Japanese features in the Momoyama Period style of architecture. Accommodations in the old part of the hotel have wide corridors, high ceilings, antique light fixtures, bamboo blinds, fireplaces (no longer in use), and comfortable old-fashioned decor. A 1984 addition offers larger, modern rooms and verandas overlooking woods or the old town (***note:*** Only the newer wing has an elevator). It's also worth dropping by just for a meal, either in the graceful **Tea Lounge** with pond views and sandwiches for lunch, or in the elegant **Mikasa** French restaurant with its soaring ceiling and original fixtures.

Nara-Koennai. www.narahotel.co.jp. ✆ **0742/26-3300.** 127 units. ¥15,000–¥22,600 single; ¥29,700–¥59,400 double. 25% discount for holders of Japan Rail Pass. From either station, an 8-min. taxi ride or by bus no. 50, 51, 53, 82, or 83 to the Nara Hotel stop. **Amenities:** 2 restaurants; bar; lounge; room service (not available in all rooms); Wi-Fi.

Seikan-so ★★ A lovely choice in inexpensive Japanese-style accommodations, this former geisha house boasts a beautiful garden, complete with azalea bushes and manicured trees—the kind of garden usually found only at *ryokan* costing twice as much. Located in quaint Naramachi about a 10-minute walk south of Nara Park, the traditional Japanese building dates from 1916 and wraps around the inner garden. Although the simple *tatami* rooms are showing their age, all is forgiven if you can reserve one of the five rooms facing the garden (those facing streetside are usually for single use). Note that there's an 11pm curfew.

29 Higashi-Kitsuji-cho. www.nara-ryokanseikanso.com. ✆ **0742/22-2670.** 8 units (none with bathroom). ¥4,320 per person. Station: Kintetsu Nara (12 min.) or JR Nara (25 min.). Bus: Loop bus no. 1 to Kitakyobate stop (1 min.). **Amenities:** Wi-Fi.

Shizuka (志津香) ★ KAMAMESHI This much loved, low-key local shop across from Nara Park and near Todaiji Temple is best known for its *kamameshi,* rice in a small metal pot and topped with other ingredients. Order from the English menu for *kamameshi* like the simple *wakadori* (chicken with vegetables) or the *Nara nanashu* (seven flavors of Nara), but don't stir the *kamameshi* right away until an *okoge* (crispy rice crust) can form where the rice meets the metal of the pot. The Tempura Gozen includes tempura and Nara-nanashu. No credit cards accepted.

59 Noborioji-cho. www.kamameshi-shizuka.jp. ✆ **0742/27-8030.** Set meals ¥1,750–¥2,300. Wed–Mon 11am–7pm (last order). On the main road between Kintetsu Station and Todaiji, across from the Nara National Museum.

Trattoria Piano ITALIAN In the center of downtown near the train stations, this small eatery offers five pastas and nine choices in pizza, both Napoli style and those with locally sourced Japanese ingredients (even the wheat for the crust is local). Cash only.

15–1 Hashimoto-cho. ✆ **0742/26-1837.** Pizza ¥850–¥1,890. Daily 11am–2:30pm and 5–11pm. Station: JR Nara (10 min.) or Kintetsu Nara (3 min.), on the corner of Sanjo Dori and a covered shopping arcade.

TEMPLES OF KOYASAN ★★★

748km (465 miles) W of Tokyo; 199km (124 miles) S of Osaka

If you've harbored visions of wooden temples nestled in among trees whenever you've thought of Japan, the sacred mountain of **Mount Koya** is the place to go. It's all here: head-shaven monks, religious chanting at the crack of dawn, the wafting of incense, towering cypress trees, tombs, and early morning mist rising above the treetops. Mount Koya—called Koyasan by Japanese—is one of Japan's most sacred places and the mecca of the Shingon Esoteric sect of Buddhism. Standing almost 900m (3,000 ft.) above the world, the top of Mount Koya is home to 117 Shingon Buddhist temples scattered through the mountain forests and to Japan's most magnificent graveyard. Fifty-two temples offer accommodations, making this one of the top places in Japan to observe temple life firsthand. Koyasan is one of my favorite destinations.

A World Heritage Site since 2004, Koyasan, located in the Kii Mountain Range, first became a place of meditation and religious learning 1,200 years ago when Kukai, known posthumously as Kobo Daishi, was granted the mountaintop by the imperial court in 816 as a place to establish his Shingon sect of Buddhism. Kobo Daishi was a charismatic priest who had spent 2 years in China studying esoteric Buddhism before returning to his native land to spread his teachings among Japanese. Admired for his excellent calligraphy, his humanitarianism, and his teachings, Kobo Daishi remains one of the most beloved figures in Japanese Buddhist history. When he died in the 9th century, he was laid to rest in a mausoleum on Mount Koya. His followers believe Kobo Daishi is not dead but simply in a deep state of meditation, awaiting the arrival of the last bodhisattva (Buddha messiah). According to popular belief, priests opening his mausoleum decades after his death found his body still warm.

Through the centuries, many of Kobo Daishi's followers, wishing to be close at hand when the great priest awakens, have had huge tombs or tablets constructed close to Kobo Daishi's mausoleum, and many have had their ashes interred here. Pilgrims over the last thousand years have included emperors, feudal lords, samurai, and common people, all climbing to the top of the mountain to pay their respects. Women, however, were barred from entering the sacred grounds of Koyasan until 1872.

Essentials

GETTING THERE Osaka is the gateway to Koyasan. **Nankai Railway's** rapid express **Koya Line** departs from Osaka's Namba Station (with a stop at Shin-Imamiya, on the Osaka Loop Line) every half-hour or hour bound for Gokurakubashi, with the trip taking about 1 hour and 30 minutes. If you want to ride in luxury, Nankai limited-express (also called super express) trains with reserved seating depart less frequently (three times in the morning) and arrive in Gokurakubashi about 1 hour and 10 minutes later (the last stretch through the mountains is beautiful). After arriving at the last stop, Gokurakubashi, you continue your trip to the top of Mount Koya via a 5-minute ride in a cable car. The entire journey from Namba Station to Mount Koya costs

¥1,380 one-way, including the cable car; if you take the faster express, it'll cost ¥780 extra. You'll save money, however, with Nankai's **Koyasan World Heritage Ticket** (available at Namba Station), which includes round-trip travel from Namba Station and the cable car, plus unlimited rides on Koya's buses for 2 days and a 20% discount to the attractions listed below. The cost is ¥2,860 if you travel by rapid express and ¥3,400 by limited-express (the return trip is by rapid express). Children pay half-fare. For information on travel to and around Koyasan, go to **www.nankaikoya.jp**.

VISITOR INFORMATION The **Koyasan Tourism Association** (www.koya.org; ✆ **0736/56-2468**) is located approximately in the center of Koyasan village, on Odawara street near Kongobuji Temple, where you can pick up a map and a bus schedule. It also offers a computer with Internet access you can use for free, a few lockers for luggage, and a 90-minute rental audio guide for ¥500 (available 3:30am–4:30pm) that's highly useful for learning more about what you're seeing throughout Koyasan, including the location of famous mausoleums and tombstones in Okunoin cemetery. You can also book *shukubo* (temple lodgings) here, but it's better if you reserve a minimum of 7 business days in advance (check http://eng.shukubo.net or call ✆ **0736/56-2616** for details). Hours for all services are daily 8:30am to 7pm (9am–5pm Dec–Feb).

GETTING AROUND Upon reaching Koyasan via cable car, you must board a **bus** that travels 2km (1¼ miles) on a narrow, winding road (no pedestrians allowed) before going through the village of Koyasan along the main street all the way to the Okunoin-guchi and Okunoin-mae bus stops, the location of Kobo Daishi's mausoleum. The bus passes most sights along the way, as well as temples accommodating visitors and the Koyasan Tourist Association office. Buses depart about 5 minutes after the arrival of every cable car; the trip to Okunoin-mae takes 20 minutes and costs ¥410. Otherwise, once you've dropped off your luggage or settled into your temple lodging, you can walk to Okunoin and other locations mentioned below. Or, rental bicycles are available at the tourist office for ¥400 for 1 hour, plus ¥100 for every 30 minutes after that (because the number of bikes is limited, you might want to reserve one in advance by calling the tourist office).

Exploring Mount Koya

THE TOP ATTRACTION The most awe-inspiring and magnificent of Koyasan's many sights, **Okunoin ★★★** is the cemetery containing the mausoleum of Kobo Daishi. The most dramatic approach to Okunoin is from the Okunoin-guchi bus stop, where the Sando pathway leads 2km (1.2 miles) to the mausoleum. Swathed in a respectful darkness of huge cypress trees forming a canopy overhead are monument after monument, tomb after tomb—some 200,000 of them, all belonging to faithful followers from past centuries. The audio guide from the tourist office (see "Visitor Information," above) will guide you to the most famous tombstones, including those of the Toyotomi, Shimadzu, Maeda, Asano, and Matsudaira clans.

I don't know whether being here will affect you the same way, but I am always awestruck by the sheer density of tombstones, the iridescent green moss, the shafts of light streaking through the treetops, the stone lanterns, and the gnarled bark of the old cypress trees. There are also many small *Jizo* statues, believed to protect children in the afterlife, wearing red bibs donated by parents who have lost a child. Altogether, the dramatic scene represents more than a thousand years of Japanese Buddhist history. If you're lucky, you won't meet many people along the way. Tour buses park at a newer entrance to the mausoleum at the bus stop called Okunoin-mae. I absolutely forbid you to take this shorter route; its crowds lessen the impact of this place considerably. Rather, take the longer Sando path from the Okunoin-guchi/Ichinohashi bus stops. Much less traveled, it's also much more impressive and is one of the main reasons for coming to Koyasan in the first place. And be sure to return to the mausoleum at night; the stone lanterns (now lit electrically) create a mysterious and powerful effect.

At the end of the pathway, about a 30-minute walk away, is the **Lantern Temple,** or Torodo, which houses about 10,000 lanterns, donated by prime ministers, emperors, and even commoners. Two sacred fires, which reportedly have been burning since the 11th century, are kept safely inside. The mausoleum itself, the Okunoin Gyobo, is behind the Lantern Hall to the left. Buy a white candle, light it, and wish for anything you want. Then sit back and watch respectfully as Buddhists come to chant and pay respects to one of Japan's greatest Buddhist leaders. Many who have successfully completed the pilgrimage to Shikoku Island's 88 Buddhist temples, often dressed in white and carrying a staff, conclude their journey here. Twice a day, at 6am and 10:30am, monks ritually offer meals to Kobo Daishi.

MORE TO SEE & DO **Kongobuji Temple** (金剛峯寺) ★★, located near the Koyasan Tourist Association in the center of town (✆ **0736/56-2011**), is the central monastery headquarters of the Shingon sect in Japan. Although Kongobuji was originally built in the 16th century by Toyotomi Hideyoshi to commemorate his mother's death, the present building dates from 1869. Pictures by famous artists from long ago decorate sliding screens and depict Kobo Daishi's trip to China. The huge kitchen, big enough to feed multitudes of monks, is also on view. The most important thing to see, however, is the temple's magnificent **rock garden,** the largest in Japan and said to represent a pair of dragons in a sea of clouds. If it's raining, consider yourself lucky—the wetness adds sheen and color to the rocks. Admission is ¥500 for adults, ¥200 for children.

A short walk farther west is the **Garan** ★ (✆ **0736/56-3215**), the first buildings constructed on Koyasan and still considered the center of religious life in the community. It's an impressive sight with a huge *kondo* (main hall), first built in 819 by Kobo Daishi; a large vermilion-colored *daito* (pagoda), which many consider to be Koyasan's most magnificent structure and which is very much worth entering for its brightly colored murals and statues (¥200 each for the *kondo* and *daito*); and the oldest remaining building on Mount Koya, the Fudodo, which was built in 1198.

All of the sites above are open daily 8:30am to 5pm (enter by 4:30pm).

Where to Stay & Eat

Although this community of 4,000 residents has the usual stores, schools, and offices of any small town, *shukubo* (temple lodgings) are where most visitors stay. I strongly urge you to do so, too, traveling only with an overnight bag if possible. Japanese almost always make reservations beforehand, and though you can do so in person upon arrival at the Tourist Association office, it's better to reserve a minimum of 7 days in advance, especially in peak season. See "Visitor Information," above, for details.

WHAT IT'S LIKE TO STAY AT A KOYASAN TEMPLE Prices for an overnight stay in one of the temples, including two vegetarian meals, range from about ¥12,000 to ¥42,000 per person, depending on the temple, room, and meal. Check-in is around 2 or 3pm (5pm at the latest) and checkout is at 9 or 10am (you can leave your luggage at the temple while sightseeing).

Your room will be *tatami* and may include a nice view of a garden. Both baths and toilets are communal in some temples (you may need to supply your own towel and toiletries), but more and more temples are adding private bathrooms (and charging much more). College students studying at Koyasan's Buddhist university and living at the temple might attend you, bringing your meals to your room (or serving in the dining hall), making up your futon, and cleaning your room. The *shojin ryori* (Buddhist vegetarian meals) are generally quite good, and because Buddhist monks are vegetarians but not teetotalers (beer and sake are made of rice and grain), alcoholic drinks are readily available at the temples for an extra charge. Meals are at set times. Dinner is at 5:30pm, and breakfast is usually served by 7:30am. The morning religious service is at 6 or 6:30am; you don't have to attend, but I strongly recommend that you do. There's something uplifting about early morning meditative chanting, even for nonbelievers; some temples include sacred fire ceremonies as well.

Unfortunately, since Koyasan became a World Heritage Site, the flood of tourists has taken its toll, with some temples seemingly more interested in cashing in than helping souls and some guests showing little respect for their surroundings; don't be one of them. Below are a few of the dozens of area temples open to overnight guests. Rates are based on two people to a room.

Bon On Shya ★ A Japanese and French couple, Takeshi and Veronique, run this small, casual cafe on Koyasan's main street. Simply outfitted with wooden tables and a play corner for children, it offers coffees, cakes (try the baked tofu cheesecake), and a daily set meal from 11:30am until they run out,

A Guest House for Budget Travelers

Koyasan Guest House Kokuu (http://koyasanguesthouse.com; ✆ **0736/26-7216**) is a compact A-frame inn that squeezes in 8 capsule beds for ¥3,500 and 3 private rooms (¥9,000 for a double), plus a cozy bar offering food and drink. Owner Ryochi Takai, a Mt. Koya native, is happy to give tips on sightseeing.

which can include rice and beans, potato salad, cake and a drink (vegan and vegetarian options available; gluten-free, too, with 24-hr. notice). Credit cards aren't accepted and there are no set hours. It's that kind of place.

730 Koyasan. © **0736/56-5535.** Set meal ¥1,200. Wed–Sun 6:30am–5pm. Bus: Odawaradori. It's identified as Bononsha on the tourist map.

Ekoin (恵光院) ★★ This 100-year-old temple, with origins stretching back almost 1,100 years when Kukai was said to have erected a stupa on this site, has nice grounds and is nestled in a wooded slope an easy walk from Okunoin. For centuries it enjoyed support of the Shimadzu clan of southern Kyushu. It's known for its excellent Buddhist cuisine (gluten-free available) and free meditation lessons at 4:30pm, usually in English. Every morning there's both a chanting service and a fire ceremony. All rooms have views of the garden (and some even have a balcony) and information on how to wear a *yukata* (cotton kimono) and take a bath.

497 Koyasan. www.ekoin.jp. © **0736/56-2514.** 37 units (34 without bathroom). ¥12,000–¥24,800 per person. Rates include 2 meals. Bus: Karukayado-mae. **Amenities:** Hot-spring bath; Wi-Fi.

Rengejoin Temple (蓮華定院) ★★ This temple, established 900 years ago but rebuilt 150 years ago after a fire, is a good place to find out about Buddhism and the significance of Koyasan. Lodging, up the hill in a newer annex, ranges from simple *tatami* rooms to those nicely decorated with painted screens and antiques, the best with views of a garden with a pond. Pluses include a lounge with TV and free Wi-Fi, as well as both evening and morning services conducted in both Japanese and English. Too bad it's on the opposite end of town from Okunoin, about a 40-minute walk away. Note that unlike the other temples listed here, no credit cards are accepted.

700 Koyasan. © **0736/56-2233.** 46 units (none with bathroom). ¥11,880–¥16,200 per person. Rates include 2 meals and exclude tax. Bus: Ishinguchi stop.

Shojoshinin (清浄心院) ★★★ Of all Koyasan's temples, this one has the most curbside appeal. Best of all, it has a great location at the beginning of the tomb-lined pathway to Okunoin, making it convenient for your late-night stroll to the mausoleum. Originating as a thatched hut built by Kobo Daishi almost 1,200 years ago and once the second-largest temple in Koyasan after Kongobuji, today it boasts attractive 150-plus-year-old buildings against a wooded backdrop, including a large wooden structure with rooms overlooking a small garden and pond. It's usually full in August and peak seasons, so make reservations early.

566 Koyasan. © **0736/56-2006.** 30 units (29 without bathroom). 10,800–¥16,200 per person. Rates include 2 meals. Bus: Okunoin-guchi. **Amenities:** Free Wi-Fi.

HIMEJI, A CASTLE TOWN ★★

640km (400 miles) W of Tokyo; 130km (81 miles) W of Kyoto; 250km (155 miles) E of Hiroshima

The main reason tourists come to Himeji, in Hyogo Prefecture, is to see its magnificent 400-year-old **castle,** which embodies the best in Japan's military architecture. If you were to see only one castle in Japan, this World Heritage Site would be my top pick. If time permits, I also highly recommend strolling the delightful nearby garden, Koko-en.

Essentials

GETTING THERE A stop on the **Tokaido/Sanyo Shinkansen** bullet train, which runs between Tokyo and Kyushu, Himeji is about 3½ hours from Tokyo, 1 hour from Kyoto, and 2 hours from Hiroshima. The fare from Tokyo is ¥15,120 for a nonreserved seat. From Osaka Station, the JR commuter Tokaido line arrives in Himeji 1 hour later; the Shinkansen from Kyoto also takes an hour.

VISITOR INFORMATION The **Himeji Tourist Information Center** (officially called the Himeji Kanko Navi Port; ✆ **079/287-0003;** daily 9am–7pm) is located at the Central (north) exit of Himeji Station. It offers maps and free Wi-Fi. For online information, see **www.himeji-kanko.jp/en**. Most people come just for the day; the station has coin lockers.

GETTING AROUND You can **walk** to Himeji's attractions. The main road in town is Otemae Dori, a wide boulevard stretching from Himeji Station north to Himeji Castle (you can walk it in about 15 min.). To the east (right) of Otemae Dori are two parallel covered shopping arcades, Miyukidori and Omizosuji. The retro-looking **Himeji Castle Loop Bus** makes runs weekdays every half-hour from 9am to 4:30pm and every 15 minutes on weekends (no weekday service Dec–Feb) from the station to the castle, Koko-en, and beyond. It costs ¥100 per ride; an all-day ticket (¥300) includes discounts to Himeji Castle and Koko-en, but frankly, you can easily walk and save money by buying a combination ticket to the castle and garden.

Exploring Himeji

Himeji Castle ★★★ CASTLE As soon as you exit from Himeji Station's north exit, you'll see Himeji Castle straight ahead at the end of Otemae Dori. Probably the most beautiful castle in all of Japan, Himeji Castle is nicknamed "White Heron Castle" in reference to its white walls, which stretch out on either side of the main *donjon* (castle keep) and resemble a white heron poised in flight over the plain. Whether it looks to you like a heron or a castle, the view of the white five-story *donjon* under a blue sky is striking, especially when the area's 1,000-some cherry trees are in bloom. This is also one of the few castles in Japan that has remained virtually as it was since its completion in 1609, surviving even World War II bombings that left Himeji in ruins. In 1993, the castle, along with Horyuji Temple in Nara, became Japan's first UNESCO's World Heritage Sites.

Originating as a fort in the 14th century, Himeji Castle took a more majestic form in 1581 when a three-story *donjon* was built by Toyotomi Hideyoshi during one of his military campaigns in the district. In the early 1600s, the castle became the residence of Ikeda Terumasa, one of Hideyoshi's generals and a son-in-law of Tokugawa Ieyasu. He remodeled the castle into its present five-story structure, though it actually has a hidden sixth floor and a basement. With its 21 gates, three moats, turrets, and a secret entrance, it had one of the most sophisticated defense systems in Japan. The maze of passageways leading to the *donjon* was so complicated that intruders would find themselves trapped in dead ends. The castle walls, made of fireproof white plaster, were constructed with square, triangular, or circular holes through which gun muzzles could poke; the rectangular holes were for archers. There were also drop chutes where stones or boiling water could be dumped on enemies trying to scale the walls. Roof eaves were designed to collect rainwater, a bonus if the castle were ever under siege.

On weekends (and some weekdays), volunteers hanging around the castle ticket office offer guided tours of the castle for free. It gives them an opportunity to practice their English while you learn about the history of the castle and even old castle gossip. But even if you go on your own, you won't have any problems learning the history of the castle—there are good English-language explanations throughout the castle grounds. With or without a guide, you'll spend at least 2 hours here. But beware, grounds are huge, with lots of stairs. ***Tip:*** A combination ticket, allowing discounted admission to both the castle and Koko-en (see below), is available at either entrance.

68 Honmachi. www.city.himeji.lg.jp/guide/castle_en.html. © **079/285-1146.** Admission ¥1,000 adults, ¥300 children. Combination ticket to Himeji Castle and Koko-en ¥1,040 adults, ¥360 children. May–Aug daily 9am–6pm; Sept–Apr daily 9am–5pm. You must enter 1 hr. before closing time. A 15-min. walk straight north of Himeji Station via Otemae Dori.

Koko-en (好古園) ★★★ PARK/GARDEN Although only laid out in 1992, this is one of my favorite gardens, occupying land where samurai mansions once stood at the base of Himeji Castle, a 5-minute walk away. It's actually composed of nine separate small gardens, each one different and enclosed by traditional walls, with lots of rest areas to soak in the wonderful views. The gardens, typical of those in the Edo Period, include an area of deciduous trees, a garden of pine trees, a bamboo grove, a garden of flowers popular during the Edo era, tea-ceremony gardens, and traditional Japanese gardens with ponds, waterfalls, and running streams. I highly recommend stopping off at the Souju-an teahouse in the Cha-no-niwa (tea-ceremony garden), where kimono-clad women serve powdered green tea and a sweet (¥500; daily 10am–4pm). Or, dine at a restaurant overlooking a carp pond (see below). In any case, don't miss this special place. If you don't stop (but how can you resist?), you can stroll all the gardens in about 45 minutes.

68 Honmachi. www.himeji-machishin.jp/ryokka/kokoen/. © **079/289-4120.** Admission ¥300 adults, ¥150 children. Combination ticket to Himeji Castle and Koko-en ¥1,040 adults, ¥360 children. Daily 9am–5pm (to 6pm May–Aug). A 15-min. walk north of Himeji Station; turn left in front of Himeji Castle (the entrance will be on your right).

Where to Eat

In addition to the choices below, consider stopping by **Kassui-ken** (© **079/289-4131**) in Koko-en garden. To be honest, this restaurant has little to recommend it but for one overwhelming feature: It overlooks a koi pond and waterfall and is certainly the most picturesque place in town to try Himeji's specialty, conger eel. If that's too exotic, it also has a few noodle dishes and beef curry, as well as set meals (¥1,350–¥2,570; no credit cards). Or stop for dessert or a refreshing drink (beer, soda, or coffee) if you avoid the busy lunchtime crowd. Last order is an hour before Koko-en closes (see above).

In the listings below, directions are from Himeji Station.

Egret Castle Mille ★ VARIED JAPANESE Great views of Himeji Castle, which is lit at night, are the trademark of this restaurant, with seating along a window-side counter or at tables. Only set Japanese meals are offered, except for one lunch option that offers an appetizer, soup, main dish like fish or steak, rice or bread, dessert, and tea or coffee.

Egret Himeji Building, 4th floor, 68 Honmachi. ✆ **079/225-0030.** Set lunches ¥1,620–¥2,700; set dinners ¥3,240–¥6,480. Mon–Fri 11:30am–2:30pm; Sat–Sun & holidays 11am–2:30pm; daily 5–9pm (last order). Walking north on Otemae Dori, turn right at the next-to-last streetlight before Himeji Castle; it's the soaring glass building on the right.

Le Chat Botté ★★★ FRENCH I don't know how chef/owner Dimitri manages, but he somehow greets customers, takes orders, cooks, and sends guests on their way, all with a friendly demeanor (his Japanese wife also helps out). The place is small, with a counter and some tables that seat only 20 or so diners. The menu, written in Japanese on a blackboard (Dimitri can translate) ranges from a simple set lunch of appetizer, soup, quiche, and tea or coffee to dinner entrees that may include French-style hamburger, roast duck with an orange sauce, salmon, or lamb. Great food and welcoming service.

71 Shiroganemachi. ✆ **079/280-3107.** Set lunches ¥1,200–¥2,000; main dishes ¥1,800–¥3,000; set dinners ¥4,000–¥6,000. Tues–Sun 11:30am–2pm; Tues–Sat 5:30–10pm. Walking north on Otemae Dori, turn left when you reach a Family Mart on your left and the large, white Yamatoyashiki department store on your right.

Menme (めんめ) ★★ UDON NOODLES The friendly husband-and-wife team here has been dishing out *udon* noodles at this same spot for more than 30 years, with tempura *udon,* curry *udon,* and other *udon* listed on the English menu. Tanimoto-san makes all of his *udon* on the spot, so though you might have to wait, it's interesting to watch the process, which he accomplishes practically at the speed of light. Though the restaurant's location draws in many passing tourists, it's also popular with locals. You'll feel very welcomed here, but note that no credit cards are accepted.

68 Honmachi. ✆ **079/225-0118.** *Udon* ¥600–¥850; set meal (Mon–Fri only) ¥730. Thurs–Tues noon–5pm. On Otemae Dori, on the left a couple blocks before reaching Himeji Castle; look for the sign board showing plates of noodles.

HIGHLIGHTS OF CHUGOKU

11

The westernmost end of Honshu, known as the Chugoku region, has long been a destination for international tourists drawn to **Hiroshima,** the first city ever destroyed by an atomic bomb and home to the thought-provoking Peace Memorial Park with its museum. Near Hiroshima is **Miyajima,** a jewel of an island considered to be one of Japan's most scenic spots and site of a shrine that's a World Heritage Site. Another worthwhile destination is **Kurashiki**—its willow-fringed canal and black-and-white granaries make this old merchant's town a photographer's dream.

KURASHIKI, MARKET TOWN OF MANY CHARMS ★★★

750km (465 miles) W of Tokyo, 235km (380 miles) W of Kyoto, 177km (110 miles) E of Hiroshima

If I were to select the most picturesque town in Japan, **Kurashiki** would certainly be a top contender. Here, in the heart of the city, clustered around a willow-fringed canal and surrounding lanes, is a small but delightful historic district perfect for camera buffs.

As an administrative center of the shogunate in the 17th century, Kurashiki blossomed into a prosperous market town where rice, sake, and cotton were collected from the surrounding region and shipped off to Osaka and beyond. Back in those days, wealth was measured in rice; large granaries were built to store the mountains of granules passing through the town, and canals were dug so that barges laden with grain could work their way to ships anchored in the Seto Inland Sea. Kurashiki, in fact, means "Warehouse Village."

It's these warehouses, still standing and now converted into restaurants, shops, and *ryokan,* that give Kurashiki its distinctive charm. Kurashiki is also known for its museums, especially the prestigious Ohara Museum of Art with a collection of European and Japanese art. For these reasons, Kurashiki, located in Okayama Prefecture, is hardly undiscovered; visitors flock here in droves, especially in summer. Despite the crowds (try to avoid coming on a weekend), Kurashiki still rates high on my list of places to see in Japan.

Essentials

GETTING THERE **By Train** Although Kurashiki has a Shinkansen station **(Shin-Kurashiki),** most Shinkansen trains do not stop there, and the station is inconveniently located about 9.5km (6 miles) west of the city center (a local train runs between Shin-Kurashiki and Kurashiki stations about every 15 min. and takes 9 min.). From most destinations, you're better off disembarking the Shinkansen in Okayama and then transferring to the **JR Sanyo Line** to **Kurashiki Station,** in the heart of the city; trains depart frequently and take about 17 minutes (fare: ¥320). From Tokyo, an unreserved seat on the Shinkansen to Okayama followed by the JR Sanyo Line to Kurashiki Station takes about 4½ hours and costs ¥16,300.

By Bus A Ryobi Bus (✆ **03/3928-6011**) departs Tokyo's Shinjuku Station nightly at 9:45pm, arriving in Kurashiki at 8:45am and costing ¥10,000 one-way.

VISITOR INFORMATION A **tourist information office** located outside Kurashiki Station to the right (✆ **086/424-1220**) is open daily 9am to 6pm. Another tourist information office, called the **Kurashiki-Kan** (✆ **086/422-0542**), is right on the canal in the historic district. Under renovation until autumn 2019, it was built in 1916 and is ironically the only Western-looking wooden building in the area. For more, go to **www.kurashiki-tabi.jp**.

ORIENTATION Kurashiki's warehouse district, called the **Bikan Historical Quarter,** is only a 10-minute walk from Kurashiki Station; take the south exit and walk south on Chuo Dori, turning left just before the Kurashiki Kokusai Hotel. In fact, you can walk virtually everywhere of interest in Kurashiki; the historic district is zoned mostly for pedestrians.

[Fast FACTS] KURASHIKI

ATM/Mail There's a post office around the corner from the tourist office, with an ATM open Monday to Friday from 9am to 7pm and weekends and holidays from 9am to 5pm. There's also a Mizuho Bank underneath the tourist office and a 7-Eleven on Chuo Dori.

Wi-Fi Free Wi-Fi is provided at more than a dozen places around the station and in the Bikan Historical Quarter, listed on a map handed out at the tourist office.

Where to Stay

EXPENSIVE

Ryokan Kurashiki (旅館くらしき) ★★★ The best lodgings to get a feeling for old Kurashiki is right in the heart of it—in one of the old warehouses on Kurashiki's picturesque willow-lined canal. This venerable *ryokan* consists of an old mansion and three converted rice-and-sugar warehouses more than 260 years old, all in its own little compound connected by a corridor of black marble polished to a sheen. Filled with antiques and curios, it has long, narrow corridors, nooks and crannies, and the peaceful sanctuary of an inner garden. There's no other *ryokan* in Japan quite like this one. Its eight rooms, which are actually two- and three-room suites consisting of a *tatami* living room and sleeping quarters with Western-style beds, are simply elegant, with antiques placed here and there, two TVs, and Jacuzzi tubs. Two are big enough for up to six people (although no children younger than 13 are allowed), and three overlook the canal. Dinner is served in your room, while breakfast (Western-style breakfasts available) is served in a delightful terrace tea lounge overlooking a small garden.

4–1 Honmachi. www.ryokan-kurashiki.jp. ✆ **086/422-0730.** 8 units. ¥32,000–¥54,500 per person. Rates include 2 meals but exclude service charge. In the Bikan Historical Quarter. **Amenities:** Restaurant; Wi-Fi.

Tsurugata (鶴形) ★★ Rustic furniture, aged wood and memorable meals of seasonal specialties are trademarks of this *ryokan,* on the canal in the Bikan Historical Quarter's oldest building, constructed in 1744. It was once a merchant's house and shop selling rice, cotton, seafood, and cooking oil. The most expensive two rooms have a view of the garden (even from their cypress tubs) with its 400-year-old pine trees and stone lanterns, while the least expensive, rather ordinary six-mat *tatami* rooms are on the second floor with views over the Bikan historic district. There is, however, one six-mat *tatami* room with both a garden view and a tub that costs slightly more. Otherwise, all rooms have private toilets, but except for the three rooms mentioned here you'll be using the common baths.

1–3–15 Chuo. ✆ **086/424-1635.** 11 units (all with toilet, 3 with bathroom). ¥21,600–¥37,800 per person. Rates include 2 meals. In the Bikan Historical Quarter, on the canal. **Amenities:** Restaurant; Wi-Fi.

MODERATE

Kurashiki Ivy Square Hotel ★★ When this 1882 brick cotton mill was converted to a hotel in 1974, much of the old architectural style was left intact, making for an interesting setting. Rooms are simple and spotlessly clean, with some facing a tiny expanse of green grass and an ivy-covered wall or a koi-filled canal. Rooms range from small, inexpensive economy rooms with very narrow beds to deluxe two-room suites with a sofa that doubles as an extra bed (note that about half of the rooms are undergoing renovation, with completion slated for March 2019). The Bikan Historical Quarter is just a minute's walk away, but the train station is a 15-minute hike away.

7–2 Honmachi. www.ivysquare.co.jp. ✆ **086/422-0011.** 161 units. ¥8,800–¥13,500 single; ¥12,600–¥29,000 double. A minute's walk south of the Bikan Historical Quarter. **Amenities:** Restaurant; bar; summer beer garden; access to nearby sports club w/gym and pool (fee: ¥800); Wi-Fi.

Kurashiki Kokusai Hotel ★★★ This has long been Kurashiki's most popular Western-style hotel—and it's easy to see why. Built in 1963, it blends into its surroundings with black-tile walls set in white mortar. The interior pays tribute to the mid-20th-century Japanese modernist style with an old-fashioned charm, retro furnishings, and huge woodblock murals in the lobby by *mingei* artist Shiko Munakata (you can see more of his work at the Ohara Museum). Locally made crafts inside the rooms lift them out of the ordinary, including Kurashiki glass lampshades and woodblock prints by a local artist. A newer annex offers slightly larger twin rooms with larger bathrooms, though I prefer the smaller but more expensive rooms in the old building facing the back with a pleasant view of the Ohara Museum, garden greenery, and the black-tile roofs of the old granaries.

1–1–44 Chuo. www.kurashiki-kokusai-hotel.co.jp. ✆ **086/422-5141.** 105 units. ¥12,000–¥15,000 single; ¥15,000–¥30,000 double. Rates exclude tax and service charge. An 8-min. walk south of Kurashiki Station, on Chuo Dori adjacent to the Bikan Historical Quarter. **Amenities:** Restaurant; bar; lounge; summer barbecue garden; Wi-Fi.

INEXPENSIVE

Toyoko Inn Kurashiki-eki Minami-guchi ★ This inexpensive business hotel has a good location between Kurashiki Station and the Bikan Historical Quarter, above a convenience store. It also tries harder than most business hotels to draw in customers, offering two guest computers in the lobby, free domestic calls from lobby phones, and free breakfast. Rooms are tiny, with most of the room taken up by double- or queen-size beds, but the price is right. Ask for a room on the 11th floor for unobstructed city views (the top 12th floor is smoking) and be sure to pick up your sleepwear in the lobby.

2–10–20 Achi. www.toyoko-inn.com. ✆ **086/430-1045.** 154 units. ¥5,300–¥6,264 single; ¥6,300–¥8,640 double. Rates include continental breakfast. A 5-min. walk south of Kurashiki Station, on Chuo Dori on the left side. **Amenities:** Wi-Fi.

Cuore Kurashiki ★★★ This is a very cool hostel hidden in the Bikan Historical Quarter. Check-in is downstairs in the super comfy cafe/bar, at the reception desk cleverly constructed out of stacked old suitcases. It's the kind of place you wouldn't mind hanging out in—quite literally, as it even has a small separate room strung with four hammocks—with its free Wi-Fi, sofas, an alcove library, bar food like pizza and fish and chis, and a full-service bar. A central glass ceiling hints at the rooms above, lined along an atrium corridor on the second and third floors (there's no elevator). In addition to three dormitory rooms, each with three bunkbeds sleeping six people (one for women only, the other two for both genders), there are single, twin, and double rooms, small but with individuality like colored walls and funky decor making each one different. The two most expensive rooms, for one or two persons, have shower, but none have toilet. The hostel also offers two one-room apartments with kitchenette, one with twin rooms and the other with a double bed plus sofa bed, a minute's walk away.

1–9–4 Chuo. www.bs-cuore.com. ✆ **086/486-3443.** 19 units (2 with bathroom, 2 with toilet, 15 without bathroom). ¥4,860–¥7,560 single; ¥8,100–¥10,80 double; ¥12,960 apartment; ¥3,780 dormitory bed. A 10-min walk south of Kurashiki Station. Walk past the Bikan Historical Quarter on Chuo Dori, turn left at Shirakabe Dori and then the first left; it's across from a children's day-care center. **Amenities:** Cafe/bar; rental bikes (¥400 all day); Wi-Fi.

Where to Eat

In addition to options below, **Ryokan Kurashiki** (Tues–Sun 11am–2pm) serves elegant, seasonal set lunches (¥1,850–¥2,500) in a tea lounge with views of its garden, while evening summer beer gardens are located in the courtyard of **Ivy Square** and on the lawn of the **Kokusai Hotel.**

EXPENSIVE

Hachikengura ★★★ FRENCH Occupying a converted rice granary that once belonged to the Ohashi family (described below in the Ohashi House review), this is my top pick for an atmospheric meal, boasting a soaring wood-beamed ceiling, tiled walls, worn wooden floor, and tables widely spaced for privacy. Traditional French cuisine, such as sautéed scallop and eggplant, lobster, or steak, is served nouvelle style and listed on the English-language menu. You can eat here more economically if you come for lunch; even the least expensive set meal is delicious. Reservations recommended.

Kurashiki Royal Art Hotel, 3–21–19 Achi. www.royal-art-hotel.co.jp. ✆ **086/423-2122** (423-2400 after 7pm). Main dishes 2,400–¥7,000; set lunches ¥2,000–¥3,000; set dinners ¥5,000–¥12,000. Daily 11:30am–1:30pm and 5:30–8:30pm (last order). Across Chuo Dori from the Bikan Historical Quarter.

MODERATE

Kiyutei (亀遊亭) ★ STEAK Enter through the front gate just off the canal, pass through the small courtyard, and dine in a room dominated by a counter with cooks grilling steaks, the specialty of the house, served with grated *daikon* (Japanese radish) or Madeira sauce. There's an English-language menu, but best is probably one of the set meals, which in addition to steaks offer fried prawns and scallops or stewed beef for dinner, or, for lunch, beef curry, grilled chicken, and a hamburger steak.

1–2–20 Chuo. ✆ **086/422-5140.** Set lunches ¥1,100–¥6,300; set dinners ¥1,800–¥7,500. Daily 11am–3pm and 5–9pm. Opposite the canal from Ohara Museum.

INEXPENSIVE

For a drink or snack, the one-room **El Greco Coffeehouse** (✆ **086/422-0297**; Tues–Sun 10am–5pm) is Kurashiki's most famous coffee shop, open since 1959 and located next to the Ohara Museum. With an ivy-covered stone facade and simply decorated with a wooden floor, wooden tables, vases of fresh flowers, and El Greco photos, it serves coffee, green tea, fruit juice, milkshakes, ice cream, and cake (cash only).

Kamoi (カモ井) ★★ VARIED JAPANESE This restaurant, occupying a 200-year-old rice granary on Kurashiki's willow-fringed canal, is sparingly decorated with stark-white walls, dark wooden beams, and hanging white paper lamps. An English-language menu has photos of sushi set meals, noodle dishes, a *tempura teishoku,* the *Kamoi teishoku* (featuring sashimi and *chirashi-zushi*—seafood rice bowl), and—my favorite—the *Kurashiki bento* with tempura, vegetables, and seasonable goodies. But what I love most is gazing out the window, watching people strolling along the canal.

1–3–17 Chuo. ✆ **086/422-0606.** Set meals ¥1,500–¥2,600. Thurs–Tues 10am–6pm (closed 2nd Mon of each month). Catty-corner across the canal from the Ohara Museum of Art.

Ristorante Rentenchi ★ PIZZA/PASTA This cozy, tiny restaurant, run by a husband-and-wife team, is a good choice for inexpensive dining near the Bikan Historical Quarter. Neapolitan-style, thick-crusted pizza from a wood-burning oven is the specialty, and the sommelier can make suggestions from a list of some 200 Italian wines. Not on the English menu are fixed-price dinners, the cheapest of which gives a choice of pizza or pasta of the day, salad, bread, dessert, and coffee or espresso.

2–19–18 Achi. ✆ **086/421-7858.** Pizza and pasta ¥1,100–¥2,800; set lunches ¥1,000–¥2,800; set dinners ¥3,000–¥5,000. Wed–Mon 11:30am–2pm and 6–10pm. On the left side of Chuo Dori when walking from Kurashiki Station, just before the historic district.

Exploring Kurashiki's Bikan Historical Quarter

Kurashiki's **historic old town** is centered on a canal lined with graceful willows and 200-year-old granaries made of black-tile walls topped with white mortar. Many of the granaries have been turned into museums, *ryokan,* restaurants, and boutiques selling hand-blown glass, Bizen pottery, papier-mâché toys, women's ethnic clothing imported from Bali and India, and mats and handbags made of *igusa* (rush grass), a local specialty. Street vendors sell jewelry, their wares laid out beside the canal, and healthy young men stand ready to give visitors rides in rickshaws.

A resident advised me that because of the crowds that descend upon Kurashiki, I should awaken early before shops and museums open and explore this tiny area while it's still under the magical spell of the early morning glow; even rain only enhances the buildings' contrasting black and white. "Real lovers of Kurashiki come on Monday," he added. "Because that's when most everything is closed, and there are fewer people." (If Mon is a holiday, however, most museums stay open and close on Tues instead.) Don't neglect the side streets between the canal and Achi Shrine on Tsurugatayama Park, especially the neighborhoods of Honmachi and Higashimachi, with cafes, antique stores, and boutiques selling clothing and crafts. I've found that early evening is also a magical time to walk the streets, especially after sunset, when many buildings along the canal are illuminated.

Ohara Museum of Art (Ohara Bijutsukan) ★★★ ART MUSEUM This is by far Kurashiki's most impressive museum, a must-see even on a short list of sightseeing. Industrialist Ohara Magosaburo, who believed that people even in remote Kurashiki should have the opportunity to view great works of art (that's his stately mansion across the canal from the museum), founded it in 1930 as Japan's first museum of Western art. The main building, a two-story stone structure resembling a Greek temple, is small but manages to contain the works of Picasso, Matisse, Vlaminck, Monet, Pissarro, Sisley, Chagall, Toulouse-Lautrec, Gauguin, Cézanne, El Greco, Modigliani, Renoir, Miró, Kandinsky, Pollack, Rothko, Jasper Johns, De Kooning, Warhol, and many more. The museum has expanded so much over the years that several annexes have been added. A *mingei* (Japan's 20th-century folkcrafts) gallery housed in a series of renovated Edo-era granaries contains works by some of my favorites, including ceramics by Hamada Shoji, Bernard Leach, and Kawai Kanjiro, and woodblock prints by Shiko Munakata, who lived in Kurashiki 3 years. It connects to the Asian Art Gallery, which displays ancient Chinese art, primarily from prehistoric times to the Tang Dynasty (A.D. 618–907). A walk through a garden brings you to an annex devoted to Japanese artists painting in the Western style and to contemporary Japanese artists like Shigeru Aoki, Ryusei Kishida, and Ryuzaburo Umehara. Allow up to 2 hours to see everything, but your ticket is good all day so you don't have to see it all at once. An audio guide (¥500) covers works in the main gallery.

1-1-15 Chuo. www.ohara.or.jp. © **086/422-0005.** Admission ¥1,300 adults, ¥800 university students, ¥500 children. Tues–Sun 9am–5pm. On the canal.

The Ohashi's House (Ohashi-ke; 大橋家住宅) ★ HISTORIC BUILDING Built in 1796 by a wealthy salt and rice merchant, this traditional mansion is typical of the era, with front rooms used for entertaining guests and conducting business (the doorsill leading to the warehouse can be removed for easy transport), and the rear used as family living quarters. An imposing front gate, usually allowed only in homes belonging to the samurai class, is proof of how important the Ohashi family was (remarkably, the Ohashi family still owns the house). Once much larger (sadly, a hotel occupies the former garden), the home's 20 remaining rooms contain some family heirlooms. Listen to a short audio introduction in English and take a 15-minute spin through if you've never seen the inside of a traditional Japanese home.

3-21-31 Achi. www.ohashi-ke.com. © **086/422-0007.** Admission ¥550 adults, ¥350 seniors and children. Daily 9am–5pm (Sat to 6pm Apr–Sept). Closed Fri Dec–Feb. Across Chuo Dori from Bikan Historical Quarter, on the left side behind Royal Art Hotel (no sign in English).

A Cycling Excursion

For some rural R & R, head north to the historic Kibiji District, once home to the ancient Kibi kingdom and known today for its huge *kofun* (burial mounds), temples, shrines, and five-story pagoda, all connected via a marked biking path that traverses this pastoral landscape. It takes about 4 hours to bike the entire 15km (10 miles) between Soja and Bizen-Ichinomiya stations, stopping at sights along the way. Kibitsu Jinja Shrine, built in an architectural style seen only here, is one of the most important stops. If you have time, fill out the shrine's application stating your desired wish and pay ¥3,000 for a special ceremony, which ends with a walk down a sloping 400m-long (1,132-ft) covered corridor to a special tatami room, where a burning fire and a 600-year-old Narukama Shinto ritual involving a boiling kettle will reveal whether your wish will come true (if you hear a roar, your wish will be granted). Otherwise, it's fun to cycle from one historic destination to the next, but what I like most about this ride is its rural setting, through villages, over rivers, past peach and bamboo groves, and along paddies (much of the bike path is actually on the same raised walkways farmers use to separate and dam their paddies and get to their fields).

Rental bikes (© **0866/92-0233**) are available daily 9am to 6pm (5pm in winter) to the right outside Soja Station, which you can reach in 11 minutes from Kurashiki Station on the JR Hakubi Line (fare: ¥240). Bikes rent for ¥400 (helmets are free) for 2 hours, but I suggest you fork out ¥1,000 for the whole day and cycle the entire pathway to Bizen-Ichinomiya Station, where you can ditch the bike and hop on the JR Kibi Linea train for an 11-minute ride to Okayama Station (fare: ¥210) and transfer there for the train back to

Kurashiki. *Caveat:* Although the bike path is well-marked in English most of the way, including path-embedded signs, I got lost trying to find Bizen-Ichinomiya Station. Villagers are apparently used to lost cyclers and soon had me merrily on my way. You'll get a cycling map when you rent your bike; the Kurashiki tourist office also has information on the Kibiji District.

HIROSHIMA, THEN & NOW ★★

894km (554 miles) W of Tokyo; 376km (235 miles) W of Kyoto

With a population of 1.19 million, Hiroshima, capital of Hiroshima Prefecture and the largest metropolis in the Chugoku region, looks just like any other city in Japan. With modern buildings and an industry that includes the manufacture of cars and ships, it's a town full of vitality and purpose, with a steady flow of both Japanese and foreign business executives in and out. But unlike other cities, Hiroshima's past is clouded: It has the unfortunate distinction of being the first city ever destroyed by an atomic bomb. (The second city—and, it is hoped, the last—was Nagasaki, on Kyushu island.)

It happened one clear summer morning, August 6, 1945, at 8:15am, when a B-29 approached Hiroshima from the northeast, passed over the central part of the city, dropped the bomb, and then took off at full speed. The bomb exploded 43 seconds later at an altitude of 600m (1,980 ft.) in a huge fireball, followed by a mushroom cloud of smoke that rose 8,910m (29,700 ft.) in the air.

Approximately 350,000 people were living in Hiroshima at the time of the bombing, and almost a third lost their lives that day. The heat from the blast was so intense that it seared people's skin, while the pressure caused by the explosion tore clothes off bodies and caused the rupture and explosion of internal organs. Flying glass tore through flesh like bullets, and fires broke out all over the city. But that wasn't the end of it: Victims who survived the blast were subsequently exposed to huge doses of radioactive particles. Even people who showed no outward signs of sickness suddenly died, creating panic and helplessness among survivors. In the years that followed, blast survivors continued to suffer from the effects of the bomb, with a high incidence of cancer, disfigurement, scars, and keloid skin tissue.

Ironically, Hiroshima's tragedy is now the city's largest tourist draw, and visitors from around the world come to see Peace Memorial Park with its haunting museum and memorials. But Hiroshima, laced with rivers and wide, tree-lined boulevards, boasts a few other worthwhile attractions as well and is the most popular gateway for trips to nearby **Miyajima,** a small island renowned for its shrine and nature (p. 319).

Essentials

GETTING THERE **By Train** Hiroshima is about 5 hours from Tokyo by **Shinkansen** bullet train (you have to change trains in Shin-Osaka or Shin-Kobe if you have a Japan Rail Pass, because only the Nozomi, which is not covered by the pass, covers the entire distance in 4 hr.) and a little less than 2

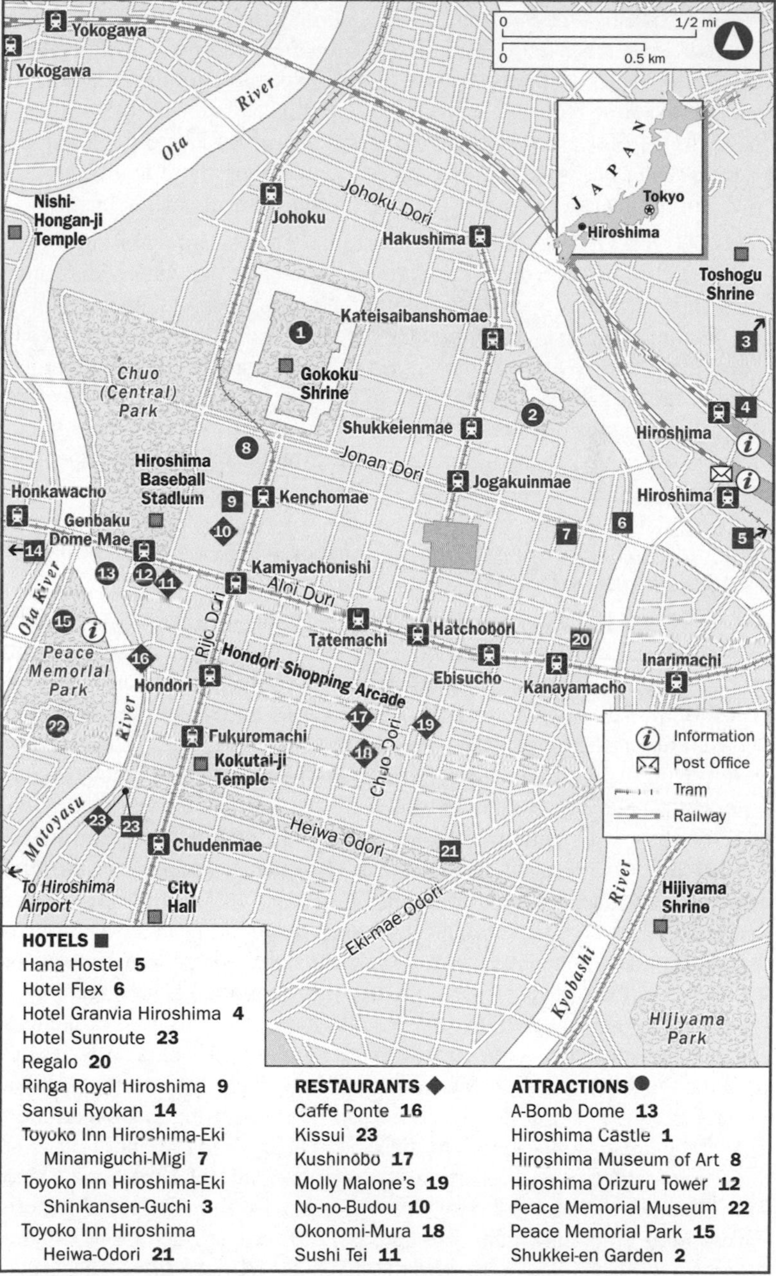

HOTELS ■

Hana Hostel **5**
Hotel Flex **6**
Hotel Granvia Hiroshima **4**
Hotel Sunroute **23**
Regalo **20**
Rihga Royal Hiroshima **9**
Sansui Ryokan **14**
Toyoko Inn Hiroshima-Eki Minamiguchi-Migi **7**
Toyoko Inn Hiroshima-Eki Shinkansen-Guchi **3**
Toyoko Inn Hiroshima Heiwa-Odori **21**

RESTAURANTS ◆

Caffe Ponte **16**
Kissui **23**
Kushinobo **17**
Molly Malone's **19**
No-no-Budou **10**
Okonomi-Mura **18**
Sushi Tei **11**

ATTRACTIONS ●

A-Bomb Dome **13**
Hiroshima Castle **1**
Hiroshima Museum of Art **8**
Hiroshima Orizuru Tower **12**
Peace Memorial Museum **22**
Peace Memorial Park **15**
Shukkei-en Garden **2**

hours from Kyoto. The fare for an unreserved seat is ¥18,040 from Tokyo and ¥10,570 from Kyoto.

By Bus **JR Buses** depart from Tokyo Station nightly at 8pm (with a stop in Shinjuku) and reach Hiroshima Station the next morning at 7:35am for ¥11,900. A **Willer Express** bus (www.willerexpress.com), departing nightly from Shinjuku at 8pm and arriving at Hiroshima Station at 8:50am, costs ¥6,000 to ¥9,400, depending on the seat and day. From Kyoto (with a stop in Osaka), Willer buses depart three times a day, taking more than 7 hours to reach Hiroshima and costing ¥4,200 and up (there are also night buses).

VISITOR INFORMATION A **Hiroshima Tourist Information Center** (✆ **082/263-5120**), at **Hiroshima Station** at the north exit where Shinkansen bullet trains arrive, is open daily 6am to midnight. A small tourist and transportation information kiosk at the station's south exit, where streetcars depart, is open daily 9am to 6pm. A third tourist office is located in **Peace Memorial Park** in the Rest House (✆ **082/247-6738**). It's open daily 8:30am to 6pm March to November (to 7pm Aug) and to 5pm the rest of the year. All three facilities have English-language maps of Hiroshima and Miyajima, including transportation maps. Be sure to pick up ***Seeking Hiroshima,*** a magazine-size encyclopedia of everything Hiroshima and Miyajima, including transportation, maps, and sightseeing. Online information on Hiroshima is available at **www.hiroshima-navi.or.jp/en/**.

GETTING AROUND One legacy of Hiroshima's total destruction was its rebirth into one of Japan's most navigable cities, with wide, open boulevards instead of the usual cramped streets. Hiroshima's main attractions, including Peace Memorial Park, Hiroshima Castle, Shukkei-en Garden, and Hiroshima Museum of Art, lie to the west and southwest of Hiroshima Station. I find it easiest to make the circuit to Hiroshima's centrally located attractions **on foot.** From Hiroshima Station, you can walk to Shukkei-en Garden in about 15 minutes, from which it's another 10-minute walk to Hiroshima Castle. You can walk onward to Peace Memorial Park in about 15 minutes, passing the Hiroshima Museum of Art and the A-Bomb Dome on the way. Just east of Peace Park is the **Hondori** covered shopping arcade and its neighboring streets, considered the heart of the city with its many department stores, shops, and restaurants.

Otherwise, the most convenient mode of transportation is **streetcar,** which costs only ¥180 one-way (children pay half-fare). A 1-day pass, which you can buy from the conductor, costs ¥600. Be sure to pick up a streetcar map from the tourist office, which also describes how to use the streetcar and how to ask for a streetcar transfer ticket *(norikae)* if transferring to another line.

There are also **sightseeing loop buses,** the "Hiroshima Meipuru-pu," with three color-coded routes departing from the backside of Hiroshima Station from about 9 to 9:30am to 5 or 5:30pm daily and traveling to Peace Memorial Park, among other attractions. The fare is ¥200 for one ride or ¥400 all day; holders of the Japan Rail Pass ride for free. Ask the tourist office for a bus map.

Finally, bikes are available from 7am to 11pm at cycle ports around town through the city's **bike-sharing system.** A 1-day pass costs ¥1,080 if you pay with a credit card via your mobile phone or with a prepaid ICOCA transportation card, ¥1,500 if paying with cash at a ticket counter. Pick up a flyer at the tourist office or go to http://docomo-cycle.jp/hiroshima/en/ for details.

[FastFACTS] HIROSHIMA

ATM/Mail Hiroshima's main post office, 2–62 Matsubara-cho (✆ **082/261-6401**), is located to the right after exiting from Hiroshima Station's south side and is open daily 7am to 9pm for mail and Monday to Friday from 9am to 4pm for money exchange. Its ATM services are available Monday to Saturday 12:05am to 11:55pm and Sunday and holidays 12:05am to 9pm.

Wi-Fi **Hiroshima Free Wi-Fi** provides free access at more than 30 spots around town. Pick up the flyer with details at the tourist office.

Where to Stay

Directions are from Hiroshima Station. The rates reflect the seasons.

EXPENSIVE

Hotel Granvia Hiroshima ★ Owned by JR West (and offering discounts to holders of the Japan Rail Pass), this hotel is convenient for short stays because it's connected to the Shinkansen (north) side of the station, where Meipuru-pu sightseeing buses depart for major attractions (streetcars, however, depart from the south side of the station). I also like its dedicated Information Center for sightseeing in the city, though the station's tourist office is also close at hand. The lodgings consist of rather small but comfortable standard rooms on the 6th to 18th floors, larger and more chic superior rooms on the 19th floor, and Granvia rooms on the 20th floor, the best of which are huge deluxe twins with separate sleeping/living areas and spacious bathrooms. None have great views, unless you count seeing the Shinkansen pulling into the station. For the time being, the Granvia has stocked each room with a complimentary smart phone, giving you access to free Wi-Fi, free local calls and to six selected countries, and a digital sightseeing guide; let's hope they keep them.

1–5 Matsubara-cho. www.hgh.co.jp. ✆ **082/262-1111.** 407 units. ¥7,700–¥21,400 single; ¥12,600–¥53,400 double. Discount for holders of Japan Rail Pass. Attached to Hiroshima Station. **Amenities:** 8 restaurants; bar; lounge; rooftop beer terrace (summer only); concierge; room service; Wi-Fi.

Rihga Royal Hotel Hiroshima ★★★ The 33-story Rihga Royal stands out as Hiroshima's tallest hotel, with a convenient location in the heart of the city between Hiroshima Castle and Peace Park and connected to a large complex that includes the Pacela shopping mall and Sogo department store. Large rooms with luxurious furnishings come with plenty of features, including magnifying mirrors and lots of counter space in the bathrooms. Rates are based on floor height and room size, but even some of the cheapest twins have views of a park across the street and the distant castle. The best views, however, are from top floors with panoramas of the Seto Inland Sea (you can even see Miyajima). A nice touch are the pictorial maps in each room describing the view, but the best view of all is from the 33rd-floor **Rihga Top** lounge (no cover charge if you sit at the bar).

6–78 Motomachi. www.rihga-hiroshima.co.jp. ✆ **082/502-1121.** 488 units. ¥14,300–¥47,500 single or double; from ¥43,000 executive double. Streetcar: 1 or 6 to Kamiya-cho-nishi (1 min.). Meipuru-pu: Kamiyacho. **Amenities:** 5 restaurants; 2 bars; concierge; executive-level rooms; health and dental clinic; health club w/gym; 25m (82-ft.) 5-lane pool, Jacuzzi, and sauna (fee: ¥3,250 for pool and sauna; ¥6,480 for everything); room service; Wi-Fi.

MODERATE

Hotel Flex ★★★ This is Hiroshima's most unconventional hotel, apparent the moment you walk in and find yourself in a cafe that doubles as the front desk and opens out onto a terrace overlooking the tree-lined Kyobashi-gawa river and promenade, with jazz playing in the background. A modern concrete structure, it offers tiny but fashionable rooms, some with relaxing river views and/or floor-to-ceiling windows and all crisply decorated with blue-and-green pillows and bed runners, stark white walls, and wooden floors. The best and most expensive are three top-floor rooms that are almost like mini-apartments without the kitchen (one even has an outdoor terrace). Unlike most hotels nowadays, however, only a minority of its rooms are nonsmoking.

7–1 Kaminobori-cho. www.hotel-flex.co.jp. ✆ **082/223-1000.** 64 units. ¥4,800–¥11,500 single; ¥7,500–¥27,500 double. Hiroshima Station (7 min.). From the station's south exit, turn right and then left after the post office; after crossing the pedestrian Ekini-shi-koka-bashi bridge and turning right to cross another bridge, it will be immediately on your right. **Amenities:** Cafe/restaurant; Wi-Fi.

Hotel Sunroute ★★★ Although most hotels in this chain are strictly business hotels, this property's excellent location, next to the river and catty-corner from the museum in Peace Memorial Park, plus two very good restaurants with great views, makes it a popular choice for tourists as well. Rooms are mostly twins, with the highest-priced twins having the additional advantage of views of the park and river (deluxe corner twins are best). Only one of the 11 double rooms faces the park, however, but those with a sofa have room to spread out. The cheapest rooms are on low floors and have no views whatsoever.

3–3–1 Otemachi. www.sunroutehotel.jp/hiroshima. ✆ **082/249-3600.** 283 units. ¥5,300–¥13,500 single; ¥7,000–¥29,160 double. Streetcar: 1 to Chuden-mae (3 min.). Meipuru-pu: The Peace Memorial Park. Southeast of Peace Memorial Park and the Heiwa-Ohashi Bridge. **Amenities:** 2 restaurants, Wi-Fi.

INEXPENSIVE

Hana Hostel ★★ This former business hotel turned backpacker hostel offers 13 small private rooms, five Western-style with private shower and toilet and the rest *tatami* rooms with either wash basin and toilet or bathroom. There are also dormitory rooms, including one with two bunk beds (and a toilet) and two for women only, making this a good choice for both families and females on a budget. Pluses include its location near Hiroshima Station, communal kitchen with free tea and coffee, a fifth-floor lounge with TV and DVDs (there's an elevator), and a rooftop terrace where you can hang out and hang laundry. If I were you, I'd ask for a room facing the front of the building, away from the train tracks, but it's still going to be noisy (pick up earplugs at the front desk).

1–15 Kojin-machi. http://hiroshima.hanahostel.com. ✆ **082/263-2980.** 16 units (4 with toilet only, 9 with bathroom). ¥3,200–¥4,480 single; ¥6,800–¥7,300 double; ¥2,500 dormitory bed. Hiroshima Station (4 min.). Turn left out of the station's south exit and follow the road that hugs the tracks, keeping left of Edi City; after passing by the road that crosses the tracks (don't cross the tracks), take the 1st right and then 1st left at the small parking lot. **Amenities:** Rental bikes (¥700 per day); Wi-Fi.

Regalo ★ Located on one of Hiroshima's many rivers, about halfway between Hiroshima Station and downtown, this nine-story hotel capitalizes on its river views with an atmospheric Italian restaurant and, across the street beside the river, an open-air-pavilion cafe. While the cheapest rooms have glazed windows facing the back and are dark, rooms only slightly more expensive have refreshing views of the river and are larger. Bedspreads instead of covered duvets, however, give the hotel an outdated appearance. Still, this establishment is a pleasant alternative to most inexpensive lodgings, with more personality than the cookie-cutter Toyoko Inn chain.

9–2 Hashimoto-cho. www.regalo-h.com/hiroshima.html. ✆ **082/224-6300.** 63 units. ¥6,500–¥9,500 single; ¥9,500–¥12,000 double. Streetcar: 1, 2, or 6 to Kanayama-cho (2 min.). Walk back toward the bridge (but don't cross it) and turn left at the river. Or a 13-min. walk from Hiroshima Station. **Amenities:** Restaurant; cafe; Wi-Fi.

Sansui Ryokan ★★★ This is a good choice for travelers who like meeting locals rather than staying in impersonal hotels. It's run by the motherly and very hospitable Kato-san, who cheerfully oversees operations, hands out maps and sightseeing brochures, has five bikes for ryokan guests (reserve in advance), and can even arrange a **tea ceremony** (¥1,500) if you make reservations 3 weeks in advance. It has a cozy communal room offering free coffee and tea; three showers for its only six *tatami* rooms; and walls covered with photos showing past happy guests. Note that rooms on the second floor are reached by steep stairs. It has a good location, only a 7-minute walk west of Peace Memorial Park. No credit cards accepted.

4–16 Koami-cho. www.sansui-ryokan.com. ✆ **082/293-9051.** 6 units, none with bathroom. ¥5,200 single; ¥9,500 double; ¥13,500 triple. Streetcar: 2 to Koami-cho (1 min.). Walk toward and turn left at the river and then the 1st left. **Amenities:** Rental bikes (¥300 per day); Wi-Fi.

Where to Eat

Although the people of Osaka claim to have made *okonomiyaki* popular among the masses, the people of Hiroshima claim to have made it an art. *Okonomiyaki* is a kind of savory Japanese pancake (or perhaps pizza) filled with cabbage, meat, and other ingredients. Whereas in Osaka the ingredients are mixed together, in Hiroshima each layer is prepared separately, which means the chefs must be quite skilled at keeping the whole thing together. Hiroshima is also famous for its oysters (among the largest I've ever seen), with thousands of rafts cultivating oysters in Hiroshima Bay and producing 20,000 tons of shelled oysters yearly.

MODERATE

Caffé Ponte ★ ITALIAN What I like most about this smoke-free restaurant is that it's easy to find (just across the river from the Rest House tourist office in Peace Park) and offers outdoor seating under white umbrellas even in winter thanks to heaters—making a meal here seem like a mini-vacation. Its English-language menu (with photos) offers lots of choices, including Hiroshima oysters, salads, pasta, pizza, fish, and a few vegetarian and gluten-free choices, as well as cocktails and other alcoholic drinks.

1-9-21 Otemachi. www.caffeponte.com. ✆ **082/247-7471.** Main dishes ¥1,380–¥2,500; set lunches ¥1,800–¥1,980; set dinners ¥3,800–¥5,800. Mon–Fri 10am–10pm, Sat–Sun and holidays 8am–10pm (7:30am–10pm daily in Aug). Streetcar: Hondori (3 min., through the covered shopping arcade) or Genbaku Dome-mae (2 min.). Meipuru-pu: Kamiya-cho. East of Peace Park, on the bank of Motoyasu-gawa river at the Motoyasu-bashi bridge.

Kissui ★★★ KAISEKI Convenient to Peace Memorial Park, with great 15th-floor views, an English-language menu, and beautifully prepared *kaiseki* meals, this is an optimal restaurant for tourists. For lunch, the Kissui Set for ¥2,800 is a great choice, but no matter what you order, you can't go wrong here unless you forget to make reservations—this place is popular. Alternatively, **Viale,** also on the hotel's 15th floor with the same open hours, offers Italian fare with the same great views.

Hotel Sunroute, 15th floor, 3-3-1 Otemachi. ✆ **082/249-3600.** Set lunches ¥2,800–¥5,300 (from ¥1,980 weekdays); *kaiseki* set dinners ¥4,620–¥11,000. Daily 11:30am–2pm and 5–8pm (last order). Streetcar: Chuden-mae (see directions in Hotel Sunroute review, above).

INEXPENSIVE

Kushinobo (串の坊) ★★★ KUSHIYAKI This is a friendly, rub-elbows-with-the-locals kind of place, lively and crowded and decorated with Japanese knickknacks. Although kushiyaki connoisseurs like ordering skewers à la carte, you're probably better off ordering one of two set meals from the English-language menu. I always get the *Kushinobo-gozen* with 10 skewers of vegetables, meat, and seafood plus pickled vegetables and soup. If you're still hungry, order more. For dipping, there's soy sauce, mustard, and coarse salt, while a ceramic fish with an open mouth serves as the receptacle for empty skewers. What I enjoy most about dining here, in addition to the food, is watching the skewers being prepared behind the counter and the friendly interactions between customers. The chef is a serious fellow, but he speaks English and somehow manages to keep all the orders straight. It's located off the east end of the Hondori covered arcade, behind Parco department store.

Parco-mae, 7-4 Horikawa-cho. ✆ **082/245-9300.** Set lunches ¥1,300–¥1,670; set dinners ¥2,450–¥2,800. Daily 11:30am–1pm and 5–9pm (last order). Streetcar or Meipuru-pu: Hatchobori (3 min.). Walk south on Chuo Dori 2 blocks to Parco department store and turn right into a covered shopping arcade; take the 1st left and then the 1st right. Look for its old-fashioned red facade.

Molly Malone's ★ VARIED WESTERN An Irish pub with good food—what more do you need? In addition to seven beers on tap (a sampler of three costs ¥1,000), it offers salads (like a spicy prawn salad), pastas (including a vegetarian choice), burgers, steak, and classic pub fare ranging from fish and chips and bangers and mash to cottage pie and Irish stew, plus a Sunday roast. Thursdays are Dice Night; you roll for the price of your drink, making it anywhere from ¥200 to ¥1,200. Add happy hour Tuesday to Saturday from 5 to 7pm, screens showing international soccer and rugby games, and free Wi-Fi, and this could be your new favorite hot spot.

Teigeki Building, 4th floor, 1–20 Shintenchi. www.mollymalones.jp. © **082/244-2554.** Main dishes ¥850–¥2,200. Tues–Thurs 5pm–1am, Fri 5pm–2am, Sat 3pm–2am, Sun and holidays 3pm–midnight. Streetcar or Meipuru-pu: Hatchobori (1 min.). Walk south on Chuo Dori Ave.; it's on the left (across from Parco) and is easy to miss. Look for the Guinness sign.

No-no-Budou (野の葡萄) ★★ JAPANESE BUFFET With an open kitchen and jazz as background music, this popular buffet restaurant in the Pacela shopping complex (next to Righa Royal Hotel) specializes in healthy, organic foods, with some 50 choices that change daily but always include Chinese and Japanese dishes, from noodles and tempura to soups and salads. An outdoor terrace has views toward the castle, but avoid the lunchtime rush.

7th floor of Pacela, 78–6 Motomachi. © **082/502-3340.** Buffet lunch ¥1,740; buffet dinner ¥2,160. Daily 11am–3pm and 5:30–9pm (last order). Streetcar: Kamiya-cho-nishi (1 min.). Meipuru-pu: Kamiya-cho. Between Righa Royal Hotel and Sogo department store.

Okonomi-Mura (お好み村) ★★ OKONOMIYAKI Open since 1963 as one of Hiroshima's most beloved establishments, this is the best place in town to witness *okonomiyaki* short-order cooks at their trade. Although the shabby building doesn't look like it contains restaurants, its name means "*okonomiyaki* village," and that's what it is—three floors of some 20 individual stalls dishing out *okonomiyaki*. All offer basically the same menu—sit down at one of the counters and watch how the chef first spreads pancake mix on a hot griddle; follows it with a layer of cabbage, bean sprouts, and bacon; and then adds an egg on top. If you want, you can have yours with Chinese noodles. Portions are huge. I suggest wandering through and choosing one that catches your fancy. No credit cards accepted.

5–13 Shintenchi. www.okonomimura.jp. © **082/241-2210.** Set meals ¥860–¥1,600. Most open daily 11am–10 or 11pm. Streetcar or Meipuru-pu: Hatchobori (2 min.). Walk south on Chuo Dori 4 blocks and turn right at Don Quijote.

Sushi Tei (すし亭) ★★ SUSHI Excellent sushi at reasonable prices is the reason this establishment is so popular. After being seated at the counter, you'll be presented with an English-language menu and an order form you fill out yourself. A fresh banana leaf serves as your plate for rolled sushi (like the avocado or crab salad roll) and sashimi. There are many Sushi Tei restaurants in town, but this one is easy to find, near the A-Bomb Dome.

1–4–31 Otemachi. © **082/545-1333.** Sushi ¥108–¥432; sushi sets ¥864–¥2,160. Mon–Sat 5pm–midnight; Sun and holidays 11:30am–10pm. Streetcar: Kamiya-cho-nishi (1 min.). Meipuru-pu: Kamiya-cho. Take the small street beside Edion and turn right; it's on the left.

Exploring Hiroshima

As you walk around Hiroshima today, you'll find it hard to imagine that the city was the scene of such widespread horror and destruction just 70-some years ago. Hiroshima doesn't have the old buildings, temples, and historic structures that other cities have, yet it draws a steady flow of travelers, including Japanese school groups, who come to see Peace Memorial Park, the city's best-known landmark. Dedicated to peace, the city also seems committed to art: In addition to art museums, you'll find statues, stone lanterns, memorials, and sculptures lining the streets.

For a bird's-eye view of Peace Memorial Park and mountains ringing the city, visit **Hiroshima Orizuru Tower** (*orizuru* means paper crane; www.orizurutower.jp/en/; ✆ **082/569-6200**), just steps from the A-Bomb Dome (see below), 1–2–1 Otemachi. Inside is the rooftop Hiroshima Hills wooden deck and the 12th-floor Orizuru Square, where you can make paper cranes and experience interactive displays; check website for admission fees and open hours. On the ground floor is a shop selling top-quality Hiroshima products, a cafe, and a tourist office open daily 10am to 6pm.

PEACE MEMORIAL PARK

Peace Memorial Park (Heiwa Koen) ★★★ lies in the center of the city. My recommendation for seeing this expansive park is to take streetcar No. 2 or 6 or the Meipuru-pu bus to the Genbaku-Domu-mae stop, just north of the park. The first structure you'll see as you alight from the streetcar or bus is the **A-Bomb Dome (Genbaku Domu),** the skeletal ruins of the former Industrial Promotion Hall, left as a visual reminder of the death and destruction caused by the atomic bomb and now on the World Heritage List. Across the river is the park; it takes 10 minutes to walk from its northern end to the museum.

Along the way you'll see many of the park's 50-some statues and memorials. Most touching is the **Children's Peace Monument,** dedicated to the war's most innocent victims, not only those who died instantly in the blast but also those who died afterward from the effects of radiation. It's a statue of a girl with outstretched arms, and rising above her is a crane, a symbol of happiness and longevity in Japan. The statue is based on the true story of a young girl, Sadako, who suffered from the effects of radiation. She believed that if she could fold 1,000 paper cranes she would become well again. But even though she folded more than 1,000 cranes, she still died of leukemia. Today, all Japanese children are familiar with her story, and around the memorial are streamers of paper cranes donated by schoolchildren from all over Japan. To the east of the statue is a former kimono shop now serving as the **Rest House,** where you'll find a branch of the Hiroshima Tourist Office. To the west is a **Cenotaph for Korean Victims.** It's a little-publicized fact that some 20,000 Koreans were killed that fateful summer day, most of them brought to Japan as forced laborers. It's significant to note that for 29 years, the cenotaph remained outside the park. In 1999, Hiroshima's mayor, calling for an end to prejudice against Korean residents in Japan, gave the memorial a new home here.

Between the Children's Peace Monument and the museum is the **Cenotaph for the A-bomb Victims,** designed by Japan's famous architect Kenzo Tange (who also designed the Tokyo Metropolitan Government offices in Shinjuku; see p. 126). Shaped like a figurine clay saddle found in ancient tombs, it shelters a stone chest, which in turn holds the names of all of those killed by the bomb and its after effects (more than 308,725 names have been registered so far). An epitaph, written in Japanese, carries the hopeful phrase, "Let all the souls here rest in peace, for we shall not repeat the evil." If you stand in front of the cenotaph, you'll have a view through the hollow arch of the Flame of Peace and the A-Bomb Dome. It is said that the **Flame of Peace** will continue to burn until all atomic weapons vanish from the face of the earth and nuclear war is no longer a threat to humanity.

East of the Peace Flame is the **Hiroshima National Peace Memorial Hall for the Atomic Bomb Victims** (www.hiro-tsuitokinenkan.go.jp; © **082/543-6271**). Its Hall of Remembrance, a 360-degree panorama re-creating the bombed city as seen from the hypocenter, is made of 140,000 tiles, the number of people estimated to have died by the end of 1945. The rest of the memorial serves as a computerized audiovisual library with information on victims, their histories, and photos. Admission is free, and it's open the same hours as the Peace Memorial Museum.

Peace Memorial Museum (Heiwa Kinen Shiryokan) ★★★ At the south end of Peace Park, this museum is the main destination in the park. It comprises two structures, the East Building and the Main Building, which tell the story of Hiroshima before, during, and after the bomb was dropped. ***Note:*** The museum's massive renovation should be nearly complete by the time you read this. The East Building's restoration has been completed, but the Main Building is closed until March 2019.

The museum concentrates on the inhumanity of atomic bombs, the A-bomb's enormous destruction (92% of Hiroshima's buildings were destroyed or burned), and the indescribable suffering on that awful day. Exhibits show in graphic detail how Hiroshima looked before and after its destruction and the effects of the blast on bodies, buildings, and materials. There are photographs of scorched earth, charred remains of bodies, and people with open wounds, while displays explain the effects of radiation, including keloid scars, leukemia, and cancer. Many personal items have been donated by families of victims and survivors, including tattered clothing, diaries, and a wristwatch stopped at exactly 8:15, accompanied by short biographies of their owners, many of them children and teenagers and many who died in the blast. Survivor accounts describe not only what they suffered the day of the blast but in the many years that followed. Other displays describe the development of the atomic bomb and the danger of nuclear proliferation.

Needless to say, visiting Peace Memorial Park is a sobering and depressing experience but perhaps a necessary one. And to think that what was dropped on Hiroshima is small compared to the bombs of today; as early as 1961, the Soviet Union had tested a hydrogen bomb 3,300 times more powerful than the atomic bomb dropped on Hiroshima. Although audio guides are available for ¥200, you won't need one, as there is plenty to see and read; plan on spending 1½ hours here to do the museum justice.

1–2 Nakajima-cho. www.pcf.city.hiroshima.jp. ✆ **082/241-4004.** Admission ¥200 adults, ¥100 high-school students and seniors; free for children. Daily 8:30am–6pm Mar–Nov (until 7pm in Aug); daily 8:30am–5pm Dec–Feb. Streetcar: Fukuro-machi (3 min.). Hiroshima Meipuru-pu: Peace Memorial Park.

More Sights & Attractions

Hiroshima Castle ★★★ CASTLE Completed in 1591 but destroyed in the atomic blast, Hiroshima Castle was reconstructed in 1958. Its five-story wooden *donjon* is a faithful reproduction of the original, but the main reason to come here is the museum housed in the castle's modern interior. Devoted to Hiroshima's history as a flourishing castle town, it can be toured in about 30 minutes and has excellent English-language presentations. It also gives a good explanation on castles in Japan, including differences in architecture between those built on hills (for defense) and those built on plains (mainly administrative; Hiroshima's is an example of a flatland castle). Videos, with English translations via earphones, describe Hiroshima's founding and the construction of Hiroshima Castle to serve as a hub for transportation, while displays explain the differences in lifestyle between samurai and townspeople, the hierarchy of the feudal administration system, and other aspects of Edo life. There's also samurai gear, swords, models of old Hiroshima and the castle, as well as a kimono and helmet and breast plate you can try on for free. The top of the *donjon* provides a panoramic view of the city.

21–1 Moto-machi. www.rijo-castle.jp/rijo/main.html. ✆ **082/221-7512.** Admission ¥370 adults, ¥180 high-school students and seniors, free for children. Daily 9am–6pm (to 5pm Dec–Feb). A 15-min. walk north of Peace Memorial Park. Streetcar: Kamiya-cho-higashi (10 min.). Meipuru-pu: Hiroshima Castle.

Hiroshima Museum of Art (Hiroshima Bijutsukan) ★★ MUSEUM This gem of a private museum, housed in a modern one-story round building surrounded by trees, is located in a park in the heart of the city. Its permanent collection of some 300 paintings, half by French painters from Romanticism to Ecole de Paris, is presented in chronological order, with about 100 on display at any one time. It's small, with only four rooms, but virtually every piece is by a well-known artist, including Delacroix, Courbet, Manet, Monet, Renoir, Sisley, Degas, Rousseau, Cézanne, Gauguin, van Gogh, Matisse, Picasso, Braque, Utrillo, Chagall, and Modigliani. An annex is devoted to special exhibits by both Western and Japanese artists. Plan on an hour here.

3–2 Motomachi. www.hiroshima-museum.jp. ✆ **082/223-2530.** Admission ¥1,000 adults, ¥500 university and high-school students, ¥200 junior-high and elementary students. Higher prices during special exhibits. Tues–Sun 9am–5pm. Streetcar: Kamiya-cho-higashi (3 min.). Meipuru-pu: Hiroshima Museum of Art. In Chuo Park, across from the Rihga Royal Hotel (Hiroshima's tallest building).

Shukkei-en Garden ★ PARK/GARDEN Shukkei-en Garden, which means "landscape garden in miniature," was first laid out in 1620 by a master of the tea ceremony, with a pond constructed in imitation of famous Lake Xi Hu in Hangzhou, China. Using streams, ponds, islets, and bridges, the feudal lord's garden was designed to appear much larger than it actually is and is best viewed on a 30-minute circular stroll. Like everything else in Hiroshima, it was destroyed in 1945, but amazingly it looks like it's been here forever. Unfortunately, like most gardens in Japan, tall neighboring buildings detract from the garden's beauty, but there are vantage points for photos where you can't see any buildings and lots of places to sit and relax.

2–11 Kaminobori-cho. http://shukkeien.jp. ✆ **082/221-3620.** Admission ¥260 adults, ¥150 university and high-school students, ¥100 children. Daily 9am–6pm (to 5pm Oct–Mar). Streetcar: Shukkeien-mae (1 min.). Meipuru-pu: Hiroshima Prefectural Art Museum. A 15-min. walk from Hiroshima Station.

MIYAJIMA, SCENIC ISLAND IN THE SETO SEA ★★★

13km (8 miles) SW of Hiroshima

Easily reached in about 40 minutes from Hiroshima, **Miyajima** is a treasure of an island only 2km (1¼ miles) off the mainland in the Seto Inland Sea. No doubt you've seen pictures of its most famous landmark: a huge red *torii,* or shrine gate, rising out of the water. Erected in 1875 and made of camphor wood, it's one of the largest *torii* in Japan, measuring more than 16m (53 ft.) tall. It guards Miyajima's main attraction, Itsukushima Shrine, designated a World Heritage Site in 1996.

With the Japanese penchant for categorizing the "three best" of virtually everything in their country—the three best gardens, the three best waterfalls, and so on—it's no surprise that Miyajima is ranked as one of the three most scenic spots in Japan (the other two are Matsushima in Tohoku; and Amanohashidate, a remote sand spit, on the Japan Sea coast). Only 31 sq. km (12 sq. miles) in area and largely steep, wooded hills, it's an exceptionally beautiful island, part of the Seto-Naikai (Inland Sea) National Park, which is mostly water, islands, and islets. Of course, this distinction means it can be extremely crowded with visitors, particularly in summer and autumn.

Miyajima has been held sacred since ancient times. In the olden days, no one was allowed to do anything so human as to give birth or die on the island, so both the pregnant and the ill were quickly ferried across to the mainland. Even today there's no cemetery on Miyajima. Covered with cherry trees that illuminate the island with snowy petals in spring, and with maple trees that emblazon it in reds and golds in autumn, Miyajima is home to tame deer that roam freely on the island.

Although you can see Miyajima in a day's trip from Hiroshima, it's such a delightful island for strolls and hikes and such a beautiful respite from city life, you'll enjoy the island much more if you stay behind after the day-trippers have left. An added benefit of a longer stay: Itsukushima Shrine is illuminated at night, a gorgeous sight overnighters should not miss (although I'm horrified by night cruises offered around the *torii*). I've therefore included a few recommendations on where to stay. Avoid Golden Week and weekends in July, August, October, and November (when maple leaves are in full color), when accommodations are usually full. In fact, if you can, avoid coming on a weekend even if you don't spend the night.

Essentials

GETTING THERE The easiest way to reach Miyajima is from Hiroshima, via JR train, streetcar, or boat. The fastest and most reliable method is the **train,** which departs from Hiroshima Station approximately every 15 minutes or less and costs ¥410 (free for JR Rail Pass holders) for the 28-minute ride to Miyajimaguchi (if you're downtown or in Peace Memorial Park, you'll find it easier to catch the train at Nishi-Hiroshima Station). Otherwise, **streetcar no. 2** takes about an hour from Hiroshima Station through town to Hiroden Miyajimaguchi, the last stop, and costs ¥260. Both the train and streetcar deposit you at Miyajimaguchi, from which it's just a 3-minute walk to the **ferry** bound for Miyajima. There are two ferry companies (JR and Matsudai) offering the 10-minute ride to Miyajima for ¥180, but if you have a **Japan Rail Pass** you can ride on the JR ferry for free.

Alternatively, boats travel from downtown Hiroshima directly to Miyajima in about 45 minutes. Operated by **Aqua Net Hiroshima** (www.aqua-net-h.co.jp; ✆ **082/240-5955**), boats depart from Motoyasu-bashi bridge, south of the A-Bomb Dome, 10 to 15 times daily depending on the season. Fare is ¥2,000 one-way; children pay half fare. Note that service is suspended during inclement weather and when the tide is low.

VISITOR INFORMATION On Miyajima island, stop off at the **Tourist Information Office** (www.miyajima.or.jp; ✆ **0829/44-2011;** daily 9am–6pm), in the Miyajima ferry terminal. It has an English-language brochure and a map. For more info, go to **www.visit-miyajima-japan.com**.

GETTING AROUND You can **walk** to all the sights, accommodations, and restaurants listed below. Omotesando Dori, the main street leading to the shrine, is lined with shops and restaurants. If you wish to visit the island's beaches, **shuttle buses** travel to the beaches year-round about once an hour for ¥300. Ask the Tourist Information Office for a schedule.

Where to Stay

EXPENSIVE

Kurayado Iroha ★★★ Located on the main Omotesando Dori pedestrian shopping street, this is modern Japanese elegance at its finest, with service so flawless you feel like staff has been waiting just for you. Before arrival you'll be asked your food preferences and allergies, and with good reason: Dinners (served in a dining room) are a feast of organic vegetables, seafood from the Seto Inland, and other local dishes; the meal typically lasts 2 hours and is a highlight of staying here. Several types of rooms, all nonsmoking, are available, with the cheapest on the second floor offering only inner courtyard or Omotesando Dori views (if you wish, you can stay in one of these *tatami* rooms for ¥21,000 for one person or ¥37,800 for two by opting only for breakfast). The other rooms have beds and face inland or toward the sea (seaside is more expensive), but the best is a combination room with both beds and *tatami* with sweeping views of the sea, including Ikutushima Shrine's torii. In any case, don't miss the top-floor indoor/outdoor baths.

589–4 Miyajima-cho. www.visit-miyajima.jp. © **0829/44-0168.** 18 units. ¥36,720–¥42,120 per person. Rates include 2 meals. A 5-min. walk from the ferry pier. **Amenities:** Restaurant (hotel guests only); Wi-Fi.

MODERATE

Momiji-so ★★ This small, Japanese-style inn, in business for 100 years, has a great location in Momijidani Park, about halfway to the ropeway to Mount Misen. *Tatami* rooms vary in size, though all have artwork, flowers, and views of the surrounding park; the best looks out over a koi pond. A plus is the outdoor **Japanese restaurant** serving noodles, barbecued conger eel on rice, and other dishes—weather permitting, you'll dine outside. Not much English is spoken, but they're used to foreigners and are very kind. No credit cards are accepted, and Wi-Fi is available only in the lobby.

Momijidani-koennai. www.gambo-ad.com. © **0829/44-0077.** 5 units. ¥9,180 per person without meals (not available peak season); ¥18,360–¥19,440 per person with 2 meals. A 25-min. walk from the ferry pier in Momijidani Park. Pickup service available.

Ryoso Kawaguchi (旅荘かわぐち) ★★★ This 300-year-old home, with whitewashed walls, wood floors, exposed beams, and nice touches like flower-filled bamboo containers, has a traditional atmosphere. *Tatami* accommodations include two airy rooms with lofts for sleeping and a two-room suite good for families. The dining room overlooks a garden courtyard, while the third-floor lounge has a view of the nearby five-story pagoda. The ninth-generation innkeepers speak English and are gracious and welcoming. No credit cards are accepted.

469 Miyajima-cho. http://ryoso-kawaguchi.jp. © **0829/44-0018.** 7 units (all with toilet, none with bathroom). ¥7,560 single; ¥14,040–¥15,120 double. Breakfast ¥1,080 extra; dinner ¥5,400 extra. A 10-min. walk from the ferry pier, on Machiya Dori. **Amenities:** Wi-Fi.

INEXPENSIVE

Miyajima Morinoyado (みやじま杜の宿) ★★ You're forgiven if you pass this place by, thinking it must be an exclusive *ryokan.* Indeed, if it weren't a municipally owned People's Lodge (Kokumin Shukusha), rates here could easily be three times as much as they are. Though modern, it has a lovely Japanese design with a lobby overlooking a carp pond. On the other hand, the many school groups and families staying here leave no doubt that it's a public lodge, and it's quite a hike from the ferry pier, on the edge of town beside Omoto Park. Both *tatami* rooms and Western-style twins—simple but spacious and spotless—are available, some with views of the bay. The public baths look onto rock gardens. Reservations should be made 11 months in advance, but sometimes there are cancellations; when I once dropped by on a weekday in June, rooms were available. Meals are served in the restaurant.

Miyajima-cho. www.morinoyado.jp. © **0829/44-0430.** 30 units (26 with bathroom, 4 with toilet only). ¥9,000–¥10,000 double room without meals; ¥12,240–¥15,220 per person with 2 meals. A 25-min. walk from the ferry pier, across from the aquarium and just before the tunnel (follow signs to OMOTO PARK).

Nakaya Bed & Breakfast ★★★ Hiroshima transplant Rie Nakaya, who speaks fluent English, lives in the front house and offers three rooms in another house out back: a Japanese-style two-room suite for three people or more, with a carved transom, a view of the pagoda over rooftops, and a toilet; a room with twin beds for one or two people; and two connecting rooms with four single beds. Only breakfast is available, but Nakaya-san is happy to provide recommendations for dinner. No credit cards.

511 Miyajima-cho. www.nakaya-bandb.com. ✆ **0829/44-0725.** 3 units (1 with toilet, none with bathroom). ¥6,000 single; ¥11,000–¥13,000 double. Breakfast ¥500 extra. A 7-min. walk from ferry pier, on Machiya Dori (a block inland from Omotesando Dori). **Amenities:** Wi-Fi.

Where to Eat

Grilled conger eel and fresh oysters (in season Nov–Mar) are two of Miyajima's specialties; it even celebrates an oyster festival in early February. Stalls along Omotesando Dori, the main street, sell oysters on the half shell. Note that the village is small, and I've included no addresses in this section (and sightseeing)—the address would only be meaningful to the postman.

Kakiya (牡蠣屋) ★★ OYSTERS Located on Miyajima's main street, this open-fronted and very narrow shop with the motto "We're so shuckin' good," is one of several selling humongous oysters cooked over a grill, along with products you might want to take home, like oyster pesto or truffle and oyster shavings. An English-language menu offers oysters prepared a half-dozen ways, including raw when in season, barbecued in the shell, and breaded and fried. It even offers wine, beer, shochu, and sake to wash it all down. How civilized! Alas, no credit cards are accepted.

www.kaki-ya.jp/. ✆ **0829/44-2747.** Oyster dishes ¥1,200–¥1,620; set meals ¥2,150–¥2,690. Mon–Fri 10am–3pm; Sat–Sun 10am–4pm. Stays open later in autumn. On Omotesando Dori, about a 6-min. walk from the ferry pier.

Miyajima Brewery ★★ OYSTERS/WESTERN & JAPANESE Offering its own brews as well as craft beers from other breweries, this third-floor eatery above a Starbucks (I know) offers excellent views of the sea with ferries coming and going. Like many restaurants in town, it specializes in oysters but also offers conger eel, a couple of salads, pasta, rice dishes, and daily specials for lunch (served until 5:30pm), with a more limited menu on weekdays and for dinner. No credit cards accepted.

https://miyajima-brewery.com. ✆ **0829/40-2607.** Main dishes ¥950–¥3,900; set lunches ¥1,800–¥3,000. Fri–Wed 11am–8pm (last order). At the end of Omotesando Dori after walking about 8 min. from the ferry pier.

Shibaisaryo Mizuha (芝居茶寮 水羽) ★ VARIED JAPANESE Occupying an old rice granary, this bustling restaurant offers set meals of local specialties like conger eel and oysters, as well as more ordinary choices like tempura and *kamameshi* (rice casserole with toppings) from an English-language menu, with a choice of table and *tatami* seating.

www.mizuhaso.com/. ✆ **0829/44-1570.** Set meals ¥1,480–¥2,400. Daily 10am–5pm. A 10-min. walk from the ferry pier, behind Itsukushima Shrine and near the five-story pagoda.

Exploring Miyajima Island

SEEING THE SIGHTS

Miyajima's major attraction, **Itsukushima Shrine★★★** (www.en.itsukushima jinja.jp/index.html; ✆ **0829/44-2020**), is a 10-minute walk from the ferry pier (turn right from the terminal), reached by walking along the seawall or via a long, narrow pedestrian shopping street called Omotesando Dori. Founded in 593 to honor three female deities, the wooden shrine is built over the water so that, when the tide is in, it appears as though the shrine is floating. A brilliant vermilion, it contrasts starkly with the wooded hills in the background and the blue sky above, casting its reflection in the waters below. If you do happen to see Itsukushima Shrine when the tide is in and it's seemingly floating on water, you should consider yourself very lucky indeed—most of the time the lovely shrine floats above a surface that's only a little more glamorous than mud. That's when imagination comes in handy (the Hiroshima tourist offices may have a tide calendar).

The majority of the shrine buildings are thought to date from the 16th century, preserving the original Shinden style of 12th-century architecture, but they have been repaired repeatedly through the centuries. Most are closed, but from 6:30am to sunset daily (usually 6pm in summer, 5 or 5:30pm in winter), you can walk along the 230m (770-ft.) covered **dock,** which threads its way past the outer part of the main shrine and one of the oldest *Noh* stages in Japan. From the shrine, you'll have a good view of the red *torii* standing in the water. Admission to the shrine is ¥300 adults, ¥200 high-school students, ¥100 children.

Another sight very worth exploring is **Daisho-in Temple ★★**, on the slope of Mount Misen (✆ **0829/44-0111;** daily 8am–5pm). One of the most famous Shingon Buddhist temples in western Japan, it has numerous worthwhile sights spread on its leafy grounds, including a mandala made of colored sand that was created by Tibetan priests; a main hall where worshipers pray for health and contentment; and a hall dedicated to Kobo Daishi, founder of the Shingon sect (his remains are interred on Mount Koya). In Henshokutsu Cave are Buddhist icons and sand gathered from all 88 pilgrimage temples on Shikoku; making a round here is considered as auspicious as visiting the temples themselves. Other halls contain deities thought to bring good health and to save humans from earthly sexual desires. Every April 15 and November 15 worshipers walk over hot coals in fire-walking festivals here; in March there's a ceremony to give thanks to retired old kitchen knives. An excellent brochure at the entrance describes the various sights, free to the public. From Daisho-in, a path leads to Mount Misen, which you can hike in about 90 minutes.

ENJOYING MIYAJIMA'S NATURAL WORLD

The other popular thing to do on Miyajima is to visit its highest peak, 535m (1,755-ft.) **Mount Misen ★★**, which seems light years away from the crowds down below. Signs direct you to Momijidani Park, a pleasant hillside park covered with maple trees (spectacular in autumn) and cherry trees (heavenly in spring) and marked by a picturesque stream. A 10-minute walk or free shuttle bus through the park brings you to the **Miyajima Ropeway** (www.miyajima-ropeway.info; ✆ **0829/44-0316**) to Mount Misen; round-trip tickets cost ¥1,800 for adults (half-fare for children). However, you might wish to buy only a one-way ticket for ¥1,000 and enjoy more scenery by walking back down; it takes about 60 to 90 minutes, down one of three different pathways. In any case, the actual summit of Mount Misen, a 30-minute walk from the cable car terminus over a strenuous up-and-down pathway, offers splendid 360-degree views of the Seto-Naikai (Inland Sea) National Park. Mount Misen is best known for Kobo Daishi's visit in 806, when he spent a 100-day retreat here and is said to have lit the Eternal Fire (located in the Kiezu-no Reikado Hall), which has reputedly been burning for more than 1,200 years and was used to light the Peace Flame in Hiroshima's Peace Memorial Park; in recent years, the Eternal Fire has come to symbolize the eternal fire of love, making it popular also with couples. Plan on at least 2 hours round-trip for the ropeway and hike to the summit, noting the last ropeway departure from Mount Misen (5 or 5:30pm most of the year). If you're hiking back down, plan on a total of 3 to 4 hours.

Miyajima is also known for its beaches. If you're looking to swim, there are two beaches west of the town and shrine: **Suginoura** and **Tsutsumigaura Natural Park** (you can also camp here; rental tents and cabins are available; https://tsutsumigaura.com/en/index.html). Ask the tourist office for a schedule of shuttle buses that will bring you to the beaches.

PLANNING YOUR TRIP TO JAPAN

12

Many first-time visitors have two main worries about a trip to Japan: the language barrier and the high cost of living. To help alleviate fears about the first, I've provided the Japanese characters for establishments listed in this book that don't have English-language signs to help you recognize their names; given brief instructions on how to reach the places I recommend; made suggestions for ordering in restaurants without English-language menus; and given prices for everything from train rides to museums.

As for costs, probably everyone has heard horror stories about Japan's high prices. In various surveys of the most expensive cities around the world, Tokyo is always among the top 10, while Osaka and other major Japanese cities have also had their spot in the top 10. But after Japan's economic bubble burst in the early 1990s, something happened that would have been unthinkable during the heady spending days of the 1980s: Japanese became bargain-conscious, ushering in a new era of inexpensive French bistros, secondhand clothing stores, 100-yen shops, and budget hotels.

The secret to seeing Japan on the cheap—or at least, to see it without breaking the bank—is to live and eat as Japanese do. This book will help you do exactly that, with tips on how to save money on everything from transportation to sightseeing, plus descriptions of affordable eateries and Japanese-style inns. While you may never find Japan as inexpensive as many other Asian countries, you will find it richly rewarding for all the reasons you chose Japan as a destination in the first place.

Another major complaint of foreign visitors to Japan is lack of convenient Wi-Fi. It is, however, getting better, and I expect Wi-Fi accessibility to only improve in light of the 2020 Olympics in Tokyo. In addition, Japan has a different phone system than the rest of the world, which makes using your own mobile phone challenging. Luckily, improvements in these areas for overseas visitors are progressing, outlined below under "Fast Facts."

Furthermore, Japan remains one of the safest countries in the world; in general, you don't have to worry about muggers, pickpockets, or crooks. In fact, I sometimes feel downright coddled in Japan. Everything runs like clockwork: Trains are on time, and the service—whether in hotels, restaurants, or department stores—ranks among the best in the world. I know if I get truly lost, someone will help me and will probably even go out of his or her way to do so. Japanese are honest and extremely helpful toward foreign visitors. Indeed, it's the people themselves who make traveling in Japan such a delight.

GETTING THERE

By Plane

Japan has four international airports. Outside Tokyo is **Narita International Airport** (**NRT;** www.narita-airport.jp; ✆ **0476/34-8000**), where you'll want to land if your main interest is in the capital or surrounding region. Much closer to central Tokyo is **Haneda Airport** (**HND;** www.haneda-airport.jp/inter/en/; ✆ **03/5757-8111**), which has long served as Tokyo's domestic airport but began accepting international flights in 2010, mostly from Asia. International long-distance flights land mostly at Narita.

Outside Osaka, **Kansai International Airport** (**KIX;** www.kansai-airport.or.jp; ✆ **072/455-2500**) is convenient if your destination is Osaka, Kyoto, or cities farther west. In between Narita and Kansai airports, outside Nagoya, is the **Central Japan International Airport** (**NGO;** www.centrair.jp/en; ✆ **0569/38-1195**), nicknamed Centrair, which serves international flights mostly from Asia.

GETTING AROUND

Japan has an extensive transport system, the most convenient segment of which is the nation's excellent **rail service. Buses** are useful for reaching places that trains don't go, like Shirakawa-go in the Japan Alps. The long-distance buses connecting major cities in western Honshu are cheaper alternatives than train.

By Train

The most efficient way to travel around most of Japan is by train. Whether you're being whisked through the countryside aboard the famous Shinkansen bullet train or winding your way up a wooded mountainside in an electric tram, trains in Japan are punctual, comfortable, safe, and clean. And because train stations are usually located in the heart of the city next to the main bus terminal or a subway station, arriving in a city by train is usually the most convenient transport. Major train stations also have tourist offices, where you can pick up brochures and maps in English and often even make reservations for local hotels free of charge. Most of Japan's passenger trains are run by the **Japan Railways (JR) Group,** made up of six regional passenger operators like JR East and JR West (plus a freight company) that together cover 20,000km (12,400 miles) and operate about 20,000 departures daily, including those of the Shinkansen. There are also private regional companies, like **Kintetsu (Kinki Nippon Railway),** operating around Osaka and Kyoto, and **Odakyu Electric Railway,** operating from Tokyo to Hakone.

SHINKANSEN (BULLET TRAIN) The Shinkansen is probably Japan's best-known train. With a front car that resembles a space rocket, the Shinkansen hurtles along at a maximum speed of 320kmph (199 mph) through the countryside on its own special tracks. Most have seat-side electric plug-ins. I've even seen *washlet* (bidet-style) toilets onboard.

> **Travel Tip**
>
> To help you reach the hotels, restaurants, and sights recommended in this book, I've included the nearest train or subway station or bus or streetcar stop, followed in parentheses by the approximate number of minutes it takes to walk from the station or bus stop to your destination.

In western Honshu, the most widely used Shinkansen routes are the Tokaido and the Sanyo lines. The Tokaido Shinkansen runs from Tokyo and Shinagawa stations west to Nagoya, Kyoto, Osaka (some go as far as Okayama), while the Sanyo continues westward from Osaka to Himeji, Kurashiki, Hiroshima, and other cities before reaching its final destination on the island of Kyushu. Each stop is announced in English through a loudspeaker and on a digital signboard in each car. Several types of Shinkansen travel along this route. The *Nozomi* Shinkansen is the fastest and most frequent train and is the only one that covers the entire 1,179km (730 miles) between Tokyo and Hakata in Kyushu; the *Mizuho* Shinkansen travels from Osaka farther into Kyushu. Frustratingly, neither the *Nozomi* nor the *Mizuho* are covered by the Japan Rail Pass (see "Japan Rail Pass," below). Instead, holders of the Japan Rail Pass must take the Tokaido line's *Hikari Shinkansen,* which makes more stops than the *Nozomi,* or the *Kodama,* which stops at every station (if your destination is a smaller city on the Shinkansen line, make sure your train stops there). Rail-pass holders wishing to travel between Tokyo and Hiroshima must take the *Hikari* or *Kodama* and transfer in Osaka, Kobe, or Okayama to the Sakura Shinkansen on the Sanyo Line. On the other hand, if you're buying individual tickets, the price is not much different whether you're traveling by *Nozomi* or a slower Shinkansen. In March 2015, the *Hokuriku* Shinkansen began service between Tokyo and Kanazawa.

REGULAR SERVICE In addition to bullet trains, there are two other types of long-distance trains that operate on regular tracks. The **limited-express trains,** or LEX *(Tokkyu),* branch off the Shinkansen system and are the fastest after the bullet trains, often traveling scenic routes; while the **express trains** *(Kyuko)* are slightly slower and make more stops. Slower still are **rapid express trains** *(Shin-Kaisoku)* and the even slower **rapid trains** *(Kaisoku).* To serve the everyday needs of Japan's commuting population, **local trains** *(Futsu)* stop at all stations.

INFORMATION For more on routes, transfers, fares, and timetables for trains and planes in Japan, there's the very useful www.hyperdia.com.

In Japan, information on JR trains, fares, schedules, and routes is also available at **Travel Service Centers** at major stations. In Tokyo, the best place for personal consulting on routes and sightseeing is at the JR East Travel Service Center in Tokyo Station (p. 58), where you can also ask for the invaluable

Japan Railway Time Table, published in English and providing train schedules for the Shinkansen and limited express JR lines throughout Japan. **Tourist Information Centers** in downtown Tokyo or at the international airports in Narita or Osaka also carry the timetable.

TRAIN FARES & RESERVATIONS Ticket prices are based on the type of train (Shinkansen bullet trains are the most expensive), the distance traveled, whether your seat is reserved, and the season, with slightly higher prices (usually a ¥200 surcharge) during peak seasons (Golden Week, July 21–Aug 31, Dec 25–Jan 10, and spring break from Mar 21–Apr 5) and a ¥200 discount during low season. Children (ages 6–11) pay half-fare, while up to two children 5 and younger travel free if they do not require a separate seat. I've included train prices from Tokyo for many destinations covered in this book (see individual cities for more information). Unless stated otherwise, prices in this guide are for adults for **nonreserved seats** on the fastest train available during regular season. Note, however, that you can save money by purchasing a round-trip ticket for long distances. A round-trip ticket by train on distances exceeding 601km (373 miles) one-way costs 10% less than two one-way tickets. No matter which train you ride, be sure to hang onto your ticket—you'll be required to give it up at the end of your trip as you exit through the gate.

You can reserve seats for the Shinkansen, as well as for limited-express and express trains (but not for slower rapid or local trains, which are on a first-come, first-served basis) at any major JR station in Japan. If you're traveling to Kanazawa on the Hokuriku Shinkansen or north of Tokyo—that is, not on the Tokaido/Sanyo route—you can also reserve online (www.eki-net.com/pc/jreast-shinkansen-reservation/English/wb/common/Menu/Menu.aspx). Reserved seats cost slightly more than unreserved seats (¥320–¥520 for the Shinkansen and express trains). It's a good idea to reserve your seats for your entire trip through Japan as soon as you know your itinerary if you'll be traveling during peak times; however, you can only reserve 1 month in advance. If it's not peak season, you'll probably be okay using a more flexible approach to traveling—all JR trains also have nonreserved cars that fill up on a first-come, first-seated basis. You can also reserve seats on the day of travel up to departure time. I rarely purchase a reserved-seat ticket when it's not peak season, preferring the flexibility of being able to hop on the next available train (sometimes I reserve a seat just before boarding). Nonreserved seats *(jiyuuseki)* are located in cars at the front or back of Shinkansen trains. To determine where you should stand to board the train, look for the platform display showing a diagram of the train cars and which ones are reserved and nonreserved. Then look for signs—either on digital boards overhead or written on the platform itself—that shows the location for each car.

In addition to purchasing Shinkansen tickets with seat reservations at JR stations, since 2017 you can also do so for bullet trains along the Tokaido/Sanyo routes by using the **Tokaido Sanyo Shinkansen Reservation App** (https://smart-ex.jp/en/) and registering a credit card. Tickets can be purchased up to 1 month in advance and can be changed up to 4 minutes before departure. You'll then use your credit card at the Shinkansen station by inserting it into a special ticket machine marked with "EX." Note, however, that you cannot use this app to make seat reservations if you're using a Japan Rail Pass.

SAVING MONEY WITH A RAIL PASS The Japan Rail Pass is without a doubt the most convenient way to travel around Japan. With the rail pass, you don't have to worry about buying individual tickets, you have unlimited travel on all JR trains throughout Japan including the Shinkansen (except regrettably, the *Mizuho* and *Nozomi*), and you can reserve your seats on all JR trains for free.

Several types of rail passes are available; make your decision based on your length of stay in Japan and the cities you intend to visit. You might even find it best to combine several passes to cover your travels in Japan, such as a 1-week Japan Rail Pass to journey around Honshu, plus a regional pass just for Kansai (see below). Information on the Japan Rail Pass is available at **www.japanrailpass.net**, which also provides links to the websites of all six JR companies with details on regional passes.

A Japan Rail Pass is available for ordinary coach class and for the first-class Green Car for travel lasting 7, 14, or 21 consecutive days. Rates for coach class are ¥29,110 for 7 days, ¥46,390 for 14 days, and ¥59,350 for 21 days. Rates for the Green Car are ¥38,880, ¥62,950, and ¥81,870 respectively. Children (ages 6–11) pay half-fare. Personally, I have never traveled in the first-class Green Car in Japan and don't consider it necessary, especially since there are no green cars on most *Hikari* and *Kodama* bullet trains between Osaka and Hiroshima.

The main thing to remember is that the Japan Rail Pass is available only to foreigners visiting Japan as tourists and in most cases *can be purchased only outside Japan* (see note below). It's available from most travel agents, including **Kintetsu International** (www.kintetsu.com/japan-rail-pass.php) and **JTB USA**

Advantages of a Japan Rail Pass

You can save quite a bit by purchasing a rail pass, even if you only plan to travel a little. How economical is a Japan Rail Pass? If you were to buy a round-trip reserved-seat ticket on the Hikari Shinkansen from Tokyo to Kyoto in regular season, it would cost approximately ¥24,480, which is not much less than a week's ordinary rail pass. Thus, if you plan to see more than just Tokyo and Kyoto, such as adding on Hiroshima or Kurashiki, it pays to use a rail pass, ***which you must buy outside Japan*** (some regional rail passes, however, described below, can be purchased in Japan if you're a tourist).

With a Japan Rail Pass, you can make seat reservations for free, which otherwise costs up to ¥520 per ride on the Shinkansen. Another advantage to a rail pass is that it offers a 10% discount or more off certain room rates at more than 50 JR Hotel Group hotels, including the Hotel Granvia in Kyoto, Okayama, and Hiroshima and the Nara Hotel. A Japan Rail Pass booklet, which comes with your purchase of a rail pass, lists member hotels (or go to www.japanrailpass.net/en/hotel.html). Note, however, that discounts are available only by booking directly with the hotel, at which time you should confirm which room type and the rate (this may require a telephone call; discounts may not be available during peak seasons). Note, too, that regional rail passes, however, do not qualify for the hotel discount.

(www.jtbusa.com). A full list of authorized travel agents, plus their addresses and contact information, is available at www.japanrailpass.net. ***Note:*** Since 2017 a pilot program allowing purchase of the Japan Rail Pass inside Japan has been extended to March 31, 2019. In any case, this pass is more expensive than the rates given above. See www.japanrailpass.net for updated information.

Upon purchasing your pass, you'll be issued a voucher (called an **Exchange Order**), which you'll then exchange for the real pass after your arrival in Japan. Note that once you purchase your Exchange Order, you have 3 months until you must exchange it for the pass itself in Japan. When obtaining your actual pass in Japan, you must then specify the date you wish to start using the pass within a 1-month period.

In Japan, you can exchange your voucher for a Japan Rail Pass at more than 40 JR stations that have Japan Rail Pass exchange offices, at which time you must present your passport and specify the date you wish to begin using the pass. You'll find exchange offices at both Narita Airport (daily 6:30am–9:45pm) and Kansai International Airport (daily 5:30am–11pm). Other exchange offices, all located in JR train stations, include those at Tokyo, Ueno, Shinjuku, Ikebukuro, Shibuya, and Shinagawa stations in Tokyo; Kyoto Station; Shin-Osaka and Osaka stations; and Nara, Kanazawa, and Hiroshima stations. Stations and their open hours are listed in a pamphlet you'll receive with your voucher, as well as at www.japanrailpass.net.

REGIONAL PASSES FOR FOREIGN VISITORS In addition to the standard Japan Rail Pass above, regional JR rail passes for ordinary coach class are available (and convenient) for travel in western Honshu, among other places. These can be purchased before arriving in Japan from the same vendors that sell the standard pass but can also be reserved online or purchased inside Japan, usually only within the area covered by the pass but also at Narita airport for some passes. These regional passes are available only to foreign visitors—you'll need to present your passport to verify your status as a "temporary visitor"; you may also be asked to show your plane ticket. Only one pass per region per visit to Japan is allowed. Children 6 to 11 years of age pay half-price for all passes; up to two children 5 years old and younger can travel free with a paying adult.

In the Tokyo area, the **JR Tokyo Wide Pass** (www.jreast.co.jp/e/tokyowidepass/index.html) is a 3-day pass for ¥10,000 that allows unlimited travel on JR trains, including Shinkansen bullet trains traveling north from Tokyo as far away as Utsunomiya (useful for trips to Nikko), Karuizawa, GALA Yuzawa (a ski resort), Mount Fuji, Izu Peninsula, Narita (including the airport), and other areas. As for non-JR passes, the **Hakone Free Pass,** offered by Odakyu railways (www.odakyu.jp/english), includes round-trip transportation from Tokyo and unlimited travel in Hakone for a specific number of days (p. 172).

If you're arriving by plane at the Kansai Airport outside Osaka and intend to remain in western Honshu, consider buying one of several different **JR-West Passes** (www.westjr.co.jp/global/en/ticket/pass/), available at Kansai Airport, Osaka JR station, Kyoto Station, and other locations, but you'll get a slight discount if purchased online in advance. The **Kansai Area Pass,** which can be used for travel between Osaka, Kyoto, Kobe, Nara, Himeji, and other destinations in the Kansai area, is available as a 1-day pass for ¥2,300, 2-day pass for ¥4,500, 3-day pass for ¥5,500, or 4-day pass for ¥6,500. Travel is restricted to JR rapid and local trains, as well as unreserved seating in the Kansai Airport Express Haruka operating between Kansai Airport, Shin-Osaka, and Kyoto (that is, Shinkansen are not included in the pass). Similar but covering a wider area, including all Shinkansen traveling between Shin-Osaka Station and Kurashiki stations (including *Nozomi* and *Mizuho*), is the **Kansai Wide Area Pass,** which costs ¥9,500 (¥9,000 online) for 5 consecutive days. The 7-day **Sanyo-San'in Area Pass** covers a larger area still, including the Shinkansen from Shin-Osaka through Hiroshima all the way to Hakata (in the city of Fukuoka on Kyushu) and to Matsue for ¥20,000, while the 7-day Kansai-Hokuriku Area Pass includes the Kansai area, Okayama, and Kanazawa for ¥16,000.

Two other non-JR passes are available for Kansai. The **Kansai Thru Pass** (www.surutto.com) is valid on city subways, private railways (*not* JR trains), and buses throughout the Kansai area, including Kansai Airport, Osaka, Kyoto, Nara, Kobe, Himeji, and Mount Koya, and provides slight discounts to hundreds of tourist facilities (usually ¥100 or 10%). Available only to tourists, it costs ¥4,000 for a 2-day pass and ¥5,200 for 3 days and can be used on non-consecutive days; it's sold at Kansai International Airport, Tourist Information Centers in Osaka and Nara, and the Kyoto Station Bus Information Center, among others, or can be purchased online.

By Bus

Buses often go where trains don't and thus may be the only way for you to get to the more remote areas of Japan, such as Shirakawa-go in the Japan Alps. They are also low-cost alternatives to trains for long-distance travel.

Some intercity buses require that you make reservations or purchase your ticket in advance at the ticket counter at the bus terminal. For others (especially local buses), when you board a bus you'll generally find a ticket machine by the entry door. Take a ticket, which is number-coded with a digital board displayed at the front of the bus. The board shows the various fares, which increase with the distance traveled. You pay when you get off.

In addition to serving the remote areas of the country, **long-distance buses** (called *chokyori basu*) operate between all major cities in Japan and offer the cheapest mode of transportation. Private companies run the majority of buses, but some do not have English-language websites. Those that do are listed on the **Nihon Bus Association** website (www.bus.or.jp), with links to companies around Japan. For routes and reservations, you should also check **www.kousokubus.net/JpnBus/en**. Otherwise, one of the largest national fleets is operated cooperatively by each of the six members of the **JR Group.** JR East (www.jrbuskanto.co.jp), for example, operates highway buses departing mostly from Tokyo Station and the Shinjuku Expressway Bus Terminal to Kanazawa, Kyoto, Osaka, and areas north of the city.

Probably the company with the best English website is **Willer Express** (http://willerexpress.com), which offers service from Tokyo, Kanazawa, Kyoto, Osaka, Nara, Kobe, Himeji, Okayama, Hiroshima, and other cities, but it also sells tickets from other bus companies. Some buses travel during the night and offer reclining seats and toilets, thus saving passengers the price of a night's lodging; double-decker buses may even have salons or bars on the first floor. Some buses are just for women, and many have a variety of seats to choose from. Long-distance buses running between Tokyo and Kyoto cost ¥3,900 to ¥9,800, depending on the seat selected (reclining seats cost more), time of day (weekdays are generally cheaper), and season. Willer Express also offers a bus pass for foreign tourists good for any 3 days of travel for ¥12,500 or 5 days for ¥15,000 within a 2-month period (passes for traveling only Monday through Thursday are cheaper).

By Car

Driving is not recommended for visitors wishing to tour Japan. Driving is British style (on the left side of the road), often a challenge for those not used to it; traffic can be horrendous; and it isn't even economical to drive. Not only is gas expensive (about ¥140 per liter/¼ gallon at press time), but all of Japan's expressways charge high tolls—the one-way toll from Tokyo to Kyoto is almost the same price as a ticket to Kyoto on the Shinkansen. And whereas the Shinkansen takes only 3 hours to get to Kyoto, driving can take about 8 hours. Driving in cities is even worse: Streets are often hardly wide enough for a rickshaw, let alone a car, and many roads don't have sidewalks so you have to dodge people, bicycles, and telephone poles. Free parking is hard to find, and garages are expensive. Except in remote areas, it just doesn't make sense to drive.

If you're undeterred, major car-rental companies in Japan include **Toyota Rent-A-Car** (https://rent.toyota.co.jp; ✆ **0800/7000-815** toll-free); **Nippon Rent-A-Car Service** (www.nipponrentacar.co.jp; ✆ **03/6859-6234** for the English Service Desk), **Nissan Rent-A-Car** (https://nissan-rentacar.com; ✆ **0120/00-4123** toll-free), and **Orix** (http://car.orix.co.jp). You'll need either an **international** or a **Japanese driving license.** Signs on all major highways are written in both Japanese and English, though some rental companies offer GPS with English voice guidance as well. It is against the law to drink alcohol and drive, all passengers must wear seat belts, and it's prohibited to use a mobile phone while driving. Although anyone 18 and older can drive in Japan, some rental companies may require a driver to have held a driving license at least 3 years.

BREAKDOWNS & ASSISTANCE The **Japan Automobile Federation (JAF;** www.jaf.or.jp) is one of several road service providers maintaining emergency telephone boxes along Japan's major arteries to assist drivers whose cars have broken down or who need help. Calls from these telephones are free and will connect you to JAF's operation center. English is spoken. The website also provides useful information on driving in Japan.

[FastFACTS] JAPAN

Area Codes The country code for Japan is 81. All telephone area codes for Japanese cities begin with a zero (03 for Tokyo, 06 for Osaka, 075 for Kyoto), but drop the first zero if calling Japan from abroad. If you're calling a Japanese cellphone from overseas, which generally starts with **090** or **080,** drop the first zero and just dial **90** or **80** after the country code.

ATMs The best way to get cash is from an ATM (automated teller machine). Because most bank ATMs in Japan accept only cards issued by Japanese banks, your best bet for obtaining cash is the ubiquitous **7-Eleven** convenience store (www.sevenbank.co.jp/english/), most of which are open 24 hours and have ATMs that accept foreign bank cards. Note, however, that not all cards, even those issued through Visa or MasterCard, are accepted. I suggest traveling with at least two cards from different issuers.

You'll also find 26,000-some ATMS operated by the **Japan Post Bank** (www.jp-bank.japanpost.jp/en/ias/en_ias_index.html), most of them located in **post offices** all over Japan and with instructions in English. Although major post offices, usually located near central train stations, have long open hours for ATMs (generally 7am–11pm weekdays and 9am–7 or 9pm on weekends, though some are open almost 24 hours a day), small post offices may have limited hours for ATMs (closing around 6 or 7pm weekdays and 5pm weekends, for example). Increasingly, you'll also find Japan Post Bank and 7-Eleven ATMs outside these businesses, including department stores, train stations and shopping malls.

Banks Banks are generally open Monday through Friday 9am to 3pm, though business hours for exchanging foreign currency usually don't begin until 10:30 or 11am (be prepared for a long wait; you'll be asked to sit down as your order is processed). All banks in Japan displaying an AUTHORIZED FOREIGN EXCHANGE sign can exchange currency and traveler's checks, with exchange rates usually displayed at the appropriate foreign-exchange counter. More convenient—and quicker—are **Travelex** (www.travelex.co.jp) foreign-exchange kiosks, with locations in many airports and cities, including Tokyo, Kyoto, Kanazawa, and Osaka.

Other places to exchange money include your hotel and **department stores,** which are often open until 7:30 or 8pm. Note, however, that hotels and department stores may charge a handling fee, offer a slightly less favorable exchange rate, and require a passport for all transactions. In a welcome development, I've noticed some hotels and department stores with money-changing machines, like Isetan at Kyoto Station, though these are still rare.

Business Hours Banks are open Monday through Friday 9am to 3pm. Neighborhood post offices are open Monday through Friday 9am to 5pm, though a large city's central post office (usually located near major train stations) has longer hours and may be open weekends as well. Keep in mind that museums, gardens, and attractions stop selling admission tickets at least 30 minutes before the actual closing time. Similarly, restaurants take their last orders at least 30 minutes before the posted closing time (even earlier for *kaiseki* restaurants). Most national, prefectural, and city museums are closed on Monday; if Monday is a national holiday, however, they'll remain open and close on the following day, Tuesday, instead. Privately owned museums, however, usually close on holidays.

Customs Visitors entering Japan must fill out a "Customs Declaration" form (handed out on incoming flights). If you're 20 or older, you can bring duty-free into Japan up to 400 cigarettes or 500 grams of tobacco or 100 cigars; three bottles (760cc each) of alcohol; and 2 ounces of perfume. You can also bring in goods for personal use that were purchased abroad whose total market value is less than

¥200,000. For more information, check the website www.customs.go.jp.

Disabled Travelers
For those with disabilities, traveling can be a nightmare in Japan, especially in Tokyo and other large metropolises. City sidewalks can be so jam-packed that getting around on crutches or in a wheelchair is exceedingly difficult; some busy thoroughfares can be crossed only via pedestrian bridges.

Toilets for the handicapped can be found across Japan, including train stations (almost every station has at least one), department stores, and attractions. Shinkansen and some limited express trains have spaces for wheelchairs and accessible toilets. Most major train and subway stations have elevators, but they can be difficult to locate. Otherwise, smaller stations, especially in rural areas, may be accessible only by stairs or escalators, though in recent years some have been equipped with powered seat lifts. While some buses are no-step conveyances for easy access (including new ones being added in Tokyo), subway and train compartments are difficult for solo wheelchair travelers to navigate on their own due to a gap or slight height difference between the coaches and platforms. In theory, you can ask a station attendant to help you board, though you might have to wait if he's busy; you can also request an attendant at your destination to help you disembark. Although city trains, subways, and buses have seating for passengers with disabilities—called "Priority Seats"—subways can be so crowded that there's barely room to move. Moreover, Priority Seats are almost always occupied by commuters, so unless you look visibly handicapped, no one is likely to offer you a seat.

As for accommodations, only hotels with 50 or more rooms are required to offer one barrier-free room (called a "universal" room in Japan and used primarily by seniors). Only a scant 1% of Japanese inns have such rooms. Lower-priced accommodations may also lack elevators.

Restaurants can also be difficult to navigate, with raised doorsills, crowded dining areas, and tiny bathrooms that cannot accommodate wheelchairs. Best bets for ramps and easily accessible bathrooms include restaurants in department stores and upper-end hotels. Even Japanese homes are not very accessible, since the main floor is always raised about a foot above the entrance-hall floor.

When it comes to facilities for the blind, Japan has a very advanced system. At subway stations and on many major sidewalks in large cities, raised dots and lines on the ground guide blind people at intersections and to subway platforms (in fact, Japan pioneered the system). In some cities, streetlights chime a theme when the signal turns green east-west, and chime another for north-south. Even Japanese yen notes are identified by a slightly raised circle—the ¥1,000 note has one circle in a corner, while the ¥10,000 note has two.

In any case, it's hoped that the 2020 Summer Paralympics will spur improvements for disabled travelers. For more information on accessibility in Japan, www.japan-accessible.com provides valuable tips on wheelchairs and accessibility for sights, neighborhoods, hotels, and more.

Doctors Many first-class hotels offer medical facilities, an in-house doctor, or a doctor on call. Otherwise, your embassy or the **AMDA International Medical Information Center** (http://eng.amda-imic.com; ✆ **03/6233-9266** in Tokyo; Mon–Fri 10am–3pm) can refer you to medical professionals who speak English.

Drinking Laws The legal drinking age is 20. Beer, wine, and spirits are readily available in department stores, grocery stores, convenience stores, and liquor stores. Many bars, especially in nightlife districts such as Shinjuku and Roppongi, are open until dawn. If you intend to drive in Japan, you are not allowed even one drink.

Electricity The electricity throughout Japan is 100 volts AC, but two different cycles are in use (which ended up playing havoc during electricity shortages after the Great East Japan Earthquake): In Tokyo and in regions northeast of the capital up through Hokkaido, it's 50 cycles, while in Nagoya, Kyoto, Osaka, and all points to the southwest, it's 60 cycles. In any case, it's close enough to the American system that I've never encountered any problems plugging in my American electronics, including laptops and camera or phone rechargers. Leading hotels often have two outlets, one for 110 volts and one for 220 volts (with the appropriate plugs used in the U.S. and Europe), so you can use most American or European appliances (electric razors, travel irons, laptops, and so forth) during your stay. Note, too, that the flat, two-legged prongs used in Japan are the same size and fit as in North America, but three-pronged appliances are not accepted. For my laptop, I bring the small two-prong attachment so I can plug into a Japanese socket, though hotels usually have them available. Some hotels even have USB ports for charging phones.

Embassies & Consulates The following embassies are located in Tokyo (visa or passport sections of most embassies are open only at certain times during the day, so it's best to call in advance). There are also Australian, British, Canadian, and U.S. consulates in Osaka.

Australian Embassy: 2–1–14 Mita, Minato-ku (http://japan.embassy.gov.au/; ✆ **03/5232-4111;** station: Azabu-Juban Station, exit 2).

British Embassy: 1 Ichibancho, Chiyoda-ku (www.gov.uk/government/world/organisations/british-embassy-tokyo; ✆ **03/5211-1100;** station: Hanzomon).

Canadian Embassy: 7–3–38 Akasaka, Minato-ku (www.canadainternational.gc.ca/japan-japon/index.aspx?lang=eng; (✆ **03/5412-6200;** station: Aoyama-Itchome).

Embassy of Ireland: Ireland House, 2–10–7 Kojimachi, Chiyoda-ku (www.irishembassy.jp; ✆ **03/3263-0695;** station: Hanzomon, exit 3).

New Zealand Embassy: 20–40 Kamiyama-cho, Shibuya-ku (www.mfat.govt.nz/en/countries-and-regions/north-asia/japan/new-zealand-embassy; ✆ **03/3467-2271;** station: Shibuya).

U.S. Embassy: 1–10–5 Akasaka, Minato-ku (https://jp.usembassy.gov; ✆ **03/3224-5000;** station: Toranomon).

Emergencies The national emergency numbers are ✆ **110** for **police** and ✆ **119** for **ambulance** and **fire** (ambulances are free in Japan unless you request a specific hospital). You do not need to insert any money or a prepaid telephone card into public telephones to call these numbers. Be sure to speak slowly and precisely.

Health After the 2011 Great East Japan Earthquake and the subsequent struggle to contain the damaged Fukushima nuclear power plant, there was widespread fear of radiation and contaminated foods. While decontamination in Fukushima Prefecture continues, rest assured that measures are in place to protect food and water safety and that Japan's standards for radioactive contamination are the same as in the U.S. In any case, Tokyo is 240km (150 miles) from the crippled Fukushima plant, and my personal take on the radiation situation is that a month's stay will have no long-term effects on my longevity. Frankly, you're likely to get more radiation on the flight to Japan than being in west Honshu.

Otherwise, it's safe to drink tap water and eat to your heart's content everywhere in Japan (pregnant women, however, are advised to avoid eating raw fish and to avoid taking hot baths). To prevent the spread of avian and H1N1 flu, all incoming passengers are monitored upon arrival at Narita Airport for fever; those with a higher than normal temperature may be quarantined. To be on the safe side, therefore, you may opt for an influenza vaccine before departing from home.

You don't need any inoculations to enter Japan. **Prescriptions** can be filled at Japanese pharmacies *only if they're issued by a Japanese doctor.* To avoid hassle, bring more prescription medications than you think you'll need, clearly labeled in their original containers, and be sure to pack them in your carry-on. To be safe, bring copies of your prescriptions with you, including generic names of medicines in case a local pharmacist is unfamiliar with the brand name. Over-the-counter items are easy to obtain, though name brands are likely to be different from those back home, some ingredients allowed elsewhere may be forbidden in Japan, and prices may be higher.

Internet & Wi-Fi Narita International Airport, Haneda Airport, and Kansai International Airport all offer free **Wi-Fi** (wireless fidelity), as well as computer terminals (¥100 per 10 min.).

With the exception of lodging in remote areas and some youth hostels, most accommodations nowadays provide free Wi-Fi in their guest rooms (some super-deluxe properties, however, charge for Wi-Fi). Throughout this book, I've indicated for each hotel and inn whether Wi-Fi is available in guest rooms. Most accommodations also have computers for guest use, usually for free.

Outside hotels, many department stores, shopping centers, restaurants (including all McDonald's), cafes (including all Starbucks), and bars offer free Wi-Fi, though you may have to ask for the password. I've also found that all but the smallest of towns, and even neighborhoods within cities, now offer free Wi-Fi hotspots to tourists, though time usage may be limited and reception can by spotty. See individual chapters for information on train station tourist offices, which provide maps or lists of Wi-Fi availability. Both JR East and JR West provide free Wi-Fi in many of their stations, including all JR stations and trains in Tokyo (Tokyo's subway stations also offer free Wi-Fi) and in major stations in the Kansai area. You should also download the Japan Connected-free Wi-Fi app (www.ntt-bp.net/jcfw/use/index.html, which connects you to Wi-Fi hotspots around Japan and also offers offline maps; it's free.

Otherwise, you can rent a mobile Wi-Fi router upon arrival at Narita, Haneda, and Kansai airports, which provides Internet access virtually anywhere. See "Mobile Phones," below, for more information.

LGBT Travelers Japan has no laws forbidding homosexual activity and there is no ban against homosexuality by either Buddhism or Japan's indigenous religion, Shintoism. Indeed, same-sex relationships have been well-documented through the ages in Japanese literature and woodblock prints. On the other hand, gays have no legal rights in Japan. Although there are many gay and lesbian establishments in Tokyo (concentrated mostly in Shinjuku's Ni-chome district; see chapter 5), the gay community in Japan is not a vocal one, and local information in English is hard to come by. A useful website for information on the gay scene in Japan, as well as gay and lesbian club listings in cities around the country, is **www.utopia-asia.com/tipsjapn.htm**. **Out Asia Travel** (www.outasiatravel.com) is a Tokyo-based gay travel agency that offers guided tours of gay nightlife districts in Tokyo, Kyoto, Osaka, and other towns, special-interest tours, individually oriented trips, and tours to other destinations in Japan and Asia.

Legal Aid Contact your embassy if you find yourself in legal trouble. The **Legal Counseling Center** (www.horitsu-sodan.jp) is operated by three bar associations that provide legal counseling in English. The fee is generally ¥5,000 for 30 minutes, plus ¥2,500 for each additional 15 minutes.

Luggage & Lockers Storage space on Shinkansen bullet trains is limited, so travel with the smallest bag you can get away with. Coin-operated lockers are located at major train stations throughout the country, but lockers are generally not large enough to store huge pieces of luggage (and those that do are often taken). Lockers generally cost ¥300 to ¥800 per day depending on the size; if you leave them overnight, you'll have to pay the next-day's charge to retrieve them. Due to increased tourism, many major stations also have check-in rooms or in-town delivery service for luggage (see individual city chapters). If your bag becomes too much to handle, you can have it sent to

Over & Out

If you're traveling with a buddy or family, consider bringing along walkie-talkies. They're cheaper than phones, could be a lifesaver if you get separated, and make it easier to rendezvous, especially in big cities.

your next or even last destination via door-to-door service offered by companies like Yamato's **TA-Q-BIN** (www.global-yamato.com/en/hands-free-travel/), available at homes, offices, upper- and mid-range hotels, and all convenience stores in Japan. At Narita and Kansai international airports, service counters will send luggage to your hotel the next day (or vice versa) for about ¥2,300 per bag.

Mail & Postage If your hotel cannot mail letters for you, ask the concierge for the location of the nearest post office, recognizable by the red logo of a capital T with a horizontal line over it. Mailboxes are bright orange-red. It costs ¥110 to airmail letters weighing up to 25 grams and ¥70 for postcards to Australia, North America, and Europe. Domestic mail costs ¥82 for letters up to 25 grams, and ¥62 for postcards. Post offices throughout Japan are also convenient for their ATMs, which accept international credit cards for money exchange.

Although all **post offices** are open Monday through Friday from 9am to 5pm, international post offices (often located close to the central train station) have longer hours, often until 7pm or later on weekdays and with open hours also on weekends (in Tokyo and Kyoto, counters are open 24 hr.). If your hotel does not have a shipping service, it is only at these larger post offices that you can mail packages abroad. For more information, visit **www.post.japanpost.jp**.

Measurements Before the metric system came into use in Japan, the country had its own standards for measuring length and weight. Rooms are still measured by the number of *tatami* straw mats that will fit in them. A six-*tatami* room, for example, is the size of six *tatami* mats, with a *tatami* roughly .9m (3 ft.) wide and 1.8m (6 ft.) long.

Mobile Phones The three letters that define much of the world's wireless capabilities are GSM (Global System for Mobiles). Unfortunately, Japan uses a system that is incompatible with GSM, and foreigners are not allowed to buy cellphones in Japan. You can, however, **bring your own mobile phone** and buy a prepaid SIM card in the arrival lobbies of Narita, Haneda, and Kansai airports from one of many companies like **Softbank** (www.softbank-rental.jp). **eConnect** (www.econnectjapan.com/) is an online service, with pickup at Narita's post office. In town, prepaid SIM cards are also available at Yodobashi and Bic camera shops. The cheapest SIM options are for data only, which means you can't make calls or send text messages.

First, however, you'll want to make sure your phone SIM is unlocked. If not, both eConnect and Softbank also rent mobile Wi-Fi routers that let you connect to the Internet virtually anywhere, allowing you to check mail and make phone calls via Skype and other Internet-based phone companies. Check their websites to see whether a router or SIM card works best for you.

You can also simply rent a mobile phone, though it's the most expensive option. Many companies at airports offer phone rentals with various packages available (check airport websites for company listings, provided under "Getting There," earlier in this chapter). **PuPuRu** (www.pupuru.com/en) offers the extra convenience of delivering a rental phone to any address in Japan (such as your hotel), with its return via a prepaid, preaddressed envelope. It also rents routers.

THE VALUE OF THE YEN VS. OTHER POPULAR CURRENCIES

Yen	Aus$	Can$	Euro€	NZ$	UK£	US$
100	A$1.21	C$1.19	€0.79	NZ$1.32	£0.69	$0.91

Money & Costs Frommer's lists exact prices in the local currency. The currency conversions quoted above were correct at press time. However, rates fluctuate, so before departing consult a currency exchange website such as **www.oanda.com/currency/converter** to check up-to-the-minute rates.

The currency in Japan is called the *yen*, symbolized by ¥. Coins come in denominations of ¥1, ¥5, ¥10, ¥50, ¥100, and ¥500. Bills come in denominations of ¥1,000, ¥2,000, ¥5,000, and ¥10,000, though ¥2,000 notes are rarely seen. Keep plenty of change handy for riding local transportation such as buses or streetcars. Although change machines are virtually everywhere, even on buses where you can change larger coins and ¥1,000 bills, you'll find it faster to have the exact amount on hand (or buy an IC card like Suica; see "Getting Around" in chapter 4).

Some people like to arrive in a foreign country with that country's currency already on hand, but I don't find it necessary for Japan. **Narita, Haneda,** and **Kansai** have exchange counters for all incoming international flights that offer better exchange rates than what you'd get abroad, as well as ATMs. I usually change enough money to last several days.

Most Japanese pay with either credit cards or cash for larger purchases. The most readily accepted cards are **American Express, Diners Club, MasterCard** (also called Eurocard), **Visa,** as well as the Japanese credit card **JCB** (Japan Credit Bank) and those from other countries. The bulk of your expenses—hotels, train tickets, major purchases, meals in many restaurants—can be paid for with credit cards. Shops and restaurants accepting credit cards will usually post which cards they accept at the door or near the cash register.

Note, however, that Japan is still largely a cash society. Some establishments may be reluctant to accept cards for small purchases and inexpensive meals, so inquire beforehand. Note, too, that the vast majority of Japan's smaller and least-expensive businesses, including many restaurants, noodle shops, fast-food joints, ma-and-pa establishments, and the cheapest accommodations, do not accept credit cards. For that reason, you'll want to have plenty of cash on hand, especially if you're traveling in rural areas where you might not have easy access to an ATM for cash withdrawals.

I also find traveler's checks still useful in Japan. Traveler's checks help you avoid annoying credit card fees and withdrawal limits, generally fetch a better exchange rate than cash, and offer protection in case of theft. *You may need your passport to exchange traveler's checks.* Note, however, that in some very remote areas, even banks won't cash them. Before taking off for small towns, be sure you have enough cash.

Newspapers & Magazines Two English-language newspapers are published daily in Japan: the ***Japan Times*** (www.japantimes.co.jp), which comes distributed also with the *International New York Times,* and the ***Japan News*** (www.the-japan-news.com), published by *Yomiuri Shimbun.* In addition, the *Asahi Shimbun* has an English website, www.asahi.com/ajw/, with news on Japan. I also like http://newsonjapan.com, which gives a roundup of the daily news—business, politics, travel, society, and more—with excerpts drawn from Japanese news sources.

Packing Tips The first thing you'll want to do is select the smallest bag you can get away with and **pack as lightly as you can.** Storage space is limited on Japan's trains, including the Shinkansen bullet train, business hotels often lack closets, and you'll have to navigate multitudes of stairs and overhead and underground passageways in virtually every train station in the country (there are elevators and escalators, but these can be difficult to find).

The most important item is **a good pair of walking shoes,** well broken in, since you will probably be walking more than you do at home. Because you have to remove shoes to enter Japanese homes, inns, shrines, temples, and even some restaurants, bring a pair that's easy to slip on and off. As for **clothes,** you'll need a coat in winter and very light clothing for the hot and humid summer months. Jackets are necessary for spring and autumn; I've seen it snow in March in Tokyo, and even May can be quite crisp. Otherwise, for sightseeing, casual wear is okay, including jeans, shorts, and sandals, but be aware that Japanese put more stock in how you dress and look than maybe back home. Because the sun rises early in summer (as early as 4am), you might also want to pack a pair of eyeshades.

It's also good to carry a supply of pocket tissues, hand sanitizer, change for local buses (faster than trying to change ¥1,000 notes), a folding umbrella, and a compass for getting your bearings and following my directions using local maps.

Pharmacies Drugstores, called ***yakkyoku,*** are found readily in Japan and contain beauty products and a great many other useful items. Note, however, that you cannot have a foreign prescription filled in Japan without first consulting a doctor in Japan, so it's best to bring an adequate supply of essential medicines with you. No drugstores in Japan stay open 24 hours. However, ubiquitous convenience stores like 7-Eleven, Lawson, and FamilyMart, open day and night throughout Japan, carry such nonprescription items as aspirin. In fact, convenience stores are your best friend, where you can get cash from an ATM, purchase concert tickets, buy beer or ready-made foods they'll heat up for you, stock up on extra socks or notepads, and use its bathroom.

Safety The tragic 2011 Great East Japan Earthquake brought world-wide attention to the fact that Japan is earthquake-prone, but in reality, most earthquakes are too small to detect (of the more than 100,000 earthquakes annually in Japan, only 1% are big enough to feel). In any case, Japan has the world's best early-warning systems for impending earthquakes and tsunamis (the death toll would have been much higher without them) and strict building codes (it's worth noting that not one skyscraper was felled by the 3/11 earthquake; the tsunami caused most of the damage). If you're around other people, you'll most likely hear everyone's phones going off at once for an earthquake alert, since most people are signed up for the warning that an earthquake may be imminent. In the event of a warning or an earthquake, there are a few precautions you should take. If you're indoors, the three rules of thumb are Drop, Cover, and Hold On. In other words, you should drop to the ground, take cover under a sturdy table, a piece of furniture or under a doorway, and then hold on until the shaking stops. Do not go outdoors—the greatest danger is from falling debris, collapsing walls, and flying glass. Never use elevators during a quake.

If you are outdoors, stay away from trees, power lines, streetlights, and the sides of buildings; if you're surrounded by tall buildings, seek cover in a doorway. If

Take a Load off Heavy Bags

If your bag becomes a burden but you don't want to mail items home, an alternative is to send a bag onward to your next or last stop by **TA-Q-BIN,** available at larger hotels, train stations, and convenience stores. Bags reach most destinations in 1 or 2 nights, with the delivery cost of an average-size bag weighing 10kg (22 lb.) about ¥1,469. I love this amazingly efficient service—it's a lifesaver! For more information, see Yamato Transport's website at www.global-yamato.com/en/hands-free-travel/. Another good website is www.luggage-free-travel.com/travel/index.php.

you're in a coastal area, move away from the beach. The authorities will issue a tsunami warning if dangerous waves seem imminent. And expect aftershocks. Although secondary shockwaves are generally not as severe as the first one, they can damage weakened structures and can occur in the first hours or days—and even months—after the first quake. In case of major emergencies, there are emergency shelters throughout Japan, mostly schoolyards and other public facilities. Other precautions include noting emergency exits wherever you stay; all hotels supply flashlights, usually found attached to your bedside table. For more on what to do during earthquakes, evacuation shelters, updates on disasters and weather warnings and advisories, see the Japan government's **Disaster Prevention Portal** at www.mlit.go.jp/river/bousai/olympic/en/index.html.

As for crime, Japan has long been recognized as one of the safest countries in the world. In all the years I've lived and worked in Japan, I've never had even one fearful encounter, and I never hesitate to walk anywhere any time of the night or day. After the 2011 tsunami, the possibility of looting occurring along the damaged coast never even crossed my mind; in fact, millions worth in yen and other valuables found in the rubble was turned over to authorities. When a friend of mine forgot her purse in a public restroom in Osaka, someone turned it in to the police station complete with money, digital camera, and passport. In other words, if you lose something, say on a subway or in a park, chances are good that you'll get it back. To find out how, go to the nearest police station or contact the local tourist office.

That being said, crime—especially pickpocketing—is on the increase, and there are precautions you should always take when traveling: Stay alert and be aware of your immediate surroundings. Be especially careful with cameras, purses, and wallets in congested areas like Narita airport, subways, department stores, or tourist attractions. Some Japanese caution women against walking through parks alone at night.

Smoking The legal age for purchasing tobacco products and smoking in Japan is 20. Smoking is banned in most public areas, including in trains and subways, train stations (although stations sometimes have a smoking room), and office buildings. In most cities, ordinances also ban smoking on sidewalks but allow it in marked areas, usually near train stations. Many restaurants have nonsmoking sections or prohibit smoking during lunch hour, though bars do not. Entirely smoke-free restaurants are on the rise, with your best bet of finding one in a hotel. Virtually all hotels have designated nonsmoking floors, though Japanese-style inns, because of their small size, sometimes do not; some business hotels also don't. On the other hand, an increasing number of lodgings are entirely smoke-free.

Taxes The tax imposed on goods and services, including hotel rates and restaurant meals, is 8% (it's expected to rise to 10% in October 2019). Hotels and restaurants are inconsistent about including the tax in their published rates, but will generally state whether tax is included or will be added on their tariff sheets and menus. Tokyo and Kyoto hotels also levy a separate accommodations tax (see chapters 4 and 8). In hot-spring resorts, a ¥150 *onsen* tax is added for each night of your stay.

In addition to these taxes, a 10% to 15% **service charge** will be added to your bill in lieu of tipping at most of the fancier restaurants and at moderately priced and upper-end hotels; in *ryokan*, the service charge can be as high as 20%. Business hotels, *minshuku*, youth hostels, and inexpensive restaurants do not impose a service charge.

As for **shopping,** a consumption tax is also included in the price of most goods. Travelers from abroad are eligible for an exemption on goods taken out of the country within 6 months, although only department stores, designer boutiques, souvenir shops, and specialty stores seem equipped to deal with the procedures. General items such as clothing and household goods are eligible, as well as consumables (cosmetics, food, and drinks), as long as you don't consume them in Japan; they will be placed in a sealed bag. In any case, stores will grant a refund on the consumption tax only when the total amount of purchases for the day at their store exceeds ¥5,000. You can obtain a refund immediately by having a sales clerk fill out a list of your purchases and then presenting the list to the tax-exemption counter of the department store; *you must present your passport.* Note that stores are allowed to charge 1.1% commission on your refund (with the 8%, you will be refunded only 6.9%). A Tax-free Proof of Purchase receipt will be attached to your passport to show when departing Japan; make sure to pack your purchases in your carry-on luggage.

Telephones Despite the proliferation of mobile phones, you can still find public telephones in telephone booths on the sidewalk, in or near train stations, in hotel lobbies, restaurants and coffee shops, and even on the bullet train (the latter require a prepaid card, sold from vending machines beside the phone). A local call costs ¥10 for each minute; a warning chime will alert you to insert more coins or you'll be disconnected. It's best, therefore, to insert two or three coins so that you won't have to worry about being disconnected; ¥10 coins that aren't used are returned at the end of the call. Most public phones accept both ¥10 and ¥100 coins. The latter is convenient for long-distance calls, but no change is given for unused minutes. Numbers beginning with **0120** or **0088** are toll-free.

Television If you enjoy watching television, you've come to the wrong country. Almost nothing is broadcast in English; even foreign films are dubbed in Japanese. But even if you don't understand Japanese, I suggest that you watch TV at least once; maybe you'll catch a samurai series or a sumo match. Commercials are also worth watching. Otherwise, most upper-range hotels offer **bilingual televisions,** whereby you can switch from Japanese to English if the program or movie was *originally in English*, though only a few (and fairly dated) English movies and sitcoms are broadcast each week. The plus of bilingual TVs is that you can listen to the nightly national news broadcast by NHK at 7 and 9pm. Otherwise, major hotels in larger cities have cable or satellite TV with English-language programs including CNN broadcasts (sometimes in Japanese only) and BBC World. Many also offer in-house pay movies. Note, however, that while upper-range hotels usually have a few choices in English and automatically charge the movie to your bill, cheaper lodgings like business hotels usually offer only one kind of pay movie—generally "adult entertainment," which can be accessed only by purchasing prepaid cards from vending machines in the corridor.

Time Japan is 9 hours ahead of Greenwich Mean Time, 14 hours ahead of New York, 15 hours ahead of Chicago, and 17 hours ahead of Los Angeles. Although there's been discussion of initiating daylight saving time, Japan currently does not use daylight saving time, so subtract 1 hour from the above times in the summer when calling from countries that have daylight saving time such as the United States.

Because Japan is on the other side of the international date line, you lose a day when traveling from the United States to Asia. (If you depart the United States on Tues, you'll arrive on Wed.) Returning to North America, however, you gain a day, which means that you arrive on the same day you left.

Tipping One of the delights of being in Japan is that there's no tipping—not even to waitresses, taxi drivers, or bellhops. If you try to tip them, they'll probably be confused or embarrassed or run down the street after you with your change. Instead, a 10% to 15% service charge is added to your bill at higher-priced accommodations and restaurants. That being said, you might want to tip, say, your room attendant at a high-class *ryokan* if you're making special requests or meals are served in your room; in that case, place crisp, clean bills (¥3,000–¥5,000) in a white envelope on the table of your room at the beginning of your stay; but it's perfectly fine if you choose not to tip.

Toilets If you need a restroom, your best bets are at train and subway stations, big hotels, department stores, convenience stores, and fast-food restaurants. Use of restrooms is free in Japan, and though public facilities supply toilet paper, it's a good idea to **carry a packet of tissues.** Many do not provide soap, so it's also wise to carry **hand sanitizer.** In parks and some restaurants in rural areas, don't be surprised if you go into a restroom and find men's urinals and private stalls in the same room. Women are supposed to walk past the urinals without noticing them.

Many toilets in Japan, especially those at train stations, are **Japanese-style toilets:** They're holes in the ground over which you squat facing forward toward the end with a raised hood. Men stand and aim for the hole. Although Japanese lavatories may seem uncomfortable at first, they're actually more sanitary because no part of your body touches anything.

Western-style toilets in Japan are usually very high-tech. Called **Washlets,** these combination bidet/toilets have heated toilet seats, buttons and knobs directing sprays of water of various intensities to various body parts, blow dryers, and even lids that raise when you open the stall. But alas, instructions are often in Japanese only. Listen to the voice of experience: Don't stand up until you've figured out how to turn the darn spray off.

Visas For most foreign tourists, including Americans, Canadians, Australians, New Zealanders, and citizens of the United Kingdom, visas are not required for stays up to 90 days.

Visitor Information

The **Japan National Tourism Organization (JNTO)** is the best source for travel information on Japan. You can reach JNTO via the Internet at **www.japan.travel** (and at **www.us.jnto.go.jp** for U.S. travelers; http://ilovejapan.ca/ for Canadian travelers; **www.seejapan.co.uk** for British travelers; and **www.jnto.org.au** for Australian travelers), where you can read up on what's new, view maps, get the latest weather report, find links to online hotel reservation companies and tour companies, and browse through information ranging from hints on budget travel to regional events. JNTO also showcases local tourism attractions, Japanese cuisine, and other topics (including yours truly, twice in 2011) on YouTube at www.youtube.com/visitjapan. I also recommend the comprehensive www.japan-guide.com, with links to many other websites.

In Japan, your best bet for general or specific information for destinations throughout Japan is at one of JNTO's three excellent **Tourist Information Centers (TICs).** They're located in downtown Tokyo, at Narita Airport (outside Tokyo), in Kyoto Tower across from Kyoto Station, and at Kansai International Airport outside Osaka (see chapters 4, 8, and 9 for locations and open hours). All distribute leaflets on attractions throughout Japan—for example, Japanese gardens, hot springs, museums, and art galleries. Be sure to ask for the invaluable *Japan Railway Time Table,* which contains timetables for Shinkansen trains and major JR train lines throughout Japan.

You'll also find locally run tourist offices in nearly every city and town throughout Japan, most of them conveniently located at or near the main train station. Look for the logo of a red question mark with the word INFORMATION written below. They can point you in the direction of your hotel, provide you with an English-language map, give information on Wi-Fi hotspots, and, in many cases, even make hotel bookings for you. I've included information on local tourist offices throughout this book (see "Visitor Information," in the regional chapters), including how to reach them after you disembark from the train and their open hours.

Water The water is safe to drink anywhere in Japan, although some people claim it's too highly chlorinated. Bottled water is also readily available.

Index

See also Accommodations and Restaurant indexes, below.

General Index

T

U

V

W

Y

Accommodations

Restaurants

Map List

Photo Credits

p. i: © onemu; p. ii: © f11photo; p. iii: © Patryk Kosmider; p. iv: © Luciano Mortula - LGM; p. v, top: © Sean Pavone; p. v, bottom: © Sean Pavone/Shutterstock.com; p. vi, top: © Phattana Stock; p. vi, middle: © yukihipo; p. vi, bottom: © julianne.hide/Shutterstock.com; p. vii, top: © Gritsana P/Shutterstock.com; p. vii, bottom left: © ANURAK PONGPATIMET; p. vii, bottom right: © Savvapanf Photo; p. viii, top: © martinho Smart; p. viii, middle: © Sean Pavone/Shutterstock.com; p. viii, bottom: © Pauline Frommer; p. ix, top: © Guitar photographer; p. ix, bottom: © Guitar photographer; p. x, top: © superjoseph/Shutterstock.com; p. x, bottom: © Sanga Park; p. xi, top left: © Kei Shooting; p. xi, top right: © Sakarin Sawasdinaka; p. xi, bottom: © f11photo; p. xii, top left: © Juri Pozzi; p. xii, top right: © Kobby Dagan/Shutterstock.com; p. xii, bottom: © Kinek00; p. xiii, top: © oleandra/Shutterstock.com; p. xiii, bottom left: © Justin.Jacobs/Shutterstock.com; p. xiii, bottom right: © fbdesigncenter; p. xiv, top: © Navapon Plodprong; p. xiv, bottom: © kawaken; p. xv, top: © StevanZZ/Shutterstock.com; p. xv, middle: © Boris-B/Shutterstock.com; p. xv, bottom: © Kuro3; p. xvi, top: © phichak; p. xvi, bottom left: © Kenneth Dedeu/Shutterstock.com; p. xvi, bottom right: © PK289

Frommer's EasyGuide to Tokyo, Kyoto & Western Honshu, 2nd edition

Published by
FROMMER MEDIA LLC

ISBN 978-1-62887-436-5 (paper), 978-1-62887-437-2 (e-book)

Editorial Director: Pauline Frommer
Editor: Alexis Lipsitz Flippin
Production Editor: Heather Wilcox
Cartographer: Roberta Stockwell
Photo Editor: Meghan Lamb
Cover Design: Dave Riedy

For information on our other products or services, see www.frommers.com.

Frommer Media LLC also publishes its books in a variety of electronic formats. Some content that appears in print may not be available in electronic formats.

Manufactured in the United States of America

5 4 3 2 1

ABOUT THE AUTHOR

Beth Reiber's career as a full-time travel writer has spanned four decades and has included 4 years living in Germany and 3 years in Japan. The author of nine guidebooks, she has been writing Frommer's guides to Japan and Tokyo for more than 30 years. Since 2009, she has been a "Visit Japan Ambassador," an honorary title awarded by the Japanese government for her contributions in promoting travel in Japan.

ACKNOWLEDGMENTS

I would like to thank the Japan National Tourism Organization for its help and behind-the-scenes support, without which this guidebook could never be as comprehensive as it is. A special thanks also to regional support, including the Tokyo Convention & Visitors Bureau, the Kyoto Convention & Visitors Bureau, and the Okayama City Tourism & Convention Promotion Division. I would also like to thank some very special people in my life: Debbie Howard, for being my best friend since we were 4 years old and for giving me a place to stay whenever I'm in Tokyo, and Jonathan Mayhew, who keeps things going when I'm on the road and keeps me centered when I'm home.

ABOUT THE FROMMER TRAVEL GUIDES

For most of the past 50 years, Frommer's has been the leading series of travel guides in North America, accounting for as many as 24% of all guidebooks sold. I think I know why.

Though we hope our books are entertaining, we nevertheless deal with travel in a serious fashion. Our guidebooks have never looked on such journeys as a mere recreation, but as a far more important human function, a time of learning and introspection, an essential part of a civilized life. We stress the culture, lifestyle, history, and beliefs of the destinations we cover, and urge our readers to seek out people and new ideas as the chief rewards of travel.

We have never shied from controversy. We have, from the beginning, encouraged our authors to be intensely judgmental, critical—both pro and con—in their comments, and wholly independent. Our only clients are our readers, and we have triggered the ire of countless prominent sorts, from a tourist newspaper we called "practically worthless" (it unsuccessfully sued us) to the many rip-offs we've condemned.

And because we believe that travel should be available to everyone regardless of their incomes, we have always been cost-conscious at every level of expenditure. Though we have broadened our recommendations beyond the budget category, we insist that every lodging we include be sensibly priced. We use every form of media to assist our readers, and are particularly proud of our feisty daily website, the award-winning Frommers.com.

I have high hopes for the future of Frommer's. May these guidebooks, in all the years ahead, continue to reflect the joy of travel and the freedom that travel represents. May they always pursue a cost-conscious path, so that people of all incomes can enjoy the rewards of travel. And may they create, for both the traveler and the persons among whom we travel, a community of friends, where all human beings live in harmony and peace.

Arthur Frommer